LANDMARK ESSAYS ON RHETORIC OF SCIENCE: ISSUES AND METHODS

Landmark Essays on Rhetoric of Science: Issues and Methods compiles the essential readings of the vibrant field of rhetoric of science, tracing the growth and core concerns of the field since its development in the 1970s.

A companion to Randy Allen Harris's foundational *Landmark Essays on Rhetoric of Science: Case Studies*, this volume includes essays by such luminaries as Carolyn R. Miller, Jeanne Fahnestock, and Alan G. Gross, along with an early prophetic article by Charles Sanders Pierce. Harris's detailed introduction puts the field into its social and intellectual context, and frames the important contributions of each essay, which range from reimagining classical concepts like rhetorical figures and topical invention to integrating such new approaches as modal materialism and the neomodern hybridization of Actor Network Theory with Genre Studies. Race, revolution, and Daoism come up along the way, and the empirical recalcitrance of the moon.

This collection serves as a textbook for graduate and advanced undergraduate courses in science studies, and is an invaluable resource for researchers concerned with science not as a special, autonomous, sacrosanct enterprise, but as a set of value-saturated, profoundly influential rhetorical practices.

Randy Allen Harris is Professor of Linguistics, Rhetoric, and Communication Design at the University of Waterloo. His other books include *Rhetoric and Incommensurability* and *The Linguistic Wars*.

THE LANDMARK ESSAYS SERIES

Landmark Essays is a series of anthologies providing ready access to key rhetorical studies in a wide variety of fields. The classic articles and chapters that are fundamental to every subject are often the most difficult to obtain, and almost impossible to find arranged together for research or for classroom use. This series solves that problem.

Each book encompasses a dozen or more of the most significant published studies in a particular field, and includes an index and bibliography for further study.

Series Editors:
James J. Murphy
Krista Ratcliffe

Landmark Essays on Bakhtin, Rhetoric, and Writing
Edited by Frank Farmer

Landmark Essays on Rhetoric and the Environment
Edited by Craig Waddell

Landmark Essays on Aristotelian Rhetoric
Edited by Richard L. Enos, Lois P. Agnew

Landmark Essays on Advanced Composition
Edited by Gary A. Olson, Julie Drew

Landmark Essays on Writing Centers
Edited by Christina Murphy, Joe Law

Landmark Essays on Rhetorical Invention in Writing
Edited by Richard E. Young, Yameng Liu

Landmark Essays on Writing Process
Edited by Sondra Perl

Landmark Essays on Writing Across the Curriculum
Edited by Charles Bazerman, David R. Russell

Landmark Essays on Rhetorical Criticism
Edited by Thomas W. Benson

Landmark Essays on Voice and Writing
Edited by Peter Elbow

Landmark Essays on Classical Greek Rhetoric
Edited by A. Edward Schiappa

Landmark Essays on Kenneth Burke
Edited by Barry Brummett

Landmark Essays on Rhetoric of Science: Issues and Methods
Edited by Randy Allen Harris

LANDMARK

ESSAYS ON RHETORIC OF SCIENCE:
ISSUES AND METHODS

Edited by

RANDY ALLEN HARRIS

Routledge
Taylor & Francis Group

NEW YORK AND LONDON

First edition published 2020
by Routledge
52 Vanderbilt Avenue, New York, NY 10017

and by Routledge
2 Park Square, Milton Park, Abingdon, Oxon, OX14 4RN

Routledge is an imprint of the Taylor & Francis Group, an informa business

Library of Congress Cataloging-in-Publication Data
A catalog record has been requested for this book

ISBN: 978-1-138-69591-7 (hbk)
ISBN: 978-1-138-69592-4 (pbk)

Typeset in Minion
by Wearset Ltd, Boldon, Tyne and Wear

This book is for
Galen Naidoo Harris

Unerring Nature, still divinely bright,
One clear, unchanged and universal light.
—Alexander Pope
Essay on Criticism

CONTENTS

PREFACE

It's déjà vu all over again.

—Yogi Berra (1998:9)

This book is a beneficially belated but timely companion to another Landmark Essays volume, *Landmark Essays on Rhetoric of Science: Case Studies*—belated, because it was always intended to accompany that volume, from its publication in 1997; timely, because it now appears in tandem with the second edition of that volume. The story of its belatedness is the story of academic publishing over the last few decades. *Case Studies* began life with the Landmark Essays series, in discussion with James J. "Jerry" Murphy, then Founder and Publisher of Hermagoras Press and still one of the most erudite and supportive of scholars. I started with *Case Studies* because of the broad consensus that the best way to advance in the field was by exempla (Melia 1984, Bazerman 1988, Prelli 1989, Myers 1990, Gross 1996 [1990], Simons 1990), but there were also landmarks in the issues and methods of the field from the earliest rhetoric-of-science days, so Jerry and I wanted to follow the first-order case-studies volume with a second-order, theory-driven volume. We just wanted to wait a year or two, for *Case Studies* to make its way, before we went ahead with *Issues and Methods*.

Case Studies made its way very well indeed, the most successful book in the series, but Hermagoras and its listings changed hands, and changed hands again, going through some bumpy times, with absurdly skyrocketing prices, and plans for this volume stalled. All the while, very impressive work continued to appear; second and third generation rhetoricians of science coming into the landscape with impressive versatility, talent, and critical sensibilities. New approaches emerged, old approaches reached greater heights, in disparate places, with no volume where they could be lined up alongside each other both for mutual reinforcement of the overall enterprise and for comparison shopping. I moped, regretting the planned delay between the two volumes.

But eventually, with the Landmark Essays series now at Routledge, Jerry took the helm again, it began expanding, and refurbishing some of the original volumes. Hence, the 2018 second edition of *Case Studies*. Hence, the new volume now in your hands, *Issues and Methods*. Among other virtues, its existence allows the inclusion of major landmarks in rhetoric of science omitted from the first volume for reasons of orientation, such as Philip Wander's "The Rhetoric of Science" and Carolyn R. Miller's "*Kairos* in the Rhetoric of Science," whose failure to republish has haunted me since the first volume went to press. But, as I noted, its belatedness is beneficial, too, allowing the inclusion of such latter-day landmarks as Jeanne Fahnestock's groundbreaking work on rhetorical figures, Celeste M. Condit's brilliant modal materialist approach, and Alan G.

Gross's pioneering expansion into scientific visuals. Rhetoric of science is boomingly hale.

One consequence of that bustling good health is that there are more issues and methods than fit between the covers of one book, so I make no claims to comprehensiveness in either area, though in most cases the loss is not particularly keen, because there are good places to go for coverage. Perhaps most prominently among the issues, incommensurability is barely mentioned—the philosophical notion that at least some symbolic constructs (in particular, competing theories of the same phenomena) have no common measure and therefore no meeting point at which they can be rationally adjudicated—as fundamentally a rhetorical issue implicating science as one might imagine, the primary warrant for a rhetoric of science, as Simons's essay in this volume suggests. But see Harris (2004), a consensus that incommensurability is not an aspect of scientific practice so much as an artifact of philosophical assumptions, an artifact that is dissolved by rhetorical perspectives, alongside Gross's sharply dissenting opinion that incommensurability limits the applicability of rhetorical investigations of science (also see Gross 2006:180–194, and, from a case-study perspective, Graham and Herndl 2013). Similarly, demarcation, the notion that science is distinct (or not) from other grand human institutions (religion, politics, folklore), is largely overlooked and never focalized in this volume—though it frequently provides the backdrop to other discussions, especially in Xiao's account of an amalgamated scientific and Daoist "holy war" in early twentieth century China. But see Charles Taylor's (1997) careful rhetorical mapping of demarcation (and, from a case study approach, Condit's (1996) revealing study of alleged genetic differences of intellect between the sexes). Issues resulting from the radically changed and changing landscape of scientific communication and knowledge making—that is, the internet with its many media and genres—are under-represented (largely by Mehlenbacher and Maddalena's essay, and the implications of Stewart's methodology), but see Gross and Buehl (2017). Reception methods are unrepresented (Paul et al. 2001, Ceccarelli 2005, White 2014), as are sampling methods (Bazerman 1988, Fahnestock 2004). The entire domain of Medical Science is absent. I have wrangled much over inclusions and omissions, but one cannot be too upset about such a robust indication of the field's spectacular good health. There's a lot going on, and there's just not enough room for all of it—medical science, especially, has no presence here because it has effectively become its own brilliant subfield, one that deserves a Landmark Essays offering of its own—but the inclusions in this volume prove an even stronger index of our well-being than the absences.

I will keep my acknowledgments brief because a genuinely reflective account of the influences funneling into this book would make for a book of their own. I want to thank Halifax's Uncommon Grounds, for the caffeine fueling this preface, and for the cozy corner in which to write it; Michael Halloran, Jerry Murphy, Alan Gross, and Jeanne Fahnestock, for their sustained support and for modeling the scholarship to which I aspire; Indira Naidoo-Harris, Galen Naidoo Harris, and Oriana Naidoo Harris, for their support and for their unbounded inspiration, and now there's Brenna; Dorthea Harris for life, the universe, and everything.

For citations, please see References after the Introduction.

1.
INTRODUCTION
by Randy Allen Harris

> I suppose that I need present no argument that we are indeed living in an age of science and technology. The very fact that we are the first people in history to have viewed, via electromagnetic signals, men driving a vehicle on the surface of the moon over 200,000 miles away in space would seem to be proof enough.
>
> —Thomas M. Sawyer (1972:390)

Rhetoric of science, now a field that science scholars in all disciplines neglect at their methodological, theoretical, and critical peril, began in the 1970s, with a clutch of papers arguing about whether it made sense to stitch those two nouns into a prepositional colligation. Sure, there was a viable rhetoric of politics, a rhetoric of film, a rhetoric of literature, a rhetoric of music, of religion, of history, of protest, of logic, of advertising, of graffiti, not to mention an elaborate rhetoric of motives—a series of expansions that eventually became known, derisively, as the "Rhetorics of *X*" excesses—but a rhetoric of *science*?[1] Surely science—the splitter-of-the-atom, the putter-of-men-on-the-moon, the treasure house of the inverse square law, the double-helix model, and $e = mc^2$—was an *X* too far. How could something as sloppy as suasion, as precious as style, as superficial as delivery, possibly gain purchase on the pristinely adamantine standards of scientific argument, penetrate those dense thickets of mathematical formalisms, disturb that ramrod posture of utter rationality? One rhetorician, highly relevant to our story, recalls his Cold War high school experience as one in which physics, chemistry, and mathematics held all the prestige, a hegemonic ethos in which "science was not merely valuable and essential for national defense, it was also a measure of intelligence" (Wander and Jaehne 2000:214).

But there were other disciplinary and cultural stories unfolding behind the critical expansion of rhetoric. As the humanities rapidly lost ground to technoscience in the post-war political and academic contexts, the world of 'facts' splitting apart from the world of 'values,' the discourse of science engulfed virtually all aspects of Cold War public talk. Non-scientists "may have wonderful insights," Abraham Maslow noted in the preface to his classic *Psychology of Being*, "but however sure *they* may be, they can never make mankind sure. They can convince only those who already agree with them, and a few more." We have to be realistic: "Science is the only way we have of shoving truth down the reluctant throat." Maslow is actually attempting to reassure worried humanists here, those "sensitive people … [who] are afraid that science besmirches and depresses, that it tears things apart rather than integrating them, thereby killing rather than creating." Maslow comes, in fact, to heal the fact/value split. But his proposal is that the world of facts should eat the world of values, that science can find the appropriate language for "problems of love, creativeness, value, beauty, imagination, ethics and joy." When Maslow itemizes those sensitive and worried people, we find all of them intimately associated with rhetoric: "poets, prophets, priests, dramatists, artists, [and] diplomats" (Maslow 1962:v).

But as Maslow urges a greater floodtide for science, washing over values and creativity, two humanities disciplines are moving in quite different directions, the history and philosophy of science. Maslow's book came out the same year as Thomas S. Kuhn's *Structure of Scientific Revolutions* (2012 [1962]) and Paul K. Feyerabend's "Explanation, reduction and empiricism" (1981 [1962]:44–96), two pivots in an emerging scholarship that revealed the pristine standards of scientific argument to be particular subsets of everyday arguing, and not infrequently only given lip service anyway; its mathematical formalisms to be a particular idiom of all symbolic activity, with uncertainties, dependencies, and limitations of their own; its ramrod posture to be only one of the many stances of science, its public-facing stance. Meanwhile, applied science was putting men on the moon, Tang on the table, and the existential dread of nuclear annihilation on the daily news. Science was certainly going to be the toughest *X* to solve for the *Rhetoric-of-X* calculus, but by the mid 1970s, as technoscience penetrated every corner of material culture, the resulting exhilarations and anxieties massing into an undeniable exigence, rhetoric was ready for science, science had been revealed amenable to rhetoric, and the colligation, *rhetoric of science*, became real.

The field emerged in two strains, first through a few scattered and unaffiliated critical studies, second out of theoretical arguments. It is anachronistic to call those early critical works *case studies*, since they weren't consciously cases of anything larger than themselves, just investigations of specific texts, motivated chiefly by the power and influence those texts exerted. But retrospectively we can see them as clear antecedents of the now impressive array of case studies that sustain, substantiate, and stimulate the rhetoric of science. The theoretical arguments, on the other hand, were not homegrown. Not unlike the cocktail-party atmosphere suggested by Kenneth Burke's parlor allegory (1941:110–111), they were overheard in knots of heated discussion among party-goers who had arrived earlier. Those partiers came from disciplines which had been quicker to let *science* satisfy the variable in their own *of-X* dilations (History of *X*, Philosophy of *X*), but they were talking about matters familiar to rhetoricians. A few of the nosier rhetoricians eavesdropped just outside those knots and heard that there was uncertainty and contention in the halls of science, that one could find contingency there, alternate rationalities, argument fields, even propaganda and persuasion.

A small clutch of rhetoricians thought they had caught the tenor of the arguments and gathered to debate the philosophical and technoscientific exigence for a new expansion. Should they saunter over and join the group of their neighbors, over by the stereo, mingling with those stiff-backed, lab-coated, math-spouting nerds? That's where the power was, they recognized, and rhetoricians have always been drawn to sources of power. The conversation, too, was reaching a critical mass for them. The second edition of Kuhn's *Structure* was out (2012 [1970]) and getting lots of play, with a long invitational Postscript doubling down on persuasion and conversion and value commitments. As one party-goer later remembered, Trevor Melia, "Kuhn's invitation to a rhetoric of science tended to get lost in the noisy philosophical debate that [followed *Structure*]. For the most part, rhetorical theorists did not respond to the rhetorical invitation; they joined the philosophical debate" (1984:303). They were hashing over the very idea of a rhetoric of science. Meanwhile, Kuhn's book became a citation behemoth and back-stopped a movement in science studies and social epistemology that Richard Rorty called *the rhetorical turn* (Simons 1990:vii), a turn that finally included a contingent of card-carrying rhetoricians in the 1980s.[2]

Our collection, which follows a 2×2 arrangement, suitably begins with essays hashing over that possibility, though we go back to Charles Sanders Peirce for an illuminating precedent. The 2×2 arrangement is artificial, in the best sense of the word, representing the main lines of development over the three-plus decades since rhetoric of science reared its disciplinary head. The two superordinate categories are **Issues** and **Methods**, each with its own pair of subcategories. Issues puts **The Very Idea**, arguments on whether it makes intellectual sense for there to be such a field as rhetoric of science, next to **Through Thick and Thin**, arguments about how fully rhetoric penetrates science, how much of a remainder, if any, is left once rhetoric has done its thing to science; or, in the stasis question that came to define this constellation of themes: is the vocabulary of rhetoric thick enough to say anything worthwhile about science? While they occupy two sections, however, the Issues are perhaps better seen as occupying different ranges of the same continuum than as qualitatively different discussions. The Very Idea essays establish their positions mostly by assembling or implicating a rhetorical vocabulary to gain purchase on scientific argumentation. The Thick and Thin essays probe that vocabulary.

A vocabulary is not just a way of talking, nor even a way of seeing or thinking—though it is certainly good for all three. A vocabulary is a way of acting. A vocabulary is a machinery, a body of instruments, a set of tools for building, taking apart, and rebuilding the world around us; often (and inextricably so for technoscience), in a reciprocal, ongoing symbolic-material intercourse. Burke has done the most to understand vocabularies as structure of action, though Kuhn was not far behind him later in his career, when he dropped *paradigm* in favor of *lexicon*.[3]

A rhetorical vocabulary is a vocabulary about vocabularies. It acts on ways of acting. The two Methods sections, accordingly, represent two ways of acting on the symbolic-material constructs of science, **Neoclassical** and **Neomodern**. The Neoclassical essays are concerned with the lexical instruments of rhetorical antiquity. The Neomodern essays draw in the instruments of other disciplines. Here too we should see our section-labels in terms of a continuum, signalling frameworks with greater or lesser proportions of ancient and modern vocabularies of analysis.

The labels that segregate the sections, then, are artificial in the sense of crafting categories that allow us to see patterns in the development of our field.

As long as I am confessing, or bragging, about artificialities, there is an artificial elephant in the metaphorical room, which should get a pat on the trunk before we move along, the volume-enforced separation between case studies, on the one hand (Harris 2018), and issues and methods, on the other, which we can temporarily designate *theory*. We can take two landmarks as exemplary on this front, John Angus Campbell's "Charles Darwin: Rhetorician of Science" (2018 [1987]), the opening essay of the *Case Studies* volume, and Carolyn R. Miller's "*Kairos* in the Rhetoric of Science" a landmark theory paper (and, therefore, included in this volume). Perhaps the titles tell all the story that needs to be told, Campbell's declaring its focus on the symbolic activities of one individual; Miller's, on the symbolic implications of one concept. But Miller's essay includes the same degree of close reading and textual analysis as Campbell's essay, featuring a contrastive study between two scientific papers at the cusp of organic chemistry and molecular biology, nine years apart. Read as a piece of rhetorical criticism, it is as revealing as anything that has been written about either of those papers. Meanwhile, Campbell's essay is framed as documentary evidence for the very idea of rhetoric of science, beginning and ending with the claim that his analysis demonstrates that rhetoric is a necessary bridge between science and culture.

Case studies are not case studies, in other words, unless they participate in a field of issues; nor can they do so without exemplifying a set of methods. They must be cases *of* something, and must deploy a methodological vocabulary. In the *Case Studies* volume, we see S. Michael Halloran arguing for the transitivity of ethos, John Lyne and Henry Howe charting the complex inter-relations between fields of discourse and scientific expertise, Michelle Sidler examining the implications of the internet for reception studies. Meanwhile, theories have to touch ground. Issues cannot be examined without illustrations, even if only through a network of scattered mentions; methods, especially, cannot be sold without demonstrations of their worth. So, in this book, in addition to Miller's contrastive analysis of two papers, we have Celeste M. Condit's account of articles in *Science* and the *New York Times*, Alan G. Gross's study of Wegener's graphics in *Origin of the Continents and Oceans*, Xiaosui Xiao's rhetorical chronicle of the 1923 Chinese campaign to assimilate western science, and Ashley Rose Mehlenbacher and Kate Maddalena's investigation of citizen science in the wake of the Fukushima disaster, among many other scattered examples (Avogadro's number, celestial navigation, intelligent design, climate change).

The *Issues and Methods* essays deploy their examples and critical analyses as data in arguments for points of theory: Miller to introduce the importance of Kairos, Condit for her modal materialist approach, Gross to demonstrate the relevance of his dual-coding approach to visuals, Xiao to show the cultural amalgamation of the discourses of religion and science, Mehlenbacher and Maddalena to argue that Rhetorical Genre Theory can explain material objects. The *Case Study* essays, on the other hand, while certainly not presented as ends in and of themselves, subordinate whatever particular points they articulate to the provisioning of a storehouse empirical accounts to undergird "the development of theories comprehending more general principles that operate across larger bodies of discourse" (Halloran 2018 [1984]:86).

Issues

> [S]cience is a partial universe of discourse, which is concerned only with facts and the relationships between them. Rhetoric is concerned with a wider realm, since it must include both the scientific occurrence and the axiological ordering of these facts.
> —Richard Weaver (1959:20)

The scientific times, they were a changin' in the mid-twentieth century. Science was no longer just a source of truth about the natural world and, downstream, of mechanisms to alter our relation to the natural world—the steam engine, the telegraph, the light bulb. It was increasingly a pervasive source of both daily convenience and existential unease.

"The sciences extend our horizons, they take us to the roots of things, they carry our knowledge beyond the stars," waxed Donald Lemen Clark in 1950, in a policy paper on the place of rhetoric in a post-war academy busily courting technoscience. "But the infinite variety of the data of experience may frustrate us and confuse us and lose us in chaos, as we know only too well in this terrifying scientific age." (1950:294). His awe and anxiety over the growing cultural power of science are characteristic of the period. So is his disciplinary dread. "Of the two," he added over the page, "rhetoric has more to lose by walking alone than do the sciences" (295). Nor did the sciences appear to want any company. Donald C. Bryant, returning from a 1955 symposium on "The Scientific World Picture and the Humanities," reported on the doubt its participants expressed

> that life for the conceivable future permits time for the humanities, doubt that we can afford the luxury of attention to the whole of man when we are so far short of securing his mere physical survival.
>
> (Bryant 1956:363)

Bryant's anxiety-riddled title was "Whither the Humanities?"

Well, there was always the help-mate role. By the middle of the last century, rhetoricians took it for granted that they were the authorities scientists should turn to for any and all discursive work. "[R]hetoric has widened its scope," Elbert W. Harrington noted, specifically about its relation to science, "and instead of being regarded as a narrow art of persuasion, is now concerned with the proper presentation of all knowledge" (Harrington 1956:27). Most composition manuals included discussions or sections that offered stylistic advice specific to various scientific modes and genres. "Students of technical and scientific subjects seem to me to be as truly acquiring practical training when they are improving their skill in writing," A. Howry Espenshade had noted, "as when they are performing experiments in the laboratory or smelting ores at the furnace" (1904:5).

So, when Don Geiger expresses worries similar to those of Clark and Bryant about the relation between science and rhetoric, he emphasizes their complementary epistemic roles: "science to find the truth, rhetoric to energize it" (1958:54). But then he complicates those roles. He first historicizes the status of the truths that science finds, noting that they all seem to have expiry dates, new truths replacing old truths as the frameworks of science shift. Then he gives more urgency to the energizing activities of rhetoric, noting the importance to human life of deliberative values and prudent action that science seems to leave at the door when it enters the lab. Geiger offers a fable: "Imagine a group of cats, near a tree," he says, as they observe "a barking dog running toward them" (59). The barking, charging dog that worries him most, that defines Clark's terrifying scientific age, that imperils man's physical survival in Bryant's terms, is the atom bomb (56–57). It was atomic-age anxiety that was most responsible for squeezing rhetoric and the humanities out of public discourse. Science had created the problem, the feeling was in many quarters; only science could solve it. Geiger's take was different. Science will give the cats beside the tree all the data they need—the weight and mass and velocity of the dog, the number and size and sharpness of its teeth, the time to arrival, down to the millisecond, the probability it will arrive in ill humor; lots and lots of facts important for deciding a course of action. But only rhetoric—equipped, as it is, beyond those flat facts—can provide the "complex act of description, evaluation, and motivation" needed to get the cats into the tree (59).

Geiger's allegory marks a particular order of response to the technoscientific cultural (and academic) eclipse of rhetoric and the humanities, another aspect of the dilation of rhetoric's scope seen in Harrington's "presentation of all knowledge," the disposition to *critique* all knowledge, and all the processes of knowledge production. Richard McKeon, in particular, fought back against the academic and public abatement of the humanities, and argued particularly for rhetoric as an architectonic art, what is now often called a *master narrative*, a superordinate structure for all knowledge. He championed the traditional arts of communication (grammar, logic, rhetoric) to govern regimes of knowledge, and he regularly probed the ethical problems of science. As early as 1937, he observed what the deflation of those great arts to mere knacks meant for the American intellectual climate. "Grammar," he wrote,

> was not limited in antiquity to the bare enumeration of the formal rules of usage. It was primarily exegetical, and training in grammar involved the study of the poets—later of the prose writers as well—with full attention to the problems of understanding a text and of imitating the qualities which analysis disclosed in it. Rhetoric, likewise, once involved not merely the enumeration of formal rules or the routine of composition but the analysis and emulation of masters of cogent expression, as logic once involved the study not merely of syllogisms and fallacies but of the great and influential examples of rational and scientific analysis.
>
> (1937:375)

The reduction to rules and routines in the communication arts meant that

> the graduates of our colleges, and even the candidates for the doctorate, are unable to write correct, expressive, and fluent English; to understand arguments and demonstrations or to formulate rational grounds on which to defend their own positions; to organize the sequence of their thoughts clearly, order them relevantly, or present them persuasively.
>
> (1937:375)

So that, in society,

> [o]ur words today convey univocal and acceptable meanings only within small groups; we have little in the way of common knowledge of the past or common intellectual background in science or art; we have built a society suspicious of reasons and at the mercy of a vast multiplication of experts; and we have constructed a model of life in which the solemn business is practical and the leisure has grown progressively more purposeless.
>
> (1937:381)

This fragmentation of modern life is especially acute because it ghettoizes the interrogation of values into an increasingly devalued humanities, leaving "scientific methods and scientific explanations value-free" (McKeon 1968:111). The value-free nature of contemporary science, properly seen, he said, was an institutional freedom from value accountability: there is no shortage of values at constant play in the sciences, giving rise "numerous occasions for rhetorical disputation in science." These disputes pivot "on the attacks and defenses of schools of thought, on the formulation of programs for extensions or curtailments of theory or research, on the praise of scientists and the celebration of scientific achievements, and the encroachment of pseudo-science, dogma, or political prescription or the withdrawal of financial support or popular enthusiasm" (McKeon 1945:283), as clear and prescient a prescription for rhetoric of science as one might want.[4]

While science features in McKeon's language of a reinvigorated humanism, it is really *techno*science that preoccupies him. The word was in very limited circulation at the time, but anxiety over the conceptual amalgam that *technoscience* references was not. "The use of the laws of phenomena in pure science," he said, are "as ways of transacting business effectively with concrete existences. Theoretic and practical are amalgamated by both becoming instances of the operation of a productive art" (1945:259). Like Geiger, Bryant, and Clark, McKeon is less worried about the theoretical pursuits of scientists than about the value-laden (but professedly value-agnostic) material outcomes of those pursuits. His view of the centrality of rhetoric as a solution to technoscientific problems achieves particular clarity in "The Uses of Rhetoric in a Technological Age" (McKeon 1987 [1971]). "We need a new architectonic productive art," he said, an art especially to govern technoscience in its educational, political, and corporate realizations, and he tags one:

> Rhetoric exercised such functions in the Roman republic and in the Renaissance. Rhetoric provides the devices by which to determine the characteristics and problems of our times and to form the art by which to guide actions for the solutions of our problems and the improvement of our circumstances.
>
> (1987 [1971]:11)

McKeon defines *architectonic art* as "an art of structuring all principles and products of knowing, doing, and making" (1987 [1971]:3)—that makes for some Big-ass Rhetoric—but it is not the most famous example of the vast expansion many rhetoricians adopted in the latter twentieth century. That honor goes to Kenneth Burke's much travelled motto, "Wherever there is persuasion, there is rhetoric. And wherever there is 'meaning,' there is 'persuasion,'" a formulation from which he was careful not exclude science. "[S]omething of the rhetorical motive comes to lurk in every 'meaning,'" he says, "however purely 'scientific' its pretensions" (1969 [1950]:172). Lurking in Burke's meaning, we see a stasis of jurisdiction, the very idea of a rhetoric of science.

Not every rhetorician eagerly strapped on the Big-ass Rhetoric sandwich board, however. Lawrence Rosenfield dismissed the expansion of rhetoric with a *reductio ad absurdum* at the conference where McKeon gave a version of his "Uses of Rhetoric" arguments. Such an approach, he said, "includes everything but tidal waves." McKeon did not grant the absurdity: "Why *not* tidal waves?" he responded. In recounting this exchange 25 years later, Lloyd Bitzer is on Rosenfield's side. "In light of [such a] conception," he says, not in a good way, it is difficult "to find instances of nonrhetorical human transactions" (Bitzer 1997:20). Also not in a good way, Edwin Black targets McKeon's architectonic view for claiming that rhetoric "is everywhere, that it saturates human activity." Big Rhetoric is a disciplinary pathology for Black, a "bloviation," a condition that causes rhetoric "to lose [the] identity it has sustained for two thousand years" (1997:23).

As we will see, rhetoric of science, the *X* too far for some rhetoricians, inevitably becomes a site for the Big Rhetoric debate.[5]

The Very Idea

> [I]t has hitherto seemed … that to talk of the style of a scientific communication was somewhat like talking of the moral character of a fish.
>
> —Charles Sanders Peirce

The notion that there might be a critical enterprise anchored in the tools of rhetoric and probing the practices of science, was unthought for much of our intellectual history, for two reasons; one, general and methodological, the other, specific and theoretical. Methodologically, rhetoric was primarily, often exclusively, a productive enterprise for much of that history. It was concerned with the generation of discourse, not with the analysis of discourse. Theoretically, rhetoric orbited around public speech, science around specialized empirical practices. Its notebooks, reports, chalkboard writings and sketchings, and other pieces of language were seen, at best, as by-products.

This account is a distortion in several respects, but the overall shape is true enough. It was not until the latter Big Rhetoric decades of the twentieth century that a broadening critical orbit around texts, materials, and practices, coinciding with an erosion of the sanctity of scientific specialization, began giving rhetoricians the very idea of a rhetoric of science.

We start off, however, with a remarkable anticipation of the confluence of these late twentieth century currents, **Charles Sanders Peirce's** 1904 essay, "**Ideas, Stray or Stolen, about Scientific Writing, No. 1**." Unpublished until 1978 (and, so far as I can tell, never followed up by a No. 2), it may feature the first appearance of our defining colligation, "rhetoric of science," and sets out a globalization program for rhetoric that takes science as its most revealing object.[6] Not even McKeon or Burke penned an itemization as comprehensive as Peirce's proposal for

> a universal art of rhetoric, which shall be the general secret of rendering signs effective, including under the term "sign" every picture, diagram, natural cry, pointing finger, wink, knot in one's handkerchief, memory, dream, fancy, concept, indication, token, symptom, letter, numeral, word, sentence, chapter, book, library, and in short whatever, be it in the physical universe, be it in the world of thought, that, whether embodying an idea of any kind (and permit us throughout to use this term to cover purposes and feelings), or being

connected with some existing object, or referring to future events through a general rule, causes something else, its interpreting sign, to be determined to a corresponding relation to the same idea, existing thing, or law.

(Peirce, this volume, 42)

Whew! Peirce's view is still centrally productive here ("rendering signs effective"), but its capaciousness is breathtaking, and his notion of productivity extends to invention, personal reasoning, and "physical effects" in the essay, to the point where analysis seems clearly to be along for the ride. The view here of Peirce's program is only partial. When followed out through his many articulations of Speculative Rhetoric, we see that it prominently "treat[s] of the formal conditions of the force of symbols, or their power of appealing to a mind" (1867:295), and that, among other goals, it seeks to "ascertain the laws by which in every scientific intelligence one sign gives birth to another, and especially one thought brings forth another" (1940 [1897]:99). Peirce envisions a rhetoric of science, in other words, not just in terms of the epistemic preoccupations that accompanied its emergence in the 1980s and 1990s, but also the ontological and material preoccupations that accompanies its growth in the 2000s.[7]

Peirce's project was urged forward by one of his most visionary readers, Burke, who was fond of seeing literary and scientific discourses as natural variations of the same cognitive affinity, most famously in his "Four Master Tropes" essay, which sets out the tropes' role in "poetic realism" and "scientific realism" (1941), and where he observes that "[v]arious kinds of scientific specialists now carry out the implications of one or another of such [explanatory] perspectives with much more perseverance than that with which a 17th Century poet might in one poem pursue the exploitation of a 'conceit'" (1941:422–423). And he often defined his dramatism against scientism, or used science to illustrate the operations of rhetoric. He can even be seen picturing empirical experimentation as a form of wholly material rhetoric, in which "the setting up of laboratory situations for testing one's hunches or one's ad hoc conclusions" is constructing

a series of devices whereby one deliberately [gives] voice to the opposition, by a selection of means that addresse[s] such questions to speechless nature as enable[s] nature to give unequivocal answers.

(Burke 1962:11–12)

Among the first to pick up directly on these literary and dramatistic implications for science was **Paul Newell Campbell**. His "**The Personae of Scientific Discourse**" casually takes up Burke's invitation to extend expressly literary language to the workings of science (also P. N. Campbell 1973), with very little sense that it is opening up a new field. "The argument that scientific discourse is rhetorical in nature is easy enough to make," he notes, because "the materials for that argument" had already been forged by scholars like Susanne K. Langer, Thomas Kuhn, and Jacob Bronowski, coordinating them with Burke (this volume, 48). (He might also have included another tri-named member of Clan Campbell in the mix, since several entries of John Angus Campbell's groundbreaking critical series on Charles Darwin had recently appeared.) P. N. Campbell's assembly of these materials into his argument is powerful in its simplicity: scientists are advocates, selecting and deflecting facts in support of a position, or a theory, or a paradigm, or an idealized science writ large; advocacy is a stance; a stance is only one aspect of the writer; an aspect of the writer, cultivated for the purposes of a text, is a persona; scientific discourse is irreducibly saturated with personae; QED.

P. N. Campbell, a rhetorician not a scientist, is unhappy ending on a *QED*, however. The rhetorical nature of science is only the first step. He follows the implications of the ritualized scientific persona—a stance combining objectivity, control, and predict-ability—into ethical realms.

P. N. Campbell's essay was one of several arguments implicating a rhetoric of science in the 1970s, but as a landmark it is—to yoke together some heterogeneous metaphors for a moment—more of a weathervane than a foundation stone. Disciplinary winds were swirling around the phrase "rhetoric of science" (see, for instance, Zappen 1975; Stephens 1975:220), but the building was not going up. Case studies were appearing, but they were not consciously tethered to a general program. Perhaps—rhetorical criticism endemically an enterprise of the particular case—"rhetoric of *science*," a general notion, just did not present itself. Brown and Crable (1973) talk only of a "rhetoric of ecology"; Anderson (1970a) is more local yet, with the "rhetoric of the *Report from Iron Moun-tain*," and J. A. Campbell (1975) writes only of "the rhetoric of *The Origin*." But **Philip C. Wander** recognized the affiliation of these studies, citing them all in his manifesto-flavored, field-denominating "**The Rhetoric of Science**" as the advance guard of an emerging movement, and it is from this paper that we can most naturally trace the disciplinary appearance of the field.

Rhetoric of science, the disciplinary colligation that unfolded an umbrella over a gath-ering of diverse critical works and theoretical speculations, was born of all the currents we have charted—the booming hegemony of science in public discourse and academic hierarchies, the creeping dread of nuclear technoscience, the patriotic fervor over NASA, the new historico-philosophical picture of science, and the growing critical capacious-ness of rhetoric—but the immediate exigence was somewhat more mundane, a political squabble in Wander's Speech Communication department at San Jose State University. "Meeting after meeting, day after day, year after year," Wander recalls, "I faced argu-ments based on 'science'" (Wander and Jaehne, 2000:214; see Paul Newell Campbell's article for similar concerns about the penetration of science into Communication departments in the same period, though his methodological concerns are more directly ethical—this volume, 56-58). In the early 1970s, Wander snapped. Wander realized that the arguments were largely appealing to a façade, began reading the history and philo-sophy of science, subscribed to the *Bulletin of the Atomic Scientists*, and drew it all together into "The Rhetoric of Science."

Unlike P. N. Campbell's casual assumption that rhetorical vocabularies were suffi-cient for the analysis of science, Wander argues the point in a way that coalesces the developing themes and shifting scholarship of the period. His principal exigence arises naturally out of Cold War topoi that rippled through the disciplinary discourses over the preceding decades, the ones we have seen in Geiger, Clark, Bryant, and McKeon: the hegemonic power of science, the fading presence of the humanities, and the related perils of a fact/value separation. "Science and all that it represents," Wander says, "stands at the center of our civilization" (this volume, 68), with a rhetoric that runs both broad and deep. Broadly, on every deliberative issue of any significance, "science, scientists, and the vocabulary of science shape the debate" (this volume, 62). Deeply, there is no principled separation of the structures of information and the structures of persuasion in scientific texts, even those as typified and fact-crammed as experimental reports. On breadth, rhetoricians are therefore obliged to engage technoscience, so that it doesn't overwhelm and submerge considerations of moral value. On depth, none of the workings of science are in principle unavailable to rhetorical analysis, since the fundamental nature of knowing is rhetorical, "the product of an evolving set of human agreements" (this volume, 62).

There is an undercurrent of suspicion in Wander, too. He gives considerable airtime to arguments that scientific rhetoric is deceptive, inbred, and intentionally opaque—traits which imperil public deliberation, and therefore imperil the public. He quotes Atomic Energy Commission attorney, Harold P. Green, on decisions about "whether certain technological goals are so worth pursuing that its members must pay the price of exposure to radiation and noise, loss of privacy, and tampering with the weather." Such decisions should be open and available but instead "are made within small, closed circles of specialists on the basis of their expert judgments and predictions of the magnitude of the social consequences and the feasibility of their being controlled through technological means" (this volume, 69).

Wander makes oddly, but revealingly, extensive use of an essay by Sociologist Andrew Weigert, "The Immoral Rhetoric of Scientific Sociology" (1970): *odd*, because it runs at cross-purposes with the approach to rhetoric that informs the bulk of Wander's paper; *revealing*, because it indexes one motivation behind the rhetoric of science movement, the omnipresent spread of technoscience. Weigert's paper participates in a microgenre of articles at the time that condemned rhetoric, in its pejorative ordinary-language sense, as a kind of distorting overlay on some purer notion of expression characteristic of science and technology—as they truly are, or would be if they could rid themselves of bad actors and slippery words (see also Douglas 1971, Cox and Roland 1973).[8] Weigert's essay is a polemic against his fellow sociologists. *Rhetoric of science* is his term for a stylistic layer of fake precision and authority over unworthy arguments, coming in a range of subtypes that include the Imperialistic Rhetoric of Theory, the Magical Rhetoric of Methodology, the Pedigree Rhetoric of Underground References, the Janus-Faced Rhetoric of Valiability (a neologism blending *validity* and *reliability*), and the grandpappy of them all, the Soteriological Rhetoric of Science—that is, a salvationist terminology: the wanton use of the vocabulary of science by sinful sociologists trying to talk their way into economic and professional heaven. Your sociologist is, after all, "a profit-seeking individual, a salaried professional" contending "within a stratified professional hierarchy with known criteria for advancement and recognition" (1970:117), criteria that hinge on an "immoral rhetoric of identity deception" (1970:111): pretending to be a scientist.

Ray Lynn Anderson puts his finger on the central factor in this notion of immorality in an important contemporary essay on science journalism. He sees the popularization of science, in the relentless cheerleading of the period, as perpetuating a dangerous ideology of progress, hero worship, and imminent bounty, beyond question or critique. This ideology calls forth "a rhetoric that lives incognito, that is persistently confounded for something other than it actually is;" a rhetoric that is, therefore, "almost by definition degenerate" (Anderson 1970b:367–368).

It is this context to which **Herbert W. Simons** responds with his "**Are Scientists Rhetors in Disguise?**"—to a "rhetoric of science literature" endemically "vituperative in [its] characterizations of scientific discourse" (this volume, 71), and his *disguise* brings along the familiar ordinary-language implications of subterfuge, misrepresentation, and manipulation. But he comes to cleanse the intersection of rhetoric and science, to make room for a theoretically informed and salutary rhetoric of science, by way of a staged forensic episode.[9] With or without the vituperation, of course, it is not surprising to find motifs of disguise and deception around the rhetorical investigation of science: the primary stylistic obligation of rhetorical activity in the most proto-typical scientific texts, arguments by scientists and for scientists, is to erase itself. As it is for rhetorical activity in all domains, "the function of [rhetorical activity in science] is the successful persuasion of readers," as Bruno Latour and Steve Woolgar put it in a highly influential and neighborly book that came out the year before Simons's exercise, "but the readers are only fully convinced when all sources of persuasion seem to have disappeared" (Latour and Woolgar 1986 [1979]:76).

Simons's argument for the prosecution of scientific deception is "that scientists are guilty of such allegedly sophistic practices as using a vocabulary of legitimating motives to mask self-serving motives or promoting partisan values in the guise of being informative"—chasing grants and institutional authority and personal aggrandizement; that is, they are "motivated [to use rhetoric] by greed, power, envy, or the need for recognition." (this volume, 72). The defense paints such motives as isolated personal weaknesses. Science itself, in the collective abstract, has no such foibles: "scientific communities as a whole maintain appropriate institutionalized commitments to the pursuit of knowledge." (this volume, 72) Simons is not just prosecutor and defender, however. He is also judge and jury.

Simons's essay sorts through foundational issues in a *dissoi-logoi* structure over the stasis of jurisdiction, and the various witnesses he deposes, including Kuhn and Burke, are worth hearing on the nature of science and the relevance of rhetoric. But the verdict he returns—spoiler alert!—is wider than jurisdiction, including definition and quality. He rules in favor of reconciliation, rather than giving a zero-sum should-it-stay-or-should-it-go judgment. Simons endorses the very idea of a rhetoric of science, but of a particular, rather conservative sort, with an assistive rather than a collaborative role. Qualitatively, he advocates rhetoric adopt "a perspective 'friendly' to science," in order to remedy the vituperation. Further, he asks rhetoricians to take on the active policing of science, protecting it against sophistically disguised violations of its ethics, becoming "defenders of its time-honored norms" (this volume, 82).

You will not be surprised to hear, however, that—in a community of rhetoricians—the case was not settled with Simons's trial. Two decades later, we can still find **Leah Ceccarelli** arguing not only for Simons's friendly version of the field, but for the very viability of the field, in "**Rhetorical Criticism and the Rhetoric of Science**." And lo, once again, up rises the specter of deception.

Ceccarelli confronts the recurrent challenges to the viability of rhetorical contributions science studies since Wander's essay, tabulating them in three columns: the recalcitrance of nature, the perfect homogeneity of scientists, and the irrelevance of the individual. All of these challenges play throughout the essays in this book, in various configurations. Ceccarelli gives us an excellent way to keep score. The first column of challenges argues that nature exerts such overpowering constraints on scientific activity as to make negligible; any rhetorical quotient one might extract from the odd text the second argues that scientists operate within a kind of fully synchronized hive mind, an "exegetical equality" of such uniformity that it traffics only in the pure communication of facts, through a pristine language of numbers and semantic essences, a purity that gives persuasion no purchase; and the third suggests that the institutions of science do all the work of invention—the technologies, the rarefied mathematics, the regimes of certification—to the point where humans, the entities for whom suasion plays a role, are less relevant than equations, or beakers, or oscillating waveforms on a seismograph. I won't spoil the suspense of Ceccarelli's answers to these challenges, but the moral of her story is too important to wait, and one that all rhetoricians would do well to embroider onto the underwear of our research, so it doesn't get lost. The force of her argument is ultimately more centrifugal than centripetal—more about how the investigation of science can inform rhetoric than about how rhetoric can inform the investigation of science—and it hinges on our reputation for deceit.

"When people outside our discipline come to recognize that rhetorical criticism is concerned not just with the deceptive nature of words but with the complex relationship between the discursive and the non-discursive," she tells us, "they will have less reason to dismiss the rhetorical study as distasteful or insignificant." Accordingly, here is our job: "to publicize rhetorical criticism as a study of the *connection* between words and substance (or between words and action), rather than celebrating rhetorical criticism as a study of the all-powerful words that fabricate reality" (this volume, 88). OK, maybe that's too many words to embroider on underwear, so let me distill them: "connection, not deception."

With Ceccarelli's essay, too, even though she is pushed to contest challenges over the very viability of rhetorical analyses of science, we can see clearly a maturing field; her commentary and citations reveal a large, if factious and censured, community of rhetorical critics and theorists probing science. While the other stases continued to roil in the literature—what *is* the rhetoric of science? How deep/big/thick is the rhetoric of science? Do the methods of rhetoric really have legitimate access to the practices and products of science?—the stasis of fact had been settled. There was a rhetoric of science; well, more reasonably, rhetorics of science.

Through Thick and Thin

You know, it's been said that rhetoric of science is nothing more than a bunch of covert neo-Aristotelians blowing hot air.

—Gordon Mitchell
(in Hansen and Michaels 2000 [1998]:131)

The roiling stases have continued to be as inseparable as they were at the emergence of the field; in particular, the debates always implicate jurisdiction in some way, with definition and quality tangled in: sure, there's a rhetoric of science, but there might as well not be, since rhetoric isn't very big, doesn't go very deep, isn't thick enough; of course, there's a rhetoric of science, and it is the paradigm case for how big/deep/thick rhetoric is, epistemically, culturally, even ontologically. Big Rhetoric, which Edward Schiappa defines as "the theoretical position that everything, or virtually everything, can be described as 'rhetorical'" (2001:260) shows up under various names in the literature, including the *globalism* or *universalism* of rhetoric, but it is Dilip Parameshwar Gaonkar who gave the roil around this position in rhetoric of science its key term in a long, closely argued, highly influential and profoundly ornery essay, "The Idea of Rhetoric in the Rhetoric of Science" (1997 [1993]). He called the critical capacities of rhetoric *thin*, too abstract and insubstantial to be of any use in understanding science (or very much else).

An early exchange in the journal *Rhetorica* lined up these two positions against one another, thin rhetoric vs. thick, though the terms were not yet in circulation. **J. E. ("Ted") McGuire** and **Trevor Melia**, offering **"Some Cautionary Strictures on the Writing of the Rhetoric of Science,"** simply use the term *rhetoric* with default thinness, pitting it against what they term *rampant rhetoricism* in one place (this volume, 101), *suicidal rhetoric* in another (this volume, 102); that is, rhetoric which has run amok among the sciences with such unsustainable recklessness that it will necessarily blow out its lungs and collapse of its own pretentions. The argument is involved and forceful, building on the intuitive toe-stubbing realness of reality, the resilience of mathematico-scientific descriptions, and the agent-removal apparatus of objectivity in the methods of science (hitting all the columns in Ceccarelli's table of challenges). How could we navigate the oceans if the stars were not stubbornly real, if our math-enwrapped descriptions of them were not predictively accurate, if our procedures of measuring, testing, and encoding the intertwined facts of the stars were not distilled to a pristine essence, the vagaries and individualities of the measurers and testers vaporized away from the reach of mere rhetoric? While McGuire and Melia pose these questions *to* rhetoricians, they do not appear to be reacting to any claims directly *from* rhetoricians, certainly not to any rhetoricians actively plying their trade investigating science. Their strictures are directed, rather, at some abstract and vulnerable class of rhetoricians who might be led into temptation by exogenous scholars drumming a libertine rhetoric of science—Richard Rorty, coiner of the phrase *Rhetorical Turn* for science studies and social epistemology; a now somewhat quaint-sounding topical cluster from 1950s and 1960s, Kuhn, Feyerabend, Imre Lakatos, N. R. (Norwood) Hanson, and Michael Polanyi; and especially the splashy contemporaneous duo of Bruno Latour and Steve Woolgar, whose *Laboratory Life* (1986 [1979]) we have already heard from, describing science as fundamentally suasive. McGuire and Melia make their argument overwhelmingly against Latour and Woolgar's "imperialistic and to some extent impertinent" program, dangerous for its reduction of the facts of the world and the accounts of science to textual inscriptions susceptible to even a thin of rhetorical vocabulary (this volume, 103).

There actually was a small but concrete class of rhetoricians at the time highly tempted by Latour, Woolgar, and the social constructivism of Strong Programme sociology—most prominently represented by Charles Bazerman and Greg Myers—but it was **Alan G. Gross** who briskly stepped to the head of the class, with his deliberative response, "**Rhetoric of Science Without Constraints**." The gauge of Gross's rhetoric is not just thick, but globally, universally, utterly thick. Gross raises the banner for a "radical rhetoric of science" (this volume, 120) and urges the rhetorical polis to war. He calls for "an all-out rhetorical assault on the great variety of scientific 'texts'—papers, proceedings, notebooks, laboratory conversations" (111), astutely mapping out its strategies with re-analyses of McGuire and Melia's evidentiary cases. "[C]elestial navigation," he argues for instance, "undermines, rather than supports," their claim for a facticity beyond rhetoric because there have been multiple incompatible accounts of those facts (114). Those accounts, rhetorical constructions the lot of them, can all get you from point A to point B. But most of them, perhaps all of them, are false in their explanation of how they do it. Whatever constraints stubborn phenomena may exert on science, they don't put it beyond the reach of rhetoric.

What the McGuire and Melia/Gross exchange illustrates more than anything is the insecurity of the emerging field, seeking justification, issues, and approval, from more established science studies disciplines. There are large intellectual issues at stake in the exchange, chiefly the three R's—Relativism, Realism, and Rationality—too large, it would seem to the debaters, for anyone else practicing that other R, Rhetoric. As in McGuire and Melia's essay, no rhetoricians of science can be found in Gross's essay either (well, except for one; Gross gives himself a citation; otherwise, it's philosophers, sociologists, and historians all the way down). "[T]he rhetoric of science is in its infancy," Melia had noted a few years earlier, "and the majority in the philosophy of science continue to take a dim view of the undertaking" (1984:312). McGuire and Melia follow the deferential mode of a constrained rhetoric of science to overcome that dim view; not Gross. Gross follows the take-no-prisoner's mode of a rhetoric without constraints. Not only did he step to the head of the class, he set about defining it. The specific response to McGuire and Melia was effectively a primer for his *The Rhetoric of Science*, notorious for the soon-sloganized observation that science is "rhetoric without remainder" (1996 [1990]:33).

That slogan got the most airtime in and around the Gaonkar Perturbations, a polylogic episode heavily implicating Gross and occupying much of the rhetoric of science issues-and-methods bandwidth in the 1990s, into the 2000s, from whence the specific too-thin-for-science accusation arose. Gaonkar's campaign begins with his "Rhetoric and its Double: Reflections on the Rhetorical Turn in the Human Sciences" (1990), centered on his "The Idea of Rhetoric in the Rhetoric of Science" (1997 [1993]), and, rounding out his thinness triptych, is tied up with a ribbon in his "Close Readings of the Third Kind: A Reply to My Critics" (1997; see also 1993). They were not kindly papers. When Gordon Mitchell said that people were going around calling rhetoricians of science a pack of neoAristotelian blowhards, he could have had Gaonkar in mind. Much additional ink was spilled, many pixels lit, many voices raised.[10] The Gaonkarian hubbub was so voluble that Gross—whose name now appears in almost every remaining paragraph of this introduction, so ubiquitous and multifarious has he become—called for "a reflective moment" along with co-conspirator, Laura Gurak: "a discursive pause in the onrush of critical activity" (2005:241). The proposal was welcomed by a range of rhetoric-of-science scholars, and a baker's dozen of them joined Gross and Gurak between the covers of a special issue of *Technical Communication Quarterly*, long a friend to rhetoric of science. They all took their moments to look back at the crush of arguments over the previous decades, and to propose routes forward.

There were calls for serious rhetorical attention to scientific visuals, which had hitherto suffered neglect in rhetoric of science; for the development of tools and frameworks for studying the impact of the internet, just beginning to reshape scientific rhetoric, along with everything else; for increased reception studies, which needed more consistency and rigor; for more flexible stylistics, the incorporation of organizational rhetoric, a richer interdisciplinarity, and the deployment of specific methodologies (genetic criticism, Foucauldian analyses). It is an important volume, coming at an important time. But **James H. Collier's** contribution stands out as quite different from the rest. His "**Rhetoric of Science and Technology: Knowing In and About the World**" calls for prolonging Gross and Gurak's critical-activity pause and broadening their urge for disciplinary self-reflection—the whole paper adopting a decidedly Gaonkarian groove. In fact, we can trace a rather curious trajectory in the suspicion of Big Rhetoric most closely associated with Gaonkar's prosecution of rhetoric of science, a trajectory from Melia (1984), through the three essays of Gaonkar, to Collier's arguments. Curious, because the trajectory is a chiastic inversion: Melia wants rhetoricians to curb their rhetoric-of-science philosophizing and adopt an empirical campaign of case studies; Collier wants rhetoricians to stop proliferating case studies and pursue a deliberative campaign of philosophical soul searching.

Collier sees case studies, which were indeed burgeoning by the early 2000s, as a particularly unfortunate way of procrastinating from the hard, necessary work of interrogating our role in science studies overall, the legitimacy of our Big Rhetoric warrants, and, especially, the soundness of a science/technology demarcation. In many ways, Collier seems not to have paid much real attention to the discipline, which had been preoccupied with these questions from the beginning, which had just come through a stretch where they appeared to be almost all anyone was talking about, which had produced the special issue in which his essay appeared, full of paused musings of the sort Collier urges, and whose case studies almost ritualistically include big-picture considerations of their implications for rhetorical theories and their place in science studies generally. But Collier's critique, and his exhortations, are important. Case studies had partially fulfilled Melia's hope for them by the early 2000s, bringing legitimacy to rhetoric of science. But they brought institutional and professional legitimacy, case studies being so well suited to graduate programs, dissertation production, professorial replication, and journal population—less so, intellectual legitimacy, particularly as measured by the silence with which they were greeted in history, and philosophy, and sociology of science. Collectively, they lacked coherence. Case studies had piled up, not stacked up.[11]

Like most of the essays in the Gross–Gurak (2005) collection, Collier's articulates developments already underway in the field, more than plotting a unique new course, but he does three things that gives his essay landmark status. First, he efficiently represents the important reflective pause of the collection. Second, he epitomizes the censures of the madly-running-off-in-all-directions ethos of the case-study approach that had set off the winter of Gaonkar's discontent. Third, by repeatedly stressing that the relevant field was not Rhetoric of Science but Rhetoric of Science and Technology, he signals a shift away from rhetorical studies of individual scientists or contained episodes toward more general issues of technoscience, a shift that brought with it a growing critical presence of materialism. And, while the field overall did not particularly need to be urged toward reflection, Collier's essay serves to urge each individual researcher to interrogate their fit with the rhetorical tradition and their contribution to science studies.

David J. Depew and **John Lyne's** essay juxtaposes nicely with Collier's, offering a clear and bracing counterpoint, if not quite an antidote, to Collier's (and Gaonkar's) disdain for rhetoric-of-science case studies. "**The Productivity of Scientific Rhetoric**" surveys the field, in a theoretically informed and explicitly evaluative way, returning a robust and sanguine account of our progress. They are not a pair of Pollyannas, Depew and Lyne, blithely ignoring inconsistencies and contradictory tensions. Rhetoric of science "studies do not follow a single program or share a specific agenda," they acknowledge. "Rhetoric is opportunistic and unruly, and we cast our nets where we think the fishing is good" (this volume, 131). But they map out the way studies have clustered around variously rich fishing grounds, such as stylistic and materialist approaches, examinations of expertise and ethos, and the roles of genres and visuals—all of which have presence in our Methods essays. They sort through Collier's piles and produce cogent stacks of case studies.

As a capstone essay in the Issues section of this book, we could do no better than a theoretically imbued analysis of Alan G. Gross's career, particularly one which interrogates the meaning of *rhetoric* in his particular uses of the phrase *rhetoric of science*. **Nathan Crick** gives us precisely this interrogation in his "**When We Can't Wait on Truth: The Nature of Rhetoric in the Rhetoric of Science**," which examines the thick/thin continuum by close attention to the overlapping careers of two towering figures in our field, Alan G. Gross and Alan G. Gross; that is, Gross 1.0 and Gross 2.0.[12] Gross 1.0 is the guy we have already heard from, the free-wheeling, rhetoric-without-remainder respondent to McGuire and Melia. He argued that a full-blooded, radical rhetoric of science must be disproved, that it had presumption on its side. Within the decade, he came to feel that the burden of proof had been met by the opposite side, especially in the arguments of Gaonkar. He did something rare and heroic in scholarship. He changed his stripes, and we get Gross 2.0, epistemically far more cautious and rhetorically far less committed than Gross 1.0, someone much more likely to be a coauthor with McGuire and Melia than their respondent. Crick's essay, too, complements Collier's piece well, since it follows Gross's career-long exercise in exactly the activities Collier urges, the careful, philosophical inquiry into how rhetoric of science participates in the rhetorical tradition, on the one hand, and contributes to the interdisciplinary field of Science Studies, on the other. But Crick is not merely filing a clinical report, the autopsy of one bifurcated rhetorician's unique program of self-dialectics. Crick is a meticulous thinker in his own right, and in some ways Gross serves more as an occasion than as a topic in the essay. Crick delivers a sophisticated probing of rhetoric's intersection with science, especially by the light of analytic philosophy, tracking Willard Van Orman Quine's thought in Gross's shifting framework.

Methods

> Rhetoric is method, not subject.
>
> —Donald C. Bryant (1953:406)

Two books, a year apart, helped establish rhetoric of science as a field, both of them with titles comprised almost entirely of that phrase, but otherwise quite different. Those differences flag two strains of subsequent research. One book was ethotically modest, and perhaps for that reason is now unfortunately somewhat neglected, but advocates a thick and deep rhetorical program. The other book's ethos is considerably more brash, quickly became notorious, has been much reworked, extending to a refracted and retitled third edition. Its rhetorical program is thinner and much broader. One, you will not be surprised to hear at this point in our chronicle, is by Alan G. Gross, the brash one, *The Rhetoric of Science* (1996 [1990]; see also 2006). The other is Lawrence J. Prelli's *A Rhetoric of Science* (1989).

Rhetoric is a field both with a long and rich tradition of methods for interrogating symbolic action and with an anxious opportunism to augment and even displace those methods with the latest developments in other fields. To the extent that the former of these tendencies dominates in works of theory or criticism, an emphasis on the tradition, leveraging the ancients, it is Neoclassical. An emphasis on externally derived approaches, borrowing from the neighbors, is Neomodern. Prelli is the prophet of Neoclassical rhetoric of science. A Neoclassical approach is "rooted in the rhetorical theory of antiquity" (Mohrmann and Leff 1974:459), and *A Rhetoric of Science* brims with stases and topoi, ethos and invention, presumption and burden of proof, instruments that were either first developed in antiquity or developed in scholarship with unbroken allegiances to that antiquity. Gross is the prophet of Neomodern rhetoric of science. A Neomodern approach (I coined the term myself; you're welcome) is an approach that leverages the instruments of other, invariably more recent, disciplines.[13] *The Rhetoric of Science* deploys social philosopher Jürgen Habermas's theory of Communicative Action, itself an adaptation of Speech Act Theory, cultural anthropologist Victor Turner's social drama framework, analytic philosopher W. V. O. Quine's linguistic epistemology, sociologist Robert K. Merton's work on the emergence and disciplining of social norms, a flock of philosophers on flavors of realism. Gross draws heavily from a contingent he terms "relevant modern thinkers." But when he singles out a few of those thinkers (Propp, Freud, Habermas, Husserl), even though, as I have heard tell, there are a few relevant modern rhetoricians (Richards, Burke, Weaver, McKeon, Ong), none of them show up in the list of people to whom we should turn for renovation (1996 [1990]:19–20).[14]

There are dangers in both Neos, classical and modern, illustrated by our two exempla. Prelli's book can often seem sluggish with fidelity to the ancients; Gross's, fickle in the pursuit of intellectual fads. Prelli's can seem blindly pious in its post-hoc translation of all descriptions into rhetorical terminology, even what has been already analyzed perfectly well in another disciplinary idiom; Gross's, skittishly inconstant in its avoidance of rhetorical categories when another disciplinary idiom flashes a smile. Dominance-submission games of some order, therefore, are inevitable. Either rhetoric comes off as Master of the Universe (er, an architectonic art), or as subservient to another field. But there are manifold virtues in both directions as well, equally well illustrated by our two exempla. Prelli's book demonstrates as clearly as anyone the thickness of rhetorical vocabulary for critically probing science; Gross's, the value of supplementing that vocabulary with those fashioned through more immediate contact with science. All of our essays in this section emulate the best of these two landmark monographs.

Neoclassical

> If rhetoric is not sovereign within its own house, but must await certification … then the project of a rhetoric of science is groundless.
>
> —John Angus Campbell and Keith R. Benson (1996:77)

What Melia called "Kuhn's invitation" to rhetoric of science (1984:303) was a compelling narrative of sciences moving through cycles of development that seemed beyond the reach of traditional science studies—a process of growth and renewal, if not exactly of progress, that irresistibly implicated rhetoric. He named it: "That process is persuasion" (Kuhn 2012 [1962]:200). The most dramatic moments in the narrative, and therefore the most invitational ones, were the revolutions, moments in which everything hung on a shifting structure of appeals. For rhetoricians, Kuhn might as well have labeled his invitation, "**Rhetoric, Topoi, and Scientific Revolutions**," but he didn't, leaving that title for **Kenneth S. Zagacki** and **William Keith's** landmark essay. They take their lead most expressly from Prelli's work on the topical logic of science, but they move easily through philosophy as well, and masterfully integrate the existing rhetorical literature. Their goal is to build a general framework that brings together the various emerging rhetoric-of-science threads, and idioi topoi give them a finer-grained tool to examine the lines of persuasion in revolutionary argumentation than anything available in Kuhn's own work. They find something rather surprising. The driving topos in episodes of scientific discontinuity, a kind of super-topos, is in fact the maintenance of continuity, a wide commitment that sponsors epideictic appeals to epistemic progress. Whatever appearance an immediate disruption may have, the argumentation seeks to render it temporary and ultimately compatible with an overall scientific project of advancing knowledge that builds on previous discoveries and insights.

Carolyn R. Miller's essay, "*Kairos* **in the Rhetoric of Science**," is a double landmark, a masterwork that is a notable advance in rhetoric of science and in rhetorical criticism at large. James Kinneavy's influential 1986 essay, "*Kairos*," required the subtitle, "A Neglected Concept in Classical Rhetoric," reintroducing the long overlooked notion of the 'opportune moment,' the idea that circumstances must be right for rhetoric to be effective. It's a commonsense notion, but despite a central presence in the ancient world, up through to the Renaissance, kairos had mostly faded away into theology by the twentieth century. When Kinneavy began talking about it, everyone could see its importance, but he deployed it largely in a pedagogical mode. That kairos has now become so central to the methodology of rhetoric criticism traces to Miller's use of it in this essay. She "transformed kairos," as Gross put it, "into a contemporary term of art" (1996 [1990]:xxii).

Back home, in rhetoric of science, Miller's essay is a jewel, a model of careful argumentation that takes up the paradigm case of James Watson and Francis Crick's (1953) "A Structure for Deoxyribose Nucleic Acid," overturning much of the conventional rhetorical wisdom around that famous paper's success (Bazerman 1988:18–48, Gross 1996 [1990]:54–65, Prelli 1989:236–255, Halloran 2018 [1984]). S. Michael Halloran, most notably, had argued that the stylistic features of Watson and Crick's paper sparked the birth of molecular biology, over another paper, one with a seemingly stronger claim (Avery et al. 1944). Oswald Avery and his co-workers had experimentally demonstrated, to a high order of certainty, that DNA was the molecular vehicle responsible for genetic transmission almost ten years before Watson and Crick's paper. But, Halloran argues, that their very different ethotic framing (plodding, cautious, against the brash, ambitious style of Watson and Crick) had precluded it from the field-creating role that Watson and Crick fulfilled. Miller reads both papers carefully against their historical circumstances and redraws the rhetorical map of the birth of molecular biology around the different moments of publication. If Avery et al.'s paper was premature, Watson and Crick's paper was overdue. Traditional philosophy of science had no sense of time, transcendent notions of rationality and logic ruling the day. That disregard lifted with the historical approach that precipitated the rhetorical turn, but it took Miller, with kairos, to find the perfect temporal probe for scientific argumentation.

When Miller published her essay, the field was still young enough that most papers wore their allegiances in their titles, one or the other or both of the words *rhetoric* and *science* making titular appearances. By the time **Jeanne Fahnestock's** essay appeared, **"Figures of Argument,"** there was much less need to justify, or defend, or advertise these allegiances. The field was now so well established that one might almost call Fahnestock's paper "accidental rhetoric of science." The phrase doesn't even appear in her essay, in part because it is hunting primarily in another deer park, in argumentation studies. The essay appeared in the journal, *Informal Logic*, a version of Fahnestock's keynote address to The Uses of Argument conference, in Hamilton, Ontario. But it just so happens to draw all of its extensive and closely examined examples from science, a rather good source of argumentation. It's a wonderful essay, elegant and compelling, but Fahnestock's real landmark, for rhetoric of science, for argumentation studies, for stylistics, and, hence, for rhetoric overall, is her groundbreaking *Rhetorical Figures in Scientific Argumentation* (1999) with its program of Figural Logic. But we couldn't include the book, so we settle on this exemplary piece. It illustrates Fahnestock's program to perfection, perhaps the most important Neoclassical methodology in the rhetoric of the twenty-first century—an argumentational conspiracy of topical invention, cognition, and rationality in terms of those ancient stylistics crystals known as *rhetorical figures*.

Early strains in rhetoric of science, as Simons's essay reminds us (see also Harris 2018 [1997]:7), were rife with themes of suspicion, accusation, and reduction; the hegemony of science in all aspects of cultural, political, and academic life provoking a humanities-fueled comeuppance. That motive quickly faded to neutrality, and its inverse, what Simons calls a *friendly* strain, is now much more common. **Gordon R. Mitchell's** contribution to this volume manifests that strain in a rather unique way. Mostly friendliness in rhetoric of science is still linked in some way to the 'energizing truth' role (Geiger 1958:54), seen, for instance, in Ceccarelli's proposal that "there are ... times when the rhetorical critic should be prepared to develop scholarly insights that can be turned to the defense of a scientific orthodoxy" (2018 [2011]:163). Mitchell, rather, turns the ancient method of dissoi logoi toward scientific decision making, in his **"Switch-Side Debating Meets Demand-Driven Rhetoric of Science."** The methodology is straightforward: pit skilled debaters against each other on either side of open scientific questions, especially those implicated by deliberative policy formation, explicitly arguing against their own convictions, forcing them to inhabit the opposing side. The rhetorical data of the exchange is then mined for lines of reasoning that can improve understanding and lead to better decision making. The method has its dangers—in fact, precisely those dangers that Ceccarelli warns about in her "Manufactured Scientific Controversy" (2018 [2011]), the dangers of denying orthodox consensus by staging debates about intelligent design or the value of vaccinations, making it appear that very well established claims are on shaky and broadly contested ground rather than being targeted by a tiny ideological, or financially motivated contingent.[15] In fact, Mitchell's involvement in one such debate, over anthropogenic climate change, fits Ceccarelli's notion of a 'manufactured controversy' rather well (Hansen and Michaels 2000 [1998]). But the crucial notion in "demand-driven rhetoric of science" for Mitchell is *demand*, which he requires be interrogated. The basic notion is that "institutional actors seek enlistment of rhetoric's expertise to tackle technical problems" (this volume, 224), but Mitchell calls for an examination of what is "driving the demand"—ideology? Economics? Threats to life, well-being, or the environment?—"before embracing invitations to contribute ... argumentative expertise to deliberative projects" (this volume, 229).[16]

Lynda Walsh and **Kenneth C. Walker** take up the same issues of uncertainty and deliberation that fuel Mitchell's work, but their Neoclassical tool is ethos, a preoccupation in rhetoric of science from its first academic moments. Even when it is unnamed (as in Simons's essay, which his title reveals is about the ethotic 'disguises' adopted by scientists) or when it is otherwise named (as in P. N. Campbell's *persona*), ethos maintains a robust presence. Still, in their **"Uncertainty, Spheres of Argument, and the Transgressive Ethos of the Science Adviser,"** Walsh and Walker have a fresh take. They revisit the conflicts of facts and values that always attend public-sphere debates implicating science, exploding a model that regards levels of certainty as somehow transitive, increased scientific certainty sponsoring increased certainty of political action, centering their analysis masterfully on the precarious performance of technoscientific expertise in a role complicated by the requirement for policy expertise.

Neomodern

Looking beyond the Classical canon, there are many ways to assemble a rhetoric.

—Lynda Walsh
(in Walsh et al. 2017:414)

Disciplines are like languages. If a new substance enters the ontology that some language manages—say, spongy blocks of coagulated soy milk enter the English-managed culinary ontology of North America—it insists on signification in that language. The most common source for a signifier is a language already managing an ontology with that substance—say, Japanese. So, English borrows *tofu*. If a new concept enters a discipline—say, a system of undifferentiated nodes in a network of relations, a way of wholly flattening the differences among humans, animals, plants, machines, objects, inert substances, and whatever else might occupy a node in the network—it insists on signification in that discipline. Most commonly, a signifier (frequently, in fact, a clutch of concepts with their signifiers) is borrowed from a theory already managing that concept—say, Actor Network Theory. So, rhetoric borrows *actant*, a concept that forces attention on the materiality of symbol users and their products, while affording egalitarian influence to the 'purely' material.

Of course, disciplines and languages invariably get their borrowings 'wrong,' in that they deviate from their original shapes and relations in various ways. The middle consonant of the word we represent as *tofu*, for instance, is pronounced in a way alien to English speakers in the original Japanese (it's a bilabial fricative, sort of like a cross between a 'w' and an 's'; take the initial mouth shape of 'w' and rush the air through it with 's'-like force, and you're maybe half the way there). So, we do our best (pronouncing instead our native labiodental fricative, forcing air through a constriction formed by the top lip on bottom teeth). It sounds wrong to a Japanese speaker, but by assimilating it to our well-oiled, pre-existing system of phonology, we give it a chance to work in a new key. We habituate it. Actant is a notion antipathetic to agency, in the traditional sense of manifesting intentionality, but rhetoric is suffused with such agency. Rhetoricians natively assume that (within the constraints and affordances of genre, particular audience expectations, communal standards of argument, available symbolic resources, and so on) rhetors are primarily agents of their rhetoric.[17] Rhetoricians also natively assume that rhetoric distributes, rather than removes, agency—conventionally, for instance, through such devices as anthropomorphism, personification, prosopopoeia, and apostrophe, but also materially through such devices as beakers, telescopes, and hadron colliders. A rhetoric of science, therefore, is often concerned (as Gross says of Darwin) with showing how scientific arguments persuade by creating "a world in which plants and animals have been brought to life, ... and made to illustrate and generate evolutionary theory" (2006:56–57). So, we habituate *actant*, assimilate it to our well-oiled, pre-existing system of analysis, give it a chance to do its work in a new key.

Neomodern rhetoric is a species of criticism that imports and habituates valuable concepts and perspectives from other disciplines. Actant is such a concept, habituated in this section of our book by Mehlenbacher and Maddalena; materiality is such a perspective, habituated in this section by those same authors as well as by Condit. Rhetorical theory, however, is such a shamelessly eager adopter of instruments from other disciplinary frameworks that its boundaries can evaporate, like someone who loves tofu so much, and udon noodles, they move to Japan; they'll still have an accent, but they will increasingly approximate the natives in their talk and action. Rhetoric's urge to adopt also leads us to work with friends and neighbors, interdisciplinarily, like someone who loves tofu and udon noodles, but also Boston beans and corn-on-the-cob, so much that they open a fusion restaurant with a Japanese friend. There's nothing wrong with either approach if it produces good results, and much especially to recommend working with friends and neighbors, but this particular collection is anchored solidly in the rhetorical tradition, so we turn, in spirit, to Leah Ceccarelli. She is our rhetoric-of-science Diogenes, taking her lantern from study to study, argument to argument, peering in and asking "Where's the Rhetoric?" (Ceccarelli 2014). If its not there, and guiding the analysis, however good the essay, you'll need to look for it in a different book.

Xiaosui Xiao's contribution to this volume challenges Ceccarelli's question at the outset, in provocative ways that mark several important departures from the rhetoric-of-science tradition. It fits comfortably into two major and longstanding themes of the field, the rhetorical negotiations between religion and science, and the accommodation of scientific claims into popular culture, but it dramatically refracts another longstanding theme. We might even call that third theme the seminal theme of our field, supplied by Kuhn, the reluctant father—rhetorical charting of revolutions. Xiao's "**The 1923 Scientistic Campaign and Dao-Discourse: A Cross-Cultural Study of the Rhetoric of Science**" looks at quite a different sort of revolution, not the jockeying between two scientific framings of specific phenomena (light, stars, matter, life), but the contention between two very broad cultural worldviews, ultimately won by the west's "omnipotent concept of science" (this volume, 256). In the end, the question of its rhetorical quotient is easy to answer: top to bottom, the essay charts a suasive campaign. But it studiously avoids the technical terminology of rhetoric, not by replacing it with the vocabulary of another discipline, but by seeking the common ground of daily usage: *audience, argument, appeal,* ultimately even *persuasion,* have their ordinary-language senses, without any associated technical apparatus. On first blush, this might seem to eliminate Xiao's essay as a methodological template. But it both represents an approach once very common in rhetorical studies, holding closely to the vernacular, and makes a crucial political point. On the second basis alone—never mind the subtle astuteness of its analysis—it qualifies for inclusion in this book.

Vernacular usage has major liabilities, of course, chiefly a lack of precision, but in the context of cross-cultural rhetoric it carries political weight. Xiao's essay is almost completely isolated in its cross-cultural dimensions, signaling an unfortunate but illuminating gap in the rhetoric of science literature.[18] The gap is unfortunate because it leaves our picture of technoscience and society insularly ethnocentric, at a time when the technologies entangled with science, and our relentless appetites for them, threaten everyone on our planet. The gap is illuminating because it reveals the insular ethnocentricity of rhetoric itself, a discipline that arose in the west and is inextricably bound not just with the education and administration of the west, and therefore with its science and technology, but also, inevitably, with its vicious, technologically fueled imperialist crushing of other worldviews and its obliteration of their peoples. "No word is innocent," Françoise Thom has said (1989:28), but not all of them are as guilty as the terms of rhetoric.

Still.

Rhetoric provides one lengthy and tested, extended and calibrated, disciplinary vocabulary of universal affinities and dispositions that manifest in all symbol systems. In this book, these affinities and dispositions are best represented by Fahnestock's compelling argument that certain linguistic arrangements conform to neurocognitive grooves, in particular the universal semiotic groove of iconicity, and that reasoning itself may rest substantially on pattern completion (this volume, 211). Antithesis, for instance, condenses contrastive and oppositional lines of reasoning (this volume, 211). *Antithesis* is among the technical term Xiao avoids in "The 1923 Scientistic Campaign," but he shows how fundamental the paradoxical expressions of the Dao were in opening Chinese culture to science. The figures, tropes, and topoi of the rhetorical tradition, with or without their cumbersome Greek and Latin labels—more mangled in our pronunciations than *tofu*—are powerful instruments of suasion and judgment; therefore, powerful instruments in the analysis of suasion and judgment. Lynda Walsh has called for rhetorical engagement with such non-western epistemic practices as "Australian Aboriginal and Polynesian ecologies, Arabic biology, Diné physics, Chinese medicine, Aztec–Mayan algorithmic calculation, and West African astronomy" (2018). These engagements would continue the cross-cultural project Xiao has initiated, which can only further test and calibrate rhetoric as critical tool for probing technoscience, and be the source of methodological innovations.

Moving down to smaller contests than Xiao's scientistic campaign, **Craig O. Stewart** provides a remarkably promising approach in his amalgamation of rhetoric and sociolinguistics, "**Socioscientific Controversies: A Theoretical and Methodological Framework.**" Steward blends G. Thomas Goodnight's influential argument-spheres model (also well represented elsewhere in this volume—Walsh and Walker, Ceccarelli, Depew and Lyne) with Norman Fairclough's more broadly influential critical discourse analysis. What Fairclough brings to the party is a sensitivity to the ideological dimensions of language. Rhetoric of science has always been quite good at tracking linguistic shifts as the claims of science move from genre to genre, sphere to sphere, but this tracking has predominantly been of veridicality and certitude, not of critical discourse analysis's stock in trade, power relations. Stewart's model maps bodies of discourse as they merge, pull apart, and mutually influence each other. It holds special potential, I believe, for the increasing multimodality of rhetorical transactions. Stewart's own analysis only extends digitally as far as blogs, which were just becoming politically and culturally influential at the time of publication—so, before microblogging had been heard of, before Facebook, before Instagram, before reddit—but the methodology is very well suited to the dynamic, ongoing, participatory intertextuality of the internet.

If there is one methodological approach that most characterizes the critical approaches of contemporary rhetoric, and not just in the study of technoscience, it is materialism, what is often called *new materialism* to set itself against earlier Marxist variants (though in the way it is practiced it has much in common with Kenneth Burke's pretty old dramatistic materialism, in which scenes and agencies are integral to currents of suasions and ideologies). **Celeste M. Condit** thoroughly habituates materialism to rhetoric, as many others do not, in her brilliant "**Race and Genetics from a Modal Materialist Perspective.**" The complication with other recent importations of materialism to rhetoric is that their reduction to the wholly physical effaces rhetoric—kairos, the pisteis, invention, topoi. That's not a bad thing in and of itself. Reductionism is a powerful way of isolating forces and phenomena one would otherwise miss. But it's not rhetoric. Language is material—dancing molecules in the air, marks on pages and cereal boxes, electronic signals in wires, digital signals in fibers, lights on screens—and its effects need to be understood as material effects, but not *only* as material effects. Language is also biological—waving cilia, activated photoreceptors, neurochemical firing patterns. Its effects include organic effects. And it is symbolic—representational, typified, value-laden, arbitrary, and motivated. Its effects include symbolic effects. Condit's materialist methodology incorporates biological and symbolic modes, and she illustrates the critical power of her framework in a penetrating account of racist hierarchies circulating through specialist and popular science. She shows how revealing material and biological vocabularies are for understanding discursive effects, but also how powerless they are for understanding values and ideologies, and therefore such consequential constructs as race and gender.

There are several authors included in this collection who, but for space considerations, could easily have multiple essays in the book, who have contributed more than one landmark to issues and methods in rhetoric of science (Celeste M. Condit, Jeanne Fahnestock, Carolyn R. Miller). But with **Alan G. Gross** a double inclusion is inevitable, and not just because, as we have heard, there are at least two Alan G. Grosses. He has repeatedly blazed new paths for us to follow, and stirred up hornets' nests to get the field buzzing. If there was a Rhetoric-of-Science Mount Rushmore, his head would be in George Washington's spot, highest, most prominent, at the front. As early as 1983, Gross realized the utter centrality of graphics for technoscientific texts, and his *The Rhetoric of Science* includes a section on visuals (1996 [1990]:74–80; see also 35–38), but he was aware these treatments were heavily logocentric and somewhat ad hoc. Rhetoric had no theory for a crucial mode of argument and suasion in science. So, with his frequent collaborator, Joseph E. Harmon, he built one (2013). "**Presence as a Consequence of Verbal-Visual Interaction: A Theoretical Approach**" compactly articulates that model, a dual-coding model, in light of Chaïm Perelman and Lucie Olbrecht-Tyteca's notion of presence (1969 [1958]:115–120 *et passim*). The codes are dual because language and images are different modalities, perceived and processed differently, but in scientific texts especially, these perceptions and processes are co-present and mutually informative, as well as combinatorically suasive. Gross's framework draws on the semiotics of the man who begins this collection, Charles Sanders Peirce, in concert with Gestalt psychology and Allan Paivio's Dual Coding Theory. On the linguistic side, his approach is largely traditional—ethos, pathos, logos; invention, arrangement, style; dialectical tools of definition and classification; logical inference and induction. Gross synthesizes them all into a new and rigorous methodology for rhetoric of science to address a decades-old need; ho-hum, just another one of Gross's habitual *tours de force*.

Our collection ends with another impressive mash-up, **Ashley Rose Mehlenbacher** and **Kate Maddalena's** essay, "**Networks, Genres, and Complex Wholes: Citizen Science and How We Act Together through Typified Text.**"[19] Just articulating the threads is exhausting, though most of them are conveniently represented in the title. The *networks* evokes Actor Network Theory, the influential framework that comes out of collaborations by Michel Callon, Bruno Latour, and others. Among other critical moves, it involves 'flattening' the analytic ontology, a euphemism for eliminating agency; or, in this case, setting agency aside for key parts of the investigation, not unlike Condit in her essay. This procedure works so well in science studies because it sets up an explanatory matrix in which all influences are equal, the imagined and professed ideal of scientists, who systematically represent their research not as the product of invention but as the inevitable consequence of data, of logical and mathematical regimes, of the ontological bias for simplicity, and so on, routinely and ritualistically denying their own agency. Scientists love to erase themselves, configuring scientific phenomena as happening almost in spite of the humans who seem accidentally to be standing around next to the oscilloscopes and coincidentally recording them, perhaps out of boredom. The stylistic effects of the erasures present such phenomena as Baconian events forcing conclusions on audiences by way of passivized, nominalized, agentless texts. Even research implicating humans strives to erase them, dissolving people into interpenetrating clusters of symptoms, prognoses, and regimes of treatment.

The *genres* evokes Rhetorical Genre Theory, an approach to conventional assemblages of language and other symbols that sees them as outcomes of social action. A genre in this sense is a recurrent pattern of response to social needs—for entertainment, for catharsis, for political information, for exhibiting data, airing speculations, and building radio telescopes. There are a *lot* of such patterns in the discourse of science, more almost every day. It was not entirely true when Maguire and Melia said it, that there are "only three main genres or literary forms through which science presents itself for publication" (this volume, 106), but it was certainly tru*er* then, before the internet, than it is now. Rhetorical Genre Theory is a natural tool for the rhetorical investigation of science because it fits scientific discourse very well, and it doesn't hurt that its prime architect is a rhetoric of science luminary, Carolyn R. Miller.

The *complex wholes* evokes Annemarie Mol's (2003) notion that objects of all sorts, from books to bodies are both Gestalts, entities whose whole transcends the collectivity of its parts, and assemblages, with parts and subsystems that are not simply the constituents of that Gestalt, but Gestalts of their own, transcendent assemblages; and, at different levels of configuration (what Burke would call circumferences) operating in multiple other wholes. Mol's paradigm case is the human body, which is a whole, transcendent object but also assembled out of other wholes—organs, glands, systems, cells, with their own constituents and multiple interactions. The *citizen science* comes from a new style of science (at least new in scale), in which non-scientists, quasi-scientists, retired scientists from other fields—a citizenry—participates in the collection, partial processing, and channeling of data in a large project. Wander's article is partly motivated by the "the rise of the expert and the decline of the citizen" (this volume, 63); these developments, one hopes, signal the return of the citizen. The *typified text* takes us back to Rhetorical Genre Theory, the form taken by recurrent social action. In the bargain, we have the overall flavor of new materialism, the presence of ontologies, and the necessary implication of the internet, the primary rhetorical locus of citizen science. I may have missed one or two fruits in their Neomodern rhetoric-of-science cornucopia, but Mehlenbacher and Maddalena bring them together with aplomb in an illustrative account of the networked, social-action, citizen-science response to the Fukushima Daiichi nuclear disaster. All in all, a comprehensive round-up of so many themes and concepts that enliven contemporary rhetoric of science that a better exemplum to close this section would be hard to imagine.

Conclusion

> The scientist cannot escape choices, whether he is addressing other scientists or a popular audience. His decisions are anchored in contexts governed by rules, conventions, and practices, whether they be those of the scientist or those of the non-scientist public.
>
> —Karl R. Wallace (1963:242)

OK, you got me. There really is only one issue in rhetoric of science. Lots of methods, but only one issue: how deep does rhetoric go? Nobody, not even Gaonkar, certainly no scientist with a moment to reflect on it, believes that everything associated with science takes place in a rhetoric-free zone, that no stylistic choices are ever made, that no audiences are ever considered, that no typified formations are ever utilized. Nobody, not even Gross 1.0, certainly no rhetorician with a moment to reflect on it, believes that everything associated with science is exhaustively accounted for with a rhetorical vocabulary, that no physical forces operate on physical objects when our backs are turned, that no stars blink, no waves wash ashore, no glands secrete without symbols and inscriptions. Materialists, for instance, who spend their time "strategically overlooking" symbols and inscriptions to find the rhetoric of mute stuff (Mehlenbacher and Maddalena, this volume, 350), know that there is something in that stuff besides rhetoric. One can hold that science is rhetoric "without remainder," that you can't find anything scientists do such that some rhetorical quotient is present, that it can never be wholly 'removed,' and equally hold that there is something else present. One can describe every aspect of a human body in a vocabulary of cells. That doesn't mean one can't describe its operations through the language of mechanics, or the language of motives. Everything apparently can be described in the language of mathematics. Everything can be assigned numbers and run through equations. But to say everything is quantifiable does not mean everything is only its quantity. There is no degree-zero rhetoric of science, nor a degree-infinite rhetoric of science.

So, the first two sections of our book are explorations of different areas on the scale of rhetoric's involvement in science, the implications of one area versus another, the constraints or affordances that warrant one area versus another, the cultural or epistemic value of the claims that can be made from one area versus another. But there are lots of methods to deploy in those areas. My own commitment is that rhetoric reaches all the way down in science (though not that it would be alone if and when it gets to the bottom), that rhetoric is big. I trust this is not a surprise. So, allow me one more argument and we can be on our way.

The chief complaint about Big-ass Rhetoric—that is, the Biggest Rhetoric, which "is everywhere, [which] saturates human activity" (Black 1997:23)—is that it renders the phrase *Rhetoric of X*, for any *X*, tautological; hence, empty. But here's the thing: whatever logicians choose to do with tautologies, they are *not* empty. In the vocabulary of logic tautologies may add nothing of value: *A is X* is always true if *X* entails *A*. But if one uses the phrase "dogs are mammals" in a sixth-grade science class, *mammal* is adding something of value when it is predicated of *dogs*. The kids, at least the budding scientists among them, will want to know why dogs are mammals. What properties do they have that make them mammals? Even such rudimentary tautologies as *X is X* do something in language, add meaning and understanding. "Boys will be boys," for instance, is always deployed to explain (or, more often, excuse) the activities of males (not always boys), for some physical or symbolic action on the premise of allegedly intrinsic boy-qualities—recklessness, crudeness, libidinousness. Or, take this one:

$$x + y = y + x$$

Move along folks. Nothing to see here, nothing new … except that the very form of the equation is an axiom, declaring that order is irrelevant when you add the same quantities, whatever those quantities might be.

How does the critique play out specifically as an issue in rhetoric of science? "If everything is rhetoric/rhetorical," a clutch of science pundits tell us, some of them represented in this book, "then it is neither informative nor interesting [to] be told that a practice/discourse/institution is rhetorical. *Si omnia, nulla* [if everything, nothing]" (Keith et al. 1999:331). But it is only uninformative or uninteresting if you're apathetic, or looking out the window, or playing with the hair of the girl at the desk in front of you. Try saying "science is rhetorical" to a sixth-grade English class, as I have, and you will hear, from budding humanists and budding scientists both, "*How* is science rhetorical?" "What properties does it have that makes it rhetorical?" "What difference does it make that science is rhetorical?" That's when the methods come out, and you show them how ethos and style and genre and ontology formations shape the way science flows through culture and constructs our possible futures.[20]

To say there is a Rhetoric of X is to claim that suasion, context, intention, style, structure, character, and affect are present in X, that X is a domain of humans and their symbols. It is not to say that there are no other vocabularies that explain dimensions of X, that there is no Logic of X, no Grammar of X, no Sociology of X, no Psychology of X, and so on. What rhetoricians of X show is the relevance of suasion for the cultural influence of X. Rhetoricians of science, between the covers of their two *Landmark* volumes, and well beyond those covers, have very impressively met that burden.

But this book—hearken ye rhetoricians of all stripes—goes further. It says not just that we can certify this particular, massively significant, pervasive, and ineluctable X, science, in a *rhetoric-of* colligation. This book, in our introductory overview and especially in the arrayed arguments collected over the following pages, along with our *Case Studies* companion (Harris 2018 [1997]), says that rhetoric of science has consistently since its emergence been the most innovative, productive, vigorous engine of theory and criticism in the field. The hermeneutics-in-the-age-of-technoscience debates, with their epistemic and ontological implications, go to the very heart of the rhetorical enterprise, its past and its future. Rhetorical Genre Theory, which has become easily the most widely adopted approach to textual dynamics, grows directly out of S. Michael Halloran's program in rhetoric of science and technology (Miller 1980). The richest critical articulation of that theory is Charles Bazerman's *Shaping Written Knowledge* (1988), the chronicle of a defining scientific genre, the experimental article; Gross, Harmon, and Reidy's *Communicating Science* (2002) also charts that story, upping both the empirical and linguistic sophistication. We know, too, that the architect of Rhetorical Genre

Theory, Carolyn R. Miller, shows up on the Neoclassical side of the rhetorical-methods ledger as well, with her highly influential critical application of kairos to the birth of molecular biology (Miller, this volume [1992]). Stylistics has been wholly reinvigorated and redefined by Jeanne Fahnestock's program of Figural Logic, brilliantly deployed first on scientific argumentation (1999; this volume [2013]). Celeste Condit's (1999) *Meanings of the Gene* may be the most exquisitely balanced amalgam of quantitative and qualitative analyses our discipline has seen. Alan G. Gross and Joseph E. Harmon's *Science from Sight to Insight* plots the way for a truly integrated rhetoric of text and image (2013; Gross, this volume [2009]). No approach has done more to investigate the reciprocal impacts of the internet on discursive formations, discursive formations on the internet, than rhetoric of science (Gross & Buehl 2015; Gross and Harmon 2016; Wynn 2017; Mehlenbacher 2019). All of these issues and methods, and more, arise from rhetoric of science. None are confined to rhetoric of science.

And—hearken ye sociologists, historians, and philosophers of science, ye science and technology scholars and students of all stripes—there's more. It is not just that there exist rhetorical vantages on this massively significant, pervasive, and ineluctable X, science. It's that these vantages generate insights not directly available to you in your home fields. The textual patterns of social action opened by Rhetorical Genre Theory, the stylistics of argumentation revealed by Figural Logic, the discursively mediated, internet-fueled rise of citizen science, the rhetorical constitution of realism and relativism, and all points between, the relentless traffic in suasions of the people, materials, and symbols that constitute technoscience in all its terror and glory; these, are a few steps away. Your fields, all of them, underwent a renovating rhetorical turn as the full implications of Kuhn's (but not only Kuhn's) work rippled through them. But, lazily content to work with general or impressionistic or second-hand notions, few of you actually turned to rhetoric. Hearken: it's not too late.

A Note on the Texts and Citations

The essays have been lightly edited to correct, modernize, or increase consistency with respect to minor issues of punctuation, spelling, and typography. We have largely retained the original citation styles of the essays, although again with occasional edits to correct errors or increase consistency where required. The URL citations have all been verified (as of 1 August 2019). Nonfunctional links in the original publications have either been updated or noted as broken.

Notes

1 The phrase "Rhetoric of *X*" was apparently coined in Robbins (1990:106), but came to play a role in debates over rhetoric of science (Gaonkar 1997 [1993]:75–76, who gives a list of such 23 such *X*'s, followed by "and so on"; Schiappa 2001:260; Collier this volume 123, 125). See Booth (2004:34–38) for a (non-derisive) list of some of the *X*'s named here; for others, see Hexter (1967; *history*), Kehl (1975; *advertising*), Friedman (1966; *logic*), D'Angelo (1974, *graffiti*), Burke (1969 [1950]; *motives*). At the 1970 Wingspread Conference on the Prospects of Rhetoric, there was an active call for an expansion of the range of artifacts for rhetoric to examine (Sloan[e] 1971).

2 While this introduction refers occasionally to the disciplinary origins of rhetoric of science, and several of our essays give helpful epitomes as well, there is no attempt in this book to give a comprehensive account of those origins. You can find a relatively full chronicle in my introduction to the companion volume, *Landmark Essays on Rhetoric of Science: Case Studies* (Harris 2018 [1997]:2–19).

3 For Burke see, in particular, "Semantic and Poetic Meaning" (1941 [1939]:138–168), for Kuhn, "Possible Worlds in History of Science" (2000 [1989]:58–89)—though Burke's entire career is obsessed with the symbolic action of terminologies and Kuhn elaborated on lexicons in multiple places after settling on them in the 1980s as the solution to the totalizing action of scientific frameworks and their mutual resultant incompatibilities (AKA 'incommensurability').

4 I don't know McKeon's career well enough to speak with any authority about stages or shifts in position, but his early remarks seem to be in the 'energizing truth' mode of rhetoric's relation to science. At other points, he sees rhetoric as implicated more deeply into scientific activity. The "scientific method itself," he says, "has borrowed now from the language of rhetoric, now from the terms of dialectic, and now from the principles of apodictic logic" (1945:283), and even seems to endorse Mill's rhetoric-as-epistemic approach to science: "the practical use of the free interplay of opposed arguments on the example of the theoretic use of the methods of rhetoric to advance toward truth in the natural sciences" (1956: 152). See Depew (2010) for an account of McKeon in relation to rhetoric of science. Depew notes, in particular, McKeon's influence on Lawrence Prelli and on the important Rhetoric of Inquiry project, and has a decidedly epistemic take on "Uses of Rhetoric."

5 The term, *Big Rhetoric*, in rhetoric of science polemics is courtesy of Deirdre McCloskey (1997), though it seems to have been coined by John McVitty in his 1991 thesis, where he offers a set of useful divisions with respect to the trivium: big grammar and little grammar, big rhetoric and little rhetoric, big dialectic and little dialectic (1991:224). Edward Schiappa (2001) provides the best account of its relation to rhetorical theory in the final decades of the twentieth century, particularly its contestations, in which rhetoric of science plays a very prominent role.

6 The essay was published, with an introduction and commentary by John Michael Krois, in *Philosophy and Rhetoric* (Peirce 1978 [1904]).

7 Peirce is not an unambiguous read. His terminological inconsistency over the sweep of his dense and involuted writings can be challenging, not the least with his treatment of rhetoric, which minimally implicates the following suite of terms: *speculative rhetoric, general rhetoric, universal rhetoric, pure rhetoric, formal rhetoric,* and *methodeutic,* which Lyne (1980) treats more or less as synonyms for the global project of understanding the universal principles of semiotic effectiveness; as well as *ordinary rhetorics,* which are localized to genres, registers, dialects, languages, and other individuated semiotic systems. Gava (2018) offers a more itemized account of Peirce's rhetorical system, in which methodeutic is the subdivision of speculative rhetoric concerned with science, though he is frank that "Peirce's ... considerations on rhetoric often sound more like programmatic proposals than like detailed analyses of the subject" (2018:222).

8 The phenomenon has not gone away. The most egregious example of which I am aware is Staponkuté (2013), "Resisting the Rhetoric of Science," an article utterly oblivious to the entire field (no citations to anyone in the discipline—by which I mean the field of rhetoric, not just rhetoric of science—and no invocation of any relevant topic or theme). It celebrates the work of two particular authors, Alphonso Lingis and William Gibson, for providing a counterforce to the hyper-rationality of scientific writing (which is what she means by *rhetoric*

of science). Rhetoric and *science* are both construed in very naive ways; no scientists are cited either, by the way. Such an article would be unfortunate enough in its own right, but the fact that it is published in a special issue devoted to rhetoric of science is atrocious (Freddi et al., 2013).

9 While his mission is an important one in the history of the field—reasserting the technical sense of *rhetoric* and staking claim for the rhetorical analysis of science in the context of this emerging *rhetoric*-as-derogative literature—and while the essay was widely influential, Simons unnecessarily marched into battle alone. He appears to have been unaware of the more salutary movement that was developing around rhetorical analyses of science. He does not cite Wander, Zappen, Anderson, either of the Campbells, or affine work such as Stephens (1975), Gusfield (1976), Finocchiaro (1977), Overington (1977), or Weimer (1977). In fact, only one rhetorician shows up in his rhetoric-of-science roll call, Jeanine Czubaroff (1974), whom he lumps in with the vituperative authors. He has her quite wrong. Czubaroff's essay is a salutary early account of rhetorical expertise formation, with a good account of ridicule as a strategy for policing the field and a well-developed exemplum featuring Noam Chomsky and B. F. Skinner; its tone and aims and disciplinary understandings are very different from those of Weigert and Douglas. Simons also includes Berger and Luckmann (1966) and Szasz (1969), different yet again, but certainly implicating rhetoric in the sciences. Kelso (1980) also takes Weigert and Douglas to be allies in the rhetoric-of-science project. One essay seemingly overlooked by everyone in this context was Richard Weaver's (1959) "Concealed Rhetoric in Scientistic Sociology," which is a more richly informed and more broadly thoughtful critique of sociology's scientific posture.

10 "The Idea of Rhetoric" easily ranks among the landmarks in the issues and methods of rhetoric of science, certainly the most cited and discussed essay of the 1990s. But it is, first, very long, and, since his argument is principally that the case-study approach to rhetoric of science has revealed its intellectual bankruptcy, much of the essay is taken up with Gaonkar's charges against individual rhetoricians of science (J. A. Campbell, Gross, and Prelli). But expurgating the essay would be unjust. Second, though, its significance is not solely, perhaps not even primarily, because of its arguments, so much as because of the responses it generated. So, beyond its own page-gobbling bulk, it would have been misrepresentative to include it without also bringing along a few of those responses, and then, to be fair, we would owe Gaonkar a chance to respond to the responses, requiring the inclusion of "Close Readings" and then, *ipso facto*, we would end up with a book of essays solely concerned with the alleged thinness of rhetoric of science, which would amount to putting new covers on *Rhetorical Hermeneutics: Invention and Interpretation in the Age of Science* (Gross and Keith 1997). If you haven't read that book, do. It is compulsory reading for any rhetorician with a serious interest in science or in the scope of rhetoric overall. If you *have* read it, you will see many connections in this volume. Gaonkar's charges get some direct airing in this book (most notably in the essay by Collier, but also in the ones by Ceccarelli and Crick), but more interestingly they are foreshadowed rather fully in the McGuire and Melia essay. Gaonkar's critique, in fact, was written "as a token of affection to Trevor Melia," Gaonkar's teacher (1997 [1993]:78), and takes its explicit lead from one of Melia's earlier essays (Gaonkar 1997 [1993]:45; see Melia 1984); even the characterization of rhetorical analysis as "thin" may have originated with Melia (1992:103). In turn, the Gross essay we include in this section anticipates the tenor of most responses to Gaonkar's "Idea." I give an overview of the Gaonkar Perturbations in Harris (2018 [1997]:18–19).

11 The terms here are from Gross (1991:35), though he uses them somewhat in reverse. Calling case studies "the lingua franca of rhetoric of science," he expresses hope that they will cease piling up and begin stacking up. See Collier (this volume, 126).

12 Alan G. Gross, a scholar whose courage of convictions I greatly admire while strongly rejecting some of those convictions, has two major career iterations, manifesting a shift in what
Perelman and Olbrecht-Tyteca (1969:232), after Heinz Pächter, would call his *hierarchy of
values.* There was a notable drop in his commitment to the explanatory capacity of rhetoric in
that hierarchy, in reaction to Gaonkar's assault on the field, which included several specific
beefs with Gross's work in particular. See the special issue of *Poroi* (Beard and Newman 2014)
on the 25th anniversary of Gross's *The Rhetoric of Science* (1996 [1990]) for much discussion
of this shift (one article of which we include here, our Crick essay). My own contribution to
that issue introduced the formalized conceit of superscripts to represent two idealized versions
of Gross's different value hierarchies, two different implied authors (i.e., *Gross[1]* and *Gross[2]*;
Harris 2014). I regard my new formalization of the conceit (i.e., *Gross 1.0* and *Gross 2.0*) as an
improvement because it allows for designating variations of implied authors with regard to
those value distinctions (i.e., the possibility of such creatures as Gross 1.8 and Gross 2.1). We
will, of course, refer to the original creature, Alan G. Gross, throughout this book, without
numeric classifiers unless explicitly referencing his relation to these values.

13 Well, I coined the term and then discovered what I should have predicted, that others had
coined it for other purposes—in theology, in architecture, in futurist studies—each use quite
different from the last. In rhetoric and related symbolic studies, to the best of my knowledge,
it hasn't appeared yet, so I hereby stake my claim.

14 These are tendencies. Both books are ecumenical. Prelli makes good use of a few exogenous
scholars, especially Robert K. Merton, and Gross is certainly not bereft of rhetoric, anchoring
his variegated criticism spiritually in "the first Sophistic" (1996 [1990]:3). But they look in
decidedly different directions, Prelli into the rooms of the rhetorical tradition, Gross out the
windows at the neighbors. That the contrast between these two landmarks is more dramatic
than this brief overview might suggest is best revealed by contrasting this quotation from the
beginning of Prelli's book with Gross's famous without-remainder remark: "I do not intend
to argue that everything in science is rhetorical, without remainder" (Prelli 1989:8). I have no
direct evidence that Gross, who must have read this line, coined his phrase in deliberate
opposition, but there is the circumstantial evidence of Gross's mischievousness. Gross 2.0, by
the way, is even more Neomodern, and certainly less radical, than Gross 1.0: *Starring the Text*
(Gross 2006), while retaining many of the analyses that ground the arguments of *The Rhetoric
of Science*, avoids the sophists and has a correspondingly less constitutive role for rhetoric; see
Harris 2014, Crick in this volume.

15 See also Fuller's (2013) challenges to Ceccarelli's position and her (2013) reply to Fuller.

16 Ceccarelli's "Manufacturing" was published a year after Mitchell's "Switch-Side" paper, but
does not notice it; nor does Mitchell notice Ceccarelli's position, though it was available in
earlier versions to which he had access (Ceccarelli 2006, 2010, the latter appearing in proceedings that Mitchell edited). He does, however, reference what he calls Ceccarelli's (2005) "dim
picture regarding the potential of the rhetoric of science for scholarly and policy impact" that
his method aims to ameliorate (this volume, 239n59). The Hansen and Michaels (2000
[1998]) debate, by the way, was decidedly not a switch-side debate.

17 Gaonkar, in a phrase that is no doubt meant to sting, certainly to trouble, terms this commitment an "ideology of human agency" (1997 [1993]:33), a phrase that has caught on, largely in
discussions of postmodern and posthuman positions in rhetoric. See Geisler (2004) for a rich
discussion.

18 I am aware of only one other essay that fits Xiao's "cross-cultural rhetoric of science" category,
Marcus Paroske's (2009) treatment of AIDS policies in South Africa. Indeed, Paroske includes

the phrase "Intercultural Rhetoric of Science" among the keywords for his article; ten years later, that phrase gets exactly two hits on Google Scholar: Paroske (2009) and the dissertation which undergirds it. "Cross-cultural rhetoric of science" gets no hits at all, and separating the terms out, just gets lots of hits where they coincidentally show up together, not designating a category in any way. See Condit's (2013) "Mind the Gaps" for an account of the "internationalism-blind approach" (2013:5) that characterizes rhetoric of science, and an urgent appeal to take off the blinders.

19 This essay was originally published under Mehlenbacher's former name, *Kelly*.

20 I also address the *si omnia nulla* complaint, using somewhat different terms, in Harris (2002:173–177).

References

Anderson, Ray Lynn. 1970a. The rhetoric of the *Report from Iron Mountain. Speech Monographs* 37:219–231.

Anderson, Ray Lynn. 1970b. Rhetoric and science journalism. *Quarterly Journal of Speech* 56.4:358–368.

Aristotle of Stagira. 1991. *On rhetoric: A theory of civic discourse.* Translated by George A. Kennedy. New York: Oxford University Press.

Avery, O. T., C. M. Macleod, and M. McCarty. 1944. Studies on the chemical nature of the substance inducing transformation of pneumococcal types: Induction of transformation by a desoxyribonucleic acid fraction isolated from pneumococcus type III. *The Journal of Experimental Medicine* 79.2:137–158.

Bazerman, Charles. 1988. *Shaping written knowledge: The genre and activity of the experimental article in science.* Madison: University of Wisconsin Press.

Beard, David E., and Sara Newman, eds. 2014. Special issue: Honoring Alan Gross—rhetorician of science. *Poroi* 9.2.

Berger, Peter L., and Thomas Luckmann. 1966. *The social construction of reality: A treatise in the sociology of knowledge.* Garden City, NY: Anchor.

Berra, Yogi. 1998. *The Yogi book.* New York: Workman Publishing.

Bitzer, Lloyd. 1997. Rhetoric's prospects: Past and future. *Making and unmaking the prospects of rhetoric.* Edited by Theresa Enos. Mahwah, NJ: Lawrence Erlbaum, 15–20.

Black, Edwin. 1997. The prospect of rhetoric: Twenty-five years later. *Making and unmaking the prospects of rhetoric.* Edited by Theresa Enos. Mahwah, NJ: Lawrence Erlbaum, 21–28.

Booth, Wayne C. 2004. *The rhetoric of rhetoric: The quest for effective communication.* Oxford: Blackwell.

Brown, William R., and Richard E. Crable. 1973. Industry, mass magazines, and the ecology issue. *Quarterly Journal of Speech* 59:259–272.

Bryant, Donald C. 1953. Rhetoric: Its functions and its scope. *Quarterly Journal of Speech* 39.4:401–424.

Bryant, Donald C. 1956. Whither the humanities? *Quarterly Journal of Speech* 42.4:363–366.

Burke, Kenneth. 1941 Four master tropes. *The Kenyon Review* 3.4:421-438.

Burke, Kenneth. 1941 [1939]. *Philosophy of literary form: Studies in symbolic action.* Baton Rouge: Louisiana State University Press.

Burke, Kenneth. 1962. What are the signs of what?: A theory of "entitlement." *Anthropological Linguistics* 4.6:1–23.

Burke, Kenneth. 1969 [1950]. *A rhetoric of motives.* Berkeley, CA: University of California Press.

Campbell, John Angus. 1975. The polemical Mr. Darwin. *Quarterly Journal of Speech* 61:375–390.

Campbell, John Angus. 2018 [1987]. Charles Darwin: Rhetorician of science. *Landmark essays on rhetoric of science: Case studies*. Second edition. Edited by Randy Allen Harris. London: Routledge, 45–58.

Campbell, John Angus, and Keith R. Benson. 1996. The rhetorical turn in science studies. *Quarterly Journal of Speech* 82: 74–109.

Campbell, Paul Newell. 1973. Poetic-rhetorical, philosophical, and scientific discourse. *Philosophy & Rhetoric* 6.1:1–29.

Ceccarelli, Leah. 2005. A hard look at ourselves: A reception study of rhetoric of science. *Technical Communication Quarterly* 14:257–265.

Ceccarelli, Leah. 2006. ISSA [International Society for the Study of Argumentation] Proceedings 2006—Creating controversy about science and technology. *Rosenberg Quarterly*. http://rozenbergquarterly.com/issa-proceedings-2006-creating-controversy-about-science-and-technology/

Ceccarelli, Leah. 2010. ISSA [International Society for the Study of Argumentation] Proceedings 2010—Controversy over uncertainty: Argumentation scholarship and public debate about science. *Rosenberg Quarterly*. http://rozenbergquarterly.com/issa-proceedings-2010-controversy-over-uncertainty-argumentation-scholarship-and-public-debate-about-science/

Ceccarelli, Leah. 2013. Controversy over manufactured scientific controversy: A rejoinder to Fuller. *Rhetoric & Public Affairs* 16.4:761–766.

Ceccarelli, Leah. 2014. Where's the rhetoric? Broader impacts in collaborative research. *Poroi* 10.1: Article 12. https://doi.org/10.13008/2151-2957.1182.

Ceccarelli, Leah. 2018 [2011]. Manufactured scientific controversy: Science, rhetoric, and public debate. *Landmark essays on rhetoric of science: Case studies*. Second edition. Edited by Randy Allen Harris. London: Routledge, 160–184.

Clark, Donald Lemen. 1950. The place of rhetoric in a liberal education. *Quarterly Journal of Speech* 36.3:291–295.

Condit, Celeste M. 1996. How bad science stays that way: Brain sex, demarcation, and the status of truth in the rhetoric of science. *Rhetoric Society Quarterly* 26.4:83–109.

Condit, Celeste M. 1999. *The meanings of the gene: Public debates about human heredity*. Maddison, WI: University of Wisconsin Press.

Condit, Celeste M. 2013. Mind the gaps: Hidden purposes and missing internationalism in scholarship on the rhetoric of science and technology in public discourse. *Poroi* 9.1: Article 3.

Cox, Barbara G., and Charles G. Roland. 1973. How rhetoric confuses scientific issues. *IEEE Transactions on Professional Communication* PC-16.3 (Sept), 140–142.

Czubaroff, Jeanine. 1974. Intellectual respectability: A rhetorical problem. *Quarterly Journal of Speech* 60.2:155–164.

D'Angelo, F. 1974. Sacred cows make great hamburgers: The rhetoric of graffiti. *College Composition and Communication* 25.2:173–180.

Depew, David J. 2010. Revisiting Richard McKeon's architectonic rhetoric: A response to "The uses of rhetoric in a technological age: Architectonic productive arts." *Reengaging the prospects of rhetoric: Current conversations and contemporary challenges*. Edited by Mark J. Porrovecchio. New York: Routledge, 37–56.

Douglas, Jack. 1971. The rhetoric of science and the origins of statistical social thought. *The phenomena of sociology*. Edited by Edward A. Tiryakian. New York: Appleton-Century-Crofts, 44–57.

Espenshade, A. Howry. 1904. *The essentials of composition and rhetoric.* Boston: D. C. Heath & co.

Fahnestock, Jeanne. 1999. *Rhetorical figures in science.* New York: Oxford University Press.

Fahnestock, Jeanne. 2004. Preserving the figure: Consistency in the presentation of scientific arguments. *Written Communication* 21.1:6–31.

Feyerabend, Paul K. 1981. *Realism, rationalism and scientific method, Philosophical papers* 1. Cambridge: Cambridge University Press.

Finocchiaro, M. A. 1977. Logic and rhetoric in Lavoisier's sealed note: Toward a rhetoric of science. *Philosophy and Rhetoric* 10:111–122.

Freddi, Maria, Barbara Korte, and Josef Schmied, eds. 2013. Special issue on Rhetoric of Science. *European Journal of English Studies* 17.3.

Friedman, N. 1966. The rhetoric of logic. *The Journal of General Education* 17.4:287–294.

Fuller, Steve. 2013. Manufactured scientific consensus: A reply to Ceccarelli. *Rhetoric & Public Affairs* 16.4:753–760.

Gaonkar, Dilip Parameshwar. 1990. Rhetoric and its double: Reflections on the rhetorical turn in the human sciences. Edited by H. W. Simons. *The rhetorical turn: Invention and persuasiveness in the conduct of inquiry.* Chicago: University of Chicago Press, 341–366.

Gaonkar, Dilip Parameshwar. 1993. The revival of rhetoric, the new rhetoric, and the rhetorical turn: Some distinctions. *Informal Logic* 15.1:53–64.

Gaonkar, Dilip Parameshwar. 1997 [1993]. The idea of rhetoric in the rhetoric of science. Edited by A. G. Gross and W. Keith. *Rhetorical hermeneutics: Invention and interpretation in the age of science.* Albany: SUNY Press, 25–85.

Gaonkar, Dilip Parameshwar. 1997. Close readings of the third kind: A reply to my critics. Edited by A. G. Gross and W. Keith. *Rhetorical hermeneutics: Invention and interpretation in the age of science.* Albany: SUNY Press, 330–357.

Gava, Gabriele. 2018. Peirce's "Ideas, stray or stolen, about scientific writing" and the relationship between methodeutic, speculative rhetoric, and the universal art of rhetoric. *Semiotica* 220:221–234.

Don Geiger, 1958. Rhetoric and science: Notes for a distinction. *Communication Education* 7.1:54–60.

Geisler, Cheryl. 2004. How ought we to understand the concept of rhetorical agency? Report from the ARS. *Rhetoric Society Quarterly* 34.3:9–17.

Graham, S. Scott, and Carl Herndl. 2013. Multiple ontologies in pain management: Toward a postplural rhetoric of science. *Technical Communication Quarterly* 22.2:103–125.

Gross, Alan G. 1983. A primer on tables and figures. *Journal of Technical Writing and Communication* 13.1:33–55.

Gross, Alan G. 1991. Response to Harris. *Rhetoric Society Quarterly* 21.4:35–36.

Gross, Alan G. 1996 [1990]. *The rhetoric of science.* Second edition. Cambridge, MA: Harvard University Press.

Gross, Alan G. 2006. *Starring the text: The place of rhetoric in science studies* [Originally published under the title *The rhetoric of science*, Harvard University Press, 1990; second edition, 1996]. Carbondale: Southern Illinois University Press.

Gross, Alan G., and Jonathan Buehl, eds. 2017. *Science and the internet: Communicating knowledge in a digital age.* London: Taylor and Francis.

Gross, Alan G., and Joseph E. Harmon. 2016. *The internet revolution in the sciences and humanities.* New York: Oxford University Press.

Gross, Alan G., and Joseph E. Harmon. 2013. *Science from sight to insight: How scientists illustrate meaning.* Chicago: Chicago University Press.

Gross, Alan G., Joseph E. Harmon, and Michael S. Reidy. 2002. *Communicating science: From the 17th century to the present.* New York: Oxford University Press.

Gross, Alan G., and Laura J. Gurak. 2005. Guest editor's introduction. *Technical Communication Quarterly* 14.3:241-248.

Gross, Alan G., and William M. Keith, eds. 1997. *Rhetorical hermeneutics: Invention and interpretation in the age of science.* Albany: SUNY Press.

Gusfield, Joseph. 1976. The literary rhetoric of science: Comedy and pathos in drinking driver research. *American Sociological Review* 41.1:16–34.

Halloran, S. Michael. 2018 [1984]. The birth of molecular biology: An essay in the rhetorical criticism of scientific discourse. *Landmark essays on rhetoric of science: Case studies.* Second edition. Edited by Randy Allen Harris. London: Routledge, 78–88.

Hansen, James E., and Patrick J. Michaels. 2000 [1998]. Full transcript of inaugural AARST Science Policy Forum [moderated by Gordon R. Mitchell]. *Social Epistemology* 14.2–3:131–180.

Harrington, Elbert W. 1956. The academic and the rhetorical modes of thought. *The Quarterly Journal of Speech* 42:25–30.

Harris, Randy Allen. 2002. Knowing, rhetoric, science. *Visions and revisions: Continuity and change in rhetoric and composition.* Edited by James D. Williams. Carbondale, IL: Southern Illinois University Press.

Harris, Randy Allen, ed. 2004. *Rhetoric and incommensurability.* Lafayette, IN: Parlor.

Harris, Randy Allen. 2014. Alan G. Gross: Floppy eared rhetorical rabbit, redux. *Poroi* 10.2: Article 7.

Harris, Randy Allen, ed. 2018 [1997]. *Landmark essays on rhetoric of science: Case studies.* Second edition. London: Routledge.

Hexter, J. 1967. The rhetoric of history. *History and Theory* 6.1:3–13.

Kehl, D. 1975. The electric carrot: The rhetoric of advertisement. *College Composition and Communication* 26.2:134–140.

Keith, William, Steve Fuller, Alan Gross, and Michael Leff. 1999. Taking up the challenge: A response to Simons. *Quarterly Journal of Speech* 85.3:330–338.

Kelso, James A. 1980. Science and the rhetoric of reality. *Communication Studies* 31.1:17–29.

Kinneavy, James L. 1986. *Kairos: A neglected concept in classical rhetoric. Rhetoric and praxis: The contribution of classical rhetoric to practical reasoning.* Edited by Jean Dietz Moss. Washington, DC: The Catholic University of America Press, 79–105.

Kuhn, Thomas S. 2000 [1989]. Possible worlds in history of science. *The road since structure: Philosophical essays, 1970–1993.* Edited by James Conant and John Haugeland. Chicago: University of Chicago Press, 59–89.

Kuhn, Thomas S. 2012 [1962, 1970, 1996]. *The structure of scientific revolutions.* Fourth edition. Chicago: University of Chicago Press , 59–89.

Latour, Bruno, and Steve Woolgar. 1986 [1979]. *Laboratory life: The construction of scientific facts.* Beverly Hills: Sage Publications.

Lyne, John. 1980. Rhetoric and semiotic in CS Peirce. *Quarterly Journal of Speech* 66.2:155–168.

McCloskey, Deirdre. 1997. Big rhetoric, little rhetoric: Gaonkar on the rhetoric of science. *Rhetorical hermeneutics: Invention and interpretation in the age of science.* Edited by Alan G. Gross and William M. Keith. Albany: State University of New York Press, 101-12.

Maslow, Abraham. 1962. *Toward a psychology of being.* Princeton, NJ: D. Van Nostrand Company.

McKeon, Richard. 1937. Education and the disciplines. *International Journal of Ethics* 47.3:370–381.

McKeon, Richard. 1945. Democracy, scientific method, and action. *Ethics* 55.4:235–286.

McKeon, Richard. 1956. Dialogue and controversy in philosophy. *Philosophy and Phenomeno-logical Research* 17.2:143–163.

McKeon, Richard. 1968. Character and the arts and disciplines. *Ethics* 78.2:109–123.

McKeon, Richard. 1987. *Rhetoric: Essays in invention and discovery*. Edited by Mark Backman. Woodbridge, CT: Ox Bow Press.

McVitty, J. Dwight. 1991. Erasmus and the rhetorical tradition. PhD dissertation, University of California, Berkeley.

Mehlenbacher, Ashley Rose. 2019. *Science communication online: Engaging experts and publics on the internet*. Columbus: Ohio State University Press.

Melia, Trevor. 1984. And lo the footprint … selected literature in rhetoric and science. *Quarterly Journal of Speech* 70.3:303–313.

Melia, Trevor. 1992. Untitled review article. *Isis* 83.1:100–106.

Mohrmann, G. P., and Michael C. Leff. 1974. Lincoln at Cooper Union: A rationale for neo-classical criticism. *Quarterly Journal of Speech* 60.4:459–467.

Mol, Annemarie. 2003. *The body multiple: Ontology in medical practice*. Durham, NC: Duke University Press.

Myers, Greg. 1990. *Writing biology: Texts in the social construction of scientific knowledge*. Madison: The University of Winconsin Press.

Overington, Michael A. 1977. The scientific community as audience: Toward a rhetorical analysis of science. *Philosophy and Rhetoric* 10:143–163.

Paroske, Marcus. 2009. Deliberating international science policy controversies: Uncertainty and AIDS in South Africa. *Quarterly Journal of Speech* 95.2:148–170.

Paul, Danette, Davida Charney, and Aimee Kendall. 2001. Moving beyond the moment: Reception studies in the rhetoric of science. *Journal of Business and Technical Communication* 15.3:372–399.

Peirce, Charles Sanders. 1867. On a new list of categories. *Proceedings of the American Academy of Arts and Sciences* 7:287–298.

Peirce, Charles Sanders. 1940 [1897]. Logic as semiotic: The theory of signs. *The philosophy of Peirce: Selected writings*. Edited by Justus Buchler. London: Routledge & Kegan Paul.

Peirce, Charles Sanders. 1978 [1904]. Ideas, stray or stolen, about scientific writing, no. 1. *Philosophy and Rhetoric* 11.3:147–155.

Perelman, Chaïm, and Lucie Olbrechts-Tyteca. 1969 [1958]. *The new rhetoric: A treatise on argu-mentation*. Translated by John Wilkinson and Purcell Weaver. Notre Dame, IN: University of Notre Dame Press.

Prelli, Lawrence J. 1989. *A rhetoric of science*. Carbondale: University of South Carolina Press.

Robbins, Bruce. 1990. Interdisciplinarity in public: The rhetoric of rhetoric. *Social Text* 25/26:103–118.

Sawyer, Thomas M. 1972. Rhetoric in an age of science and technology. *College Composition and Communication* 23.5:390–398.

Schiappa, Edward. 2001. Second thoughts on the critiques of Big Rhetoric. *Philosophy & Rhetoric* 34.3:260–274.

Simons, Herbert W., ed. 1990. *The rhetorical turn: Invention and persuasion in the conduct of inquiry*. Chicago: University of Chicago Press.

Sloan[e], Thomas, et al. 1971. Report of the Committee on the Advancement and Refinement of Rhetorical Criticism. *The prospect of rhetoric: Report of the National Development Project*. Edited by Lloyd F. Bitzer and Edwin Black. Englewood Cliffs, New Jersey: Prentice-Hall, 220–27.

Staponkutė, Dalia. 2013. Resisting the rhetoric of science. *European Journal of English Studies* 17.3:295–307.

Stephens, James. 1975. Rhetorical problems in Renaissance science. *Philosophy & Rhetoric* 8.4:213–229.

Szasz, Thomas. 1969. *Ideology and insanity.* Garden City, NY: Anchor.

Taylor, Charles A. 1997. *Defining science: A rhetoric of demarcation.* Madison, WI: University of Wisconsin Press.

Thom, Françoise. 1989. *Newspeak: The language of soviet communism.* Translated by Ken Connelly. London: Claridge Press.

Wallace, Karl. 1963. The substance of rhetoric: Good reasons. *The Quarterly Journal of Speech* 49.3:239–249.

Walsh, Lynda. 2018. CFP: Global rhetorics of science. *Warp weft and way: Chinese and comparative philosophy.* http://warpweftandway.com/cfp-global-rhetorics-of-science-sept-1-deadline/

Walsh, Lynda, Nathaniel A. Rivers, Jenny Rice, Laurie E. Gries, Jennifer L. Bay, Thomas Rickert, and Carolyn R. Miller. 2017. Forum: Bruno Latour on rhetoric. *Rhetoric Society Quarterly* 47.5:403–462.

Wander, Philip C., and Dennis Jaehne. 2000. Prospects for "a rhetoric of science." *Social Epistemology* 14.2/3:211–233.

Watson, James D., and Francis H Crick. 1953. Molecular structure of nucleic acids: A structure for deoxyribose nucleic acid. Nature 171.4356:737–738.

Weaver, Richard. 1959. Concealed rhetoric in scientistic sociology. *The Georgia Review* 13.1:19–32.

Weigert, Andrew J. 1970. The immoral rhetoric of scientific sociology. *The American Sociologist* 5.2:111–119.

Weimer, Walter B. 1977. Science as a rhetorical transaction: Toward a nonjustificational conception of rhetoric. *Philosophy and Rhetoric* 10.1:1–29.

White, William J. 2014. Disciplinarity and the rhetoric of science: A social epistemological reception study. *Poroi* 10.2: Article 6.

Zappen, James P. 1975. Francis Bacon and the rhetoric of science. *College Composition and Communication* 26.3:244–247.

PART 1

ISSUES

The Very Idea

2.
IDEAS, STRAY OR STOLEN, ABOUT SCIENTIFIC WRITING, NO. 1
by Charles Sanders Peirce

Scientific journals are publishing, nowadays, many discussions concerning two matters which the late enormous multiplication of true scientific workers has raised to vital importance; namely, the best vocabulary for one or another branch of knowledge, and the best types of titles for scientific papers. Both are plainly questions of rhetoric. To a good many persons of literary culture it has hitherto seemed that there was little or no room in scientific writings for any other rule of rhetoric than that of expressing oneself in the simplest and directest manner, and that to talk of the style of a scientific communication was somewhat like talking of the moral character of a fish. Nor can one fairly say that this view of the humanists has been a particularly narrow view, since by a good many persons trained to the scientific life a coupling of the ideas of rhetoric and of science would hitherto equally have been regarded as a typical example of incongruity. Yet now and here we come upon this phenomenon of two questions of rhetoric agitating the surface of the scientific deep; and looking a little beneath, we surprise the severest sciences doing homage to rules of expression as stringent and strange as any of those by which the excellence of compositions in Chinese or in Urdu is judged. A proposition of geometry, a definition of a botanical species, a description of a crystal or of a telescopic nebula is subjected to a mandatory form of statement that is artificial in the extreme. Evidently, our conception of rhetoric has got to be generalized; and while we are about it, why not remove the restriction of rhetoric to speech? What is the principal virtue ascribed to algebraical notation, if it be not the rhetorical virtue of perspicuity? Has not many a picture, many a sculpture, the very same fault which in a poem we analyze as being "too rhetorical." Let us cut short such objections by acknowledging at once, as an *ens in posse*, a universal art of rhetoric, which shall be the general secret of rendering signs effective, including under the term "sign" every picture, diagram, natural cry, pointing finger, wink, knot in one's handkerchief, memory, dream, fancy, concept, indication, token, symptom, letter, numeral, word, sentence, chapter, book, library, and in short whatever, be it in the physical universe, be it in the world of thought, that, whether embodying an idea of any kind (and permit us throughout to use this term to cover purposes and feelings), or being connected with some existing object, or referring

Charles Sanders Peirce. "Ideas, Stray or Stolen, about Scientific Writing. No. 1" Autograph manuscript, undated. Harvard University Houghton Library Collection, Charles S. Peirce papers, Series: I. Manuscripts, Sub-Series: D. Logic Item, Identifier: MS Am 1632, (774).

to future events through a general rule, causes something else, its interpreting sign, to be determined to a corresponding relation to the same idea, existing thing, or law. Whether there can be such a universal *art* or not, there ought, at any rate to be (and indeed there is, if students do not wonderfully deceive themselves) a science to which should be referable the fundamental principles of everything like rhetoric,—a *speculative rhetoric*, the science of the essential conditions under which a sign may determine an interpretant sign of itself and of whatever it signifies, or may, as a sign bring about a physical result. Yes, a physical result; for though we often speak with just contempt of "mere" words, inasmuch as signs by themselves can exert no brute force, nevertheless it has always been agreed, by nominalist and realist alike, that general ideas are words,—or ideas, or signs of some sort. Now, by whatever machinery it may be accomplished, certain it is that somehow and in some true and proper sense general ideas do produce stupendous physical effects. For it would be a miserable logomachy to deny that a man's purpose of going down to his office causes him to go there; well, a purpose is a general idea, and his going is a physical fact. If it be objected that it is not the general ideas, but the men who believe in them, that cause the physical events, the answer is that it is the ideas that prompt men to champion them, that inspire those champions with courage, that develop their characters, and that confer upon them a magical sway over other men. It is necessary to insist upon the point for the reason that ideas cannot be communicated at all except through their physical effects. Our photographs, telephones, and wireless telegraphs, as well as the sum total of all the work that steam engines have ever done, are, in sober common sense and literal truth, the outcome of the general ideas that are expressed in the first book of the *Novum Organum.*

The speculative rhetoric that we are speaking of is a branch of the analytical study of the essential conditions to which all signs are subject,—a science named *semeiotics*, though identified by many thinkers with logic. In the Roman schools, grammar, logic, and rhetoric were felt to be akin and to make up a rounded whole called the *trivium.* This feeling was just; for the three disciplines named correspond to the three essential branches of semeiotic, of which the first, called *speculative grammar* by Duns Scotus, studies the ways in which an object can be a sign; the second, the leading part of logic, best termed *speculative critic*, studies the ways in which a sign can be related to the object independent of it that it represents; while the third is the speculative rhetoric just mentioned.

In a publication like this, all scientifically thorough discussion of any but the smallest points would be out of place. We have no room for more, nor has the average reader,—reading the journal during his journey up-town, let us suppose,—leisure for anything more than such ideas, serious or light, as might be struck out in conversation between two clever, but two probably tired and hungry, companions. Of the writer it is to be expected that he should have carried through as exhaustive a study as possible of every point he touches; and certes he should not make a secret of any truth merely because its study is difficult. Only, when he comes to deliver his ideas, good manners require that he should dismount from any high horse, and submit his conclusions as views that the reader is free to accept or reject, as may seem good to him. If the proposition that the circle cannot be squared happens to be pertinent to the matter in hand, by all means let him enunciate it. But, seeing that he cannot demonstrate it here, let him not have the air of denying the reader's perfect logical right to entertain the contrary hypothesis. Nor should the writer aver his own belief in the theorem, since the peculiar notions of an anonymous individual have no interest for the public. He may, at most, report that the impossibility of the circle's being squared is a proposition that has recommended itself to men generally esteemed competent; whereupon the reader of good sense will feel sure, as well he may, that no such intimation would have appeared in these columns unless the proposition had been a fruit ripened under the blaze of arduous investigation. But the day of editorial omniscience is past.

Of the three branches of semeiotics, the two first, the speculative grammar and critic, have been greatly elaborated. The speculative rhetoric has been comparatively neglected; yet enough has been done by two or three analysts to give results comparable in extent and value with the pure scientific contents of an ordinary text book on logic,— enough, therefore, to afford no little guidance in forming opinions about ordinary rhetoric, and to give a notion of what the general character of its influence upon ordinary rhetoric is likely to be. It must not be supposed that there is anything of the nature of metaphysical speculation in this speculative rhetoric. *Speculative* is merely the Latin form corresponding to the Greek word *theoretical,* and is here intended to signify that the study is of the *purely* scientific kind, not a practical science, still less an art. Its most essential business is to ascertain by logical analysis, greatly facilitated by the development of the other branches of semeiotics, what are the indispensible conditions of a sign's acting to determine another sign nearly equivalent to itself. A few examples have been remarked of artificial signs automatically reproducing themselves without being intended to do so. An engraving may make a vague copy of itself upon the tissue-paper guard placed over it. But these are confined to too narrow a class to illustrate anything more than the possibility of such a thing. The reproduction of signs in intended ways is, of course, common enough, but is as mysterious as the reciprocal action of mind and matter. Some of the requisites of communication which analysis has signalized are obvious enough; others are not so. Thus, it is said to be a necessary result of the analysis that the object represented by the sign, and whose characters are independent of such representation, should itself be of the nature of a sign, so that its characters are not independent of *all* representation. This is intelligible from the point of view of pragmatism, according to which the objects of which ordinary general propositions have to be true, if they are to be true at all, are the body of future percepts. But percepts are themselves signs, whether veracious or not. The fact that the characters of the future percepts are independent of what they have been expected to be does not in the least prevent their being signs. This result of analysis, that every object represented must be of the nature of a sign, is important (if accepted as true) for certain kinds of composition. Another remarkable result is that an entirely new sign can never be created by an act of communication, but that the utmost possible is that a sign already existing should be filled out and corrected. Thus, tell me that there is a diamond mine at a place I never heard of and of whose whereabouts I have not the slightest idea, and you tell me nothing; but tell me that I can find it by following out a path, the entrance to which I know well, and you are simply filling out my knowledge of that path. So you can convey no idea of colors to a man born blind; yet a certain optical investigator of high repute, domestic and foreign, is color-blind; and although the word *red* cannot have the same meaning to him that it has to the rest of us, yet he really knows more about the sensation than you and I are likely to do, in that he knows very exactly its relations to the sensations that he does possess. A writer who should lose sight of this principle would be in danger of becoming quite unintelligible. It is needless to go further to show that the sort of help that one who wishes to learn to write well can promise himself from the study of speculative rhetoric will not consist in any hitherto unheard of devices for conveying ideas to the reader's mind, but rather in clearer notions of the lineage and relationship of the different maxims of rhetoric, such notions carrying with them juster judgments of the several extents and limitations of those maxims.

It would be needless, we trust, to interpose any warning against inferring that a theory of rhetoric is false because a given advocate of it exhibits little grace, dexterity, or tact in the handling of language. For we all know how seldom an author treating of a particular kind of skill is found to be remarkably endowed himself with the skill he discourses about. Many a time, it has been precisely his consciousness of natural deficiency in that respect that has led him to study the art.

The general trend of the modifications that would be introduced into ordinary rhetoric by regarding it as a structure reared upon the foundation of the abstract study aforesaid would be determined in great part by the circumstance that the immediate basis of this ordinary rhetoric would be conceived to be merely one of a large number of special studies, or rather as one group of a large number of groups of special studies. For the specialization would be of three modes; first, according to the special nature of the ideas to be conveyed; secondly, according to the special class of signs to be interpreted,— the special medium of communication; and thirdly, according to the special nature of the class of signs into which the interpretation is to take place. The leading division of the first mode would be into a rhetoric of fine art, where the matter is of feeling mainly, a rhetoric of practical persuasion, where the chief matter is of the nature of a resolve; and a rhetoric of science, where the matter is knowledge. The rhetoric of science would be subdivided into a rhetoric of the communication of discoveries, a rhetoric of scientific digests and surveys, and a rhetoric of applications of science to special kinds of purposes. The rhetoric of communications of discoveries will vary again according as the discoveries belong to mathematics, to philosophy, or to special science; and further varieties, by no means insignificant will result from the subdivision of the sciences. One principal kind of rhetoric resulting from the second mode of specialization would be the rhetoric of speech and language; and this again would differ for languages of different families. The rhetoric naturally adapted to a Semitic tongue must be very different from a rhetoric well suited to Aryan speech. Moreover, each Aryan language has, or ought to have, its special rhetoric differing from that of even closely allied languages. German and English are marked instances of this. The rules of the common run of the books, based upon rules of Greek and Latin rhetoric, are adapted to English compositions of highly artificial styles alone. Fancy writing a fairy tale in periodic sentences! One effect of basing rhetoric upon the abstract science would be to take down the pretensions of many of the rhetorical rules and to limit their application to a particular dialect among the dialects of literary English,—that one which is founded on classical studies. At the same time, it would emphasize the necessity of the studies of Greek and Latin as the only way of gaining a mastery of an extremely important dialect of our language. The principal kind of rhetoric resulting from the third mode of specialization is the rhetoric of signs to be translated into human thought; and one inevitable result of basing rhetoric upon the abstract science that looks on human thought as a special kind of sign would be to bring into high relief the principle that in order to address the human mind effectively, one ought, in theory, to erect one's art upon the immediate base of a profound study of human physiology and psychology. One ought to know just what the processes are whereby an idea can be conveyed to a human mind and become embedded in its habits; and according to this doctrine, all the rules of ordinary rhetoric ought to be hinged upon such considerations and not upon the gratuitous assumption that men can only think according to a certain syntax-type of sentence that happens to be very common in the languages most familiar to most of us, but into which other sentences can be jammed only by Procrustean barbarities.

3.
THE *PERSONAE* OF SCIENTIFIC DISCOURSE
by Paul Newell Campbell

The concept of *persona* is, of course, entirely familiar to those of us who are in Theater or who work with literature. The term is used to mean the imaginary, the fictive being implied by and embedded in a literary or dramatic work. To rhetoricians the concept is also familiar, but less so, perhaps, because it is so easy to assume that an essay or article or speech reflects the ideas, attitudes, and beliefs of an actual human being. And to scientists the concept is, as far as I can tell, very nearly alien; that is, I know of no scientists who argue that their treatises, monographs, etc., should be critically viewed as dramatic forms that present for inspection characters as well as concepts, *personae* as well as problems and solutions.

In what follows, I shall argue that *personae* are indeed implied by and discoverable in every scientific discourse, and I shall try to show that the existence of *personae* is exceedingly important to the critical stance one takes toward such discourse. The argument will be presented in four stages: first, a summary of various comments on scientific discourse as rhetorically grounded, as a rhetorical form; second, a proposal that, like every discursive form that is based on rhetoric, or that is itself rhetorical, scientific discourse involves *personae*; third, a comparison of the concept of *persona* and the three terms commonly associated with science—"objectivity," "predictability," and "control"—concluding that these key terms or god-terms[1] create major conflicts; and fourth, an indication of the sort of change in critical attitude called for by the personae of some scientific discourse in the field of Communication.

Scientific Discourse as Rhetoric

The argument that scientific discourse is rhetorical in nature is easy enough to make, for the materials for that argument have been provided by rhetoricians, philosophers, scientists, and literary critics.

As a philosopher, Susanne K. Langer points out that science is not interested in facts or specific instances as such, but only in facts or instances *as illustrations* of some scientific theory or point of view. And she adds that facts or instances that illustrate nothing are simply not considered "scientific"; further, when confronted with a unique event, or even one that is extremely rare, scientists will choose to substitute for that event a fiction, even a denial of its occurrence, rather than to redo the very body of science itself.[2]

P. N. Campbell. "The Personae of Scientific Discourse." *Quarterly Journal of Speech*, Volume 61, Number 4, 1975, pp. 391–405.

Certainly an approach that treats facts only as illustrations of theories is committed to the theories the facts illustrate. And to be committed to certain theoretical points of view is, of course, to advocate precisely the views to which one is committed; it is a rhetorical stance. A nonrhetorical stance, were such an attitude possible, would require one to prefer no particular point of view and to hold all facts or instances as equally significant, and this science does not do.[3]

As a philosopher of science, Thomas Kuhn argues that the scientific endeavor can be roughly divided into two sorts: normal science and scientific revolutions. Normal science occurs when a "paradigm" is accepted by some significant part of the scientific community. "Paradigm" is a key term in Kuhn's argument, and he means by it those achievements that are "sufficiently unprecedented to attract an enduring group of adherents away from competing modes of scientific activity," that are "sufficiently open-ended to leave all sorts of problems for the redefined group of practitioners to resolve," and that, as a result, "provide models from which spring particular coherent traditions of scientific research."[4] A paradigm can provide an extremely powerful and profitable guide for further research, and as long as it does, normal science continues. But there comes a point at which normal science encounters problems it cannot resolve, and at that point a new paradigm must be chosen. Kuhn emphasizes the fact that the choice of new paradigms "is not and cannot be determined merely by the evaluative procedures characteristic of normal science, for these depend in part upon a particular paradigm, and that paradigm is at issue;" rather, "like the choice between competing political institutions, that between competing paradigms proves to be a choice between incompatible modes of community life;" but because each paradigm is used by the group arguing for its acceptance, such arguments are circular, and "whatever its force, the status of the circular argument is only that of persuasion. It cannot be made logically or even probabilistically compelling for those who refuse to step into the circle."[5] Of course, once the choice of a new paradigm is made, normal science takes over again.

These aspects of science, as described by Kuhn, are strikingly rhetorical in nature. A paradigm, an achievement that lures its followers away from the ideas and acts to which they had committed themselves, that offers the prospect of rewarding work, and that provides a model to be followed in that work certainly appears to be functioning rhetorically. The arguments advanced in favor of this or that paradigm in times of crisis are, I suppose, the most obviously rhetorical of the elements Kuhn deals with, but the suasory nature of science as a whole becomes clear when one realizes that, after the adoption of a particular paradigm, the scientists' work follows the model, the point of view, the outlook implicit in that paradigm. All that happens is that what was contested, what was questioned at one stage is accepted without question at a later stage; an explicit bias, an explicitly rhetorical viewpoint becomes an implicit bias and point of view, as witnessed by Kuhn's contention that "the textbooks from which each new scientific generation learns to practice its trade" are produced during periods of normal science and, rather than being objective and neutral, are "persuasive and pedagogic."[6]

As a scientist and philosopher of science, Jacob Bronowski stresses the idea that science is dependent on certain human values and that the very practice of science is infused with these values. For instance, "in a world in which state and dogma seem always either to threaten or to cajole, the body of scientists is trained to avoid and organized to resist every form of persuasion but the fact. A scientist who breaks this rule, as Lysenko has done, is ignored. A scientist who finds that the rule has been broken in his laboratory, as Kammerer found, kills himself."[7] In addition, Bronowski argues that science depends on mutual trust, since the scientist's work is usually based on the work of other scientists, that science especially prizes and rewards original and bold speculations, and that the scientific community must be a democracy in which individuals respect and honor their colleagues.[8]

No matter how idealistic these claims may seem (and one would not have to browse through too many issues of the *New York Times* to find instances in which "scientists" do not live up to Bronowski's standards), there is, I think, no doubt that these are the ways scientists *should* behave. And it may well be that these are the minimal conditions science must meet; that is, if they are not met, what has been done is simply not science. Thus, the scientific endeavor is rhetorical in that it explicitly urges its practitioners to adopt certain behaviors and attitudes. It rewards certain things and punishes others, and in the process of dealing out these rewards and punishments, scientists act rhetorically toward other scientists. And while they may "resist every form of persuasion but the fact" (though the view of facts as a means of persuasion seems peculiarly rhetorical), when they teach or advocate originality of thought, a democratic structure of the scientific community, and respect and honor for the efforts of co-workers, they are inevitably engaged in persuasion.

As a rhetorician and literary critic, Kenneth Burke establishes the rhetorical nature of the scientific outlook in these few words: "Even if any given terminology is a *reflection* of reality, by its very nature as a terminology it must be a *selection* of reality; and to this extent it must function also as a *deflection* of reality."[9] Say what one will of the accuracy, precision, logic, etc., of the scientific statement made, unless one is willing to argue that that statement includes everything that could conceivably be said, and said from every conceivable vantage point—unless one is willing to argue that—, one must grant that what has been told is a partial story. And the partial story told is obviously one that is advocated, for it is senseless to choose a certain story about a certain object/event and to claim at the same time that some other story is preferable. Hence, by definition, the scientific statement is rhetorical.

According to these, and other, theorists, scientific discourse is necessarily rhetorical in nature. We may wish to say that it differs in various ways from other discursive forms, but we cannot say that it is nonrhetorical.

Personae and Scientific Discourse

A great many critics and theorists whose primary concerns are dramatic and literary find the concept of the *persona* invaluable, for it is just too awkward to argue that the character of Ophelia or Willy Loman or the irate monk of "Soliloquy in a Spanish Cloister" is part of, or is directly related to, the character of Shakespeare or Miller or Browning. And what can one say of the very different characters created by many authors? Or of characters created by authors of whom we know little or nothing? If we are to avoid the sort of psychological determinism that underlies the view that the speaker or character of a work is necessarily similar to the author of that work, it seems that we must turn to the notion of *persona* (or implied author, or speaker) and that we must mean by that notion an imaginary being implied by the work, but a being who has no necessary resemblance to the author—quite as the gentle, whimsical, country philosopher of nearly all of Robert Frost's poetry seems to have little in common with the actual Robert Frost.

For those who wish to draw a sharp dividing line between literary or poetic and rhetorical works, the concept of *persona* will, of course, belong to poetic, not to rhetoric, because one of the major arguments used to separate the two is based on the presumed directness of contact between rhetor and audience and the absence of such direct contact (hence, the presence of a *persona*) between poet and audience. However, that sharp dividing line is difficult to maintain, primarily because so very many of the rhetorical works we consider to be important are noteworthy for their poetic or literary or aesthetic qualities, and secondarily because rhetors seem to assume and to change personalities in ways that are, perhaps, less dramatic than, but nonetheless quite reminiscent of, the poets. And once the barrier between rhetoric and poetic is breached, and the search for shared characteristics encouraged, we find that, not only are there marked poetic qualities in the most highly regarded rhetoric, but that there is a rhetorical dimension in every literary work—a dimension that is brought into being by the techniques via which the work achieves its effects.[10] The very existence of those techniques underlines the importance of *personae* in literature, for those techniques *are* the process by which the *personae* enact and demonstrate the attitudes that we call the effects of works of literature. But since many of the same techniques used in literature are also employed in rhetoric, it would seem the *personae* are to be found in both poetic and rhetoric. And so they are.

Far from being solely a literary product, the *persona* is "*the created personality put forth in the act of communicating*"[11] (italics added). For example, newspaper articles involve points of view, attitudes, value judgments, intimacy or remoteness in relation to people and events, i.e., they involve *personae*.[12] It is quite as ill advised to assume that an editorial or a feature story reflects the real character of its real author as it is to make that assumption about a short story, for both may easily be the result of artifice. And, of course, it does not stop with newspapers. People who regularly speak to large audiences enact roles, don masks, create *personae*. Martin Luther King, Jr. used a prophet *persona* in many of his speeches; he, apparently deliberately, played the role of prophet, though that is certainly not to say that the actual Reverend King was a prophet.[13]

It appears, then, that rhetorical events necessarily involve *personae*, and that leads directly to the issue of the *personae* of scientific discourse, since I have already argued that such discourse is rhetorical in nature. Thomas Kuhn seems to me to be describing precisely the *personae* of scientific discourse when he says that during periods of crisis "the competition between paradigms is not the sort of battle that can be resolved by proofs," that, indeed, "the proponents of competing paradigms must fail to make complete contact with each other's viewpoints" for at least three reasons: first, they "will often disagree about the list of problems that any candidate for paradigm must resolve" because "their standards or their definitions of science are not the same"; second, although "they ordinarily incorporate much of the vocabulary and apparatus, both conceptual and manipulative, that the traditional paradigm had previously employed …, they seldom employ these borrowed elements in quite the traditional way," for the "old terms, concepts and experiments fall into new relationships one with the other" as their very meanings change—so that, for example, to make the transition from the Newtonian to the Einsteinian universe, "the whole conceptual web whose strands are space, time, matter, force and so on, had to be shifted and laid down again on nature whole"; third, "the proponents of competing paradigms practice their trades in different worlds," i.e., though they "are looking at the world, and what they look at has not changed …, they see different things, and they see them in different relations one to the other," which is why a law that cannot even be demonstrated to one group of scientists may occasionally seem intuitively obvious to the other" and also "why, before they can hope to communicate fully, one group or the other must experience the conversion that we have been calling a paradigm shift," since "only men who had together undergone or failed to undergo that transformation would be able to discover precisely what they agreed or disagreed about."[14]

Although Kuhn never uses the term *persona*, he seems to me to be describing differences in attitude, belief, and outlook that can only be called "personal" or "personalized"—not necessarily personal in the sense of resting on sheer idiosyncrasy or whimsey (although he leaves open even that possibility),[15] but personal in the sense of depending on one's beliefs about what science should accomplish, on the values one places on the scientific process, and on the meanings of the most fundamental concepts one employs and the resultant perceived realities one confronts. If two people "are looking at the world" but "see different things … in different relations one to the other," and if they then advocate their own views as the right or appropriate views, I take it we have clear-cut examples of rhetorical discourse which embody *personae*. And though Kuhn has been describing scientific revolutions, I would repeat my contention that normal science includes these same attitudes and beliefs, i.e., these same *personae*, but includes them as implicit and noncontroversial elements.

I have already hinted at Bronowski's idealized scientist, and it is just that ideal being that, for Bronowski, is the ultimate *personae* of science. Consider these comments:

> Yet the values [the scientists] seldom spoke of shone out of their work and entered their ages, and slowly re-made the minds of men. Slavery ceased to be a matter of course. The princelings of Europe fled from the gaming table. The empires of the Bourbons and the Hapsburgs crumbled. Men asked for the rights of man and for government by consent.
>
> By the beginning of the nineteenth century, Napoleon did not find a scientist to elevate tyranny into a system; that was done by the philosopher Hegel. Hegel had written his university dissertation to prove philosophically that there could be no more than the seven planets he knew. It was unfortunate, and characteristic, that even as he wrote, on 1 January 1801, a working astronomer observed the eighth planet Ceres.
>
> Men have asked for freedom, justice and respect precisely as the scientific spirit has spread among them. The dilemma of today is not that the human values cannot control a mechanical science. It is the other way about; the scientific spirit is more human than the machinery of governments. We have not let either the tolerance or the empiricism of science enter the

parochial rules by which we still try to prescribe the behavior of nations. Our conduct as states clings to a code of self-interest which science, like humanity, has long left behind. Science has nothing to be ashamed of even in the ruins of Nagasaki. The shame is theirs who appeal to other values than the human imaginative values which science has evolved. The shame is ours if we do not make science part of our world, intellectually as much as physically, so that we may at last hold these halves of the world together by the same values.[16]

In these remarks Bronowski is describing the spirit, the *persona* of science. Idealized though this *persona* may be, even Bronowski leaves room for human frailty, although he prefers it to be as remote as possible, as indicated by this admission: "Perhaps the techniques of science may be practiced for a time without its spirit, in secret establishments, as the Egyptians practiced their priestcraft."[17] But what is of primary interest to me in these excerpts is that Bronowski has not only dealt with the *persona* of science, but has taken at least a small step in the direction of describing a specific *persona*. In many poetic and rhetorical acts, *personae* range all the way from monsters who would destroy us all to gentle, loving angels who minister to our needs. But Bronowski has limited the traits that make up his ideal *persona*: truthfulness, trust, concern for "freedom, justice, and respect," accuracy, originality, fearless independence, absolute honesty—these constitute the *persona* Bronowski perceives.

To balance this view, one may turn to Theodore Roszak who launches a vigorous attack on science and scientists. His attack is centered on "the deep personality structure of the ideal scientist" because he contends that that personality is also the personality of the culture in which we exist: "The mentality of the ideal scientist becomes the very soul of the society. We seek to adapt our lives to the dictates of that mentality"—a mentality, a *persona* that has three major characteristics, described by these phrases: "the alienative dichotomy," i.e., the psychic process via which the scientist closes off, removes, safeguards the self, the "In-Here" from any intimate involvement in the "Out-There"; "the invidious hierarchy," i.e., the psychic process via which the In-Here becomes "a place where it is desirable and secure to be," which is "the center of reliable knowledge," and from which one "learns, plans, controls, watches out cunningly for threats and opportunities," and the Out-There becomes "a place that is untrustworthy, perhaps downright dangerous," and steeped in "unpredictability [and] stupidity"; and the "mechanistic imperative" (the conclusion that follows from the preceding premises), i.e., the psychic process via which the self, the In-Here, always beset by "its claims in behalf of sensuous contact, fantasy, spontaneity, and concern for the person," institutes the search for "a superior command and control center that will take over whenever the In-Here's capacity to achieve perfect impersonality breaks down"—in other words, a search for a self-embedded device that "will never lose control of itself, never weaken, never turn unpredictably personal, for it will never have been a person in the first place."[18]

This, too, is an idealized, a negatively idealized, being. But just as with Bronowski's *persona*, Roszak's is a creature committed to certain attitudes and beliefs, i.e., a rhetorical creature. To accept either *persona* is to accept an outlook, a set of guidelines for one's supposedly scientific work.

Here, then, are two very different theorists both describing what I believe can appropriately be termed *personae* of science. Further, each of them argues that the *persona* of science is not just any and every *persona*, but is one that displays certain characteristics, although they disagree almost entirely about those characteristics. Or do they? Certainly the disagreement seems nearly total, at least at first glance. Yet Bronowski makes this very interesting comment about his own argument: "Now that the crux of my argument has ben accepted, I would, were I beginning again, give some space also to a discussion of *those values which are not generated by the practice of science—the values of tenderness, of kindliness, of human intimacy and love. These form a different domain from the sharp and, as it were, Old Testament virtues which science produces, but of course they do not negate the values of science*" (italics added).[19] While it would, I think, be foolish to argue that this comment eliminates all important differences between Roszak's cold, withdrawn, hostile *persona* and Bronowski's clear-eyed, honest, striving figure, the gap between the two does seem to me to be somewhat narrowed. If the *persona* of science does not depend on the values of tenderness, kindliness, and love, as Bronowski says it does not, then we have moved some distance toward Roszak's unconcerned, manipulating, machine-minded being. And those "Old Testament" virtues may, perhaps, be understood to include a certain strong determination, even fierceness—though presumably not the icy ruthlessness that Roszak would have. Also, the absence of tenderness, kindliness, intimacy, and love may not, as Bronowski claims, "negate the values of science," but it seems fair to ask what is meant by respect for one's colleagues, concern for freedom, justice, etc., if kindliness and tenderness and love are lacking.

Of course, two divergent, even extreme, views are present here, and, at best, it is likely to be difficult to determine which, if either, should prevail if the argument is restricted to the grounds staked out by the parties to this conflict. Thus, I shall assume that the existence of *personae* in scientific discourse has been established, or, at least, has been nearly enough established to warrant a closer and different examination of the nature and characteristics of such *personae*, and I shall try to conduct that examination on sheerly terminological grounds.[20]

"*Personae*," "Objectivity," "Predictability," and "Control"

The key-terms traditionally associated with science are "objectivity," "predictability," and "control," for they have been thought to indicate those qualities that are fundamental to the scientific endeavor. But if, as I am arguing, the concept of *persona* is essential to scientific discourse, a terminological conflict is at hand; "*persona*" and "objectivity" are often, if not always, mutually incompatible as god-terms, and "predictability" and "control" work well with "*persona*" only in certain limited ways.

To be objective, to objectify, is to treat something as an object, as external, as impersonal. Scientists can make a strong argument for the need for objectivity: only by disentangling whatever it is one wishes to study from the traces of personal values, emotions, biases, etc., is it possible to see clearly and to agree about anything at all; if my, and your, and her, and his values and beliefs are to be included in what is observed, we shall never reach agreement about that which we study simply because our emotions and beliefs and values always color what we see in individual tones; hence, what is studied must be removed from personal likes and dislikes, from individual value systems, because in order to agree on the nature of the reality we are studying we must first place it in a neutral position in which it looks the same to each of us, and second, we must place ourselves in neutral positions from which we look at it with the same eyes—otherwise we have no methodology, no science, nothing at all.

It is, as I say, a strong argument, especially so, buttressed as it is by common sense and experience: after all, we are not interested in the scientists' feelings about things, but in the facts, in the truth; and there is that remarkable list of successes—moon shots, nuclear explosions, TV, etc., etc., etc.

And there are similarly strong arguments for "predictability" and "control." Clearly there are various forms of study, and one may study, say, the past, or some segment of the past, but if the method of study includes nothing that allows one to predict future events, future behavior, or even the outcome of future studies of the same segment of reality, what is going on is not science. History, perhaps. Or critical inquiry. But not science. And closely allied to "predictability" is "control," for only by controlling those changeable and changing aspects of what is studied, those variables, can one determine which of them is exerting what influences on which of the others and on the entire reality being observed. Without control, we can study only a chaotic mass of interpenetrating influences, and thus, without control, one will never be able to attain the specificity necessary for predictions.

Again, common sense and experience seem to assent strongly. We expect accuracy and precision from the scientist, and without control they seem impossible of achievement; and we want the scientist to tell us what will work, to be able to predict what will happen when we do such and such.

But there is another view of the matter, and it can be put simply: the one who controls and predicts distorts and removes from time; the *persona* who objectifies devalues. The argument that what is studied must be separated from personal values and that personal values must be removed from the method of study is an interesting one, but it is only part of the story. If one assumes that the removal of values is possible and that such a removal has somehow occurred prior to any given scientific study, one may, of course, use that study as evidence of the worth or importance of that removal-of-values. But if one accepts the notion of the *persona*, that removal-of-values is an act committed in *that given study.*[21] And like a person, a *persona* bears the responsibility for her, or his, or its *acts*. To use a deliberately absurd example, if an attempt is made to measure the volume of the yells of individuals who have their toes stepped on, the *persona* of the study, i.e., of the resulting discourse, bears the responsibility, not only for such niceties as the accuracy of the acoustical determinations, but for the pain and injury suffered by those experimented upon. The *persona* has chosen to act as she or he did, and as with any other act, the moral valuation thereof must be levied against the agent.

It is the *personae* of scientific discourse who are responsible for the objectivity achieved in such discourse (or the claimed achievement of objectivity). While the motives of actual persons are very often tangled, sometimes at odds with the quality of the acts they underlie, frequently difficult to perceive with any clarity at all, the motives of *personae* are always implicit in the acts themselves and must be inferred directly there-from. It is not enough to claim that removing objects/events from individual value systems (others' or the scientist's) is necessary for clarity and agreement, or that assuming a neutral, nonevaluative stance is essential to science. In addition, one must accept the responsibility for doing away with values in relation to the reality studied. Except in the most unusual cases, the values are there to start with and are removed in the act of scientific study; it is rarely, if ever, the case that one begins with unvalued reality. The value of avoiding stepped-on toes, for instance, is so obvious it constitutes an extreme of one sort. But let me now turn to a very different kind of extreme: The various acts that have resulted in the litter of man-made objects on the moon began with the moon as valued object. It may be that the change from the romantic, mysterious symbol of song and poetry to a sort of airport littered with *mechanical* refuse (one assumes the bags of feces and urine quickly sizzled away in the fierce daytime heat) is of little importance. Perhaps only a limited number of moon-lovers would agree with Robert Graves who said, when interviewed by Edwin Newman a few years ago, that going to the moon was the second worst crime that had occurred in human history (the first was the cutting of the Gordian Knot), because it showed a contempt for the mysterious and the unknown. Still, whatever change is involved, and however few feel as Graves did, the responsibility for that change and for those feelings must be borne by the makers of moon shots. For they have, obliquely and indirectly, perhaps, devalued the moon.

And so it is with the *personae* of every scientific discourse: to the extent that they are neutral and objective, they devalue what they study. *Personae*, like persons, exist in a dramatic universe in which values, positive or negative, are always present, and, therefore, they cannot perceive, or feel, or observe in a neutral, value-free manner. To consider some object/event as unimportant, or dispensable, or destructible via experiment is to regard that something as worthless or as worth less than something else, and to so consider it is to devalue it and to bear the responsibility for the act of devaluing. That responsibility calls for an appraisal of the ethics of the act and the ethics of the actor. Such ethical appraisals are the critical acknowledgement of the *persona*, and the absence of those appraisals implies an absence of the *persona*. Hence, "*persona*" and "objectivity" clash precisely in the presence of the ethical judgments called for by the very existence of the *persona* vs. the absence of the ethical judgments required by the very nature of the impersonal, neutral, objective act.

The term "predictability" poses a different problem. The scientist means by that term the ability to describe procedures that will produce certain results. To use a hypothetical example (that may well be an actual one by now), if the procedures for mixing some bonding agent with sand can be laid down with such precision that that mixing markedly reduces tidal erosion, the scientist is said to have predicted accurately, and she or he accepts the responsibility for such accurate predictions. But if those same procedures result in the inability of certain fish to lay eggs in that sand, and thereby lead to the death of a particular species of fish, the scientist still considers that she or he has predicted accurately, for *the responsibility for such results or for such accuracy of prediction has never been accepted*. In other words, the scope of the scientist's predictions is artificially and arbitrarily limited. But in saying that I have called forth a further question:

What are the limits of the predictions for which the scientist is responsible in a given case? Or, to put it differently, who shall judge the appropriateness of the limits that are set?

The answer to the first question is that, in a given act or in a given discourse, the *persona* is responsible for predictions of those consequences that can reasonably be said to follow from that act. The terminological conflict between "*persona*" and "predictability" is located just here, for a *persona* cannot simply *say* that his or her predictive responsibility ends at such and such a point. A *persona* must demonstrate that there is no likely reason to fear or desire further consequences of this or that sort, hence no need to widen the limits of her/his responsibility. And that leads directly to the answer to the question as to who shall judge the appropriateness of the limits set: Judgment shall be made by the informed public, including other scientists, and that judgment shall be made on the basis of the *persona's* description of the actual process of setting such limits. It is the absence of such a description that is the locus of the most frequent clashes between "*persona*" and "predictability," for neutral, impersonal discourse may be held to require no description of the process of deciding on the limits of responsibility, while a *persona* is, by definition, a creature who must demonstrate his or her ethical views of her or his own acts. And in scientific studies of human beings the *persona* has a special responsibility for determining and describing as accurately as possible what is likely to happen to those who are studied. For the consequences that *are* likely, the *persona* cannot avoid responsibility merely by omitting a description of those consequences or of the process by which she or he decided not to predict their occurrence.

Finally, "control." To control is, essentially, to take out of time, out of change. It is here that Roszak's attack, violent as it is, seems to me most telling. As I have said, scientists are concerned with two kinds of control: control of themselves and of the phenomena they study. But how does one go about controlling phenomena and/or one's observations of them? Only by denying their uniqueness. Only by detaching them from the thicket of changes, of varying factors in which they are entangled. The observations must be controlled by separating them from the values, biases, and prejudices that are fleeting or formidable aspects of the observer, and that is to say that the observer must be made stable, made orderly, placed beyond the reach of the changes that are innate in the process of living through time. But to impose any order or system of controls on a human being is to outlaw those human qualities that are, by definition, spontaneous, disordered, uncontrolled. It is, in Roszak's terms, to separate the In-Here from the Out-There. And it is much the same with the phenomena observed: in order to control them, one denies their uniqueness and abstracts qualities that are said to be held in common by some group or category. In other words, one removes them from time, and, via abstraction, distorts them.

But the recognition of *personae* in scientific discourse would call for an admission of the humanness of the observation made, of the point of view or frame of reference underlying that observation, and a similar admission of the distortion involved in the act of observing. For example, it is not enough to claim to study, say, student reactions to stress by counting numbers of errors on true-false tests given with and without the threat/reward of a course grade. The *persona* of such a study must account for her or his ability (or, apparent ability) to ignore those reactions to stress other than incorrect answers. In addition, the *persona* must describe the sort of distortion involved in defining student reaction to stress as the number of errors on a true-false test.

Personae and Scientific Discourse in Communication

In trying to deal with scientific discourse from this, or any other, point of view, it is tempting to concentrate on examples more or less like the ones I have used thus far—examples that are blatantly rhetorical, biased, poetic, personal, unethical, etc. And one can easily find well known examples of this sort: for instance, Kepler's metaphysical comparison of the sun, the fixed stars, and the space between them with God the Father, the Son and the Holy Ghost; or, in a case somewhat similar to the Kammerer tragedy referred to by Bronowski, the recent falsification of data at the Memorial Sloan-Kettering Cancer Center in New York, in which neither the head of the Center nor the falsifier of the data committed suicide, and the falsifier was given a year's leave-of-absence with pay in order to undergo psychotherapy.[22] But there are, I'm afraid, neither Keplers nor Kammerers in the field of Communication. And though our researchers and our research are far more modest than either of these, it is the scientific discourse of our own field that I shall be concerned with in this final section.

First of all, a very large amount of the research in Communication deals directly with people (and, I suppose, all of it deals indirectly or directly with people). Rocks, atoms, spatial relationships, etc., may be thought to be simple, inanimate objects or events, but in our field we are most frequently concerned with people, and the *persona* of any scientific discourse must acknowledge the humanity of the people who are studied or observed. Unfortunately, that does not always happen. For instance, we say we are interested in studying something called "trust" in the behavior of small groups. To study it, we choose students, tell some of them that the university has commissioned an important study, that their ability to communicate will be judged, and that they are to discuss what action, if any, the university should take in relation to, say, the Black Student Union. Others of these students we instruct to behave as cooperative or competitive plants who will deliberately use deceit in various ways to enhance or destroy that something called "trust."[23] The students to whom we lie, we call "naive subjects," and I suggest that that label is singularly inappropriate. They are in no sense "naive"; rather, they are *trusting*, and we deceive them—not once, but over and over. We tell them the university commissioned the study (a lie), that the discussions they will conduct are important to the university (a lie), that they are not to be treated differently from other students in the study (a lie), and even, via a plant, that, because they will be graded, they know they must do well in the discussions (a lie). How is it that we have the right to so treat other human beings? And what is there that is neutral or objective in this entire procedure? Has not the experimenter intruded time after time into the "real" situation?

Or, we say we are interested in some aspect of conflict, say, power, and we use games and Game Theory as investigative tools. But it soon develops that simply "winning," or imaginary rewards, are not prized highly enough. Not prized highly enough, that is, to allow us to predict as we wish to, so we use different kinds of controls. We introduce "real" rewards in the form of a point on a mid-term examination awarded for every fifteen game points. But that is still not enough, so we use a different group of subjects, not students this time, but inmates of a federal prison, and now when game points are exchanged for examination points, the prisoners' ability to travel to nearby colleges for study-release time and, in certain cases, their ability to qualify for parole are involved.[24] Real rewards, indeed! One wonders in what sense the prisoners found it all a game. And one is surely entitled to ask what right the experimenter has to exercise such power, especially in a situation in which, as the experimenter admits, two of the inmates almost come to blows, retire bitterly from the "game," and can hardly be interviewed afterward.

Or, we say we are interested in certain kinds of very commonly used language, and we arbitrarily choose (or accept someone else's choice of) "opinionated" and "non-opinionated" statements, the former term meaning statements that show the speaker's attitudes toward an idea or belief *and* toward those who agree or disagree with that idea or belief, the latter meaning statements that indicate the speaker's attitude toward the belief and nothing further. Then we create messages, assign them high and low credibility sources, and set about testing for attitude change. As samples of the two sorts of language, we use "I believe the U.S. should withdraw from Viet Nam," "I can't abide that policy," "The Ku Klux Klan is one of the strongest forces supporting law and order in many areas" (*all nonopinionated*), and "Only a warmonger would oppose the withdrawal of the U.S. from Viet Nam," "No self-respecting person can abide that policy," "The Ku Klux Klan is one of the strongest forces supporting law and order in many areas. Those who do not support the KKK are mainly people who do not support law and order" (*all opinionated*).[25] Of course, Burkeans, logicians, close textualists, and theorists of other types will find much to criticize here, but I am concerned with two things: First, there is the assumption that, when I am presented with the above group of "nonopinionated" statements and am told they were uttered by someone I respect, I will *not* find that the statements imply any attitude toward *me*. Is there not an oddity here? If I revere the KKK, respect George Wallace, and hear him praise the KKK and denounce its enemies, can it be seriously argued that I do not perceive him to be praising *me*, as well as the KKK, and denouncing *my* enemies, as well as those of the KKK? Well, yes, it can be so argued, if one ignores the *personae* of the "opinionated" and "nonopinionated" state-ments, although ignoring them is made far more difficult by the assignment of high and low credibility sources. And that leads me to the second problem. There is the assump-tion here that the experimenter somehow automatically has the right to find out what sources (and it would make a difference if they were called "human beings," would it not?) the students respect or disdain, what ideas they embrace or reject, and then to create artificial statements designed to clash with the students' beliefs and to tell the stu-dents those statements were uttered by persons they hold in high or low regard. I suspect that, for some, the issues in this example will appear less dramatic than those in the two preceding cases, perhaps because this third instance can seem similar to the critical inquiry that is the stock in trade of the professor. Yet I am troubled by *our* apparent belief that we can experiment with *student* beliefs in this manner, for I perceive a truly painful dilemma here: either the student does not take seriously the false wedding of statement and source, the deliberate deception involved in putting words that bolster the students' beliefs in the mouths of persons they dislike (or vice versa)—either the student does not take all this seriously, or she/he does take it seriously; in the former case, we may safely undertake the experiment, for we will not be toying irresponsibly with ideas the student holds dear, since the student considers the whole business unimportant—only, in that case, there is no validity to the experiment; and in the latter case, we may not safely undertake the study, for the students' beliefs will be directly, perhaps permanently, altered, and altered in ways that cannot be ethically justified, since, by definition, the whole matter of pairing topic, source, high vs. low credibility, is carried out in a random fashion.

And the list could go on and on and on. I have chosen these three examples of actual studies because they seem to me to be representative of a great deal of the scientific discourse in communication. And I wish to argue that in these and a very great many similar studies, the avoidance of ethical appraisals by both critics and authors themselves is made possible by the presumed absence of *personae.* Only as "impersonal," "detached," "factual," "objective," "neutral" discourse can such studies be argued to merit no ethical evaluation.

Of course, there is a sense in which all this is an old story. We have heard frequently of the danger of "value-free" science. Charles Hampden-Turner, for example, has vigorously criticized "the capacity of 'scientific methodology' to *generate* and then '*discover*' unethical behavior," and he has concluded that, "since experimental procedures delude, render helpless, and set out to *predict* and *control* the obedient reactions of subjects, the 'discovery' of behavior they have 'scientifically' engendered is hardly an earth shaking surprise" (italics added); and he says bluntly, objective experiments "do their best to suppress ... the ethical nature of man."[26] And Abraham Maslow has denounced objectivity as the process of "looking at something that is not you, not human, not personal, something independent of you the perceiver. ... You, the observer, are, then, really alien to it, uncomprehending and without sympathy or identification. ..."[27] And there are many similar comments—comments that probably should not be ignored even by those who study such seemingly impersonal things as light, neutrinos, anti-matter, etc., and comments that must not be ignored by those who study people. What I hope to add to such coments is the notion that we can escape the need for ethical criticism only by avoiding the concept of the *persona.* But when we do avoid that concept, the dramatic nature of the discourse in question changes sharply, and in a manner quite familiar to those who work in Theater or with literature.

To be objective about what one studies is, so the scientist will argue, to treat it without bias, to view it neutrally so far as values are concerned. But this bias-free, neutral view is *dramatically impossible to enact.* The very term "neutral" is suffused with the negative: it means "*not* taking either side in a dispute," "*not* actively committed for or against," "*not* partisan," etc. No actor can perform objectivity or neutrality toward anything, because no actor can perform the negative, in this sense; what an actor *can* perform is an active, positive attitude of concern, disdain, care, contempt, etc., but there is a world of difference between these qualities and objective neutrality. The actor can show that something is unimportant, that she or he values something very little or a great deal; the actor can dismiss with whimsical changes of mood, can show only the barest feeling for something, can show lack of awareness of one thing by demonstrating awareness of something else. In brief, the actor can only *act;* she or he can never not-act.

What is true of the actor is also true of our language, for on one level our language, our discourse, is a dramatic, a presentational form that excludes the negative.[28] At bottom, our discourse is always poetic and rhetorical, always formally expressive, attitudinal, and hortatory; i.e., we are always symbolizing for the joy of symbolizing, and we are always taking points of view and expressing attitudes, never taking no-point-of-view or expressing nonattitudes.[29] Thus, our discourse, scientific or otherwise, can only display those attitudes we do, in fact, demonstrate, for on the level on which to discourse is to perform, to enact, we can enact only those attitudes, beliefs, biases, opinions that constitute the *personae* of such discourse.[30]

The scientist who strives for objectivity, for neutrality, must perforce disregard the concept of *persona* simply because that concept brings with it the very values, prejudices, attitudes, the scientist wishes to avoid. But to one who views such discourse from a literary or dramatic viewpoint, the scientist's is an exercise in perfect dramatic futility: disclaim the prejudiced, the attitudinal, the opinionated as the scientist may, the *persona* cannot be disclaimed; to discourse is, before anything else, to act, and the very nature of the act implies an actor; thus, when a scientific discourse admits to no concern, no regard for what is studied—especially for persons who are studied—the dramatic or literary critic is likely to perceive that discourse as implying a *persona* (as every discourse does), but a persona displaying positively and actively the coldness, the disdain, the alienation that Roszak, and Maslow, and Hampden-Turner, and many others, have described.

It is a matter of the self-reflexive nature of language. All discourse is a multilevel process, and the deepest of those levels is the aesthetic or dramatic presentation of selves—selves chosen from the cluster of more, or less, habitually performed roles called 'the self' and enacted for poetic-rhetorical purposes. Such selves are *personae;* they are to be found in every discursive form, including the one we call scientific; and they require ethical appraisal, particularly when they presume to study, to manipulate, to experiment with people.

Notes

Mr. Campbell is Professor of Theatre and Drama at the University of Kansas. A brief version of this paper was presented at the Speech Communication Association Convention in Chicago, December, 1974.

1 The label is Kenneth Burke's. He describes it in various works; my favorite is *The Rhetoric of Religion: Studies in Logology* (Berkeley: Univ. of California Press, 1970), pp. 1–42, but especially pp. 24–27.

2 Susanne K. Langer, *Philosophy In A New Key: A Study in the Symbolism of Reason, Rite, and Art* (New York: Mentor Books, 1964), pp. 231–232.

3 For those who feel that this paragraph comes uncomfortably close to Russell's notion of the logical paradox that occurs when one attempts to create a class of all classes, I would point out that rhetoric is here viewed as one dimension of language. That is, scientific (or poetic, or philosophical) discourse includes a rhetorical dimension but is neither limited to nor equated with rhetoric.

4 Thomas S. Kuhn, *The Structure of Scientific Revolutions* (Chicago: Univ. of Chicago Press, 1962), p. 10.

5 Ibid., pp. 93–94.

6 Ibid., p. 1.

7 Jacob Bronowski, *Science and Human Values,* rev. ed. (New York: Harper & Row, 1965), p. 59.

8 Ibid., pp. 56–62.

9 Kenneth Burke, "Terministic Screens," *Language as Symbolic Action: Essays on Life, Literature, and Method* (Berkeley: Univ. of California Press, 1968), p. 45.

10 This point is discussed in detail by Wayne Booth, *The Rhetoric of Fiction* (Chicago: Univ. of Chicago Press, 1961), p. 105 and section II.

11 Walker Gibson, *Persona: A Style Study for Readers and Writers* (New York: Random House, 1969), p. xi.

12 Ibid., Chapter 2.

13 John Rathbun, "The Problem of Judgment and Effect in Historical Criticism: A Proposed Solution," *Western Speech,* 37 (1969), 146–159.

14 Kuhn, pp. 147–149.

15 Ibid., pp. 151–152, 154.

16 Bronowski, pp. 69, 70, 73.

17 Ibid., p. 73.

18 Theodore Roszak, *The Making of a Counter Culture* (Garden City, New York: Doubleday, 1969), pp. 217–227.

19 Bronowski, p. xiii.

20 In the preceding and following sections, I am concerned with language, with science as discourse. Although I do not think that science can exist apart from discourse, there may be those who wish to view science as an event, the discursive product of which is but one aspect of the entire process. To those who view science in that manner, I would suggest that the concept of the *persona* retains its power in the nondiscursive or nonlinguistic areas of science. That is, the very appearance of the scientist before her or his subjects immediately implies a *persona,* and such an appearance can only enhance the *personae*-laden nature of whatever data are involved in or result from the research process. Pertinent here are the widely cited studies on experimenter bias: an early and important study in this group is Robert Rosenthal and Lenore F. Jacobson, "Teacher Expectations for the Disadvantaged," *Scientific American,* Apr. 1968, pp. 19–24.

21 This statement follows Burke's act-agent ratio, i.e., the sense in which the act contains the agent. See Kenneth Burke, A *Grammar of Motives,* bound together with *A Rhetoric of Motives* (Cleveland: Meridian, 1962), pp. 3–20.

22 See feature articles by Jane E. Brody, *New York Times,* 18 April 1974, p. 20, cols. 3–4, and 25 May 1974, p. 1, col. 3.

23 Dale G. Leathers, "The Process Effects of Trust-Destroying Behavior in the Small Group," *Speech Monographs,* 37 (1970), 180–187.

24 Thomas M. Steinfatt, David R. Seibold, and Jerry K. Frye, "Communication in Game Simulated Conflicts: Two Experiments," *Speech Monographs,* 41 (1974), 24–35.

25 R. Samuel Mehrley and James C. McCroskey, "Opinionated Statements and Attitude Intensity as Predictors of Attitude Change and Source Credibility," *Speech Monographs,* 37 (1970), 47–52.

26 Charles Hampden-Turner, *Radical Man* (Garden City, New York: Anchor Books, 1971), pp. 5–6, 113.

27 Abraham Maslow, *The Psychology of Science* (New York: Harper & Row, 1966), p. 49, cited in Roszak, p. 219.

28 Langer, p. 222.

29 Burke, *Language as Symbolic Action,* pp. 9–13. Burke's treatment of the negative is far more complex than Langer's, but while it is a simplification, I think it is fair to say that Burke finds that language always and positively displays attitudes, urges points of view, and offers the enticements of form.

30 It follows from this statement that when our studies include discourses as objects of study as well as methods of study, as is the case with credibility research, matters are further complicated. Both the *personae* of the discourses studied and the *persona* of the study itself interact with whatever scales of measurement are used, so that, as David Mortensen puts it, such research is unable to decide what to do with Nietzsche's first question, "Who speaks?"

4.
THE RHETORIC OF SCIENCE
by Philip C. Wander

At any given moment, what we know to exist in the world is the product of an evolving set of human agreements. Thus, in a given society, there may exist any number of conflicting interpretations of reality. Multiple, competing realities, however, create problems for those members of society who have vested interests in one interpretation over another. As a consequence, each society evolves a body of rules by which one version of reality may be legitimated and other, competing versions discredited. Because the knowledge that reality is a human construct is liable to subvert the social order nominally secured through a particular interpretation, official reality and the rules by which it is validated are everywhere cloaked with an air of mystification. Eric Goode expresses the point quite well: "The one selected view of the world must be seen as the *only possible* view of the world; it must be identified with the real world. All other versions of reality must be seen as whimsical and arbitrary and, above all, in *error*." At one time religion defined reality and secured the rules for its validation through God's vicar on earth and through interpretation of holy text. "Views in competition with the dominant one were heretical and displeasing to the gods—hence Galileo's 'crime,' " but now the style is to invest our "fictitious necessities" with what Goode calls an "aura of scientific validity." He continues: "Nothing has greater discrediting power today than the demonstration that a given assertion has been 'scientifically disproven.' "[1] Given this power, it is hardly surprising that on every great issue in modern society, science, scientists, and the vocabulary of science shape the debate.

Burdened by the historical split between science and the humanities and caught up in the mystique of modern science with its guarantee of knowledge and power and promise for the future, the rhetorical critic has been slow to treat this topic.[2] Its place in the deliberation of public policy, however, obliges the critic to concern him or herself with science: how it is used in debate; how it relates to other sources of information; what occurs when there is conflicting scientific evidence. There is yet another area within science amenable to rhetorical investigation. This has to do with the efforts made by scientists to persuade one another. Grant proposals, journal articles, and convention papers are designed to influence a professional audience (granting agencies, journal editors, and so on). In order to be successful, they must convince this audience that the research topic is worthy of study, the appropriate tools were used, and used correctly, and that the researcher knew what he or she was doing, This essay explores the ambiance

Philip C. Wander. "The Rhetoric of Science." *Western Speech Communication*, Volume 40, Number 4, 1976, pp. 226–235.

between rhetoric and science, integrates some recent research pertinent to study in this area, and indicates some possibilities for future work in the rhetoric of science.

Science and Public Policy Deliberation

Public deliberation tends increasingly to technical language and to statistical computation: the "input," "output," and "feedback" of computer technology, "infrastructure," "debriefing," megadeath estimates of the loss of human life in a nuclear war,[3] the proportion of the work force unemployed, quantity of energy reserves in the United States and the projected demand, predicted gross national product and rate of inflation. This is a mode of discourse. There are other modes (legal, moral, and religious as well as scientific) preferred at different times in different contexts, each with its own vocabulary and characteristic set of facts and inferences (precedents and interpretations, principles and imperatives, texts and revelations). Reliance on technical language in public debate is rhetorically significant, for in a democracy, whatever its practical imperfections, the people have a right, on the important public issues, to know the relevant social and economic facts as well as the policy conclusions to be drawn from them. When the language of public debate becomes too specialized, the laity is encouraged to remain silent. This is true when Latin was the official medium of intellectual exchange; it is also true with science. Not only can a technical vocabulary confuse the issues for the layman when it becomes official parlance, but it can also work to relieve the expert of his or her responsibility for informing the public. Those technically best equipped in modern society to speak out on affairs, the independent scholars in the various sciences, are becoming stultified by the language of their field. This is the situation Gunnar Myrdal was addressing, when he declared: "I must ... register my dissatisfaction with a trend among economists and social scientists generally to abandon the great tradition, adhered to through generations by even the greatest scholars, to speak to the people in simple terms that laymen can understand. They are increasingly addressing only each other. This trend of false 'scientism' is a foregoing of our responsibility for the formation of public opinion. ..."[4] When the jargon of science is officially employed, it intimidates the layman. When it is voluntarily adopted, it represents a desertion of a particular audience, that of the common citizen.

Symptomatic of the rise of the expert and the decline of the citizen in our society is the number of decisions which are made by committees of specialists. A report prepared by the Committee of Science in the Promotion of Human Welfare of the American Association for the Advancement of Science drew attention to the increased interaction between science and public policy and the problem of distinguishing scientific problems from those which ought to be resolved by social processes. One instance of this confusion, cited in the report, had to do with the radiation standards set by the Federal Radiation Council. Standards of acceptability, the Committee declared, are basically social judgments resting on the balance between the dangers and the benefits of nuclear operations, judgments which ought to be, the Committee held, wholly vulnerable to political debate, but which might not be because their appearance in the guise of a scientific decision shields them from such scrutiny.[5]

While the language of science can affect public debate over vital issues, through the reticence of non-experts to speak, and through the bottling of important information in verbal technicalities, it is the popular awe of science which makes of it such an important topic in public deliberation.[6] Every new public program must contain some scientific justi-fication. The debate over each new weapons system for the past quarter century has centered not only on military need, but also on technological feasability. The whole notion of a new weapons system depends on being able to talk about it as something which we need which is practically within our grasp. Presentations before congressional committees replete with blueprints, projections, and cost estimates are consummate rhetorical acts.

Far more public and more dramatic in its execution, however, has been the use of science in justifying massive public expenditures on the space program. Gordon J. F. MacDonald, associate director for the Institute of Geophysics and Planetary Physics at UCLA and vice president for research at the Institute for Defense Analysis, Arlington, Virginia, reflected on the curious relationship between science and the space agency:

> It must be remembered that NASA is at present concerned with science only in a limited way. The office in NASA charged with carrying out the science program received only about 15 percent of the space budget. Major space accomplishments are not measured in terms of science alone. In one sense, science rides the coattails of goals resulting from complex con-siderations of prestige, politics, and economics. However, in another sense, science is used as the underlying justification for the total program.[7]

In the areas of public policy, the use of science as a rhetorical topic for legitimizing the expenditure of billions of dollars of public funds is a fact—that is the way, though not the only way, every proposal, whether attacked or recommended, is argued, and in this context science or the use of science in public deliberation begs rhetorical investigation.

Science and the Rhetoric of Scientists

We have, thus far, discussed only generally the way science affects our talking about the world. We have not specifically considered the way scientists actually talk, for anyone can use the idiom to talk about factors in the relative decline of whatever. The archetypal speaking situation for the scientist occurs in addressing an audience of fellow scientists, and the archetypal form of discourse is the research report. This too may be examined rhetorically. A scientific research report is not just a giving of information; it is a persua-sive act as well. In order to grasp what this means, we must again consider the institu-tional context of science. In itself, a research paper is of little value. It is not likely to be widely read, nor, if read, carefully studied. Why? Because it has not undergone the acid test of scientific research, peer group review. Nearly every journal requires that a submis-sion be evaluated by one or more people (referees) who are themselves experts in the subject area. One scholar has called this review the "lynch pin" of science.[8] What this means as a practical matter is that one audience a scientist addresses, if he or she wishes to publish, is the editorship of the appropriate professional journals. Certainly it is an audience which must be persuaded before a research report will ever reach the larger professional audience which reads the journals. In a note on the writing of research reports appearing in *Science*, John H. Wilson, a member of the staff of the Technical Information Division, Lawrence Radiation Laboratory, decrys the fact that researchers do not want to write clear, literate papers which will be instantly clear to all readers. They want instead, Wilson observes, "to get a paper published that will impress their peers, and if nobody else understands, so much the better."[9] There are, of course, some agreements that any writer, whatever his specialty will wish to make with his or her audience: that the subject is worth talking about; that the speaker knows what he or she is talking about; and that the findings ought to be integrated in some way into the existing fund of personal or human knowledge. The question is what are the strategies that scientists employ in their efforts to impress their peers. This question, however, must be asked about a particular point in time, because the way in which research findings are justified varies over time.

At the turn of the century, Karl Pearson submitted a paper on biology to the Royal Society which was published a year later, in 1901, but only after the Society had passed a rule that henceforth mathematics and biology were to be separated. Pearson was offended by this treatment, and he wrote his friend, Sir John Galton, asking him whether he thought that he should resign from the Society in protest. Galton replied that he should not. Together they later founded the journal, *Biometrick*, which has as its expressed purpose to encourage the use of statistics in biological studies.[10] Our interest here has nothing to do with the *utility* of statistical reasoning in the conduct of biological research; it has to do with the *appropriateness* of statistical reasoning in professional publications. To be sure, the use of statistics in biological sciences does not now meet with the baffling and hostile response that Pearson and before him Mendel met from their contemporaries; in fact, the appearance of statistics has come to be considered evidence of one's actually being engaged in worthwhile scientific work.

An essay on the use of statistical reasoning in sociological research appeared in the February, 1970 issue of *The American Sociologist* entitled, "On Being Scientific: Changing Styles of Presentation of Sociological Research."[11] What the author, James L. McCartney, had to say on the subject is pertinent to our discussion:

> We suspect that the increasing use of statistical measures in sociological research is related to problems that sociologists encounter when seeking funding for their research. The major supporters of sociological research (governmental and private) seek useful knowledge from their expenditures, and much of the successful research they have supported in other disciplines makes considerable use of statistical reasoning. In essence, sociologists no doubt feel they must structure a research proposal so as to demonstrate its scientific merit, and use of statistics is one of the more evident indices of scientific merit. If this argument is correct, then one result should be that research which utilizes statistical reasoning is more likely to be supported than research which does not. A broader implication for sociology is that specialties which receive substantial funding are more likely to expand than specialties which receive little funding.

McCartney establishes, through a rather elaborate scheme of charts and percentages, a measure of quantitative evidence to support his hypotheses. But again, our interest is with the rhetorical significance of statistical reasoning, more specifically with its strategic value in light of the predispositions of a particular audience, those whose organizational role it is to distribute grants for scientific research. On this view it would make sense to talk about a rhetoric of grant proposals.

But there are, apart from the use of statistics, a number of other rhetorical strategies appearing in the literature of the social sciences. This is the subject of an article by Andrew J. Weigert, which also appears in the *American Sociologist*.[12] Although the work is entitled, "The Immoral Rhetoric of Scientific Sociology," it does not have to do, as one might suspect, with military-oriented research in sociology. What Weigert has in mind is a fundamental methodological distinction between the scientist, who makes an argument, consciously persuading to some end and the scientist who seeks to advance knowledge. The immorality, in Weigert's view, lies in posturing as a scientist while actually functioning as a rhetor. In order to develop this point, he displays what he considers to be among the more obvious schemes employed in social science publications to persuade an audience rather than to proclaim the truth of the matter. There is, he allows, a "rhetoric of theory" which must pretend to explain all that it intends to explain, a "pretension" which emphasizes supporting and de-emphasizes contrary evidence. There is a "factual rhetoric of empiricism," of which he writes:

> What formal scientific criteria govern the decisionmaking procedure that is essential to the selection of stimuli from among literally infinite possibilities? The decisions are sometimes made on the basis of authority and prestige of previous users ...; availability; time and money at the researcher's disposal; past experience with the items; touchiness of subject matter; necessity to mislead subjects. These are real, but hardly scientific, criteria. When the study is presented for public perusal, however, the real reasons may not appear; only the telescoped rationalization will. (p. 114)

There is also a "pedigree rhetoric of underground references," referring to the practice of thanking certain people for criticizing the draft, often quite prominent people in a given field, of reading papers at conventions before publishing them and then noting the fact in a footnote, and the widespread practice of citing one's earlier work, all of which, if it does not enable the editor to identify the author, asserts a certain eminence in the field.

Lest we draw the wrong conclusion about this excellent article, Weigert believes in the possibility of doing genuinely scientific work in sociology. To this end he has catalogued those rhetorical strategies in social science research which, while working to secure assent, do not advance science. While Professor Weigert is at pains to establish rhetoric as a legitimate method of investigation, a splendid ambition one is forced to admit, and while his effort is, on the whole, quite exemplary, he does not, I believe, push it far enough. As a result he is left with a perplexing duality between informative (scientific) and persuasive (rhetorical) discourse. The problem is that the two cannot be distinguished structurally: the form which today is used to proclaim truth, may tomorrow, in a different context with a different audience, be used to persuade. The form remains constant; the intent varies. The same problem occurs when an audience which ought to have been informed but, given the purpose and the structure of the discourse, acts as if persuaded.

The question reaches all the way back into antiquity. In Plato's republic, the orator would be a noble fellow, a trained philosopher, and the audience composed of people willing to have their opinions shaped by such a leader. In order to make it easier for those whose eye, clouded by practical matters, is not on the true Reality, Plato removed those speakers who might counterfeit the utterance of philosophers, or who might otherwise charm through beauty of expression, the poets and, alas, the rhetoricians. Aristotle, on the other hand, was more interested in day-to-day affairs when considering the subject of rhetoric. If we are to evaluate rhetoric, he tells us, it should be joined with the action it recommends. Rhetoric is like a knife; in the hands of a thief, it can kill; in the hands of a surgeon, it can save. In assessing the power of utterance, one must consider not only the reputation of the speaker, but also its moral and ethical consequences in this world. Professions of spiritual insight provided by the speaker are, following Aristotle, simply one among many available means of persuasion. In the Platonic tradition, however, it makes sense to ask why we do not dispense with rhetoric. Substituting "science" for "dialectic" as the ultimate method of arriving at truth, we may ask, with Professor Weigert, why not rid ourselves of rhetoric altogether and simply do science? The answer, I think, pivots on the measure of wisdom we are willing to attribute to ourselves, or, if stricken with humility, how much we are willing to attribute to those who claim or who have been certified knowledgeable by some external agency: God, graduate school, or journal editor.

Modern science, with its various specialties, encourages a certain amount of humility. People become experts on some particular method or object of research. Within a given field, two certified research scholars may barely understand one another's work; within the broader area of "science," the social psychologist may be unable to read even the first line of a paper written by a particle physicist. In fact, a physicist trained ten years ago may or may not be able to grasp contemporary work in his or her own specialty, so fast is the change of theory and method in the most advanced fields of study. Therefore, the body of knowledge one can point to at any given moment and call "scientific" rests almost entirely on one's faith in the research reports of myriad others, in the conduct and communication of that research, and finally in one's own abilities to interpret the work accurately. Thus, the ethos of the speaker/writer, enhanced by having been certified by a graduate school and a journal editor, remains crucial in science as in other human activities.[13] Even in science, Walter Ong observes, the word is an invitation to belief, and the belief *that* something is true is secondary to a belief *in* the word of those sharing the information.[14]

Conclusions

If it makes sense to talk about the rhetoric of science in research reports, and we have just argued that this is so, then how much more sensible to treat it in public deliberation. These two approaches to the study of science recommend a number of possibilities for rhetorical studies. One could, for example, compare the discourse of scientists; Einstein and Oppeheimer[15] come immediately to mind, speaking before professional and lay audiences on the same subject. Many prominent scientists over the last quarter century have spoken out on policy issues on the basis of their expertise. The *Bulletin of the Atomic Scientists*, founded by Einstein, Oppeheimer, Fermi, and others, was created in the belief that scientists needed a forum from which to speak to a larger audience. They believed that the issues raised by science transcended purely professional concerns.

The invocation of science by lay people debating specific issues also offers research possibilities. Nuclear testing, the SST, the anti-missile defense system, the use of nuclear energy, each of these debates turns largely on scientific findings and the interpretation of these findings. What happens when scientific evidence conflicts; what changes occur in the use of such evidence, in the nature of the evidence, in its interpretation? Another approach to the use of science by lay people might include the image of science as it appears on television, in newspapers, film, in science fiction novels (see Ray Lynn Anderson's work). Historical research can retrieve and explicate important scientific texts (John Angus Campbell's work with the *Origin of the Species* provides a brilliant model here) in light of its immediate audience, in light of contemporary attitudes toward science.

When scientists address their peers, they also use rhetorical strategies, and this too offers a fruitful area of investigation, especially when the discourse treats socially significant issues. William Stanton's book, *The Leopard's Spots: Scientific Attitudes Toward Race in America, 1815–1859*, is a remarkable work along this line. Janice Law Tucker's informative essay, "Sex, Science, and Education," *American Quarterly*, 26 (1974), 352–66, should also be examined. The rise and fall of particular strategies in scientific treatises, quotations from the *Bible* in early ethnological studies, the introduction of "observation" stories, the emergence of statistical reasoning in the social sciences, would be relevant. The "persona" implicit in scientific publications (see Paul Newell Campbell's essay [in this volume, 46-61]), the "second persona," the rhetorical situation prompting a particular bit of research, these concepts lend themselves to a rhetorical analysis of science.

A rhetorical investigation into science is not desirable in and of itself, and if all it represents is an *entre* into the bickering between scientists and humanists, or a new field within which to display professional skills, then I have not said what I intended to say. The issues reach beyond provincial quarrels and professional posturing.[16] Science and all that it represents stands at the center of our civilization. There is an increasing interest, both within and without the academy, in the rhetoric of science, and I believe, despite the irony implicit in the request, that there is a need for further research in this area.

Notes

1 Eric Goode, "Marijuana and the Politics of Reality," *Journal of Health and Social Behavior*, 10 (1969), 83–4. Goode's essay draws extensively on Peter Berger and Thomas Luckmann's book, *The Social Construction of Reality* (New York: Archer Books, 1966).

2 See, for example: John Angus Campbell's impressive work on Charles Darwin, "Darwin and *The Origin of the Species*: The Rhetorical Ancestry of an Idea," *Speech Monographs*, 37 (1970), 1–14; "Charles Darwin and the Crisis of Ecology, A Rhetorical Perspective," *Quarterly Journal of Speech*, 60 (1974), 442–49; "Nature, Religion, and Emotional Response: A Reconsideration of Darwin's Affective Decline," *Victorian Studies*, 18 (1974), 159–74; "The Polemical Mr. Darwin," *Quarterly Journal of Speech*, 61 (1975), 375–90; Ray Lynn Anderson, "The Rhetoric of the 'Report from Iron Mountain,' " *Speech Monographs*, 37 (1970), 219–31; Ray Lynn

Anderson, "Rhetoric and Science Journalism," *Quarterly Journal of Speech*, 56 (1970), 358–68; William R. Brown and Richard E. Crable, "Industry, Mass Magazines, and the Ecology Issue," *Quarterly Journal of Speech*, 59 (1973), 259–72; Paul Newell Campbell, "The *Personae* of Scientific Discourse," this volume [1975], 46–61.

Chaim Perelman and L. Albrechts-Tyteca in their book, *The New Rhetoric* (Notre Dame: Univ. of Notre Dame Press, 1969), treat examples from arguments in science throughout. More recently, Wayne C. Booth addresses the issue in *Modern Dogma and the Rhetoric of Dissent* (Notre Dame: Univ. of Notre Dame Press, 1974), pp. 14–21, 88–135. For a literary-historical treatment of the subject, see: William Powell Jones, *The Rhetoric of Science: A Study of Scientific Ideas and Imagery in Eighteenth-Century English Poetry* (London: Routledge & Kegan Paul, 1966).

3 On the jargon of nuclear policy makers and its effect on policy thinking and formulation, see: Fred Ikle, "Can Nuclear Deterrence Last Out the Century," *Foreign Affairs*, 51 (1973), 280–81.

4 Gunnar Myrdal, "Too Late to Plan?," *Bulletin of the Atomic Scientists*, 24 (January 1968), p. 9.

5 Citing this and other instances, Harold P. Green considers the larger legal and political implications:

> Unquestionably, a democratic society should be able to make the determination that certain technological goals are so worth pursuing that its members must pay the price of exposure to radiation and noise, loss of privacy, or tampering with the weather. It is questionable, however, whether meaningful determinations of this kind, based on candid disclosure of the facts and adequate public discussion, are in fact being made as a predicate of government-sponsored technological programs. On the contrary, our decisions are made within small, closed circles of specialists on the basis of their expert judgments and predictions of the magnitude of the social consequences and the feasibility of their being controlled through technological means. "The New Technological Era: A View from the Law," *Bulletin of the Atomic Scientists*, 23 (November 1967), p. 12.

6 In Harris polls in 1966, 1971, and 1972 on the question of the public's confidence in those who run science, those expressing a "great deal" and "only some" confidence ranged from a low of 74 percent in 1972 to a high of 84 percent in 1973. Those expressing "hardly any or no" confidence never reached over 10 percent. In 1973, a Harris poll of the public indicating "confidence" in sixteen institutional areas, "science" ranked second only to "medicine." Etzioni and Nunn conclude from their examination of these and other survey data that "since science seems to command more confidence than many other institutions, particularly government and education, science cannot hope to gain legitimation from public officials and educational leaders. Indeed, government and education may, in future years, turn to scientists for legitimation, since only those who are trusted can lend trust." Amitai Etzioni and Clyde Nunn, "The Public Appreciation of Science in Contemporary America," *Daedalus*, 103 (1974), 194–95.

7 Gordon J. F. MacDonald, "Science and Space Policy: How Does It Get Planned?," *Bulletin of the Atomic Scientists*, 23 (May 1967), p. 3.

8 John M. Ziman, *Public Knowledge: The Social Dimension of Science* (Cambridge: Cambridge Univ. Press, 1966), p. 148.

9 John H. Wilson, "Better Written Journal Papers—Who Wants Them?," *Science*, 165 (September 1969), p. 986.

10 See: Bernard Barber, "Resistance by Scientists to Scientific Discovery," *Science*, 134 (September 1961), pp. 596–602.

11 James L. McCartney, "On Being Scientific: Changing Styles of Presentation of Sociological Research," *The American Sociologist*, 5 (1970), 30.

12 Andrew J. Weigert, "The Immoral Rhetoric of Scientific Sociology," *The American Sociologist*, 5 (1970), 111–19. In a survey of "hard" and "soft" scientists on the criteria used to evaluate a scientific article (N=191, "hard"=105, "soft"=86), Janet M. Chase rank-ordered the criteria provided in her survey based on the proportion of her respondents marking it "essential":

  1. Logical rigor—59%
  2. Replicability of research technique—53%
  4. Originality—42%
  5. Mathematical Precision—30%
  6. Coverage of significant existing literature—25%
  7. Compatability with generally accepted disciplinary ethics—22%
  8. Theoretical significance—16%
  9. Pertinence to current research in discipline—12%
  10. Applicability to "practical" or applied problem in the field—6%

  She comments: "Perhaps the most intriguing aspect of the rankings is the closeness between 'clarity and conciseness of writing style' and 'originality,' ranked third and fourth, respectively. This finding indicates definitely that technical considerations of publications are at least equally as important in judging the worth of scientific information as the end goal of adding to the existing body of knowledge." "Normative Criteria for Scientific Publication," *The American Sociologist*, 5 (1970), 262–65.

13 "... the system of monitoring scientific work before it enters into the archives of science means that much of the time scientists can build upon the work of others with a degree of warranted confidence. It is in this sense that the structure of authority in science, in which the referee system occupies a central place, provides an institutional basis for the comparative reliability and cumulation of knowledge." Harriet Zuckerman and Robert K. Merton, "Patterns of Evaluation in Science: Institutionalisation, Structure and Functions of the Referee System," *Minerva*, 9 (1971), 99–100.

14 Walter Ong, "Voice as Summons for Belief," *Literature and Belief*, ed. M. J. Abrams (New York: Columbia Univ. Press, 1965), pp. 80–107.

15 For an excellent historical analysis of Oppenheimer, and the political influences on science during and after WWII, see: Joseph Haberer, *Politics and the Community of Science*, (New York: Van Nostrand Reinhold, 1969), pp. 217–98.

16 For this perspective, see the symposium on the public disenchantment with the social sciences in the *American Scholar*, 45 (1976), 335–60.

5.
ARE SCIENTISTS RHETORS IN DISGUISE?
An Analysis of Discursive Processes within Scientific Communities
by Herbert W. Simons

Emboldened by recent attacks on scientific orthodoxies, rhetorically minded critics of science have been vituperative in their characterizations of scientific discourse, particularly the writings of social scientists. An image appearing repeatedly in the "rhetoric of science" literature has been that of the scientist as a rhetor in disguise—one who falsely pretends to the status of nonrhetor and thereby renders his rhetoric deceptive; one, moreover, who is not above engaging in such allegedly sophistic practices as masking self-serving motives behind a vocabulary of legitimating motives or subtly promoting partisan values in the guise of being informative.

Thus by Andrew Weigert's account, behavioral sociologists are guilty of an "immoral rhetoric of identity deception."[1] According to Weigert, journal editors and readers are courted by means of various impression-management techniques, and weaknesses in research or theory are covered over or rationalized away. Grant-givers are wooed by appeals to prejudice and by the framing of social problems in the distinctive jargon of the discipline. And students are indoctrinated by means of exaggerated claims, in survey, theory, and methodology texts, about the discipline's capacities and achievements. The themes of status enhancement and duplicity are sounded once again in Jack Douglas's castigation of social scientists for relying uncritically upon a "rhetoric of statistics," in Jeanine Czubaroff's illustrations of "the rhetoric of academic respectability," in Berger and Luckmann's depiction of medical jargon, white coats, and framed diplomas as the rhetorical stock-in-trade of physicians, and in Thomas Szasz's references to psychiatric labels as a justificatory rhetoric of rejection and oppression.[2]

What are we to make of these characterizations of scientists and of scientific discourse? Clearly they stand in marked contrast to the traditional view of science as falling outside the province of rhetoric. Less clear, however, is whether they add up to an inherent case against science in general, or even against the discourse of social scientists. Are the indictments offered by rhetorically minded critics valid in principle or do they apply only to atypical practices by isolated scientists?

One way to gain clarity on the issue of inherency is to cast "pro" and "con" positions in the form of a debate, and that is what I shall be doing in this paper. By juxtaposing competing views the debate format should also permit differentiation between easily

Herbert W. Simons. "Are Scientists Rhetors in Disguise? An Analysis of Discursive Processes within Scientific Communities." In Eugene E. White, ed. *Rhetoric in Transition: Studies in the Nature and Uses of Rhetoric.* University Park: The Pennsylvania State University Press, 1980, pp. 115–131.

refutable claims and counterclaims and those which resist clear resolution. In this way it should serve to advance the questions, even if in the process it also makes it more diffi-cult to render clear-cut, unequivocal conclusions.

What would it take to mount an inherent case, one that establishes in principle that scientists are rhetors in disguise? In other words what is the affirmative's burden of proof in this debate?

To begin with, the affirmative must successfully undermine the traditional notion that scientists are in some way different from ordinary rhetors—different by dint of their alleged capacity to provide objective, unambiguous, uncontestable tests of assertions (as opposed to the plausible arguments traditionally associated with rhetorical discourse). To do so it must cut to the heart of the claim to scientific objectivity, the presumed capa-city of scientific communities as a whole to correct for the foibles and passions of indi-vidual scientists. While critics can undoubtedly point to subjective elements in the discourse of individual scientists, defenders of science might concede the point, as Karl Popper has done, and nevertheless insist that what sets scientific discourse apart from that of ordinary rhetors is the error-correcting *process of exchange* that takes place within scientific communities. Here Popper refers to the normatively sanctioned use of a com-monly understood technical language, the insistence by the group as a whole that theoretical statements be framed in such a way that they can be tested by observations and experiments, and, above all, the unrestrained criticism of any and all ideas, includ-ing those which emanate from the highest authorities.[3] Once Popper's view of science as a communal enterprise is given credence, it becomes logically inappropriate to conclude that scientific discourse is inherently rhetorical simply by citing evidence of passion, prejudice, or other subjective elements in the discourse of individual scientists. In place of an *act-centered* view of scientific discourse a *process-centered* view is needed, one that shows scientific assertions to be eminently contestable or ambiguous (i.e., rhetorical) even after they have been honed and refined by exchanges within scientific communities.

The notion of rhetoric as a communal process figures prominently with respect to the second burden which the affirmative must carry in this debate, that of showing that scientists are guilty of such allegedly sophistic practices as using a vocabulary of legiti-mating motives to mask self-serving motives or promoting partisan values in the guise of being informative. Even assuming that all of the charges cited earlier are valid, it is unclear whether they add up to an inherent case. Just as evidence of subjectivity in the discourse of individual scientists does not in itself refute the Popperian notion of scient-ific objectivity as a communal product, evidence of sophistic practices by individual sci-entists is an insufficient basis upon which to condemn entire scientific communities.

Beyond evidence of sophistic practices, compelling arguments are needed as to why, in principle, these misdeeds are bound to occur. Barring that, defenders of science might reasonably acknowledge misdeeds while insisting that no serious harm is done so long as scientific communities as a whole maintain appropriate institutionalized commitments to the pursuit of knowledge. To return to charges leveled by critics, some individual sci-entists may be motivated by greed, power, envy, or the need for recognition, but the norms and practices of any given scientific community might well provide an effective counterforce to these motives. Similarly some individual scientists may exaggerate discoveries and even fabricate them, demean critics and even slander them, ingratiate themselves with institutional superiors and even pander to them, inject personal values into their arguments and even deliberately polemicize: in the long run, however, any given scientific community might well survive these allegedly sophistic practices by dint of an overarching, institutionalized commitment to public testing of testable ideas in a free marketplace of ideas. Unless it can be shown that deceptions, evasions, and distortions *follow* in some way from the very nature of scientific communities, science in its collective, Popperian sense must stand acquitted of the charge of sophistry.

Thus far I have attempted to fix the burden of proof for rhetoricians of science (the affirmative in the debate) in establishing that scientists are inherently rhetors in disguise. In so doing I have stressed the need for a process-centered view of scientific discourse, as opposed to an orientation focused on individual acts. At this point we may let the promised debate begin. In constructing the debate I have attempted to act as an honest spokesman for both sides by giving strong voice to each. Following the debate I offer a "judge's verdict," consisting of an attempted reconciliation of extreme views as well as a list of questions that continue to nag.

The Debate: Resolved that Scientists are Rhetors in Disguise

The Affirmative

There are two major issues in this debate. First, are scientific communities incapable of providing objective tests of assertions? Second, do patterns of sophistic practices follow in some way from the very nature of scientific communities?

Objective Tests of Assertions. Since the communal aspect of science figures so prominently in the defense of the notion of scientific objectivity, it is worth emphasizing that the tests made by scientists may be considered unambiguous or uncontestable only if one buys the value and belief premises that scientific communities share in common. That science is not value free has been attested to by many scientists themselves. Alfred Whitehead observed some time ago that "without judgments of value there would be no science." And John F. A. Taylor remarked about the scientific commitment to objectivity itself that "the rule which guarantees the disinterestedness of inquiry is not itself neutral with respect to the matter of disinterestedness."[4] In his excellent treatise on *A Sociology of Sociology*, Friedrichs suggested that scientists

> shoulder the responsibility of settling upon one of a number of logical systems, none of which is able to validate itself in terms of itself. ... If a sociologist follows an essentially Aristotelian logic, he will paint social experience in colors quite different from those that would come through given an initial commitment to a dialectical logic—pigments that impinge upon issues of ideology.[5]

The general point, made by mathematician Kurt Gödel, is that "no single logistic system ... can tenably claim to embrace only logical truth *and* the whole of logical truth." It follows, of course, that science's assumptive underpinnings are not themselves scientifically demonstrable. Rather, as Willem F. Zuurdeeg has suggested, science functions "within a larger framework which is convictional." The process by which consensus is reached on the so-called transcendent values of science is inherently rhetorical, as Thomas Farrell has argued.[6] And that consensus is also limited. From a perspective outside the scientific, religious revelation or mystical intuition or extrasensory perception may appear to be far truer paths to knowledge than those accepted as a matter of scientific faith.

Even assuming that the foregoing philosophical considerations were somehow irrelevant to the scientific quest, it would still be true that scientists cannot provide objective tests of assertions, at least at the level of paradigm choice. In addition to agreeing on philosophical premises, scientific communities are committed to roughly the same criteria for evaluating theories: problem-solving ability, manageability, and parsimony. But there are inevitably sharp disagreements between adherents to competing paradigms about the relative weights to be assigned to each criterion and about how they should be interpreted in any given case. Moreover, as Thomas Kuhn has argued in his now familiar treatise, *there are no neutral algorithms in terms of which such disagreements can be resolved.*

> When paradigms change, there are usually significant shifts in the criteria determining the legitimacy both of problems and of proposed solutions. ... To the extent ... that two scientific schools disagree about what is a problem and what is a solution, they will inevitably talk through each other when debating the relative merits of their respective paradigms. In the partially circular arguments that regularly result, each paradigm will be shown to satisfy more or less the criteria that it dictates for itself and to fall short of those dictated by its opponent. There are other reasons, too, for the incompleteness of logical contact that consistently characterizes paradigm debates. For example ..., paradigm debates always involve the question: Which problems is it more significant to have solved? Like the issue of competing standards, that question of values can be answered only in terms of criteria that lie outside of normal science altogether, and it is that recourse to external criteria that most obviously makes paradigm debates revolutionary.[7]

There is a sense, too, in which paradigm debates are about different realities. That is why Kuhn insists,

> Communication across the revolutionary divide is inevitably partial. ... Equally, it is why, before they can hope to communicate fully, one group or the other must experience the conversion that we have been calling a paradigm shift. Just because it is a transition between incommensurables, the transition between competing paradigms cannot be made a step at a time, forced by logic and neutral experience.[8]

The rhetorical implications of Kuhn's "revolutionary" thesis have been understood, although hardly appreciated, by Israel Scheffler:

> In place of the notion of Peirce that scientific convergence of belief is to be interpreted as a progressive revelation of reality, we are now to take such convergence as a product of

rhetorical persuasion, psychological conversion, the natural elimination of unreconciled dissidents, and the retraining of the young by the victorious faction. Instead of reality's providing a check on scientific belief, reality is now to be seen as a projection of such belief, itself an outcome of non-rational influences. The central idealistic doctrine of the primacy of mind over external reality is thus resuscitated once again, this time in a scientific context.[9]

To round out the argument of this subsection, we would suggest further that scientists who share commitments to a given paradigm still do not have complete and unambiguous rules for testing assertions within the framework of that paradigm. As Koch has argued,

> The scientific process is, in principle and at all stages *under-determined by rule.* ... Among the re-analyses of inquiry that are now shaping up there is no point-for-point consensus, but most agree in stressing the absurdity in principle of any notion of *full formalization,* in underlining the gap between any linguistic "system" of assertions and the unverbalized processes upon which its interpretation and application (not to mention its formulation) are contingent, in acknowledging the dependence of theory construction and use at every phase on sensibility, discrimination, insight, judgment, guess.[10]

A major stumbling block to full formalization is language itself. Kenneth Burke has maintained that any symbolic construction, however it reflects reality, is necessarily "a selection of reality; and to this extent it must function also as a deflection of reality."[11]

Notwithstanding the heroic efforts of logical positivists, the persuasiveness of theoretical claims is still highly dependent on stylistic choices, particularly in the social sciences. Try as they might, for example, psychologists have been unable to avoid the use of central metaphors such as "drive" and "attraction" in motivational theories.[12]

And values are reflected in stylistic choices as well. Whether one describes the "high" produced by LSD as "mind expanding" or "mind destroying" matters not; a value judgment is being reflected either way. Nor are such judgments avoided by the use of mechanistic reductions: treating reasons as "causes" and symbolic actions as "behaviors"; denying mind, will, spirit, and other mentalisms. Implicit in these reductions is a commitment to what Koch calls "metaphysical materialism."[13]

Sophistic Practices. Thus far the affirmative has tried to show that scientists misrepresent the process of exchange within scientific communities when they insist that it yields objective tests of assertions. That discourse, rather, is inherently rhetorical: it appeals to subjectively shared premises rather than indubitably true premises; it contains extrafactual, extralogical arguments rather than purely factual, purely logical arguments; and it yields judgments, however credible, rather than certainties.

At this point we will argue that Popper's reference to the "communal" or "institutional" aspect of science does not save science from the kinds of sophistic practices cited by Weigert, Douglas, Czubaroff, Berger and Luckmann, and Szasz. Rather, we will maintain that various communities of science permit and partially encourage these misdeeds. An outstanding example is provided by the recent history of social psychology. We think it outstanding, not because we have reason to believe the discipline is unique (at least among the social sciences), but only because social psychologists have been unusually candid of late in detailing its record. Thus McGuire has conceded that the claims of progress during the fifties and sixties were largely illusory. Greenwald has found support for mainstay propositions disappearing from view. Schlenker has acknowledged that current theories have not proven highly useful in applications to real world problems. And Katz has characterized as "surprisingly small" the number of experimental studies supplying new information to a cumulative body of knowledge.[14]

Of special interest to rhetoricians is the persuasion/attitude change area within social psychology. Here Fishbein and Ajzen have concluded that despite the hundreds of studies conducted in the area, we are left with virtually no empirical generalizations about message or source effects that are not circular, trivial, or false.[15] They have taken their colleagues to task rather severely for having inconsistently operationalized independent variables while neglecting the need for distinctions among dependent variables; for using single item measures of attitude in hastily prepared questionnaires; for failing to report statistically nonsignificant findings while highlighting significant findings; and for drawing unqualified generalizations in reviews of literature from studies yielding inconsistent findings. To this list may be added the heavy reliance on theatrically staged deception experiments, appreciated more for their "cuteness" than for their capacity to generate consistent results. Also mentioned by critics, among other concerns, have been the persistent use of semantic differential measures, few of which were factor analyzed; the tendency to justify negative findings from loosely designed studies by means of ad hoc explanations; and the willingness to generalize from restricted samples (usually composed of college students).[16]

With such evidence of shoddy designs, discrepant results, and failures to replicate, why were the severe problems in this area not exposed earlier? Why, instead, did the textbook writers and grant applicants of the fifties and sixties boast of "ironclad laws," "relevant theories," and "formulas for persuasive success"?[17] Why did researchers of the fifties and sixties persist in reporting studies that violated established scientific canons?

A state of pervasive innocence is, of course, one explanation for these actions; self-deception is another. Still another perspective on the matter seems at least partially valid, and that is the kind of rhetorical perspective offered by critics such as Weigert. From that perspective these actions are best described as willful and self-serving forms of selling, displaying, indoctrination, and ingratiation, no different from those actions practiced by ordinary rhetors such as advertisers and politicians. Let none of us profess shock at this interpretation for as Albert Einstein once remarked, "If an angel of God were to descend and drive from the Temple of Science all those … motivated by display and profit, I fear the Temple would be nearly emptied."[18]

But more to the point of this paper, during the fifties and sixties where were the journal editors, foundation consultants, advisors to book publishers, and other guardians of the social psychology community? The answer is that by their own examples as theorists and researchers, and by their actions as "gatekeepers" of knowledge, they were helping to lead the charge. Thus, for example, it remains common practice for journals to refuse to publish studies containing statistically nonsignificant findings. And foundations effectively discourage attempts at replication by declaring that they will fund "original" research. Similarly the tendency to generalize broadly from restricted samples persists with few official objections. As Paul Meehl noted, researchers continued to produce shoddy deception experiments because "cuteness" and "cleverness" were rewarded by the discipline.[19]

The general point to be made from this extended example is that there is a range of practices at variance with established scientific canons which scientific communities tolerate and may even encourage. Such violations of idealized norms as plagiarism or outright lying are censured, to be sure, but there appear to be informal norms within scientific communities that give license to less extreme violations of the formal code. Here we will offer a general explanation for this tendency which, although fragmentary and speculative, seems highly plausible.

First, science in the collective sense requires organization. In addition to being employed by various organizations, scientists organize themselves into professions and coordinate their activities through professional associations: chemical societies, communication associations, and the like.

Literature concerning the sociology of professions suggests that professions are by no means all bad. A profession, by definition, is more than a mere trade or occupation, for example. On the basis of his own review of the literature, Pavalko states that professions are distinguished by their public-service character, the abstract and highly specialized expertise they require (and which individual professionals acquire through long and arduous training), their strong sense of subcultural identity, and by their commitment to a calling as well as a well-defined code of ethics.[20]

Yet there is a counterside to professionalization which, although necessary to the functioning of professional collectivities, can be dysfunctional with respect to the advancement of science. Some inkling of what we are getting at was provided by William Goode when he suggested that "no occupation becomes a profession without a struggle."[21] More specifically, every professional collectivity is a permeable social system which influences and is in turn influenced by external systems (e.g., government agencies, foundations, the "public") as well as subsystems within it (individual members, interest groups, subdisciplines). The status and even the very survival of the professional system are dependent upon its interactions with other systems. For example, it must recruit new members from the external system and compete, in the process, with other collectivities for the best available talent. It must have other resources (time, money, equipment) to conduct its work as well as freedom from external interference. And the professional system must be responsive to the multiple needs of its internal subsystems: for example, individual professionals who have families to feed and careers to advance.

Elsewhere Simons proposed a theoretical framework for understanding and analyzing the rhetoric of social movements.[22] He argued that as a voluntary collectivity operating within a larger system, every social movement has to fulfill certain *rhetorical requirements*. Moreover these requirements (goal demands, value demands, membership demands, power demands, organizational demands) tend to be incompatible, thus giving rise to *rhetorical problems*. Social movements, therefore, devise *rhetorical strategies* to ameliorate these problems and fulfill their requirements. And, as is commonly the case, these strategies remedy some problems but create others in the process.

It should be apparent that a theoretical extension of the "requirements-problems-strategies" framework to the rhetoric of scientific professions is being proposed here. Scientific professions are not social movements, to be sure, and their rhetorical needs and remedies will perforce be somewhat different. But they are voluntary collectivities, and they are obligated to do more than produce scientific discoveries. Rhetorically speaking they are required to recruit and indoctrinate new members, justify their claims to special expertise before accrediting agencies, plead for freedom from political regulations or other such pressures, mold and reinforce the sense of collective identity among individual members, and, in general, legitimate the profession and its activities before outsiders and insiders. These requirements are not always compatible with the need for scientific advancements, as when inflated claims about scientific method in textbooks must be unlearned by recruits if they are to produce major scientific achievements. They lead, nevertheless, to sophistic practices which gain informal acceptance within scientific communities. It should be apparent that these practices are part of a pattern, one which can be explained, rather than explained away, by viewing scientific discourse as a collective process.

The Negative

Objective Tests of Assertions. In maintaining that scientists are incapable of providing unambiguous tests of assertions, rhetoricians of science reveal unambiguously their own subjectivist colors. In so doing they further undermine their case. For, as Israel Scheffler argues,

> Objectivity is relevant to all statements which purport to make a claim, to rest on argument, to appeal to evidence. Science ... is not uniquely subject to the demands of objectivity; rather, it institutionalizes such demands in the most systematic and explicit manner. But to put forth *any* claim with seriousness is to presuppose commitment to the view that evaluation is possible, and that it favors acceptance: it is to indicate one's readiness to support the claim in fair argument, as being correct or true or proper. For this reason, the particular claim that evaluation is a myth and fair argument a delusion is obviously self-destructive. If it is true, there can be no reason to accept it; in fact, if it is true, its own truth is unintelligible: what can truth mean when no evaluative standard is allowed to separate it from falsehood?[23]

Scientific communities share philosophical commitments to certain belief and value premises, it is true, but these premises ought not to be regarded as mere prejudices. Unlike religious revelation or mystical intuition (cited as alternative "paths to knowledge" by the affirmative), the utility of these premises is demonstrated daily by the concrete achievements of those who adhere to them. Paradoxically it is the commitment to such values as the public testing of testable ideas that permits science to be value free in its daily operations. Let religious revelation or mystical intuition yield knowledge of how to build a bridge, then these so-called paths to knowledge will be taken seriously. Until then scientists will remain content with their own philosophical premises.

As for the claim that the switch to a new paradigm is akin to a "religious conversion"—a matter of "persuasion" rather than "proof"—Kuhn grossly overstated his case at some points and backed off from it considerably at others. In his postscript, for example, Kuhn admitted that all talk of "faith" to the contrary, scientists are "fundamentally puzzle-solvers." That is, "the demonstrated ability to set up and to solve puzzles presented by nature is, in case of value conflict, the dominant criterion for most members of a scientific group." Although value conflicts remain ("puzzle-solving ability proves equivocal in application"), communication between rivals is difficult, and the new paradigm is resisted at first by adherents to the old, eventually the new paradigm proves decisive to the scientific community as a whole because of its superior ability to solve scientific puzzles.[24]

The general point, then, is that debates between so-called incommensurables are capable of objective resolution. As Scheffler states:

> Lack of commensurability, in the sense here considered, does not imply lack of comparability. Even works of art may be reasonably discussed, criticized, compared, and evaluated from various points of view; the incommensurability of these works does not establish that such critical discussion must consist of empty rhetoric alone. Comparison is not limited to an effort at what Kuhn calls "communication across the revolutionary divide"; it need not translate, step by step, one paradigm into some other, any more than art criticism need translate one work into another. Having appreciated the differing potentials of competing paradigms, the scientist, like the critic or indeed the historian, may step back and consider the respective bearings of the paradigms with regard to issues he holds relevant. Such consideration is itself not formulated within, nor bound by, the paradigms which constitute its objects. It belongs rather to a second-order reflective and critical level of discourse. This is the level on which paradigm debates take place, and the incommensurability of their objects is no bar to their reasonableness or objectivity.[25]

If rhetoricians were as inclined to read Kuhn's critics as they are to read Kuhn, they would recognize that his thesis is fuzzy, inconsistent, and, in any case, not at all damaging to the basic notions of scientific objectivity and progress. Were they to read Kuhn open-mindedly, they would recognize that he was not characterizing science as subjective or relativistic. And were they more attuned to evidence than conjecture, they would discover, as sociologists of science have done, that there has been far less crisis, alienation, and conflict among scientists at the point of fundamental innovation than Kuhn had intimated.[26]

Let us turn now to the affirmative's remaining objection in this series, the claim that the scientific process is "underdetermined" by rules, even within the framework of a given paradigm, and that the vagaries of language in particular constitute an inherent impediment to objective resolution of competing assertions.

There is once again an ironic and self-defeating twist in the rhetorician's use of language to prove that all claims which rely on language for support are inconclusive. We will concede, however, that the absence of full formalization of rules presents an obstacle to verification and that problems of language are often acute, especially in the social sciences. But these problems are not inherent. When the locus is shifted from the individual scientist to the scientific community as a whole, the objection fades in significance. While one scientist's formulation "deflects" from a given reality, another's "reflects" that reality, and the scientific community, by its method of free criticism, stands ready to provide the necessary tests and correctives to both. For example, it may reject "mind expanding" and "mind destroying" as descriptors of LSD effects, insisting on less emotionally charged terms as well as operational definitions.

Sophistic Practices. Let us turn, finally, to the question of scientific communities being "required" to countenance, let alone encourage, sophistic practices incommensurate with scientific achievement.

To begin with, the affirmative has not presented a case against science as a whole. At best the affirmative's arguments can be said to apply to the "softer" social sciences such as social psychology, for at no point has the affirmative offered evidence of a pattern of sophistic practices within the better established sciences such as physics or chemistry. And it is doubtful whether they could. Having initially conjectured about the existence of positively sanctioned norm violations in the "hard" sciences, sociologists of science have looked at the evidence and have found, to quote a recent review, that "the mechanisms of social control in science work on the whole according to the institutional norms in spite of individual deviations."[27]

Before buying the affirmative's case as applied to communities of social scientists, we had best look more carefully at what they have called sophistic practices. Surely the affirmative has been ungenerous in characterizing every suspect practice as "willful," "self-serving," or a "misdeed." Undoubtedly some are errors and no more than that. Others, such as the tendency to exaggerate accomplishments in grant applications, are rather innocuous; foundations routinely expect boastful claims and discount them as part of the grantsmanship "game." Still other practices that might initially appear to be unjustifiable could be defended on extrinsic grounds. For example, although the disinclination by journal editors to publish statistically nonsignificant findings may distort the overall research picture, it could be argued that studies with nonsignificant findings tend to be methodologically defective, and that, in any case, it would be financially unfeasible to publish all or most of them.

To be sure, there are deviations from idealized norms in every field, and the affirmative's brief history of the social psychology discipline suggests that during the fifties and sixties, the community as a whole was extremely lax in permitting, sometimes even encouraging, unjustifiable practices. However, by their own admissions of error present-day social psychologists further strengthen our case. Scientific communities are not "required" to lend support to distortions, exaggerations, and misrepresentations; on the contrary, the current acknowledgments of past mistakes are proof that even in a relatively "soft" discipline, the community's error-correcting norms eventually prove triumphant. These days social psychologists are going so far as to wonder aloud whether, given the ephemeral nature of their data, they can ever be more than contemporary historians of passing cultural fancies. In place of the bland assurances of previous days, they are setting less ambitious goals for their theories and incisively criticizing the studies and generalizations of the past. Indeed the prevailing talk is of a "crisis of confidence" in social psychology, as scholars confront squarely the problems of individual differences, situational complexity, and intercultural variation.[28] Surely there is little evidence in all this of a discipline continuing to countenance practices incommensurate with scientific achievement.

Rhetoricians perform a useful service when they call attention to the pressures scientists are under to communicate sophistically and to the deceptions and misrepresentations themselves. But sophistic practices are hardly a "requirement" of scientific professions or a pattern of behavior characteristic of scientific professionals. Although some deviations from idealized norms may be countenanced for a time, the error-correcting norms of the scientific community eventually prove triumphant.

The Judge's Verdict

Given a view of scientific discourse as a process of exchange within scientific communities, has it been shown in this debate that scientists are in principle rhetors in disguise? Does the process of exchange yield objective tests of assertions or is that process inherently rhetorical? Do the communities of science provide safeguards against sophistic practices, or do they actively permit and encourage them?

After reviewing the "pros" and "cons" in this debate, the scientifically orthodox will undoubtedly be left with the conviction that although the scientific donkey may have been pinned with an unbecoming rhetorical tail, it is still capable of carrying a heavy load. Many rhetoricians will be convinced, to the contrary, that science is rhetorical through and through, and that by its denials and deceptions, the donkey appears as an ass of a different kind.

My point in utilizing a debate format to examine the issues has been that the arguments of both sides have merit to a degree; consequently, I will approach this "judge's verdict" in a spirit of reconciliation. With the affirmative I maintain that the donkey is rhetorical through and through. With the negative I conclude that the donkey is still capable of carrying a heavy load.

Because "rhetoric" tends to be a "devil" term in our culture—often preceded by "mere," "only," "empty," or worse—scientists understandably recoil from it, insisting instead that their discourse is purely "objective." Yet in the classical, nonpejorative sense "rhetoric" refers to reason-giving activity on judgmental matters about which there can be no formal proof. The classical conception permits and even encourages the eulogistic sense of rhetoric as *good* reason-giving on matters of judgment. In the final analysis that is what defenders of science *mean* by "scientific objectivity." Though some positivists still stipulate full formalization of rules as a necessary condition of objectivity, most philosophers of science have begged off from it, as Scheffler did when he equated scientific objectivity with "reasonableness" in his comparison between scientific judgment-making and art criticism. The negative could not fully refute the claim that science is grounded on scientifically undemonstrable premises; that it has no neutral algorithms for evaluating competing paradigms; and that it is "underdetermined" by rules within the framework of a given paradigm. But they could rightly insist that the process of free criticism which Popper alluded to often yields good reasons in support of assertions that survive the scientific community's screening procedures.

To be sure, practices by some scientists are sophistic, and I believe my "requirements-problems-strategies" framework may help us to understand why they are employed and why they are sometimes countenanced by scientific communities. However, as the negative has reminded us, we had best use the term "sophistic" with extreme caution, restricting it to acts that are manifestly willful, self-serving, and in clear violation of established scientific canons. Because some acts are harmful while others are relatively innocuous, we might also attempt to differentiate among them on an "ethical values scale," rather than lump them together as the affirmative has in this paper.

The differences between opposing sides in this debate might be further reconciled by distinguishing two senses of the term "scientific community." There is, on the one hand, the ahistorical sense of "scientific community," and as we have seen in the case of social psychology, these communities may be temporarily caught up in the needs of their members or in the needs of the community as a whole to demonstrate its legitimacy. There is also the sense of "scientific community" as a relatively enduring, institutional-ized collectivity and, as history has repeatedly shown, these communities have been capable of surmounting such extreme pressures as papal decrees and totalitarian dictates. In the case of social psychology we have seen that its rhetoric could undergo an abrupt transformation in a brief period of time.

The foregoing also suggests what may be the most appropriate stance of the rhetori-cian of science in his capacity as critic of discourse. Following Burke some rhetorical critics have been prone to label all science as "magic," "ideology," or "secular theology." There is merit in a skeptical posture (Nietzsche's "art of mistrust") but rather than carping at science in general, rhetorical critics would be more persuasive were they to reserve their slings and arrows for more limited and vulnerable targets such as individual practitioners or communities in the time-bound sense. Of special concern should be willful violations of scientific canons, and here critics can stand not as enemies of science, but as defenders of its time-honored norms.

From a perspective "friendly" to science, there is also much theoretical work to be done. How in particular do paradigms gain acceptance? By what stratagems and through what channels are theoretical innovations diffused? In the absence of fully formalized rules, what role is played by exemplars and by enthymematic appeals? How is the language of one paradigm translated into the language of another? "Just because it is asked about tech-niques of persuasion … in a situation in which there can be no proof," said Kuhn, "our question is a new one, demanding a sort of study that has not previously been under-taken."[29] Rhetoricians of science should be in an ideal position to pursue these issues.

Notes

1 Andrew Weigert, "The Immoral Rhetoric of Scientific Sociology," *American Sociologist* 5 (May 1970): 111–19.

2 Jack D. Douglas, "The Rhetoric of Science and the Origins of Statistical Social Thought: The Case of Durkheim's *Suicide*," in Edward A. Tiryakian, ed., *The Phenomenon of Sociology* (New York: Appleton-Century-Crofts, 1969), pp. 44–57; Jeanine Czubaroff, "Intellectual

Respectability: A Rhetorical Problem," *Quarterly Journal of Speech* 59 (1973): 155–64; Peter L. Berger and Thomas Luckmann, *The Social Construction of Reality: A Treatise in the Sociology of Knowledge* (Garden City, N.Y.: Anchor, 1967), p. 88; Thomas Szasz, *Ideology and Insanity* (Garden City, N.Y.: Anchor, 1969).

3 The traditional distinction between rhetorical discourse and scientific discourse is described well (but not supported) by Ch. Perelman and L. Olbrechts-Tyteca. See *The New Rhetoric: A Treatise on Argumentation,* pp. 1–4; Karl Popper, "The Sociology of Knowledge," in James E. Curtis and John W. Petros, eds., *The Sociology of Knowledge: A Reader* (New York: Praeger, 1970), p. 653–54. Said Popper, "If scientific objectivity were founded upon the individual scientist's impartiality or objectivity, then we should have to say good-bye to it."

4 *Aims of Education* (New York: Macmillan, 1938), p. 229; "The Masks of Society: The Grounds for Obligation in the Scientific Enterprise," *Journal of Philosophy* 15 (June 1958): 496.

5 Robert W. Friedrichs, *A Sociology of Sociology* (New York: Free Press, 1970), p. 152.

6 *Encyclopaedia Britannica*, 1961, s.v. "Logic, History of," (quoted in Friedrichs, p. 150); Willem F. Zuurdeeg, *An Analytical Philosophy of Religion* (Nashville: Abingdon, 1958); Thomas B. Farrell, "Knowledge, Consensus, and Rhetorical Theory," *Quarterly Journal of Speech* 62 (February 1976): 1–14.

7 Thomas S. Kuhn, *The Structure of Scientific Revolutions*, 2nd ed. enlarged (Chicago: University of Chicago Press, 1970), pp. 109–10.

8 Kuhn, pp. 149–50.

9 Israel Scheffler, *Science and Subjectivity* (Indianapolis: Bobbs-Merrill, 1967), pp. 73–74.

10 Sigmund Koch, "Psychology and Emerging Conceptions of Knowledge as Unitary," in T. W. Wann, ed., *Behaviorism and Phenomenology: Contrasting Bases for Modern Psychology* (Chicago: University of Chicago Press, 1964, pp. 21–22.

11 "Terministic Screens," *Language as Symbolic Action: Essays on Life, Literature, and Method* (Berkeley: University of California Press, 1968), p. 45.

12 See K. B. Madsen, *Theories of Motivation* (Cleveland: Howard Allen, 1961).

13 Koch, p. 6.

14 William J. McGuire, "The Yin and Yang of Progress in Social Psychology: Seven Koan," *Journal of Personality and Social Psychology* 26 (1973): 446–56; Anthony G. Greenwald, "Consequences of Prejudice Against the Null Hypothesis," *Psychological Bulletin* 82 (1975): 1–20; Barry R. Schlenker, "Social Psychology and Science: Another Look," *Personality and Social Psychology Bulletin* 2 (Fall 1976): 387; Daniel Katz, "Some Final Considerations About Experimentation in Social Psychology," in C. G. McClintock, ed., *Experimental Social Psychology* (New York: Holt, Rinehart and Winston, 1972), p. 557.

15 Martin Fishbein and Icek Ajzen, *Belief, Attitude, Intention, and Behavior: An Introduction to Theory and Research* (Reading, Mass.: Addison-Wesley, 1975). See esp. pp. 11–12, 53–59, 114–17, and 513–19.

16 See Daniel Katz, "Social Psychology: Comprehensive and Massive," *Contemporary Psychology* 16 (1971):277; Gary Cronkhite and Jo Liska, "A Critique of Factor Analytic Approaches to the Study of Credibility," *Communication Monographs* 43 (June 1976): 91–107; Paul E. Meehl, "Theory Testing in Psychology and Physics: A Methodological Paradox," *Philosophy of Science* 34 (1967): 114. See also Clyde Hendrick, "Social Psychology as History and as Science: An Appraisal," *Personality and Social Psychology Bulletin* 2 (Fall 1976): 392–403. Psychologists often justify the use of restricted samples on grounds that they are studying "basic psychological processes," common to all persons, and can thus predict from the few to the many. But, as Hendricks has pointed out, the notion of "basic psychological processes" and others in

social psychology is probably chimerical. Moreover, even if such processes could be identified, they would have little predictive value as guides to the control of human behavior (see pp. 394–96).

17 It should be noted that traces of this kind of exaggeration are even manifested in Herbert W. Simons's *Persuasion: Understanding, Practice and Analysis* (Reading, Mass.: Addison-Wesley, 1976).

18 Weigert suggests that, in general, rhetorical perspectives enable us to understand the discourse of any intellectual elite "as that of a rhetoric of legitimacy, value, and means for the in-group, and a rhetoric of problem discovery, problem-solving, and functional indispensability for the out-group" (p. 112). See also Friedrichs, p. 141.

19 Meehl, p. 114.

20 Ronald M. Pavalko, *Sociology of Occupations and Professions* (Taska, Ill.: F. E. Peacock, 1971), pp. 15–27.

21 Quoted in Friedrichs, p. 89.

22 "Requirements, Problems and Strategies: A Theory of Persuasion for Social Movements," *Quarterly Journal of Speech* 56 (1970): 1–11.

23 Scheffler, p. 21.

24 Kuhn, pp. 205, 152, 168.

25 Scheffler, pp. 82–83.

26 See, for example, Margaret Masterman, "The Nature of a Paradigm," in Imre Lakatos and Alan Musgrave, eds., *Criticism and the Growth of Knowledge* (Cambridge, Mass.: Harvard University Press, 1970); Dudley Shapere, "The Structure of Scientific Revolutions," *Philosophical Review* 73 (1964): 383–94. See also Kuhn, pp. 205–7; Joseph Ben-David and Teresa A. Sullivan, "Sociology of Science," in Alex Inkeles, ed., *Annual Review of Sociology* (Palo Alto, Calif.: Annual Reviews, 1975), p. 215.

27 Ben-David and Sullivan, p. 207.

28 See Kenneth J. Gergen, "Social Psychology as History," *Journal of Personality and Social Psychology* 26 (1973): 309–20. Studying the past: An excellent example, once again, is Fishbein and Ajzen. Their critique of research on persuasion has led them to the development of a theory of persuasion that abandons any pretense of yielding concrete predictions about source or message effects. See also McGuire: "The temple bell has tolled and tolled again, disturbing the stream of experimental social psychology research and shaking the confidence of many of us who work in the area" (p. 446). Also see A. R. Buss, "The Emerging Field of the Sociology of Psychological Knowledge," *American Psychologist* 30 (1975): 988–1002; Allen C. Elms, "The Crisis of Confidence in Social Psychology," *American Psychologist*, pp. 967–76.

29 Kuhn, p. 152.

6.
RHETORICAL CRITICISM AND THE RHETORIC OF SCIENCE
by Leah Ceccarelli

In 1976, Philip Wander published an article in *WJC* with the title "The Rhetoric of Science." Pointing out that "the rhetorical critic has been slow to treat this topic" because of "the mystique of modern science" and "the historical split between science and the humanities," Wander noted that scholarship on the rhetoric of science was just beginning to appear in our disciplinary journals (62). He then sketched the outlines of this newly emerging subfield of rhetorical inquiry. According to Wander, there were two ways in which science would be amenable to rhetorical investigation. First, the place of science in public policy deliberation "obliges the critic to concern him or herself with science: how it is used in debate; how it relates to other sources of information; what occurs when there is conflicting scientific evidence" facing decision makers in the public sphere (62–63). Second, the "efforts made by scientists to persuade one another," such as "grant proposals, journal articles, and convention papers [that] are designed to influence a professional audience," open science to the scrutiny of rhetorical critics (63).

In the years that followed Wander's article, work in both the external and internal rhetoric of science grew; however, the second grew faster than the first, and the professional discourse of scientists soon became entrenched as the "prototypical" form of text studied in the subfield (Harris 294–96). It is likely that rhetorical critics who were interested in science turned their attention to the discursive practices that go on *inside* scientific communities because they considered artifacts from the inner sanctum to be the "hard case" for a rhetoric of science, which, once made, would open the external texts of science to rhetorical study as well.

They had good reason to think that their task would not be easy. Some scholars have argued that the discourse of science differs significantly from the discourse of the public sphere that the rhetorician is accustomed to studying, and because of this, rhetorical criticism is bound to fail when it is turned on textual artifacts produced in the specialized technical sphere of science. The three characteristics of scientific discourse that are most often isolated in describing its resistance to rhetorical scrutiny are the "recalcitrance of nature" that guides scientific textual inscriptions, the "exegetical equality" of scientific discursive practices, and the "institutionally driven" nature of scientific text production processes.

Leah Ceccarelli. "Rhetorical Criticism and the Rhetoric of Science." *Western Speech Communication,* Volume 65, Number 3, 2001, pp. 314–329.

A close look at work that has been done in the "rhetoric of science" subfield will show that each of these three alleged differences between scientific discourse and public discourse is illusory. However, rhetorical critics should not dismiss these matters out of hand, for when scrutinized further, it turns out that each of them stands in for a more serious issue about the relationship between text and context in the broader field of rhetorical criticism. In this paper, I will examine each topic as it relates to the rhetoric of science. I will then explore the larger implications that spin from each topic when considered from the perspective of the broader field of rhetorical criticism. With these implications in mind, I will offer a recommendation in each case for how rhetorical critics might further develop their critical practice.

Before closing, I will examine a final concern that has been raised about work on the rhetoric of science—that scholarship in the subfield dangerously globalizes rhetorical theory. Those who express this concern accept the claim that rhetorical criticism *can* be applied to scientific discourse, but they are not sure that such a study *should* be undertaken by scholars of rhetorical inquiry. As with the other objections against a rhetorical study of science, I will not leave this as a matter for the sole consideration of specialists in the subfield; instead, I will explore the implications of this critique for rhetorical critics of all stripes. In both cases—with respect to the possibility and the desirability of a rhetorical study of scientific texts—I will engage in an exploration of research that has been done and an investigation into what might yet be done in order to address some larger issues that are of general interest to scholars in the field of rhetorical inquiry.

The Recalcitrance of Nature

The difference most often noted between scientific texts and public discourse is the closer connection that seems to exist between scientific texts and material reality. According to some scholars, the "recalcitrance of nature" will always keep rhetoricians from creating an adequate rhetorical reading of scientific texts. For example, Michael Bokeno points out that the rhetorician's claim that knowledge is socially constructed does nothing to account for the explanatory and predictive success of science (297). J. E. McGuire and Trevor Melia concur, arguing that "Science is the result not only of textual representation, but also of extra-textual interventions with nature. That is, scientific texts, unlike other texts, are not only the product of libraries, but also and notably of laboratories" (108).

The nature of the relationship between a text and its subject matter is the issue here. Are scientific texts *mere* rhetoric, constructing knowledge from socially inflected discursive practices, or are scientific texts a reflection of some deeper reality over which rhetoric can make no claim? The philosophical debate has raged for many years, with no end in sight; in fact, each side has stopped trying to persuade the other, proclaiming that the issue has been settled in its favor.[1]

But despite the entrenched positions of opponents in the so-called "science wars," the question is ultimately a false dilemma for the working rhetorical critic. When engaged in critical practice, rhetorical scholars are neither radical relativists nor strident realists; instead, they must always strike a middle ground position between these two extremes. Texts from either the technical or public sphere, *when scrutinized through the lens of rhetorical inquiry,* are neither reducible to "mere" words nor understood as straightforward reflections of some deeper reality; instead, the scholarly practice of rhetorical criticism always treats texts as a convergence of discursive opportunities and material constraints.

This is just as true for public texts submitted to rhetorical analysis as it is for scientific texts. Despite the contention of McGuire and Melia, texts that are traditionally studied by rhetorical critics, like political speeches, are not "only the product of libraries." Rhetorical critics recognize that discourse in the public sphere is always shaped by a combination of situational constraints. Without assuming the ontological reality of such "recalcitrances" as political situation, biographical circumstance, and socio-historical setting, rhetorical critics of public address use these "facts" as constraints to shape their readings of public texts.

Likewise, without assuming the ontological reality of laboratory or field observations, rhetorical critics of scientific texts use certain "facts" as constraints to shape their readings. For example, consider Alan Gross, who once countered McGuire and Melia's "Cautionary Strictures on the Writing of the Rhetoric of Science" with the call for a "Rhetoric of Science Without Constraints." Although Gross supports a radical relativist position in his theoretical writings, when performing rhetorical criticism of scientific texts, he assumes the "existence" of laboratory findings that limit the arguments offered by scientists. In a reading of Watson and Crick's "A Structure for Deoxy Ribose Nucleic Acid," Gross acknowledges that a two-dimensional X-ray diffraction photograph and "previously isolated chemical facts" constrained the scientists' textual model building (*The Rhetoric of Science* 63–64). In a reading of Newton's first paper on optics, Gross acknowledges that "the crucial experiment clearly and unequivocally shows" that white light can be separated into rays that make up the colors of the spectrum (*The Rhetoric of Science* 119–20). When performing a rhetorical reading of a text, even a rhetorician who leans toward a radical relativist position is forced to suspend his disbelief.[2]

It is not some special characteristic of the scientific text that forces Gross to recognize material constraints in his rhetorical analysis. Rather, it is a special characteristic of *rhetorical inquiry,* which, recognizing the interconnection of words and things, is designed to be sensitive to the recalcitrances of nature, just as it is designed to be sensitive to the possibilities of language. In short, the concern of some that the rhetorician might do a disservice to science by failing to recognize the constraints of extra-textual entities in the construction of scientific knowledge claims is unwarranted. Texts in both the public and technical spheres are constructed from the interaction of words and things, and rhetorical criticism, with its attention to both discursive possibilities and situational constraints, is well prepared to examine this relationship.

This issue of how texts relate to their subject matter is important to all rhetorical critics, not just to those examining scientific texts, because we must all contend with the complex relationship between the textual and the extra-textual. I believe that if we were to do more to explicitly recognize the way in which linguistic and material factors cooperate to shape a rhetorical reading, we might help our discipline improve its position in the larger public and academic communities. Every day in the popular press and in the scholarship of those who are unfamiliar with the rhetorical tradition, the term "rhetoric" is used in a pejorative sense, set in opposition to the terms "substance" or "action." If we rhetoricians did more to publicize rhetorical criticism as a study of the *connection* between words and substance (or between words and action), rather than celebrating rhetorical criticism as a study of the *all-powerful* words that fabricate reality, or allowing rhetorical criticism to be dismissed as the study of *mere* words divorced from reality, we might find ourselves in a better position with respect to the larger community in which we work.[3] When people outside our discipline come to recognize that rhetorical criticism is concerned not just with the deceptive nature of words but with the complex relationship between the discursive and the non-discursive, they will have less reason to dismiss the rhetorical study as distasteful or insignificant. Rather than describing our critical practice as "rhetorical" without explaining what we mean by that, or dropping the term "rhetoric" to avoid the negative connotations that come along with it, we can rehabilitate the public image of rhetorical criticism in a way that will make both scientists and public actors more receptive to our critical readings of their texts.

Exegetical Equality

The second characteristic of scientific texts that allegedly makes them different from public texts is their remarkable ability to communicate clearly to their target audience. According to McGuire and Melia, many of the specialized textual norms of the scientific community work together to create a message that cannot be misread, embodying "in its very structure the possibility that *all* expert members of the scientific community are equal to it exegetically" (107). The standardized form of scientific writing purportedly creates a text that requires no special interpretive powers to decode its message; all scientists read that text in the same way. According to Gyorgy Markus, this superior communicative quality makes scientific texts different from public texts, and explains why there is no need for a hermeneutics of natural sciences (9–10). As Paul Ricoeur puts it, scientific language seeks not only to reduce polysemy, but to eradicate it: "All readers are, in a sense, one and the same mind, and the purpose of [scientific] discourse is not to build a bridge between two spheres of experience, but to insure the identity of meaning from the beginning to the end of an argument" (127–29).

The nature of the relationship between a text and its audience is the issue here. Are scientific texts transparent to their audiences? If so, can rhetorical critics, who are trained to interpret public texts that are embedded with complex meanings, say anything of interest about these terminologically sophisticated but exegetically shallow texts produced by science? If the nature of the relationship between scientific texts and their audiences is radically different from the nature of the relationship between public texts and their audiences, then rhetorical critics may be ill equipped to study scientific texts.

Once again, a look at some work that has been done in the "rhetoric of science" subfield can help us to answer these questions. Several close readings of scientific texts have indicated that despite assumptions to the contrary, multiple meanings *are* embedded in scientific discourse; in fact, the hidden polysemy of scientific texts may actually contribute to their effectiveness. For example, my rhetorical analysis of Theodosius

Dobzhansky's *Genetics and the Origin of Species* and Erwin Schrödinger's *What is Life?* indicates that the very *lack* of exegetical equality is what allows some scientific texts to be so persuasive with scientific audiences (*Shaping Science*). John Angus Campbell's work on Darwin's *Origin of Species* also "challenges the received notion that clarity or univocacy is the norm or goal of scientific language" ("On the Way to the Origin" 22; see also "The Polemical Mr. Darwin" 384–85). And Michael Bishop's recent study of Newton's *Optics* discovers "semantic flexibility," rather than rigid precision of meaning, forcing Bishop to conclude that "scientific expressions (like many others) are often supple and open-ended. The possibility of expressing a partially indeterminate concept is an important (and neglected) element of scientific practice" (225).

So once again, an alleged difference between scientific texts and public texts is found to be more a product of "the mystique of science" and "the historical split between science and the humanities" than an actual phenomenon of the texts under study. Scientific texts, like public texts, are hermeneutically complex. That is not to say that there is *no* difference between the way that scientists interact with texts and the way that public audiences interact with texts. Some of the most vocal supporters of the rhetoric of science project have admitted that the reading practices of scientists differ from the reading practices of public audience (Fuller 309–10; Gross, *The Rhetoric of Science*, reprint ed., xvii). But, as Davida Charney has shown through her experimental study of scientific readers, the differences are ones that do nothing to diminish a rhetorical criticism. Charney has shown that scientists read their discourse "rhetorically ... In other words, they read their literature the way scholars in the humanities might read *PMLA*" (228). While graduate students in the sciences often try "to do no more than comprehend the text and integrate it with their prior knowledge," professionally advanced scientific readers are "prone to treat the text rhetorically, as probabilistic argument about facts and values" (228). The reading practices of scientists are therefore perfectly intelligible to the rhetorical critic, perhaps more so than the reading practices of public audiences, whose actual relationship with texts the rhetorical critic has done little to reveal.

The larger issue in rhetorical criticism raised by this mediation on the relationship between a scientific text and its audience regards the question of how audiences interpret the texts they encounter. For many years, the rhetorical critic has been satisfied with asking how audiences were *invited* to respond to texts. But discovering how an ideal reader was constructed in the text only tells us how an implied author envisioned his or her audience, not how audiences actually interpreted the text. This focus on the ideal reader becomes especially problematic when one considers the fact that an interpretation of the audiences present but not addressed, or addressed but not persuaded, might provide a more useful understanding of the power dynamics at play in important historical moments (Condit 335). If we are interested in the way that a text achieves or does not achieve its end of persuasion, or if we are interested in how a discourse participates in the development of cultural truths, we need to pay more attention than we presently do to the relationship between texts and their audiences.

Elsewhere, I have introduced a revised critical method that connects texts with their receptional context by producing a close reading not only of the primary artifact, but of the textual fragments that preserve evidence of audience response ("Polysemy" 400–02,

404–07). My claim, which is not as radical as it may seem, is that rhetoricians should do more to uncover the ways that actual audiences interpret texts. I am not arguing that rhetorical critics should adopt a social scientific methodology to study audiences; instead, I am suggesting that we apply the critical practices we have already perfected on primary texts to the inscribed responses of readers who encountered those texts.[4] In many cases, evidence about reception exists, but is not examined by rhetorical critics who restrict their attention to the artifact itself and to its broader historical context.[5] By paying more attention to the relationship between text and audience, we can do more to substantiate our claims about the influence of rhetorical action, and can thereby increase the usefulness of our critical practice.

Institutionally Driven

The third characteristic of scientific texts that purportedly makes them unfriendly to rhetorical criticism is the institutional nature of their production. According to Dilip Gaonkar, rhetorical criticism is tied by its classical roots to the "ideology of human agency," and because of this, it is particularly "disadvantaged in doing interpretive work with institutionally driven discursive formations such as modern science" ("Close Readings" 343). Presumably, the scientific text is different from the archetypal model of public address in that the former is not composed by an intentional agent seeking to influence others, but is instead produced by a "matrix of technologies … that elude the reach and the imprint of the subject" ("Close Readings" 337). Says Gaonkar, "the vexatious fact remains that rhetoric, conceived primarily as a transaction by and between discrete individuals, cannot unlock the grammar of massive social formations such as 'modern science' that are propelled by 'system imperatives' " ("Close Readings" 337–38).

   The nature of the relationship between a text and its author is the issue here. Are scientific texts constituted through institutional imperatives rather than crafted by individual agents? If so, then perhaps rhetorical criticism, which typically "binds speaker, strategy, discourse, and audience in a web of purposive actions," is inadequate to explain the production of scientific discourse (Gaonkar, "Idea" 263).[6]

   Some scholars of the rhetoric of science respond to this question by contesting Gaonkar's portrayal of scientific discourse. They argue that scientific texts, like public texts, are the result of *both* authorial cunning and institutionalized discursive patterns, and they suggest that any assumption to the contrary is evidence once again of "the mystique of modern science" being used to falsely differentiate the humanities from the sciences. Gaonkar's vision of a scientific discourse that is produced solely through the synergy of systemic forces is too limited. As John Angus Campbell puts it, all speakers can be described accurately as "the point of origin" or "the point of articulation" or "as a tensional fusion of both" ("Strategic Reading" 123). Campbell's work on Darwin's *Origin* indicates that the production of at least one important scientific text was both inadvertent and intentional, both influenced by its position in a cultural matrix and a unique innovation by a talented rhetor upon what had come before ("On the Way" 22). Alan Gross makes a similar point with his study of modern peer review in science; he shows that today's scientific writers are indeed human agents responsible for their actions ("What If" 145).[7] His rhetorical study, tied tightly to the "ideology of human agency," disputes sociological studies of science that focus exclusively on the "limitations of individual wills and the degree to which those wills are constituted by cultural imperatives" ("What If" 145). According to both Campbell and Gross, a rhetorical criticism infused with the ideology of human agency allows us to recognize the importance of *both* scientific rhetor and scientific institution in the production of scientific discourse. In fact, it is especially important that rhetorical criticism be added to the already growing sociological study of science, because otherwise, scholars may fail to recognize how scientific texts are made up of *both* the carefully crafted rhetorical strategy and the articulatory practices of a cultural conjuncture.

The larger issue raised in the field of rhetorical criticism by this question about the relationship between scientific rhetor and text concerns the degree to which a rhetorical critic should be expected to trace the variety of influences that work to shape textual production. If a rhetorical critic focuses exclusively on the text itself, and assumes that what is found there is the infallible sign of a consciously deliberating agent with "a tangible power to influence and refigure the ideological terrain" from which s/he originated, the critical project is misguided (Gaonkar, "Epilogue" 273). On the other hand, if a rhetorical critic focuses exclusively on the intertextual matrix from which a text emerged, and assumes that what is found there is the infallible sign that human agency is powerless before the institutional forces that impel discourse along certain fixed paths, the critical project is also distorted. Once again, it seems that a balanced negotiation between text and context is required if we are to make the most of our critical practice.

James Jasinski is thinking of this issue when he recommends that we improve the practice of rhetorical criticism by reading the text within and against its intertextual background, charting the relationship between text and "performative traditions" (212). The rhetorical critic following this recommendation assumes that text production is not simply the inspiration of a genius rhetor, nor is it a process of following rules or precepts that dictate discursive practice; instead, it is an orchestration of both invention and tradition (214–16). Because Jasinski's recommendation to negotiate between contextual constraint and textual strategy merges the cultural critic's desire to uncover the hidden institutional constraints on discursive action with the textual critic's desire to uncover the hidden genius in the persuasive design of the text, it becomes a promising way of achieving an equilibrium between two competing interests in the larger discipline. It is an improvement to critical practice that I wholeheartedly support.

Globalization

The recalcitrance of nature, the alleged exegetical equality of scientific texts, and the institutionally guided nature of scientific text production are all weaker barriers to a rhetorical study of scientific texts than some have assumed. Perhaps because of this, most have accepted the claim that rhetorical criticism *can* be applied to the discourse of science. But some are still unsure about whether or not it *should* be. These scholars are concerned that because the discipline has expanded the range of its critical scrutiny, turning away from its traditional restrained subject matter of discourse in the public sphere, it is changing to fit its new expanded role, and in so doing, is losing its theoretical bite.

Those who express this apprehension about the rhetorical study of science are concerned that in trying to explain too much, rhetoricians are being forced to globalize rhetorical theory, making it fatally thin. In order to accommodate the "rhetoric of science," the field of rhetorical inquiry is being forced to adopt a sterile theoretical perspective that can be used to describe all discourse but is no longer specific enough to say anything of interest about any particular discourse. As Thomas Farrell warns, with the expansion of rhetoric's range, we will have "so much to study, so little to say" (82). According to this view, the more rhetoric is generalized to explain many different genres, the less susceptible it will be to falsification and the less capable it will be of maintaining its role as a vital, non-trivial academic enterprise.[8]

This concern is a very real one for those who adopt a view of theory as a unified conceptual scheme that is progressively built by academic workers; from this perspective, the expansion of rhetoric outside its traditional domain of public discourse can only work to shorten the list of generalizable characteristics. To find the presence of rhetoric in all discourse genres, the theoretical vocabulary will have to be made so "thin" that it will lose any disciplinary force (Gaonkar, "Idea" 263). Rhetoricians will be forced to analyze symbolic action that cuts across all levels of human activity, and the only theory that can be produced will be a sort of general symbolic grammar. Those concerned about the consequences of globalization say that rhetoricians might have produced a useful theory of the speech that occurs in the restricted space of the public sphere, but a rhetorical theory that encompasses *all* communication will have to be so general as to be useless for most practical purposes.

Once again, a look at the literature of the subfield shows that the worst fears of critics are not realized in practice. For example, Jeanne Fahnestock shows that rhetorical theories developed in one sphere of activity can be just as useful in explaining discourse in another. She identifies several traditional figures of speech (antithesis, incrementum, gradatio, antimetabole, ploche, and polyptoton) in the discourse of science, and does not distort the classical rhetorical theory of figuration to do so. In fact, Fahnestock finds that she is better able to exemplify the way in which the figures function by turning to scientific arguments, which give their "main lines of reasoning a high profile," than by relying solely on the oral public discourse for which the theories were first developed (xi). Likewise, rhetorical theories productively inform several studies of Watson and Crick's "A Structure for Deoxy Ribose Nucleic Acid." Rhetorical critics explain the design of this text through theories pertaining to voice, ethos, irony, kairos, stasis, and narrative (see Bazerman 18–55; Halloran; Gross, *The Rhetoric of Science* 54–65; Miller; Prelli 236–57; Fisher). While they do not all agree about how this prototypical scientific text should be interpreted and judged, they all find intriguing things to say about its production and its influence without diluting the rhetorical theory through which they view it.

Of course, rhetoricians of science are not the only contemporary rhetorical scholars to enlarge the scope of the art. The range of artifacts considered by critics has expanded enormously from the traditional terrain covered by the discipline; today, rhetorical critics are just as likely to study television programs, monuments, and web sites as they are to examine public speeches.[9] Like rhetorical critics of scientific texts, these rhetoricians have found the terminology and perspectives of the rhetorical tradition useful in interpreting, explaining, and judging the artifacts they study, and they have had little difficulty adapting rhetorical theories to these new uses.

However, the fact that rhetorical theory has not yet been rendered so diffuse as to be useless does not guarantee that it will remain a vital art in the future. In my opinion, there are two things that rhetorical critics can do ensure that our field is not trivialized now that we have expanded our sights to include the study of nontraditional communication genres: we can recognize our unique ability to explain influence through the identification of important microscopic features of texts, and we can affirm a nonhierarchical conception of theory that allows for a variety of insights to be linked in web-like fashion rather than force-fitted into a hierarchically arranged globalized system.

First, if we can no longer differentiate our work from that of other disciplines by the domain of human communication we study, we can still differentiate ourselves by the *way* we study communication. I think we should recognize and celebrate the fact that we have a unique perspective to offer the academy: we illuminate intriguing structures of influence beneath the surface of the text (and we do so regardless of where the text originated).

Rhetoricians who recognize the danger to the discipline of a globalized rhetorical theory are fond of quoting the Latin phrase "*Si omnia, nulla*" (Keith et al. 331). But this maxim does not always hold when it comes to the creation of powerful disciplinary identities. Sometimes, the power of a discipline is directly related to the ubiquity of its object of study. An analogy helps to make this point more clear. A molecular biologist would say that the fact that biological molecules are everywhere and everything in organisms, and the fact that molecular biologists can help us understand these molecules, is the very reason the field of molecular biology has become so powerful today. Molecules are omnipresent, but because they are not observable by the naked eye, they must be studied by specialists who are educated in the various ways of revealing their secrets. Likewise, rhetorical structures are present in all forms of text, but they are rarely recognized by the layperson; the rhetorical critic has the specialized training to identify these structures and explain their function.

It is true that some types of biological molecule differ slightly from one species to the next, others are fairly uniform across species, while yet others are unique to one species alone; likewise with the rhetorical patterns that critics discover within different genres of discourse: some are uniform across genres or are closely related to each other, while others are unique to the genre in question. Just as molecular biologists study molecules in different species of animal, so too should rhetorical critics study persuasion in different genres of text. And just as an analysis of the function of biological molecules can tell much about how organisms work, so too can many practical insights be gathered from a recognition of specific rhetorical constructions found in the close study of different textual artifacts. Rhetorical criticism, because it uncovers pervasive and important but subtle and otherwise unrecognized persuasive structures that may differ from one text to the next, avoids becoming trivialized when it expands its field of potential artifacts.

The second approach we can take to counter the danger of globalization is to abandon any lingering scientistic attachment to the "strong version" of theory, in which academic workers seek to develop a hierarchically unified conceptual scheme, and instead promote a more pragmatic and humanistic conception of theory. Rather than trying to construct a generalized theoretical system that explains all discourse in broad but unremarkable vertical strokes, rhetoricians should use their critical faculty to recognize analogic characteristics of texts in a horizontal move from one particular to the next (Leff, "Things Made by Words" 223–31). Rather than apply a global vocabulary to the study of large discursive formations in the hopes of building a single, unified, "one-size-fits-all" theory of persuasion, rhetorical critics should choose which aspects of a fairly loose rhetorical lexicon to use to best illuminate a specific text, and work to build a pool of findings that are united opportunistically in the person of the sensitive and well-read rhetorician. With a perspective toward theory based in the arts and humanities, we can apply rhetorical criticism to a variety of artifacts from both public and technical spheres while avoiding the reduction of our insights to a single globalized, but rather trivial, theoretical structure.

Conclusions

The question of whether or not rhetorical criticism can and should be applied to the scientific text concerns the proper scope of the art. This question can best be answered by examining work that has been done over the last twenty-five years by scholars who have attempted to use rhetorical criticism to reveal interesting things about texts from the inner sanctum of science. These studies show that while there are certainly differences between the scientific text and the public text, those differences are small enough, and the critical practice of rhetorical inquiry is flexible enough, to make rhetorical criticism a useful tool to employ in the study of scientific discourse. Rhetorical criticism is fully competent to scrutinize texts that entangle the possibilities of language with the recalcitrances of nature; it is helpful in uncovering the exegetical complexity that is hidden beneath the surface of the seemingly transparent scientific text; and it does a fine job of revealing the subtle ways in which scientific discourse is both institutionally driven and carefully crafted by human agents. As long as we take a perspective toward theory that is grounded in the arts and humanities, the study of scientific texts will result not in trivially global pronouncements, but in specific developments in our understanding of human communication.

This reflection on the contested status of a "rhetoric of science" should be of interest not only to those who examine texts from the technical sphere, but to all rhetorical critics. First, each purported difference between the scientific text and the public text raises a broader issue about critical practice in the larger field: what is the relationship between texts and their subject matter, or between texts and their audiences, or between texts and their authors? Second, reflection on the desirability of a rhetorical study of scientific texts forces us all to ask some serious questions about our disciplinary identity and the nature of our contribution to the mission of the academy.

Some of these questions resonate with the central problem engaged in the 1990 *Western Journal of Communication* "Special Issue on Rhetorical Criticism": what is the proper relationship between text and context in the rhetorical critic's art? In this paper, I have argued that today's rhetorical critics should seek to balance between the competing extremes of a too exclusive focus on text or a too expansive a focus on context. We can achieve this balance by focusing on the *connections* between text and subject matter, between text and audience, between text and author, and between text and theory.

For example, rather than perpetuate a formalist study of the internal dimensions of an isolated text, the rhetorical critic can vow to make connections between text and intertext, uncovering fragments of reception that indicate how audiences interpreted the primary text and fragments of production that indicate how authors both reproduced and altered the institutional and cultural resources available to them. At the same time, rather than abandon our discipline's unique ability to grapple with the particular and the consequential, the rhetorical critic can vow never to defer the text in an exclusive focus on context that makes her scholarship into a work of amateur cultural history and leaves little trace of the microscopic reading of texts that so distinguishes our scholarship. A focus on the *connection* between text and context demands a careful examination of a primary text and the intertextual fragments that surround it. It also demands a recognition that the rhetorical is made up of the interpenetration of the discursive and the non-discursive, and the intentional and the involuntary, as these seemingly competing forces come together in a particular, situated, persuasive artifact.

Notes

1 Examples of the anti-realist position in the rhetoric of science are set forth in Gross, *The Rhetoric of Science*, and in Myers. Examples of the realist position taken by some scientists can be found in Gross and Levitt, and in Sokal and Bricmont.

2 When asked to bracket the *philosophical* issue and talk about the *practice* of rhetorical criticism with respect to the realism/anti-realism debate, Alan Gross acknowledges that a scholar must at the very least hold to Arthur Fine's conception of "common sense reality" (which one assumes to exist but which cannot be characterized independently of the observer) when writing a rhetorical analysis. He made this comment at the 1992 National Communication Association Convention presentation of his "Rhetoric of Science Without Constraints" paper.

3 The study of the connection between words and matter is a Ciceronian view of rhetoric, the celebration of the all-powerful words that fabricate reality is a sophistic view of rhetoric, and the dismissal of rhetoric as mere words rather than reality is a Platonic view of rhetoric. As rhetorical critics, I think we often unwittingly promote a sophistic or Platonic view of our field when we seek to uncover the "deceptive rhetoric" employed by hegemonic social institutions or particularly loathsome political figures.

4 This approach has certain affinities with the new audience studies in the criticism of popular culture, and with recent scholarship by rhetorical critics on interpretive shifts through history. For examples of the former, see Stromer-Galley and Schiappa; Lewis; and Radway. For examples of the latter, see Mailloux; Watson; and Leff, "Lincoln Among the Nineteenth-Century Orators." My approach differs from the new audience studies in popular culture criticism in that I ask the rhetorical critic to apply *rhetorical* methods to the study of reception, rather than methodologies with which she is unaccustomed. My approach differs from the

study of receptional changes over time in that I do not ask the rhetorical critic to seek a dominant reading for each particular age, but instead, I ask her to uncover how different interpretive communities may have interpreted a text at a particular moment in history. More discussion of the benefits and limitations of this approach can be found in the last chapter of my book.

5 For example, consider the various rhetorical studies of Lincoln's second inaugural address published in the first issue of *Communication Reports*. Evidence of reception exists (see Ceccarelli, *Polysemy* 400–02), but was not examined by several rhetorical critics who made very different claims about the meaning of the text.

6 For evidence that Gaonkar's point about scientific discourse is taken seriously in the field, see the responses of various scholars in *Rhetorical Hermeneutics*.

7 The study to which he refers is Gross, *The Rhetoric of Science*, 129–43.

8 Dilip Gaonkar makes the more general argument that the contemporary interpretive turn in rhetorical inquiry leads to a globalized rhetorical practice. However, in his discussion of the writings of Alan Gross and Lawrence Prelli, he suggests that it was their effort to expand rhetoric in order to accommodate scientific texts that made their readings global and thus trivial (Gaonkar, "Idea" 261–66, 282–90).

9 The call for an expansion in artifacts was made by the National Development Project on Rhetoric in 1971; see Sloan[e] et. al. For some examples of contemporary rhetorical criticism that moves beyond the restrained scope of public address, see Dow; Blair; and Warnick.

Works Cited

Bazerman, Charles. *Shaping Written Knowledge: The Genre and Activity of the Experimental Article in Science.* Madison: U of Wisconsin P, 1988.

Bishop, Michael. "Semantic Flexibility in Scientific Practice: A Study of Newton's Optics." *Philosophy and Rhetoric* 32 (1999): 210–32.

Blair, Carole. "Reflections on Criticism and Bodies: Parables from Public Places." *Western Journal of Communication*, 65 (Summer 2001): 271–294.

Bokeno, R. Michael. "The Rhetorical Understanding of Science: an Explication and Critical Commentary," *Southern Communication Journal* 52 (1987): 285–311.

Campbell, John Angus. "The Polemical Mr. Darwin." *Quarterly Journal of Speech* 61 (1975): 375–90.

——. "On the Way to the Origin: Darwin's Evolutionary Insight and Its Rhetorical Transformation." *The Van Zelst Lecture in Communication, May 24, 1990.* Evanston: Northwestern University School of Speech, 1991.

——. "Strategic Reading: Rhetoric, Intention, and Interpretation." *Rhetorical Hermeneutics: Invention and Interpretation in the Age of Science.* Ed. Alan G. Gross and William M. Keith. Albany: SUNY, 1996. 113–37.

——, ed. *Rhetorical Criticism.* Spec. issue of *Western Journal of Communication* 54 (1990): 249–376.

Ceccarelli, Leah. "Polysemy: Multiple Meanings in Rhetorical Criticism." *Quarterly Journal of Speech* 84 (1998): 395–415.

——. *Shaping Science with Rhetoric: The Cases of Dobzhansky, Schrödinger, and Wilson.* Chicago: University of Chicago Press, 2001.

Charney, Davida. "A Study in Rhetorical Reading: How Evolutionists Read 'The Spandrels of San Marco'." *Understanding Scientific Prose.* Ed. Jack Selzer. Madison: U of Wisconsin P, 1993. 203–31.

Condit, Celeste. "Rhetorical Criticism and Audiences: The Extremes of McGee and Leff." *Western Journal of Communication* 54 (1990): 330–45.

Dow, Bonnie. *Prime-Time Feminism: Television, Media Culture, and the Women's Movement Since 1970.* Philadelphia: U of Pennsylvania P, 1996.

Fahnestock, Jeanne. *Rhetorical Figures in Science.* New York: Oxford UP, 1999.

Farrell, Thomas. "From the Parthenon to the Bassinet: Death and Rebirth Along the Epistemic Trail." *The Quarterly Journal of Speech* 76 (1990): 78–84.

Fisher, Walter R. "Narration, Knowledge, and the Possibility of Wisdom." *Rethinking Knowledge: Reflections Across the Disciplines.* Ed. Robert F. Goodman and Walter R. Fisher. New York: SUNY, 1995. 169–92.

Fuller, Steve. " 'Rhetoric of Science': A Doubly Vexed Expression." *Southern Communication Journal* 58 (1993): 306–11.

Gaonkar, Dilip Parameshwar, "Epilogue. The Oratorical Text: The Enigma of Arrival." *Texts in Context: Critical Dialogues on Significant Episodes in American Political Rhetoric.* Ed. Michael C. Leff and Fred J. Kauffeld. Davis: Hermagoras, 1989. 255–75.

———. "The Idea of Rhetoric in the Rhetoric of Science." *Southern Communication Journal* 58 (1993): 258–95.

———. "Close Readings of the Third Kind: Reply to My Critics." *Rhetorical Hermeneutics: Invention and Interpretation in the Age of Science.* Ed. Alan G. Gross and William M. Keith. Albany: SUNY, 1996. 330–56.

Gross, Alan G. *The Rhetoric of Science.* 1990. Cambridge: Harvard UP, 1996.

———. "Rhetoric of Science Without Constraints." This volume [1991], 111–122

———. "What If We're Not Producing Knowledge: Critical Reflections on the Rhetorical Criticism of Science." *Rhetorical Hermeneutics: Invention and Interpretation in the Age of Science.* Ed. Alan G. Gross and William M. Keith. Albany: SUNY, 1996. 138–55.

Gross, Alan G., and William M. Keith, eds. *Rhetorical Hermeneutics: Invention and Interpretation in the Age of Science.* Albany: SUNY, 1996.

Gross, Paul R., and Norman Levitt. *Higher Superstition: The Academic Left and Its Quarrels with Science.* Baltimore: John Hopkins UP, 1994.

Halloran, S. Michael. "The Birth of Molecular Biology: An Essay in the Rhetorical Criticism of Scientific Discourse." *Landmark Essays on Rhetoric of Science: Case Studies,* second edition. London: Routledge, 2018 [1984]. 78–88.

Harris, Randy Allen. "Rhetoric of Science." *College English* 53 (1991): 282–307.

Jasinski, James. "Instrumentalism, Contextualism, and Interpretation in Rhetorical Criticism." *Rhetorical Hermeneutics: Invention and Interpretation in the Age of Science.* Ed. Alan G. Gross and William M. Keith. Albany: SUNY, 1996. 195–224.

Keith, William, Steve Fuller, Alan Gross, and Michael Leff. "Taking Up the Challenge: A Response to Simons." *Quarterly Journal of Speech* 85 (1999): 330–34.

Leff, Michael. "Things Made by Words: Reflections on Textual Criticism." *Quarterly Journal of Speech* 78 (1992): 223–31.

———. "Lincoln Among the Nineteenth-Century Orators." *Rhetoric and Political Culture in Nineteenth-Century America.* Ed. Thomas W. Benson. East Lansing: Michigan State UP, 1997. 131–55.

Lewis, Justin. *The Ideological Octopus: An Exploration of Television and Its Audience.* New York: Routledge, 1991.

Mailloux, Stephen. *Rhetorical Power.* Ithaca: Cornell UP, 1989.

Markus, Gyorgy. "Why Is There No Hermeneutics of Natural Sciences? Some Preliminary Theses." *Science in Context* 1 (1987): 5–51.

McGuire, J. E., and Trevor Melia. "Some Cautionary Strictures on the Writing of the Rhetoric of Science." This volume [1989], 101–110.

Miller, Carolyn. "*Kairos in the Rhetoric of Science.*" This volume [1992], 184–202.

Myers, Greg. *Writing Biology: Texts in the Social Construction of Scientific Knowledge.* Madison: U of Wisconsin P, 1990.

Prelli, Lawrence. *A Rhetoric of Science: Inventing Scientific* Discourse. U of South Carolina P, 1989.

Radway, Janice. *Reading the Romance: Women, Patriarchy, and Popular Literature.* Chapel Hill: U of North Carolina P, 1984.

Ricoeur, Paul. "Creativity in Language: Word, Polysemy, and Metaphor." *The Philosophy of Paul Ricoeur: An Anthology of His Work.* Ed. Charles E. Reagan and David Stewart. Boston: Beacon, 1978: 120–33.

Sloan[e], Thomas, et al. "Report of the Committee on the Advancement and Refinement of Rhetorical Criticism." *The Prospect of Rhetoric: Report of the National Development Project.* Ed. Lloyd F. Bitzer and Edwin Black. Englewood Cliffs, New Jersey: Prentice-Hall, 1971. 220–27.

Sokal, Alan, and Jean Bricmont. *Fashionable Nonsense: Postmodern Intellectuals' Abuse of Science.* New York: Picador USA, 1998.

Stromer-Galley, Jennifer, and Edward Schiappa. "The Argumentative Burdens of Audience Conjectures: Audience Research in Popular Culture Criticism." *Communication Theory* 8 (1998): 27–62.

Wander, Philip C. "The Rhetoric of Science." This volume [1976], 62–70.

Warnick, Barbara. "Masculinizing the Feminine: Inviting Women On Line Ca. 1997." *Critical Studies in Mass Communication* 16 (March 1999): 1–19.

Watson, Martha Solomon. "The Dynamics of Intertextuality: Re-reading the Declaration of Independence." *Rhetoric and Political Culture in Nineteenth-Century America.* Ed. Thomas W. Benson. East Lansing: Michigan State UP, 1997. 91–111.

Zarefsky, David ed. *Lincoln's Second Inaugural Address.* Spec. issue of *Communication Reports* 1 (Winter 1988): 9–37.

PART 1

ISSUES

Through Thick and Thin

7.

SOME CAUTIONARY STRICTURES ON THE WRITING OF THE RHETORIC OF SCIENCE

by J. E. McGuire and Trevor Melia

The proliferation of papers, programs, and now a journal issue dedicated to the "rhetoric of science" is eloquent testimony to the vitality of what may be called the "rhetorical turn."[1] The fact that the present writers, working respectively from within a department of Communications and a department of the History and Philosophy of Science, have for some time been laying the ground work for a joint program in the Rhetoric of Science is evidence of the extent to which they subscribe to the intellectual currents which motivate the rhetorical turn.

Nevertheless, the peculiar nature of "science" itself, the practice thereof, and even its rendition as text, compel us to offer some cautionary strictures against the too easy assumption that scientific texts are as susceptible to rhetorical analysis as are texts in other disciplines. We are aware, of course, that such cautions go somewhat against the tide of opinion, both of some other writers in the present issue of *Rhetorica* [Volume 7, Number 1, in which this article was first published], and increasingly in the humanistic disciplines generally. Lest we be suspected of a hankering for the restoration of an unfashionable and discredited "scientism," we offer a caveat and a concession.

First, the strictures referred to here are directed at rhetorical analyses of the output of the contemporary "hard sciences," physics, astronomy and mathematics particularly. We doubt that texts in these exemplary sciences can be exhaustively accounted for in rhetorical-hermeneutical terms alone. The texts of the so-called social or human "sciences," whose very subject is what Kenneth Burke has called the "symbol using animal," are much more likely to surrender to sheerly linguistic analysis. Second, we are bound to acknowledge the extent to which even the "hard" sciences have been rendered permeable by the speculation of Kuhn, Lakatos, Feyerabend, Hanson, Polanyi, Rorty, Latour and Woolgar *et al.* We are also disciplined by the sometimes penetrating, and always recondite, "textualizing," of the contemporary continental philosophers— Derrida, Barthes, Foucault and Ricoeur, etc. In short, we want to acknowledge the problem of paradigms, of incommensurability, of tacit dimensions, of mirrors, of the metaphorical foundation of science, and of the omnipresent hermeneutical circle. We think it would be a mistake, however, to replace an arrogant scientism with a rampant rhetoricism.

J. E. McGuire and Trevor Melia. "Some Cautionary Strictures on the Writing of the Rhetoric of Science." *Rhetorica: A Journal of the History of Rhetoric*, Volume 7, Number 1, 1989, pp. 87–99.

Our cautionary strictures proceed from two separate but closely related concerns. First, we maintain that scientific texts encounter a special "recalcitrance" from the world they hope to describe. And insofar as Bruno Latour and Steve Woolgar are often cited as successfully denying any such special status for the products of "Laboratory Life" we shall examine their claims carefully.[2] Second, following Gyorgy Markus in his interesting paper "Why is there no Hermeneutics of Natural Sciences?", we will support the claim that there is a special relationship among the author, text, and reader of the texts of natural science.[3]

Our cautionary stance is anticipated by no less an advocate of the "linguistic turn" and adversary of scientism, than Kenneth Burke. Burke, who like Einstein, has relativized much that hitherto has been taken to be absolute, is frequently mistaken for an absolute relativist. But, like Einstein, Burke is perhaps better understood as a great but subtle defender of classical faith. Just as Einstein insisted on one "absolute"—the velocity of light—so Burke, as most scholars now acknowledge, has maintained that "Dramatism" is not itself a metaphor. What is less recognized is that Burke has implicitly at least argued for the special nature of scientific texts. We refer to his neglected doctrine of "recalcitrance." After, affirming that our "discoveries" inevitably reflect our point of view, Burke goes on to caution:

> But the discoveries which flow from the point of view are nothing other than revisions made necessary by the nature of the world itself. They thus have an objective validity.

and

> ... the point of view, in seeking its corroboration or externalization, also discloses many significant respects in which the material of externalization is recalcitrant. And our 'opportunistic' shifts of strategy, as shaped to take this recalcitrance into account, are objective.[4]

To be sure as the "materials of externalization" differ so do the orders of "recalcitrance." Texts dealing with theology or its "coy counterpart" metaphysics, according to Burke, meet only the recalcitrance implicit in language itself. Texts dealing with human relations inevitably reflect their "materials of externalization" by displaying a normative component. And insofar as all science is at one level "social" we anticipate such a socially negotiated normative component. The greatest recalcitrance is met by texts directly describing *scene* and is not fully accounted for in sheerly linguistic or rhetorical terms.[5] Thus, commenting on D. H. Lawrence's disposition of some lunar realities, Burke observes: "Lawrence's assertions are too often distorted by precisely the order of knowledge which he is condemning. The 'facts' which he tells us about the moon, in bald opposition to the astronomer's facts, are simply bad astronomy."[6]

The sentence taken from the appropriate section of the newspaper that asserts an intimate connection between the phase of the moon and the affairs of people born under the sign of Taurus begs for rhetorical analysis. The text that claims that the moon *causes* the ebb and flow of the tides may also arouse hermeneutical suspicion. It is a suicidal rhetoric of science, however, that fails to recognize that she/he who would deny that the phases of the moon are correlated with movements of the tides faces a special recalcitrance.

Latour and Woolgar in their increasingly influential *Laboratory Life* offer an account in which such "recalcitrance" is dissolved in "text." Plausibly enough, they propose to treat the laboratory as if it were an institution within an alien scientific culture. More specifically, they see themselves as practicing the methodology of the "anthropology of science" with a view to discovering how it is that the "realities of scientific practice become transformed into statements about how science has been done."[7] Unfortunately, in so doing, they commit the original sin of anthropology—cultural imperialism. They seem determined to see and to highlight that which is familiar and to understand that which is unfamiliar in familiar terms—viz. as text and writing. Indeed, there is a certain sort of hubris in walking into an alien culture, of which they claim to know nothing, taking a single event from the most taxonomical of sciences (biology), and proceeding to dismantle the entire scientific culture by showing that it is in fact a self-deluded copy of their own linguistic culture. This is like describing native magic as bad science, or the clearing between grass huts in terms of the playing fields of Eton—imperialistic and to some extent impertinent.

Latour and Woolgar do claim, of course, that their anthropological perspective on science "entails a degree of reflexivity not normally evident in many studies of science."[8] That is, they hold that the methods they use in studying the practices of the laboratory are similar to those of the practitioners of science themselves. But they give no indication of how this is so, and, on the face of it, to claim that the techniques of scientific research are, in general, similar to those of anthropology is dubious.

In their assumed role of anthropological observers, Latour and Woolgar view the Salk laboratory as an extended "text" exhibiting a wide range of linguistic practices and using artifacts as "inscription devices." The notion of an "inscription" refers to more than a linguistic act, such as writing; it refers to all traces, spots or points on screens or scales, and to histograms, recorded numbers, spectra, and peaks on diagrams, and so on. An "inscription device" is an apparatus used such that it provides some sort of symbolic output. Accordingly, an apparatus that "transforms pieces of matter into written documents" is an "inscription device." It is thus "any item of apparatus or particular configuration of such items which can transform a material substance into a figure or diagram which is directly usable by one of the members of the office space."[9] So a scale on an apparatus is an "inscription device" if it provides information about a new compound—a machine if it weighs something or a checking device when it is used to verify an operation. In short, an apparatus is used as an "inscription device" when it is used in an argument such as that involved in the construction of a bioassay profile.

In accordance with this perspective, Latour and Woolgar develop a sophisticated form of linguistic constructionism. Construing the laboratory as a locus of activity, involving communication, persuasion, and the use of apparatuses as "inscription devices," they focus their anthropological investigation on the sociological and the linguistic features of laboratory activities. The laboratory is presented as a "system of literary inscription, an outcome of which is the occasional conviction of others that something is a fact." But what is the status of the fact to which they have been persuaded?

We might think that a fact is something recorded in a scientific article that has "neither been socially constructed nor possesses its own history of construction." Latour and Woolgar think this is a wrong-headed conception of the origin of facts. And they wish to examine how talk of facts appears "to remove the social and historical circumstances on which the construction of a fact depends."[10]

This seems benign enough. But the writers are committed to more than the obvious claim that facts are socially and linguistically constructed in virtue of the directed activities of laboratory research. They claim that facts *are* social constructs. This commitment is unambiguously stated in the following passage:

> Specific to this laboratory is the particular configurations of apparatus that we have called inscription devices. The central importance of this material arrangement is that none of the phenomena "about which" participants talk could exist without it. Without a bioassay, for example, a substance could not be said to exist. The bioassay is not merely a means of obtaining some independently given entity; the bioassay constitutes the construction of the substance.—It is not simply that phenomena *depend on* a certain material instrumentation; rather, the phenomena *are thoroughly constituted by* the material setting of the laboratory. The artificial reality, which participants describe in terms of an objective entity, has in fact been constructed by the use of inscription devices.[11]

Accordingly, facts do not obtain in a theory-independent reality, but are constituted and constructed by the social and linguistic processes of the laboratory. Indeed, substances could not be said to exist independently of configurations, such as a bioassay, which supervene on items displayed on inscription devices. Thus, facts, far from being objective realities that are discoverable, are themselves constructed by the methodologies of inscription devices.

Latour and Woolgar are nevertheless at pains to deny that facts are just artifacts of social and linguistic practice. They wish to reconcile two facets of "fact" talk: (a) that the term connotes the making or constructing of something, and (b) that "fact is taken to refer to some objectively independent entity which, by reason of its 'out thereness' cannot be modified at will and is not susceptible to change under any circumstances."[12] Repeatedly the authors claim that they are not anti-realists in the sense that substances, and the facts that pertain to them, do not exist; but rather that they do have objective existence, but only *as* constructs. How is this view to be maintained? And how do they combine the claim that facts are not independent of their modes of construction while denying that they are merely artificial?

What the authors claim is that it "*is not just that facts are socially constructed. We also wish to show that the process of construction involves the use of certain devices whereby all traces of production are made extremely difficult to detect.*"[13] Specifically, they claim that an important inversion takes place in the dialectics of science, an inversion in statements and what statements are about. In the early stages of the dialectical process, there are only statements or linguistic exchanges among scientists, that is, agreements and disagreements. Moreover, the conditions of the construction of these statements are manifestly visible and seem necessary for purposes of persuasion. However, once wide-spread communal agreement is reached, the inclusion of these conditions as a means of persuasion are no longer necessary; indeed, they seem to threaten the "fact-like" status of the statements themselves. At this point what a statement is about takes on a life of its own. It is as if the "statement had projected a virtual image of itself which exists outside the statement." More and more reality is then attributed to what the statement is about, and less and less to the statement itself. "Consequently, an inversion takes place: the object becomes the reason why the statement was formulated in the first place."[14] If the function of literary inscription is the successful persuasion of readers, such that they are most completely convinced when all forms of persuasion disappear, then the "result of the construction of a fact is what appears unconstructed by anyone; the result of rhetorical *persuasion* in the agnostic field is that participants are convinced that they have not been convinced,"[15] Indeed, on this view, the various social and linguistic activities that sustain the argument, and which are eventually seen by the participants as irrelevant to the "facts," are the same conditions that constitute and generate the "factual" quality of a given statement itself.

Facts, then, are epiphenomenal projections of the constructive techniques that generate them, and their "objectivity" is a function of the dialectical inversion characteristic of scientific practice. It may seem otherwise to some, especially to practicing scientists. Forgetting the "constructive" process that constitutes "facticity," scientists and their readers often revert unconsciously to the notion that facts are "out there," and that their existence is revealed by the techniques of scientific discovery. But this is an illusion—Latour and Woolgar insist—an illusion because those statements warranted by scientific consensus as "fact-statements" stand alone long after their constructive procedures have become invisible.

Whatever the merits of this argument, to which we shall return, Woolgar and Latour neglect a feature of scientific texts that has engaged the attention of Gyorgy Markus. He points out that disputes about scientific texts are rarely characterized (as they are in other disciplines) by hermeneutic suspicion. Faced with refutation, writers of scientific texts rarely argue that they have been misunderstood by their critics. Rather, the dispute is said to be not about meanings intrinsic to the text, but about how the text relates to extra-textual matters—in short, about recalcitrance.

Whatever the disposition of the notion of "recalcitrance," the fact that scientific texts command an unusually high degree of assent from their target audience cannot fail to command the attention, and to arouse the interest, of rhetoricians. It is our contention that this disproportionate consensus is accounted for not only by the special relations obtaining between scientific texts and what such texts hope to describe, but also that there is intrinsic to these texts a special nexus between author, text, and reader (A-T-R).

If a paper in the scientific journal *Nature* is consulted, the informed reader is immediately impressed with the text's encoded, bounded, autonomous and self-sufficient system of meanings. Moreover, the text can be placed at once in a recognizable world of rigor and consistency. Not only are the investigators involved in the production of the paper acutely aware of the terms and definitions employed, but where possible they use quantitative and mathematical methodologies. And if the paper falls under the sciences of zoology and biology, again there is an impressive level of taxonomic rigor controlled by practice and theory. Here, then, is a world of meaning and system which is highly immune to the vagaries of the larger culture within which the science is pursued. What is there in the text, and in the text alone, is all that a reader may take from it legitimately.

In giving this general (and somewhat impressionistic) account of a scientific text, we do not wish to imply that a given text automatically engenders only one set of meanings. More than one interpretation is of course possible; however, the range of possible interpretations is severely delimited. Moreover, the business of interpretation is strictly confined to the possibilities of significance that inhere in the text itself. And consequently it is to that text, and not to the general culture, that anyone must turn who would understand a piece of science.

The notions of textual autonomy and self-sufficiency of meaning become clearer if we consider scientific texts in the context of the A-T-R relationship. In this regard, Markus discusses some interesting features of these texts. He argues that scientific texts are depersonalized, decontextualized, and desubjectivized. His main point is that although the dynamics of producing a scientific paper are highly formalized, standardized, and ritualized, the "author *inscribed* into the texts of contemporary natural sciences is (as a norm) a completely depersonalized one."[16] The "inscribed author" of the text functions in scientific space as a normative construct both with respect to authorial responsibility for the text and to its audience reception. Thus "depersonalization" points to the fact that a scientific text largely obliterates the presence of the *real* author(s) in virtue of the normative features intrinsic to its style, format, and content. Moreover, there are in fact only three main genres or literary forms through which science presents itself for publication: the "scientific paper," the "comprehensive textbook" and the "theoretical monograph." These are highly standardized formats. For example, the "scientific paper," the chief vehicle for announcing discovery, invariably reflects the following sequence of sections: Abstract—Introduction—Materials and Methods—Results—Discussion—References. This implies a definite way that the paper should be understood. For instance, the Abstract purports to summarize the paper's content without remainder, thus largely immunizing that content from its literary and argumentative features. After discussing the sequence of sections in a scientific paper Markus says:

> —the "inscribed author" of the natural scientific text appears as an anonymous performer of methodologically certified, strictly regulated activities and a detached observer of their results—without any further personal identifying marks beyond possession of required professional competence.[17]

It is through this depersonalization that the experimental or theoretical paper possesses its fundamental characteristic, that of being a *report.*

Thus regarded, in the continuum between "language speaking for itself vs. facts speaking for themselves," the scientific text fits close to the factual end. So much so, that if a reported experiment is rejected by the scientific community, the experimenters are not viewed as having "got it wrong" or as having "reasoned incorrectly." On the contrary, they are regarded as being unlucky to get a result that could neither be foreseen, nor explained, given the present state of theory and practice in the scientific community. As Markus observes this depersonalized authorial role often combines with diminished authorial responsibility (in the cognitive sense) for the content of the published report.

These considerations have important implications for rhetoric. First, it is clear that if scientific texts are "normatively depersonalized," the degree of consensus or dissensus they can achieve in the scientific community arises from the special features of the A-T-R relationship. This means that if depersonalization of the inscribed author diminishes significantly the responsibility of the real author for the text, the desubjectivation that results measurably reduces *real* authorial control and manipulation over *meaning*. Consequently, a scientific text is considered equally available to all experts in the field, and no-one is thought to have "privileged" access to its meaning anymore than those who produce the text are charged with misunderstanding it or with misinterpreting its significance.

Given the efficacy of our case thus far, we can make an important observation: the research report, the main scientific genre of present-day science, embodies in its very structure the possibility that *all* expert members of the scientific community are equal to it exegetically. This "exegetical egalitarianism" that a scientific text provides, has important lessons for a rhetoric of science, indeed, for rhetoric in general. In the first place, the strategy of normatively "depersonalizing" a scientific text is a deliberate rhetorical move. Indeed, in the very process of minimizing those literary features that carry rhetorical nuance, the scientific community establishes a positive rhetoric for disguising the rhetorical. Second, since scientific texts uniquely provide a close connection between rhetorical "depersonalization" and "exegetical egalitarianism," these texts best exemplify a central claim of deconstructionism.

This is the claim that the reader is written by the text, a view based on the perspective that texts are the intrinsic bearers of their own authentication, independently of authorial intention and purpose. If texts have a life of their own, and through their dynamic, endlessly disseminate multiple meanings which tend to preclude the possibility of possessing a core significance, then, anything goes exegetically, and no exegesis is to be preferred over any other. This is, at least, a reasonable interpretation of much that passes as deconstructionist practice.

Whether such an interpretation of deconstruction is correct or sustainable is not a matter for consideration here. What interests us is the claim that texts are intrinsically open to "exegetical egalitarianism." It seems to us, however, that only scientific texts (and especially the scientific research report) can satisfy this claim in any straightforward and relatively non-controversial way. Only they, by sanctional fiat and canonical practice, are normatively "depersonalized" and "desubjectivized"; only they are normatively autonomous and intrinsically self-sufficient in their meanings. Hence only they are accessible to a communal practice of "exegetical egalitarianism." Ironically enough, it is the scientific text that the deconstructionist in practice avoids like the plague.

We have, then, a social and linguistic account from Latour and Woolgar of how scientific texts come to have a "factual quality." But the concept of the "desubjectivized," "decontextualized," and "normatively depersonalized" scientific text is open to an interpretation of "facticity" consistent with their approach. After all, the replacement of the real author(s) by the "normatively constructed author," the consequent diminishing of authorial responsibility for the content of the text, and its openness to "exegetical egalitarianism," are each in their way facets of deliberate social practice. As much, then, as Latour and Woolgar, Markus, despite his advocacy of the special features of scientific texts, appears committed to the view that "recalcitrance" injected into those texts by their "facticity" is a matter of their social construction. Are we back again to the view that scientific texts are susceptible to rhetorical analysis under the same assumptions as guide rhetorical analysis of texts in other disciplines?

We think not. Science is the result not only of textual representation, but also of extra-textual interventions with nature. That is, scientific texts, unlike other texts, are not only the product of libraries, but also and notably of laboratories.

It is one thing to stress the social, the artifactual, and the conventional aspects that characterize the purposive production of scientific knowledge. It is quite another to claim that warranted scientific knowledge and talk about the "factual quality" of consensual statements are at bottom about the activities of scientific knowers and not about states-of-affairs in nature. There would appear to be a fallacious shift in reasoning. Latour and Woolgar begin with a perfectly sound methodological question: How is scientific knowledge about facts generated *in* the cognitive community of the laboratory? But they conclude that that knowledge is no more than a function *of* the special linguistic and social activities of that community, that scientific facts *are* social constructs predicated on social action. From methodological premises about how people behave we can scarcely derive ontological conclusions about what is the case in nature. This is to confound *how* knowledge is produced with what that knowledge is *about*.

But talk about "aboutness" is the crux of the issue. Latour and Woolgar (and those who would interpret Markus in a constructionist fashion) claim that the "factual quality" which certain texts exhibit is due to the role they play in the consensual context of scientific discourse. It is not because they are "about" something extra-textual that they have factual status. It is rather because they occupy a special place in the adopted scientific consensus.

It is incumbent on those who take this line, however, to show how the explanatory and empirical features of scientific practice are to be accounted for in terms of social theory. That is, they must account for the explanatory and predictive successes of science and its ability to discover novel and new phenomena, without appeal to any factors that are not intrinsic to social theory. Of course, the constructionist can claim that scientific facts are items that exist in the constructed space of the social discourse of science. But this in itself does not easily explain the ability that science provides to interfere with, and to manipulate, certain processes and entities long after the theories that predicted them and designed the techniques necessary for these types of *actions* have been abandoned. Nor does it readily account for the explanatory power available on the perspective that science actually talks about theory-independent entities. For example, there are many rigorously independent ways of calculating Avogadro's number: It is difficult to think that this ability supervenes on social construction alone. Thus, there are reasons to doubt that constructionism can give a compelling account of what makes science explanatorily adequate. It may well include in its account of science the empirical adequacy of a scientific theory, e.g., its success in prediction. But it is difficult to see how repeated predictive success of this sort is fully explained merely on the ground that the theory continues to be embedded in the right sorts of social adaptations practiced in the laboratory. Latour and Woolgar do not deny, of course, that science investigates physical things. What they do say is that facts as social constructs are not warranted because they are *about* those things. But on the view we are discussing, the "recalcitrance" accounted for by scientific texts arises specifically because those texts are *about* extra-textual entities, the characteristics of which fall under the explanatory scope of the theories the texts advocate.

We want also to hold that there are grounds for a minimal realism, at least about certain sorts of scientific "entities," if not about all the features of scientific textualizing as such. In other words, while we agree with Rorty about the dangers lurking in such metaphors as "representing" and "mirroring," and we do not endorse the notion of the "World in itself," and the idea that the mind copies the world which admits description by One True Theory; we also agree with Ian Hacking in his *Representing and Intervening*[18] that science does more than retrieve meanings that are inscribed in texts. That science actively intervenes in nature testifies to an irreducible difference between the texts of science and those of other disciplines. Science not only encodes relationships linguistically and theoretically between the inscriptional items of an apparatus; it also predictively and creatively interferes and intervenes with nature. In so saying, we are not claiming that scientific entities are there, to be discovered by just anyone. Many scientific effects do not exist without the intervention of certain kinds of laboratory apparatus. But those effects are there, and they are real, because they have to do with the world and not with our conventions. And this is so in regard to two separate cases: the case where an experimental apparatus directed by theory creates a preordained effect, and the case where a phenomenon is unexpectedly detected by the use of an apparatus alone, e.g., X-rays. In both cases there are no prior grounds, let alone social conventions, for suspecting the existence of what is brought about by the resources of the laboratory.

Our point, however, can be made without resorting to the incunabula of Latour and Woolgar's *Laboratory Life*. That navigators can meet in mid-ocean by reference to such symbolic constructs as latitude and longitude may seem to the unwary to prove the power of social convention. After all, the lines of latitude and longitude are not there to be discovered. The deeper non-textual fact is that these lines are derived from the motions of celestial bodies. The mid-ocean meeting is indeed testimony to the power of human symbolism; but it is also a testament to a crucial relationship between the symbolism and what is symbolized. Lovers aboard our mid-ocean ship, content to remain at sea, may wish to be guided by D. H. Lawrence's pliant and poetic moon even if it is, as Kenneth Burke maintains "bad astronomy." The ship's navigators duty bound to "make port," had better be steering by a far more "recalcitrant" moon.

Notes

1 This paper was first delivered at such a program—The Eastern Communication Association, Baltimore, MD, April, 1988.

2 See Bruno Latour and Steve Woolgar, *Laboratory Life: The Construction of Scientific Facts* (Princeton: Princeton University Press, 1986)

3 Gyorgy Markus, "Why is there no Hermeneutics of the Natural Sciences," *Science in Context*, I.I (1987) pp. 5–51.

4 Kenneth Burke, *Permanence and Change* (Los Altos: Hermes Publications, 1954), p. 257.

5 Burke's concept of *scene* is complex, but at its simplest it denotes human context—nature—and it is so used here. The "Three types of Recalitrance" will be the subject of an extended treatment in a forthcoming article. [This article was never completed.]

6 *Ibid.*, p. 251.

7 Latour and Woolgar, *Op. Cit.*, p. 29.

8 *Ibid.*, p. 30.

9 *Ibid.*, p. 51.

10 *Ibid.*, p. 105.

11 *Ibid.*, p. 64. Emphasis is Latour's and Woolgar's.

12 *Ibid.*, p. 175.

13 *Ibid.*, p. 176. Emphasis is Latour's and Woolgar's.

14 *Ibid.*, p. 176.

15 *Ibid.*, p. 76 and p. 240.

16 Markus, *Op. Cit.*, p. 12

17 *Ibid.*, p. 13

18 Ian Hacking, *Representing and Intervening* (Cambridge: Cambridge University Press, 1983).

8.
RHETORIC OF SCIENCE WITHOUT CONSTRAINTS
by Alan G. Gross

Eventually the breakthrough came that made modern navigation possible: the discovery of longitudes and latitudes. These are thin black lines that go around the Earth in a number of locations, so that all you have to do is follow them, and you have a surefire way of getting wherever it is they go. Of course they are difficult for the untrained eye to see . . .

Dave Barry

In 1979, Bruno Latour and Steve Woolgar crossed the invisible line that divided the social from the scientific, opinion from knowledge. The subtitle of *Laboratory Life: The Social Construction of Scientific Facts* implicated the social in the formation of these very facts. But the title left ambiguous the exact degree of causal involvement: did social action just contribute, or was it the sole cause of scientific knowledge? When *Laboratory Life* was republished, its authors deleted from their subtitle a single word: *social*. In a postscript, they asserted that this deletion was a necessary consequence of the book's thesis: "by demonstrating its pervasive applicability, the social study of science has rendered 'social' devoid of any meaning."[1] Another line had been crossed: not just the social structure of science, but science itself, scientific knowledge, was fully explainable within the framework of their strong constructivism.

A constructivism so imperial implies an equally ambitious rhetoric of science. The two have a common birth: the relativism of the first sophistic. If man is the measure of all things, his perceptions are criterial: it is he who determines what exists and what does not. If Latour and Woolgar's research site, the brain hormone TRF, is typical of science, and if TRF does not exist apart from the communicative and manipulative activities that call it forth, rhetorical analysis is central to the sociology of science. Science becomes a literary activity, its operations producing a variety of "texts"—graphs, meter readings, laboratory conversations, lectures, papers, review articles, press conferences. Each must be interpreted. When interpretations differ, there is but one means of settlement: persuasion, the art of rhetoric. A strong constructivism makes rhetorical analysis methologically imperative.

Radical relativism applied to science is so counterintuitive that the realist feels impelled to single out some obvious fact of the matter on which to rest his case. Dr. Johnson reportedly kicked a stone; in "Some Cautionary Strictures on the Writing of the

Alan G. Gross. "Rhetoric of Science without Constraints." *Rhetorica: A Journal of the History of Rhetoric,* Volume 9, Number 4, 1991, pp. 283–299.

Rhetoric of Science," J. E. McGuire and Trevor Melia [this volume, 101–110—RAH] adopt an analogous strategy. They adduce in favor of their modest realism three durable empirical regularities: the moon's effect on the tides, Avogadro's number,[2] and the predictable configuration of heavenly bodies that makes modern celestial navigation possible. In their view these are three typical results of science, three metonyms for the pervasive facticity of all scientific knowledge.

McGuire and Melia claim that the best explanation for the pervasive facticity of science is a reality independent of anyone's perception. They believe that constructivists point the causal arrow in the wrong direction: gravity, molecules, and magnetic fields do not exist because we perceive them; we perceive them because they exist. By taking thought, realists claim, you can neither alter the tides, nor obtain a new Avogadro's number, nor orient your compass in the vicinity of a marlinspike. You can make this world work for you, but only if you work with it. Choose otherwise, and you will bump your head, or worse. You will experience what McGuire and Melia call, after Kenneth Burke, a "recalcitrance": the underlying causal basis of the world we mutually perceive. Rhetorical interaction may contribute to the proliferation of scientific knowledge, even within science; but it provides no explanation for that knowledge itself.

McGuire and Melia's moderate view is of the kind that seems generally to prevail. They accept the importance of rhetoric in getting science across, even to scientists. But they stop short where scientific knowledge begins; they defer to science. Reasonably so; is there a cognitive enterprise in the West, or anywhere, that is more successful? Nevertheless I will argue that McGuire and Melia are mistaken, that there is no line that can be successfully drawn between rhetoric and scientific knowledge. Further, I will contend that recalcitrance and realism explain nothing about science; worse, they add unnecessarily to the burden of explanation. Finally, I will maintain an apparent paradox: if there is a case against a radical rhetorical stance, a case in McGuire and Melia's favor, it is best discovered by means of the radical rhetorical analysis they abjure.

What are the stakes in this intellectual debate? By means of the rhetorical analysis of the hard sciences—biology, chemistry, and physics—rhetoric of inquiry inserts itself into the inner sanctum of epistemological and ontological privilege. If no aspect of these sciences is proof against this analysis, the case for the rhetorical construction of all knowledge is immeasurably strengthened.

Three Necessary Distinctions

Those who wish to draw a line between science and rhetorical analysis routinely point to the durability of empirical regularities like those mentioned by McGuire and Melia. To argue counterintuitively, to argue against the position that these regularities describe one natural limit to such analysis, three distinctions must be made: between prediction and truth, between prediction and explanation, and between an explanation and its target. Placed side by side, the astronomical systems of ancient Babylonia, ancient Greece, and Newton will illustrate that these empirical regularities are not explanations but calls for explanation, not science but calls for science. They will also demonstrate that prediction, however accurate, neither explains anything, nor says anything about truth.

In *The Exact Sciences in Antiquity*, Otto Neugebauer recounts the impressive achievements of ancient Babylonian mathematical astronomy. By 300 B.C., this science was fully developed, "a consistent mathematical theory of lunar and planetary motion,"[3] capable of predicting such phenomena as new moons. To construct their lunar calendar, to determine the varying length of the lunar month, the ancient Babylonians had to be aware of at least five independent, contributary causes: the relative motions of the sun and moon, their relative velocity, the variation in the angle between the horizon and the ecliptic, and the deviation in the latitude of the moon as measured against the ecliptic.[4] "All these effects," Neugebauer says,

> act independently of each other and cause quite irregular patterns in the variation of the length of the lunar months. It is one of the most brilliant achievements in the exact sciences of antiquity to have recognized the independence of these influences and to develop a theory which permits the prediction of their combined effects.[5]

But Babylonian lunar theory is not a theory in our sense. In the first place, their mathematical astronomy operates without an underlying physical model, a three-dimensional picture of three-dimensional objects like the earth and the moon. This absence means that Babylonian astronomy says nothing about the varying configurations of the actual objects—the physical earth, the physical moon—from whose relative motions the data for its calculations are derived. In our current explanation of solar eclipses, a physical model is presupposed: we say that at certain relative distances the moon passes across the sun's disk; as it does so, it casts its shadow over a portion of the earth's surface. If we know the distances and relative sizes of the three bodies involved, we can calculate the dates of solar eclipses. Because the Babylonians do not understand astronomy in this way, "[their] texts do not suffice to say anything more than that a solar eclipse is excluded or that a solar eclipse is possible."[6]

Babylonian astronomy also functions without a kinematic model. This means that Babylonian astronomy is not a science of motion: the apparent movements of celestial bodies are not analyzed in terms of their possible components. For us, as for the Babylonians, celestial objects change their position recurrently and regularly. But the Babylonians are indifferent to the movements that lie behind these changes; they track not motion, but changes in position.

In contrast to the Babylonian, ancient Greek astronomical theory presupposes both a physical and a kinematic model. The underlying physical model is one of nested spheres, with the earth at the center and the *primum mobile* imparting motion from the periphery. In the kinematic model, observed celestial positions are resolved into combinations of circular motions. In their aggregate, these combinations account for the apparent motions of the celestial bodies. Throughout Hellenistic and medieval times, there is some question whether the component motions of the Ptolemaic system are real; however, their nature and variety effectively preclude their integration into the dominant paradigm, Aristotelian physics. Indeed, it is doubtful that these various circles moving at varying speeds—deferents, epicycles, eccentrics, equants—could be integrated into *any* coherent physics. The physical and the kinematic models are only loosely connected:

both presuppose a stationary central earth, but in the first the earth is a real presence, in the last, a theoretical construct. No physical model of nested spheres can comfortably accommodate the family of kinematic models of which Ptolemaic astronomy largely consists.

Newtonian celestial mechanics differs from Babylonian or Ptolemaic astronomy in its fundamental aim. It is a dynamic theory based on laws of motion that purport to be actual, laws that apply universally. The solar system is one model, one realization, of a theory whose central terms—force, acceleration, and mass—are defined only within that theory. It is these that actually produce the motions of celestial bodies. Newton makes astronomy not an independent science, but a branch of physics; his is not a theory of the solar system, but of all systems in which physical objects interact. Whatever its configuration, the solar system would still "obey" Newton's laws.

Side by side, these three astronomical systems dramatize the differences between explanation and its target, between prediction and truth, and between prediction and explanation. Each system predicts the position of celestial bodies, their common target, but predictions are not explanations; rather, they call for an explanation. In each system, we must also separate the accuracy of predictions from the truth of their underlying system of generation. According to current physics, none of these systems is correct, though all predict celestial appearances with varying degrees of accuracy. In all cases, the predictions of a "false" theory may be as accurate as those of a "true" one. Finally, explanation is very different from prediction. All three systems predict, but only Newton's actually explains, in the sense that his predictions flow coherently from the dynamic theories of his physics.

With these three distinctions in mind—between explanation and its target, between prediction and truth, and between prediction and explanation—we are now in a position to analyze McGuire and Melia's examples: celestial navigation, Avogadro's number, and the effect of the moon on the tides.

Drawing the Line at Empirical Regularities

In celestial navigation, the navigator calculates his position according to the apparent movements of heavenly bodies seen from a stationary earth: the exact configuration within the celestial sphere visible above his head acts as his guidance system. To do so properly, its stars must be brought down to earth: their relative celestial positions must be transformed into the terrestrial longitudes and latitudes. However accurate the navigator's predictions, his theory is false, knowingly so: the earth is not stationary, the celestial sphere an illusion. In fact, modern celestial navigation and the traditional navigation on the Puluwat Atoll in the Carolines are both based on false theories that yield true predictions. The Puluwatans navigate accurately by means of "a special logical construct or cognitive map based on the concept of a moving island [and a stationary canoe]."[7] If false theories yield accurate predictions, we surely cannot argue that accurate predictions point to the truth of underlying models or explanations. The efficacy of celestial naviga-tion undermines, rather than supports, the case for realism.

McGuire and Melia's second and third examples—Avogadro's number and the effect of the moon on the tides—form a pair: the first a physical constant, the second a constant physical relationship. Both are well attested empirical regularities. Science can consist either in these regularities (perhaps described mathematically) or in their explanation. If explanation is the stuff of science, scientific knowledge is clearly contingent: in the case of Avogadro's constant, the explanations of Newtonian mechanics and quantum mechanics differ; in the case of the effect of the moon on the tides, the explanations of Newton and Einstein differ. If we assume that the quantum and relativistic explanations are correct, rather than those of classical mechanics, is it because they are merely *later* or because they are also *better?* Claiming the first, we concede the question to relativism; claiming the second, we beg the question of realism. If instead we argue that science is only the set of its current empirical regularities and their accompanying techniques, preferably mathematical, we may seem on firm ground. But science then becomes an aggregate of practical knowledge closer to carpentry than to classical physics. Presumably, this ground is not what McGuire and Melia have in mind.

Moreover, even this ground is less firm than it appears. Although the targets of scientific explanation are more durable than the explanations themselves, they also alter over time: after Newton, motion was no longer a target; after phrenology, cranial irregularies. Moreover, even within science, constants can change their character: after quantum electrodynamics, *c*, the *constant* speed of light, turns out to be an average, not a constant. A skeptic might question whether, under their various descriptions over time, Avogadro's number, the cycles of the tides, or the configurations of celestial bodies remain unaltered targets.

In sum, scientific explanations alter profoundly over the centuries, an alteration that effectively undermines the putative truth value of currently approved theories. Prediction, however accurate, tells us nothing about truth. And the targets of explanation shift from time to time. Is there any sense, then, in which we can say that science describes and explains an unchanging, underlying causal reality? In these matters, people decide, not nature; indeed, it is people who decide what nature is. These decisions fall well within the provinces of sociology and rhetoric.

Drawing the Line at Well-Attested Theoretical Unobservables

McGuire and Melia draw the line a second way. They refer favorably to Ian Hacking's *Representing and Intervening*, a book that endorses the reality of well-attested unobservable entities. Hacking's principal example is the electron. Since light cannot penetrate into the subatomic world, no one will ever be able to "see" electrons. Still, electrons leave clear tracks, tracks from which we can derive their properties: the spin of an electron is a property so reliably present that it can be used as a tool in experiments, a tool as dependable as the equipment we *can* see. Hacking's example is PEGGY II, a polarizing electron gun used to investigate the properties of weak neutral currents.[8]

Hacking characterizes electrons as "a family of causal properties": presumably, such properties as mass, spin, and charge. It is these "in terms of which gifted experimenters describe and deploy electrons in order to investigate something else."[9] When such properties are used in the further exploration of physical reality, as in PEGGY II, we have engineering in the service of science: the use of spin as a tool is *a fortiori* a proof of the existence of electrons. Such properties, moreover, are relatively resistant to theory change. From Thomson's to quantum physics, the interpretation of the mass-to-charge ratio has undergone a profound change. But the electron remains as real as ever. This point of view is indifferent to "whether electrons are clouds or waves or particles."[10] This choice concerns their sense. It is not the sense, but "the reference that fixes the sameness of what we are talking about."[11] Because of this continuity of reference "the incommensurabilist would be out of his mind if he said that Thomson measured the mass of something other than the electron—our electron, Millikan's electron, Bohr's electron."[12]

Hacking's rhetoric conceals an equivocation between the reference of middle-sized objects, available to our senses, and that of unobservable entities, available only through instrumental mediation. Each causal property of the electron is observed not directly, but as marks on graphs, smears on photographs, or readings on meter dials: Thomson discovered the electron by measuring its mass-to-charge ratio in a cathode ray tube rigged as a deflection meter. Thomson saw not an electron, not a mass-to-charge ratio, but the consistent deflection of cathode rays in a darkened room. If this is so, to say that mass and charge exist, to say that, in this case, electrons *caused* the observed deflections, is to make use of theory: it is theory that turns arresting curiosities into properties, properties into entities. The interpretation of deflection as a ratio of causal properties, and the assignment of the properties evident in that ratio to the electron—*both* of these decisions are theory-driven. If an unobservable survives major theory change, it is not because its existence was established experimentally, as opposed to theoretically; rather, it survives because some theories are more durable than others; some smaller theories manage to outlive the more encompassing intellectual constructions into which they have been incorporated.

A theory of the equipment fixes the reference of the causal properties of unobservables; the reference of the unobservable themselves, on the other hand, is fixed by definition, by allocating causal properties within a theory that accounts for them. If we insist on fixing the reference of unobservables directly, that is, without the mediation of theory, we cannot explain what scientists were talking about when they referred to such discarded entities as phlogiston and the ether. Indeed, Hacking admits this as a problem in his system.[13] According to Hacking's theory, each of these discarded entities was always an empty set with null extension: scientists were literally referring not to phlogiston or the ether, but to nothing. In each case, the same nothing.

There is a better story near at hand. In the late nineteenth and early twentieth centuries, the luminiferous ether was an unobservable entity with well known causal properties. The ether was as real for physicists then as the electron is for physicists now: the wave theory of light depended absolutely on the existence of a medium rigid enough to transmit transverse waves, though rare enough to count as "empty space." Of electrons, Hacking says: "So far as I'm concerned, if you can spray them then they are real."[14] But Michelson felt just this way about the ether. In his first interferometer paper, he says: "the undulatory theory of light assumes the existence of a medium called the ether, whose vibrations produce the phenomena of heat and light, and which is supposed to fill all space."[15] The interferometer was designed to detect the motion of the earth by means of fringe shifts in wave patterns of light; the rigidity of the ether was built into the device.

If we assume, says Michelson, "that the ether is at rest, the earth moving through it, [then] the time required for light to pass from one point to another on the earth's surface, would depend on the direction in which it travels."[16] The fringe shifts—signs of the motion of the earth—should have been detected. But they were not. Since his experiment failed, Michelson felt that "the hypothesis of a stationary ether is ... shown to be incorrect."[17]

In other words, it was ultimately irrelevant to the existence of the ether that its well known causal property, its rigidity, had been built into the device: you cannot make unobservables into tools; you can only build into your experimental device causal properties that a particular theory attributes to a particular unobservable entity. Analogously, when we spray electrons, we say nothing criterial about their existence: we confirm only the causal property we call *spin*. Because of the way in which unobservable entities are constituted by scientific practice, they may turn into fictions, a process from which electrons cannot be automatically excluded.

Robbed of its causal properties, its reason for being, the ether simply ceased to exist. Its rigidity was superfluous in relativity theory: a medium of transmission was no longer needed. What had been a medium was now an environment, the field. Light was no longer waves; it was photons, self-motile, zero-mass particles that had some wavelike properties. When an old theory is discarded, its entities may be discarded along with it; if so, their causal properties, those still acknowledged by the new theory, will be redistributed in accordance with that theory. Some similar fate may well await the electron in some future science, its spin, mass, and charge reinterpreted and reassigned within a new ontology.

The tracks that electrons make are real enough, as real, if you will, as the tracks the stars make: the line between observation and detection cannot be cogently drawn.[18] But for science it is not the tracks that matter; it is their selection as a target of explanation, and their interpretation within some current theory. Both selection and interpretation are well within the boundaries of social action and rhetorical analysis.[19]

The Explanatory Power of "Recalcitrance"

Realists and their opponents agree that people cannot walk through walls. This limit, this "recalcitrance," has a scientific explanation, one that covers not only the phenomenon mentioned, but whole classes of phenomena. And classes of these classes. Concerning quantum theory, Feynman says:

> think about the mess at the beginning of this century, when there was heat, magnetism, electricity, light, X-rays, ultraviolet rays, indices of refraction, coefficients of reflection and other properties of various substances, all of which we have since put together into one theory, quantum electrodynamics.[20]

These explanations are rightly, and highly, valued; they represent the best of science as we know it.

McGuire and Melia wish to explain why these explanations work; they wish to explain the success of current physics in a manner analogous to the way current physics explains physical objects and events. Current physics works, in their view, only because it is in close touch with the various "recalcitrances" that together constitute the shape of the only world that is, the underlying causal structure of the world of appearances.[21]

For realists like McGuire and Melia, recalcitrance founds an argument that differentiates social from natural facts. We ignore a social fact like the monetary system at our peril; in doing so, however, we are constrained only by the prior actions and agreements of others like ourselves. But while we may have to agree that there is an Avogadro's constant, that it is a certain number, and that it is important to science, current actions or agreements cannot change that number without reference to the natural world. And Avogadro's number is just a metonym for all scientific knowledge, none of which can be altered without reference to the natural world.

But to serve as a cause of the phenomenal world, "recalcitrance" must be capable of independent characterization. On this point, "recalcitrance" suffers from the same disabilities as an analogous concept, Kant's noumenon. Unlike the phenomena, which are objects of our perception, noumena (and recalcitrances) "exist" only outside space and time. As a result, they cannot act as causes and they cannot be known: "the concept of a noumenon is . . a merely *limiting concept*, the function of which is to curb the pretensions of sensibility; and it is therefore only of negative employment ... it cannot affirm anything positive beyond the field of sensibility."[22] To conceive of noumena (or recalcitrances) is to think of a real world object, say a chair, and systematically to empty the idea of that chair of all temporal, sensory, and geometrical properties. Recalcitrance (or the noumenon) is the limit of that process; in other words, nothing. But nothing can cause nothing; nothing can explain nothing.

"Recalcitrance" solves no problems, scientific or philosophical. Worse, it generates explanatory burdens no relativism need share: not only must recalcitrance describe the indescribable; it must make sense out of the jumble of discontinuous, seemingly incompatible, ontologies variously espoused throughout the history of science. Is light a wave or a particle? Or is it, as we now believe, a particle with wavelike properties? The rhetorical relativism I advocate allows scientists to decide, sociologists and rhetoricians to explain their decisions.[23]

"Recalcitrance" and the Myths of Science

Despite these arguments, metaphysical realism persists; we have not heard the end of noumena or recalcitrances. The persistence of such concepts depends heavily on a widespread myth about science: that its success hinges in large part on decisive confrontations between theories and the world that theories are "about."[24] A well-known example of such a purported encounter is the verification of general relativity, one of whose predictions is the bending of star light in the vicinity of the sun.

This deviation can be observed only during a solar eclipse. Here is Einstein's account:

> We are indebted to the Royal Society and to the Royal Astronomical Society for the investigation of this important deduction. Undaunted by the war and by difficulties of both a material

and a psychological nature aroused by the war, these societies equipped two expeditions—to Sobral (Brazil), and to the island of Principe (West Africa)—and sent several of Britain's most celebrated astronomers (Eddington, Cottingham, Crommelin, Davidson), in order to obtain photographs of the solar eclipse of 29th May, 1919. The relative discrepancies to be expected between the stellar photographs obtained during the eclipse and the comparison photographs amounted to a few hundredths of a millimetre only. Thus great accuracy was necessary in making the adjustments required for the taking of the photographs and their subsequent measurement.

The results of the measurements confirmed the theory in a thoroughly satisfactory manner.[25]

But the situation was far more problematic than Einstein reveals. The measurement of stellar deviation of under two seconds of arc during an eclipse is "the absolute measurement of a very small quantity during a particular short time interval under usually quite difficult conditions of a temporary field-station in some more or less remote part of the world." Einstein had predicted a deviation of 1.74 seconds; the actual results of repeated expeditions range from 0.93 to 2.73, a range so wide that the difference between extremes is larger than the predicted quantity.[26]

But even had these measurements converged, verification would not cease to be problematic. There is no question of applying general relativity directly, of measuring stellar positions, and plugging measurements directly into formulae. For the purpose of "calculational convenience," a set of idealized initial conditions is postulated at every stage; at each stage, when there is a failure of fit, the blame is placed not on the theory, but "on the idealized initial conditions": deviations count not against the theory, but against its verifiers.[27]

After tabulating the results of the various expeditions, Sciama says:

> It is hard to assess their significance, since other astronomers have derived different results from a rediscussion of the same material. Moreover, one might expect that if observers did not know what value they were "supposed" to obtain, their published results might vary over a greater range than they actually do; there are several cases in astronomy where knowing the "right" answer has led to observed results later shown to be beyond the power of the apparatus to detect.[28]

Such problematic results are not confined to astronomy. The general success of the methods of science, as reflected in the routine confirmation of theory by observation and experiment—this myth cannot survive detailed investigation of actual practice. Peter Galison on the establishment of the value of *g*, Gerald Holton on Millikan's oil-drop experiments, Andrew Pickering on the discovery of the quark[29]—each of these marvelously detailed accounts can comfortably sustain a radical social and rhetorical reading. The long chains of inference that mark scientific practice at its creative edge suggest that the confirmation of theories of great generality, theories far removed from the reality they purport to describe and explain, are little endangered by experience.

In the accounts of Holton, Galison, and Pickering, we see "aboutness" constructed before our eyes. Not by any special perceptual intuition, but by means of "the many strands of instrumental and theoretical beliefs that are locked into the practice of experi-mentation,"[30] physicists determine that the electrons' charge has an integral character, that their g-factor is 2 (a key test of quantum theory), that quarks exist.

In Einstein's case, rhetoric conceals the uncomfortable truth: an "important deduc-tion" is investigated by "celebrated astronomers" who, "undaunted" by the requirement of "great accuracy," produce "thoroughly satisfactory" results. In reality, so unsatisfac-tory were these results that there were, between 1919 and 1952, *twelve additional attempts* to measure the bending of stellar light in the solar field, attempts that consistently failed to resolve the equivocation inherent in the original results. This repeated failure did not seriously impede the acceptance of general relativity.[31] Nor should it.

Relativism: Neither Incoherent nor Anti-Rational

In his *Critique of Pure Reason*, Kant showed that the affirmation of causal foundations, and its contrary, their denial, are equally false. Both assume the ability to escape the world of experience within which, and *only* within which, meaning, and predication, are possible. We cannot predicate causation apart from the network of causation *within* the world. The notion of a cause *of* the world, McGuire and Melia's claim for "recalcitrance," is a quasi-empirical claim at the very least, and is incoherent; its denial therefore is equally incoherent.[32] On the other hand, the relativism that radical rhetorical analysis presupposes is perfectly coherent; it neither affirms nor denies foundations. It is not metaphysically, but methodologically, ambitious.

A radical rhetoric of science is not antirational either. Because conceptions of ration-ality are part of the social world of science, a rhetoric that barred them from its analysis would be pointlessly impoverished. Of course, appropriate methodological cautions must be exercised. It must not be assumed that scientists consciously hold the beliefs inferred from their work, nor that the beliefs they profess actually drive their practices. Most important, their conceptions of rationality should be analyzed "independently of any favorable or unfavorable appraisals of those beliefs based upon their meeting or not meeting the requirements of some preferred conception of scientific rationality."[33] A radical rhetoric of science may also use normative conceptions of rationality as analytical probes, as frameworks for its own judgments. Such theoretical use will be legitimate so long as normative concepts are employed only to *characterize* the enterprise on which they are focused: "the appraising force typically implied by [the] employment [of these concepts] in making value-judgments" must be suspended.[34]

Conclusion

The radical rhetoric of science I advocate does not foreclose on the possibility that McGuire and Melia are correct, that there is a limit to rhetorical analysis. But the persua-siveness of any demarcation between rhetoric and science does not depend on *a priori* considerations; instead, it relies on the ultimate failure of radical rhetorical analysis. But the failure of an analytical system implies its use: an all-out rhetorical assault on the great variety of scientific "texts"—papers, proceedings, notebooks, laboratory conversations.

If, in consequence of such an assault, the machinery of rhetorical analysis breaks down at any point, a demarcation between rhetoric and science will have been made, *at precisely that point.* It is a demarcation both realist and relativist must acknowledge on pain of irrationality. McGuire and Melia cannot be right before the fact; they must turn out to be right.

Notes

1 (Beverly Hills: Sage, 1979; Princeton: Princeton Univ. Press, 1986), 281.
2 The hypothesis that equal volumes of different gases under like conditions contain the same number of molecules.
3 2d ed. (Providence: Brown Univ. Press, 1957), 97.
4 The ecliptic is the apparent annual path of the sun and the planets among the stars.
5 Ibid., 108–9.
6 Ibid., 119.
7 Thomas Gladwin, *East is a Bird: Navigation and Logic on Puluwat Atoll* (Cambridge: Harvard Univ. Press, 1970), 181.
8 (Cambridge: Cambridge Univ. Press, 1983).
9 Ibid., 272.
10 Ibid., 272.
11 Ibid., 81.
12 Ibid., 84.
13 Ibid., 86–87.
14 Ibid., 23; emphasis omitted.
15 A. A. Michelson, "The Relative Motion of the Earth and the Luminiferous Ether," *American Journal of Science*, 3d series, vol. 22, 120ff; reprinted in L. S. Swenson, Jr., *The Etherial Aether: A History of the Michelson-Morley-Miller Aether-Drift Experiments, 1880–1930* (Austin, Texas: Univ. of Texas Press, 1972), 249.
16 Ibid.
17 Ibid., 257. As it turned out, Michelson's experiment was not crucial: it took a half-century of experimental work, by Michelson, Morley, and Miller, to put the ether finally to rest. Nor did so eminent a physicist as Lorentz see the point in discarding so summarily an unobserved entity with well-understood causal properties, an entity that, according to Maxwell, was the best confirmed in natural philosophy (Larry Laudan, "A Confrontation of Convergent Realism," in *Scientific Realism*, ed. Jarrett Leplin [Berkeley: Univ. of California Press, 1984], 226). Lorentz offered instead an alternate interpretation of Michelson's experiments, one that preserved the reality of ether by giving it an additional property, on analogy with its known effect on electrical and magnetic forces. When Michelson's equipment moved against the ether wind, Lorentz said, the arm perpendicular to that wind shortened slightly because its motion against a stationary incompressible medium altered its balance of molecular forces (H. A. Lorentz, "Michelson's Interference Experiment," in *The Principle of Relativity: A Collection of Original Memoirs on the Special and General Theory of Relativity*, ed. A. Sommerfeld; trans., W. Perrett and G. B. Jeffery. New York: Dover, 1952 [1895], 3–7). This FitzGerald-Lorentz contraction survived relativity theory, where it emerged in a new guise as an entailment of Einstein's fundamental postulates.
18 Arthur Fine, *The Shaky Game: Einstein, Realism, and the Quantum Theory* (Chicago: Univ. of Chicago Press, 1986), 146–47.

19 For a discussion of these matters in another context, see Alan G. Gross, "Reinventing Certainty: The Significance of Ian Hacking's Realism," *Proceedings of the 1990 Annual Meeting of the Philosophy of Science Association*, vol. 1. (East Lansing: Philosophy of Science Association, 1990), 421–31.

20 Richard P. Feynman, *QED: The Strange Theory of Light and Matter* (Princeton: Princeton Univ. Press, 1985), 149.

21 McGuire and Melia *say* that they "do not endorse the notion of the 'World in itself', and the idea that the mind copies the world." But this does not discharge their burden of proof: they still must define the "special recalcitrance" of science, the presumed cause of their "scientific effects" (op. cit., 109).

22 Immanuel Kant, *Critique of Pure Reason*, trans. Norman Kemp Smith (New York: St. Martin's, 1965), A255/B310–11.

23 Of course, scientists can explain their decisions themselves; if they do, these explanations will also be targets of sociological and rhetorical analysis.

24 There is another underlying myth, one I have not questioned so far, the myth that science is, by and large, successful. But the history of science is not, for the most part, a history of success: "overwhelmingly, the results of the conscientious pursuit of scientific inquiry are failures: failed theories, failed hypotheses, failed conjectures, inaccurate measurements, incorrect estimations of parameters, fallacious causal inferences, and so forth" (Fine, 119). Those who think otherwise should be compelled to read the *Proceedings* of the Royal Society—the whole set.

25 Albert Einstein, *Relativity: The Special and General Theory*, trans. Robert W. Lawson (New York: Crown, 1961), 128.

26 D. W. Sciama, *The Physical Foundations of General Relativity* (New York: Double-day, 1959), 70–71.

27 Robert Laymon, "The Path from Data to Theory," in *Scientific Realism*, ed. Jarrett Leplin (Berkeley: Univ. of California Press, 1984), 114, 117.

28 Sciama, 70.

29 Peter Galison, *How Experiments End* (Chicago: Univ. of Chicago Press, 1987); Gerald Holton, *The Scientific Imagination: Case Studies* (Cambridge: Cambridge Univ. Press, 1978); Andrew Pickering, *Constructing Quarks: A Sociological History of Particle Physics* (Chicago: Univ. of Chicago Press, 1984). *G* is the ratio of the angular momentum of an electron to its magnetic moment.

30 Galison, *How Experiments End*, 74.

31 For an extended discussion of these matters, see Alan G. Gross, *The Rhetoric of Science* (Cambridge: Harvard Univ. Press, 1990).

32 Kant's argument from the Antimonies has been subjected to steady critique, but Henry E. Allison makes a cogent case for this set of inferences. See his *Kant's Transcendental Idealism: An Interpretation and Defense* (New Haven: Yale Univ. Press, 1983), 35–61.

33 Russell Keat, "Relativism, Value Freedom, and the Sociology of Science," in *Relativism: Interpretation and Confrontation*, ed. Michael Krausz (Notre Dame: Univ. of Notre Dame Press, 1989), 292.

34 Ibid., 282.

9.
RECLAIMING RHETORIC OF SCIENCE AND TECHNOLOGY
Knowing In and About the World
by James H. Collier

"The aim of philosophy … is to understand how things in the broadest possible sense of the term hang together in the broadest possible sense of the term."
—Wilfrid Sellars, "Philosophy and the Scientific Image of Man"

In the rhetoric of science and technology (RST), we have called for a pause at the end of the day. In so doing, we call upon philosophy. Under the incessant pressure that disciplinarity exerts, a newer field such as RST can become distracted; it can lose its commitment to understanding how things "hang together." In RST, what disciplinary conditions interfere with its ability to philosophize? How might it once again do philosophy? And why would it even want to?

In this essay, I will argue that some dominant disciplinary practices in RST indeed circumvent philosophical deliberation. Here, I will discuss three: the profusion of case studies, the indiscriminate reliance on contextualization, and the globalization of rhetoric. The boundless supply of case studies, the infinite combination of contexts for studying science and technology, and the enumerable rhetorics of X (Goankar, "Idea" 75) portend no shortage of research sites and perspectives for up and coming scholars. In this sense, RST seems like an active discipline with a bustling research agenda. However, I will argue, RST currently lacks the philosophical vision to synthesize its knowledge into a coherent story about science and technology.

The philosophical growth of RST may have been impeded by its separation from Science and Technology Studies (STS), one of its early travelers. The declining presence of STS in RST signals at once RST's disciplinary consolidation and dwindling of possibilities for synthesizing what we know about science and technology from its scientific and humanistic study. RST needs philosophy to understand science and technology "in the broadest possible sense." But, more urgently, RST needs philosophy in order to understand itself.

James H. Collier. "Reclaiming Rhetoric of Science and Technology: Knowing In and About the World." *Technical Communication Quarterly*, Volume 14, Number 3, 2005, pp. 295–302.

Tending your Own Garden

Case studies are common currency in RST (as well as STS). Case studies signify a coalesced, active field of inquiry to researchers, administrators, and funding agencies. Fuller characterizes the embrace of case studies in RST as "a kind of Kuhnian normal science," in which practitioners toil on a defined set of problems in a predictable, forward-moving fashion ("Globalization" par. 5). Following Fuller's logic, RST "converts the concepts of classical rhetoric into analytic techniques that can be unleashed on virtually any unsuspecting text to produce a distinctly 'rhetorical' brand of research" (par. 5). Gaonkar ("Idea" 41) also notes that the RST case study is a methodological commonplace: "A case study typically takes some structured episode (say, a controversy) or some specifiable dimension (say, writing) of scientific practice and analyzes it from a rhetorical perspective. ... [O]ne can always find a hesitant gesture towards generalization ... about an inward connection between science and rhetoric derived from a certain version of philosophical anthropology ... that makes rhetoric simultaneously unavoidable and erasable" ("Idea" 41). Although the case study may have helped RST to achieve disciplinary legitimacy, the case study seems unable to offer unique conclusions about its object of study.

Case studies are an efficient scholarly technique for building disciplines. Legitimate disciplines need graduate programs. Case studies can be molded to fit the closely monitored timetable for getting a graduate degree. Given the general methodological flexibility of the case study—elastic historical beginning and end points, for example—the breadth and depth of the case study can be made to fit the genre of theses, dissertations, and the next generation of academic books. Case studies are empirical, get positive results, and can be tailored to the requisite graduate student or assistant professor timetable. The humanities look more scientized, which academic administrators often recognize as valid knowledge production and which they fund. The work gets published. It can fit publishers' demands, is marketable, and fits in what is recognizable in terms of disciplinary progress as seen in the social sciences.

The ethos of case studies in science studies is that the researcher's approach reveals something real, and somehow buried (or tacit), about the object of study. The *locus classicus* of the science studies case study, initially rendered as fiction, is Bruno Latour and Steve Woolgar's *Laboratory Life*. *Laboratory Life* showed the sustained social and material conditions necessary for the production of scientific knowledge. Latour and Woolgar's blend of authoritativeness (in part from associating with Jonas Salk), thoroughness, and mysteriousness made the book ripe for critical response (see the postscript for the second edition) and imitation. *Laboratory Life* would come to represent the genre of the sophisticated, but doable, case study. Interdisciplinary researchers adapted the case study to satisfy the varied constraints imposed by the diverse political economies of academic research.

In STS, Malcolm Ashmore's *The Reflexive Thesis*, a case study about the Sociology of Scientific Knowledge (SSK) through the process of his own academic credentialing, shows how a cleverly conceived case study can be successfully deployed no matter the academic genre. The unmistakable innovation of Ashmore's work offers a sure sign of the viability and entrenchment of STS research. In RST, Leah Ceccarelli's *Shaping Science with Rhetoric* offers a somewhat more earnest, traditional take on the case study. Still, the work's plasticity—as dissertation; as comprised of related but autonomous cases suitable for journal articles; as coherent book; as methodological innovation (examining a case of failed rhetoric for example)—marks the maturity of RST.

I take the work of Ashmore and Ceccarelli as an apparent historical indicator of the next generation of scholarship in their respective fields. Dissertations in STS and RST, respectively, had become heralded books. That the dissertations were case studies, albeit markedly different approaches, suggested a lesson for scholars in the field and administrators of rising graduate programs. The features of the case study could be manipulated to produce good, widely valued work. Consequently, academic researchers set forth to ethnographically toil in the fields and bring back their stories.

What is the problem with being an honest toiler in the STS and RST fields? The absence of a moment of synthesis. As Fuller points out: "The case study method so cherished by science studies practitioners often appears as carping from the sidelines; the research is so focused on particular cases, it seems to have no implications for the 'big picture.' Yet the public understanding of science seems to demand such a picture … the overall impression is that science studies has abdicated any responsibility for constituting the future of science" (qtd. in Atkinson-Grosjean, par. 10).

Context and Globalization

Like case studies, contextualization is a salient feature of scholarship in RTS. Context is invoked as a way of more broadly understanding a given object of study. In *The Structure of Scientific Revolutions*, Kuhn ushered in the historical turn in the philosophy of science, and in doing so unwittingly ended positivism. For many scholars, Kuhn seemed to teach a methodological lesson: science is best understood scientifically, through empirical social science. However, once science became the object of study for history and sociology, context-based studies of science and technology mushroomed. While many researchers tend to privilege historical contexts as a way to set the stage for their accounts, they rarely discriminate among the number and kinds of contexts within which an object of study can be placed—the more contexts, the more knowledge, the better and more comprehensive the account. The problem with this assumption is obvious. For any given object of study, the number of contexts one might consider seems practically infinite and remarkably indiscriminate.

In appropriating interdisciplinary pluralism from STS, the additional problems of fragmentation and globalization have been visited on RST. For rhetoric, the object of study can change constantly. While science and/or technology can be the object of study, the number of "coarticulations"— "the rhetorics of X" (Gaonkar, "Idea" 75)—ceaselessly multiply. Gaonkar lists twenty-three such coarticulations ("Idea"). Those who now care to count will likely find exponentially more. Rhetoric's globalization (Schiappa, "Second Thoughts") brings attendant disputes regarding its disciplinary status. Examples include Simons ("Globalization") and Fuller ("Globalization"); Cherwitz, Hikins, and Schiappa et al.; and Simons ("Rhetorical") and Keith et al. Each of these debates addresses issues elaborated by several prominent scholars (Gross and Keith), extended by Gaonkar ("Idea"), and raised by Melia. Contemporary arguments regarding rhetoric's scope and purpose reach back at least to the postwar period. Gross and Keith designate Bitzer and Black's *The Prospect of Rhetoric* as an historical endpoint. I cite this long history to suggest the constancy of disputes over the status of rhetoric's globalization and object of study, which brings us back to the case study, that handy tool of globalization.

While these debates continue, so, too, do the case studies. At best, the attention of RST is divided between "general essays and case studies" ("Idea" 41). And while general studies attempt to sort out "how [RST] is positioned in relation to the received traditions in science studies … [they] invariably conclude by calling for more case studies. …" (Gaonkar, "Idea" 41). RST lacks a meta-theory for sorting out, comparing and contrasting, and evaluating the significance of case studies. Meta-theory would be especially helpful as we pause to consider whether rhetoric of technology is to be a separate field of inquiry (Miller, "Learning"; Bazerman, "Production"), or if rhetoric can account for artifacts in the networked continuum of "technoscience" (see Latour, *Science*). The assumption appears to be that the coarticulation itself—a rhetoric of … science, technology, science and technology, or technoscience—smoothes out the ontological difference in the objects of study. In the quest for academic legitimacy, we keep piling up case studies.

Rhetoric in and about the World

Where do we find models of deliberation for RST and STS? Do we look to the past in order to recuperate what we find there, or do we look to the present with an eye toward the future, considering what we might now know, and to develop a procedure for shaping knowledge? (Either can be idealized.) Do we look to the past, to the Athenian forum to find, and model, participatory democracy (Leff)? Do we look to the Enlightenment tradition of Mill, Dewey, and Popper (Fuller, "Rhetoric")? Do we look to the United States constitutional convention (Fuller and Collier)? Do we turn to Habermas, Rorty, or Rawls for direction? Do we look to the Discussion Movement and the Forum Movement (Keith, "Democratic")? Do we look to science as an exemplar of the Athenian polis (Zilsel; see Fuller, "Rhetoric")? Do we look to computers and cyberspace (Doheny-Farina; Gurak, *Persuasion*; Welch; and Warnick)? What if, instead, we looked inward, at academic disciplines (Fuller and Collier)?

Disciplines pose a unique problem in trying to understand knowledge as both in and about the world. Disciplinary knowledge is embodied in the world. It is subject to numerous caprices, not the least of which is the political economy of academia and our often vague approaches to given objects of study. In fully (even reflexively) disclosing the embodiment of our knowledge, we face criticism of our knowledge about the world—its basis, its veracity, its coherence. Given the complex and variable interactions of rhetoric, science, and technology, we are subject to charges (leveled by other experts—scientists, computer programmers, philosophers) of illogic, wrong-headedness, or sophistry. We may choose to embrace these criticisms—the reflexive turn in STS, the opening *apologia* of bringing together science and rhetoric in RST—or divide our attention, allowing disciplinary spokespeople to hash out the theoretical controversies while practitioners produce case studies. Yet managing these tensions is the task of how a discipline tells its story, its disciplinary history.

Once bounded, a field of study gets busy reproducing and sustaining itself. The apparent pluralistic virtues of interdisciplinarity gives RST both a ready-made argument for disciplinary agnosticism and the ability to hold off decisions about where it will locate. Does RST belong to NCA [National Communication Association] rhetoricians or is it a global citizen free to roam (Simons, "Globalization" versus Fuller, "Globalization"; and Simons, "Rhetorical" versus Keith, Fuller, Gross, and Leff)? Is contemporary rhetorical theory becoming a master trope provincially worried about its disciplinary impact and not its veracity (Cherwitz and Hikins)? Or is rhetoric a "vocabulary for redescribing communicative phenomena" (Schiappa et al.)? Rhetoric contemplates a disciplinary home—Communication, English, Composition, Technical Communication—while considering its own disciplining as RST or, perhaps, "captology" (not to be confused with captation; see Fogg; Latour, *Science*).

While motion and not method seems the current occupation of rhetoric, the ability to philosophize in a synthetic manner is swept aside. The question is not whether we can recuperate classical or modern rhetoric. We need a synthetic moment, a moment not at which we talk at each other, but where we collectively philosophize about the conduct of our inquiry. To some extent, STS took responsibility for this discussion, at least until *l'affaire Sokal*. In the wake of the Sokal hoax, STS and RST got religion in the form of pragmatism (Fuller, "Globalization"). And penance was performed by doing case studies.

For RST and STS, the project of theorizing how the knowledge production can be explicitly both in and about the world has been addressed by Fuller' project of social epistemology. Fuller's "alternative 'grand narrative' " (Atkinson-Grosjean) regarding science's future has been variously explored in his voluminous work. Here, I wish only to point out the need for RST to consider the normative implications of its work both in a disciplinary framework and about science and technology. While the mere mention of norms leaves many scholars cold, the explicit criteria, or rules, for a discussion of the future of RST and SRS requires, in part, a pause from the harried labors of discipline building. STS, for example, tried to reflexively consider its future on the fly and ran head-long into the science wars. I believe that by collectively, as it were, going meta—general essayists and case studies researchers in RST and STS alike—we may pause and collectively respond to the work that has gone before under the umbrella of the study of science. By "Going Meta," I am not necessary referring to political confrontations of the type analyzed by Simons. Rather, at this pause, I am calling for the collective negotiation of the narrative we have constructed about science and technology. And we need to do so while being cognizant of the stories we tell.

Final Thoughts

In RST and STS, what do we know, and on what basis? It is time to adjudicate the knowledge that we purport to create. We need to negotiate social and philosophical syntheses. At one point STS promised a synthesized, interdisciplinary approach to the public understanding of science and technology. That promise has not been fulfilled. And, in the incessant pressure that disciplinarity exerts, we have lost the deliberative process in RST. Debates over globalization and disciplinarity focus on matters of producing and distributing the research. We try to find occasion for deliberation, but it tends to be ceremonial rather than a fundamental, normative feature of our practice. As we pause to consider the possibilities of RST, let us take up the deliberative process on the parapet where we can see the horizon.

Works Cited

Ashmore, Malcolm. *The Reflexive Thesis: Wrighting Sociology of Scientific Knowledge.* Chicago: U of Chicago P, 1989.

Atkinson-Grosjean, Janet. "Science Studies: Beyond the *Social Text* Hoax" *21stC* 2.3 (1997): 14 Dec. 2004.

Bazerman, Charles. "The Production of Technology and the Production of Human Meaning." *JBTC* 12.3 (1998): 381–87.

Bitzer, Lloyd F., and Edwin Black. *The Prospect of Rhetoric: Report of the National Developmental Project.* Englewood Cliffs: Prentice-Hall, 1971.

Ceccarelli, Leah. *Shaping Science with Rhetoric: The Cases of Dobzhansky, Shrödinger, and Wilson.* Chicago: U of Chicago P, 2001.

Cherwitz, Richard A., and James W. Hikins. "Climbing the Academic Ladder: A Critique of Provincialism in Contemporary Rhetoric." *QJS* 864 (2000): 375–85.

Doheny-Farina, Stephen. *The Wired Neighborhood.* New Haven: Yale UP, 1996.

Fahnestock, Jeanne. *Rhetorical Figures in Science* New York: Oxford UP, 1999.

Fogg, B. J. *Persuasive Technology: Using Computers to Change What We Think and Do.* San Francisco: Morgan Kaufmann, 2003.

Fuller, Steve. "The Globalization of Rhetoric and Its Discontents." *Poroi* 2.2 (2003): 14 Dec. 2004 https://doi.org/10.13008/2151-2957.1050.

——. " 'Rhetoric of Science:' Double the Trouble?" *Rhetorical Hermeneutics: Invention and Interpretation in the Age of Science.* Eds. Alan G. Gross and William M. Keith. Albany: State U of New York P. 1997. 279–98.

Fuller, Steve, and James H. Collier. *Philosophy, Rhetoric and the End of Knowledge: A New Beginning for Science and Technology Studies.* 2nd ed. Mahwah: Erlbaum, 2004.

Gaonkar, Dilip. "The Idea of Rhetoric in the Rhetoric of Science." *Rhetorical Hermeneutics: Invention and Interpretation in the Age of Science.* Eds. Alan G. Gross and William M. Keith. Albany: State U of New York P. 1997. 25–85.

——. "The Idea of Rhetoric in the Rhetoric of Science." *Southern Speech Communication Journal* 584 (1993): 258–95.

Gross, Allen G., and William Keith. Eds. *Rhetorical Hermeneutics: Invention and Interpretation in the Age of Science.* Albany: State U of New York P, 1997.

Keith, William. "Democratic Revival and the Promise of Cyberspace: Lessons from the Forum Movement." *Rhetoric and Public Affairs.* 5.2 (2002): 311–26.

Keith William, Steve Fuller, Alan Gross, and Michael Leff. "Taking Up the Challenge: A Response to Simons." *QJS* 85.3 (1999): 330–38.

Kuhn, Thomas. *The Structure of Scientific Revolutions.* 2nd ed. Chicago: U of Chicago P, 1970.

Latour, Bruno. *Science in Action.* Cambridge: Harvard UP, 1987.

Latour, Bruno, and Steve Woolgar. *Laboratory Life: The Social Construction of Scientific Facts.* Beverly Hills: Sage, 1979.

Leff, Michael C. "Modern Sophistic and the Unity of Rhetoric." *The Rhetoric of the Human Sciences.* Eds. John S Nelson, Alan Megill, and Donald N. McCloskey. Madison: U of Wisconsin P, 1987. 19–37.

Meila, Trevor. "And Lo the Footprint … Selected Literature in Rhetoric and Science." *QJS* 70.3 (1984): 303–13.

Miller, Carolyn R. "Learning from History: World War II and the Culture of High Technology." *JBTC* 12.4 (1998): 288–315.

Schiappa, Edward. "Second Thoughts on the Critiques of Big Rhetoric." *Philosophy and Rhetoric* 34.3 (2001): 260–74.

Schiappa, Edward, Alan G. Gross, Raymie E. McKerrow, and Robert L. Scott. "Rhetorical Studies as Reduction or Rediscription? A Response to Cherwitz and Hikins." *QJS* 88.1 (2002): 112–20.

Sellars, Wilfrid. "Philosophy and the Scientific Image of Man." *Frontiers of Science and Philosophy.* Ed. Robert Colodny. Pittsburgh: U of Pittsburgh P (1962): 35–78.

Simons, Herbert "The Globalization of Rhetoric and the Argument from Disciplinary Consequence." *Poroi* 2.2 (2003): 3 Jan. 2005 https://doi.org/10.13008/2151-2957.1049.

——. "Going Meta: Definition and Political Applications." *QJS* 80.4 (1994): 468–81.

——. "Rhetorical Hermeneutics and the Project of Globalization." *QJS* 85.1 (1999): 86–100.

Warnick, Barbara. *Critical Literacy in a Digital Era: Technology, Rhetoric, and the Public Interest.* Mahwah: Erlbaum, 2002.

Welch, Kathleen E. *Electric Rhetoric: Classical Rhetoric, Oralism, and a New Literacy.* Cambridge: MIT P, 1999.

Zilsel, Edward. "The Genesis of the Concept of Scientific Progress." *Journal of the History of Ideas* 6.1 (1945): 35–50.

10.
THE PRODUCTIVITY OF SCIENTIFIC RHETORIC
by David J. Depew and John Lyne

1. Rhetoric and Contemporary Studies of Science

The rhetoric of science is so far a small but proud scholarly field that seeks simultan-eously to contribute to rhetorical studies and to secure a place for rhetoric in the conver-sation of–to use a broad and not exclusively owned term–science studies. We want to be mindful of both of those fronts. The approach of rhetorical studies to argumentation, including scientific argumentation, recognizes that, no matter how valid their reasoning or how strong their evidence, speakers must command authority with audiences and that audiences bring a lot of baggage with them to the context-dependent rhetorical situ-ations in which they encounter rhetorical activity. Accordingly, rhetoricians of science take seriously the role of rhetorical choices, including the use of tropes and figures, nar-rative accounts, genre expectations, and terministic framing to shape conversations about science.

The field owes its gratitude to pioneers such as John Angus Campbell, Lawrence Prelli, Alan Gross, Randy Allen Harris, Jeanne Fahnestock, Carolyn Miller, and others who made this or related points at a time when the reflective study of science was still dominated by history and philosophy of science. Within the narratives of these more prestigious disciplines, the scope of rhetoric was pretty much confined to public com-munication of scientific results. The epistemic grounds of scientific claims were located elsewhere.

Since then, studies of science have taken so decidedly a discursive and social turn that logical-formalist philosophies and internalist histories of science are no longer taken seriously by nearly anybody (with certain exceptions that both these authors know all too well). This development raises two interlinked questions. One is whether the social-discursive turn in the study of science has taken full advantage of rhetorical theory and criticism in articulating its alternative to philosophy of science. The other is whether we rhetoricians of science have taken full advantage of the opening created by the broader discursive-social turn to articulate, deploy, and advertise our distinctive yet varied approach.

If one were to cast a net in the waters of rhetorical studies of science and technology, one would capture quite a range of projects in the last several decades. These include but

David J. Depew and John Lyne. "The Productivity of Scientific Rhetoric." *Poroi*, Volume 9, Number 1, 2013, Article 4.

are not limited to: (1) rhetorical analysis of major scientists; (2) the rhetoric of scientific genres; (3) rhetoric within specific scientific fields; (4) the rhetoric of science-related controversies; (5) inventional practices in science; (6) controversy-strewn episodes in the history of science; (7) public appropriations of scientific terms; (8) language and figures within science; (9) incommensurability and demarcational relationships among disciplines; (10) rhetoric and philosophical rationality; (11) the uses of scientific expertise; (12) the rhetoric of medicine, (13) rhetoric and materiality; (14) the rhetoric of risk; (15) visual rhetorics of science; and (16) the mythic rhetorics of science and religion.[1] Collectively, these writings represent contributions to the theory, criticism, and history of rhetoric. And we can be proud of the many variations on a theme. But the studies do not follow a single program or share a specific agenda. Rhetoric is opportunistic and unruly, and we cast our nets where we think the fishing is good. Is this a problem? This is a fair and timely question. What would it mean to be part of a unified agenda, and what principles might provide that unity? Or, by contrast, might we embrace the concept of *repertoire* and still remain aspirational? Is that enough?

Perhaps it is an aspiration to find a common framework that leads us to draw upon other fields. Many among us want to make common cause with Bruno Latour, for example, and it is encouraging that this most prominent proponent of social studies of science does himself make use of the term *rhetoric* to describe the transactions that resulted in, for example, the pasteurization of France or the exportable, packaged bits of sellable knowledge generated by words as much as by deeds at places like the Salk Laboratories (Latour, 1988). Let us quote Latour in reference to the R-word. "Rhetoric," he observed, "is a fascinating albeit despised discipline, but it becomes still more important when debates are so exacerbated that they become scientific and technical" (Latour, 1987, p. 30). We note, too, that Latour's own rhetoric is fascinating to us. For instance, his thought experiment of ontological egalitarianism in which things as well as persons take part in the wrangling of a great parliament may have helpfully challenged the assumption that persons alone are articulate and things just get pushed around (Latour, 1993, 2007). Even as this exercise strains credulity, it leads to valuable insights. Still, Latour's inventional spark is so bold that its very success has caused him difficulties in convincing people that his case studies support local, context-dependent forms of scientific empiricism and realism. This is not the wholesale social constructionism most of his readers, especially the lazy ones, expect to hear.

We largely agree with Latour about going local and about robust contextualization. We also sympathize with his exasperated assurances that science does not either in fact or in his view reduce to textualism. Yet, here is a point at which the rhetorical perspective leads us to the contentious but attractive claim that the rhetoric of science contextualizes science better than does the sociology of science because the latter tends to reduce arguments to context rather than defining context by argument. This is for the rhetoric of science a key point. It means that context is a very flexible concept; it embraces the discursive as well as the material. In this and related matters, perhaps we rhetoricians of science can engage the social studies of science to mutual benefit, and in the process fulfill the expectations that led our founders to form this association.

Perhaps Kenneth Burke's pentadic devices for distributing agency would add something of value to Latour's argument. One of those five terms is "scene." G. Thomas Goodnight's threefold distinction between personal, technical, and public spheres of discourse, which is itself a rhetorical reconstruction of Habermas's theory of communicative action, can help frame the scene in which the kinds of transactions Latour posits take place (Goodnight, 1982). If you see it this way you will observe that only under very particular, very contingent, and very hard to sustain conditions, such as those that obtained in post-War America, can modern societies support the degree of phase separation among these three discursive spheres that grants serene autonomy to the technical sphere in ways philosophers of science tend to take for granted. Why otherwise would the intrusions of creationists and climate science deniers seem like, well, intrusions? Rhetoricians know better. The boundaries between discursive spheres are not natural. They are constructed and maintained by ongoing rhetorical activity, and even at their best, they leak at the seams.

If there is one theorem that we rhetoricians of science have sustained in ways that have suffered little back talk, it is that demarcation or boundary-work between science and society; between science, non-science, junk science, and pseudo-science; and between various scientific fields themselves is irreducibly rhetorical. We are thinking of the work of Charles A. Taylor (1997) and of Thomas Gieryn (1999). Efforts of philosophers to try to find purely logical, Bayesian probabilistic, and other methodological ways of demarcating have been in vain. Still, the main implication of recognizing that demarcation is essentially rhetorical is both inescapable and hard to hear even for some of its supporters. Unless you define the technical sphere in a way that is both question-begging and hopelessly unreal, it must be admitted that there is nothing in principle that prevents junk science and pseudo-science from being hatched in and passed out by reputable technical sphere venues. Nor is there anything in principle that prevents public sphere discourse from putting the burden of proof on what comes out of the mouths of scientists.

Both of these things in fact happen. It was not scientifically scrupulous progressives or scientists themselves, for example, but benighted big city Catholic politicians who did the discursive spade work that put the brakes on the eugenic laws in this country.[2] The laws were not only supported by scientists and political progressives; they had been proposed by them in the first place.

Rhetoricians are well-equipped to study cases like these because there is in them a strong sense of how contexts, events, politics, and traumas are integral and intertwined factors in the trajectories of scientific research programs. At present, many in our field are worried, with good reason, about how good science is being blocked by political opposition. We do not want to forget, however, that it has sometimes been scientists who have blocked good sense. One sometimes hears that we needn't worry about such misadventures as eugenic laws anymore because that was the result of bad science, while we, unlike the people of a century ago, practice good science and would never make such mistakes. (Well, at least we wouldn't use *eugenics* as an authorizing term if we did.) Such complacency does not seem to be justified by history. Nor is the view that deviations like that can go on only for a while, since there is a built-in mechanism in scientific rationality that inevitably corrects for ideologically-inspired errors like eugenics laws or Lysenkoism in Stalin's Russia. That isn't quite how it happened in either case.

2. Optimism about Science—and about Democratic Discourse

Reflecting on histories like these, some science studies folks (largely constructionists) have drawn on what they call "the pessimistic induction," according to which science never gets good enough to rise above the weak forms and norms of evidence that presumably haunt public and personal spheres of discourse. If this is so, the hope of the middle class regimes that first took power in America and Europe in the 1830s that science would serve as a corrective for the democratic institutions they were promising to erect would indeed be in vain. Irrationality would reign. Historically, in fact, we find just such bursts of irrationality accompanied by epistemic pessimism, even nihilism, at times and places where pseudoscience thrives and democracy collapses, as it did in Germany in the 1930s.

But what if rhetoricians of science made it their special charge to point out that this may be a false dichotomy? And conversely, what if public discourse is not always and antecedently dismissed as deficient in rationality? Even if its forms and norms of rationality are different from those of science, is it not possible, indeed likely, that public argumentation is rational enough to mix it up with science in productive, if also messy, ways? What if scientists, in order to live up to their loudly proclaimed devotion to rational inquiry, were asked reflectively to confront and reject their own prejudices, as feminist philosophers of science have, for example, been asking them to do with some success in recent years?

In that case, might one draw a different, more optimistic induction from the histories that on scientistic assumptions stimulate the pessimistic induction? Consider the case of eugenics again. If in the end things did go well, we think it was because criticism in democratically structured public venues inspired criticism in technical ones, which eventually destroyed the genetics arguments on which eugenics was predicated and prepared the ground for the reception of these arguments. It was because scientists shared the intuitions of untutored publics that they looked for and found empirical arguments that validated their intuitions. Their critique, first intimated by advocates of religion, then supported by scientists committed to liberal egalitarianism, turned into a tidal wave in the wake of revelations about Nazi science. Celeste Condit has shown that, aside from serving as a stigmatizing term, use of the term *eugenics* virtually ended—but, we add, it did so completely only when the story of its rise and fall was told in public venues by people like Daniel Kevles in the 1980s.

In sum, because we rhetorical scholars are not antecedently contemptuous of public sphere and personal sphere forms of discourse, we are more upbeat about truth-finding, or at least falsehood-extinguishing, in technical sphere venues. Maybe our civic instincts make us comfortable with the idea that science is too important to be left to the scientists. While there is no magic guarantee that errors will be flushed out of science, we believe that the arc of a vigorous cross-sphere practice of rhetorical criticism of scientific claims, evidence, assumptions, and implications tends to bend toward truth, albeit situated and localized truth—just as Martin Luther King reminded us that the long arc of democracy bends toward justice. To those skeptical of appeals to truth and justice on such a large scale, let us at least offer this alternative: Good rhetoric, like good science, helps in rooting out falsity and injustice, which are far more plentiful.

3. Discovery and Proof: An Inventional Continuum

What justifies our optimism that rhetoric can be as good for science as it can be for justice? It is partly because, along with Fahnestock (2013), Prelli (2013), and others, we think that rhetoric (both as advocacy and as criticism) is an *organon*, a tool that is productive of knowledge. It extends the tentacles of conceptual grasp. It is as epistemic in its force as the rhetoric-baiting Plato and the anti-rhetorical Platonists after him took logic and mathematics alone to be.

Here we give a tip of the hat to Richard McKeon's call for rhetoric to be an architectonic productive art, even if, localists that we are, we do not share the grandeur of his ambition (Depew, 2010; Hauser & Cushman, 1973; McKeon, 1971). During the post-War heyday of the philosophy of science, it was big news to assign to rhetoric, as he did, a role not just in marketing scientific discoveries to non-expert audiences but, more deeply, in inventing ideas that it also plays a role in subjecting to confirmation and falsification. McKeon made that case by pointing out that the logical empiricist and the Popperian distinction between the context of discovery and the context of justification is a riff on the ancient rhetorical distinction between invention and arrangement. As Jeanne Fahnestock pointed out in her excellent earlier review, Iowa's Project on the Rhetoric of Inquiry (POROI), with which both of us have been associated, was and is more or less dedicated to reviving rhetorical invention in and especially across fields of inquiry, including science (Fahnestock, 2008).

Considered rhetorically, invention in science, as in other forms of inquiry, can't be thought of in isolation from justification at all; rather, the two comprise at most dialectical poles in the dynamics of inquiry. Invention is a shared social practice, not the private, purely psychological process to which philosophers invidiously confined it in order to put the accent instead on logical justification. When one invents, it is with an eye toward how the invented argument, framing, or interpretation might hold up under the scrutiny of an audience. And sometimes that audience, including the internalized audience that any well-socialized inquiry leans upon, sends the inquirer back to the drawing board. Indeed, the critical audience (e.g., another scientist or an external critic) might not just challenge an explicit argument but also, for example, challenge the use of a dominant metaphor, which then puts it within the space of investigation and productive inquiry. While we understand that a metaphor is never precisely true or false, a metaphor that is apt for a particular phenomenon under inquiry can open whole new vistas, while a bad one can really gum up the works. So metaphors too can be, and often are, challenged and tested.

All of this makes the activity of inquiry less like a monologue than a dialogue. The scientist is, so to speak, putting down steppingstones as he or she goes, with each step testing them with one foot. Those scientific ideas that make themselves clear enough to count as testable hypotheses do so in and through debates about their merits. The process of stating a claim is inseparable from justifying it. What philosophers like to call justification, as opposed to discovery, is the perspicuous deductive display after the fact, rather like what rhetoricians once called arrangement. It may seem otherwise, as when we hear about crucial experiments like Michelson-Morley that dispose of an issue once and for all. But closer inspection shows that in such cases what has happened is that critical discussion has reached a point of satiation, that is, a point at which prior discourse has generated a well-formed issue that precludes the usual posing and talking past each other. The crucial experiment is both invented and tested within a field of argument, in this case whether a light-carrying medium, the ether, exists or does not. The same experiment in a different rhetorical situation would mean very little.

The rhetorical productivity that we have inadequately described comes into focus as soon as we recognize that knowledge production necessarily takes place in the space of implicit or explicit controversies (Goodnight, 1982). All controversies, whether they are scientific, political, or religious, find their natural medium in rhetorical argumentation, both on the side of advocating claims and on the side of criticizing them. This point turns out not to be trivial. It implies, for one thing, that the meaning of claims and the persuasiveness of evidence for and against them are essentially entangled with the claims they contest and the evidence for and against them. This is primarily what we mean by the localness of inquiry. Controversies are rhetorically situated.

4. Embedded Rhetoricity

What do we see when we look closely at such scenes of contestation? We see the productive interplay of competing accounts, models, configurations, narratives, metaphors, emphases, and authorizing terms. Let us look a bit more closely at a few of these.

Working as both of us do in the rhetoric of evolutionary biology, along with our esteemed colleagues John Angus Campbell and Leah Ceccarelli, we see the rhetoricity of ostensibly demonstrative scientific prose everywhere. Let's look at a couple of the ways this happens in a field that raises passions because it overlaps not only public and technical spheres of argumentation but also engages the personal sphere as well, where the meaning of life and the value of interpersonal relationships make themselves most felt.

Selective Examples as Good Evidence

Ever since Aristotle, let us recall, we have known that examples play a key evidential role in rhetorical argumentation as is very prominent in evolutionary biology. Evolutionary arguments rest, in fact, on persuasive examples: archaeopteryx, black and grey pepper moths, the heterozygotic superiority of blood cells that confer some immunity to malaria, and others. We are aware that these examples, which appear over and over again in textbooks, stand in for, and offer promissory notes on behalf of, many other similar cases that, authors assure us, will eventually turn up to confer general significance on the examples. We are aware, too, that, while similar cases often do show up, they are seldom enough to turn a case study into a general model or even less often to turn a good model into a law-governed theory. Neo-positivist philosophers of science like Alexander Rosenberg (1994) worry about this enough to conclude that evolutionary biology, let alone the social sciences, is not and never can be law-like enough to be a real science.

As rhetoricians of science, however, we have a more equable attitude. We are not in the least scandalized by the fact that examples are perspicuous and paradigmatic because they are described in terms of images, analogies, metaphors, and other tropes. Why, in a specific context of inquiry, did Dawkins have to say that DNA is "selfish" if he wanted to make the point stick with those he was addressing that it is more explanatory and more parsimonious to look at natural selection as operating on behalf of genes than on behalf of the organisms that contain them? There are, or at least were in the 1970s, good reasons for saying this. The characterization made certain newly discovered facts intelligible. At the same time, selfishness and Darwinism, when combined, bring a lot of extra baggage with them too. Examples are perspicuous only when criticism blunts their tendency to become excessively persuasive, as this one did when Dawkins took it so seriously that he thought he had to defend materialism and atheism in order to protect his interpretation when its *kairotic* moment had passed (Depew, 2012).

Authorizing Terms

Persuasive examples, we think, are closely tied, when their force is spelled out, to authorizing terms. Here we encounter an issue about which the two of us talk a lot. The connection between local cases and high-level theories is so open that authorizing terms like "Darwinism" are not forced conclusions, but independent variables. Why do evolutionary scientists think they have to call what they are doing "Darwinism," especially since that term packs so much baggage that the insistence of scientists on it does more than anything else to keep creationism or intelligent design alive in the space of controversy as alternative authorizing terms? One of us tends to think that the ideograph "Darwinism" has been so poisoned by its history that it might be better to give it up altogether. What would be lost, he asks, if the scientific community took, say, a "Lamarckian" turn? Would this not let us see what experimental biologists are showing all the time these days? Genomes, it seems, are surprisingly sensitive to environmental changes. With more ease than would have been thought possible in the heyday of Francis Crick's "central dogma" (right: *dogma*) of molecular biology, they can intensify the rate at which genetic variation, the fuel of natural selection, occurs and can even hatch up regulatory sequences, micro-RNAs, epigenetic markers, and other bits of ontogenetic machinery to respond to environmental changes (Jablonka & Lamb, 1995).

Still, we have to admit that Lamarckism lugs along some baggage too, such as Lysenkoism. Accordingly, the other of us is inclined to follow the lead of Theodosius Dobzhansky, whose genial and inviting rhetoric has been studied by Leah Ceccarelli (2001), in hoping to show the public that natural selection is actually a benign process that does not carry the negative connotations associated with so-called "social Darwinism." Which of us is right? We are not sure. What we are sure of is that this discussion puts the phenomena we are studying in the right, that is, the rhetorical, light. In that light, "Darwinism" and "Lamarckism" are authorizing terms.

Presumption and Burden of Proof

No one, we hope, will construe our remarks as anti-science. So we take the opportunity to express our agreement with Celeste Condit that rhetorical scholars, in opposing scientism and its philosophical defenders, are ill advised to buy into an anti-science stance. Just as we do not think creationists should colonize evolutionary biology by making it conform to their worldview, neither do we think that literary humanists should be allowed to do something similar. We are afraid that social constructionism has fallen into that trap, and that this has been encouraged by certain trends in rhetorical theory. We hope we have given you reasons to see why we think we have evaded that approach.

We may put our point differently by noting something else about the rhetorical character of scientific argumentation. Since it is embedded in rhetorical occasions, scientific criticism, whether by scientists or informed others, is permeated by judgments about where presumptions and burdens of proof lie at any given time. These always favor maintaining or restoring a certain judicious balance between innovation and tradition. Accordingly, being a rhetorician who is pro-science does not require granting presumption to the latest thing to come out of scientific fields, especially fields that are clearly in an incipiently inventive stage. Among these are behavioral and cognitive genetics. The impulse to extend evolutionary biology to these topics runs very deep. But the track record of earlier attempts to bring these topics under scientific, even techno-scientific, control is very poor, and the burden of proof remains on them.

The assumption that this burden is currently shifting is based on the idea that we now know enough about genetics to do the job. This assumption is probably wrong; or, even if it is right, it shows that we also need to know a lot about other things as well, such as development and its intersection with culture. So caution is advisable. Caution is particularly advisable because public sphere books and articles tend to place too great a value on particular discoveries that might have, we are always told, revolutionary implications. The language of a "gene for this" or a "gene for that" falls into this class of journalistic effects. In the technical sphere, however, things seldom, if ever, work that way. The latest and biggest thing soon turns into a single data point in an array that continues to change. The lesson is that rhetoricians of science must know enough about what is going on in the technical sphere to be able to address, and judge properly, its relevance to the public sphere. Rhetoric is about judgment—in science as in other dimensions of discourse.

5. Inventing on all Cylinders

Our emphasis on the productive role of rhetoric in the sciences has so far focused on how criticism fosters the growth of knowledge. But the productivity of rhetoric so considered also affects how we should think of inventing new hypotheses. That is, the rhetorical dimension of scientific activity makes us look to the question of how invention is *doing work* within science in ways that support many of the traditional aspirations of science in modernizing societies.

Ever since the early days of rhetorical theory, topical and stasis theory has proven to be one useful way of thinking about invention. It has proven no less fertile in the sciences. Francis Bacon's view of scientific method was in fact an extension of the a-technical rhetorical proofs to scientific inquiry in a context of political improvement. Baconians might from the start have been more attuned to rational-discursive or technical rhetorical proof as well—*ethos, pathos,* and *logos*—and hence to the integral role of discourse of science that we have advocated. The motto of the Royal Society, *nullius in verba,* may be well taken as dissociating science from the decorative rhetoric of the day. But it is not in the least true about the role of rhetorical argumentation in science as it subsequently developed in modern societies. It has been full of *ethos, pathos,* and *logos.* Thankfully, the palette is slowly expanding in rhetoric of science work today and more generally in the work of contemporary science studies.

In the view we are advocating, invention, as we have already said, is not sudden inspiration. It is a process in which leads and topics are explored in as creative and systematic a way as Edison, for example, explored them (Bazerman, 2002). Because the inventional process is a critical, context-dependent practice, it does not stand in contrast to discovery or of proof. It *is* a process of discovery and proof. Since on this point we want once again not to play into the hands of those who might dismiss us as advocating some kind of effete textualism, we might picture a kind of spectrum on which discovery lies at one end and invention at the other, with most cases closer to one end than the other. In saying that a previously unknown species has been "discovered," we register that something ontological does indeed seem to be at stake, pulling us back from going as far as Latour when he maintains that microbes did not exist until Pasteur discovered them (Latour, 1988). Invention in our usage does not carry that force or implication. What it carries is the implication that when something gets called a discovery, a process of discourse has been found so persuasive that talk moves on to other things in which the discovery is taken for granted—although in principle it is re-visitable.

Below are a few dimensions of the inventive process as productive work in evolutionary biology, and *mutatis mutandis,* in science generally.

Inventing Counter-Examples

In debates over biological evolution, the use of carefully selected examples has often performed extensive rhetorical work in the advocacy of different explanatory models, as we have noted. As we say, the textbooks provide ample testimony of examples that have become so obligatory that they have exemplary status as standing for other similar things. Their persuasive function is that of metonyms or synecdoches: stand-ins for an entire underspecified class of other such things presumed to be "out there." One might think of this process as inventional and the corresponding practice of offering counter-examples as critical. But our way of thinking about invention suggests that there are just as many productive, inventive possibilities in scouting out counter-examples. Generating counter-examples is close to the core of scientific inquiry. It breaks up the rush to generalization that is inherent in using examples as paradigm cases. It is no surprise that Dawkins's selfish genes provoked researchers to find cases of group selection as counter-examples and that finding them has led to new truths about the biological, and especially the human, world.

Inventing (and Expanding) the Scope and Texture of Context

Not all rhetorical criticism should be tied to current circumstances. This is why Isocratean rhetoric, structured as it is by the pressing concerns of the *kairos* moment, is probably not enough for a satisfactory rhetoric of science. Nor is the kind of political reductionism we find in Shapin and Shaffer's *Leviathan and the Air Pump* (1989). In the context of the sciences, the pertinent circumstances are not just today and tomorrow. Rather, they pertain to a long-range trajectory in the pursuit of inquiry and should not be tied too closely to the ups and downs of political life. Nor should science be measured by how fast it produces technologies either, as seems to be the current *Zeitgeist*. What used to be called basic research, for instance, is now often called "curiosity science." This is a very powerful act of renaming, because it makes concern for the long-term future seem like a kind of diversion, and thereby re-contextualizes those concerns. The concern with local context does not in the least contravene science's orientation toward the long run.

Inventing Names

The phrase "curiosity science" points to our next type of invention. Naming, mis-naming, and re-naming can be very powerful indeed. As Kenneth Burke (KB) put it, "A way of seeing is a way of not seeing" (Burke, 1984, p. 49). Burke was right about this point. Did you notice how fast some of the fast food chains capitulated when a particular substance in their hamburger patties was re-named "pink slime"? That was a brilliant rhetorical move, and a good counter-example to deterministic ways of thinking. Did you notice how support for the inheritance tax went down once it was re-named a "death tax"? Are these not in some ways similar to (and also different from) certain rhetorical moves emanating from the sciences—we're looking at you, "selfish gene" and "the Modern Synthesis"—even if there are generally more stringent checks on unfettered invention and more specificity to the available means of persuasion in those provinces? Names can be, as Fahnestock (2008) says of rhetorical figures in science, "figures of thought" (see also Fahnestock, 2013).

Here is a case very much to KB's point. Public attention has recently been called in a most dramatic way to that part of the genetic material that does not code for DNA, which is to say, most of it. The term "junk DNA" was coined in 1972 and has fanned out, first among prominent biologists and subsequently widely across the general culture. Yes, this name was chosen to reflect a view, widely adopted at the time, that non-coding parts were also nonfunctional parts. In that sense and context, the term arguably did productive work in crystallizing the theoretical outlook that led to full understanding of the so-called genetic code, "coding" and "programming" being metaphorical terms that advanced this very local research program. But as that view gradually lost scientific credibility by its very success, leading to the epigenetic revolution that is upon us now, whole segments of the evolutionary biology community, in thrall to a name, remained largely blind to a revolution within the most respected precincts of molecular biology itself that has pointed to the importance of (noncoding) regulatory genes. The term "junk" continues to sustain a blinkered view of what genes are all about. This orthodoxy has borne down on many scientists as well as on that part of the public who read about such things. Change the names and you invent a better, truer future. Naming is framing. (The term, "dark matter" has been used in reference to noncoding genetic material. We are intrigued by the overtones and possible rhetorical destiny of that term.)

But naming has more systemic uses as well. One of these is in the maintenance of authorizing terms, the terms under which research programs are legitimated. On the matter of supporting a program by advocating for a term, Dawkins could not have said it better: "My contribution to the idea of the selfish gene," he wrote, "was to put rhetoric into it and spell out its implications" (Dawkins, 1995, p. 76). Dawkins here offers a stunningly direct acknowledgement of—indeed, an embrace of—the rhetoricity of his project. This process of embracing a term and then justifying it occurs right in the thick of scientific theorizing, which Dawkins's inventional process also did, in addition to reaching a broader public. These discursive processes are going on all the time. So, for instance, as "autopoetic" theory bids for respectability in evolutionary theory, it relies on the name to do a lot of the work of coalition-making, opponent-defining, and concept-aligning, even as its arguments are not static. In that sense, the term is a call to "think this way." Advocates will search for reasons to support that way of thinking, and opponents will put forth reasons for not thinking that way. That's how it goes.

Inventing within a Dialogical Frame

Let us bring to bear on the topic of invention our earlier insistence that science takes place within the space of implicit or explicit controversies. This being so, we should resist the tendency to think of scientific rhetoric as something that is monological, or something merely to be mapped, or something apprehended as text. Scientific arguments move forward by encounters with professional resistance, alternatives, counter-interpretations, arguments about the reproducibility of results, theoretical or conceptual adjustments, biases, cultural and ideological resistance, and funding issues. They also move on the harnessed energy of theories, programs, technological promises, reputations, funding, and aspirations. These things constitute the rough ground that is presupposed in the discourse of science. We should be alert to the events and traumas that affect the movement of science as it responds to them. One of the challenges for competing accounts, in evolutionary biology and elsewhere, is to find ways of putting the dominant metaphors into some kind of dialogical relationship. This represents an inventional challenge for evolutionary biology particularly, and other fields generally.

6. Need we be Unified?

Celeste Condit (2013) has acted to stimulate democratic debate. In her survey, it is the *purpose* of studying the rhetoric of science and technology—not, as in ours, the *process*—that is given primacy; explicitly so in two of the categories of work covered in her overview: the purpose of building theory and the purpose of improving scientific rhetoric. These are purposes that we both can and in our way do sign on to, as we have been trying to suggest. The other two categories Condit has identified and summarized starkly as "science bad" and "science too powerful," might better be described as matters of "attitude" rather than purpose, and her point about the attitude rhetoricians of science should take toward them is our point too. Implicit in these two attitudes is oppositional motivation, and so it seems to have answered in advance and hence slightly begged, the question, "To what end?" or perhaps "In the service of what?" is this work undertaken?

Condit is no doubt right, however, to surmise that some members of our community share in the view of science against which she warns us. Here it seems that we rhetoricians of science and technology may have differences among us as a community of inquiry that have not been very well thematized and debated in our field. It is a situation we might rectify. As nothing unifies like an attack from the outside, Condit (2013) points to a looming threat from the outside as a motivation to pull us together. We believe her concerns are well justified. If the very conditions under which we work are endangered, then rallying to preserve and protect values even more basic then the value of rhetoric of science is—as the physician might say—"indicated."

There is also risk in defining our purpose in political terms. Here we need to tread carefully. Nothing undercuts the credibility of scientific claims faster than when the messenger is seen as acting with political intent. Witness the extraordinary hit that belief in global warming took in public opinion after the "climategate" emails were politically exploited. And there are similar risks within academic institutions. We believe, for example, that the normative meta-theory adopted by advocates of STS has come at some cost to their credibility in some quarters (Collin, 2010). If we sign on to a set of political objectives in studying the rhetoric of science, do we risk activating *ethos*-damaging blowback? And, if so, is that a risk worth taking?

As diversity seems to be a good thing in both ecology and evolution, it might have some advantages for those who have been constructing an environmental niche for rhetoric of science. Work thus far has been highly varied in character. Perhaps that pluralism should be embraced rather than taken as a sign of weakness. Steve Fuller's view that we need a strong program in rhetoric of science, analogous to the strong program of social studies of science and technology, has some appeal (Fuller, 1995). We have done little, however, to relieve his predictable exasperation about the fact that we haven't endorsed this view or this analogy in this position paper. As a rhetorical framing, a strong program should beat out a weak program every time. But if we take the metaphor of niche construction as a heuristic, diversity need not equate to weakness. Fuller, after all, would have us follow him into places we might not want to go.

7. Parting Thoughts

Michael Pollan (2007) wrote a well-regarded book, *The Omnivore's Dilemma,* for which the title sets up his central question: Since humans can eat just about anything, how do we—meaning those of us who have the option of choosing—decide what to eat? How we answer that question has implications not just for our health, but for our environment, our ethics, and our politics as well. The contemporary rhetorician has a similar dilemma. When the world is your field, it's hard to know what to feast upon. We exaggerate slightly, if at all, in suggesting that rhetoric has taken the world and all that's in it—and potentially in it—as our field of concern.

The rhetoric of science has always lent itself to interdisciplinarity, but at times it seems to have its sights set on omni-disciplinarity. If other fields offer powerful explanations for the way things work—sociology, psychoanalysis, philosophy, neuroscience—then many of us want to harness power like that. From a historical viewpoint this is to be expected, as conceptions and practices of rhetoric have over the centuries been shaped by the social, political, and epistemic biases of their times. Moreover, rhetoric tends to gravitate to the centers of power and to adapt according to what that power is—the church, the king, the assembly, public opinion, funding agencies, and so on—for that is where it can matter most. We should therefore expect that the very powerful forces of science are magnets for rhetoric. But as rhetoricians we should want to be careful not to give up on the idea that there is power in rhetorical invention, for good or for ill, that it should be studied and engaged, and that this study need not be outsourced to other disciplines. If we succumb to determinisms that relegate discourse to the level of epiphenomena, we would do well to get on the wagon of some other field, such as sociology, economics, psychoanalysis, or neuroscience. But otherwise not.

Now rhetoric invites these fields, and practically all others, to help it see the terrain on which discursive interventions occur. But at the same time, it need not fade into the woodwork as it draws on the expertise of other fields. POROI was more or less founded on that understanding. It was an assumption of those who founded ARSTM, too, and we believe it is a shared assumption of most of those interested in the rhetoric of science and technology, including authors who, like ourselves, have worked collaboratively with folks from other disciplines. We have advocated for more attention to how rhetoric can be productive within science. Our perspective is that this process does not happen in a hermetically-sealed technical sphere, just as its consequences certainly do not confine themselves there. And that means that our perspective is very much pro-science—and just as much pro-rhetoric.

Notes

1 The original version of this essay included an Appendix with examples of publications fitting into each of these 16 categories. We have left the appendix out of this version for reasons of space and cost.

2 See Kevles (1985, pp. 118–119). The Catholic hierarchy opposed eugenics not on scientific but on ethical and theological grounds. It thus put a view into circulation in the American public sphere that later found support from scientists. There were, of course, geneticists who dissented

from eugenic programs, both positive and negative, in the 1920s and 1930s because they didn't think you could isolate environmental and genetical factors in human populations. Or even if you could, they doubted that you could objectively determine which traits are to be selected for and against. But these objections were pragmatic, not principled. There was a huge institutional connection between genetics and eugenics that was not fully broken even when Theodosius Dobzhansky provided compelling arguments in the 1940s that eugenics is not only impractical but biologically incoherent. Unlike the Galileo case, the Catholic Church got this one right, albeit not on scientific grounds. Other churches, especially those affected by modernist progressive movements, did not, including the Episcopalians and Methodists. This case does not mean that publics are presumptively right. They are most certainly not when it comes to creationism. But that's just the point. You never can tell until you look at the particulars in all their complexity.

References

Bazerman, C. (2002). *The languages of Edison's light.* Cambridge, MA: MIT Press.

Burke, K (1984). *Permanence and change* (third edition). Berkeley, CA: University of California Press.

Collin, F. (2010). An alternative road for science and technology studies and the naturalization of philosophy of science. In F. Collin (Ed.), *Science studies as naturalized philosophy* (pp. 197–233). New York: Springer.

Condit, Celeste M. (2013). "Mind the gaps": Hidden purposes and missing internationalism in scholarship on the rhetoric of science and technology in public discourse. *Poroi* 9, 1, Article 3.

Ceccarelli, L. (2001). *Shaping science with rhetoric: The cases of Dobzhansky, Schrodinger, and Wilson.* Chicago, IL: University of Chicago Press.

Dawkins, R. (1995). A survival machine. In J. Brockman (Ed.). *The third culture: Beyond the scientific revolution* (pp. 74–95). New York: Simon & Schuster.

Depew, D. (2010). Revisiting Richard McKeon's architectonic rhetoric. In M.J. Porrovecchio (Ed.), *Reengaging the prospects of rhetoric* (pp. 37–56). New York: Routledge.

———. (2012). The rhetoric of evolutionary theory. *Biological Theory,* 6, 1–10. doi: 10.1007/s13752-012-0054-2.

Fahnestock, J. (2008). Rhetoric in the natural sciences. In A. Lunsford, K. Wilson, & R. Eberly (Eds.), *SAGE handbook of rhetorical studies* (pp. 175–196). Thousand Oaks, CA: Sage.

———. (2013). Promoting the discipline: Rhetorical studies of science, technology, and medicine. *Poroi* 9, 1, Article 6.

Fuller, S. (1995) The strong program in the rhetoric of science. In H. Krips, J. E. McGuire, T. Melia (Eds.), *Science, reason, rhetoric* (pp. 95–117). Pittsburgh, PA: University of Pittsburgh Press.

Gieryn, T. (1999). *Cultural boundaries of science: Credibility on the line.* Chicago, IL: University of Chicago Press.

Goodnight, G.T. (1982). The personal, technical, and public spheres of argumentation. *Journal of the American Forensics Association,* 18, 214–227.

Hauser, G., & Cushman, D. (1973). McKeon's philosophy of communication: The architectonic and interdisciplinary arts. *Philosophy and Rhetoric,* 6, 21–34.

Jablonka, E., & Lamb, M. (1995). *Epigenetic inheritance and evolution: The Lamarckian dimension.* New York: Oxford University Press.

Kevles, D. (1985). *In the name of eugenics.* Berkeley, CA: University of California Press.

Latour, B. (1987). *Science in action: How to follow scientists and engineers through society.* Cambridge, MA: Harvard University Press.

——. (1988). *The Pasteurization of France.* Cambridge, MA: Harvard University Press

——. (1993). *We have never been modern.* Cambridge, MA: Harvard University Press.

——. (2005). *Reassembling the social: An introduction to actor-network theory.* New York: Oxford University Press.

McKeon, R. (1971). The uses of rhetoric in a technological age: Architectonic productive arts. In L. Bitzer & E. Black (Eds.), *The prospect of rhetoric* (pp. 44–63). Englewood Cliffs, NJ: Prentice-Hall.

Pollan, M. (2007). *The omnivore's dilemma: A natural history of four meals.* New York: Penguin.

Prelli, Lawrence J. (2013). The Prospect of Invention in Rhetorical Studies of Science, Technology, and Medicine. *Poroi* 9,1, Article 2.

Rosenberg, A. (1994). *Instrumental biology, or the disunity of science.* Chicago, IL: University of Chicago Press.

Shapin, S., & Shaffer, S. (1989). *Leviathan and the air pump.* Princeton, NJ: Princeton University Press.

Taylor, C.A. (1997). *Defining science: A rhetoric of demarcation.* Madison, WI: University of Wisconsin Press.

Note: The original publication included an appendix listing examples of all the types of rhetoric-of-science research the authors discuss. We have left the appendix out of this version for reasons of space and cost.

11.
WHEN WE CAN'T WAIT ON TRUTH
The Nature of Rhetoric in *The Rhetoric of Science*
by Nathan Crick

We readily concede that the law courts and the political forum are special cases of our everyday world, a world in which social reality is uncontroversially the product of persuasion. Many of us can also entertain the possibility Aristotle could never countenance: the possibility that the claims of science are solely the products of persuasion

(Gross, 1996, 3).

As you phrase it, oratory is the craft that exercises its influence through speech. Somebody might take you up, if he wanted to make a fuss in argument, and say, 'So you're saying that arithmetic is oratory, are you Gorgias?' I am sure, however, that you are not saying that either arithmetic or geometry is oratory

(Plato, 1997, 450e).

None of this suggests that science is *only* rhetoric; no sane person could reach so bizarre a conclusion

(Gross, 2006, 78).

When Alan G. Gross's *The Rhetoric of Science* was published in 1990, it helped resurrect a long-standing philosophical question: What is the relationship between rhetoric and truth? This is the question which inspired one of Plato's most influential dialogues, the *Gorgias*, which dramatizes Socrates's encounter with the aging Sophist in a raucous street brawl. Gorgias had just finished a lengthy oration, and, when pressed by Socrates, brags of the immense scope and power of his art, encompassing as it does every activity which depends on speeches and persuasion for its actualization. As the Sophist summarizes the power of oratory: "It encompasses and subordinates to itself just about everything that can be accomplished" (Plato, *Gorgias*, 456b). In short, Gorgias begins the dialogue by setting out the proposition that truth is a product of persuasion without remainder. Socrates, however, will have none of this, and soon forces Gorgias into retreat. First, Gorgias admits that there are two types of persuasion, "one providing conviction without knowledge, the other providing knowledge" (Plato, *Gorgias*, 454d). Second, he reduces the scope of rhetoric to decisions which take place "in law courts and in those other large gatherings" in which members of the public deliberate about "matters that are just and unjust" (Plato, *Gorgias*, 454b). Although it will soon become apparent that rhetoric,

Nathan Crick. "When We Can't Wait on Truth: The Nature of Rhetoric in The Rhetoric of Science." *Poroi*, Volume 10, Number 2, 2014, Article 8.

according to Socrates, does not even have authority there (Plato, *Gorgias*, 502e), the opening dialectic clearly sets out the terms of the debate, with one side granting rhetoric a significant, constitutive role in production of knowledge and the other side considering it a form of flattery capable only of persuading the masses concerning subjects they know nothing about.

Reminiscent of Plato's dialogue, Gross frames his book from the opening page as a revival and defense of the sophistical position associated with Gorgias. There, Gross introduces the guiding principle of the text, that "rhetorically, the creation of knowledge is a task beginning with self-persuasion and ending with the persuasion of others" (Gross, 1996, 3). He goes on to make explicit his debt to the sophistical tradition, writing that "this attitude toward knowledge stems from the first Sophistic, an early philosophical relativism made notorious by Socrates" (Gross, 1996, 3). Aristotle had tried to restrict the scope of rhetoric to judicial and political forums, but Gross feels this compromise to be unwarranted: "If scientific texts are to be analyzed rhetorically, this Aristotelian limitation must be removed; the spirit of the first Sophistic must roam free" (Gross, 1996, 3). This removal of the Aristotelian limitation allows him to use Aristotle's *Rhetoric,* rather than any sophistical tract, as the "master guide to the exegesis of scientific texts" (Gross, 1996, 18). For instance, Gross uses the *Rhetoric* to explore the function of style, analogy, arrangement in scientific argument, to demonstrate that "*ethos, pathos,* and *logos,* are naturally present in scientific texts," and to show that "as a fully human enterprise, science can constrain, but hardly eliminate, the full range of persuasive choices on the part of its participants" (Gross, 1996, 16). Here Gorgias is brought to life again to stimulate critical investigation into the relationship between rhetoric and truth.

Yet the productive controversy that the original publication of *The Rhetoric of Science* helped stimulate, and which Gross is rightly proud of provoking, also had the consequence of forcing him into partial retreat from the rhetorical tradition that he featured so strongly in the text. In the new 1996 preface to the original 1990 text of the *The Rhetoric of Science,* Gross still holds to the fundamental position that "Rhetoric has a crucial epistemic role in science" and "that science is constituted through interactions that are essentially rhetorical" (Gross, 1996, x). However, at the same time he defends the place of rhetoric in science, he admits, on reflection, the "relative intellectual vacuity of classical rhetorical theory" (Gross, 1996, xix). The resulting complete revision of the book in 2006, renamed *Starring the Text: The Place of Rhetoric in Science Studies,* significantly reduces the presence of classical rhetoric while at the same time tempering what he calls "radical epistemological inferences that were designed to provoke thought" (Gross, 2006, ix). In their places is a much stronger presence of the theories of language put forward by W.V.O. Quine, Donald Davidson, Nelson Goodman, and Hilary Putnam, that are used to give a "rhetorical account of truth" (Gross, 2006, 41). It is thus to the tradition of analytic philosophy, and not to classical rhetoric, that Gross looks for defense of a rhetoric of science when it needs defending.

Yet this repositioning of rhetoric still leaves the Socratic question unanswered: what, exactly, is the nature of this art that is said to be "constitutive of scientific knowledge"? (Gross, 2006, 8). Gross mounts a strong case that "rhetoric is indeed epistemic in the deepest sense," but often at the expense of explicit reference to that tradition (Gross,

2006, 13). But by leaving the classical vocabulary behind, Gross appears to leave himself without any clear definition of the nature of rhetoric itself. For instance, it is not exactly clear what Quine, Davidson, Goodman, or Putnam would make of having their theories of language and truth be described as "rhetorical." What could this mean? Gross offers the following answer based on their insights:

> When scientific truth is a consensus concerning the coherence of a range of sentences, rather than the fit between the facts and reality, conceptual change need no longer be justified on the basis of its closer approximation to that reality. It is instead the natural result of the persuasive process that is science, a persistent effort to renew consensus, despite a constant influx of potentially disruptive sentences (Gross, 2006, 44).

If we take this passage at its word, rhetoric represents the conscious effort to create, transform, and maintain consensus concerning a range of sentences by either producing or responding to other sentences that might disrupt that consensus. Yet since all language, under a coherence view of truth, is tasked with either disrupting or producing consensus, there is no such thing as a non-rhetorical language. The only difference between scientific and political rhetoric, therefore, is in the subject matter of those sentences and the nature and scope of the audience charged with coming to consensus. The task of the rhetorician, from this perspective, thus changes from identifying and analyzing particular texts that are distinguished by their rhetorical character to disclosing the implicit rhetorical qualities that are inherent in even the most technical, scientific tract that are many steps removed from the law court or assembly.

The enduring question that persists in the wake of *The Rhetoric of Science*, even after the passing of two decades, is what remains of rhetoric when it redescribes its aims and foundations through the discourse of analytical philosophy. I argue in this essay that the turn toward analytical philosophy, represented here chiefly in the work of Quine, offers a highly sophisticated holistic epistemology at the expense of stripping rhetoric of its character as a situated art whose aim is the constitution of judgment. What remains of rhetoric in this context is thus precisely what Gross later judged it to be—a relatively vacuous vocabulary for identifying tropes, figures, and enthymemes. However, this vacuity is not intrinsic to language of classical rhetoric, but is a result of reorienting rhetoric from problems of public judgment to questions of epistemological validity. In summary, by reading Gross's work alongside that of Quine and the extant speeches of Gorgias, I suggest that analytic philosophy, while an important resource for our understanding of the nature of scientific theorizing, is an inadequate theoretical basis for the rhetoric of science, and that a "full" rhetoric of science must return to Gross's original project of enlivening classical texts to produce new insights into contemporary problems.

The Search for a "Full" Rhetorical of Science

Why *The Rhetoric of Science* remains such a provocative text is precisely the boldness of its claim. Siding with the Platonic Gorgias, Gross sweeps away the constraint of realism in order to make way for what he calls a "fully rhetorical" account of science and of knowledge. With the false veneer of realism stripped away, rhetoric thus becomes synonymous with any and all conscious efforts, whether in science or in public, to discursively invent, articulate, and argue for an account of things that we are supposed to take to be true. Realism, that is to say, prevents a fully rhetorical description of science whenever it posits that "after analysis, something unrhetorical remains, a hard 'scientific' core" of "untranslatable scientific meaning" (Gross, 1996, 33). Once this hard scientific core is revealed, through the work of Quine et al., to be just one more utterance within a man-made fabric of linguistic statements that impinges on experience only along the edges, the possibility opens up of the ability to reconstruct science "rhetorically, without remainder" (Gross, 1996, 33). Gross thus argues for a view of rhetoric that does not simply appear in certain scientific contexts or situations, but is ubiquitous in every claim put forward by a scientist. The task of the rhetoric of science is clear: to use classical rhetorical terminology, such as *ethos, logos, pathos*, style, analogy, and arrangement, to redescribe all those scientific activities previously given only a rational account based on the presuppositions of realism. This is an ambitious, interesting, and partially successful enterprise. It proposes that: "If a rhetorical reconstruction describes rhetorically every aspect that a rational reconstruction describes rationally, a complete rhetoric of science becomes possible" (Gross, 1996, 34).

The revised book, *Starring the Text: The Place of Rhetoric in Science Studies*, exchanges this provocative tone for a more tempered position. As indicated by the title, Gross no longer wishes to make sweeping assertions, Gorgias-style, that all science is a product of persuasion and rhetoric without remainder. Instead, in a context in which the discipline of "science studies" have come into its own, he wishes to advocate that rhetoric has a unique perspective on science, is "one discipline among many joined in a common enterprise," and has for its contribution the ability to "star" the "texts, tables, and visuals of science" in order to make "their hermeneutic unraveling central" (Gross, 2006, ix). *Starring the Text* thus advances a perspectival account of the rhetoric of science, suggesting that if we look at scientific texts rhetorically, we are able to gain new insights into them that would be left unrecognized when taken simply to be dispassionate representations of experience, reality, or other approaches in the meta-field project of science studies. Therefore, counter to the radical claims of his first book, he writes:

> None of this suggests that science is *only* rhetoric; no sane person could reach so bizarre a conclusion. These chapters can show no more than that, like sociology, history, and philosophy, rhetoric is a discipline; moreover, its disciplinary status entitles us to speak of all the written and visual records of the sciences from a rhetorical perspective (Gross, 2006, 78).

Classical terminology is still vital to this project, but understood as a way of looking at texts, not as a means to give a totalizing account of all of the complex practices of science that hitherto have lacked clear rhetorical counterparts.

However, this retreat from the provocative sophistical nature of the first book—a quality that made the initial text such an effective vehicle to spark productive controversy—does little to alter its fundamental view of rhetoric itself. It remains what it was in the first text: a handbook of techniques that can be used to advocate for a position that lacks sufficient rational certainty or empirical verifiability to defend itself without those techniques. In effect, then, Gross actually accepts, in both books, the Platonic position that the difference between rhetoric and non-rhetoric is the difference between a discourse grounded in opinion (and therefore reliant on appeals to emotion, authority, and style to flatter the ignorant) and a discourse grounded in knowledge of the real (and therefore dependent only on appeals to reason to inform the wise). But Gross differs from Plato by accepting Quine's position that there is no such thing as a discourse grounded in knowledge of the real. Therefore, although he acknowledges that science is not *only* rhetoric, this is simply meant to acknowledge that "texts depend heavily on a set of practices well outside the scope of rhetorical analysis" (Gross, 2006, 21). With respect to the *texts* of science, however, he still agrees with Gorgias, who in his *Encomium of Helen* suggested studying the "arguments of astronomers, who replace opinion with opinion: displacing one but implanting another, they make incredible, invisible matters apparent to the eyes of opinion" (Gorgias, DK11, trans. Gagarin and Woodruff, 1995). Or, as Gross says of Newton, "To move from the early papers to the *Opticks* is not to move from one science to another but from one rhetoric to another" (Gross, 2006, 74). The task of the rhetoric of science, that is to say, remains to redescribe rhetorically everything in science that we thought was purely rational. In this light, the dominant method throughout both books remains the same: to show through case studies how what we commonly think of as a purely rational procedure by which scientists make inferences about reality is actually a rhetorical exercise to gain acceptance by an audience for the validity of an utterance by using the full resources of persuasion.

Here are some examples. Regarding taxonomy: "Potential species are brought to life by giving them presence, by placing these purposeful collections of living things at center stage in audience consciousness" (Gross, 2006, 57). Regarding Newton: "The rhetorical value of meticulous detail extends to measurement. Everywhere in *Opticks*, measurement, so important in the early papers, increases in importance; in seemingly every case, measurements previously made are remade" (Gross, 2006, 74). Regarding Copernicus: "I shall how in *Narratio Prima*, Rheticus justifies his choice of the Copernican over the Ptolemaic hypothesis. To do so, he goes beyond argument and evidence" (Gross, 2006, 112). In each of these examples, Gross takes texts presumed to be "rational" and shows how "rhetorical *ethos, pathos,* and *logos* are naturally present in scientific texts," thus proving that "science can constrain but hardly eliminate the full range of persuasive choices on the part of its participants" (Gross, 2006, 29). Human beings, that is to say, are not mechanical logical machines; they encounter the world *as* human beings with all their capacities, desires, limitations, and assumptions, and their language about the world is always weighted, strategic, and intentional.

Consistent with the tenor of most contemporary history of science, Gross makes the important point that truths are not so much discovered as fought over, that the caretakers of knowledge in any age are bound up with structures of power and authority, and that the scientific community often accepts arguments in the short term (or even the long-term) for reasons other than pure rationality. To the extent that readers still might hold to the myth of the dispassionate, objective scientist who encounters "reality" empirically and then infers a rational "truth" based on that reality, all of these examples may come as a revelation. To them, Gross makes a further political point with respect to the authority often granted to science based on this myth. There is politics in the authority that Gross sees at work in "debates over fluoridation, the SST, and nuclear power" (Gross, 1996, 190). For him, it is important in these cases to "remind ourselves that the real issue is not the effect of particular initiatives; it is the arrogance of experts, their attempt to circumvent in their own interests the checks and balances of an open society" (Gross, 1996, 192). Thus, one of the important contributions of Gross's work is simply to make science fallible, and to show that "the sciences create bodies of knowledge so persuasive as to seem unrhetorical—to seem, simply, the way the world is" (Gross, 1996, 207). That is why the last sentence of *The Rhetoric of Science* takes aim at realism, arguing that for rhetoricians, "Realism must remain an analytical target, a rhetorical construct like any other" (Gross, 1996, 207). From this perspective, the reason for Gross's insistence on a "full" rhetoric of science becomes clear: to leave any scientific "core" left behind is to leave in place the authority of expertise granted by realism that corrodes the public sphere and renders rhetoric a marginal art.

Despite the consistent assault on the tenets of metaphysical realism, Gross nonetheless draws back from a Gorgias-style sophistical relativism that denies nature's existence, knowability, and communicability. A rhetoric of science does not deny the validity of what we today consider "brute facts" such that "planes fly" or "men can't have babies" (Gross, 2006, 42). As he explains, "No theory of physics can ignore flight; no theory of biology can turn its back on sex; no optics can dismiss refraction" (Gross, 2006, 42). For instance, he acknowledges that observation sentences such as " 'On day y, planet x exhibits a retrograde motion of z degrees of arc' " were taken to be brute facts by the likes of Ptolemy, Copernicus, Kepler, and Newton because they were recurrent and reliable generalizations about specific appearances (Gross, 2006, 43). Far from denying the reality of things, he asserts that "what is stable in science is the much-denigrated world of appearances, embodied in observation sentences, the only world with which science must square itself" (Gross, 2006, 43). Here we have what sounds like a traditional assertion of logical empiricism: the view that language, while never being able to precisely "mirror" reality, nonetheless can reach reliable characterizations of reality based on repeated observations of particular phenomena captured in precise language. From this perspective, rhetoric would seem to be limited to its traditional concern with how facts come to bear on issues of practical and ethical judgment rather than arguing about whether or not planet x exhibits retrograde motion of z degrees of arc.

Still, Gross does not leave the sophistical spirit behind. It reappears again in the view that facts are by their nature linguistic and therefore are not essentially bound to this much-denigrated world of appearances. Although Gross asserts that the rhetoric of science cannot deny or be skeptical of much that we consider "brute fact," he nonetheless asserts that "The claim of rhetorical analysis is that the phrase *brute facts* is an oxymoron" (Gross, 2006, 42–3). For the world of appearances does not carry meanings on its surface that are simply translated naturally into the language of the mind once they are experienced. As Gross makes clear, "facts are not in the world but in our heads; they are by nature linguistic—no language, no facts. By definition, a mind-independent reality has no semantic component. It can neither mean nor be incorporated directly into knowledge. Incorporation by reference is the only possibility" (Gross, 2006, 43). In short, "while our sentences about the world are *caused* by objects and events in the world, it is we and not the world who attribute *meaning* to those objects and events" (Gross, 2006, 42). From Gross's perspective, rhetoric leaves the law court and assembly and becomes part and parcel of every effort to make meaning of the world of experience.

The problem is that when rhetoric becomes detached from its traditional habitation within moments of contingency, urgency, and judgment, it also loses its very character *as* rhetoric. In the case of Gross, this means that rhetoric ceases to be grounded in the perspective of Aristotle or the Sophists and instead is determined by the premises of analytic philosophy—in particular, the philosophy of Quine. Accordingly, in order to show just what kind of rhetoric Gross's rhetoric of science is, I turn toward the work of Quine to explore the nature and consequences of his notions of under-determination, holism, and ontological relativity. I suggest that Quine's position leads to extremely fruitful insights concerning the "reality" of the objects of science and the central importance of language, experience, utterance, and behavior within any scientific inquiry, and that any rhetoric of science can take valuable lessons away from a study of the holistic tradition of analytic philosophy. However, I also argue that simply grafting a classical rhetorical vocabulary onto Quine's philosophy leads to the "thin" style of analysis that Gross seeks to avoid and that a "full" rhetoric of science must ground itself in the rhetorical attitude embodied in the classical tradition and its concern for judgment, not simply about matters of consensual belief but about matters of action as well.

Quine on the Pragmatics of Language

To understand what Gross means by a "fully" rhetorical account of science, we must turn to the work of W.V.O. Quine. For although the original text of *The Rhetoric of Science* underwent considerable modification in its new form as *Starring the Text*, one thing has remained unchanged: its reliance on premises of analytical philosophy largely centered on the work of Quine. In the original text, Gross quotes a passage from Quine's most famous essay, "Two Dogmas of Empiricism," to "make a point that is central to a view of scientific truth compatible with rhetorical analysis" (Gross, 1996, 202). The quoted passage runs as follows:

> Total science, mathematical and natural and human, is … underdetermined by experience. The edge of the system must be kept squared with experience; the rest, with all its elaborate myths or fictions, has as its objective the simplicity of laws (Quine, 1980, 45, quoted in Gross, 1996, 202).

Here we find expressed three of Quine's most foundational principles, that of under-determination, holism, and ontological relativity. The first posits that no truth claim ever possesses sufficient empirical verification to render it impervious to argument; the second asserts that any truth claim only finds its meaning within a totality of the discourse that gives it its meaning; and the third argues that the meaning of any "object" encountered in sensory experience is only defined relative to a background language. Taken together, Gross asserts, these three principles carve an "intellectual space for the rhetoric of science" (202).

The emphasis I am giving to Quine may seem disproportionate to his physical presence in *Starring the Text*, appearing as he does on only two pages. Yet these two pages summarize the view of both rhetoric and science that pervades the entire text. Whereas Quine only features prominently in *The Rhetoric of Science* in the closing pages of the epilogue, his work, moreover bolstered by quotes from Davidson, Putnam, and Goodman, form the basis of the third chapter in *Starring the Text* that articulates "the kind of rhetoric science is" (Gross, 2006, 32). As Gross puts it most succinctly: "From the point of view of rhetoric, the truths of science are not beyond argument; rather, they are the achievements of argument; science rests on facts and theories that have been argued into place" (Gross, 2006, 43). Importantly, this statement is not simply an assertion of relativism or skepticism. It is an assertion that grows out of the epistemological and ontological premises of Quine's analytic philosophy, according to which sense experiences only acquire meaning by being embodied in observation sentences and incorporated within a logical system of naming and predication. In Gross's view, "Scientific knowledge represents a consensus concerning the coherence and empirical adequacy of scientific utterances," while rhetoric represents the practice of disrupting and reconstituting that consensus through argument (Gross, 2006, 43). Quine's analytic philosophy thus provides a thick foundation on which the rhetoric of science can stand. Instead of being an afterthought, Quine forms the theoretical basis of the entire book.

One likely reason Gross found Quine's work particularly salient for rhetoric is the fact that it was popularized by Richard Rorty in his highly influential 1979 book, *Philosophy and the Mirror of Nature*, which used Quine's brand of analytic philosophy (suitably adumbrated by Donald Davidson) to advance a neo-pragmatic understanding of language and truth that Rorty admits bumps up against rhetoric. Like Gross, Rorty finds in Quine's holism a clear rejection the "quest for certainty" and the conception of knowledge "as accuracy of representation," and a clear embrace of the "commitment to the thesis that justification is not a matter of a special relation between ideas (or words) and objects, but of conversation, of social practice" (Rorty, 1979, 170). Rorty realizes, of course, that Quine, unlike himself, is no post-modernist, and that in blurring the "line between science and philosophy" Quine assumes that "he has thereby shown that science can replace philosophy" (Rorty, 1979, 171). However, Rorty, unlike Quine, sees no justification why science should be the choice over "the arts, or politics, or religion" (Rorty, 1979, 171). With certainty reduced to the pragmatic utility of background languages, Rorty sees the field now cleared for any humanistic endeavor, including rhetoric, to take up the mantle of knowledge and carry it forward. After all, for Rorty, to advocate holism is to advocate conversation, and "the ability to sustain a conversation, is to see human beings as generators of new descriptions rather than beings one hopes to be able to describe accurately" (Rorty, 1979, 378). Thus, Quine's principles of holism and under determination free us from the chains of mind-as-mirror-of-nature realism that bind us and allows a flourishing of new, more humanistic, descriptions of ourselves and our world. This is Rorty in a nutshell.

Quine's apparent, but unacknowledged rhetorical sensibilities would naturally make him attractive to rhetorical scholars, particularly those within the rhetoric of science who wish to use his scientific ethos to build bridges across disciplines. In order to explore the possibilities and limits of adopting his perspective in rhetoric, I will focus primarily on exploring the significance of two of his most famous essays, "The Two Dogmas of Empiricism" and "Ontological Relativity." These make the most provocative and rhetoric sounding claims. For within this framework, questions of ontology—that is, of "being"—are minimized, and questions of epistemology—that is, of "knowing"—are equated with questions of semantics. Science thus ceases to become the study of "reality" and the representation of that reality in a discourse of "truth." Instead, science becomes a systematic incorporation of observation sentences within a complex logical system of fictions whose only goal is to square itself with the empirical edges of the system. Here, it seems, is a view of science that opens the possibility of what Gross refers to as alternately a "complete" and a "full" rhetorical description of science (Gross, 2006, 64).

Quine's most famous essay, "The Two Dogmas of Empiricism," lays out his vision of holism that effective destroys empiricism's two dogmas and puts in their place a coherence view of truth. The first dogma is a belief that one can make a cleavage between *analytic* and *synthetic* truths. *Analytic* truths refer to those truths that are true only in reference to the semantic rules of a language or a logic (akin to symbolic systems such as mathematics). *Synthetic* truths refer to matters of fact, presumably empirical, that refer to actual existences (such as "there are brick houses on Elm Street"). The second dogma is the belief in epistemic *reductionism,* or "the belief that each meaningful statement is equivalent to some logical construct upon terms which refer to immediate experience" (Quine, 1980, 20). However, the belief in epistemic reductionism rests upon the belief that there exists analytic and synthetic truths, or the "feeling that the truth of a statement is somehow analyzable into a linguistic component and a factual component" (Quine, 1980, 41). Quine concludes that "the two dogmas are, indeed, at root identical" (Quine, 1980, 41). Reductionism defends the abstract-sounding claims of science (i.e. "human beings have evolved through natural selection") by asserting that these beliefs are grounded in verifiable empirical claims (i.e. "a fossilized skull with a human sized brain capacity was found in this rock formation"), which is simply another way of saying that analytic truths are built up from the bricks of synthetic truths.

Because the dividing line between rhetoric and science is often drawn at the line between *hard fact* and *mere opinion,* it is easy to understand how Quine can be read as emancipating the rhetorical perspective when he proceeds to completely undermine these two dogmas of empiricism. In Quine's view, the analytic/synthetic distinction on which reductionism has been based has "been the root of much nonsense" (Quine, 1980, 42). The strategy Quine employs to counter both dogmas is rather simple. It involves an extension of the continued trend to see meaning, definition, and reference in terms of more and more complex structures built from atomistic bits. Moving from the "impossible term-by-term empiricism of Locke and Hume," we first recognized that "the statement, rather than the term" should be used as the "unit accountable to an empiricist critique" (Quine, 1980, 42). But Quine urges that "even in taking the statement as unit we have drawn our grid too finely" (Quine, 1980, 42). Indeed, from Quine's perspective, "the unit of empirical significance is the whole of science" (Quine, 1980, 42). Science is not made up of "the statements of science taken one by one," but of the entire system of interconnections taken as a whole (Quine, 1980, 42). In fact, our individual statements themselves acquire their meaning from the "total system," much in the way we would think that the identification of an atom is meaningless without having accepted the total system of atomic theory (Quine, 1980, 44). In this way, Quine undermines a kind of naïve belief in induction, or the sense in which simply accumulating simple perception somehow adds up to a general theory like building a brick wall out of bricks. In reality, the "bricks" that make up the facts of a scientific theory are defined only after accepting a certain theory of bricks that is tied up with a blueprint for building walls.

Rhetorically, one natural consequence of accepting Quine's holism is to undermine traditional realism, whether scientific or Platonic, which often was used to distinguish rhetoric from "reality." This realism often takes the form of the correspondence theory of truth in which, in Gross's words, "truth is the correspondence between the sentences we form and the states of affairs in the world" (Quine, 1980, 41). But in Quine, the eradication of the synthetic/analytic distinction also undermines the integrity and autonomy of the empirical facts that make the correspondence theory plausible. Since the parts take their value from the larger whole, "Any statement can be held true come what may, if we make drastic enough adjustments elsewhere in the system" (Quine, 1980, 43). Science is no longer an accumulation of bricks (i.e., stable observational facts), but is "a man-made fabric which impinges on experience only along the edges" (Quine, 1980, 42). If this is the case, it is difficult to know where science ends and rhetoric begins—at least insofar as we understand the distinction between the two discourses to be distinguished by their ability to represent reality accurately without distortion, uncertainty, or ulterior motives, a criteria that goes back to Plato (or even before Plato to Parmenides).

But this leveling of distinctions between genres of discourse is not restricted to rhetoric and science in Quine. His work levels the distinction between any and all discourses that purport to say anything about what exists, how it exists, or how we know it exists. For instance, Quine famously dissolves the ontological differences between the objects of religion and the objects of physical science. Because, for him, any isolated statement of fact is meaningless outside of a larger theory, "Physical objects and the gods differ only in degree and not in kind"; they are "conceptually imported into the situation as convenient intermediaries—not by definition in terms of experience, but simply as irreducible posits" (Quine, 1980, 44). The question is not whether gods or atoms are *actually there*; the question is how well we can integrate observation sentences about them into our larger vocabulary in a coherent manner. Quine believes in physical objects and not Homer's gods, but he does so *not* because he can reach out and grasp their metaphysical being—i.e., not because they are more "real"—but because "the myth of physical objects is epistemologically superior to most in that it has proved more efficacious than other myths as a device for working a manageable structure into the flux of experience" (Quine, 1980, 44). It is just here that Quine cops to American pragmatism. In other words, Quine measures the epistemological superiority of any theory by how many observation sentences about sense stimuli can be effectively integrated into a coherent network of utterances that we have warrant to believe to be "real."

Whatever vestiges of the correspondence theory of truth may have been left behind after the assault by "Two Dogmas" are finally stripped away in his essay "Ontological Relativity." Here, Quine explicitly rejects the "copy theory" of language on which the correspondence theory of truth is based, a theory of language that holds to "the myth of a museum in which the exhibits are meanings and the words are labels" (Quine, 1969, 27). That is to say, if the "museum myth" was true, we could point to a thing and state its name and everyone would understand what we meant by that term. However, the "museum myth" is exactly that—a myth. Instead of having a one-to-one correspondence of language to object, we have the "inscrutability of reference," or the situation where a single word can mean many things under many conditions, and just what exactly one is talking about is often unclear (Quine, 1969, 47). In short, we have a situation where "There is no fact of the matter" (Quine, 1969, 47). What there *is* is a flux of sensory experience that makes sense to us only through the invocation of what Quine calls a "background language" that provides the context for any utterance (Quine, 1969, 48). In other words, "It makes no sense to say what the objects of a theory are, beyond saying how to interpret or reinterpret that theory in another" (Quine, 1969, 50). Ontological relativity, in sum, is a doctrine that denies that the being of entities is somehow intrinsic to the entities themselves or the sensory experiences they produce, but is relative to a theoretical language in which those entities are interpreted and defined.

Lastly, if Quine still seems to be speaking a language somewhat far from the sphere of rhetorical practice, he appears to correct it in his provocative espousal of what he calls a "thorough pragmatism" with respect to our understanding of the relationship between science, language, and sensory stimulation (Quine, 1980, 46). In his very spare form of pragmatism, "we recognize that there are no meanings, nor likeness, nor distinctions of meaning, beyond what are implicit in people's dispositions to overt behavior" (Quine, 1969, 29). Specifically, the behavior Quine is interested in is a type of utterance made in response to a particular sensory stimulation. That is why he defines an observation sentence (quoted by Gross, 2006, 42) as an utterance "on which all speakers of the language give the same verdict when given the same concurrent stimulation" (Quine, 1969, 86–7). For instance, on perceiving something white, small, and furry with two long years, one might say "Lo! A Rabbit!" and receive assent from other speakers based on an implicit agreement on the validity of a background language concerning rabbits. Pragmatically, what matters is not the correspondence between our utterance and "reality" but whether our utterance expedites our dealings with sense experiences and can be ultimately validated by the behavior and utterances of those around us. It is in this latter respect that Quine translates questions of epistemology into questions of communication. Epistemology is less about what we *know* to exist and more about what we can effectively *say* what exists by gaining assent from others through our utterances.

Understanding Quine's perspective helps make sense of Gross's contradictory-sounding statements that, on the one hand, science is solely the product of argumentation while, on the other hand, it is not *only* rhetoric. Following Quine, science can in one way be said to be solely a product of argumentation in so far as any apparent "fact" is amenable to revision, incorporation, or rejection by making adjustments elsewhere in the discursive system. As Quine writes, "Even a statement very close to the periphery can be held true in the face of recalcitrant experience by pleading hallucination or by amending certain statements of the kind called logical laws" (Quine, 1980, 43). Yet, as indicated by this passage, defending a statement in the face of recalcitrant experience (or attempting to refute the truth of the statement consistently verified by experience) requires a considerable amount of rhetorical labor. For the most part, Quine suggests that usually it is pragmatically useful simply to accept the habitual utterances of one's peers as valid if one wishes to get along in the world. To put it in rhetorical terms, while it is always theoretically possible to make the weaker argument the stronger, pragmatically it is not always the most prudent option.

Finding Rhetoric in the Rhetoric of Science

If Quine helps us make sense of the apparent paradox of Gross's acknowledging and denying the existence of brute facts, he does little to clarify what the meaning of the modifier "rhetorical" might mean in his system. It is true that Quine eradicates the correspondence theory of truth and acknowledges the importance of background languages, utterances, and argumentation in scientific inquiry. But never does he refer to any of this as particularly rhetorical. Instead, he privileges philosophy—or rather the philosophy of logic—the dominant art insofar as logic is concerned with the cognitive and semantic relationship between words and objects. Of course, like Rorty, Gross argues that Quine's personal desire for science and logic to be the master disciplines can easily be overridden. His annihilation of the correspondence theory of truth opens the field for rhetoric as much as it does for science, art, religion, and culture. But as this essay will show, constructing a vision of the rhetoric of science based on Quine's premises alone comes with a significant price, which is the abandonment of the traditional orientation of rhetoric toward practical judgment within kairotic moments that arise in the contexts of political action and meaning.

The problem with Gross's use of Quine to assault the citadel of realism is not in its emancipatory aim. That is a well-aimed project. The problem is that the effort to reinterpret all of science as rhetoric comes with a price of stripping rhetoric of its character as a situated art. The irony of Gross's use of logicians like Quine to provide a foundation for the rhetorical analysis of science is that it presumes a definition of rhetoric drawn almost exclusively from the philosophy of science. What Gross actually does is less to redescribe science rhetorically than to redescribe rhetoric epistemologically. He sees a "full" rhetoric of science as going beyond its traditional interest in the popularization of science, science education, or the intersection of science with public policy and embracing the idea that "knowledge is rhetorical" (Gross, 2006, 7). But this is a way of saying that the task of rhetoric is not to advocate for a particular action within a context of judgment but to articulate and advance knowledge claims whose primary end is the creation of warranted beliefs about objects, laws, and processes. Yet since this is precisely what Quine sees as the goal of logic, then logic and rhetoric become effectively interchangeable arts. For Gross to use Quine to argue for a rhetorical analysis of science is to suggest replacing the word "logic" with the word "rhetoric" in his philosophy while leaving the rest of it effectively unchanged.

This colonization of rhetoric by logic in Gross is easy to miss, however, especially in *The Rhetoric of Science*, because it is masked by his surface use of classical rhetorical terminology and his insistence that Aristotle's *Rhetoric* is his "master guide" (Gross, 1996, 18). It soon becomes clear, however, that the *Rhetoric* is not, in fact, his master text, for no sooner is Aristotle introduced than Gross insists that "the *Rhetoric* must be updated," meaning in effect that rhetoric and science must be seen as differences of degree and not kind (Gross, 1996, 18). The first update we have already explored—the explicit incorporation of "relevant modern thinkers" such as Quine (Gross, 1996, 19). But two more changes stand out.

First, Gross erases the distinction between syllogistic and enthymematic reasoning, which for Aristotle meant the difference between a complete and self-contained logical argument and an incomplete argument that began with uncertain premises and relied on audience participation for its completion. Gross insists that the differences are "not in kind but only in degree" (Gross, 1996, 12). Following Quine, Gross argues that "no deductive logic is a closed system, all of whose premises can be stipulated; every deductive chain consists of a finite number of steps between each of which an infinite number may be intercalated" (Gross, 1996, 12). Consequently, the protest that rhetoric has no business in science because scientific argument does not employ enthymemes is swept away. For Gross, all arguments are enthymematic because all arguments are underdetermined and therefore are capable of rhetorical analysis. And it is important for Gross to have realized the implications of this revised logic for our understanding of scientific argumentation.

But an enthymeme is defined by more than simply its relative probabilities as opposed to its certainty. In fact, Aristotle places greater emphasis on the fact that enthymemes, as opposed to syllogisms, are persuasive precisely because they invite audience participation (Garver, 1994). And it is this characteristic, and not the certainty of the premises, which has long been the identifying quality of the enthymeme. Lloyd Bitzer, for instance, argues extensively against the position that the relative completeness of an argument is what distinguishes an enthymeme from a syllogism. Instead, he argues that the defining quality of an enthymeme is the fact that it involves the "joint efforts of speaker and audience" which "intimately unite speaker and audience and provide the strongest possible proofs" (Bitzer, 1991, 408). Thomas Conley, meanwhile, defines an enthymeme as an argument whose success "is dependent on the ability of speakers and audiences to apprehend and interpret connections and differences" (Conley, 1984, 182). Consequently, even enthymemes that have certain premises remain enthymemes insofar as they bind speaker and audience together in an act of co-creation within a specific moment.

So it is really Gross's third update of Aristotle that is far more provocative and controversial with respect to our understanding of the place of rhetoric in the rhetoric of science. This update encourages rhetoricians to expand the notion of audience beyond its situated character, relying instead on the pragmatic fiction of what Chaim Perelman and L. Oblbreachts-Tyteca called the "universal audience," or what Gross calls that "ideal aggregate that can refuse a rhetor's conclusions on the pain of irrationality" (Gross, 1996, 18). Scientists, he explains, usually do not write to specific individuals but to an abstract audience whose standards of argumentation they have internalized and that they take to exist not in a specific place and time but in all places and at all times. Of course, Gross realizes (just as all scientists realize) that such an ideal audience does not exist empirically. But he nonetheless claims with considerable warrant that "all scientists attribute to imagined colleagues standards of judgment presumed to be universal: not in the sense that everyone judges by means of them, but in the sense that anyone, having undergone scientific training, must presuppose them as a matter of course" (Gross, 1996, 19). The replacement of a real audience with a normative "universal audience" therefore allows rhetoricians to interpret scientific texts from the same universal stand-point without having to consider the specific contributions that a situated audience makes in order to render judgment on a particular state of affairs.

The use to which the universal audience can be put within the rhetoric of science is made more explicit in *Starring the Text*. There, Gross outlines a method of rhetorical criticism that allows for the interpretation of texts from the imagined perspective of the universal audience rather than any specific empirical one. Indeed, "It is by means of this universal audience that the natural sciences come within the sphere of rhetoric" (Gross, 2006, 56). The universal audience, Gross writes, "is simply one that must be presup-posed; it is the audience that scientists must see themselves as addressing when they write or speak" (Gross, 2006, 56). In the case of evolutionary taxonomy, for instance, the universal audience is the one that the scientist holds in his or her mind when trying to win them over. A rhetorical analysis would thus "show how scientists create a world that persuades their fellows, a world in which plants and animals have been brought to life, raise to membership in a taxonomical group, and made to illustrate and generate evolutionary theory" (Gross, 2006, 56–7). But by "fellows," Gross clearly means to refer to all possible scientists who study evolutionary taxonomy, both in the present and in the future—and for good reason. What persuades a certain group of scientists at a certain time may not persuade a different group at a later time, and vice versa. Since the text can endure through time in a way that an arguer cannot, positing a universal audi-ence allows rhetoricians to concentrate on the text itself rather than restricting interpre-tation to a specific audience in history.

As reasonable as this method of updating Aristotle appears, it immediately comes in tension with the situated character of rhetoric when Gross proposes *stasis* theory as a method of rhetorical criticism of science. Stasis theory, of course, represented a way of determining what is at stake in a forensic courtroom, asking questions of fact, definition, quality, and jurisdiction in order to determine what would be the best defense for a client. By shedding the criteria of certainty of premises and participation of a situated audience, Gross is able to draw a parallel between the method by which we consider whether treason occurred and asking, in science, "What entities really exist? Does phlo-giston? Do quarks?" (Gross, 2006, 22). Just as the jury of Greek heroes decides on the guilt of Palamedes after his trial, so too with Einstein and atoms: "Before Albert Ein-stein's papers on Brownian movement, the existence of atoms was in question; after, their existence was regarded as confirmed" (Gross, 2006, 22). The fact that the trial of Palamedes ended in a specific judgment by a particular audience on a specific occasion (his guilt and execution) whereas the "trial" of atoms is an ongoing affair before a universal audience is not a factor in Gross's account. In the updated Aristotle, it is not particular judgments by situated audiences that matter but provisional consensus about knowledge claims arrived at in the ongoing deliberations of a particular epistemic community.

This is why in the updated Aristotle, it is actually Quine, not Aristotle, who becomes the master guide of rhetorical analysis of science. The reason is that Quine is also unconcerned with matters of particular judgment that call audiences to action. The only "action" Quine is interested in is the act of consensual utterance, of saying "yay" or "nay" to statements like "Lo! A rabbit!" He is not interested in prosecuting the rabbit, hunting the rabbit, killing the rabbit, experimenting with the rabbit, genetically modifying the rabbit, or buying the rabbit as a pet for his kids. For in each of these situations, one must make a practical judgment about the rabbit in relationship to the desires of an audience and the constraints of an immediate situation. Once the demand for *praxis* becomes paramount, all manner of motivations, like anxiety, credibility, love, hate, passion, trust, and urgency, suddenly become highly influential—as Aristotle recognized by making *ethos* and *pathos* constitutive modifiers of *logos* in rhetorical argumentation. For Quine, all of these motivations, while obviously important *in the moment*, are ephemeral and distracting from the purely epistemological question of whether or not we have sufficient warrant to categorize a certain nexus of sensory stimuli as a "rabbit" or some other object. Thus, as David Depew has observed, in contradistinction to pragmatists like John Dewey, who "tried to naturalize the intention-laden and meaning-full world that humans share in their daily life ... Quine's naturalism extended no further than 'extensionalist' ontologies that allow the inferential apparatus of propositional logic to map onto the physical world that impinges on agents in such a way that bits of behavior are elicited and shaped in response to it" (Depew, 1995, 115). In other words, Quine was largely uninterested in the mundane world of practice that so infatuated the earlier pragmatists. For Quine, it was obvious that this or that person may refer to this or that nexus of sensory stimuli in all manner of ways, sometimes for strategic purposes, sometimes for humor, and sometimes because they are operating under hallucination. But none of this matters for logic. What matters is the clarity and long-term reliability of a denotative designation across multiple circumstances and communities. But that is something other than the art that we tend to associate with rhetoric.

The *Kairos* of Classical Rhetoric

If there is anything distinctive about the classical rhetorical tradition, it is its attention to the power of the persuasive word when spoken in a timely moment of choice. It is this difference in the context of the speech act, and not the difference between the "truth" of what he said, that distinguishes rhetoric from logic. One sees the difference between the two arts in Gorgias's *Defense of Palamedes*. Palamedes defends himself against charges of treason and appeals to his audience of Greek heroes by appealing to their fear of making the wrong decision. He says: "If it were possible to make the truth of actions clear and evident to listeners through words, a decision based on what has been said would now be easy. But since this is not so, safeguard my body, wait for a while longer, and make your decision with truth" (Gorgias, DK11, trans. Gagarin and Woodruff, 1995). Here is the difference between the two arts. Logic, unconstrained by situated demands of judgment, hypothetically has the luxury of waiting not only longer but forever. The day of judgment never comes with logic, only the day of revision and reconsideration. But rhetoric must throw its full force behind a judgment in the moment, rallying whatever resources it can to advocate for a choice here and now. The stakes are high in rhetoric, as Palamedes warns his audience: "If you kill me unjustly, it will be evident to many; for I am not unknown, and your wickedness will be known and evident to all Greeks. For this injustice you, not the accuser, will be blamed in everyone's eyes, since the outcome of the trial is in your hands" (Gorgias, DK11, trans. Gagarin and Woodruff, 1995). Palamedes can make this argument because a sentence of guilt made in his trial is irreversible. Later logical analysis of evidence may find him innocent, but it cannot bring back his life. That is something that must be defended with rhetoric and with all resources he can muster.

From the classical perspective, rhetoric arises whenever we feel the pressure to make a choice under constraints and uncertainty. In those situations, all realists, materialists, idealists, and relativists embrace rhetoric not because they want to but because they must. Thomas Farrell, channeling the non-updated spirit of Aristotle, aptly describes the context under which rhetoric arises:

> When we have some stake, or interest, in the array of things around us, for instance, we are not likely to be concerned with an underlying cause or a larger, more inclusive general opinion. For the particularity of things has become a provocation. We cannot leave well enough alone. We also disagree about things. We may try to ignore them. We may take issue as regards what they mean. Eventually—perhaps sooner than we wish—we may have to own up to them, make judgments about them, and act on them. This is the tension that Aristotle captures with his rhetorical mood of *contingency*. Here we suddenly have the unsettledness of appearances, wherein differences are crystallized in opposed directions which may be resolved one way or the other (Farrell, 1993, 27).

For Aristotle, then, it is the mood of *contingency* that calls forth rhetoric as a productive art, just as it is the identification of texts that move people to action within contingent situations that calls forth rhetoric as a suitable mode of criticism. According to him, the subjects of rhetorical deliberation "are such as seem to present us with alternative possibilities" (Aristotle, *Rhetoric* 1357a5, trans. Roberts, in Aristotle 1984). Aristotle treated rhetoric as an art of putting people in a frame of mind that makes certain possibilities more attractive than others in moments of choice, thereby making any rhetorical criticism grounded in Aristotle an art of retrospectively determining why specific texts had the power to move real audiences in particular ways within in those moments.

Aristotle, in short, makes the art of rhetoric an explicitly *situated* art. Rhetoric for him is inextricably bound to the contingency of the moment, the motivations of an audience, and the imperatives of judgment. It is only within these situated moments that the full power of such rhetorical proofs as *ethos, pathos,* enthymeme, and style become instruments for achieving a practical and political aim. That such proofs inevitably find their way into even the most technical exposition is beyond a doubt, as Gross aptly demonstrates. Language being a human art, it will always convey some aspect of our humanity, including our biases, our desires, and our fears, and so even the most "dispassionate" scientist is not immune to its appeals. What makes scientific discourse different from rhetoric has little to do with the degree of "persuasiveness" of any text looked at only *as* a text. The difference is found in the contexts in which those texts operate. Most scientific texts operate in contexts in which no practical judgment is called for beyond a consideration of new truth claims and a reconsideration of old ones within the pages of academic journals. Rhetoric, by contrast, operates in context in which our choices make differences that cannot be so easily undone and that directly bear on matters of practice. Scientific argument thus becomes rhetorical when those judgments about "truth" intersect the realm of prudential judgment. It is at this point that scientists, often involuntarily, find themselves thrust into a public scientific controversy that makes hitherto obscure technical debates matters of rhetorical deliberation (Crick and Gabriel, 2010). It is thus the context in which scientific arguments are deployed, and not the specific content or epistemological validity of those arguments, that makes them rhetorical and thereby amenable to rhetorical analysis.

Yet the majority of case studies Gross investigates tend to downplay if not overlook entirely the situatedness of any discourse. Instead, they focus on showing how "rhetoric" (understood as any effort at constructing a persuasive argument) is somehow present in situations that we would not otherwise think of as a rhetorical—i.e., situations in which there is no clear judgment to be made. But little of this analysis, it turns out, requires any knowledge of rhetoric. The analysis of both Descartes and Newton is actually a philosophical critique of their metaphysics and methods. The reading of Darwin's notebooks indicates the importance of making diagrams in the generation of tentative theories. The complex political climate in which Copernicus published his theories is reduced to a single non-rhetorical problem: "to make coherent physical sense of the apparent behavior of celestial objects" (Gross, 2006, 112). The existence of peer review proves quite emphatically the lack of situatedness in science insofar as any claim "is neither scientific nor knowledge until it is the conviction, not merely of the individual or even a small group of like-minded adherence but of a broad consensus of practitioners" (Gross, 2006, 98). The debate over cold fusion hammers home that point that even the strong emotions tied up with intellectual rivalries between disciplinary communities can be overriden by "means of experimental disconfirmation" pursued rigorously and methodically by those communities (Gross, 2006, 133). In none of these cases does the incorporation of the rhetorical tradition add anything substantial to the analysis, a claim verified by the fact that beyond the use of the word "rhetorical," Gross incorporates none of the tradition to illuminate any aspect of these artifacts or situations. If anything, it demonstrates Quine's point that logic, at least once suitably relativized, is sufficient to understand the scientific process without any need for its rhetorical counterpart.

From a classical standpoint, however, if there is no judgment to be made and no action to be done, then all the strategies of rhetoric are so much wasted breath. For instance, what use is it to deliver an impassioned defense of one's innocence at a prehearing in which the only concern is for the admissibility of facts in a court trial? Even if an audience was persuaded by one's innocence, that is not the task at hand. But for a universal audience tasked with determining the epistemological validity of a scientific claim across time, the actual trial never comes. One simply has a never ending series of pre-hearings concerning the admissibility of facts and their relevance to theoretical assertions. In contradistinction, what makes the cases of historical figures like Darwin or Copernicus so fascinating for rhetoric was how their work had to overcome significant institutional, political, and religious resistance to even have their truth claims given a hearing. To the extent that their works overcame that resistance and influence the action of specific individuals, they are rhetorical. But insofar as their works contributed to the long-term development of established scientific theory based on a sustained investigation by a community of inquirers into validity of their truth claims with respect to accumulated empirical evidence, they are works of logic. This distinction has nothing to do with which discipline is more "true seeking" than the other or which text more "persuasive." It has everything to do with whether or not we are more interested in the relationship between words, objects, and meanings than we are in the relationship between speech, action, and power.

A Classical Rhetoric of Science

The irony of trying to "find" rhetoric in science is that rhetoric rarely needs to be found. Its very nature as persuasive art is to always be out front and to be experienced as a challenge, not just to a community of minds, but to an audience of actors. And it is important to emphasize that Gross, too, celebrates this characteristic of rhetoric as a situated, quasi-political drama. In the chapter on "Science and Society," Gross turns to the action by West Virginia miners who fought to have black lung disease redefined in their interests in order to change both their working conditions and their ability to acquire compensation in the event of acquiring the disease. The problem they confronted was that black lung had been defined in such a way that it was difficult for miners to prove the causation that would lead to compensation. As Gross writes, "Until phosphorus necrosis, asbestosis, or byssinosis is defined by a medical science driven by the cognitive technical interest, neither match workers, tile workers, nor cotton workers can sicken and die of it; therefore their complaints are without an object" (Gross, 2006, 155). Here is a case in which the conclusions of science are perceived to influence the lives of individuals, directly or indirectly, and thereby become relevant to ethical and political judgment.

Notably, Gross identifies the specific point—a "breach"—at which what had been largely a question of logic and epistemology suddenly erupted into a public scientific controversy that involve multiple rhetorical actors. This event was a mine explosion in 1968 which led to a "breach in the existing moral order—public anger among the miners followed by political action" (Gross, 2006, 153). Specifically, the miners unleashed a "fiery rhetoric aimed at the reform of the existing moral order," and through such "histrionics" as mock funerals in the displays of diseased lungs to the press and legislators, the miners "initiated an insurgency that eventually provided more liberal compensation for Black Lung" (Gross, 2006, 154). Notable about Gross's analysis, too, is the attention he gives to specific (i.e., non-universal) audiences who were mobilized to act in response to particular rhetorical appeals made in the heat of the moment:

From their early insurgency in the cold fields of West Virginia to their successful fight in Washington, the miners would have achieved little were it not for outside funding and the help of sympathetic legislators, physicians, and news media, competent attorneys working for a pittance, VISTA volunteers, and community organizers. It is these professionals who gave the miner's organization its leadership and its focus. Without the deep-seated and general discontent of the miners, it is true, these outsiders would have achieved nothing, but there is no denying either that the power of the workers was mediated at each step by those willing to defy the interests of the class from which they came (Gross, 2006, 157).

How different from the context in which Gross analyzes the work of Copernicus, Darwin, or Descartes! Here is a drama of multiple actors interacting within a moment of particular judgment in which science comes to bear as a warrant for decision-making. Only in this case, the scientific consensus was challenged by a rhetoric of social action by ordinary citizens faced with urgent problems, a rhetoric that made legislators, business leaders, and scientists make specific choices that determined both the course of future research and the policies that are out of those research agendas.

What Gross makes vividly clear in this case study is the fact that most rhetorical actors do not need to go through a long detour through analytic philosophy to call into question the realist doctrine of "brute facts." In a rhetorical situation, all audiences take as "brute facts" those appearances that help their cause, just as all audiences take as "fictions" those accounts that are used to override their interests and refute their positions. The history of the word "fact" is, in fact, bound up with such selections (Poovey, 1998). The miners certainly would have little patience for Quine's effort to problematize their utterance "Lo! Black Lung disease!" by showing how it was underdetermined by experience and relative to some background language. What they wanted was safer working conditions and compensation for what they believed to be a disease caused by excessive inhalation of coal dust. Similarly, an industry funded scientist might actually fully acknowledge that science is a man-made fabric that impinges reality only along the edges, but once thrown into the context of political deliberation, would speak the language of "brute facts" simply because her conclusions were being challenged by a motley crew of miners, attorneys, and activists. For what matters in rhetorical action is not some abstract belief about the existence of objects. What matters is how any belief can be used to leverage judgment in a particular case.

Gross argues in the closing pages of *Starring the Text* that rhetoric is not simply after the advancement of knowledge claims within some ongoing ideal speech situation; it deals with "symbolic interaction in the sphere of social action" (Gross, 2006, 179). To find a place for rhetoric in science studies is therefore to find those places in which science intersects with the sphere of social action. This does not mean simply restricting rhetorical studies of science to science policy, however. It occurs at any point within scientific inquiry—even the most theoretical—in which specific audiences are tasked with making judgments and performed actions that turn a situation this way rather than that way, and when those judgments are influenced by a whole range of rhetorical appeals that are brought to bear on a moment of choice. For as Aristotle wrote, "The duty of rhetoric is to deal with such matters as we deliberate upon without arts or systems to guide us," and "the subjects of our deliberation are such as seem to present us with alternative possibilities" (Aristotle, *Rhetoric* 1357a1–5, trans. Roberts, in Aristotle 1984). These deliberations happen at all levels of human practice, for social action does not mean non-scientific action. It simply means action performed alongside interested others for the pursuit of aims, interests, and resources that are more than simply episte-mological. And that we feel warranted to pursue this type of inquiry today without apology is in large part due to the work of Alan Gross, who accomplished that most dif-ficult and laudable of intellectual goals that Aristotle also attributed to the Sophists—the beginning of something new.

To pursue the rhetoric of science is to find those moments within a process of inquiry in which actors are presented with alternative possibilities and must make practical judg-ments without other arts or systems to guide them. These are moments when an individual scientist must decide to pursue one or another course of inquiry, when institutions must open or close their doors to particular ideas that have an impact on the world of practice, when citizens must mobilize to make their voice heard against institutional forms of power that use knowledge as a weapon, when public intellectuals are called upon to take their sci-entific ideas to a recalcitrant public uninterested in challenging long-held beliefs, when sci-entists appeal to their peers within crisis moments of their discipline, when scientific claims become warrants for practice, and when political practice threatens to overturn the asser-tions of science. These are moments of drama, of conflict, of heroism, of tragedy, of battle, of victory, of invention, of uncertainty, of possibility, and of beauty. The duty of rhetoric is to illuminate these moments in the practice of science in order to show that the achieve-ment of knowledge is always a struggle and that rhetoric appears at those moments in which a battle must be won so that truth (at least as we conceive it) can have a chance to prevail in a world in which we live, move, and have our being.

Reference List

Aristotle. *Rhetoric. The Rhetoric and the Poetics of Aristotle.* Trans. Roberts, W. Rhys. Ed. Edward P.J. Corbett. New York: The Modern Library, 1984.

Bitzer, L. "Aristotle's Enthymeme Revisited." *Quarterly Journal of Speech* 45 (1991): 399–408.

Conley, T. M. "The Enthymeme in Perspective." *Quarterly Journal of Speech* 62 (1984): 1–14.

Crick, N. and J. Gabriel. "The Conduit Between Lifeworld and System: Habermas and the Rhet-oric of Public Scientific Controversies." *Rhetoric Society Quarterly* 40.3 (2010): 201–223.

Depew, D. "Introduction." In Hollinger, R. and D. Depew (Eds.) *Pragmatism: From Progressivism to Postmodernism.* Westport, CT: Praeger, 1995.

Gagarin, M and P. Woodruff. (Trans.) (Eds.) *Early Greek Political Thought from Homer to the Sophists.* Cambridge: Cambridge University Press, 1995.

Garver, E. *Aristotle's Rhetoric: An Art of Character.* Chicago: University of Chicago Press, 1994

Gross, A. *The Rhetoric of Science.* Second edition. Cambridge, MA: Harvard University Press, 1996.

——. *Starring the Text: The Place of Rhetoric in Science Studies.* Carbondale: Southern Illinois University Press, 2006.

Farrell, T. B. *Norms of Rhetorical Culture.* New Haven: Yale University Press, 1993.

Plato. *Gorgias. Plato: Complete Works.* Trans. Donald J. Zeyl. Ed. John M. Cooper. Indianapolis: Hackett Publishing, 1997.

Poovey, M. *A History of the Modern Fact: Problems of Knowledge in the Sciences of Wealth and Society.* Chicago: University of Chicago Press, 1998.

Quine, W.V. *From a Logical Point of View: Nine Logico-Philosophical Essays.* Cambridge: Harvard University Press, 1980.

———. *Ontological Relativity and Other Essays.* New York: Columbia University Press, 1969.

Rorty, R. *Philosophy and the Mirror of Nature.* Princeton: Princeton University Press, 1979.

PART 2

METHODS

Neoclassical

12.
RHETORIC, TOPOI, AND SCIENTIFIC REVOLUTIONS
by Kenneth S. Zagacki and William Keith

Rhetorical scholars have become increasingly interested in the persuasive tactics and strategies that arise out of the communication that occurs in the course of doing science.[1] Philosophically, two primary ways of approaching this intrinsic rhetoric of science, and the practice of science itself, have emerged. One is to look at the community and practice of science as relatively stable, a progressive vision of scientists gradually making discoveries and weeding out error, passing along their knowledge and techniques to students.[2] But a second approach, made popular by Thomas Kuhn and his followers, holds that periods of stability are temporary and fragile and the history of science is less like steady progress than like a series of revolutions (twists and turns), where old facts, and the theories that permit them, are simply replaced by new ones, and students are trained to ignore the old structures or consider them 'wrong'.[3]

This latter view has been very controversial since many unpleasant epistemic conclusions are held to follow from it, conclusions that seem to attack the very foundation of Reason itself. Many rhetoricians have embraced Kuhn to support their general claim that revolutionary scientific change is mediated through rhetorical activities—and in some cases, that scientific knowledge is itself rhetorically constituted.[4] Yet, while the rhetorical activities of scientists have been explored, the nature of revolutionary rhetorical topoi and the situational/historical contingencies that give rise to them have not been fully delineated. In the following essay, we argue that stages of scientific revolution are accompanied by particular rhetorical exigencies, which themselves give rise to rhetorical topoi that advance the process of scientific argument and change. We contend that at least four crucial exigencies demand fitting rhetorical response during the development of scientific revolutions: the technical exigence of *uncertainty*, the problem of creating appropriate scientific *personae* during revolutions, the exigence of *preserving* revolutionary ideas, and the problem of *transforming* revolutionary change into establishment practice.

We believe that a historical understanding of scientific revolutions grounded in topical theory is especially consistent with the tradition of rheorical criticism, insofar as the rhetorical analyst studies discourse not for itself but to discover how discourse reflects its historical, ideational, and political contexts and the ways in which discourse is

William Keith and Kenneth S. Zagacki. "Rhetoric, Topoi, and Scientific Revolutions." *Philosophy & Rhetoric*, Volume 25, Number 1, 1992, pp. 59–78.

adapted to these contexts.[5] Such a comprehensive perspective will also help to integrate some of the diverse threads in the rhetoric of science literature and to extend systematically our understanding of that important rhetorical domain. We begin with a discussion of rhetorical topoi in science, and then illustrate the rhetorical, topical dimensions of various stages of revolutionary transition.

I. Topical Thinking in Science

Lawrence Prelli has provided an extensive treatment of the relationship between rhetorical topoi and science, although he has not investigated directly the underlying topoi of scientific revolutions.[6] For Prelli, scientists make systematic rhetorical decisions, based upon knowledge about fitting rhetorical ends and potentially relevant topoi that indicate what can or cannot be said concerning scientific claims in different situations. While these criteria in themselves are not logically determined in any formal sense, they are not illogical. Prelli claims that scientific rhetoric "is strategically *created* with a view to securing acceptance as reasonable by a special kind of audience. It is based on a particular kind of topical logic" (emphasis his).[7] Scientists cannot simply discover what they believe are important findings and expect other scientists to recognize the implications of these results. A critical purpose of scientific rhetoric is to identify ways in which one's work modifies the problems that members of the addressed scientific community perceive as pertinent. Thus, Prelli defines topoi as "repeatable and acceptable themes that deal with shared beliefs, values, and opinions … . [that] have to do with situationally appropriate scientific thoughts and actions."[8] Scientific topoi are requisites of doing science, revealed in the communicative choices and the persuasive tactics employed by scientists.

Prelli groups the topoi of science into four central headings—the problem-solving, the evaluative, the exemplary, and the ethotic.[9] The practice of science mandates that scientific discourse solves significant problems. But only discourse that reveals "experimental competence" and "predictive power," or addresses "significant anomalies," is accepted as a legitimate instance of scientific problem-solving. Evaluative topoi "suggest lines of argument in which rhetors test the special values of experimental, theoretical, or methodological claims."[10] Hence, in order to evaluate one set of claims against another, scientists employ evaluative topoi—such as "internal consistency," "simplicity," and "fruitfulness"—that demonstrate that a scientific discourse is a more reasonable and productive explanation of extant problems than current views. Exemplary topoi include such discursive strategies as examples, analogies, and metaphors, which can be enlisted to support scientific arguments. Finally, topoi that enhance a scientist's ethos include "universality," "skepticism," "disinterestedness," and "communality." But what specific rhetorical problems and situations confront practicing scientists during scientific revolutions? What rhetorical strategies and topoi do they use to address them? We consider these questions below.

II. The Topoi of Scientific Revolutions

A. The Problem of Uncertainty

Philosopher and historian of science I. Bernard Cohen divides the progress of a revolution in science into four stages: the intellectual revolution, the revolution of commitment, the revolution on paper, and the revolution in science.[11] The "intellectual revolution" is the primal creative activity in which the individual scientist and/or his immediate working colleagues create, discover, or intuit a relatively complete (revolutionary) idea. While this idea arises out of current theories and paradigms, it transforms or alters them in some significant way.[12] The process of rhetorical, topical thinking begins in Cohen's second stage, the "revolution of commitment." This stage consists of the personal or group recording of the revolutionary idea, in the form of "an entry in a diary or notebook, a letter, a set of notes, a report, or the draft of a full account which might eventually be published as an article or book."[13] The group or the individual scientist may be considered committed because they have taken the trouble to put their thoughts in a relatively permanent form.

In the "revolution of commitment," rhetorical questions regarding the validity of the discovery and ways of determining its validity permeate the scientist's every decision. Indeed, the basic rhetorical problem of the "revolution of commitment" is coping with various kinds of *uncertainty*, by grappling with the significance of the new insight. The creative thinker of Stage One has had an idea that seems right, a provisional bit of certainty. As a rhetorical exigence, uncertainty invites a way of thinking and discoursing about the new insight, even if such talk is confined to one's intra-group deliberations. The exigence of uncertainty directs that before the scientist proceeds to Stage Three, he or she must assume that a certain ambiguity exists concerning the new finding, and then search for reasons that might reduce the ambiguity in a way that the scientific community deems reasonable. In fact, the exigence of uncertainty may initiate the process of rational deliberation over the precise nature of the insight. Therefore, the exigence of uncertainty creates many technical problems concerning the factual nature of the discovery: "What are the facts?" "How can I find out?" "What do they mean?" These questions can be explored through *problem-solving* topoi (e.g., experimental procedures that will confirm and replicate the existence of the phenemenon), which themselves warrant judgments about the facts, the meaning of the facts, and the best way of investigating the facts.

Still in Stage Two, the scientist must evaluate, however provisionally, the historical relevance of the insight, which itself remains cloaked in uncertainty. Thus, the scientist may enlist salient *evaluative* topoi for interpreting the meaning of the facts in terms of the received view. Various strategies suggest themselves: The researcher may discount the idea or result, or try to reconcile it within existing theory. These two responses take their author out of the process of making a revolution, though it is perfectly possible that revolutionary significance will be assigned to their idea or result by someone else. A third response to the insight might be "It's revolutionary!" This possibility and the self-conscious notion of winning academic glory through "revolutionary" insights is probably a recent, post-Einsteinian phenomenon. In fact, it is possible now that "revolutionariness" enters at Stages One and Two: an idea conceived just to be revolutionary. The "giants" in the history of science are generally successful revolutionaries, so those who aspire to gianthood might do well to cast themselves as revolutionaries.[14]

If scientists are willing to recognize their ideas as revolutionary, they again face the technical exigence of uncertainty: "What are the facts?" "What do they mean?" and "How can they be reconciled within (or from without) the context of existing theory and research?" Many *problem-solving, evaluative,* and *ethotic* topoi are available to help resolve these questions. These topoi concern the nature of experimentation, the formal features of potential theoretical explanations, and the long-term (personal and scientific) impact of these explanations. Possible analyses include: satisfying one's own, or some external, epistemic or experimental standards; fortifying against coming trials and the effects to the researcher's reputation if the new theory is found wanting; and anticipating attacks on the theory, the motives behind them, and the experimental and theoretical evidence that must be marshalled in support of the theory.

In general, then, the ways in which scientists during Stage Two cope with the technical exigency of uncertainty through topical mechanisms arise from their perceptions of the prevailing views of scientists; this exigency functions like Perelman and Olbrechts-Tyteca's "universal audience" in that it prompts further inquiries about what people will say about or think of this new insight as the revolution unfolds. In other words, the "universal audience" provides the revolutionary scientist with the initial stance of reasonable doubt and the consequent topoi for determining the factual significance of the insight.[15] Before they commit their insights to public scrutiny, working scientists are in a very important sense acting rhetorically, as they discuss findings with colleagues or outline notes and reports that will appear more formally in Stage Three. Little is certain at Stage Two, and scientists are far from the coherence they will someday be assigned in textbook accounts of their activities. So their rhetorical behavior must adapt to this stage by summoning particular topoi which assure or deny the importance of the discovery.

B. The Problem of Creating a Revolutionary Persona

The third stage of the scientific revolution, the "revolution on paper," occurs when the ideas that the scientist has committed to paper are circulated in the scientific community and become accessible (and critique-able) as part of the public, scientific domain. Of course, a revolution at this stage is not complete simply because of presentation to the "outside world": frequently "the intellectual revolution is not complete until the scientist fully works out his [sic] ideas on paper."[16] The central rhetorical problem of Stage Three concerns creating an appropriate scientific *persona*.[17] We suggest three personae scientists may adopt to present their claims publicly—the revolutionary, the conciliator, and the conservative. We begin with the revolutionary.

1. The Revolutionary Persona

In order to overcome uncertainty, the scientists have had to display enough methodological precision or sophistication to overcome doubt. But simply displaying the results of experimental investigation to substantiate the (at least temporary) certainty of new findings do not situate scientists in relation to their discoveries; nor does it clarify the significance of the insights for the received view. Scientists make revolutionary claims, thereby announcing the overall significance of their work. These claims—and the revolutionary persona within which they are framed—can be manipulated in two ways: One may be compelled to be revolutionary or one may be seeking revolution. A scientist who claims to be compelled to be revolutionary might employ the *evaluative* topos of the significant anomaly to fashion her- or himself as an ordinary scientist, doing routine scientific work (i.e., Kuhn's "normal" science), when along came this extraordinary anomaly that simply could not be dismissed. After attempting to reconcile this anomaly with existing views, the scientist may admit that it could not be reconciled, and therefore challenged existing orthodoxy. This researcher could also draw upon the *evaluative* topos of fruitfulness, along with what we would call the *evaluative* topos of *scientific creativity;* these topoi show how his or her results and explanations are carefully construed within present scientific practice, how these findings might be productive of further insights, and how they can be creatively pursued within the bounds of legitimate science. The scientist would therefore argue that "I'm not being revolutionary because I want to be, but because the facts and the practice of science compel it; and I'll follow the facts and the procedures of science wherever they take me, no matter how difficult, just as the creative practice of science dictates."

We can see this more moderate approach to framing a revolutionary persona in the comments of chaos researcher Ralph Abraham. Abraham, like many chaos scientists, encountered stiff resistance to his revolutionary ideas. Yet he describes himself and fellow physicist Robert Shaw as researchers *compelled* to be revolutionary, and emboldens this persona by linking it to the *evaluative* topoi of fruitfulness and scientific creativity:

> All you have to do is put your hands on these knobs, and suddenly you are exploring in this other world where you are one of the first travelers and you don't want to come up for air ... . [Robert Shaw] had the spontaneous experience where a little exploration reveals all the secrets. ... All the important concepts ... would just naturally occur to you. You would see it and start exploring.[18]

Abraham would have us believe he stumbled upon his revolutionary findings. Clearly, he was not looking to be revolutionary. But so provocative were his initial observations—and because the topoi of science required him to pursue such provocative findings—neither he nor any other reputable scientist could possibly ignore them; in fact, so important were these findings that they quite "naturally" led to new insights. Once he became engrossed in observation, Abraham had no desire "to come up for air," to escape from the intoxicating lure of scientific (revolutionary) discovery. What scientist would not be persuaded, after venturing on Abraham's exciting intellectual journey, to announce revolutionary results? Perhaps more important for Abraham's rhetorical purpose, after hearing Abraham's drama, what scientist would not be willing to consider his or her findings for the dramatic insights they might entail?

The scientist seeking revolution might characterize him- or herself in a more radical fashion. This researcher could draw on the *evaluative* topos of scientific creativity, on what we call the *problem-solving* topos of *methodological relevance*, on Prelli's significant anomaly or his *ethotic* topos of disinterestedness. These topoi can portray the received view as absurdly inadequate, while demonstrating how dogged allegiance to the received view is "anti-scientific" since it stifles fresh thinking and leaves difficult problems unsolved. This researcher may emphasize the need to discover dramatically different explanations, or highlight the problems associated with holding dogmatically to traditional methods and concepts. Radical proposals, it could be maintained, not only address significant anomalies but force one to re-examine one's fundamental assumptions or to question the very methods of inquiry themselves—assumptions and methods that may be preventing scientists from seeing the phenomenon in innovative and perhaps more realistic ways. This researcher's radical persona might thus advocate revolutionary views which share little with the status quo and enlist the above-mentioned topoi to justify her or his departure. Additionally, this scientist might entertain any number of *exemplary* topoi, such as metaphors, analogies, or what we would identify as *rhetorical contrast*, to highlight the differences between the new theory and received views. Yet she or he might also try to preserve credibility (as reasonable and scientific) by including certain other *evaluative* and *problem-solving* topoi—such as simplicity, experimental competence, or predictive power—that demonstrate commitment to the norms of the scientific enterprise.

This more radical revolutionary persona is exemplified in the work of paleontologists Niles Eldridge and Stephen J. Gould. These scientists, as John Lyne and Henry Howe remind us, aggressively assaulted Darwinism's dependence on induction and other of its scientific tenets in a 1972 paper introducing the theory of punctuated equilibria. The overall strategy of Eldridge and Gould seemed grounded in the *exemplary* topos of rhetorical contrast. As Lyne and Howe explain, new scientific theories excite our attention partly because of the contrast they pose to existing theories. "The theory of punctuated equilibria drew criticism for posing that contrast too sharply, and yet this was also a source of its rhetorical potency … . it made itself attention-worthy by positioning itself in dialectical opposition to accepted views."[19] In a later paper, Gould alone was adamant about the problems with Darwinism's inductive procedures. He developed a "revolutionary manifesto," based in the *problem-solving* topos of methodological relevance and the *ethotic* topos of disinterestedness. He noted how Darwinists resorted to restrictive, perhaps inappropriate, inductive methods to solve conceptual problems, and were not disinterested at all; rather, when confronted with new explanations, Darwinists dogmatically invoked traditional (inductive) explanations and methods that served to perpetuate their power and official standing in the scientific community, but most important, prevented them from seeing how evolution actually worked.[20]

2. The Conciliatory Persona

Sometimes, as Cohen explains, there is a long delay between the revolution on paper in Stage Three and a truly large-scale revolution in science; often, the revolution in science never comes about. Delays occur for various reasons: new theories are met with great skepticism and even downright hostility; a lag between the introduction of theoretical predictions and accepted experimental procedures to test them; a scientist lacks orthodox credentials; and theories are debated and reformulated for many years until finally accepted.[21] These delays have important rhetorical consequences. Harsh reactions to revolutionary ideas, for instance, often cause scientists to shift from a radical into a more conciliatory persona. Rather than advocating a dramatic overthrow of existing dogma, the conciliator argues that her or his findings, while extraordinary, can still be explained within extant theory and research. Certainly, the theory promoted by the conciliator may in retrospect be considered revolutionary; but at the moment of use the conciliatory persona is meant to ameliorate the harsh reception of one's ideas by playing down their radical nature.

As Alan G. Gross has shown, after encountering severe resistance to his initial revolutionary portrayal of optics theory, Newton constructed a more conciliatory persona in his *Opticks* by locating his discoveries firmly within the preceding optics tradition. Newton directed several *exemplary* topoi toward this goal, including the use of particular organizational patterns, experimental references, and stylistic devices. As Gross explains, Newton's conciliatory response "employed a Euclidean arrangement to create an impression of historical continuity and logical inevitability ... . [and] by piling experiment on experiment, and, in each experiment, detail on detail, he created in this work an overwhelming presence for his experimental method. Finally ... he initiated a cascade of rhetorical questions, whose cumulative effect was both to sanction his science and license his speculations."[22]

3. The Conservative Persona

That skepticism and hostility frequently confront new ideas also reveals that while scientists are rewarded for being "revolutionary," there is significant weight afforded those "guardians" of the old view. Scientists, in this sense, adopt a third revolutionary persona, the *conservative* defender of the scientific status quo. As Cohen observes, "New and revolutionary systems of science tend to be resisted ... because every successful scientist has a vested intellectual, social, and even financial interest in maintaining the status quo. If every revolutionary new idea were welcomed ... utter chaos would be the result."[23] The conservative persona may be congenial, though it is typically harsh.

The opposition mounted against Velikovsky's radical cosmological physics is a good example of both a harsh and courteous reaction. In 1973, at a meeting of the American Association for the Advancement of Science, a fierce debate was held and five scientists attacked Velikovsky's system, with only Velikovsky holding on in defense. Six years later, astrophysicist Robert Jastrow remarked ruefully that only three of ten Velikovsky predictions had been corroborated—the rest were directly contradicted. Jastrow lamented this state of affairs since "nothing could be more exciting than to witness a revolution in scientific thought in our own lifetime." "Unfortunately," he concluded, "the evidence does not support this possibility."[24] Jastrow both praises and blames Velikovsky. And his comments reflect the use of certain *ethotic* and *evaluative* topoi to fashion a conservative persona: He recognizes the value of, even admires the attempt at being revolutionary, and thus evokes what we refer to as the *ethotic* topos of *revolutionary consent*, where science and "revolutionariness" are seen as part and parcel of one another; yet he also realizes that, when evaluating new revolutionary theories, these theories must be experimentally rigorous, meet particular evidentiary guidelines, and unfold within the parameters of scientific practice as presently conceived. In short, he reaffirms the value of change and the credibility associated with those bold enough to seek it, while maintaining the rigorous evaluative standards that sanction change in the first place.

C. The Problem of "Preserving" Revolutionary Ideas

Other sources of delay during Stage Three, such as the lag between the time a scientist achieves enough credibility to assert him- or herself and between the period radical predictions or findings can be assimilated to accepted technological and experimental procedures, reveal another exigence particularly characteristic of this stage—the need for scientific rhetoric to be "preservative." Preservative rhetoric "insure[s] that epistemic judgments are maintained in the marketplace of ideas where they may be subjected to the scrutiny of others … . [rhetoric] keeps alive ideas whose time has not yet come," for technical or other reasons.[25]

Rhetorical scholars have described several *exemplary* topoi for preserving scientific ideas during Stage Three. Lyne and Howe illustrate the preservative power of lively images and "picturing strategies" in the rhetoric of Gould and Eldridge, whose early revolutionary account of fossil gaps represented "a coherent idea, resplendent in its newness and apparent power"—an idea that allowed for a "rhetoric of punctuational inquiry" to be "forged."[26] Gould's subsequent revolutionary manifesto revealed the use of "appealing new imagery of organic, non-deterministic processes," that also helped to express and preserve his revolutionary insights.[27] Darwin clearly hoped his lively presentation of evolutionism would yield subsequent debate about and eventually the acceptance of his theory. Yet he also recognized the need to exploit the *exemplary* topoi of pre-established Baconian science and natural theology (i.e., their formal, stylistic features)—a rhetorical move that, as John Angus Campbell tells us, demonstrated "the intelligibility of [an evolutionary] worldview everyone thought" these pre-existing categories excluded.[28] This strategy, Campbell argues, preserved for Darwin a serious reading by an otherwise skeptical audience.

Some "preservative" decisions stem from the individual scientist's desire to claim personal responsibility for a discovery, which presumably would ensure a glorious place in the history of science. Maurice Finocchario has shown how the French chemist Lavoisier, feeling he had made a revolutionary advancement in combustion research but not knowing precisely what that advancement was, wished to preserve credit for discovering something. Lavoisier thus employed what we would call the *exemplary* topos of *ambiguity* in a sealed note he submitted to the Academy of Sciences in Paris. Later, when the note was opened, Lavoisier hoped his message to be ambiguous enough to claim credit for any number of explanations proffered during the interim between the submission and the opening of the note.[29] Preservative rhetoric designed, in part, to guarantee credit for new discoveries has been identified by Gross in the work of DNA scientists. These researchers resorted to metaphors and analogies not so much to establish truth claims about DNA coding (as more tightly argued, less analogical presentations would do), but to emphasize "the heuristic, as distinct from the probative value of analogy in the sciences."[30] Gross's analysis illustrates the preservative power of *exemplary* and *evaluative* topoi: *Exemplary* topoi like metaphorical and analogical explanation convey the meaning of basic scientific breakthroughs; *evaluative* topoi like fruitfulness and heuristics stake claims about what scientists suspect to be true about a potentially productive line of research and guarantee the prospects of further scientific inquiry—the essential insights of which may at some point be attributed to them.

D. The Problem of Transforming Revolutions into Establishment Practice

Scientific revolutions overall are never really consummated until the fourth stage, which Cohen calls "revolution in science." At this point the formerly revolutionary ideas become part of the theoretical status quo. As Cohen observes, the ideas become entrenched and defended by members of the status quo, indicating that the revolution was successful: "Even after publication, no revolution in science will occur until a sufficient number of other scientists become convinced of the theories or findings and begin to do their science in the revolutionary new way."[31] The "revolution in science" is really the stage of success. Revolutions that make it through this stage are transformed and go from being revolutions to being part of the scientific establishment—they become textbook science. As Latour notes, science-in-use becomes "readymade" or "Black Box" science, pre-packaged and no longer in doubt.[32] The uncertainty and persuasive struggles that characterize the previous three stages are gone; the rhetoric of the Fourth Stage concerns this essential problem, common to all revolutions: keeping the substance of the revolution intact while transforming the rhetoric of the revolution into the rhetoric of the establishment. Three rhetorical strategies can be used to accomplish this end: characterizing the old view, assigning an appropriate history to the new view, and making the new view accessible. We begin by examining characterizations of the old view.

The theory overthrown by the successful scientific revolution remains a thorn in the new view: "Are we really sure about this change?—we thought we were right before." In a certain sense, scientists must collectively admit they were wrong. Thus, while the old view must be characterized in such a way that it no longer appears to be a significant competitor with the new theory, the dignity of science must also be preserved. Several topical mechanisms permit this, including what we call the *ethotic* topoi of *progress and truth in science* and *fallibilism*. If science makes progress toward discovering truer versions of reality, then there is bound to be change, and if there is bound to be change, then scientists will turn out to be wrong part of the time. Therefore, this line of reasoning concludes that there is scientific virtue in being wrong or being "fallible." In fact, this willingness to be wrong is sometimes said to be the hallmark of the scientific enterprise, since doing so diminishes personal biases while opening the possibility for the advancement toward truth.

But despite protestations, nobody, apparently, likes to have been wrong, even collectively. Therefore rhetoric about the overthrown theory may also try to explain why it was wrong. One way to accomplish this is to employ what we label the *evaluative* topos of *experimental correspondence*. Here, revolutionaries point out that the old theory's empirical assumptions no longer corresponded to experimental data, and therefore required a new set of assumptions or theoretical concepts. It can also be argued that the old view's philosophical suppositions regarding the nature of reality worked well, given access to whatever level of reality the view described. However, exploration into more sophisticated dimensions of the world requires more complicated theoretical suppositions. Still another version of this topical response is to attribute the problems with the old view to technological limitations. Scientists, the argument goes, were doing the best they could under the circumstances, as in "Newton's theory worked well enough, given the measurements he was able to make, but now we have much more precise measurements, and consequently see the inadequacy of his view." Newton escapes censure as unscientific, even though his system has been eliminated from competition with current ones.

In any case, transition to a new theory seems in accordance with the logic (the topoi) of doing science, insofar as one's theoretical preferences are guided by the rational criteria of what passes as scientific decision-making and experimentation. One cannot be a scientist, the argument goes, and work in any other way. Werner Heisenberg's description of the quantum revolution exemplifies this topical reasoning. For him, quantum theory represented a radical "change in the concept of reality." And so, this conceptual change required "a real break in the structure of modern science" from Newton.[33] Heisenberg explains further that:

> ... the hopes which had accompanied the work of the scientists since Newton [to work under one grand, Newtonian paradigm] had to be changed. Apparently, progress in science could not always be achieved by using the known laws of nature for explaining new phenomena. In some cases new phenomena that had been observed could only be understood by new concepts which were adapted to the new phenomena in the same way as Newton's concepts were to the mechanical events.[34]

In this characterization of scientific revolution, the sacred status in the history of science for Newton and other scientists is preserved, while the new theory is seen to fit nicely into this tradition. Indeed, as if to legitimate further the Quantum revolution, Newton is pictured to have followed the same topical logic as contemporary scientists, even though he was exploring a wholly different level of reality. For quantum researchers "adapted" their concepts to quantum phenomena just as Newton's concepts were scientifically "adapted to the mechanical events." Newton, Heisenberg suggests, dealt appropriately with the level of reality to which he had direct and only access. On Heisenberg's account, had Newton been privy to quantum results (or to modern technology), he, too, would have made a splendid and very willing quantum scientist.

Another means of characterizing previous views as erroneous is to include what we call the *evaluative* topos of *external influence*. In this scenario, the failure of the old view is blamed on external problems, such as political institutions, human gullibility or super-stition, or lacking knowledge of scientific method. This topical approach reflects what Steve Fuller calls the distinction between the internal dimension of science (scientific research and reporting) and its external dimension (everything else). Scientists, argues Fuller, claim that the more free science is from any external influence, the more likely it is to arrive at truth. For scientists, error in science is attributed to external factors; quality science concentrates on internal problems.[35] But the very recognition of external con-straints supplies scientists in Stage Four with a means of rejecting preceding theories. The popular fiction that "the Catholic Church enforced the heliocentric view for religious reasons until Copernicus bravely dared look at the sky" is one such rhetorical characterization, as is the common explanation of why educated and sensible people believed in witches until relatively recently—they were mired in superstition.

Once the old view has been featured, the new view must also be put in its proper place. Positioning the new view into perspective primarily entails replacing the messy, disorganized process by which the new theory was discovered and justified, with a more elegant narrative. The stylistic technique of *narrative* itself can supply an *exemplary* topos from which both the rightness and the inevitability of the new view might be stressed. The story of the discovery and its acceptance can thus be told in a way compatible with the aims and goals of science, as currently practiced. Perhaps the numerous rhetorical tactics discussed by Latour for the building of "black boxes" in science (e.g., stratifica-tion, captation) also act as *exemplary* topoi, directing attention away from the sometimes turbid activities of scientific discovery and toward the tacit assumption that this dis-covery proceeded according to accepted scientific principles and methods.[36] Addition-ally, various *evaluative* and *problem-solving* topoi can be employed to underline the role of pure science (not external factors) on revolutionary change. Thus, while eighteenth century scientists were likely to attribute the success of a revolution to their more penetrating understanding of God's domain, the rhetoric of modern scientists is more likely to relegate revolutionary success by deploying *evaluative* and *problem-solving* topoi (e.g., scientific creativity and appeals to scientific method), a sort of "back to basics" in science.

Finally, consolidating a revolution requires, as Cohen argues, that adherents to the revolutionary view take over the organs of power in science, by gaining control "of the scientific press, the educational system, and the seats of power—in scientific academies and laboratories or on major scientific committees which make policy and apportion resources."[37] One way to accomplish this is to find means of communicating the new insight in standard forms, usable by all those working in a field, and usable by outside interest groups, even by the educated public. As Latour suggests, complex scientific research must be "translated" to "networks" (e.g., corporations, research foundations, governmental organizations), who can help financially to sustain research under the new paradigm.[38]

Possibly the most important rhetorical tactic for communicating a set of findings and for gaining adherents, scientific or otherwise, is one cited by Kuhn in his discussion of paradigms: the need for central examples and metaphors that anchor an entire per-spective, what Prelli has called *exemplary* topoi. Most lay people understand atomic/

molecular theory through ball and stick models; recent breakthroughs in astrophysics rely upon "string" metaphors to convey ideas about physical forces; more recent developments in "chaos" theory focus on everyday occurrences like dripping faucets, weather patterns, and heartbeats; and as both Prelli, and S. Michael Halloran and Annette Norris Bradford have shown, DNA researchers have used "coding" metaphors for comprehending and teaching sophisticated genetics.[39] Despite their inadequacy with respect to certain highly abstract or mathematically based notions, these *exemplary* topoi provide a potent way of communicating essential insights about atomic structure, physical force, probability and chaos, DNA and heredity. And they are nearly as important in the scientific community as outside of it, since until the new view has been in place long enough to be taught in graduate schools, working scientists will have to teach it to themselves, or get brief instruction at conferences.

III. Implications and Conclusions

By no means does the present analysis exhaust the number of rhetorical exigencies, strategies, or topoi extant in scientific revolutions. But a topical scheme allows us to move beyond the mere categorizing of scientific topoi and to understand the essential historical/situational exigencies and other rhetorical problems accompanying scientific change; it also integrates the diverse rhetoric of science literature into a coherent, theoretical framework. Several implications stem from a topical reading of revolutionary science. The first concerns the observation that scientists work from a sort of master topos, what we would call the topos of *continuity in science*, in order to manipulate the reception of their work. Certainly, scientists may use continuity as a marker of scientific progress over competing theories. Yet by playing down the contrast between a new theory and its established competitor, the topos of continuity may provide scientists with a way to argue for the rightness of their views and the relative correctness of the views they wish to supercede, without upsetting the stability of the addressed scientific community. But scientists may also appeal to a more abstract notion of continuity—what we have called the topos of *progress and truth in science*—even while arguing for the discontinuous nature of their work. In these cases, theories may be made to look discontinuous with the immediate received view but continuous with the overall tradition of scientific progress. In other words, scientists find it necessary, advantageous even, to claim revolutionary, discontinuous stature for their theories, and various rhetorical strategies allow them to do so. But even here scientists are compelled to conform to a higher principle of continuity—the continuity of a scientific tradition deeply steeped in beliefs about their ability to achieve progress and truer approximations of reality.

Our topical investigation, then, suggests that scientists tell each other the same old stories, based on progress and truth, about why and how science changes, and about what they do with change once it occurs. Scientists argue for the rightness of their theories, in a fundamental sense; they also argue about the value of being wrong when either they or the theories they have overturned turn out to be incorrect. This state of affairs may seem curious, in light of the transformation Kuhn and post-Kuhnian philosophy of science is supposed to have worked. Nevertheless, inspection of scientific revolutionary rhetoric suggests that *continuity,* and *progress and truth* have become key rhetorical topoi for delineating the presence of legitimate scientific revolutions and for revealing that these revolutions came about through orderly means, fully consistent with the institution of science itself. Perhaps this is the real source of the resistance to Kuhn and similar philosophers of science: By dismantling the concept of scientific progress, they have taken away some of the most important rhetorical topoi for legitimating scientific change.

A second implication is that the inspection of revolutionary topoi should prompt the revision of ideas about the range of responses available to scientific revolutionaries and the reactions to revolutionary work. Revolutionaries in science confront various rhetorical exigencies and have many different topoi for doing so. Even responses to failed revolutionary rhetoric, though usually conservative, contain leeway for rebuttal. Failed revolutions present opportunities to assail the vanquished while reaffirming the principles of the victors. Perhaps Thomas Lessl's thesis that attempts to challenge existing scientific "orthodoxy" are described as "heresies" should be amended: challenges to scientific orthodoxy are only heresies when they are unsuccessful, because there is an abundance of rhetoric and rhetorical topoi designed to accommodate the successful revolution. One does not become a heretic for disagreeing but for failing to integrate this disagreement into relevant topical replies. Those, like Velikovsky, who are not sufficiently insiders to take advantage of the scientific rhetoric that enables revolution, will receive a moral as well as an intellectual rejection.[40] This is because, in science, it is acceptable to be wrong—even zealously wrong—as long as certain institutional frameworks have not been challenged. When these challenges are perceived by members of a scientific community, then perhaps the rhetoric of heresy or orthodoxy is engaged. Successful revolutionaries may be in fact those who select topoi that both strongly advance their argument yet do not appear to challenge the scientific establishment in unacceptable ways. Thus there is a sense in which the scientist *qua* scientist has a moral commitment to truth.[41] Those whose views—or practices—seem to challenge this commitment may appropriately receive censure within the scientific community. Censure of this type (or the corresponding praise that goes with Nobel prizes, etc.) is a rhetorical manifestation of the value commitments of the scientific community, and points to our final implication, the *epideictic* function in scientific rhetoric.

As illustrated, at moments of revolutionary change, scientists have a rhetorical requirement to maintain community and their own place in it—to speak about replaced theories but not necessarily to speak ill of them. Scientific rhetoric about external influences on research reveals similar epideictic traits. Thus, given the commitments of scientists, it is unlikely that for any audience they would be willing to claim that theories have changed due to fashion, economics, or politics. Even if these things do play a role in scientific revolution, the nature of the entire project would be undermined should scientists claim there is nothing more to it. This is not to ignore the fact that scientists mention important external factors upon their work. However, while external factors are included in discussions of scientific revolutions, the primary reasons given for undertaking scientific projects and for the occurrence of subsequent revolutionary breakthroughs are, in the rhetoric of scientists, scientific. We are not trying to be skeptical, as if to say "Why don't scientists just admit it's all politics." We are contending that regardless of one's philosophical views on Truth or the ontological reality of subatomic particles, scientists require an epideictic rhetoric to preserve the piety of science—so members of an overthrown paradigm might get along with members from another, and so that their work can be seen as the grand, progressive enterprise scientists and the larger culture take it to be.

Notes

1 For an overview of the rhetoric of science literature, see R. Michael Bokeno, "The Rhetorical Understanding of Science: an Explication and Critical Commentary," *Southern Speech Communication Journal* 52 (Spring 1987): 300–21; Bruno Latour, *Science in Action* (Cambridge MA: Harvard University Press, 1987).

2 See, for example, George Sarton, *The Study of the History of Science* (Cambridge MA: Harvard University Press, 1936); see also Karl Popper, *Conjectures and Refutations: The Growth of Scientific Knowledge* (New York: Harper & Row, 1963).

3 Thomas S. Kuhn, *The Structure of Scientific Revolutions* (Chicago: University of Chicago Press, 1970).

4 See Walter R. Carleton, "What is Rhetorical Knowledge? A Response to Farrell—and More—and More," *Quarterly Journal of Speech* 64 (Oct. 1978): 313–28; and "Social Knowledge II," 329–34.

5 See Roderick P. Hart, "Contemporary Scholarship in Public Address," *Western Journal of Speech Communication* 50 (Summer 1986): 283–95.

6 Lawrence J. Prelli, *A Rhetoric of Science: Inventing Scientific Discourse* (Columbia SC: University of South Carolina Press, 1989). For a related topical analysis of scientific rhetoric, see Alan G. Gross, "Discourse on Method: The Rhetorical Analysis of Scientific Texts," *Pre/text* 9 (1988): 169–85.

7 Prelli, 119.

8 Prelli, 258.

9 The original publication, following Prelli, used the word *ethical* as the adjectival form of *ethos*. Because of its ambiguity with the sense of *ethical* from philosophy (namely, to signal, in a largely approbative way an action or belief in accord with the principles of some system of ethics) we have substituted Brinton's (1986) *ethotic*, now widely adopted in argumentation studies, where it denotes "the kind of argument or technique of argument in which ethos is invoked, attended to, or represented in such a way as to lend credibility to or detract credibility from conclusions which are being drawn" (Brinton 1986:246) (RAH).

10 Prelli, 199.

11 Bernard Cohen, *Revolution in Science* (Cambridge MA: Harvard University Press, 1985).

12 Cohen, 28–29.

13 Cohen, 29.

14 Cohen takes into account the values engaged by the process of discovery making. Being revolutionary, he contends, does not always have the stigma it does in politics and religion and often results in many significant social and economic rewards.

15 See Chaim Perelman and L. Olbrechts-Tyteca, *The New Rhetoric: A Treatise on Argumentation*, John Wilkenson and Purcell Weaver, trans. (Notre Dame IN: University of Notre Dame Press, 1971).

16 Cohen, 31.

17 For an examination of the scientific persona, see Paul Newell Campbell, "The *Personae* of Scientific Discourse," this volume [1975], 46–61.

18 Quoted in James Gleick, *Chaos: The Making of a New Science* (New York: Viking, 1987), 247.

19 John Lyne and Henry Howe, " 'Punctuated Equilibria': Rhetorical Dynamics of a Scientific Controversy," in Randy Allen Harris, ed., *Landmark Essays on Rhetoric of Science: Case Studies,* second edition. (London: Routledge, 2018 [1986]). 138

20 Lyne and Howe, 138.

21 Cohen, 31–39.

22 See Alan Gross, "On the Shoulders of Giants: Seventeenth-Century Optics as an Argument Field," in Randy Allen Harris, ed., *Landmark Essays in Rhetoric of Science: Case Studies,* second edition. (London: Routledge, 2018 [1988]). 69

23 Cohen, 35.

24 Quoted in Cohen, 33.

25 See Richard A. Cherwitz and James Hikins, *Knowledge and Communication* (Columbia SC: University of South Carolina Press, 1986), 98.

26 Lyne and Howe, 136.

27 Lyne and Howe, 138.

28 John Angus Campbell, "Scientific Revolutions and the Grammar of Cultures: The Case of Darwin's *Origins,*" *Quarterly Journal of Speech* 72 (Nov. 1986): 352.

29 See Maurice Finocchario, "Logic and Rhetoric in Lavoisier's Sealed Note: Toward a Rhetoric of Science," *Philosophy and Rhetoric* 10 (Spring 1977): 111–22.

30 See Alan Gross, "Analogy and Intersubjectivity: Political Oratory, Scholarly Argument and Scientific Reports," *Quarterly Journal of Speech* 69 (Feb. 1983): 43.

31 Cohen, 31.

32 See Latour, *Science in Action.* Ready-made science is the science of textbooks, where everything is known, coherent and non-fuzzy. Latour also calls this "black-box science," since one does not need to inquire about how it was discovered, how many mistakes were made on the way to it, the alternatives it replaced, etc.

33 See Werner Heisenberg's *Physics and Philosophy: The Revolution in Modern Science* (New York: Harper & Row, 1958).

34 Heisenberg, 97.

35 See Steve Fuller, *Social Epistemology* (Bloomington IN: Indiana University Press, 1989).

36 See Latour, 21–62. Kuhn points out that the choice between Copernican and Ptolemaic systems was not at all the simple matter of simplicity and truth that it was later made out to be. In fact, the two theories were nearly equal in both simplicity and explanatory strength. See *The Copernican Revolution* (Cambridge MA: Harvard University Press, 1957).

37 Cohen, 11.

38 See Latour, 103–78.

39 See Prelli, 205–17; see also S. Michael Halloran and Annette Norris Bradford, "Figures of Speech in the Rhetoric of Science and Technology," in Robert J. Connors, Lisa S. Ede, and Andrea A. Lunsford, eds. *Essays on Classical Rhetoric and Modern Discourse* (Carbondale: Southern Illinois University Press, 1984): 181–92.

40 See Thomas Lessl, "Heresy, Orthodoxy, and the Politics of Science," *Quarterly Journal of Speech* 74 (Feb. 1988): 18–34.

41 For a clear statement of this value-orientation in science, see Willard Van Orman Quine and J. Ullian, *The Web of Belief* (New York: Random House, 1978), chapter 1.

13.
KAIROS IN THE RHETORIC OF SCIENCE
by Carolyn R. Miller

If there is a canonical text in this still-early period of the rhetorical criticism of science, it is the 1953 *Nature* paper in which James D. Watson and Francis H. C. Crick proposed the double-helix structure for DNA. The founding text of molecular biology, it has been much commented on by scientists themselves and has already been subjected to rhetorical analysis no fewer than four times: by Charles Bazerman, Alan G. Gross, S. Michael Halloran, and Lawrence J. Prelli.[1] Bazerman's study is a close textual reading with careful attention to the effects of language; Halloran and Prelli both use the categories of classical rhetoric, such as *stases, topoi,* and *ethos*; and Gross's brief discussion examines the persuasive effects of the basic descriptive strategies used. To varying extents, all four critics also take explicit notice of the historical and scientific background of the paper, recounting for their readers the situational context—the competition with Linus Pauling, the difficult relationship with the London lab of Maurice Wilkins and Rosalind Franklin, the excitement and haste with which the paper itself was prepared.

Understanding the relationship between historical context and particular characteristics of discourse is essential to a specifically rhetorical interpretation of a scientific or any other text. This claim is an argument for the centrality of *kairos* to rhetoric. As the principle of timing or opportunity in rhetoric, *kairos* calls attention to the nature of discourse as event rather than object; it shows us how discourse is related to a historical moment; it alerts us to the constantly changing quality of appropriateness. As James Kinneavy has pointed out, *kairos* was important in both Sophistic and Platonic rhetoric but has been neglected in the contemporary revival of classical rhetoric. In bringing *kairos* to our attention, Kinneavy notes that current rhetoric has a close analogue to it in the concept of "situational context," which is important in many contemporary fields of inquiry; still, he says, "rhetoric desperately needs the notion of *kairos*" ("*Kairos*" 83).

The relevance of *kairos* to the rhetoric of science can be suggested by a further look at Halloran's discussion. He compares Watson and Crick's paper with one published by Oswald Avery and two colleagues in 1944, nine years earlier, a paper that identified DNA as the "active principle" in the genetic transformation of bacteria and is now understood as the first demonstration that DNA is the genetic substance.[2] Avery's paper, however, did not significantly influence researchers in genetics at the time (Wyatt). Halloran attributes this failure in part to its style: dense, painstaking, depersonalized, characterized

Carolyn R. Miller. "*Kairos* in the Rhetoric of Science." In Steven P. Witte, Neil Nakadate, and Roger Cherry, eds. *A Rhetoric of Doing: Essays Honoring James L. Kinneavy.* Carbondale: Southern Illinois University Press, 1992, pp. 310–327.

by the *ethos* of "a cautious skeptic who is forced somewhat unwillingly to certain conclusions" (77). He calls the paper as a whole "rhetorically weak" (82 n. 15).

But there is another way to understand both the reception of Avery's paper and its rhetorical features, an understanding that has to do with *kairos*. Gunther Stent, a molecular biologist and historian of molecular biology, has called Avery's work "premature," noting that "geneticists did not seem to be able to do much with it or build on it. That is, in its day Avery's discovery had virtually no effect on the general discourse of genetics." Stent defines as "premature" a discovery whose "implications cannot be connected by a series of simple logical steps to canonical, or generally accepted [scientific] knowledge" ("Prematurity" 84).[3] The canonical knowledge was that genes had to be proteins (Judson 30, 36) and that DNA was a "stupid molecule" (qtd. in Judson 59), that is, one whose structure was so simple that it couldn't carry genetic information. According to Horace Freeland Judson's history, the resistance to hypotheses other than protein was particularly strong at the Rockefeller Institute, where Avery was working (40).[4] In addition, it was widely assumed that bacteria were a special biological case from which it would be rash to generalize to other forms of life (Wyatt 87). Avery's style of cautious skepticism seems, then, to be appropriate; it would not have been opportune for him to press the implications of his discovery harder (even though, according to Rollin D. Hotchkiss, Avery "was well aware of the implications of DNA transforming agents for genetics and infection" ["Avery" 6]). Similarly, the coy[5] self-assurance of Watson and Crick can be seen as opportune, rather than as sheerly idiosyncratic, as Halloran implies: they had just won a public race, they were outsiders who weren't even supposed to be running, and the initial genetic significance of their structural discovery was indeed obvious to knowledgeable observers and didn't need to be spelled out. In fact, the assimilation of this work was so rapid that we might think of it as being quite the opposite of premature: it was *overdue*.[6] Avery was working at one end of a nine-year "revolution" in the understanding of genetic mechanism, Watson and Crick at the other.[7] The *kairos* in each case was quite different.

This nine-year episode in the history of a scientific specialty illustrates the way that rhetorical situations change in science. Science itself is often seen as a program for change, the supreme engine of progress. Because *kairos* emphasizes change, or the way one time is different from another, it seems to me that it might be a particularly useful critical concept for exploring the rhetoric of science. This essay will make that case first by examining how aspects of *kairos* apply to science and then by developing more fully the ways in which recent thinking about the enterprise of science is consistent with a rhetoric that features *kairos*, using the cases of Avery and of Watson and Crick to illustrate the discussion.

Aspects of *Kairos*

Kairos is one of those ancient Greek terms that doesn't translate simply to contemporary English, and we can find at least two distinct aspects of its meaning, two metaphors embedded in it, a temporal one and a spatial one, both of which are applicable to science. To elucidate these, I'll begin with the contemporary notion of *situational context*, as the structural description of a moment in time. Each rhetorical situation presents a different sort of opportunity, a different *kairos*: in Lloyd Bitzer's widely used terms, each has a different exigence, a different audience, different constraints. Bitzer's objectivism insists that the situation exists independent of the rhetor; thus a *kairos* presents itself at a distinct point in time, manifesting its own requirements and making demands on the rhetor, which the rhetor must discern in order to succeed. But Richard Vatz offers another perspective, suggesting that situations are created by rhetors; thus, by implication, any moment in time has a *kairos*, a unique potential that a rhetor can grasp and make something of, defining (at least in part) the terms for his or her success.

These two perspectives on situation can be clarified by contrasting the two Greek terms for time, *chronos*, the quantitative term, and *kairos*, the qualitative term. In his discussion of these terms as dimensions of historical knowledge, John E. Smith defines *chronos* as duration, measurable time, the background that *kairos* presupposes ("Time, Times" 2). Against that background, *kairos* appears as a critical occasion for decision or action (or revelation, as in the biblical uses of the term), an occasion that is objectively presented or divinely ordained. Kairos, according to Smith, "involves *ordinality* or the conception of a special temporal position, such that what happens or can happen at 'that time' and its significance are wholly dependent on an ordinal place in the sequences and intersections of events" ("Time, Times" 1–2).

Kairos is often translated as "the right time": one waits for a specific moment, and success depends on discerning it. But one might also ask "right for what?" "success at what?" If a particular moment in time is right for some action, the next moment, while wrong for that action, is right for another. In 1953, the time was right—even overdue— for a bold Nobel-winning claim about the structure of DNA; in 1944, the time was right for elaborating the phenomenon of bacterial transformation, but the time was not yet right for identifying DNA as the active substance in heredity.[8] For Avery, the time was right for scientific caution and exploration, not for bold claims. Bitzer would say that *kairoi* are important exigences punctuating *chronos*, special moments of opportunity that present themselves every now and then, like the chance to win a Nobel Prize. Vatz would hold that *every* moment along the continuum of *chronos* has its *kairos*, which can be seized and developed in some way with imagination; Nobel Prizes, after all, aren't the only forms of success in science.[9]

Scott Consigny's resolution of the two perspectives on rhetorical situation emphasizes both the concrete particularities of persons and events that constitute any situation and their "troublesome disorder," which "the rhetor must structure" (178); he emphasizes, that is, both the constraints that give any situation its particular qualities and the activity of the rhetor in turning those qualities into rhetorical resources. Consigny's mediation does not favor either concrete situation or creative rhetor, nor does it subordinate them to a third perspective; rather it requires a dynamic interplay between objective and subjective, between opportunity as discerned and opportunity as defined. *Kairos*, I submit, also permits this interplay by including both objective and subjective dimensions of a moment in time.

Another important aspect of *kairos* derives from a spatial metaphor, rather than from the temporal. An analogous spatial metaphor is at the root of *opportunity*, in the

Latin *porta*, "entrance" or "passage through" (Onians 347–48). The original Greek uses of *kairos*, in both archery and weaving, refer to a "penetrable opening, an aperture" (Onians 345) through which an arrow or a shuttle must pass for success. As an opening, *kairos* becomes for rhetoric a discursive void, much like Bitzer's definition of exigence as "an imperfection marked by urgency … something waiting to be done, a thing which is other than it should be" (6). But we should remember that an opening can be constructed as well as discovered.

In fact, John Swales has claimed that constructing an opening is the basic rhetorical task of the introduction section of scientific research articles. His analysis of the discourse structure of forty-eight introductions from physical, biological, and social science articles (*Aspects*, "Research") led him to postulate what he has since called the "create-a-research-space" model for introductions (Swales and Najjar 178). The model consists of four "rhetorical moves": (1) establishing the field, (2) summarizing previous research, (3) preparing for present research, and (4) introducing the present research. The third move is the crucial one, which is usually made by "indicating a gap in the previous work" and often contains some "negative element." In the fourth move, "the *gap* is turned into the research space for the present article" (179). *Kairos* as spatial opening is thus central to the rhetoric of the scientific article, and again, the work that it does is to obliterate the distinction between objective and subjective: the opening must be one into which the writer can successfully place his or her own conception of what has been done and, at the same time (and place), one that readers will agree exists. *Kairos* as opening is actively constructed by writers and readers and is simultaneously accepted as really existing (or not) in a way that matters for subsequent actions.

Putting together the two metaphoric dimensions of *kairos*, the temporal and the spatial, we might come up with a definition much like that of Eric Charles White, who portrays *kairos* as "a passing instant when an opening appears which must be driven through with force if success is to be achieved" (13). This formulation, like Consigny's, allows for both objective and subjective dimensions, so long as we permit the appearance of the opening and the terms of success themselves to be matters of rhetorical negotiation. Indeed, Consigny claims that it is the capacity of rhetoric as "art" that achieves the suspension of the opposing perspectives. As an art, rhetoric engages the phenomena of concrete experience and itself is engaged by the force of human motivation; it is thus the site of interaction between situation and rhetor. That interaction, as Consigny indicates, is characterized by struggle, because situations are usually not "well-posed problems" (176) but rather "incoherent" and "indeterminate" (177); we can think of rhetors similarly, not as coherent unities but as tangles of inconsistent motives and capacities. The art of rhetoric must be an instrument by which one indeterminacy struggles with another.

This account is reminiscent of that of the earliest rhetoricians, the Sophists, for whom *kairos* was a key concept. The Sophists, too, conceived of situation as an indeterminate confusion in which opposing statements (*dissoi logoi*) could be made, in which a rhetor could attain probable knowledge but never certainty, and in which the art of rhetoric that helped in this process was itself necessarily unsystematic. The judgment of history on this rhetoric has been harsh, in large part because of the ascendance of a philosophical tradition that valorizes universal knowledge over the situated and certainty over the probable—a tradition, in short, that has elevated science precisely because it seems to achieve these ends. Smith, for example, although promoting the value of *kairos*, expresses concern about the "dangers surrounding the engaged response to the particular time and circumstance at hand," dangers that are usually summarized in the label "relativism" ("Time and Qualitative Time" 16).

Both relativism and Sophism have been undergoing revaluation recently, and neither is the simple epithet it once was. The rediscovery of *kairos* is doubtless a part of the general rehabilitation of Sophistic thinking. A rhetoric that involves *kairos*, as Smith suggests, is necessarily relativist; conversely, it may also be the case, as Michael Carter has suggested, that a relativist rhetoric requires *kairos* (105). This is so because *kairos* provides both an opportunity and a requirement for taking action within "the contradictory multiplicity of the real world," as Mario Untersteiner puts it (113). He describes how *kairos* operated in the thought of two of the Sophists. For Protagoras, drawing on the Pythagorean tradition, *kairos* provided a principle of harmony that resolves conflict: "A prerequisite for a sound decision is *kairos*, a harmony of the conflicting elements" (Untersteiner 72 n. 18). For Gorgias, *kairos* provided a moment of decision when conflict is simply superseded by willed choice, by the "imposition of one of the two alternatives" (161). *Kairos* breaks up the conflict and creates something new, which is the conviction that one of the conflicting elements is more powerful: "one has only to fix one's attention—or rather, allow one's attention to be fixed—on one of the two alternatives, and at once, irrationally, action is not only possible but necessary" (160). Untersteiner characterizes action in such circumstances as essentially tragic. White, on the contrary, characterizes it as inventive, even playful: "Understood as a principle of invention, or a prescription concerning the way thought should encounter reality, one might say that *kairos* therefore counsels thought to act always, as it were, on the spur of the moment" (13).

The implications of *kairos* for the rhetoric of science inspire great caution. Can a relativist epistemology account for the demonstrable success of scientific knowledge in predicting and controlling natural phenomena? I won't presume to answer that question here, but I can show that postpositivist thinking about science is remarkably congruent with a rhetoric in which kairos is central. I shall develop this claim below by examining recent discussions of science and scientific discourse for the two metaphoric dimensions of *kairos*: first, the changing quality of moments in time, moments that constitute the contexts for scientific discourse; and second, the creation and use of conceptual space in which scientific work can be taken as a contribution and by which its success is evaluated.

Science as Change Over Time

Traditionally, science is figured for us not merely as an enterprise that changes over time but as one that promotes change in a particular direction. Key terms in the conceptualization of science are *growth* and *progress*. Over time, knowledge about the natural world not only changes but grows, and it not only grows but improves or advances. This model has been a powerful one ever since Bacon, whose *Advancement of Learning*, however, has less to say about where knowledge is going than about what keeps it from going there. In *New Atlantis* Bacon does define the purpose of Salomon's House, the imaginary research institute devoted to the advancement of learning, as "the knowledge of causes, and secret motions of things; and the enlarging of the bounds of human empire, to the effecting of all things possible" (210). Knowledge advances by becoming more complete and more effective: it is not a far step from this to the positivist program of explanation, prediction, and control. And Bacon states explicitly in *Novum Organum* that "knowledge and human power are synonymous" (107).

Although positivist philosophers say remarkably little about the goal and conduct of science over time, being interested exclusively in the structure of scientific knowledge and its justification, they presuppose the Baconian inductionist model of change—simple accretion over time—a model that emphasizes quantitative time, chronos. Carl G. Hempel, for example, says only that science answers the "deep and persistent urge ... to gain ever wider knowledge and ever deeper understanding of the world" (2). And in characterizing science as the paragon of progress, Charles Coulston Gillispie reminds us that "every college freshman knows more physics than Galileo knew" (8). Over time, then, science changes by being able to explain more phenomena more completely and more accurately; accuracy is shown by the ability to predict new phenomena and relationships (or laws). According to Frederick Suppe, "the only aspects of the growth of scientific knowledge relevant to [positivist] philosophy were the inductive justification or confirmation of knowledge claims and the incorporation of older theories into more comprehensive theories via intertheoretic reduction" (704). Science is not conceived diachronically, as a process or enterprise, but synchronically—in Rudolf Carnap's words, as a set of "statements expressing ... regularities as precisely as possible" (3).

To retain its focus on science as a synchronic system of statements, positivist philosophy relied on a distinction between the context of discovery, or science as it happens, and the context of justification, or post facto analysis, declaring the former outside the bounds of philosophy (Suppe 125). "The resulting view of scientific knowledge," according to Suppe, "was a static one which, ignoring the dynamics of scientific progress ... led to a highly distorted portrait of science" (704). This static view is achieved at the explicit and deliberate expense of history and individual experience. *Kairos* can play little part in such a science, since it assumes that all scientific statement-making takes place in a single, austere, generic situation, that of adding a true statement to the set of true statements. One opportunity cannot be much different from another. Statements are not events but accumulated objects.

We now have a number of alternatives to positivist conceptions of science, alternatives that introduce a role for *kairos*. Although Suppe characterizes these alternatives generally as *Weltanschauung* philosophies, there are significant differences among them with respect to their conceptions of scientific change; I will examine here differences among the ideas of Karl Popper, Thomas Kuhn, and Stephen Toulmin. Popper is committed to the "criterion of progress" (217), to the notion that scientific knowledge not only accumulates but improves. "Continued growth," he says, "is essential to the rational and empirical character of scientific knowledge"; however, "it is not the accumulation of observations which I have in mind when I speak of the growth of scientific knowledge, but the repeated overthrow of scientific theories and their replacement by better or more satisfactory ones" (215). He contrasts this conception explicitly with the ideal of science as an axiomatized deductive system, an ideal that we have seen is static. Popper's science is dynamic; it is movement toward the truth: "We simply cannot do without something like this idea of a better or worse approximation to truth," of "better correspondence" between theory and facts (232).

Popper gives us a science in which net change over time is in one direction, toward the truth. However, knowledge changes not by steady accumulation but by advancing and retreating, by a series of what Popper calls conjectures and refutations, by being always prepared to give up a position that is no longer tenable and to hazard another advance, based on new evidence and criticism. Thus, the state of knowledge that a scientist addresses constantly changes: we might say that there are two generic rhetorical situations, described by Popper's title, *Conjectures and Refutations*. In addition, this model puts the scientist-rhetor into the picture, as the one who does the conjecturing and refuting. We thus have science as a changing human activity for which *kairos* can become a description of its state at any given time.

A more complex and more rhetorical version yet is that of Thomas Kuhn, one that makes *kairos* a richer and more central concept for scientific rhetoric. Kuhn begins his *Structure of Scientific Revolutions* by questioning the view of science as a "stockpile" of observations and laws (2).[10] Although he does believe that progress is central to science (161–62), he rejects both the accumulation model of progress and the notion that progress means getting "closer and closer to the truth" (170). Scientific knowledge evolves not "toward-what-we-wish-to-know" but "from-what-we-do-know" (171). Kuhn substitutes an existing human consensus for Popper's objective state of nature and implies that the changing beliefs of a community define the opportunities for discourse. If Popper provides a rhetor for science, Kuhn provides an audience, whose changing group commitments define the *kairos*, the qualitative dimension of each particular moment.

Kuhn's familiar description of how those commitments change gives us a four-phase model of change over time: normal science, accumulation of anomaly, crisis (or proliferation of theories), and revolution (theory-choice), leading to a new period of normal science governed by a new "paradigm," or constellation of intellectual commitments.[11] Normal, puzzle-solving science is cumulative, in the way of Baconian positivism (*Structure* 52); in solving well-defined puzzles with well-understood methods, normal science makes progress both "obvious and assured" (*Structure* 163) because progress is defined by the commitments that permit the work to be done. And a scientific revolution also produces progress, again by definition, since the group that chooses the new paradigm *must* see it as progress. In one view, it would seem that *kairos* has a clear role to play in revolutionary science but not in normal science. In this view, the Bitzerian one, a *kairos* develops with the accumulation of anomaly and, during a crisis, demands resolution. It is thus tempting to describe Watson and Crick as responding to a *kairos*, but not Oswald Avery, who conceived of his work (at least at first) as the normal elaboration of an established phenomenon (Judson 36). This interpretation also justifies the award of the Nobel Prize to Watson and Crick but not to Avery.

But we can also see in Kuhn's model a justification for Vatz's version of *kairos*, a version that would emphasize the different sorts of scientific and rhetorical opportunities available during periods of normal science and anomaly accumulation, as well as crisis and theory-choice. This version emphasizes the creative work that is to be done in puzzle solving or in pursuing the implications of an anomaly. Success for Avery is to be thought of as willingness to challenge the force of an existing paradigm or as tenacity and meticulousness in observing anomalous phenomena, not as boldness in resolving a crisis with a synthesizing hypothesis.

Stephen Toulmin credits Kuhn with "re-emphasizing the close connections" between the intellectual content of a scientific discipline and the individuals and groups who do the work of the discipline and hold the intellectual commitments of which it consists (116). But he faults Kuhn for the ultimate irrationality of his relativism (102) and for historical inaccuracy (103), especially for being unable to account for gradual change. Instead of a revolutionary account, then, Toulmin offers an evolutionary one, which focuses not on discontinuous replacement of one conceptual system by another but on the progressive transformation of "conceptual populations" (122).

Toulmin's theory is Darwinian, taking innovation and selection as a general model of historical explanation (135). Scientific change proceeds by the development of conceptual variants and their selection on the basis of their explanatory utility at the moment. Toulmin also notes that there are two sorts of related change in science, which he calls the disciplinary and the professional. He holds that "any well-structured rational enterprise has two faces. We can think of it as a discipline, comprising a communal tradition of procedures and techniques for dealing with theoretical or practical problems; or we can think of it as a profession, comprising the organized set of institutions, roles, and men whose business it is to apply or improve those procedures and techniques. And these two faces represent alternative views of the same historical changes, as seen from different directions" (142). These two faces can be separated, he says, only at the price of oversimplification (143):

> The historical transformation by which the content of a scientific discipline evolves is intelligible only in terms of the current explanatory ambitions of the relevant professional guild. Yet, in its turn, the character of those ambitions can itself be explained only by using terms drawn from the vocabulary of the discipline. … In this dialectical manner the task of defining the current ideals of a science with all the necessary precision implicitly mobilizes the whole of its historical experience. (154)

Although Toulmin's account seems to resemble Popper's in its use of a twofold model of change (innovation and selection are similar to conjecturing and refuting), looked at another way, it provides no generic phases of change at all. Rather, it emphasizes that each point in scientific time is in important respects unprecedented, that the current state of conceptual commitments, their histories, relevant explanatory goals, and available conceptual variants combine to produce unique rhetorical requirements.

A remark by Hotchkiss reflects this perspective on *kairos*. In justifying Avery's restraint in discussing the genetic implications of his work, Hotchkiss tells us that "it was not in the ethos of that time for an explorer to announce the 'path to the summit' before he had at least tested it" ("Identification" 326). The suggestion here is that a period in scientific time has an *ethos*, just as much, perhaps, as an individual rhetor has; in other words, part of the quality of a time that *kairos* represents is an *ethos*. Halloran's discussion focuses on the concept of *ethos*, specifically on the sharply different dramatizations of the scientist's role offered in the papers by Avery and Watson and Crick. He claims that the confident entrepreneurial voice in the paper by Watson and Crick "contributed to the speed with which their model of DNA gained prominence as a theory" (78) and that, as noted earlier, the painstaking impersonality of Avery's paper contributed to its failure to influence other scientists. But he doesn't offer an explanation as to *why* one of these voices should lead to scientific success and the other to scientific obscurity. Indeed, Hotchkiss implies that in Avery's time, the Watson-Crick *ethos* would have led to rhetorical failure. Whether or not that is true, both Kuhn's and Toulmin's models of change make of *ethos* a phenomenon that acquires its character only against a set of expectations that are part of a historical moment. Thus Watson and Crick's *ethos* cannot be *absolutely* successful, just as Avery's cannot be necessarily a failure.

Kuhn's model, with its rather distinct stages, suggests that *ethos* itself may evolve predictably in concert with the stages of scientific progress. I have intimated as much above in suggesting that Avery's cautious tone was more appropriate for a period when anomalies were just beginning to be noticed against a framework of fairly solid expectations, and that Watson and Crick's confident gentility was more appropriate for a period when an explanatory synthesis was awaited. Kuhn's model also helps put into perspective some other contrasting features of these two papers, which I have not yet mentioned. Avery's paper is twenty-one pages long and lists twenty-nine references; it was received by the *Journal of Experimental Medicine* three months before it was published. Watson and Crick's paper is less than a page and a half long, lists six references, and was sent to *Nature* just three weeks before it was published. We might suspect that the two papers belong to quite different genres, which are defined in part by the rhetorical action achievable within the differing scientific situations. Avery's paper is a report, with exhaustive experimental protocols for both isolating and then identifying the transforming principle by the successive elimination of possibilities,[12] a rhetorical action designed to emphasize the credibility of observational results. Watson and Crick's paper is what has come to be known as a "short communication," a genre designed to provide rapid publication that can stake a proprietary claim on fast-breaking developments. This original paper was followed a month later by a longer one (four pages and five references) detailing the genetic implications of the DNA model (which had been only alluded to in the original paper) and several months later by a much longer discussion (nine pages and twenty-six references), giving experimental and theoretical details. Avery probably could not have gotten a "short communication" published; there simply was no exigence for such a move. And if Watson and Crick had waited to prepare an exhaustive presentation of the reasoning and evidence supporting their model, they might well have gotten scooped and lost their claim to priority. Kuhn's insight, that scientific change consists of the repeated restructuring of commitments, provides a basis for understanding why reasoning carefully from evidence and precedent may be an appropriate rhetorical strategy at one time and staking claims briefly and with minimal evidence appropriate at another. The persuasive task is much different in a time when a paradigm is just beginning to be challenged than it is in a period when everyone believes a new one is needed.

Science and Conceptual Space

John Swales's model of research article introductions provides a particularly vivid illustration of the spatial aspect of *kairos* in science. But the "create-a-research-space" model is also related to other recent lines of thinking about the role of problems in science. In Swales's model, the "gap" or "inadequacy" in previous knowledge becomes the "research space" for current work: a problem or exigence, in other words, becomes an opportunity, a *kairos*. In this sense, *kairos* becomes a fundamental and quite literal *topos* for the development of a scientific argument.

Although Popper ultimately views science as progressing toward the truth, he also characterizes it as "progressing from problems to problems—to problems of ever increasing depth." He explains what scientific problems are:

> Problems crop up especially when we are disappointed in our expectations, or when our theories involve us in difficulties, in contradictions; and these may arise either within a theory, or between two different theories, or as the result of a clash between our theories and our observations. ... [O]bservations may give rise to a problem, especially if they are *unexpected*; that is to say, if they clash with our expectations or theories. ... [E]very worthwhile new theory raises new problems; problems of reconciliation, problems of how to conduct new and previously unthought-of observational tests. And it is mainly through the new problems which it raises that it is fruitful. (222)

Kuhn distinguishes between problems of the sort that Popper describes, conflicts that challenge established knowledge and lead to reformulations of that knowledge, and *puzzles*, conflicts that are expected, even defined by current knowledge. Puzzles, as Kuhn puts it, are challenges not to the theory but to the ingenuity of the scientist (*Essential Tension* 270–71 n. 6). And it is model problem-solutions of this latter sort that constitute the primary pedagogical strategy in the sciences: textbooks "exhibit concrete problem solutions that the profession has come to accept as paradigms, and then they ask the student ... to solve for himself problems very closely related in both method and substance." Education in the sciences, he holds, "remains a dogmatic initiation in a pre-established tradition" (*Essential Tension* 229), yet "the ultimate effect of this tradition-bound work has invariably been to change the tradition. Again and again the continuing attempt to elucidate a currently received tradition has at last produced ... tradition-shattering novelties." This is so because "no other sort of work is nearly so well suited to isolate for continuing and concentrated attention those loci of trouble or causes of crisis upon whose recognition the most fundamental advances in basic sciences depend" (*Essential Tension* 234).

The fundamental commitment to tradition that Kuhn emphasizes is always in basic conflict with "tradition-shattering novelties"; this conflict is the "essential tension" of scientific research that Kuhn describes in an essay of that name, the tension between tradition and innovation, or what he also calls "convergent thinking" and "divergent thinking." The scientific community's intellectual commitment to previously established knowledge and methods, which Kuhn condenses into the term *paradigm*, appears in Swales's model in moves one and two. Novelty is a problem, creates anomaly and thus tension, only against a background of established thinking, a tradition. The difference between novelty and tradition opens up a "problem space," a kairotic opportunity for scientific work.[13]

Several recent studies also use the concept of "tension" to describe the problems that scientists are trying to solve as readers and writers. Greg Myers's essays on two biologists writing grant proposals and journal articles provide detailed examples of the ways that tradition and innovation contend with each other. He finds a tension between authority and humility within the persona of proposal writers and a corresponding tension between the original and the canonical in the writers' efforts to define their claims: the proposed work "must be original to be funded, but must follow earlier work to be science" ("Social Construction" 229). In his study of the same two biologists preparing articles for publication, Myers also finds "a tension inherent in the publication of any scientific article that makes negotiation between the writer and the potential audience essential" ("Texts" 595). In the particular cases he examines, both researchers attempt to define problem spaces that their reviewers do not discern: one biologist was "answering a question that had not been asked" and the other was "giving a new answer to a question that had already been answered" (598). If the claim is the answer to a question, a piece that fits into the research space defined in the introduction, then it is not only the claim that must be negotiated but also the problem space itself.

Thomas Huckin's current study of scientific discourse also describes a "tension" between news value and credibility, or in Kuhn's terms between innovation and tradition. The reading patterns of his informants (six scientists) are "dominated by the search for new information" (5). He identifies this reading goal as "surprise value," taking the term from Kinneavy's discussion of semantic and pragmatic unpredictability in *A Theory of Discourse* (92–95, 134–39). Huckin suggests that the discourse pattern described by Swales helps manage the tension that surprise value creates by both establishing the writer's credibility (his or her familiarity with previous work) and offering something of value, something worth reading for. He finds a corresponding discourse pattern in the discussion section, which consists of the same four moves as in the introduction but in reverse order, so that the writer in effect reasserts his or her "membership in the … community by trading surprise value for community knowledge" (4). But the nature of this trade changes with circumstance. Thus Watson and Crick could afford high surprise value and Avery could not because of how much community knowledge each paper had to offer in exchange: Watson and Crick were well supplied with strong expectations, a situation that permits brevity and allusion, but Avery had only communal knowledge that contradicted his findings.

Avery's work illustrates the tension between tradition and innovation by suggesting the limits of innovation within the scope of any one piece of work. In presenting strong evidence that DNA is the substance causing bacterial transformation, a novel finding that contradicted the weight of scientific expectation, the paper allows itself no space for speculation about genetic mechanism. Indeed, Avery is reluctant even to connect the concepts of transformation and genetic transmission, although they both appear. In the opening paragraphs, transformation is presented as a special case of hereditary change, but after that, the focus is on the unidentified "substance" and the "reaction" it evokes. Any interpretation, Avery says, "must of necessity be purely theoretical" (154). He cites three interpretations sanctioned by earlier work, of which one is genetic (155), and his own characterization of what he has observed is almost a textbook definition of genetics: "the experimentally induced alterations are definitely correlated with the development of a new morphological structure and the consequent acquisition of new antigenic and invasive properties. Equally if not more significant is the fact that these changes are predictable, type-specific, and heritable" (154). But he makes no claim about the nature of genetic material or its relation to transformation. The prior commitment to protein as the only possible candidate for the genetic material was apparently too strong, in Avery's judgment, to challenge directly *before* his observations about transformation had become themselves a part of that tradition. Avery's caution, then, reflects not only a personal quality and not only the *ethos* of the time but also the inertial weight of communal scientific commitment.

The handling of tradition by Watson and Crick is quite different, of course; they seem to ignore it altogether. Their failure even to cite Avery's work has elicited some comment.[14] One can interpret this failure as simple lack of generosity or scientific propriety, which may indeed have been involved. But another explanation has some bearing here, Peter Medawar's contention that it was understandable historical "insensibility." "The history of science," he says, "bores most scientists stiff" because it is already comprehended in the present state of knowledge (3). It is of little concern to a scientist engaged in solving a problem how that problem came to be. That DNA was an important and problematic substance was a presupposition that Watson and Crick adopted without looking back. As Medawar puts it, "A scientist's present thoughts and actions are of necessity shaped by what others have done and thought before him; they are the wavefront of a continuous secular process in which The Past does not have a dignified independent existence" (3). Avery's attention to his predecessors was necessitated by his need to retain credibility for his surprising results; Watson and Crick's negligence was made possible by their assurance that the problem they were working on already had the attention of the relevant scientific world.

Toulmin's discussion of the development of scientific disciplines also relies on the definition of a scientific problem as a "gap." The gap lies between, he says, the explanatory ideals that scientists hold, which are "defined by their current ideals of natural order, or models of complete intelligibility" (152), and their current capacities, that is, the concepts and methods by which they can " 'account for' the relevant features of the natural world" (152). As he puts it, "The gap between these two things, i.e., the difference between explanatory ideals and actualities, is a measure of the explanatory distance this particular science still has to go … to fulfil its current intellectual ambitions" (174). This kind of conceptual gap exists at all times, not just at moments of crisis. Further, the nature of the gap is a matter of social construction, since explanatory ideals and capacities are themselves socially constructed. Thus, like Vatz's creative rhetor, the scientist has some power to define the gap, or *kairos*. Swales's characterization of scientific article introductions as primarily "exercise[s] in public relations" or even "pleas for acceptance" ("Research" 82) is consistent with this version.[15]

In Watson and Crick's *Nature* paper the research space is created by presuming moves one and two in Swales's scheme and dwelling on moves three and four. First (moves one and two), it is assumed that the structure of DNA is both unknown and worth knowing. These assumptions are implicitly attributed to readers, even in the opening sentence: "We wish to suggest a structure for the salt of deoxyribose nucleic acid" (737): only readers who already have reasons for wanting to know the structure need read on. Watson and Crick also refer to the structures already proposed by two other groups of researchers, efforts that confirm their presumptions. Second (move three), Watson and Crick find those proposed structures inadequate: one is characterized as "unsatisfactory" for stereo-chemical reasons and the other is said to be "ill-defined." The "research space" thus created has a fairly specific shape: the structure of DNA must be consistent with established expectations (Bazerman shows how many of these expectations are embedded even in the chemical name of DNA; 28–29), and it must also overcome the inadequacies of the earlier proposals. In move four, however, Watson and Crick go *beyond* the solution required by the gap they have defined by claiming that their structure has "novel features of considerable biological interest" (second sentence, first paragraph) and that it is "radically different" from the other two proposals (first sentence, fourth paragraph). Their claim, then, is not merely to have solved the problem as generally understood but to have posed new problems.

Oswald Avery's 1944 paper is offered as a contribution to a much different research space, one that has nothing to do with DNA. The "gap" is implied rather than shown by negative terms: it is the mere existence of a "striking" "phenomenon" that is well documented and widely acknowledged but not understood (137), the transformation of one strain of *Pneumococcus* into another. In Swales's terms, Avery dwells on moves one and two, nearly omits move three, and in move four, introducing the present research, presents his paper as an attempt to isolate and identify the active principle of transformation: "The present paper is concerned with a more detailed analysis of the phenomenon of transformation of specific types of Pneumococcus. The major interest has centered in attempts to isolate the active principle ... and to identify if possible its chemical nature" (138). The paper is an answer to the basic scientific question "How does this phenomenon happen?" or "What is the substance responsible?" which Hotchkiss claims was Avery's characteristic question ("Avery" 2). But the answer to the question itself creates a much greater research space, one that Avery was not willing to take responsibility for. As Judson comments, "Avery opened a new space in biologists' minds, a space that his conclusions, so carefully hedged, could not at once fill up" (40). The contrast with Watson and Crick, whose claim overflows the research space, is especially stark. But in Avery's case, opening the space in the first place, challenging the tradition, is a prerequisite achievement.

Toulmin describes another kind of "space" that can provide the opportunity for discourse, a social space he calls a "forum." It is only through the operation of these social spaces, Toulmin claims, that "the original ideas of individuals ... get into professional circulation" (209). A forum is where tradition and innovation come together, where convergent and divergent thinking must somehow become accommodated to each other. It is in a forum and for a forum that the public relations work that Swales mentions becomes necessary, as one portrayal of the disciplinary *kairos* is put forward for acceptance, rejection, or modification by the profession (that is, incrementally, by other individual portrayals). One of Avery's problems may have been that he had no real forum: his work was premature also in the sense that there was no field of molecular biology yet. Wyatt outlines the many forums in which Avery's findings would have had some relevance (biochemistry, the phage group, genetics, microbiology, and bacteriology), noting that Avery's citation patterns indicate that "he intended [the paper] to be found, seen and read by those interested in pneumococci, not genetics" (87). If Wyatt is correct, this intention is another indication of Avery's general conservatism in his definition of the *kairos* in which he was working.

A forum is also where, in Toulmin's account, the disciplinary and the professional dimensions of a rational enterprise engage each other, where it becomes clear that the rhetoric of science has an audience and a set of social constraints as well as an intellectual content. The efforts of scientists to seize or construct an opportunity to connect their beliefs about their science to those of other scientists are at the same time efforts to change the social relationships and decisions of the forum, even efforts to advance their own careers (they advance themselves by advancing their claims). *Kairos*, then, can be understood as operating in two arenas: it is both a conceptual or intellectual space, understood as the opportunity provided by explanatory problems, and a social or professional space, understood as the opportunity provided by a forum of interaction. Both of these spaces change constantly and are always subject to appropriation and redefinition. Avery's work should remind us, however, that such changes can meet with great resistance.

Final Remarks

In an interview about a paper that he was starting to write, a scientist demonstrates an understanding of *kairos* that is instructive for rhetoricians:

> This one is very special to me, and it's not just because I want to add another paper to my bibliography ... I think it's going to be a classic study, and so I'm excited about writing it. ... I have thought about it. I sort of held it, oh like a little jewel in the back of my head, uh, it ... gives me a lot of pleasure just to think about it, and the time is right. (Rymer 221)

I have attempted here to show that *kairos* is a concept that can be fruitful for the rhetorical study of scientific discourse. It compresses into one handy Greek term a variety of related but distinguishable rhetorical considerations. Most important, I believe, *kairos* teaches us some things about the complex nature of rhetorical context, or situation. I have argued that *kairos* shows two distinct but related aspects of context: the temporal, which we may consider as the diachronic context, and the spatial, or synchronic context. *Kairos* also holds in productive suspension the apparently objective and subjective dimensions of context, emphasized, respectively, by Bitzer and Vatz. In science these appear as the traditional and innovative dimensions of scientific argument and as the intellectual and social dimensions of scientific work. The examples of Avery and of Watson and Crick show us how important these dimensions are to understanding scientific discourse.

Kairos also illuminates the conceptual frameworks of Kuhn and Toulmin in a new way. Although presented as incompatible views of science, the revolutionary and the evolutionary, these frameworks can also be seen as two perspectives on the same phenomenon. Kuhn's view is more objectivist, emphasizing the public, repeatable patterns of scientific change and the extent to which a scientist's discourse must contend with the weight of tradition, with the "objective" constraints imposed by group commitments. Toulmin's evolutionary view is more subjectivist, emphasizing the unique qualities of moments in scientific time, the unprecedented nature of scientific change, and the extent to which discourse must take responsibility for shaping perceptions of problems. Choosing between these views is not necessary if we see them as complementary aspects of *kairos*.

I do not believe that this Sophistic concept is dangerous to science. Instead, *kairos* emphasizes for us the real work of science—the constant struggle for problems that are testable and interesting, for connections between concepts and observations, for innovation balanced with credibility, for the attention of other scientists, for coherence, for expression, for concurrence of referees and editors, for readership and citation. As Charles Bazerman has shown us in *Shaping Written Knowledge*, science is an *agonistic* enterprise—it is epistemic struggle, the making of opportunities for belief. The nature of that struggle changes over time; each moment on the continuum of scientific effort has its own quality, its own *kairos*. This view makes the achievements of science the more remarkable, and it helps us characterize more precisely, and understand better, the very different achievements of scientists like Oswald Avery and Watson and Crick.

Notes

1 The present essay will make a fifth time. This canonization is a bit unfortunate, since Watson and Crick's paper is such an atypical scientific report.
2 Avery's coauthors were Colin M. MacLeod and Maclyn McCarty. For syntactic convenience, throughout this essay I will treat the authorship of the paper as singular. This treatment is consistent with scientific commentary on the paper, which indicates that it owes most to Avery's scientific thought and intellectual style.
3 Stent's assertion has been contested by several other scientists; see Judson 627–28 (note to p. 57). Delbrück, Luria, and Chargaff (Judson 60, 62, 94) declare themselves to have been decisively influenced by Avery's work, but Luria simultaneously confesses that he and other workers in the area (the "phage group") were "not thinking biochemically, but we were somehow—and probably partly unconsciously—reacting negatively to biochemistry. And

biochemists. As such. As a result, for example, I don't think we attached great importance to whether the gene was protein or nucleic acid" (Judson 62–63). The tone of the comments is a bit testy at times, and one can't help suspecting that the strong reactions to Stent's term are somewhat self-defensive. Stent was in part characterizing his own failure to accord Avery a place in an historical account he had previously published, but he also points to a 1950 symposium on genetics in which Avery's work was referred to only in passing by one person of twenty-six. Hotchkiss ("Identification") and Wyatt continue the debate, Hotchkiss maintaining that Avery's work "was certainly not being ignored" (326) and Wyatt that "neither the geneticists nor the phage group ... appeared to be greatly influenced by the news" from Avery's lab (87).

4 Also, an embarrassing error about the structure of enzymes that had been made in Germany in the 1920s was "on *everybody's* mind," according to one of Avery's colleagues (Judson 40), reinforcing a general conservatism.

5 The word is used by Crick in characterizing how others had described their famous concluding sentence, "It has not escaped our notice ..." (766).

6 In his introduction to the Norton Critical Edition of *The Double Helix*, Stent remarks about Watson and Crick's *Nature* report that "as soon as the contents of that article become known—and they become widely known almost immediately—most biologists interested in the mechanism of heredity quickly realized that the time had come to think about genetics in terms of large molecules that carry hereditary information" (xi). In an interview with Judson, Luria said that Watson and Crick's structure "had embedded in it—one saw it immediately— the properties of the gene" (63).

7 Delbrück has characterized Watson and Crick's work as a "denouement" to the work that Avery had done (Judson 60). In 1972 Wyatt stated that "it is generally accepted that molecular biology began with the paper by Avery, MacLeod and McCarty in 1944" (86). Halloran rejects this dating of the revolution in genetics from Avery's work just because "Avery's work did not have an immediate revolutionary effect" (76). I am urging a larger view of scientific change that focuses on the development of a complex of beliefs rather than the response to any single paper.

8 Which Avery does not do. His conclusion is that DNA is "the fundamental unit of the transforming principle of Pneumococcus Type III" (156).

9 Judson does suggest, in line with Halloran's assessment, that "Avery's public caution stands in awkward contrast to the self-assurance of Watson and Crick nine years later. The cost may have been great. The Nobel Prize selectors had their attention drawn to Avery's work. They waited for the second round of discoveries" (41). And, in a footnote to that passage, he quotes a member of the Nobel Foundation as saying, "That Avery never received the prize is lamentable, and had he not died when he did [1955] I think he would almost certainly have gotten it" (626).

10 Kuhn compares his views to Popper's in "Logic of Discovery or Psychology of Research" (*Essential Tension* 266–92); the major difference is Popper's reluctance to accept the need for psychological and sociological explanations for what he sees as the logical and objective phenomena that constitute the history of science.

11 Interestingly, Kuhn's model of scientific change appears in two accounts of the history of molecular genetics. In *The Coming of the Golden Age* (a book subtitled *A View of the End of Progress*), Stent describes this history as consisting of four periods, classic, romantic, dogmatic, and academic. The book was published in 1969, after Kuhn's first edition, but makes no reference to Kuhn. The four stages do not match Kuhn's precisely, but the general shape of the history he tells is consistent with Kuhn's account. Sociologist Nicholas Mullins documents

"The Development of a Scientific Specialty: The Phage Group and the Origins of Molecular Biology." He uses retrospective papers by the scientists involved to show the social relationships and structures that developed at each of the intellectual stages in the development of the specialty, stages that are based on Kuhn's.

12 Halloran identifies the argumentative strategy as the "method of residues" (76).

13 In their work on novelty in academic writing, Kaufer and Geisler describe the mental work such an opportunity requires of an author as both constructive (acquiring consensual knowledge, or tradition) and contrastive (staking and supporting a claim against the consensus).

14 Wyatt creates a citation map of the field from Avery's precursor to Watson and Crick, showing, among other things, how few of their immediate precursors Watson and Crick did cite (89).

15 Swales himself finds Toulmin's account of problems unsatisfactory because it privileges the weight of communal knowledge over the author's need to advance his or her own research career (Swales and Najjar 177). This is indeed a matter that requires delicate negotiation, as the fate of Avery's work shows, but Toulmin is not attempting to discuss the ways in which individual scientists use explanatory goals or current capacities as rhetorical resources.

Works Cited

Avery, Oswald T., Colin M. MacLeod, and Maclyn McCarty. "Studies on the Chemical Nature of the Substance Inducing Transformation of Pneumococcal Types." *Journal of Experimental Medicine* 79 (1944): 137–57.

Bacon, Francis. *Advancement of Learning, Novum Organum, New Atlantis*. Great Books of the Western World 30. Ed. Robert Maynard Hutchins. Chicago: Encyclopedia Britannica, 1952.

Bazerman, Charles. *Shaping Written Knowledge: The Genre and Activity of the Experimental Activity in Science*. Madison: U of Wisconsin P, 1988.

Bitzer, Lloyd. "The Rhetorical Situation." *Philosophy and Rhetoric* 1 (1968): 1–14.

Carnap, Rudolf, *An Introduction to the Philosophy of Science*. Ed. Martin Gardner. New York: Basic, 1966.

Carter, Michael. "*Stasis* and *Kairos*: Principles of Social Construction in Classical Rhetoric." *Rhetoric Review* 7 (1988): 97–112.

Consigny, Scott. "Rhetoric and Its Situations." *Philosophy and Rhetoric* 7 (1974): 175–86.

Crick, Francis. "The Double Helix: A Personal View." *Nature* 248 (26 Apr. 1974): 766–69. Rpt. Stent, *Double Helix* 137–45.

Gillispie, Charles Coulston. *The Edge of Objectivity: An Essay in the History of Scientific Ideas*. Princeton: Princeton UP, 1960.

Gross, Alan G. *The Rhetoric of Science*. Cambridge: Harvard UP, 1990.

Halloran, S. Michael. "The Birth of Molecular Biology: An Essay in the Rhetorical Criticism of Scientific Discourse." *Landmark Essays in Rhetoric of Science: Case Studies*, second edition. London: Routledge, 2018 [1984]. 78–88

Hempel, Carl G. *Philosophy of Natural Science*. Englewood Cliffs, NJ: Prentice-Hall, 1966.

Hotchkiss, Rollin D. "The Identification of Nucleic Acids as Genetic Determinants." *The Origins of Modern Biochemistry: A Retrospect on Proteins. Annals of the New York Academy of Sciences* 325 (1979): 321–42.

——. "Oswald T. Avery, 1877–1955." *Genetics* 51 (1965): 1–10.

Huckin, Thomas N. "Surprise Value in Scientific Discourse." Conference on College Composition and Communication. Atlanta, Mar. 1987. ERIC ED 284 291, 1987.

Judson, Horace Freeland. *The Eighth Day of Creation: The Makers of the Revolution in Biology.* New York: Simon and Schuster, 1979.

Kaufer, David S., and Cheryl Geisler. "Novelty in Academic Writing." *Written Communication* 6 (1989): 286–311.

Kinneavy, James L. "*Kairos:* A Neglected Concept in Classical Rhetoric." *Rhetoric and Praxis: The Contribution of Classical Rhetoric to Practical Reasoning.* Ed. Jean Dietz Moss. Washington, DC: Catholic U of America P, 1986. 79–105.

———. *A Theory of Discourse: The Aims of Discourse.* Englewood Cliffs, NJ: Prentice-Hall, 1971.

Kuhn, Thomas S. *The Essential Tension: Selected Studies in Scientific Tradition and Change.* Chicago: U of Chicago P, 1977.

———. *The Structure of Scientific Revolutions.* 2d ed. Chicago: U of Chicago P, 1970.

Medawar, Peter B. "Lucky Jim." *New York Review of Books* 28 Mar. 1968: 3–5. Rpt. Stent, *Double Helix* 218–24.

Mullins, Nicholas C. "The Development of a Scientific Specialty: The Phage Group and the Origins of Molecular Biology." *Minerva* 10 (1972): 51–82.

Myers, Greg. "The Social Construction of Two Biologists' Proposals." *Written Communication* 2 (1985): 219–45.

———. "Texts as Knowledge Claims: The Social Construction of Two Biology Articles." *Social Studies of Science* 15 (1985): 593–630.

Onians, Richard Broxton. *The Origins of European Thought about the Body, the Mind, the Soul, the World, Time, and Fate.* 1951. New York: Arno, 1973.

Popper, Karl R. *Conjectures and Refutations: The Growth of Scientific Knowledge.* New York: Basic, 1962.

Prelli, Lawrence J. *A Rhetoric of Science: Inventing Scientific Discourse.* Columbia: U of South Carolina P, 1989.

Rymer, Jone. "Scientific Composing Processes: How Eminent Scientists Write Journal Articles." *Writing in Academic Disciplines.* Ed. David A. Jolliffe. Vol. 2 of *Advances in Writing Research.* Norwood, NJ: Ablex, 1988. 211–50.

Smith, John E. "Time and Qualitative Time." *Review of Metaphysics* 40 (1986): 3–16.

———. "Time, Times, and the 'Right Time': *Chronos* and *Kairos.*" *Monist* 53 (1969): 1–13.

Stent, Gunther S. *The Coming of the Golden Age: A View of the End of Progress.* Garden City, NY: Natural History Press, 1969.

———. "Prematurity and Uniqueness in Scientific Discovery." *Scientific American* 227 (Dec. 1972): 84–93.

———, ed. *The Double Helix: A Personal Account of the Discovery of the Structure of DNA.* By James D. Watson. New York: Norton, 1980.

Suppe, Frederick. *The Structure of Scientific Theories.* 2d ed. Urbana: U of Illinois P, 1977.

Swales, John. *Aspects of Article Introductions.* Birmingham: Language Studies Unit, University of Aston in Birmingham, 1981.

———. "Research into the Structure of Introductions to Journal Articles and Its Application to the Teaching of Academic Writing." *Common Ground: Shared Interests in ESP and Communication Studies.* Ed. Ray Williams, John Swales, and John Kirkman. New York: Pergamon, 1984. 77–86.

Swales, John, and Hazen Najjar. "The Writing of Research Article Introductions." *Written Communication* 4 (1987): 175–91.

Toulmin, Stephen. *Human Understanding: The Collective Use and Evolution of Concepts.* Princeton: Princeton UP, 1972.

Untersteiner, Mario. *The Sophists.* Trans. Kathleen Freeman. Oxford: Blackwell, 1954.

Vatz, Richard E. "The Myth of the Rhetorical Situation." *Philosophy and Rhetoric* 6 (1973): 154–61.

Watson, J. D., and F. H. C. Crick. "A Structure for Deoxyribose Nucleic Acid." *Nature* 171 (25 Apr. 1953): 737–38. Rpt. Stent, *Double Helix* 237–41.

White, Eric Charles. *Kaironomia: On the Will-to-Invent.* Ithaca: Cornell UP, 1987.

Wyatt, H. V. "When Does Information Become Knowledge?" *Nature* 235 (14 Jan. 1972): 86–89.

14.
FIGURES OF ARGUMENT
by Jeanne Fahnestock

In 1865 the chemist August Kekule published an article in French and German introducing the structure of benzene as a particular arrangement of carbon atoms, an arrangement that, many years later, Kekule claimed to have visualized while dozing on and off in his easy chair before a fire. But when Kekule made a case for this structure in the *Bulletin de la Société Chimique de France* and the *Annalen der Chemie*, he did not offer his daydream as support for his claim. But neither did he offer detailed experimental data and a chain of inferences leading up to his insight. Instead, he argued by gesturing to the obviousness of his claims and the ease of reaching them, and by using the semantic resources of a particular rhetorical device to make his claims plausible. Thus the actual text of Kekule's argument suggests a different version of his methods and perhaps even of his original inventive resources. And it provides evidence for how reasoning and composing practices characterized in the rhetorical tradition can appear in the sciences, though they are not limited to scientific arguments.

Kekule introduces his views as based on a hypothesis that he says, constructing his audience, almost all chemists admit: the atomicité of elements, their ability to behave like discrete units. In *The Architecture of Matter*, Toulmin and Goodfield point out that Kekule never actually committed himself to more than a descriptive notion of the atom, though it is difficult to keep that reservation in mind while reading his text (264–265).

Calling the status of his argument "theorizing," Kekule expresses the hope that he will "see this theory rapidly confirmed or refuted by numerous experiments [experiences]" (Kekule, 1865,98)[1] He therefore offers only a plausible extrapolation, beginning from the assumption that substances with at least six carbon atoms must have something in common, some type of core. In accounting for this core, he assures his readers that his hypothesis is so simple, it will be unnecessary to insist on it at length. Proposing that carbon atoms can bind to each other, Kekule reaffirms, from his own earlier work, that this binding can produce chains when one carbon joins with either one or two neighbors. Concentrating on chains of just six atoms, he then proposes the existence of two kinds: *une chaine ouverte* and *une chaine fermée* (Kekule, 1865, 100). The former does not bind to itself; the latter does, closing into what could be called a circle, though the words *circle* or *ring* never appear in the article nor does any visualization of the benzene ring that is now so common. An open chain of six carbon atoms would contain eight "non-saturated" affinity units, he claims, and a closed chain six, leading to differences in

Jeanne Fahnestock. "Figures of Argument (OSSA 2005 Keynote Address)." *Informal Logic*, Volume 24, Number 2, 2004, pp. 115–135.

the compounds that could be formed.[2] In short, Kekule's plausible proposal in this paper, called one of the most successful predictions ever made in science, has at its core a pair of semantic opposites, open and closed, deployed in claims with contrasted corresponding properties.

If Kekule's paper argues for a plausible pair of opposites that awaits confirmation, another famous argument delivered in the same year is characterized by its meticulous presentation of experimental results: namely Gregor Mendel's paper on plant hybridization. Yet this argument too is driven by oppositions in both its data presentation and its reasoning. Deceptively chronological, Mendel's single scientific publication offers a statistical accounting of seven characters of pea plants followed through several generations and interpreted in a way to reveal the laws of genetic combination that now go by his name. However the hallmark of Mendel's work is not his careful empiricism; his many predecessors in plant hybridization did far more breeding experiments than he did. It is rather his imposition of antitheses in both constructing his categories of observation and in interpreting his results. Always somewhat confusing, even suspicious to later generations, was Mendel's luck or cunning in selecting traits of pea plants that bred true and were not the products of linked genes or mosaic expression. But Mendel chose traits that he could, as he explains, separate easily; or, to put this constraint another way, he chose traits that he could describe separately: yellow versus green, wrinkled versus smooth, tall versus short, a selection driven in part by the available terms (Mendel, 1866, 7–8). Mendel's conceptual leap was then his imposition of the terms *dominant* and *recessive* on these contrasted traits, defined by antitheses as follows: a dominant trait is the only one that appears in the first generation of hybrids from a cross and a recessive trait is the one that reappears in the first generation from the hybrids (Mendel, 1866, 10–11).[3] The hybridizer cannot know ahead of time which is which. Having been a student of mathematics and physics at the University of Vienna, Mendel knew how to impose the combinatorial principles for two items randomly assorted in what in retrospect could be called a coin toss with genes.

Less well remembered about Mendel's work is that he named a second order of antitheses, two contrasted types of dominants, parental and hybrid (Stamm-Merkmal and Hybriden Merkmal, p 15). When he crossed plants that were dominant by phenotype, some of course yielded, and would continue to yield, only offspring expressing the dominant trait, while others yielded offspring showing the same statistical variation in traits as the first generation from the hybrids (3/4 dominant, ¼ recessive). This difference would have been striking for Mendel given that he was looking at pea shape and color in pods on a single plant as expressions of traits in a subsequent generation, so he could, again invoking opposites, distinguish between plants that had phenotypically different peas in their pods, and those that did not. It was the imposition of this second antithesis that allowed Mendel to make predictions on the outcome of future crosses, and so claim that he had discovered the "laws" of hybridization. It is to this day doubtful that Mendel really had a conception of unitary material genes in gametes, but then he really did not need such a conception to manipulate the patterns of opposites that he had established.

Moving backward in time almost eighty years before Kekule and Mendel, Lavoisier delivered to the *Academie des Sciences* his only paper in geology, but it was one which made as stimulating a contribution as his work in chemistry. Lavoisier had been part of a project to map the mineralogical resources of France, and when he finally reported on this work, he began his paper by first reminding his audience that, given the evidence of marine bodies of all types in these strata, it was impossible to doubt that the sea had once covered a great part of the globe. But he became convinced of the following distinctions in his observations. His actual wording deserves quotation at some length, first, because it demonstrates the combination of providing the argument and gesturing toward it as in Kekule, second, because of the interpenetration of the language of description and that of the subsequent claim, as in Mendel, and, finally, simply because Lavoisier is such an elegant writer.

> But if after the first view one follows with a more profound examination the arrangement of the banks and the materials which compose them, one is astonished to see there at one time all that characterizes order and tranquility, and at the same time all that announces disorder and movement. Here one finds a mass of shells thin and fragile; the majority are neither worn down nor abraded; they are precisely in the state in which the animal abandoned them in losing life; all those of an elongated figure are bedded horizontally; almost all are in the situation determined by the position of their center of gravity: all the circumstances which surround them suggest a profound tranquility and, if not an absolute repose, at least of gentle movements depending on their will.
>
> Some feet above or below the place this observation was made presents a spectacle entirely opposite: One no longer sees any trace of beings living or animated; one finds, in that place rounded pebbles of which the angles have been abraded by a rapid movement continued for a long time; it is the image [tableau] of a sea in anger, which comes to break against the shore, and which rolls with a crash the considerable mass of the shingle. How to reconcile these observations so opposite? How do effects so different appear from the same cause? How has the movement which has abraded quartz, rock crystal, the hardest stones, which has rounded their angles, respected light and fragile shells? (translated from Lavoisier, 1789, 186–187)[4]

This passage is a tour de force of rhetorical stylistics. It hinges on an antithesis which is then beautifully amplified, leading to a paradox expressed in repeated rhetorical questions.

It is, however, unlikely that Lavoisier's field observations were in fact presented to him in such stark contrast. No accusation is intended here that he falsified his perceptions, but when he expressed them, the structures available to him, no doubt from his considerable rhetorical training, led him to frame his observations in etched oppositions, order versus disorder, tranquility versus movement. (The term *tranquillité* has its sense as stillness emphasized when it is paired against movement, so a better English translation, sensitive to the underlying figure, would probably be *stillness versus movement*). Lavoisier claims that his opposed observations, "Ce contraste de tranquillité et de mouvement, d'arrangement et de désordre, de séparation et de mélange" (187) did not seem explicable at first until by dint of seeing and re-seeing, it seemed possible to explain in "une manière naturelle et simple," the "principle laws which nature has followed in the arrangement of horizontal beds" (187–188).

There must exist in the mineral realm two sorts of beds very distinct, the one formed in the full sea and at a great depth, and that I will name in imitation of M.Rouelle, pelagian beds, the other formed at the shore which I will name littoral beds; that these two species of beds must have distinctive characters which do not permit them to be confounded, that the first must present a mass of calcareous materials, of animal debris, of shells, of marine bodies accumulated slowly and peaceably, during an immense succession of years and centuries, that the other, on the contrary, must present above all image of movement, destruction and tumult (translated from Lavoisier, 1789, 189–190)[5]

Lavoisier's conclusion is the outcome of antithetical reasoning and phrasing; the two are indistinguishable. In Toulmin's terms, both data and claim have the same verbal signature. The passage presenting the two types of beds, pelagian and littoral, deep sea versus shore, has the force of a characterization by definition based on the description of their distinctive features. The plausibility of Lavoisier's argument, his characterization of it as "natural and simple," depends on the audience's willingness to accept the occurrence of opposites as plausible so that, in a very literal sense from Aristotle's terms expressing the first of the twenty-eight lines of argument in the *Rhetoric*, opposite lies with opposite (Aristotle, 1991, 241; Freese, 1926, 296).

Another century before Lavoisier, in the early 1600s, William Harvey used the same figural logic to shape his observations, experiments and premises in arguments for the circulation of the blood, overturning the long-held belief that the body produced and absorbed its blood in a one-way flow. Again, the story is sometimes told that Harvey's breakthrough was shaped by his metaphorical insight that the heart is a pump, though this claim need not be labeled a metaphor to begin with because Harvey could have meant, literally, the heart *is* a pump. But such an image, metaphor or identification never appears in his published argument, *De Motu Cordis*. (It does appear on a separate page inserted in lecture notes, but the date of this notation is problematic [Whitteridge, 1971, 169–170].) What appears instead in Harvey's text is a very rich use of other figures of speech to express his arguments. A device called the *antimetabole* is critical in Harvey's expressed reasoning, but in subsidiary arguments Harvey uses antitheses supported in part by observations from his own dissections and those of his recent predecessors among the anatomists. Because of the distinctive syntactic and semantic profile of the antithesis, it is possible to use parallel phrasing and one set of opposing terms to predispose an audience toward seeing the other pair of terms in the phrases as opposites. In Harvey's case, the two terms being separated and pushed apart are "veins" and "arteries," terms which were sometimes used interchangeably by earlier anatomists. Arguing against traditional learning, here is how Harvey emphatically claimed their difference.

Though vein and artery were not unreasonably both styled veins (as Galen noted) by the ancients, one of them, namely the artery, is a vessel which carries blood from the heart to the component parts of the body, while the other is a vessel which carries blood from those component parts back to the heart.) The one is a channel from, the other a channel to, the heart. The latter channel contains cruder, worn-out blood that has been returned unfit for nutrition; the former contains mature, perfected, nutritive blood (Harvey, 1990, 47; Harvey, 1628, 42).[6]

The antitheses in this passage that encourage the reader to accept the opposed or at least differentiated nature of the veins and arteries are based on the reciprocal relation of the heart versus the rest of the body, on motions to and from the heart, and on the opposite nature of the blood they carry, i.e. crude versus perfect, worn-out versus mature, non-nutritive versus nutritive. While Harvey was on sound anatomical ground with his arguments for the direction of flow, the veins having semilunar valves permitting only one-way movement, he was carried by the figure into less certain territory with his claims about the nature of the blood.

Harvey's arguments were written in Latin, and his antitheses are expressed more crisply in that language. Examples such as Harvey's can be multiplied in early modern texts from natural philosophy, but they persist even today in arguments across the sciences.

The Antithesis in Contemporary Scientific Arguments

The expectation that nature offers opposite entities with opposite properties has proved surprisingly durable and fruitful in scientific invention and in the subsequent arguing for that invention in texts. Take a recent example from molecular biology. In the field of gene regulation scientists had established that the DNA inside a cell's nucleus is wrapped around histones and they identified certain enzymes that could add methyl groups to these histones, contributing to the regulation of the encircling genes. But they also predicted that there had to be "enzymes that did the opposite" (Couzin, 2004, 2171); Why there would be this expectation is of course rooted in precedents in biological systems predicting a reversible mechanism in this case; the argument from precedents here is field specific. But there is also that same presumption of the likelihood of opposites tapped by Kekule, Mendel, Lavoisier and Harvey. For decades, molecular biologists had a name in waiting, histone demethylase, for an enzyme that eluded discovery until last year.

The ubiquity of such paired opposites as the core of scientific arguments is of course thanks to the importance of what Mill called the method of difference in research design (Mill, 1874, 280–281). A sampling of articles from one volume of *Science* in 2001 reveals research reports on predator naïve versus predator experienced moose, on contrasted molecular switches at the center versus the membrane periphery of cells, on bosons that clump together and fermions that avoid each other, and on Antarctic temperatures that show a long-term pattern of increasing while Greenland temperatures show a simultaneous pattern of decreasing (Fahnestock, 2004, 25–27). Another addition to this list, from the social sciences, is the case made by researchers at the University of Alberta reported in the *Science Times* that parents observed in supermarkets prefer their pretty children to their ugly children (Bakalar, 2005, F7). Here perhaps the presumption of opposites has run amok with research that is "pretty ugly," but this example leads to another point. The cases offered so far of scientific arguments expressed in antitheses are cherry-picked successes. But nature need not cooperate with the use of antitheses as an invention device any more than an audience has to be captivated by it. There have probably been more failed than successful scientific arguments based on antitheses – phlogisticated versus dephlogisticated air, continuous versus discontinuous evolution, and others long forgotten. The antithesis is a linguistic prompt, an invention device for a potential line of argument. No more, and no less.

The recent examples of scientific arguments hinging on antithesis, and the unrolling lineage behind them – Kekule, Mendel, Lavoisier, Harvey – can be linked to the tradition of argument invention and expression as it was revived and revised in the fifteenth and sixteenth centuries. In what follows, the historical roots for these figure-based arguments in natural philosophy are traced to the new, rhetorically-inflected dialectical treatises of the 1500s. The interanimation of rhetoric and dialectic in this period has received considerable attention from historians (e.g., Gilbert, 1960; Howell, 1961; Vasoli, 1968; Jardine, 1974; Kristeller, 1979; Mack, 1993) and it is the subject of a recent collection of essays edited by Van Eemeren and Houtlosser (2002). An historical argument about sources does not, however, entirely explain the persistence of these forms; their enduring appeal can instead be traced to the more general role of iconicity in persuasiveness, as illustrated by arguments epitomized by parallelism, the root of the figures antithesis and antimetabole. While a cognitive rationale for the persuasiveness of these devices is possible, such a rationale would not be possible for all the stylistic devices marked in the rhetorical tradition. An overview of the types of figures, using the categories of contemporary linguistics, suggests that they re-inscribe in isolated devices the variables of situated argument. Ignored today, the figures were prominent in early works of natural philosophy, thanks primarily to the very different attitude toward language in the early modern period which justified a stylistic approach to argument that we tend to find problematic.

Early Modern Dialectic

The invention and expression of lines of argument like the antithesis was the deliberate subject matter of the early modern arts curriculum. The revised dialectic that along with grammar and rhetoric took its place in the trivium under the humanist educational reforms of the sixteenth century is usually discounted in the history of logic. In actually trying to defend this period, E.J. Ashworth conceded that "historians of logic have regarded the early modern period with unremitting gloom," seeing the fifteenth and sixteenth centuries as a "period of unchecked regression, during which [logic] became an insignificant preparatory study, diluted with extra-logical elements... ." (Ashworth, 1968, 179).

But this sixteenth-century humanists' dialectic, filled with "extra-logical" elements, was the system taught to many of the first generation of natural philosophers, to Harvey at Cambridge, to Kepler at Tübingen, to Gilbert, to Huygens, to Hooke, to Newton. Key texts in this tradition are Rudolph Agricola's *De Inventione Dialectica*, written in 1479 but first published in 1515 (Cogan, 1984, 163), and Philip Melanchthon's *Erotemata Dialectices*, which went through three expanding versions in 1521, 1527 and 1547 (Melanchthon, 1963a, 509–510; the earlier editions had different titles). Their "degenerate" version of dialectic persisted through the seventeenth century with many imitators including, for example, Robert Sanderson's *Logicae Artis Compendium*, first published in

1615 and in print well into the eighteenth century (Howell, 1961, 299–307). It was the third edition of Sanderson that Newton's uncle gave him when the family decided to send him to Cambridge and that Newton reportedly read during the summer before he matriculated. It was the first book he attended lectures on and discussed with his tutor, though he had already mastered it (Brewster, 1965, 21).

Early modern dialectic differs somewhat from its predecessors because its authors redefined its goals and changed its emphases. For Agricola and Melanchthon, dialectic is not primarily an art of disputation or questioning. It is a general art of teaching, and to that end it provides guidelines for analyzing and inventing convincing arguments (McNally, 1967, 393–395). Furthermore, it concerns all subjects humans are to be taught. For Melanchthon, who quickly incorporated insights from Vesalius and Copernicus into the Wittenberg curriculum (Kusukawa, 1995, 114–120; 170–173), the things to be taught included not only "the recognition of God, the perception and duties of the virtues," but also "the consideration of nature" (Melanchthon, 1963a, 513–514). This reconceived dialectic takes on then the first of the three Ciceronian offices of the orator — teaching, and its goal is to produce extended discourse, not short answers in an exchange. The texts that could be produced according to the revised art included texts in natural philosophy, of which Melanchthon himself wrote two (Kusukawa, 1995, 92–95; 145–148).

As a general art of teaching, including advice on how to construct good arguments on any subject, early modern dialectic emphasized invention. That emphasis is especially obvious in Agricola's textbook which dispenses with the traditional parts of scholastic logic and features the topics as they were presented in rhetoric textbooks. Rhetoric's inventional schema, however, were always particular to arguments in the three essentially civic speech genres, deliberative, forensic and epideictic. But dialectical treatises were completely general in their suggestions of the subject matter of arguments. The humanist treatises in particular display an indifference to subject matter, mixing examples we would now separate between ethics and the natural sciences. So, for example, to illustrate the distinction between simple and complex questions, Melanchthon offers the following: "Whether a heavenly object is a comet or a star" and "whether a Christian can become a soldier" (Melanchthon, 1963a, 517; these are complex questions because they involve two terms rather than one such as "What is virtue?" and they both concern "hot" issues at the time). The bottom line is a new integration in these treatises: the inventional emphasis of rhetoric is combined with the subject generality of dialectic. The natural philosophers of the sixteenth and seventeenth centuries, exposed to the application of the topics to issues in natural philosophy, did not need a separate theory of argumentation to handle subjects in physics or astronomy since the texts in which they studied the invention of probable argument moved seamlessly from one field to another.

Melanchthon's texts also reveal another dimension of the mix between rhetoric and dialectic at the time because he wrote treatises for both arts, each taken through several versions and each version through several editions, and he explicitly connected the two claiming, "So great is the resemblance between Dialectics and Rhetoric that scarcely any distinction can be observed between them" (La Fontaine, 1968, 82). And in the section of the final version of his *Rhetoric* devoted to the figures of speech, where an emphasis on argument might be least expected, he adds, "The zealous reader will observe that all the figures, especially those that enhance a speech, have their origin in the *places of dialectic*" (La Fontaine, 1968, 263; "locis dialecticis" is incorrectly translated "dialectical expressions" by La Fontaine). In his strongest claim for the connection, Melanchthon goes on to observe that the same expressions are at one and the same time adornment and argument (264). Melanchthon delivered on this declaration by organizing the figures in the third edition of his rhetoric according to the topics (Melanchthon, 1963b, 479–480; 482–483ff).

Overall, the humanist's attention to language is the connecting matrix across the three related arts of the trivium. In their pedagogical alembic, the arts of grammar, rhetoric and dialectic overlapped considerably, so that the exercises in reading and parsing under the grammarian were reinforced by the compositional and analytical exercises under the teachers of rhetoric and dialectic. Students would continually encounter the same forms. They would mark a figure like antithesis in their reading, they would practice it as a syntactic scheme in their composing, and they would learn that predicating opposites was a way to distinguish species (the goal of the arguments by Kekule, Mendel, Lavoisier and Harvey). And it is important to remember that the language medium for all this tuition was Latin, a second language for everyone in the early modern period, whose study usually began at the age of seven. The role of stylistic formalism in a laboriously acquired and primarily written second language is easy to imagine (see Costello, 1958, 180).

Perceptual Rationale for the Appeal of the Figures

It is hardly surprising then that early modern natural philosophy texts feature figured arguments. But the figures originated in classical treatments and survive past any influence of rhetorical training. So some account seems necessary in terms of perception and cognition to explain the persistence of these forms. Stephen Toulmin has again set the direction of this line of inquiry in the discussion of language universals that concludes *Human Understanding* (1972). Are we dealing with linguistic universals here, with concepts whose slow pace of change looks like stasis? And again following the direction of Toulmin's inquiry, can the effect of the figures be explained in terms of what is known, albeit fragmentary, about language processing from neuroscience?

One explanation for the effectiveness of the figures is offered briefly in Christopher Tindale's *Rhetorical Argumentation* (2004) where he describes them as either constituting or emphasizing arguments (81–82), and suggests that, for a figure like antimetabole, the audience is persuasively involved because of their "experiencing the rhythm of the discourse," and 'seeing' the reversal (83). Tindale concludes that there is "something distinct about the arguments drawn from the figures" (86), that they engage the audience "at a quite deep, often emotional level, before reason moves in as an organizing force" (86).

Though a dissociation of these devices from reasoning may be unnecessary, nevertheless locating the effect of at least some of the figures in the "rhythm," that is in the sound dimension of prose, provides a starting point for investigating their enduring persuasiveness. What are the sources of this rhythm? The antimetabole and the antithesis, for example, are built from parallel cola or clauses; the sound similarities between the cola would indeed constitute a perceivable pattern and this pattern, along with certain semantic features, can have a certain force and memorability.[7]

For a perceptual rationale behind this memorability, we can find a starting point in the school of Gestalt psychology, whose "laws" have been absorbed as a set of commonplaces in current theories of perception: the laws of closure, similarity, proximity, symmetry, continuity, and finally, the law of prägnanz according to which human perception is seen as governed, overall, by an innate drive to make visual experiences regular, orderly, simple, and symmetrical (Boeree, 2000). Of course in the case of figures, the input is aural, not visual. But the point holds: humans prefer patterns in perceptions and work to complete them, and perhaps, from this perspective, reasoning and pattern completion are not all that far apart.

How would such a propensity for pattern detection and completion operate at the level of sentences or propositions? To explore how patterns depending on similar units or sounds are a feature of some of the figures of speech, we can go back to Aristotle, Book III of the *Rhetoric*, where, in his discussion of effective prose style, he first drew attention to *parisosis* or what we would call *parallelism* between cola or clauses (243).

Two consecutive clauses can be parallel in several ways: First they can be roughly the same length in number of syllables or have the same pattern of stressed syllables; hence they can present sound similarities to the ear. Such sound similarities are not trivial since there is substantial evidence from neurolinguistics, based on imaging and studies of brain damaged patients, that the prosodic contour of a phrase, which carries its affective dimension, is decoded separately in the brain from the syntax and semantics (Fahnestock, 2005, 164–68). Hence the prosodic contour of an utterance is a distinct feature. Rhetorical manuals marked out this kind of sound parallelism as *isocolon*, and they advised that in prose, as opposed to poetry, the adjacent cola (clauses) need only be approximately equal.

Next, two consecutive sentences can be parallel not in length but by virtue of having the same grammatical structure, that is, the same placement of subject, verb, object, etc., in relation to modifying phrases and dependent clauses. And within those same grammatical structures, the words used can reflect patterns of organization in the lexicon; that is, the chosen terms can come from the same semantic field or be paired as synonyms or matched as opposites. The sum of all these sources of parallelism would be clauses featuring exact repetition, since precisely repeated phrases necessarily have the same syllable length, grammatical form, and semantic features. Rhetorical manuals paid a great deal of attention to patterns of repetition, whether in the beginnings or endings or within or between clauses.

Taken in pairs, parallel clauses with the same grammatical structure and with repetition can produce an impression of coordination, leveling or similarity between statements. To begin with the obvious, they can effectively express a comparison, though of course two parallel clauses are by no means the only way to express a comparison. A comparison can be sandwiched into a single sentence or developed across pages of text.

But two adjacent clauses featuring the constraints just mentioned can be taken to epitomize a comparison (Fahnestock, 1999, 23–24). A verbal epitome is the most succinct and yet complete expression of a line of argument, as in the following fabricated example:

> Clinton sent troops to intervene in Haiti
> Reagan sent troops to intervene in Grenada.

These two sentences repeat all but their first and last words, and the words not repeated come from the same semantic categories: US presidents and Caribbean Islands. Whatever the factual nuances avoided here, the parallelism makes these statements comparable if not equal. One could back away from the repetition but retain the same grammatical structure and still preserve the sense of comparability: *Reagan sent troops to intervene in Grenada and Clinton used the military to control the Haitian situation.* Again, such parallelism epitomizes likeness. A real example occurs in Clinton's speech praising the Marines who defended their comrades in Mogadishu: "That's the kind of soldiers they are. That's the kind of people we are" (Clinton, 1993).

In a theory of figuration that is part of a theory of argument, figures are defined as apt or epitomizing iconic forms for the arguments they express (on iconicity see the excellent article by Leff and Sachs, 1990). Nothing of course stops us from going beyond two and piling up more parallel clauses as in the following passage from the second chapter of John Stuart Mill's *On Liberty*.

> History teems with instances of truth put down by persecution. If not suppressed forever, it may be thrown back for centuries. To speak only of religious opinions: the Reformation broke out at least twenty times before Luther, and was put down. Arnold of Brescia was put down. Fra Dolcino was put down. Savonarola was put down. The Albigeois were put down. The Vaudois were put down. The Lollards were put down. The Hussites were put down. Even after the era of Luther, wherever persecution was persisted in, it was successful (27).

Here, one could say that Mill has constructed a comparison among seven items. But of course his persuasive purpose in this passage is to offer a summation supported by a series of examples, and these individual instances have been constructed into examples on the basis of parallel predication. So here is the next obvious use of parallelism (with in this case a heavy dose of epistrophe, i.e. repeated endings): parallelism, especially with repetition, is the epitomizing or iconic form for example sets that support a summation or generalization.

Appearing in a text published in England in 1859, Mill's passage builds on the assumptions, beliefs and even anxieties of its contemporary audience. But Mill's argument is also crafted stylistically for effectiveness with any reader of English. The passage uses formal or figural persuasiveness to induce adherence by pattern completion. To support his general claim about the usual success of persecution, each of the instances Mill cites must be immediately accepted as an uncomplicated particular case supporting the overall point. Accepting the examples as support is encouraged in the first place by parallelism in their presentation. Seven sentences share the same grammatical structure and vary tightly between six to eight syllables, establishing and sustaining a relentless rhythm. By at least the second example, the repetition has set up a pattern and hence an expectation in the reader that the pattern will be continued, as gestalt psychologists noticed.

Furthermore, it is necessary to Mill's argument here that each instance of persecution be roughly equivalent to the others. As Perelman and Olbrechts-Tyteca (1969) point out, when arguers cite supporting examples for a generalization, they tend to reduce or skeletalize the specific instances so that only their common feature has rhetorical presence (358). What would detract from Mill's point here is any sophisticated second thinking about the individual examples that began to make distinctions among them – whether, for instance, the cases of Savanarola and the Albigensians were really equivalent. Instead, the homogeneity of the individual cases is constructed by the repetition so that they can be expressed as equal items in a minimal listing. The equivalence in the examples is also achieved by Mill's use of the passive construction (*were/ was put down*) minus an agent and their forcefulness is further enhanced by the phonetic brutality of the repeated "put down." Consider the loss of force and clarity if Mill had ended each sentence with an attribution of agency in a "by" phrase (e.g., *Savanarola was put down by the Venetian Doge. The Albigeois were put down by a papal army.*) There would be a gain in historical accuracy, but as the tails of the sentences began to wag out of control, the focus on the point of commonality in the examples would diminish.

Example sets phrased as a sequence of parallel predications were used to illustrate induction in early modern dialectical treatises. Melanchthon's example concerns three types of wine (1963a, 620): It was translated into English in Thomas Wilson's *The Rule of Reason*: "Rhenyshe wine heateth/Malmesey heateth/Frenchewine heateth, neither is there any wyne that doth the contrary: Ergo all wine heateth" (1970 [1551], n.p.). The same verbal epitome is used in early editions of the venerable Irving Copi, where induction is characterized as probable argument and no clause claiming the absence of contrary examples is offered: "All cows are mammals and have lungs/All horses are mammals and have lungs/All men are mammals and have lungs. /Therefore probably all mammals have lungs" (Copi, 1972, 25). A contemporary logic text like Groarke and Tindale's uses a somewhat different canonical instance of an inductive argument: "The group of microchips examined is a representative sample of the chips sent. All of the microchips examined are made to specification. All of the microchips sent are made to specification" (2004, 292). But every one of the "microchips examined" would have to sustain a parallel claim (e.g., "Microchip #234 was made to specification," "Microchip #235 was made to specification," etc.).

Rather than fit instances of parallelism with existing argument types, it might also be interesting to ask the bottom-up question, "Given a particular stylistic structure, what kind of argumentative work can it perform?" The set of potential rhetorical arguments is perhaps larger than typically appreciated (see Tindale, 1999, 113, 200). Here, for instance, are sentences in sequence from Dr. Martin Luther King Jr.'s *I've Been to the Mountaintop*: "The nation is sick. Trouble is in the Land. Confusion all around" (King, 1968, 2). This series exhibits approximate isocolon (5, 6, and 6 syllables), and it seems likely that the final sentence was reduced to a fragment so that it would fit the pattern.

Isocolon alone imposes only the constraint of sound parallelism by syllable length; it is a very minimal figure and probably rarely noticed. Yet here it underscores *restatement* as these three sentences essentially repeat the same point.

Another possibility epitomized by parallelism is the *replacement* relation, which is in effect a single antithesis, deploying both isocolon and grammatical parallelism. Here is an example from a Stephen Jay Gould essay in which the second proposition fills the place emptied by the first: "This is not an essay about optimism; it is an essay about tragedy" (1993, 282).

And finally here is the presentation of *alternatives* in parallel phrasing with repetition, again from Clinton's address to the nation on Somalia, "Do we leave when the job gets tough, or when the job is well done?" (1993). To present alternatives is to present roughly equivalent options; hence the epitomizing force of parallelism.

Antimetabole:

There are semantic constraints on all the arguments using parallelism cited above. In comparisons or example sets, the terms filling the grammatical slots should belong to the same semantic category, or at least the audience should believe or come to believe that that constraint has been fulfilled. Once the semantic constraints on parallel clauses are changed, a different set of arguments is epitomized.

Beginning with parallel clauses, instead of repeating terms in the same order we can switch their order. This manipulation creates the figure *antimetabole* which has given us everything from Jesus' revolutionary claim that "The Sabbath was made for man, not man for the Sabbath" (Mark 2:27) to Seven-Up's memorable ad line, " "You like it; it likes you." The antimetabole can iconically express corrective inversions, identity claims and claims of reciprocal causality (Fahnestock 1999, 131–155).

And this particular figure had a special place in Aristotelian dialectic as the test phrasing for a statement about a unique property or a definition as opposed to a statement about a genus or an accident. Claims that fell into the former set were convertible; that is, they could sustain an antimetabole. Those in the latter presumably were not. Aristotle's example in the *Topics* shows the convertibility of a property of man: "For if he is a man, he is capable of learning grammar, and if he is capable of learning grammar, he is a man" (Barnes 1984, I, 170).

If we encounter an antimetabole in an early modern work in natural philosophy, from a mind trained in the stylistic identification of argument forms, we can almost be certain that its author is testing a proposition of a certain kind by its convertibility. When Newton wrote his 1672 paper on the spectrum created by a prism, he used the following formulation as the second in a list of claims:

> To the same degree of refrangibility [i.e. bending] belongs the same colour, and to the same colour ever belongs the same degree of refrangibility. The least refrangible rays are all disposed to exhibit a red colour, and contrarily those rays which are disposed to exhibit a red colour are all the least refrangible. So the most refrangible Rays are all disposed to exhibit a deep Violet Colour, and contrarily those which are apt to exhibit a violet colour, are all the most Refrangible (Newton, 1672, 3081).

This statement follows item #1 in which Newton claims, "Colours are not Qualifications of Light, ... but Original and connate properties" (3081). Readers as familiar with Sanderson's *Logic* as Newton, where the requirement of convertibility is mentioned in the first few pages, would recognize item #2 as support for item #1 (Sanderson 1631, 6, 18). This scholastic formalism could be just an interesting side note but it is arguably much more; it can be seen as the inventional prompt for what Newton reports as his *experimentum crucis* (3078). Because Newton knew the kind of reciprocal claim he had to support, he designed his critical experiment to demonstrate the persistent degree of refrangibility associated with a particular color. In this experiment involving two prisms, the first separates by refrangibility into color and the second uses isolated color to show the same degree of refrangibility. It is otherwise somewhat confusing to see why Newton makes this experiment the crucial one, rather than the other antimetabolic demonstration that white light is split into colored light, and colored light recombined into white light, as reported toward the end of the paper (3086). But here he is testing a definition which should also be as convertible as a claim about properties.

Antithesis:

Still another permutation on a pair of grammatically parallel clauses is possible with another semantic variation. In the classical understanding of word families, great emphasis was placed on pairs of opposites. In Aristotelian semantics as given in the *Categories* and used in the *Topics*, there are four types: contraries, contradictories, correlatives, and privatives (Barnes 1984, I, 18, 189–190). In parallel clauses, key words in the subject and predicate can be matched as opposites, producing the figure of speech antithesis. With this new constraint, the syntactic frame of parallelism expresses not comparability but contrast. *The New Testament*, betraying its origins in Greek rhetorical practices, is filled with these: "For as by one man's disobedient act many were made sinners, so by the obedient act of one shall many be made righteous" (Romans 5.19). Aristotle pays special attention to parallelism that predicates opposite of opposite, giving it a special place in the *Rhetoric* both as the first of the twenty-eight lines of argument in Book II, chapter 23, and as an especially engaging phrase structure in Book III, chapters nine and ten. In Book II, Aristotle recommends trying out a predication where opposite lies with opposite to see if one has a premise that would be acceptable to one's audience as in his example, Temperance is beneficial because excess is harmful. Constructing a memorable premise in a parallel statement deploying opposite wording works because it satisfies the widely held belief that opposite things should have opposite qualities.

The use of the antithesis to make distinctions by predicating opposite features is illustrated in the opening examples from Kekule, Mendel, Lavoisier and Harvey for whom, as for Newton in the case of the antimetabole, a figure of speech had heuristic power, dictating ahead of time the kind of claim that the evidence had to support. Hence figural epitomes prompt invention and suggest a direction for observations and experiments which may or may not be refuted later.

Other Figures in the Tradition

The figures attended to here that depend on parallel phrasing and certain semantic constraints (parallelism, antimetabole, antithesis) can be connected as epitomes, as "prefab" iconic forms, to certain durable lines of argument taught explicitly in dialectic and rhetoric. But the figure manuals offer many more than three figures of speech; the Roman *Rhetorica ad Herennium* specifies sixty-three and some Renaissance figure manuals offer over two hundred. Does each epitomize or prompt the invention of different lines of argument?

To even begin to address this question requires appreciating the systematics of the figures as it has been worked out over the centuries. Despite expansions and differences from manual to manual, three basic and very different categories of figures, first set up by Quintilian, persist: schemes, tropes and the lamentably labeled "figures of thought" [*figura sententiae*] (Quintilian 1986, III, 350–357). One way to understand these categories is to look back from the perspective of contemporary linguistics and use its subdisciplines of phonology, morphology, semantics, syntax, and pragmatics to help sort out the figures. There are in fact figures that can be placed in each of these divisions of contemporary language study. Some schemes concern sound patterns (e.g., *isocolon, alliteration, assonance, homeoteleuton*), and others specify word or more particularly morpheme construction (*paronomasia, agnominatio*). With a baffling desire for precision, figure manuals specify all the ways to alter words by adding, deleting, transposing or substituting letters or syllables. So the sound dimension and the inner construction of words, the territory of phonology and morphology, are amply covered in rhetorical stylistics. (For a dictionary of figures with definitions from classical and early modern rhetorical treatises, see Sonnino 1968.)

Under semantics, the category of the tropes needs no introduction since its most important member, metaphor, has come in some cases to displace not only all of rhetorical stylistics, but all of rhetoric. That metaphors, or more specifically what Aristotle calls in the *Poetics* "proportional metaphors," are arguments from analogy has been frequently illustrated (Corbett 1984, 251–252). The other figures originally identified as tropes concern some type of displaced reference. These include not only metaphor, metonymy and synecdoche, as forms of renaming according to various principles of substitution, but also devices like antonomasia, antiphrasis, litotes and hyperbole which deliberately rename or misname to create a shared awareness between a speaker and listener on the intention for the substitution and hence the implicated value.

Schemes involve syntax by specifying the precise order of clausal constituents and the placement of phrases. Under this category are all the figures of repetition which are so notable in oratory in the grand style like Martin Luther King Jr's. And to this category also belong the three discussed above – parallelism, with or without isocolon, antimetabole and antithesis.

The final category, figures of thought, corresponds to pragmatics, the subdiscipline of linguistics that concerns features of language determined by context and use. Figures of speech in this third category constitute a very large group of devices that construct or manage the speaker/audience relationship in terms of parameters including their social distance, their group identities, their states of mind and emotion both initially and dynamically in the unfolding of an argument, and in terms especially of their state of agreement on the argument itself. So for example when Kekule said that his argument was obvious and needed little explanation, he was attempting to "preconstruct" his reader's attitude toward his argument. One of the durable devices in this category is *licentia* or "frank speech," the device by which a speaker acknowledges the power or superior position of an addressee but nevertheless claims to boldly tell the addressee something that he or she would rather not hear, what we now call speaking truth to power ([Cicero] 1981, 349). All these devices either foreground, construct or attempt to manage an unfolding speaker/audience relationship. Some of the figures selected by Tindale in *Rhetorical Argumentation* fall into this pragmatic category (e.g., *praeteritio, prolepsis* [Tindale 2004, 78–85]), and it was this category that expanded greatly in early modern treatises which anatomized a very large set of possible speaker/audience interactions and speech acts the rhetor might perform. So for instance, the greatest of the early modern English style manuals, Henry Peacham's *Garden of Eloquence*, includes the figure *ara*, "a form of speech by which the orator detesteth and curseth some person or thing, for the evils which they bring with them, or for the wickedness which is in them" and in Peacham's specification of its use, "This figure is the fit instrument of speech to express the bitterness of the detestation within us against some evil person, or evil thing" (Peacham 1954 [1593], 64). *Ara* has its partner, mentioned next, in *eulogia*, "A forme of speech by which the orator pronounceth a blessing upon some person for the goodness that is in him or her" (65). The former is usually directed at a third party, the latter to the audience.

In the context of a fully rhetorical view of argument, all these devices may have persuasive force; they are all figures of argument from a rhetorical perspective of the three appeals. Knowing them ahead of time, as those trained in the rhetorical tradition did, could certainly prompt their deployment in a specific situation. But only some of them epitomize the lines of argument used to make a case, to invent the logos.

Conclusion

The tradition of rhetorical stylistics and the analysis of actual arguments, as expressed, the suggestions of neuroscience and the principle of iconicity all elevate forms of expression as important elements in argument. This view of language could inspire again the centuries-old distrust of eloquence that is a hallmark of both the seventeenth-century reformers who wanted to abandon natural language in favor of a perfect symbol system, and the twentieth-century postmoderns who despair over language and the supposed indeterminacy of meaning. Toulmin has reminded us of this destructive perspective in *Return to Reason* and of the concomitant idealization of a mathematical standard of reasoning. But to the sixteenth-century humanists, at the moment of fusion between rhetoric and dialectic, language was still an instrument of power that merited celebration not suspicion. Henry Peacham, author of perhaps the best treatise on style in English, calls figured language, in his highest terms of encomium, the most excellent gift of divine goodness making humans "next to the omnipotent God in the power of persuasion" (Peacham 1954, 3–4). With perhaps less than this pitch of enthusiasm, we can still appreciate the role of craftsmanship in using language and the role of some of the figures as prepared linguistic grooves of argument and ideation. We are in a position to teach our students not only an awareness but perhaps once again a mastery of these forms and their inventive possibilities.

Notes

1 "Il me parait opportun maintenant de publier les principes fondamentaux d'une théorie que j'ai concue, il y a assez longtemps déja, sur la constitution les substances aromatiques, et qui se base unqiuement sur des hypotheses que presque tous les chimistes admettent maintenant, à savoir: l'atomicité des elements en general, et la tétratomicité du carbone en particulier." (Kekule, 1865, 98); "… c'est ensuite l'espoir de voir cette théorie rapidement confirmée ou refute par les nombreuses experiences quo sont en voie d'exécution." (98).

2 "… une groupe, lequel, considéré come *une chaine ouverte*, aura encore *huit* affinités non saturées. Si l'on admet, au contraire, que les deux atomes qui terminent cette chaine se combinent entre eux, on aura une *chaine fermée* possédant encore *six* affinities non saturées" (Kekule, 1865, 100): The pairs of terms to be taken as opposed (ouverte/fermée and huit/six) were italicized in the original. Kekule does continue in the article to explain families of substances in terms of these types of chains.

3 "In der weiteren Besprechung werden *jene Merkmale, welche ganz oder fast unverändert in die Hybride-Verbindung übergehen,* somit selbst die Hybriden-Merkmale repräsentiren, *als dominirende,* und *jene, welche in der Verbindung latent werden, als recessive* bezeichnet" (Mendel, 1866, 9–10; italics added). In the original printing, the words *dominirende* and *recessive* are printed with extra spacing between the letters, and so stand out distinctly in the text, but this effect may be an accidental byproduct of left and right margin justification. The most frequently used English translation of Mendel's paper does not preserve the minimally parallel phrasing of the original.

4 "Mais si à ce premier coup d'oeil on fait suivre un examen plus approfondi de l'arrangement des bancs et des matières qui les composent, on est étonné d'y voir à la fois tout ce qui caractérise l'ordre, la tranquillité, et en même temps tout ce qui annonce le désordre et le mouvement.
Ici se trouvent des amas de coquilles parmi lesquelles on en voit de minces et de fragiles; la plupart ne sont ni usées, ni frottées; elles sont précisément dan l'état où l'animal les a laissées en perdant la vie: toutes celles qui sont de figure allongée sont couchées horizontalement; presque toutes sont dans la situation qui a été déterminée par la position du centre de gravité: toutes les circonstances qui les environnent attestent une tranquillité profonde et, sinon un repos absolu, du moins des mouvements doux et dépendants de leur volonté.
Quelques pieds au-dessus ou au-dessous du lieu où cette observation a été faite se présente un spectacle tout opposé; on n'y voit aucun trait d'êtres vivants ou animés; on trouve, à la place, des cailloux arrondis dont les angles ont été usés par un mouvement rapide et longtemps continué; c'est le tableau d'une mer en courroux, qui vient se briser contre le rivage, et qui roule avec fracas des amas considérables de galets. Comment concilier des observations si opposées? Comment des effets si différents peuvent-ils appartenir à une même cause? Comments le mouvement qui a usé le quartz, le crystal de roche, les pierres les plus dures, qui en a arrondi les angles, a-t-il respecté des coquilles fragiles et légères?" (Lavoisier, 1789, 186–187)

5 "Ces premières réflexions nous conduisent à une conséquence natruelle, c'est qu'il doit exister dans le règne minéral deux sortes de bancs très distincts, les uns formés en pleine mer, et à une grande profondeur, et que je nommerai à l'imitation de M. Rouelle, bancs *pélagiens*, les autres

formés à la côte, et que je nommerai bancs littoraux; que ces deux espèces de bancs doivent avoir des caractères distinctifs, qui ne permettent pas de les confondre; que les premiers doivent présenter, les amas de matières calcaires, des débris d'animaux; de coquilles, de corps marins accumulés lentement et paisiblement, pendant une succession immense d'années et de siècles; que les autres, au contraire, doivent présenter partout l'image du mouvement, de la destruction et du tumulte" (Lavoisier, 1789, 189–190).

6 "Vena & arteria ambae à veteribus venae non immerito dictae, ut Galenus annotavit; eo quod haec, videlicet arteria, vas est differens sanguinem, è corde in habitum corporis; illa sanguinem ab habitu rursus in cor: haec via à corde; ad cor usque, illa: illa continet sanguinem crudiorem, effeotum, nutritioni iam redditum inidoneum; haec, coctum, perfectum, alimentativum" (Harvey, 1661 [1628], 60; this passage from a later revised edition places a colon between each complete antithesis and the semicolon between each half of an antithesis).

7 To briefly illustrate the potential of these figures to express arguments in a memorable manner, the many figured phrases quoted in *Return to Reason* (2001) can be cited: To note just antimetaboles: Toulmin observes that Euclidean models focus attention on "doing your sums right" and not on "doing the right sums (66); he recalls the Kantian epigrams, "precepts without concepts and concepts with precepts," and "Idealism without Realism is naïve, Realism without Idealism is sterile" (146); he cites Raymond Greene's aphorism about people who put too much emphasis on their work: "Their work eats them up. Whereas they, of course, ought to eat up their work" (113); he quotes Imre Lakatos, "In theoretical arguments, truth flows downward from general statements to particular ones. Empirically the contrary holds good: Truth flows upward from particular examples to broader generalizations" (108).

References

Aristotle. 1991. *On Rhetoric: A Theory of Civic Discourse*. Trans. G.A. Kennedy. New York: Oxford University Press.

Ashworth, E. J. 1968. "Propositional Logic in the Sixteenth and Early Seventeenth Centuries." *Notre Dame Journal of Formal Logic* IX.2: 179–192.

Bakalar, N. 2005. "Ugly Children May Get Parental Short Shrift." *The New York Times (Science Times)*. May 4: F7.

Boeree, C. G. 2000. *Gestalt Psychology*, www.ship.edu/~cgboeree/gestalt/html. Accessed 1/15/2005. [Link broken as of 2019 publication—RAH].

Barnes, J., ed. 1984. *The Complete Works of Aristotle*. The Revised Oxford Translation. Princeton, NJ: Princeton University Press.

Brewster, D. 1965 [1855]. *Memoirs of the Life, Writings, and Discoveries of Sir Isaac Newton*. Vol. I. New York and London: Johnson Reprint Corporation.

[Cicero]. 1981. *Rhetorica ad Herennium*. Cambridge, MA: Harvard University Press.

Clinton, W. J. 1993. "U.S. Military Involvement in Somalia." Address to the Nation, Washington DC, 7 October 1993. http://dosfan.lib.uic.edu/ERC/briefing/dispatch/1993/html/Distpatch v4no42.html.

Cogan, M. 1984. "Rodolphus Agricola and the Semantic Revolutions of the History of Invention." *Rhetorica* 2.2: 163–194.

Copi, I. M. 1972. *An Introduction to Logic*. 4th ed. New York: Macmillan.

Corbett, E.P.J., ed. *The Rhetoric and Poetics of Aristotle*. New York: Modern Library.

Costello, W. T. 1958. *The Scholastic Curriculum at Early Seventeenth-Century Cambridge*. Cambridge, MA: Harvard University Press.

Couzin, J. 2004. "Long-Sought Enzyme Found, Revealing New Gene Switch on Histones." *Science* 306.5705: 2171.

Eemeren, F.H. van and P. Houtlosser, eds. 2002. *Dialectic and Rhetoric: the Warp and Woof of Argumentation Analysis*. Dodrecht: Kluwer.

Fahnestock, J. 1999. *Rhetorical Figures in Science*. New York: Oxford.

Fahnestock, J. 2003. "Verbal and Visual Parallelism." *Written Communication* 20.2: 123–152.

Fahnestock, J. 2004. "Preserving the Figure: Consistency in the Presentation of Scientific Arguments." *Written Communication* 21.1: 6–31.

Fahnestock, J. 2005. "Rhetoric in the Age of Cognitive Science." In R. Graff, A.E. Walzer, J.M. Atwill, eds. *The Viability of the Rhetorical Tradition*. Albany, NY: SUNY Press, pp. 159–179.

Freese, J. H. Trans. 1926. *Aristotle: Art of Rhetoric*. Cambridge, MA: Harvard University Press.

Gilbert, N. W. 1960. *Renaissance Concepts of Method*. New York: Columbia University Press.

Groarke, L. A. and C. W. Tindale. 2004. *Good Reasoning Matters! A Constructive Approach to Critical Thinking*. Ontario: Oxford.

Gould, S. J. 1993. *Eight Little Piggies: Reflections in Natural History*. New York: Norton.

Harvey, W. 1661. *Exercitatio Anatomica de Motu Cordis et Sanguinis in Animalibus*. London: R. Daniels.

Harvey, W. 1990. *The Circulation of the Blood and Other Writings*. Trans. K. J. Franklin. London: Everyman.

Howell, W.S. 1961. *Logic and Rhetoric in England, 1500–1700*. New York: Russell and Russell.

Jardine, L. 1974. *Francis Bacon: Discovery and the Art of Discourse*. Cambridge: Cambridge University Press.

Kekule, A. 1865. "Sur la constitution des substances aromatiques." *Bulletin de la Société Chimique* 3:98–110.

King, Jr, M. L. 1968. "I've Been to the Mountaintop." (www.americanrhetoric.comspeeches/mlkivebeentothemountaintop.htm)

Kristeller, P.O. 1979. *Renaissance Thought and Its Sources*. Ed. Michael Mooney. New York: Columbia University Press.

Kusukawa, S. 1995. *The Transformation of Natural Philosophy*. Cambridge: Cambridge University Press.

La Fontaine, M.J. 1968. "A Critical Translation of Philip Melancthon's *Elementorum Rhetorices Libri Duo*." [Latin text with English translation and notes.] Unpublished thesis. University of Michigan.

Lavoisier, A. L. 1789. "Observations Générales sur Les Couches Modernes Horizontales qui ont été deposes par la Mer et sur les Conséquences qu'on peut tirer de leurs Dispositions Relativement à L'Ancienneté du Globe Terrestre." *Memoires Academie des Sciences*, pp. 186–204.

Leff, M. and A. Sachs. 1990. "Words the Most Like Things: Iconicity and the Rhetorical Text." *Western Journal of Speech Communication* 54 (Summer 1990): 252–273.

Mack, P. 1993. *Renaissance Argument: Valla and Agricola in the Traditions of Rhetoric and Dialectic*. Leiden: Brill.

McNally, J. R. 1967. "Rudolph Agricola's *De Inventione Dialectica Libri Tres*: A Translation of Selected Chapters." *Speech Monographs* 34.4:393–422.

Melanchthon, P. 1963a. *Erotemata Dialectices*. In C.G. Bretscneider, ed. *Opera quae supersunt omnia*. XIII: 509–752. New York: Johnson Reprint Corporation.

Melanchthon, P. 1963b. *Elementa Rhetorices*. In C.G. Bretschneider, ed. *Opera quae supersunt omnia*. XIII: 415–506.

Mendel, G. 1866. "Versuche über Pflanzen-Hybrdien." Separatabdruck aus dem IV. Bande der Verhandlungen des naturforschenden Vereines. Brünn: Gastl.

Mill, J.S. 1978 [1859]. *On Liberty.* Indianapolis: Hackett.

Mill, J.S. 1874. *A System of Logic, Ratiocinative and Inductive: Being a Connected View of the Principles of Evidence and the Methods of Scientific Investigation.* New York: Harper.

Newton, I. 1672. "New Theory about Light and Colors [sic]." *Philosophical Transactions* 6: 3075–3087.

Peacham, H. 1954 [1593]. *The Garden of Eloquence.* Gainesville, FL: Scholars' Facsimiles.

Perelman, C. and L. Olbrechts-Tyteca. 1969. *The New Rhetoric: A Treatise on Argument* Trans. J. Wilkinson and P. Weaver. Notre Dame, IN: University of Notre Dame Press.

Quintilian. 1986. *Institutio Oratoria.* Vol. III. Trans. H. E. Butler. Cambridge MA: Harvard University Press.

Sanderson, R. 1631. *Logicae Artis Compendium.* 3rd ed. Oxford: Lichfield.

Sonnino, L. 1968. *A Handbook to Sixteenth-Century Rhetoric.* New York: Barnes and Noble.

Tindale, C.W. 1999. *Acts of Arguing. A Rhetorical Model of Argument.* Albany: SUNY Press.

Tindale, C. W. 2004. *Rhetorical Argumentation: Principles of Theory and Practice.* Thousand Oaks, CA: Sage Publications.

Toulmin, S. and J. Goodfield. 1962. *The Architecture of Matter.* Chicago: University of Chicago Press.

Toulmin, S. 1972. *Human Understanding: The Collective Use and Evolution of Concepts.* Princeton: Princeton University Press.

Toulmin, S. 2001. *Return to Reason.* Cambridge, MA: Harvard University Press.

Vasoli, C. 1968. *La dialettica e la retorica dell'Umanesimo.* Milano: Feltrinelli.

Whitteridge, G. 1971. *William Harvey and the Circulation of the Blood.* London: MacDonald.

Wilson, T. 1970 [1551]. *The Rule of Reason.* Amsterdam: Theatrum Orbis Terrarum.

15.
SWITCH-SIDE DEBATING MEETS DEMAND-DRIVEN RHETORIC OF SCIENCE
by Gordon R. Mitchell

Recently, U.S. intelligence officials have sought to improve intelligence analysis by borrowing core principles from the field of rhetoric. U.S. Intelligence Community Directive 205 on "Analytic Outreach," signed into effect by Director of National Intelligence John McConnell in July 2008, seeks assistance from experts outside the intelligence community to "closely review analytical assumptions, logic and, where appropriate, evidence" in intelligence assessments. The directive indicates that outside experts also may be "commissioned separately to examine an alternative view or approach to an issue; to argue the pros and cons to a judgment involving uncertainty, ambiguity, or debate."[1] This description evinces a marked sensitivity to the value of rhetoric, since as David Zarefsky observes, "rhetoric's responsibility is to enable people to judge whether a claim is reasonable and just," especially when called "to make decisions under conditions of uncertainty, when the right course of action is not self-evident but we nevertheless must act."[2] Indeed, it appears that the intelligence community is attempting to refurbish its analytic tradecraft by hitching its wagons to the heuristic engines of rhetorical practice.

Such efforts are being driven not only by recommendations from executive directives, blue-ribbon committees, and legislative decrees,[3] but also by scholarly commentary. Consider Douglas Hart and Steven Simon's proposition that one major cause of the intelligence community's misjudgments on Iraq in 2002–2003 was "poor argumentation and analysis within the intelligence directorate." As a remedy, Hart and Simon recommend that intelligence agencies encourage analysts to engage in "structured arguments and dialogues" designed to facilitate "sharing and expression of multiple points of view" and cultivate "critical thinking skills."[4]

The U.S. intelligence community's Analytic Outreach initiative implements what Ronald Walter Greene and Darrin Hicks call "switch-side debating"—a critical thinking exercise where interlocutors temporarily suspend belief in their convictions to bring forth multiple angles of an argument. Drawing on Foucault, Greene and Hicks classify switch-side debating as a "cultural technology," one laden with ideological baggage. Specifically, they claim that switch-side debating is "invested with an ethical substance" and that participation in the activity inculcates "ethical obligations intrinsic to the technology,"[5] including political liberalism and a worldview colored by American

Gordon R. Mitchell. "Switch-Side Debating Meets Demand-Driven Rhetoric of Science." *Rhetoric and Public Affairs*, Volume 13, Number 1, 2010, pp. 95–120.

exceptionalism. On first blush, the fact that a deputy U.S. director of national intelligence is attempting to deploy this cultural technology to strengthen secret intelligence tradecraft in support of U.S. foreign policy would seem to qualify as Exhibit B in support of Greene and Hicks's general thesis.[6]

Yet the picture grows more complex when one considers what is happening over at the Environmental Protection Agency (EPA), where environmental scientist Ibrahim Goodwin is collaborating with John W. Davis on a project that uses switch-side debating to clean up air and water. In April 2008, that initiative brought top intercollegiate debaters from four universities to Washington, D.C., for a series of debates on the topic of water quality, held for an audience of EPA subject matter experts working on interstate river pollution and bottled water issues. An April 2009 follow-up event in Huntington Beach, California, featured another debate weighing the relative merits of monitoring versus remediation as beach pollution strategies. "We use nationally ranked intercollegiate debate programs to research and present the arguments, both pro and con, devoid of special interest in the outcome," explains Davis. "In doing so, agency representatives now remain squarely within the decision-making role thereby neutralizing overzealous advocacy that can inhibit learned discourse."[7]

The intelligence community and EPA debating initiatives vary quite a bit simply by virtue of the contrasting policy objectives pursued by their sponsoring agencies (foreign policy versus environmental protection). Significant process-level differences mark off the respective initiatives as well; the former project entails largely one-way interactions designed to sluice insight from "open sources" to intelligence analysts working in classified environments and producing largely secret assessments. In contrast, the EPA's debating initiative is conducted through public forums in a policy process required by law to be transparent. This granularity troubles Greene and Hicks's deterministic framing of switch-side debate as an ideologically smooth and consistent cultural technology. In an alternative approach, this essay positions debate as a malleable method of decision making, one utilized by different actors in myriad ways to pursue various purposes. By bringing forth the texture inherent in the associated messy "mangle of practice,"[8] such an approach has potential to deepen our understanding of debate as a dynamic and contingent, rather than static, form of rhetorical performance.

Juxtaposition of the intelligence community and EPA debating initiatives illuminates additional avenues of inquiry that take overlapping elements of the two projects as points of departure. Both tackle complex, multifaceted, and technical topics that do not lend themselves to reductionist, formal analysis, and both tap into the creative energy latent in what Protagoras of Abdera called *dissoi logoi*, the process of learning about a controversial or unresolved issue by airing opposing viewpoints.[9] In short, these institutions are employing debate as a tool of deliberation, seeking outside expertise to help accomplish their aims. Such trends provide an occasion to revisit a presumption commonly held among theorists of deliberative democracy—that debate and deliberation are fundamentally opposed practices—as the intelligence community's Analytic Outreach program and the EPA's debating initiatives represent examples where debating exercises are designed to facilitate, not frustrate, deliberative goals.

The move by the respective institutions to tap outside resources for support also implicates the long-simmering theoretical discussions in the rhetoric of science, where Dilip Gaonkar charges that scholars such as John Campbell, Lawrence Prelli, and Alan Gross err by utilizing concepts from classical Greek rhetoric as a hermeneutic metadiscourse for interpreting scientific texts.[10] In Gaonkar's telling, the "hegemonic" project to "globalize" rhetoric by bringing all textual artifacts (even hard science) under its scope is an ill-fated exercise in supply-side epistemology. Yet the intelligence community's Analytic Outreach project and the EPA's debating initiatives entail a demand-driven rhetoric of science, where institutional actors seek enlistment of rhetoric's expertise to tackle technical problems. Rather than rhetoric pushing its epistemology on science, here we have science pulling rhetoric into its interdisciplinary orbit.[11] Could it be that the "thinness" of the productivist classical Greek lexicon, for Gaonkar a liability in rhetorical criticism, here becomes a strength supporting the type of practice-oriented scholarship that Zarefsky envisioned growing out of his theory of argumentation as "hypothesis testing"?[12] The following analysis, which considers in turn the intelligence community and EPA debating initiatives, engages this question.

Evidence and Argument Fields in Intelligence Community Deliberations

"The axiom of all rhetoric" is the "principle of insufficient reason," says Hans Blumenberg.[13] In this formulation, when a pressing situation calls for action, but all the facts are not yet in, rhetoric lends practical guidance to those seeking to navigate uncharted waters. In Lloyd Bitzer's shopworn terminology, such "rhetorical situations" are meaning vacuums that invite, even "call" discourse to the scene as "fitting" remedies for the "imperfect" state of affairs.[14] Yet the current era of "content abundance"[15] seems to invert this commonly held sense of the rhetorical situation, as we struggle to stay afloat in the wake of new waves of facts, figures, and testimony churned out by today's proliferating sites of knowledge production.[16] According to Richard Lanham, "we're drowning" in this endemic state of surplus information, struggling to marshal sufficient attention to make sense of it all.[17] To capture this sense of inundation, Damien Pfister coins the term "hyperpublicity" to describe the "massive expansion in the capacity of personal media to record, archive, and make searchable thoughts, events, and interactions in publicly accessible databases." In this meaning-saturated environment, which has "double potential to enrich and threaten public life,"[18] the challenge has less to do with figuring out how to make practical decisions based on scarce shreds of evidence (rhetoric filling a lack) and more to do with sorting through ever-expanding mounds of evidence whose relevance to pressing decisions may not be immediately apparent (rhetoric responding to a surplus).

The official U.S. intelligence community routinely faces such inverted rhetorical situations when it is called upon to deliver consensus judgments such as National Intelligence Estimates. To reach such judgments, analysts must comb through terabytes of digital data from SIGINT (signals intelligence gathered from satellites and other monitoring devices), HUMINT (human intelligence drawn from informants and agents), as well as a burgeoning supply of "open source" intelligence (data in the public domain). As the community is composed of 16 separate agencies and entities that each serve different customers and pursue distinct approaches to intelligence analysis, heterogeneous perspectives often complicate the process of sorting the proverbial wheat from the chaff. As Simon and Hart explain, "the basic problem stems from moving knowledge created using evidence and analysis in one group or organisation into another. This is not a trivial undertaking, because the process, language and ultimate purpose of the created knowledge often differ radically between the originating and receiving organisations." As a result, "analyses involving jihadist perceptions or technical details concerning chemical, biological or nuclear weapons can often generate interpretive or semantic differences between originating and receiving organisations as to what a word, measurement or outcome actually means."[19] Here, centrifugal forces of professional specialization and horizontal knowledge diffusion scatter the pool upon which analysts draw data. Simultaneously, centripetal forces oblige these same analysts to synthesize vast sums of diverse information and render coherent arguments on complex and multifaceted issues. This challenge stems from a tension borne from the push brought about by the splintering of the intelligence community into disparate agencies, on the one hand, and the pull of institutional directives requiring coordination of intelligence products, on the other.

Surmounting this complex epistemological dilemma requires more than sheer information processing power; it demands forms of communicative dexterity that enable translation of ideas across differences and facilitate cooperative work by interlocutors from heterogeneous backgrounds. How can such communicative dexterity be cultivated? Hart and Simon see structured argumentation as a promising tool in this regard. In their view, the unique virtue of rigorous debates is that they "support diverse points of view *while* encouraging consensus formation." This dual function of argumentation provides "both intelligence producers and policy consumers with a view into the methodologies and associated evidence used to produce analytical product, effectively creating a common language that might help move knowledge across organisational barriers without loss of accuracy or relevance."[20] Hart and Simon's insights, coupled with the previously mentioned institutional initiatives promoting switch-side debating in the intelligence community, carve out a new zone of relevance where argumentation theory's salience is pronounced and growing. Given the centrality of evidentiary analysis in this zone, it is useful to revisit how argumentation scholars have theorized the functions of evidence in debating contexts.

In the words of Austin Freeley, "evidence is the raw material of argumentation. It consists of facts, opinions and objects that are used to generate proof."[21] Here, evidence becomes the "factual foundation for the claims of the advocates."[22] When an interlocutor attempts to forward claims based on data, "the process of advancing from evidence to conclusion is argument."[23] What are the different types of evidence? Which are most persuasive in certain situations? How can evidence be misused? What *doesn't* count as legitimate evidence? In the field of argumentation, scholars have long grappled with these questions, often by developing idiosyncratic taxonomies of evidence usage.[24] So, for example, one textbook breaks down types of evidence into three categories—examples, statistics, and authority—and three sources—original, hearsay, and written.[25] An earlier effort identifies three "forms of data that provide proof for a claim" as unwritten, ordinary, and expert.[26] In a blistering critique, Dale Hample questions the usefulness of these projects: "The typologies—for they are indeed plural—differ from textbook to textbook and have never been defended as having any phenomenal reality for anyone not taking an argumentation exam."[27] One factor accounting for the limited conceptual appeal of these evidence taxonomies is that such schemes are tied tightly to the practical activity associated with their development—intercollegiate debating. Since as Dean Fadely points out, the "bedrock of contest debate" is evidence,[28] it is only natural that many of these taxonomical efforts are designed to support student classroom work. For example, the preface to Robert and Dale Newman's 1969 *Evidence* explains, "This book is designed primarily for students of exposition, discussion, persuasion, and argument who must buttress their speeches or essays with evidence."[29] Such a pedagogical orientation underwrites the practical dimension of evidence studies, where the emphasis rests on cultivating invention skills sufficient to enable students to research, deploy, and defend evidenced claims in argumentative situations.[30]

A related strand of scholarship concerns the mobilization of argumentation theory to critique evidentiary practices used in the conduct of public affairs. This critical orientation is also manifest in Newman and Newman's 1969 *Evidence* text, which features analyses of the authenticity, credibility, and factual grounding of evidence provided by government officials, journalists, and experts discussing public policy issues. Later, Robert Newman's article "Communication Pathologies of Intelligence Systems" would deploy this same framework to show how intelligence failures ranging from the Bay of Pigs to Vietnam were rooted in systematic institutional pressures that distorted communication between intelligence analysts and policymakers, causing them to mishandle evidence.[31]

As one traces the evolution of evidence studies beyond the debate-contest-round context, a host of other argument-informed analyses come into view. Some of these projects measure empirically the psychological dimension of evidence uptake by audiences,[32] whereas others, often working under the banner "informal logic," explore the field dependency of evidence norms. Where analytical treatments by logical empiricists such as Carl Hempel sought to develop universal accounts of evidence that would hold fast across object domains, argumentation scholars, led by Stephen Toulmin, have posited that the domains in which argument takes place structure expectations and norms regarding evidence.[33] Thus, answers to questions like "which type of evidence is most persuasive" pivot depending on the argument field in which the argument takes place. Hearsay testimony, for instance, may be persuasive evidence for a journalist working on a story about a recent crime. Yet that same testimony will likely receive less sympathetic treatment in a courtroom trial where a prosecutor attempts to present it as evidence against a suspect accused of committing the crime. These dimensions of contingency and interpretation are largely absent in formal logic, where field invariant rules govern connections between claims and their supporting evidence. As Chaim Perelman and Lucie Olbrechts-Tyteca show in *The New Rhetoric*, the conceptual scaffolding of argumentation is well equipped to shed light on precisely those situations where deductive forms of reasoning and formal logic fail to deliver.[34]

The field-dependent approach to the study of evidence is straightforward when invention and critique are approached within the horizon of a distinct field. One first discerns the local norms governing evidence in the particular field in which an argument takes place, then applies those norms to the task at hand, whether it be creation of novel argumentation or analysis of extant arguments already on record. Yet things grow complicated when the discursive milieu spans two or more argument fields, especially when those fields feature incompatible conventions regarding evidence. Consider that the Central Intelligence Agency's (CIA) prioritization of the warning function in intelligence analysis predisposes CIA analysts to deploy different evidence standards than the State Department's Bureau of Intelligence and Research, where analysts are trained to prioritize accurate prediction over threat warning.[35] One factor accounting for the intelligence failure prior to the 2003 Iraq War was an inability by intelligence analysts and policymakers to appreciate fully how the disparate assessments regarding Saddam Hussein's arsenal of unconventional weaponry could be understood as products of the distinct argument fields producing the assessments.

Some of the specific projects underway in the intelligence community stemming from Director McConnell's Analytic Outreach initiative show how the leadership is banking on the process of argumentation to help prevent a repeat of the 2003 Iraq War intelligence failure.[36] For instance, Dan Doney, one of McConnell's deputies, is spearheading a project named BRIDGE that "provides a platform for debating alternative viewpoints and comparing evidence across agencies, specialties, and borders of all kinds."[37] As Doney explains, "BRIDGE is designed to enable crowd-sourcing of intelligence applications—following the iPhone AppStore model—by providing a low barrier-to-entry platform to stimulate innovation and enable analysts to discover next generation capabilities that have value to their mission."[38] One cannot help but recall Greene and Hicks's formulation of debating as a technology after reading a summary of the first wave of applications featured in the BRIDGE program. The first web-based "app," named Collaborative Analysis of Competing Hypotheses, enables analysts to "gather evidence collaboratively and think more critically about the plausible scenarios, mitigating bias" and to "hone in on differences, making debate more constructive and encouraging deeper reasoning." Another online app, HotGrinds, supports "semantic search, expertise identification, and management overviews of debate" that "provide greater collective awareness and enhanced collaboration."[39] The key premise underlying specific design features of this software is that through online connectivity, analysts will be empowered to redouble their capacity for collaborative deliberation.

The watchwords for the intelligence community's debating initiative—collaboration, critical thinking, collective awareness—resonate with key terms anchoring the study of deliberative democracy. In a major new text, John Gastil defines deliberation as a process whereby people "carefully examine a problem and arrive at a well-reasoned solution after a period of inclusive, respectful consideration of diverse points of view."[40] Gastil and his colleagues in organizations such as the Kettering Foundation and the National Coalition for Dialogue and Deliberation are pursuing a research program that foregrounds the democratic *telos* of deliberative processes. Work in this area features a blend of concrete interventions and studies of citizen empowerment.[41] Notably, a key theme in much of this literature concerns the relationship between deliberation and debate, with the latter term often loaded with pejorative baggage and working as a negative foil to highlight the positive qualities of deliberation.[42] "Most political discussions, however, are debates. Stories in the media turn politics into a never-ending series of contests. People get swept into taking sides; their energy goes into figuring out who or what they're for or against," says Kettering president David Mathews and coauthor Noelle McAfee. "Deliberation is different. It is neither a partisan argument where opposing sides try to win nor a casual conversation conducted with polite civility. Public deliberation is a means by which citizens make tough choices about basic purposes and directions for their communities and their country. It is a way of reasoning and talking together."[43] Mathews and McAfee's distrust of the debate process is almost paradigmatic amongst theorists and practitioners of Kettering-style deliberative democracy.

One conceptual mechanism for reinforcing this debate-deliberation opposition is characterization of debate as a process inimical to deliberative aims, with debaters adopting dogmatic and fixed positions that frustrate the deliberative objective of "choice work." In this register, Emily Robertson observes, "unlike deliberators, debaters are typically not open to the possibility of being shown wrong. ... Debaters are not trying to find the best solution by keeping an open mind about the opponent's point of view."[44] Similarly, founding documents from the University of Houston–Downtown's Center for Public Deliberation state, "Public deliberation is about choice work, which is different from a dialogue or a debate. In dialogue, people often look to relate to each other, to understand each other, and to talk about more informal issues. In debate, there are generally two positions and people are generally looking to 'win' their side."[45] Debate, cast here as the theoretical scapegoat, provides a convenient, low-water benchmark for explaining how other forms of deliberative interaction better promote cooperative "choice work."

The Kettering-inspired framework receives support from perversions of the debate process such as vapid presidential debates and verbal pyrotechnics found on *Crossfire*-style television shows.[46] In contrast, the intelligence community's debating initiative stands as a nettlesome anomaly for these theoretical frameworks, with debate serving, rather than frustrating, the ends of deliberation. The presence of such an anomaly would seem to point to the wisdom of fashioning a theoretical orientation that frames the debate-deliberation connection in contingent, rather than static terms, with the relationship between the categories shifting along with the various contexts in which they manifest in practice.[47] Such an approach gestures toward the importance of rhetorically informed critical work on multiple levels. First, the contingency of situated practice invites analysis geared to assess, in particular cases, the extent to which debate practices enable and/or constrain deliberative objectives. Regarding the intelligence community's debating initiative, such an analytical perspective highlights, for example, the tight connection between the deliberative goals established by intelligence officials and the cultural technology manifest in the BRIDGE project's online debating applications such as Hot Grinds.

An additional dimension of nuance emerging from this avenue of analysis pertains to the precise nature of the deliberative goals set by BRIDGE. Program descriptions notably eschew Kettering-style references to democratic citizen empowerment, yet feature deliberation prominently as a key ingredient of strong intelligence tradecraft. This caveat is especially salient to consider when it comes to the second category of rhetorically informed critical work invited by the contingent aspect of specific debate initiatives. To grasp this layer it is useful to appreciate how the name of the BRIDGE project constitutes an invitation for those outside the intelligence community to participate in the analytic outreach effort. According to Doney, BRIDGE "provides an environment for Analytic Outreach—a place where IC analysts can reach out to expertise elsewhere in federal, state, and local government, in academia, and industry. New communities of interest can form quickly in BRIDGE through the 'web of trust' access control model—access to minds outside the intelligence community creates an analytic force multiplier."[48] This presents a moment of choice for academic scholars in a position to respond to Doney's invitation; it is an opportunity to convert scholarly expertise into an "analytic force multiplier."

In reflexively pondering this invitation, it may be valuable for scholars to read Greene and Hicks's proposition that switch-side debating should be viewed as a cultural technology in light of Langdon Winner's maxim that "technological artifacts have politics."[49] In the case of BRIDGE, politics are informed by the history of intelligence community policies and practices. Commenter Thomas Lord puts this point in high relief in a post offered in response to a news story on the topic: "[W]hy should this thing ('BRIDGE') be? … [The intelligence community] on the one hand sometimes provides useful information to the military or to the civilian branches and on the other hand it is a dangerous, out of control, relic that by all external appearances is not the slightest bit reformed, other than superficially, from such excesses as became exposed in the COINTEL-PRO and MKULTRA hearings of the 1970s."[50] A debate scholar need not agree with Lord's full-throated criticism of the intelligence community (he goes on to observe that it bears an alarming resemblance to organized crime) to understand that participation in the community's Analytic Outreach program may serve the ends of deliberation, but not necessarily democracy, or even a defensible politics. Demand-driven rhetoric of science necessarily raises questions about what's driving the demand, questions that scholars with relevant expertise would do well to ponder carefully before embracing invitations to contribute their argumentative expertise to deliberative projects. By the same token, it would be prudent to bear in mind that the technological determinism about switch-side debate endorsed by Greene and Hicks may tend to flatten reflexive assessments regarding the wisdom of supporting a given debate initiative—as the next section illustrates, manifest differences among initiatives warrant context-sensitive judgments regarding the normative political dimensions featured in each case.

Public Debates in the EPA Policy Process

The preceding analysis of U.S. intelligence community debating initiatives highlighted how analysts are challenged to navigate discursively the heteroglossia of vast amounts of different kinds of data flowing through intelligence streams. Public policy planners are tested in like manner when they attempt to stitch together institutional arguments from various and sundry inputs ranging from expert testimony, to historical precedent, to public comment. Just as intelligence managers find that algorithmic, formal methods of analysis often don't work when it comes to the task of interpreting and synthesizing copious amounts of disparate data, public-policy planners encounter similar challenges.

In fact, the argumentative turn in public-policy planning elaborates an approach to public-policy analysis that foregrounds deliberative interchange and critical thinking as alternatives to "decisionism," the formulaic application of "objective" decision algorithms to the public policy process. Stating the matter plainly, Majone suggests, "whether in written or oral form, argument is central in all stages of the policy process." Accordingly, he notes, "we miss a great deal if we try to understand policy-making solely in terms of power, influence, and bargaining, to the exclusion of debate and argument."[51] One can see similar rationales driving Goodwin and Davis's EPA debating project, where debaters are invited to conduct on-site public debates covering resolutions crafted to reflect key points of stasis in the EPA decision-making process. For example, in the 2008 Water Wars debates held at EPA headquarters in Washington, D.C., resolutions were crafted to focus attention on the topic of water pollution, with one resolution focusing on downstream states' authority to control upstream states' discharges and sources of pollutants, and a second resolution exploring the policy merits of bottled water and toilet paper taxes as revenue sources to fund water infrastructure projects. In the first debate on interstate river pollution, the team of Seth Gannon and Seungwon Chung from Wake Forest University argued in favor of downstream state control, with the Michigan State University team of Carly Wunderlich and Garrett Abelkop providing opposition. In the second debate on taxation policy, Kevin Kallmyer and Matthew Struth from University of Mary Washington defended taxes on bottled water and toilet paper, while their opponents from Howard University, Dominique Scott and Jarred McKee, argued against this proposal. Reflecting on the project, Goodwin noted how the intercollegiate debaters' ability to act as "honest brokers" in the policy arguments contributed positively to internal EPA deliberation on both issues.[52] Davis observed that since the invited debaters "didn't have a dog in the fight," they were able to give voice to previously buried arguments that some EPA subject matter experts felt reticent to elucidate because of their institutional affiliations.[53]

Such findings are consistent with the views of policy analysts advocating the argumentative turn in policy planning. As Majone claims, "Dialectical confrontation between generalists and experts often succeeds in bringing out unstated assumptions, conflicting interpretations of the facts, and the risks posed by new projects."[54] Frank Fischer goes even further in this context, explicitly appropriating rhetorical scholar Charles Willard's concept of argumentative "epistemics" to flesh out his vision for policy studies:

> Uncovering the epistemic dynamics of public controversies would allow for a more enlightened understanding of what is at stake in a particular dispute, making possible a sophisticated evaluation of the various viewpoints and merits of different policy options. In so doing, the differing, often tacitly held contextual perspectives and values could be juxtaposed; the viewpoints and demands of experts, special interest groups, and the wider public could be directly compared; and the dynamics among the participants could be scrutinized. This would by no means sideline or even exclude scientific assessment; it would only situate it within the framework of a more comprehensive evaluation.[55]

As Davis notes, institutional constraints present within the EPA communicative milieu can complicate efforts to provide a full airing of all relevant arguments pertaining to a given regulatory issue. Thus, intercollegiate debaters can play key roles in retrieving and amplifying positions that might otherwise remain sedimented in the policy process. The dynamics entailed in this symbiotic relationship are underscored by deliberative planner John Forester, who observes, "If planners and public administrators are to make democratic political debate and argument possible, they will need strategically located allies to avoid being fully thwarted by the characteristic self-protecting behaviors of the planning organizations and bureaucracies within which they work."[56] Here, an institution's need for "strategically located allies" to support deliberative practice constitutes the demand for rhetorically informed expertise, setting up what can be considered a demand-driven rhetoric of science. As an instance of rhetoric of science scholarship, this type of "switch-side public debate"[57] differs both from insular contest tournament debating, where the main focus is on the pedagogical benefit for student participants, and first-generation rhetoric of science scholarship, where critics concentrated on unmasking the rhetoricity of scientific artifacts circulating in what many perceived to be purely technical spheres of knowledge production.[58] As a form of demand-driven rhetoric of science, switch-side debating connects directly with the communication field's performative tradition of argumentative engagement in public controversy—a different route of theoretical grounding than rhetorical criticism's tendency to locate its foundations in the English field's tradition of literary criticism and textual analysis.[59]

Given this genealogy, it is not surprising to learn how Davis's response to the EPA's institutional need for rhetorical expertise took the form of a public debate proposal, shaped by Davis's dual background as a practitioner and historian of intercollegiate debate. Davis competed as an undergraduate policy debater for Howard University in the 1970s, and then went on to enjoy substantial success as coach of the Howard team in the new millennium. In an essay reviewing the broad sweep of debating history, Davis notes, "Academic debate began at least 2,400 years ago when the scholar Protagoras of Abdera (481–411 BC), known as the father of debate, conducted debates among his students in Athens."[60] As John Poulakos points out, "older" Sophists such as Protagoras taught Greek students the value of *dissoi logoi*, or pulling apart complex questions by debating two sides of an issue.[61] The few surviving fragments of Protagoras's work suggest that his notion of *dissoi logoi* stood for the principle that "two accounts [*logoi*] are present about every 'thing,' opposed to each other," and further, that humans could "measure" the relative soundness of knowledge claims by engaging in give-and-take where parties would make the "weaker argument stronger" to activate the generative aspect of rhetorical practice, a key element of the Sophistical tradition.[62]

Following in Protagoras's wake, Isocrates would complement this centrifugal push with the pull of *synerchésthé*, a centripetal exercise of "coming together" deliberatively to listen, respond, and form common social bonds.[63] Isocrates incorporated Protagorean *dissoi logoi* into *synerchésthé*, a broader concept that he used flexibly to express interlocking senses of (1) *inquiry*, as in groups convening to search for answers to common questions through discussion;[64] (2) *deliberation*, with interlocutors gathering in a political setting to deliberate about proposed courses of action;[65] and (3) *alliance formation*, a form of collective action typical at festivals,[66] or in the exchange of pledges that deepen social ties.[67]

Returning once again to the Kettering-informed sharp distinction between debate and deliberation, one sees in Isocratic *synerchésthé*, as well as in the EPA debating initiative, a fusion of debate with deliberative functions. Echoing a theme raised in this essay's earlier discussion of intelligence tradecraft, such a fusion troubles categorical attempts to classify debate and deliberation as fundamentally opposed activities. The significance of such a finding is amplified by the frequency of attempts in the deliberative democracy literature to insist on the theoretical bifurcation of debate and deliberation as an article of theoretical faith.

Tandem analysis of the EPA and intelligence community debating initiatives also brings to light dimensions of contrast at the third level of Isocratic *synerchésthé*, alliance formation. The intelligence community's Analytic Outreach initiative invites largely one-way communication flowing from outside experts into the black box of classified intelligence analysis. On the contrary, the EPA debating program gestures toward a more expansive project of deliberative alliance building. In this vein, Howard University's participation in the 2008 EPA Water Wars debates can be seen as the harbinger of a trend by historically black colleges and universities (HBCUS) to catalyze their debate programs in a strategy that evinces Davis's dual-focus vision. On the one hand, Davis aims to recuperate Wiley College's tradition of competitive excellence in intercollegiate debate, depicted so powerfully in the feature film *The Great Debaters*, by starting a wave of new debate programs housed in HBCUS across the nation.[68] On the other hand, Davis sees potential for these new programs to complement their competitive debate programming with participation in the EPA's public debating initiative.

This dual-focus vision recalls Douglas Ehninger's and Wayne Brockriede's vision of "total" debate programs that blend switch-side intercollegiate tournament debating with forms of public debate designed to contribute to wider communities beyond the tournament setting.[69] Whereas the political *telos* animating Davis's dual-focus vision certainly embraces background assumptions that Greene and Hicks would find disconcerting—notions of liberal political agency, the idea of debate using "words as weapons"[70]—there is little doubt that the project of pursuing environmental protection by tapping the creative energy of HBCU-leveraged *dissoi logoi* differs significantly from the intelligence community's effort to improve its tradecraft through online digital debate programming. Such difference is especially evident in light of the EPA's commitment to extend debates to public realms, with the attendant possible benefits unpacked by Jane Munksgaard and Damien Pfister:

> Having a public debater argue against their convictions, or confess their indecision on a subject and subsequent embrace of argument as a way to seek clarity, could shake up the prevailing view of debate as a war of words. Public uptake of the possibility of switch-sides debate may help lessen the polarization of issues inherent in prevailing debate formats because students are no longer seen as wedded to their arguments. This could transform public debate from a tussle between advocates, with each public debater trying to convince the audience in a Manichean struggle about the truth of their side, to a more inviting exchange focused on the content of the other's argumentation and the process of deliberative exchange.[71]

Reflection on the EPA debating initiative reveals a striking convergence among (1) the expressed need for *dissoi logoi* by government agency officials wrestling with the challenges of inverted rhetorical situations, (2) theoretical claims by scholars regarding the centrality of argumentation in the public policy process, and (3) the practical wherewithal of intercollegiate debaters to tailor public switch-side debating performances in specific ways requested by agency collaborators. These points of convergence both underscore previously articulated theoretical assertions regarding the relationship of debate to deliberation, as well as deepen understanding of the political role of deliberation in institutional decision making. But they also suggest how decisions by rhetorical scholars about whether to contribute switch-side debating acumen to meet demand-driven rhetoric of science initiatives ought to involve careful reflection. Such an approach mirrors the way policy planning in the "argumentative turn" is designed to respond to the weaknesses of formal, decisionistic paradigms of policy planning with situated, contingent judgments informed by reflective deliberation.

Conclusion

Dilip Gaonkar's criticism of first-generation rhetoric of science scholarship rests on a key claim regarding what he sees as the inherent "thinness" of the ancient Greek rhetorical lexicon.[72] That lexicon, by virtue of the fact that it was invented primarily to teach rhetorical performance, is ill equipped in his view to support the kind of nuanced discriminations required for effective interpretation and critique of rhetorical texts. Although Gaonkar isolates rhetoric of science as a main target of this critique, his choice of subject matter positions him to toggle back and forth between specific engagement with rhetoric of science scholarship and discussion of broader themes touching on the metatheoretical controversy over rhetoric's proper scope as a field of inquiry (the so-called big vs. little rhetoric dispute).[73] Gaonkar's familiar refrain in both contexts is a warning about the dangers of "universalizing" or "globalizing" rhetorical inquiry, especially in attempts that "stretch" the classical Greek rhetorical vocabulary into a hermeneutic metadiscourse, one pressed into service as a master key for interpretation of any and all types of communicative artifacts. In other words, Gaonkar warns against the dangers of rhetoricians pursuing what might be called supply-side epistemology, rhetoric's project of pushing for greater disciplinary relevance by attempting to extend its reach into far-flung areas of inquiry such as the hard sciences.

Yet this essay highlights how rhetorical scholarship's relevance can be credibly established *by outsiders*, who seek access to the creative energy flowing from the classical Greek rhetorical lexicon in its native mode, that is, as a tool of invention designed to spur and hone rhetorical performance. Analysis of the intelligence community and EPA debating initiatives shows how this is the case, with government agencies calling for assistance to animate rhetorical processes such as *dissoi logoi* (debating different sides) and *synérchesthé* (the performative task of coming together deliberately for the purpose of joint inquiry, collective choice-making, and renewal of communicative bonds).[74] This demand-driven epistemology is different in kind from the globalization project so roundly criticized by Gaonkar. Rather than rhetoric venturing out from its own academic home to proselytize about its epistemological universality for all knowers, instead here we have actors not formally trained in the rhetorical tradition articulating how their own deliberative objectives call for incorporation of rhetorical practice and even recruitment of "strategically located allies"[75] to assist in the process. Since the productivist content in the classical Greek vocabulary serves as a critical resource for joint collaboration in this regard, demand-driven rhetoric of science turns Gaonkar's original critique on its head.

In fairness to Gaonkar, it should be stipulated that his 1993 intervention challenged the way rhetoric of science had been done to date, not the universe of ways rhetoric of science might be done in the future. And to his partial credit, Gaonkar did acknowledge the promise of a performance-oriented rhetoric of science, especially one informed by classical thinkers other than Aristotle.[76] In his Ph.D. dissertation on "Aspects of Sophistic Pedagogy," Gaonkar documents how the ancient sophists were "the greatest champions" of "socially useful" science,[77] and also how the sophists essentially practiced the art of rhetoric in a translational, performative register:

> The sophists could not blithely go about their business of making science useful, while science itself stood still due to lack of communal support and recognition. Besides, sophistic pedagogy was becoming increasingly dependent on the findings of contemporary speculation in philosophy and science. Take for instance, the eminently practical art of rhetoric. As taught by the best of the sophists, it was not simply a handbook of recipes which anyone could mechanically employ to his advantage. On the contrary, *the strength and vitality of sophistic rhetoric came from their ability to incorporate the relevant information obtained from the on-going research in other fields.*[78]

Of course, deep trans-historical differences make uncritical appropriation of classical Greek rhetoric for contemporary use a fool's errand. But to gauge from Robert Hariman's recent reflections on the enduring salience of Isocrates, "timely, suitable, and eloquent appropriations" can help us postmoderns "forge a new political language" suitable for addressing the complex raft of intertwined problems facing global society. Such retrospection is long overdue, says Hariman, as "the history, literature, philosophy, oratory, art, and political thought of Greece and Rome have never been more accessible or less appreciated."[79]

This essay has explored ways that some of the most venerable elements of the ancient Greek rhetorical tradition—those dealing with debate and deliberation—can be retrieved and adapted to answer calls in the contemporary milieu for cultural technologies capable of dealing with one of our time's most daunting challenges. This challenge involves finding meaning in inverted rhetorical situations characterized by an endemic surplus of heterogeneous content.

Notes

1 John McConnell, "Analytic Outreach," Intelligence Community Directive Number 205, July 16, 2008, p. 2, 3, *www.fas.org/irp/dni/icd/icd-205.pdf* (accessed November 1, 2009). As cyberintelligence expert Jeff Carr observes, the BRIDGE program—one component of

McConnell's Analytic Outreach initiative—"provides a platform for debating alternative viewpoints and comparing evidence across agencies, specialties, and borders of all kinds." Jeff Carr, "Building Bridges with the U.S. Intelligence Community," *O'Reilly Radar* weblog, April 22, 2009, *http://radar.oreilly.com/2009/04/building-bridges-with-the-us-i.html* (accessed October 20, 2009). For a typology of forms of alternative analysis in intelligence tradecraft, see Roger Z. George, "Fixing the Problem of Analytical Mindsets: Alternative Analysis," in *Intelligence and the National Security Strategist: Enduring Issues and Challenges*, ed. Roger Z. George and Robert D. Kline (Washington, DC: National Defense University Press, 2004), 311–26.

2 David Zarefsky, "The Responsibilities of Rhetoric," in *The Responsibilities of Rhetoric*, ed. Michelle Smith and Barbara Warnick (Long Grove, IL: Waveland Press, 2010), 15.

3 McConnell's debate initiative stems directly from recommendations by the Silberman-Robb Commission's 2005 report on Iraq WMD intelligence, which calls for implementation of a "formal system for competitive and even explicitly *contrarian* analysis. Such groups must be licensed to be troublesome." The Commission on the Intelligence Capabilities of the United States Regarding Weapons of Mass Destruction, "Report to the President of the United States," March 31, 2005, 170, *www.gpoaccess.gov/wmd/index.html* (accessed November 1, 2009 [Link broken as of 8 August 2019—RAH]). Section 1017 of the *Intelligence Reform and Terrorism Prevention Act of 2004* also calls for a redoubled commitment to "red team" competitive intelligence analysis as a key reform plank. See *Congressional Record*, December 7, 2004, H10930–H10993.

4 Douglas Hart and Steven Simon, "Thinking Straight and Talking Straight: Problems of Intelligence Analysis," *Survival* 48 (2006): 50.

5 Ronald Walter Greene and Darrin Hicks, "Lost Convictions: Debating Both Sides and the Ethical Self-Fashioning of Liberal Citizens," *Cultural Studies* 19 (2005): 100–126, 110, 111.

6 Exhibit A, for Greene and Hicks, is the American intercollegiate policy debate community's project of cultivating undergraduate student citizenship by having debaters debate both sides of the 1954 college debate topic on the U.S. recognition of Communist China. For commentary on Greene and Hicks's claims regarding this point, see Eric English, Stephen Llano, Gordon R. Mitchell, Catherine E. Morrison, John Rief, and Carly Woods, "Debate as a Weapon of Mass Destruction," *Communication and Critical/Cultural Studies* 4 (2007): 221–25. Greene and Hicks offer a response in their paper, "Conscientious Objections: Debating Both Sides and the Cultures of Democracy," presented at the Sixteenth NCA/AFA Conference on Argumentation, Alta, UT, July 30–August 2, 2009.

7 John W. Davis, "Using Intercollegiate Debate to Inform Environmental Policy Discourse in America," Concurrent Session Program Description, U.S. Environmental Protection Agency, Community Involvement Training Conference, Seattle, Washington, August 18–20, 2009, online at *www.epa.gov/ciconference/proceedings.htm* (accessed November 1, 2009 [Link broken as of 8 August 2019—RAH]).

8 Andrew Pickering, *The Mangle of Practice: Time, Agency, and Science* (Chicago: University of Chicago Press, 1995).

9 Rosamond Kent Sprague, ed., *The Older Sophists*, 2nd ed. (Indianapolis: Hackett, 2001); see also John Poulakos, "Rhetoric and Civic Education: From the Sophists to Isocrates," in *Isocrates and Civic Education*, ed. Takis Poulakos and David J. Depew (Austin: University of Texas Press, 2004), 81–82; and Edward Schiappa, *Protagoras and Logos: A Study in Greek Philosophy and Rhetoric* (Columbia: University of South Carolina Press, 1991).

10 Dilip Parameshwar Gaonkar, "The Idea of Rhetoric in the Rhetoric of Science," in *Rhetorical Hermeneutics*, ed. Alan G. Gross and William M. Keith (Albany, NY: State University of New York Press, 1997), 25–85.

11 For a programmatic analysis exploring possible contours of an applied research program in the rhetoric of science utilizing a public debate methodology, see Gordon R. Mitchell and Marcus Paroske, "Fact, Friction, and Political Conviction in Science Policy Controversies," *Social Epistemology* 14 (2000): 89–107. Paroske illustrates how this research approach can yield insight in extended case studies. See Marcus Paroske, "Deliberating International Science Policy Controversies: Uncertainty and AIDS in South Africa," *Quarterly Journal of Speech* 95 (2009): 148–70.

12 See David Zarefsky, "Argument as Hypothesis-Testing," in *Advanced Debate: Readings in Theory, Practice and Teaching*, ed. David A. Thomas and John P. Hart (Skokie, IL: National Textbook Company, 1979), 427–37.

13 Hans Blumenberg, "An Anthropological Approach to the Contemporary Significance of Rhetoric," in *After Philosophy: End or Transformation?*, ed. Kenneth Baynes, James Bohman, and Thomas McCarthy (Cambridge: Massachusetts Institute of Technology Press, 1987), 447.

14 Lloyd F. Bitzer, "The Rhetorical Situation," *Philosophy and Rhetoric* 1 (1968): 1–14; see also Richard E. Vatz, "The Myth of the Rhetorical Situation," *Philosophy and Rhetoric* 6 (1973): 154–61; Scott Consigny, "Rhetoric and Its Situations," *Philosophy and Rhetoric* 7 (1974): 175–85; and Kathleen M. Hall Jamieson, "Generic Constraints and the Rhetorical Situation," *Philosophy and Rhetoric* 6 (1973): 162–70.

15 Michael Jensen, "Scholarly Authority in the Age of Abundance: Retaining Relevance within the New Landscape," Keynote Address at the JSTOR annual Participating Publisher's Conference, New York, May 13, 2008, http://www.michaeljonjensen.com/jstor.htm (accessed November 1, 2009 [link updated and accessed 9 August—RAH]).

16 Damien Pfister, "Toward a Grammar of the Blogosphere: Rhetoric and Attention in the Networked Imaginary" (Ph.D. diss., University of Pittsburgh, 2009). Pfister draws on an early essay by Herbert Simon arguing that too much information undermines attention. Herbert A. Simon, "Designing Organizations for an Information-Rich World," in *Computers, Communications, and the Public Interest*, ed. Martin Greenberger (Baltimore: Johns Hopkins University Press, 1971).

17 Richard Lanham, *The Economics of Attention: Style and Substance in the Age of Information* (Chicago: University of Chicago Press, 2006), xi.

18 Pfister, "Grammar of the Blogosphere," 384.

19 Hart and Simon, "Thinking Straight," 46, 47.

20 Hart and Simon, "Thinking Straight," 53. On rhetoric's role as a medium of translation in medical research, see Gordon R. Mitchell and Kathleen M. McTigue, "Promoting Translational Research in Medicine through Deliberation," paper presented at the Justification, Reason, and Action Conference in Honor of Professor David Zarefsky, Northwestern University, Evanston, IL, May 29–30, 2009.

21 Austin J. Freeley, *Argumentation and Debate: Critical Thinking for Reasoned Decision Making*, 9th ed. (Belmont, CA: Wadsworth, 1996), 107; see also James H. McBurney, James M. O'Neill, and Glen E. Mills, *Argumentation and Debate: Techniques of a Free Society* (New York: Macmillan, 1951), 73.

22 David L. Vancil, *Rhetoric and Argumentation* (Boston: Allyn and Bacon, 1993), 48.

23 A. Craig Baird, *Argumentation, Discussion and Debate* (New York: McGraw-Hill, 1950), 90.

24 For a review of the literature on empirical dimensions of evidence's role in argument, especially regarding perceptions of evidence strength by interlocutors, see Rodney A. Reynolds and J. Lynn Reynolds, "Evidence," in *The Persuasion Handbook: Developments in Theory and Practice*, ed. James Price Dillard and Michael W. Pfau (Thousand Oaks, CA: Sage, 2002), 427–44.

25 Trischa Goodnow Knapp and Lawrence A. Galizio, *The Elements of Parliamentary Debate: A Guide to Public Argument* (New York: Longman, 1999), 17–18.

26 Baird, *Argumentation, Discussion and Debate*, 95.

27 Dale Hample, *Arguing: Exchanging Reasons Face to Face* (Mahwah, NJ: Lawrence Erlbaum, 2005), 200.

28 Dean Fadely, *Advocacy: The Essentials of Argumentation and Debate* (Dubuque, IA: Kendall Hunt, 1994), 55.

29 Robert P. Newman and Dale R. Newman, *Evidence* (New York: Houghton-Mifflin, 1969), vii.

30 On the general topic of how the communication field's pedagogical roots inflect communication theory, see Richard Graff and Michael Leff, "Revisionist Historiography and Rhetorical Tradition(s)," in *The Viability of the Rhetorical Tradition*, ed. Richard Graff, Arthur E. Walzer, and Janet M. Atwill (Albany: State University of New York Press, 2005), 11–30.

31 Robert P. Newman, "Communication Pathologies of Intelligence Systems," *Speech Monographs* 42 (1975): 271–90.

32 Dale Hample, "Testing a Model of Value Argument and Evidence," *Communication Monographs* 44 (1977): 106–20; Hans Hoeken, "Anecdotal, Statistical and Causal Evidence: Their Perceived and Actual Persuasiveness," *Argumentation* 15 (2001): 425–37.

33 Carl G. Hempel, "A Purely Syntactical Definition of Confirmation," *Journal of Symbolic Logic* 8 (1943): 122–43.

34 Cháim Perelman and Lucie Olbrechts-Tyteca, *The New Rhetoric: A Treatise on Argumentation*, trans. John Wilkinson and Purcell Weaver (Notre Dame, IN: University of Notre Dame Press, 1969).

35 Greg Thielmann, "Intelligence in Preventive Military Strategies," in *Hitting First: Preventive Force in U.S. Security Strategy*, ed. William W. Keller and Gordon R. Mitchell (Pittsburgh: University of Pittsburgh Press, 2006), 153–74.

36 John A. Kringen, "How We've Improved Intelligence: Minimizing the Risk of 'Group-think,' " *Washington Post*, April 3, 2006, A19.

37 Carr, "Building Bridges."

38 Dan Doney, quoted in Carr, "Building Bridges."

39 Carr, "Building Bridges."

40 John Gastil, *Political Communication and Deliberation* (Thousand Oaks, CA: Sage, 2008), 8.

41 For an illuminating collection of case studies in this burgeoning area of scholarship, see John Gastil and Peter Levine, ed., *The Deliberative Democracy Handbook* (San Francisco: Jossey-Bass, 2005).

42 One notable exception is Christopher F. Karpowitz and Jane Mansbridge's chapter, "Disagreement and Consensus: The Importance of Dynamic Updating in Public Deliberation," in *The Deliberative Democracy Handbook*, ed. John Gastil and Peter Levine (San Francisco: Jossey-Bass, 2005).

43 David J. Mathews and Noelle McAfee, *Making Choices Together: The Power of Public Deliberation* (Dayton, OH: Kettering Foundation, 2003), 10.

44 Emily Robertson, "Teacher Education in a Democratic Society: Learning and Teaching the Practices of Democratic Participation," in *The Handbook of Research on Teacher Education*, 3rd ed., ed. Marilyn Cochran-Smith, Sharon Freiman-Nemser, and D. John McIntyre (London: Routledge, 2008), 32.

45 University of Houston, Downtown Center for Public Deliberation, "What is Public Deliberation," www.uhd.edu/academics/humanities/news-community/center-public-deliberation/Pages/uhd-cpd-what-is.aspx (accessed October 20, 2009 [Link updated and accessed 8 August 2019—RAH]).

46 On vapid presidential debates, compare George Farah's *No Debate: How the Republican and Democratic Parties Secretly Control the Presidential Debates* (New York: Seven Stories Press, 2004) with former intercollegiate debaters Newton N. Minow and Craig L. LaMay's more measured, yet still critical account. See Minow, LaMay and Vartan Gregorian, *Inside the Presidential Debates: Their Improbable Past and Promising Future* (Chicago: University of Chicago Press, 2008). Deborah Tannen's *The Argument Culture* (New York: Ballantine Books, 1999) catalogs an array of combative, headstrong episodes of argumentation that are sometimes characterized as legitimate "debates" in popular culture and politics.

47 This line of thinking is intended to endorse neither complete erasure of the theoretical differences between debate and deliberation, nor denigration of deliberation on its own terms. Rather, it signals receptivity to theoretical frameworks, such as James R. Crosswhite's "rhetoric of reason," that foreground the multifaceted dimensions of argumentative practice, some which are more consistent with deliberative objectives than others. See James Crosswhite, *The Rhetoric of Reason: Writing and the Attractions of Argument* (Madison: University of Wisconsin Press, 1996).

48 Dan Doney, quoted in Carr, "Building Bridges."

49 Langdon Winner, *The Whale and the Reactor: A Search for Limits in an Age of High Technology* (Chicago: University of Chicago Press, 1986), 19.

50 Thomas Lord, comment on Carr, "Building Bridges," April 22, 2009 on line at *http://radar. oreilly.com/2009/04/building-bridges-with-the-us-i-html#comment-2058136* (accessed November 1, 2009).

51 Giandomenico Majone, *Evidence, Argument, & Persuasion in the Policy Process* (New Haven, CT: Yale University Press, 1989), 12–20, 5, 2.

52 Ibrahim Goodwin, personal correspondence with Gordon Mitchell, July 21, 2009.

53 John Davis, personal correspondence with Gordon Mitchell, June 7, 2009. In personal correspondence with Gordon Mitchell on August 4, 2009, debater Seth Gannon reinforced this notion: "Our EPA audience expressed great thanks for a debate on the merits of their policies that was invested only in the debate process and not any particular interests."

54 Majone, *Evidence, Argument and Persuasion*, 5.

55 Frank Fischer, *Citizens, Experts and the Environment: The Politics of Local Knowledge* (Durham, NC: Duke University Press, 2000), 257; Charles Arthur Willard, *Liberalism and the Problem of Knowledge: A New Rhetoric for Modern Democracy* (Chicago: University of Chicago Press, 1996). Fischer goes on to spell out one implication flowing from this line of thinking, that policy analysts "must develop a quite different set of skills. … Beyond a competent grasp of empirical-analytic skills, he or she requires as well the ability to effectively share and convey information to the larger public. In this sense, the analyst is as much an educator as a substantive policy expert. The pedagogical task is to help people see and tease out the assumptions and conflicts underlying particular policy positions, as well as the consequences of resolving them in one way or another" (Fischer, *Citizens, Experts and the Environment*, 261). For related analysis of this theme in the context of a programmatic effort to integrate argumentation theory with science studies, see William Rehg, *Cogent Science in Context: The Science Wars, Argumentation Theory, and Habermas* (Cambridge: Massachusetts Institute of Technology Press, 2009).

56 John Forester, *Critical Theory, Public Policy, and Planning Practice: Toward a Critical Pragmatism* (Albany: State University of New York Press, 1993), 59. Specifically, Forester suggests "spreading design responsibility" and "promoting critically constructive design and policy criticism" as mechanisms for policy planners to incorporate argumentation into their

professional practices (29). In the context of scientific inquiry, Steve Fuller makes similar points. See Steve Fuller, *Social Epistemology* (Bloomington: Indiana University Press, 1991); Steve Fuller, *The Governance of Science: Ideology and the Future of the Open Society* (Buckingham, UK: Open University Press, 2000).

57 As Jane Munksgaard and Damien Pfister observe, when pursued in the context of public debate, "switch-sides debating represents the ultimate consideration of various perspectives. Students must do intensive research and reading to inform themselves of various sides of an issue ... credibly advance those views as advocates, and rebuild their positions through cross-examination and rebuttal. Switch-sides debating displays the possibilities of intellectual engagement as a process of understanding, not combat. Careful consideration of others' opinions reshapes the metaphor of argument as war into a metaphor of collaboration." See Jane Munksgaard and Damien Pfister, "The Public Debater's Role in Advancing Deliberation: Towards Switch-Sides Public Debate," in *Critical Problems in Argumentation*, ed. Charles Willard (Washington, DC: National Communication Association, 2003), 506.

58 See Randy Allen Harris, ed., *Landmark Essays on Rhetoric of Science: Case Studies* Second edition. (London: Routledge, 2018).

59 Such grounding may help ease disciplinary anxieties raised by commentators such as Leah Ceccarelli, who paint a dim picture regarding the potential of the rhetoric of science for scholarly and policy impact beyond the field of communication. See Leah Ceccarelli, "A Hard Look at Ourselves: A Reception Study of Rhetoric of Science," *Technical Communication Quarterly* 14 (2005): 257–65.

60 John W. Davis, "Words as Weapons," Debate Solutions website, December 5, 2007, *static. wamu.org/d/programs/kn/08/01/words_as_weapons.pdf* (accessed October 20, 2009 [Link updated and accessed 8 August 2019—RAH]).

61 Sprague, *The Older Sophists*; see also John Poulakos, "Rhetoric and Civic Education," 81–82.

62 Schiappa, *Protagoras and Logos*, 100, 117–23, 103–16.

63 Ekaterina Haskins, *Logos and Power in Isocrates and Aristotle* (Columbia: University of South Carolina Press, 1997), 88.

64 Isocrates, *Panathenaicus*, trans. George Norlin, Loeb Classical Library, Vol. 2 (London: William Heinemann, 1929), 14, 76.

65 Isocrates, *Nicocles*, and *On the Peace*, trans. George Norlin, Loeb Classical Library, Vol. 2 (London: William Heinemann, 1929), 19, 2, 9.

66 Isocrates, *Panathenaicus*, and *Panegyricus*, trans. George Norlin, Loeb Classical Library, Vol. 1 (London: William Heinemann, 1928), 146, 81.

67 Isocrates, *Panegyricus, Helen*, and *Against Callimachus*, trans. Larue Van Hook, Loeb Classical Library, Vol. 3 (London: William Heinemann, 1945), 43, 40, 45; see also Takis Poulakos, *Speaking for the Polis: Isocrates' Rhetorical Education* (Columbia: University of South Carolina Press, 1997), 19; Haskins, *Logos and Power*, 8; and Kathleen E. Welch, *Electric Rhetoric: Classical Rhetoric, Oralism and a New Literacy* (Cambridge: Massachusetts Institute of Technology Press, 1999).

68 *The Great Debaters*, dir. Denzel Washington (Chicago: Harpo Films, 2007). Timothy M. O'Donnell provides insightful commentary on the historical and prospective significance of this film in " 'The Great Debaters': A Challenge to Higher Education," his January 7, 2008, article for *Inside Higher Education*, www.insidehighered.com/views/2008/01/07/great-debaters-challenge-higher-education [Link updated and accessed 8 August 2019—RAH]; as well as his "The Pittsburgh Debaters," an article published in *The Pittsburgh Post-Gazette*, December

30, 2007, www.post-gazette.com/opinion/2007/12/30/Sunday-Forum-The-Pittsburgh-debaters/stories/200712300169 (accessed October 20, 2009 [Link updated and accessed 8 August 2019—RAH]).

69 Douglas Ehninger and Wayne Brockriede, *Decision by Debate* (New York: Dodd, Mead, 1963). For related commentary on the entwinement of debate tournament competition and public debating, see Gordon R. Mitchell and Takeshi Suzuki, "Beyond the *Daily Me*: Argumentation in an Age of Enclave Deliberation," in *Argumentation and Social Cognition*, ed. Takeshi Suzuki, Yoshiro Yano, and Takayuki Kato (Tokyo: Japan Debate Association, 2004), 160–66; Joe Miller, *Cross-X* (New York: Farrar, Strauss and Giroux, 2006), 470–78.

70 See Davis, "Words as Weapons."

71 Munksgaard and Pfister, "Public Debater's Role," 507.

72 Gaonkar, "The Idea of Rhetoric." For a survey of early rhetoric of science scholarship, see Harris, *Landmark Essays.*

73 Edward Schiappa, "Second Thoughts on the Critiques of Big Rhetoric," *Philosophy and Rhetoric* 34 (2001): 260–74; see also Herbert W. Simons, ed., *The Rhetorical Turn: Invention and Persuasion in the Conduct of Inquiry* (Chicago: University of Chicago Press, 1990).

74 Government initiatives calling on rhetorical scholars to support collective deliberation around issues of science and technology are taking place in other contexts as well. For example, the Institute for Civic Discource and Democracy (ICDD), a multi-disciplinary group launched from the Speech Communication Department at Kansas State University, is engaged in research, teaching, and outreach focused on deliberative processes such as the "Great Plains States Wind Energy Consortium" and the "Agricultural Decision Making under Uncertainty" project. In both cases, communication scholars were recruited as collaborators because the respective grant agencies (Environmental Protection Agency and National Science Foundation) stipulated that projects should include deliberative elements that engage people who would be using/adapting the discoveries generated by scientific research. ICDD's role would be to construct and convene deliberations while also researching the content and processes employed during those deliberations.

75 Forester, *Critical Theory*, 59.

76 Gaonkar, "The Idea of Rhetoric," 78, n.3.

77 Dilip Parameshwar Gaonkar, "Aspects of Sophistic Pedagogy" (Ph.D. diss., University of Pittsburgh, 1984), 121.

78 Gaonkar, "Aspects of Sophistic Pedagogy," 248, emphasis added.

79 Robert Hariman, "Civic Education, Classical Imitation, and Democratic Polity," in *Isocrates and Civic Education*, 228, 217.

16.
UNCERTAINTY, SPHERES OF ARGUMENT, AND THE TRANSGRESSIVE ETHOS OF THE SCIENCE ADVISER
by Lynda Walsh and Kenneth C. Walker

1. Introduction

Uncertainty as a topic of argument stands in a special relationship to ethos—persuasive performances of authority and character—because there must always be an un/certain "I" or "we." Uncertainty is the goad that drives us to locate ourselves and others on the map of the cosmos, and argumentation is the *techne* we have developed to manage this cosmology. This was the essential insight behind Thomas Goodnight's (1982) Spheres of Argument model. Goodnight (1982) reasoned that "all argumentation is involved in the creative resolution or the resolute creation of uncertainty" (p. 215) but noted that these arguments appeared to be grounded in three distinct spheres: personal, technical, and public. Managing uncertainty in the personal sphere involved appeals to individual experience or perception and often took place on an intimate scale; managing uncertainty in the technical sphere required the standards and forums of a profession; managing uncertainty in the public sphere recruited shared political values and took place in ostensibly open forums such as courts, legislatures, and rallies (Goodnight, 1982, p. 216). Goodnight pointed out that a single issue, such as a murder trial, could recruit reasons from multiple spheres even if it took place in a forum characteristic to one of them (a courtroom); he also demonstrated how an issue, such as a sick child, could initiate in the personal sphere and then move through technical (medical) and public (policy) spheres over time as attempts to resolve its uncertainties recruited larger and larger working groups.

While the spheres model has generated many productive studies of uncertainty, and while Goodnight (1982) hinted that these studies "may illuminate the values, character, and blindspots of an era, society, or person" (p. 216), the role of ethos in the model remains largely unexamined, particularly as it mediates public and technical spheres of

Lynda Walsh and Kenny Walker. "Uncertainty, Spheres of Argument and the Transgressive Ethos of the Science Adviser." In Jean Goodwin, Michael F. Dahlstrom, and Susanna Priest, eds. *Ethical Issues in Science Communication: A Theory-Based Approach.* Proceedings of the Third Summer Symposium on Science Communication, Iowa State Symposium on Science Communication Volume 3, Ames: Iowa State Digital Press, 2013, pp. 325–335.

argumentation.[1] This is an oversight worth addressing for a few reasons. Chief among Goodnight's (1982) concerns was the "erosion" of the public sphere by privatized technical activity (p. 221); meanwhile, the ethos of the science adviser—a scientist called upon for expert advice in public debates—appears as a salient mediator between technical and public spheres; therefore, the science adviser's ethos seems like a good place to start searching for specific mechanisms of erosion. At the same time, if arguments about uncertainty entail ethos (the un/certain speaker), and there are three spheres of uncertainty, it stands to reason that ethos may perform differently in these spheres. This insight concords with the oldest known definition of ethos as custom, habit, or dwelling place—in other words, a role traditionally associated with a procedure or forum for managing uncertainty (Hyde, 2004). However, we must remember that ethos is also character—that combination of good sense (*phronesis*), moral excellence (*arête*), and goodwill (*eunoia*) that warrants the claims a person makes about the world (Aristotle, trans. 2007, 2.1378a5). So, when a science adviser expresses uncertainty, she both *articulates her character* and *locates herself in a particular forum* of argumentation.

These warranting and orienting functions of ethos usefully complicate Goodnight's model by directing our attention to how character performances and forum-specific roles interact to integrate spheres of argumentation. They also help explain the otherwise unpredictable reception of science advisers in the public sphere, a reception that tends to oscillate between "doctor worship" and witch-hunt (Wood, 1964, p. 43). In this paper we clarify the interactions of uncertainty type, forum of argumentation, and character performance in the reception of science advisers, using several historical cases as touchstones. Understanding these interactions, we contend, can help explain the erosion of the boundaries between public and technical spheres and can help science advisers select more effective ethotic performances in public debates.[2]

2. Ethos and the Spheres

In his flagship article, Goodnight (1982) does not provide a full-fledged theory of how the spheres of argument stay integrated in a polity, yet this integration is key to the "so what?" of his model: namely, that public deliberation is disappearing into personal and technical spheres. What are the channels that enable this erosion? Goodnight (1982) mentions a "disagreement" as one channel that opens *kairos* after *kairos* in sphere after sphere until the uncertainty at stake is resolved or loses its exigence (p. 218); however, Goodnight seems to believe disagreements refresh rather than sap public argumentation. Another, more suspect channel is the mass media, via which "deliberation is replaced by consumption" (Goodnight, 1982, p. 223); but while it is easy to see how media consumption might expand personal grounds of evaluation at the expense of public grounds, it is harder to see how it would expand the purview of the technical sphere.

A more likely agent responsible for sequestering public argumentation in technical forums is hinted at in Goodnight's (1982) lengthy quotations from Charles Beard, the preeminent historian of early 20th century American technocracy: the technocratic science adviser. Not only do science advisers physically travel back and forth from technical to public forums of argumentation, but technical arguments crucially depend on their ethos. When a science adviser says "I believe humans are causing climate change because my models all point to industry as the prime driver of warming," certainly the reasons ("my models point to industry …") and the grounds (evidence showing that the scientists' models do in fact point to industrial drivers) of that argument are technical. Nonetheless, this argument only coheres if the audience buys its warrant, which is something like "my models are reliable *techne* for determining climate change." Since the science adviser made the models, the warrant really comes to roost in the character of the adviser herself, in her technical ethos.

Here is the crux of the matter: the adviser's technical ethos has two parts—a role that is bound to technical forums for managing uncertainty; and a character that, while it was developed in technical forums, nonetheless travels with her like a lab coat from sphere to sphere in the course of her daily life. Because technical character can travel in this way, it helps integrate public and technical spheres of uncertainty management: we call on technical experts to help resolve uncertainties in public debate, and this conversation keeps the spheres of argumentation connected and porous.

However, the eminent portability of ethos-as-character can create conflicts with ethos-as-role in a particular forum. We are all familiar with these kinds of clashes: consider the eye-rolling that commences when a psychologist friend starts pontificating about the behavior of the people at a party (technical ethos performed in a personal forum), the snickering about the personal tics of a politician (personal ethos performed in a public forum), the denunciations following a scientist expressing their political views at a professional meeting (personal ethos performed in a technical forum). These clashes of character and forum are easy to recognize in our daily lives, but we have yet to treat them seriously in the public reception of science advisers. The first step is understanding how types of uncertainty—personal, technical, and political (public)—condition the expected roles of scientists in those forums. The next step will be to consider what happens when science advisers carry all three of their characters—personal, technical, and political—into public forums.

3. Ethos and Uncertainty in Science Advising: Forum

Uncertainty is a boundary object not just between academia and the polis but even among the academic disciplines that work on the problem. Unique definitions of uncertainty populate the literature on systems modeling, cognitive psychology, linguistics, philosophy, rhetoric, sociology, and political science—and yet scholars of scientific argumentation who work with sources from several or all of these disciplines often persist in using the term as if it has a single, consensual definition. While this kind of willful misunderstanding has been shown to be helpful in scaffolding collaboration across political borders (Shackley & Wynne, 1996; Zehr, 1999), we must be able to recognize the characteristics of different spheres of uncertainty argumentation because they yield different consequences for the ethotic performances of science advisers.

3.1 Personal Uncertainty

Personal uncertainties revolve around expressions of commitment to particular claims about the world. Cognitive psychologists, epistemologists, linguists, and rhetoricians have studied personal uncertainty in scientific argument, and they have focused in particular on hedging (e.g., "*We believe* the results are robust" v. "the results are robust" (Hyland, 1998)), claim strength (e.g., "Evapotranspiration is *the primary* predictor of plant resilience" v. "*We found* evapotranspiration to be *a significant* driver of plant resilience *within the study area*" (Latour & Woolgar, 1986, pp. 75–90)), and accommodation (e.g., the tendency of scientific arguments to move up-stasis, generalize, and emphasize novelty as they recruit wider publics; cf. "Scientists have discovered an antioxidant peptide in mussels" v. "Scientists find cure for cancer!" (Fahnestock, 1986)).

These expressions of personal un/certainty are regulated by norms, the most famous formulation of which is Merton's (1973) CUDOS: Communism (the scientist should relate herself to scientific knowledge not as an individual owner but as a member of a community); Universalism (the scientist's nationality or ethnicity should not perturb the knowledge s/he acquires); Disinterestedness (the scientist's personal agendas should not taint the knowledge s/he acquires); and Organized Skepticism (the scientist's job is to question rather than to commit herself to scientific knowledge). Mertonian norms prohibit strong expressions of personal commitment to beliefs about nature or to policy predicated on these beliefs. These are norms, not descriptions: in practice, individual scientists have been observed to be selfish, parochial, biased, and dogmatic (Barnes, 1970; Mitroff, 1974). But that does not stop them from giving lip-service to the norms and enforcing them on their colleagues.

3.2 Technical Uncertainty

Technical uncertainties concern scientists' instruments and techniques—which we will combine under the heading *techne*—for constructing knowledge about nature. Technical uncertainties include those about whether *techne* are sensitive enough to register the phenomena of interest (metrical uncertainty), uncertainties about whether models are taking into account all the important drivers of a particular phenomenon (structural uncertainty), and uncertainties about how to interpret model results (translational uncertainty; Rowe, 1994). These uncertainties frequently catalyze public debates about associated risks, especially regarding climate change and nuclear energy. Into these debates the scientist is called as an adviser on the warrant of her technical character.

Technical character and the *techne* of uncertainty reduction (models, etc.) exist in a kind of ethotic symbiosis: the reliability of the *techne* stand on the reputation of the scientist; meanwhile, the scientist's reputation stands on the strength of the *techne* she has developed for reducing uncertainty. This symbiotic relationship can result in *techne* standing in as a proxy for technical character in public debates about uncertainty. Carolyn Miller (2003) found in her study of the Rasmussen report that when audiences asked for judgments about risks, science advisers tended to defer to their models. The models thus stood in for the advisers' technical character and gave them deniability in the case of error or disaster (Miller, 2003, p. 184). Miller called this proxy function "technical ethos"; we will temporarily rename it "*techne*-ethos" to avoid confusion with the terminology of Goodnight's model.

3.3 Political Uncertainty

Political uncertainties—those negotiated in the public sphere—do not concern questions of knowledge but questions of right action based on shared values. So, we are not dealing here with comprehension but with conviction; not *scientific certainty*, which is a patent impossibility, but *political certainty*, which is temporarily and provisionally achievable in policy. And yet the two categories are conflated all the time in policymaking (Pielke, 2007, p. 35). Both scientists and politicians present the reduction of scientific uncertainty as a means to political certainty, a myth that covers up the role that political values *must* play in constructing political certainty. This myth scaffolds the continued collaboration of politicians and scientists (Shackley & Wynne, 1996, p. 280); it is also the chief facilitator of the problem that most worried Goodnight (1982)—the cooption of public argumentation by the technical sphere.

4. Ethos and Uncertainty in Science Advising: Character

Now that we have reviewed the way that spheres of uncertainty argumentation shape the roles science advisers are expected to play in personal, technical, and public forums, we can turn to considering the interaction of these forum-specific roles with the advisers' performances of character.

Generally speaking, scientists' character performances are well-received if they take place in the forum that originally shaped them, e.g., technical character in technical forums, personal character in personal forums. But something odd happens to scientists in public forums: performances of political character (i.e., arguments grounded in appeals to shared values and warranted by citizenship) are not predictably felicitous; in fact, they're often strongly censured. Why?

The obvious answer is that we seem to expect science advisers to continue to perform technical character in political forums: after all, technical expertise formed the grounds for their public calling in the first place. But a logical fallacy hides in this reasoning: the warrant provided by technical expertise does not support political arguments. Political arguments—in Goodnight's (1982) model—engage political, not technical, uncertainties; are grounded in shared values, not *techne*; and are warranted by political character, not technical character. For example, in an argument about whether cap-and-trade violates the spirit of free-market capitalism, the warrant is "free-market capitalism is important to preserve," a value that a science adviser's methods and models have no traction on and that does not reference her expertise.

Yet, we continue to call scientists into public debates and to insist against logic and practical experience that the reductions in technical uncertainty they can provide will automatically yield reductions in political uncertainty. This insistence is not founded in technical ignorance but on a model of argumentation that pre-dates Goodnight's (1982) model and does not distinguish between technical and public spheres. This Enlightenment model for integrating science and policy tapped natural philosophers (the precursors of our scientists), who were fast discovering the laws that governed all of nature (including human society), as those best qualified to make policy. This technocratic or progressive model unproblematically derived values from facts, conflated technical and political certainties, and called on the science adviser to serve as both arbiter of information and evaluative decision maker (Ferris, 2010, p. 104; Shapin, 2008, p. 24).

But the progressive model is not the only model that dictates the roles our science advisers should play in public forums. A powerful competitor arose in response to abuses of technocracy: the is/ought model, articulated on grounds first laid by David Hume (1740/2010), pursues the logical conundrum articulated above in our discussion of the differences between technical and political uncertainty—namely, that you cannot derive what you "ought" to do from what "is" the case with nature or society; a value structure must always be interpolated before policy can be made (Shapin, 2008, p. 11). This is the model that split the technical and political spheres. Under the is/ought model, scientists are admonished to do their work in the technical sphere and then somehow pass the results through the membrane separating that sphere from the public sphere to politicians. The politicians then attach shared values to the technical information and make policy on that foundation.

Both models still operate, waxing and waning with the political tides and creating an unpredictable ethotic atmosphere for science advisers. When progressive administrations are in power, or when there is a strong national consensus on an issue, the progressive model of science-policy integration dominates, and science advisers achieve powerful policymaking positions that license their performances of political character. However, if they refuse to make policy recommendations in these milieu for some reason—perhaps the habitual practice of CUDOS or fear of reprisal from peers in the technical sphere—they can be censured for obstructing policymaking or lose ground to other scientists who are willing to advocate policy (Brooks, 1964, pp. 85–86; Pielke, 2007, p. 16). While surely exasperating to the science adviser, these pressures are appreciable from the politician's perspective: if you have reached out in a crisis for advice to someone you believe has special access to knowledge, someone whom you have given millions of dollars to secure this knowledge, you don't want to hear "We don't have enough data to say for sure" or "We don't know." You want answers.

When conservative administrations come to power, on the other hand, or when issues seriously divide public opinion, science advisers are predictably censured for performing personal or political character, as such performances are considered to have transgressed the scientist's proper sphere (technical), *even when the adviser has been called into a political forum.* The science adviser wears the stereotype of CUDOS into public forums like a lab coat, and politicians and citizens are just as likely as peers to punish a science adviser's expressions of emotion, personal values, or loyalty to a particular party (Porter, 1995, p. 7).

In a pluralist democracy such as the United States, the political footing for science advisers becomes even more unstable when, say, a progressive executive squares off against a conservative Congress—a charged environment of conflicting values. In these situations, a science adviser can find herself, on a relatively short time span, welcomed into the public sphere on the progressive model and then charged with trespassing on the is/ought model. Such was Robert Oppenheimer's experience between his appointment to the Atomic Energy Commission's advisory committee by Truman in 1947 and the stripping of his security clearance by Eisenhower in 1954; similarly, Michael Mann was appointed to the UN Intergovernmental Panel on Climate Change (IPCC) in 1998 but, beginning in 2005, investigated by Congress (and six other agencies) after the publication of the infamous "hockey stick" graph in the IPCC's *Third Assessment Report* (2001).

To cope with this volatile ethotic environment, science advisers have chosen a range of ethotic strategies, but most fall into two categories: foregrounding technical character (*techne*-ethos), and foregrounding political character (prophetic ethos). We will briefly examine some illustrative historical cases in these categories: there are no salient examples of science advisers hewing to the personal rigors of CUDOS because refusing to make policy recommendations on the grounds of Disinterestedness and Organized Skepticism virtually guarantees that a scientist won't last as a science adviser (Jasanoff, 1994, p. 16; Pielke, 2007, pp. 4–5).

4.1 Foregrounding Technical Character (*Techne*-Ethos)

Some science advisers choose to foreground their methods and models as proxies for performances of technical character in public forums. Miller (2003) was the first to document such a case, as mentioned above. Jamieson (2000) observed that economists pushed criticism of their work off on their models, which were amenable to quick repair and improvement in a way that their technical reputations were not (p. 319). Walsh (2013) found that a similar strategy involving climate visualizations helped IPCC scientists deflect attacks on their technical character (pp. 179–180). However, these studies also noted side effects: first, deploying *techne*-ethos as a shield can lead stakeholders to believe that the *techne* somehow work independently of the scientist who created them, that they channel natural truths directly and unproblematically; this misconception Walsh (2014) has labeled the "myth of natural inscription." As a result of this myth, a second side effect emerges: stakeholders come to believe that *techne*, not people, make policy—thus complicating justice and accountability in science policymaking.

4.2 Foregrounding Political Character (Prophetic Ethos)

Science advisers can respond to the volatility of the public sphere by foregrounding their political character and calling for policy change on the basis of their special access to knowledge in the technical sphere. Walsh (2013) calls this performance of political character by scientists "prophetic ethos." There are multiple historical examples of science advisers performing prophetic ethos with variable success.

Frequently, science advisers are censured for performances of prophetic ethos, particularly under conservative administrations or in periods of high political uncertainty.

Robert Oppenheimer embraced prophetic ethos in the wake of the bombing of Hiroshima and Nagasaki, sitting on a number of government advisory boards and giving press interviews in which he intoned aphoristic warnings such as "the physicists have known sin," and "we [the U.S. and U.S.S.R.] can be likened to two scorpions in a bottle, each capable of killing the other, but only at the risk of his own life" (Bird & Sherwin, 2006, pp. 323, 465). As indicated above, a change in administrations put Oppenheimer in front of an ethics panel that ended his career as a federal science adviser. Along the same lines, climatologist James Hansen has performed prophetic ethos for the last 25 years, during which he testified before Congress on the dangerous "greenhouse effect," was arrested for sit-in protests of coal mining operations, and published books with titles like *Storms of My Grandchildren: The Truth About the Coming Climate Catastrophe and Our Last Chance to Save Humanity.* Hansen has experienced a mixed reception of this prophetic performance: on the one hand, he is one of the most recognized public figures associated with climate change debates, and he is credited with putting global warming on the national radar. On the other hand, he has claimed to be repeatedly and systematically censored by Bush administration officials, and he cast his retirement from NASA as a response to these pressures (Gillis, 2013).

In other instances, science advisers have managed to avoid censure and even catalyze policy by performing prophetic ethos. For example, in the *kairos* surrounding the publication of *Silent Spring,* Goodnight (1982) and Walker (2013) both observed how Rachel Carson leveraged growing public awareness of a crisis in the use of pesticides, a crisis that had been sequestered until very recently in the technical sphere, in government labs and the confidential internal reports of chemical companies. Against the technocratic ethos of these experts, Carson performed a prophetic ethos, speaking on behalf of silenced mothers and crop-workers. She positioned herself as the people's science adviser, helping them retake the halls of government from the usurping technocrats. She testified before two federal committees and was credited in the eventual banning of DDT (though she had never explicitly advocated a ban) and the formation of the Environmental Protection Agency (which she did explicitly advocate).

Likewise, atmospheric physicists F. Sherwood Rowland and Mario Molina (1994) illustrate a case in which the very scientists who discovered the chemical reactions depleting the ozone were also among the first to call for action to stop it and to avert immanent threats. Like Carson, Rowland and Molina took their jeremiad to various polities and were heavily criticized by peers, industry, and politicians for doing so, yet they prevailed and even augmented their technical characters through the political fight.

While these prophetic performances succeeded in many ways, it is clear that they did not bootstrap the agency necessary to catalyze international policy; rather, this agency flowed from a whole series of events that increased political certainty on the issues involved. Carson's performance rode a cresting wave of public fears about chemical and nuclear contaminants, benefited from the media attention already attracted to these fears, and was warmly received by an incoming progressive administration. She also escaped typical channels of censure since she was an independently funded scholar. Rowland and Molina's performance took advantage of a series of heat waves, vivid images of the ozone "hole," and existing cancer frameworks, to name a few amplifiers.

All of these factors were clearly beyond the science advisers' control. Thus, while these successful performances of prophetic ethos are instructive, they are not necessarily replicable.

5. Conclusion

Our examination of the interaction of forum and character in the ethotic performances of science advisers suggests a new explanatory account of Goodnight's (1982) concerns about the cooption of public argumentation by the technical sphere. First, the spheres model is substantially enabled by the is/ought model for science-policy integration, which "divided the waters" of the technical and public spheres in response to ethical abuses by technocrats. As a result, the public-forum role assigned to science advisers brings with it two incompatible spheric models—one that insists upon and one that refuses to recognize the segregation of the political from the technical. Finally, the conflation of technical and public uncertainties inherent to the progressive model licenses illogical but persuasive technical warrants for public arguments; this rhetorical situation encourages politicians either to cloak their advocacy positions in *techne* (Pielke, 2007, p. 89), or to abdicate technical issues to science advisers, and thus to the technical sphere (Lapp, 1965, p. 227).

This account is productive for re-considering the integration—both salubrious and problematic—of the spheres of argumentation, but a question remains: what is the best ethotic stance for a science adviser in public debates about uncertainty? It should be clear by this point that there is no one-size-fits-all ethotic solution to this dilemma. There can be no ethos without *kairos*, and so a performance of technical ethos that is felicitous for one crisis, time, and forum will not remain so when those kairotic factors shift. That being said, as we enumerated the challenges science advisers have faced in selecting effective ethotic strategies, we also observed some felicitous patterns: 1.) When technical uncertainties are at stake in public debates, shifting the warrant of argument to *techne* (the reliability of models and methods) appears to insulate science advisers' character from attack, even as it reinforces the conflation of technical and political uncertainties; 2.) Under progressive administrations, prophetic performances of political character by science advisers tend to be rewarded, and policy gets made (and often, but not always, the opposite also holds); and 3.) When stakeholders believe that a public crisis has been illegitimately sequestered in the technical sphere, or when a broad consensus begins to emerge on a technical issue, a science adviser may effectively perform prophetic ethos to galvanize popular support for policy change.

These are observations, not recommendations, but they do support our contention that scientists must consider the types of uncertainty at stake—personal, technical, and/ or political—as well as the forum they are arguing in when selecting an appropriate ethotic stance; the stakes are particularly high for science advisers arguing in public forums.[3] This is the principal counsel we can offer science advisers—along with the recommendation to study cases of uncertainty management that bear on their particular situations before stepping into a public forum to argue about their work.

Notes

1 Doxtader (2000) addresses ethos as a "moderator" and anchor of public sphere argumentation but does not consider it as an integrator of Goodnight's spheres.

2 The original publication used the word *ethical* as the adjectival form of *ethos*. Because of its ambiguity with the sense of *ethical* from philosophy (namely, to signal, in a largely approbative way an action or belief in accord with the principles of some system of ethics) we have Brinton's (1986) *ethotic*, now widely adopted in argumentation studies, where it denotes "the kind of argument or technique of argument in which ethos is invoked, attended to, or represented in such a way as to lend credibility to or detract credibility from conclusions which are being drawn" (Brinton 1986:246) (RAH)

3 This caution particularly applies to readers of Pielke's (2007) *Honest Broker* framework. Pielke creates a two-by-two matrix defined by "Views of Science" (as integrated in a "linear" fashion with policy or as an iterative negotiation of scientific opportunity and social need) and "Views of Democracy" (Madisonian pluralist advocacy or Schattschneiderian voting on options selected by technocrats). The result is four "ideal" roles a science adviser can play: the pure scientist, the science arbiter, the issue advocate, and the honest broker. Pielke argues that all four ideal roles should be in circulation for science policy to function well in a democracy, but he's partial to the honest broker—while warning that organizations, not individuals, are best suited for this role and that even honest broker organizations are likely to lose political competitions with issue advocates, who are happy to comply with politicians' demands to narrow and simplify rather than expand and enrich policy landscapes. He provides a heuristic for science advisers to select the appropriate role: in cases of "values consensus and low uncertainty," advisers should serve as pure scientists or science arbiters. In all other cases (lack of consensus and low uncertainty, lack of consensus and high uncertainty, consensus and high uncertainty), he encourages advisers to choose between issue advocate and honest broker, depending on whether they want to narrow or expand policy options. The difficulty for rhetoricians wishing to apply Pielke's heuristic to historical cases is that it is not rhetorical; thus, it brackets out the role of ethos and *kairos*. First, it doesn't acknowledge the kairotic instability of the science advisers' public role. We have seen in the cases reviewed that the is/ought model and progressive model can conflict in defining this role on short time scales and even between agencies with which the science adviser has to work—and yet forum and *kairos* are bracketed out of Pielke's heuristic and its generative framework. Second, the heuristic does not acknowledge the unique category of personal uncertainties (expressions of commitment), lumping them in with political uncertainties (expressions of citizenship/articulations of shared values) and thus conflating political certainty with political consensus. A group can have consensus on the range and strength of its shared values and still be unable to commit to taking action if there is no exigence, no kairotic moment. Pielke assumes a high level of exigence in all science policy issues, but this is not always the case. A science adviser's sense of exigence, and thus her level of personal commitment to a policy option, clearly makes a difference when she is trying to choose between issue advocacy and honest brokerage.

References

Aristotle (2007). *On rhetoric: A theory of civic discourse*. G. A. Kennedy (Trans). New York, NY: Oxford University Press.

Barnes, B., & Dolby, R. G. A. (1970). The scientific ethos: A deviant viewpoint. *European Journal of Sociology, 9*, 3–25.

Bird, K., & Sherwin, M. (2006). *American Prometheus: The triumph and tragedy of J. Robert Oppenheimer*. New York, NY: Vintage Books.

Brinton, Alan. (1986). Ethotic argument. *History of Philosophy Quarterly, 3*, 3, 245–258.

Brooks, H. (1964). The scientific adviser. In R. Gilpin & C. Wright (Eds.), *Scientists and national policy-making* (pp. 73–96). New York, NY: Columbia University Press.

Doxtader, E. W. (2000). Characters in the middle of public life: Consensus, dissent, and ethos. *Philosophy & Rhetoric, 33*(4), 336–369.

Fahnestock, J. (1986). Accommodating science: The rhetorical life of scientific facts. *Written Communication, 3*(3), 275–296.

Ferris, T. (2010). *The science of liberty: Democracy, reason, and the laws of nature*. New York, NY: Harper Perennial.

Gillis, J. (2013, April 1.). Climate maverick to retire from NASA. *New York Times*. Retrieved from www.nytimes.com/2013/04/02/science/james-e-hansen-retiring-from-nasa-to-fight-global-warming.html [Link updated and accessed 8 August 2019—RAH]

Goodnight, T. (1982). The personal, technical, and public spheres of argument: A speculative inquiry into the art of public deliberation. *Journal of the American Forensic Association, 18*, 214–227.

Hyde, M. J. (2004). Rhetorically, we dwell. In M. J. Hyde (Ed.), *The ethos of rhetoric* (pp. xiii–xxviii). Columbia, SC: University of South Carolina Press.

Hume, D. (2010). *Treatise of Human Nature*. In C. Choat (Ed.), *Project Gutenberg*. (Original work published 1740) Retrieved from www.gutenberg.org/files/4705/4705-h/4705-h.htm #2H_4_0085

Hyland, K. (1998). *Hedging in scientific research articles*. Philadelphia, PA: John Benjamins.

Jamieson, D. (2000). Prediction in society. In D. Sarewitz, R. A. Pielke Jr., & R. Byerly Jr. (Eds.), *Prediction: Science, decision making, and the future of nature* (pp. 315–325). Washington, D.C.: Island Books.

Jasanoff, S. (1994). *The fifth branch: Science advisers as policymakers*. Cambridge, MA: Harvard University Press.

Lapp, R. (1965). *The new priesthood*. New York, NY: Harper & Row.

Latour, B., & Woolgar, S. W. (1986). *Laboratory life: The construction of scientific facts*. Princeton, CT: Princeton University Press.

Merton, R.K. (1973). The normative structure of science. In N. Storer (Ed.), *The sociology of science: Theoretical and empirical investigations* (pp. 267–278). Chicago, IL: University of Chicago Press.

Miller, C. R. (2003). The presumptions of expertise: The role of ethos in risk analysis. *Configurations, 11*(2), 163–202. doi:10.1353/con.2004.0022

Mitroff, I. I. (1974). Norms and counter-norms in a select group of the Apollo moon scientists: A case study of the ambivalence of scientists. *American Sociological Review, 39*(4), 579–595.

Pielke, R.A., Jr. (2007) *The honest broker: Making sense of science in policy and politics*. New York, NY: Cambridge University Press.

Porter, T. (1995). *Trust in numbers: The pursuit of objectivity in science and in life*. Princeton, NJ: Princeton University Press.

Rowland, F.S. & Molina, M. (1994). Ozone depletion: 20 years after the alarm. *Chemical and Engineering News, 72(33)*, 8–13.

Rowe, W. D. (1994). Understanding uncertainty. *Risk Analysis, 14*(5), 743–750.

Shackley, S., & Wynne, B. (1996). Representing uncertainty in global climate change science and policy: Boundary-ordering devices and authority. *Science, Technology and Human Values, 21*(3), 275–302.

Shapin, S. (2008). *The scientific life.* Chicago, IL: University of Chicago Press.

Walker, K. (2013). "Without evidence, there is no answer": Uncertainty and scientific ethos in the *Silent Spring(s)* of Rachel Carson. *Environmental Humanities, 2,* 105–121.

Walsh, L. (2009). Visual strategies to integrate ethos across the "is / ought" divide in the IPCC's Climate Change 2007: Summary for policy makers. *POROI, 6*(2), 33–61.

Walsh, L. (2013). *Scientists as prophets: A rhetorical genealogy.* New York, NY: Oxford University Press.

Walsh, L. (2014). "Tricks," hockey sticks, and the myth of natural inscription: How the visual rhetoric of climategate conflated climate with character. In Nocke, T., Schneider, B. (Eds.), Image politics of climate change: Visualizations, imaginations, documentations (pp. 55-81). Bielefeld, Germany: Transcript Verlag.

Wood, R. C. (1964). Scientists and politics: The rise of an apolitical elite. In R. Gilpin & C. Wright (Eds.), *Scientists and national policy-making* (pp. 41–72). New York, NY: Columbia University Press.

Zehr, S. C. (1999). Scientists' representations of uncertainty. In S. M. Friedman, S. Dunwoody, & C. L. Rogers (Eds.), *Communicating uncertainty: Media coverage of new and controversial science* (pp. 3–22). Mahwah, NJ: Lawrence Erlbaum Associates.

PART 2

METHODS

Neomodern

17.

THE 1923 SCIENTISTIC CAMPAIGN AND DAO-DISCOURSE
A Cross-Cultural Study of the Rhetoric of Science
by Xiaosui Xiao

In the 1970s the intellectual waves stirred by philosophers, sociologists, and historians of science such as Thomas S. Kuhn, Stephen Toulmin, Robert Merton, Barry Barnes, David Bloor, Bruno Latour and Steve Woolgar, and Gerald Holton virtually washed out the "Berlin Wall" that had separated science from rhetoric from the time of Aristotle, and a new discipline called "the rhetoric of science" soon arose and began to bloom.[1] The young field had boundless prospects in the twenty-first century, a seemingly more exciting age of science. There are so many things in the scientific world that can be looked at from a rhetorical perspective if one begins to see scientists as persuaders. Recently, a prominent and promising trend of study has emphasized the specific contexts against which scientific argumentation is judged as persuasive. Lawrence Prelli, for instance, focused on the special culture of scientific communities, in which reasonable and persuasive scientific discourse was "perceived as identifying, modifying, or solving problems that bear on a specific community's maintenance and expansion of their comprehension of the natural order." Alan Gross's study of Newton's successful campaign for his radically new physics of light supported this view of science as a communal and cultural practice. The key to Newton's triumph, according to Gross, was the rhetorical invention of his "essential continuity" with the presumptions underlying the work of fellow physicists. Other rhetoricians look at the larger socio-cultural milieu. In his examination of Darwin's *Origin of Species*, John Angus Campbell convincingly showed that the prevailing intellectual trend of the mid-nineteenth century was toward Baconian science, and Darwin's "deference" to this trend basically explained the great success of Darwin's scientific revolution.[2]

This approach to the rhetoric of science, however, has not gone much beyond the contexts of Western cultures, although many of the typical cases for the rhetorical study of science, such as those of Galileo, Bacon, Newton, Darwin, and Einstein, have had worldwide influence. The past century has witnessed the rapid spread of the "gospel" of Western science in the East, which has brought about changes in the mindsets and lives of people in the East. A more challenging question for the rhetorician of scientific discourse thus becomes: How did this scientific gospel from the West come to be received as gospel by a non-Western and basically non-scientific nation?

Xiaosui Xiao. "The 1923 Scientistic Campaign and Dao-Discourse: A Cross-Cultural Study of the Rhetoric of Science." *Quarterly Journal of Speech*, Volume 90, Number 4, 2004, pp. 469–492.

The successful 1923 campaign to introduce an omnipotent concept of science in China is an excellent case for studying the rhetoric of scientific popularization in a cross-cultural context.[3] The campaign promoted popular conversions to the "god" of science among Chinese intellectuals at a time when these converts did not have much training in the logic or methods of science and who, for the most part, had been remote from the activities of any scientific community. Chinese intellectuals made their own judgments about the voice of reason, of course. The persuasiveness of the campaign, thus, has to be explained in terms of appeals appropriate to a different cultural and intellectual context.

Although early movements toward modern science in the West, as Edwin Arthur Burtt observed, took place in a cultural and intellectual context dominated by neo-Platonic and Christian-theological discourses,[4] the 1923 campaign must be examined in the context of the Chinese tradition of discourse on Dao. The tradition of "Dao-discourse" points to a sacred, profound, and long-standing form of discursive practice in traditional China geared to expounding and propagating the subtle meaning of Dao. As a core subject of discussion in Chinese culture, Dao generally was perceived as the ideal state of morality and society and as the "universal law" that governed both the natural world and human life.[5] In a narrow sense, Dao-discourse referred to a conscious disquisition on the subject of Dao. Lao Zi's *Daode jing* is by far the earliest known work of this kind, yet the topic must have attracted great attention in earlier times. Confucius himself was a fanatical audience of Dao-discourse; he said he would not regret dying in the evening if he heard the Dao in the morning.[6] After Lao Zi, all great Chinese thinkers continued to explore this subject through the ages. Zhuang Zi's (399–295 B.C.E.) "The Dao of Heaven," Liu An's (179–122 B.C.E.) "Teaching on the Essence of Dao," Yang Xiong's (53 B.C.E.–A.C.E. 18) "Asking about Dao," Guo Xiang's (251–312) "A Note on the Dao of Heaven," Ge Hong's (284–363) "The Meaning of Dao," Wang Tong's (584–618) "On the Kingly Dao," Han Yu's (768–824) "The Essence of Dao," Zhang Zai's (1020–1077) "The Dao of Heaven," Wang Tinxiang's (1474–1544) "The Substance of Dao," Wang Fuzhi's (1619–1692) "On the Dao of Heaven," and contemporary discourses such as Jin Yuelin's *A Treatise on Dao*, Feng Youlan's *A New Perspective on the Essence of Dao*, and Tang Junyi's *On the Essence of Dao* are but some modal disquisitions.[7] The study of Dao-discourse, however, should not be confined to these special and direct deliberations. According to Zhang Liwen et al., Chinese scholars have taken different approaches in their talk about Dao at different times, for instance by speaking of it in terms of "Heaven," "the Ultimate," "the Great Void," "Buddha-hood," "the Principle of Heaven," "Mind," and "*Qi*" (Vital Force).[8] Discussions on these related subjects should be considered indirect examples of Dao-discourse. The practice of Dao-discourse also should include religious discussions on subjects such as infinity, eternity, immorality, and God, which, to traditional Chinese audiences, concern nothing more than certain aspects of Dao. That is why all religious preaching in China has been generally called "the preaching on Dao" (*chuan Dao*). Having realized the spiritual power of Dao-discourse, the Christianized Jews who first came to China during the Song period (960–1279) translated "God" as "Dao." Consequently, as J. R. Stevenson observed, they "passed on to later members of their community a term that, with its strong flavor of immanence, radically changed the character of their transcendental God."[9]

I recommend that we view the early-twentieth-century Chinese campaign for science as a continuation of this sustained practice of Dao-discourse, which aimed at establishing an omnipotent concept of science. Modern scientists who speak about science have hesitated to use the term "Dao," however, because the term was too mysterious and surrounded by superstition for them to use it to describe the "laws" of nature. As this study will reveal, however, champions of science still followed the conventions of Dao-discourse, especially when addressing the "grant laws" of their scientific universe.

This particular approach to the modern Chinese campaign for science was reasonable in that Chinese socio-cultural and intellectual context. The 1923 scientific campaign differed from scientific campaigns in the West because it did not compete with other scientific viewpoints. Instead, it challenged traditional Chinese metaphysics for the position of the sole legitimate voice of Dao. Thus, whether the campaign spoke more scientifically than its metaphysical counterparts is not the relevant question of this study; rather, how did it come to be more persuasive than its competitors in the context of early-twentieth-century practice of Dao-discourse?

The discourse on Dao differs from discourse on any ordinary thing because it requires the adoption of particular modes of expression. This essay argues that the persuasiveness of the scientific campaign was owing primarily to the campaigners' application of the language of traditional discourse on Dao to preach the Dao of their scientific universe and, more fundamentally, to their style of scientific preaching, which reconfirmed the traditional assumptions of the almighty Dao while it was under serious threat.

This case extends our understanding of the rhetoric of scientific dissemination in a cross-cultural context. For the most part, rhetoricians who study scientific discourse have ignored the less scientific East, making the East a safe breeding ground for the modern myth of the scientific "gospel." Many, including Eastern scholars, have seen the last century's popularization of science in the East as an inevitable process in which Western scientific ideas shed their "irresistible" light of reason on the benighted and superstitious East.[10] A cultural approach, such as this one, to the study of the rhetorical process of scientific popularization in the East, one of the most fundamental processes in the twentieth-century East, can help us to understand not only the history of science in an Eastern culture. Examining this cultural process in light of the perspective of the tradition of Dao-discourse also can offer insight into the long-lasting consequences of the 1923 scientific movement in China. In particular, it helps to explain why this movement led China to a new myth, a new form of doctrinairism, and a new version of dogmatism—exactly the sorts of things that science aims to avoid.

The following examination begins with an account of the emergence of the 1923 scientific campaign as an active response to the challenge of traditional metaphysics. The account is followed by a brief review of the development of the tradition of Dao-discourse to provide a broader context for understanding this campaign. The ensuing analysis focuses on how the advocates of science made use of the conventions of this discursive tradition to justify their scientific worldview. The conclusion addresses the implications of this case for a cross-cultural study of the rhetoric of science and discusses its far-reaching effects on the contemporary intellectual history of China.

Science vs. Metaphysics

On February 14, 1923, at the time when Chinese started to see "science" as synonymous with modern civilization, Professor Zhang Junmai of Qinghua University in Beijing used a campus speech to ask a serious question of the Chinese public: Can science govern a view of life? According to Zhang, a view of life necessarily must be "subjective, intuitive, synthetic, freely willed, and unique to the individual." In contrast, Zhang saw science as "objective, determined by the logical method, analytical, and governed by the laws of cause and effect and by uniformity in nature."[11] The questions of one's philosophy of life, therefore, could not be answered by science, especially those questions relating to the psychological and ethical dimensions of human experience. Zhang's lecture was published, leading Ding Wenjiang, a geologist who regarded science as omnipotent, to respond with an essay criticizing Zhang's view.[12] Ding's critique prompted a public debate that included leading Chinese scholars and thinkers of the time.[13] To one defender of science, the debate was nothing less than "the first great battle in the thirty years since China's contact with Western culture."[14] It was described as a holy war against the "metaphysical ghosts."[15] At the end of the controversy, as Li Zehou observed, the pro-science, anti-metaphysics group had gained overwhelming support from the young intelligentsia while the "metaphysical ghosts" were reviled.[16]

The triumph of science in this debate marked the dawn of a *scientific* era in China, an era that Larry Laudan saw as characterized by "the belief that science and science alone has the answers to all our answerable questions."[17] Before the debate, most Chinese considered science as just a useful "implement" (*qi*) for gaining wealth and power. In the 1910s, a first few radical patriots started to speak of science as a savior. As Chen Duxiu put it, "only 'Master Democracy' and 'Master Science' can rescue China from all its political, ethical, educational, and ideological darkness."[18] Even then, however, science still was considered merely a pragmatic means to solve pressing problems. It was not until the debate, in which science was reevaluated according to certain time-honored values, that science was seen as the universal Dao (Way) instead of as just one expedient path.

How did science, representing an imported system of values, win the debate? Scholars have focused on three explanations. First, in the early twentieth century, China's worsening socio-political situation spurred intellectuals to call for revolutionary change to a new moral-spiritual orientation.[19] Second, the endeavor by the pro-science group to establish a practical system of knowledge as a guide for one's view of life found solid support in the pragmatic modes of thinking common among Chinese.[20] Third, the pro-science stress on empirical evidence, rather than metaphysical speculation, added weight to their arguments, because "[t]he modern world demanded objectivity as the criterion for judgment of truth, honesty, reliability, and hence respectability."[21]

These accounts reveal the complex nature of the eloquent campaign for science, but they neglect one of its important and profound characteristics—the fanatical tendency toward what Hu Shi called a "nationwide worship" of science.[22] The religious zeal shown in this successful campaign against the "metaphysical ghosts" suggests that another process of persuasion must have been at work, in addition to the arguments in support of pragmatism and scientific discourse.

The hidden process of persuasion comes to light only if what became a *scientistic* campaign in the early twentieth century is placed in the context of the tradition of discourse on Dao. Placing the scientistic campaign in that context reveals the essence of the campaign to be an admirable effort to maintain this tradition of discourse in the face of a severe crisis for the tradition.

The Riddles of the Sphinx

In China at the time of Confucius and Lao Zi, metaphysical speculation did not start from a clear distinction between worlds, such as the world of darkness and the world of light, the realm of Matter and the realm of Form, or the earthly kingdom and the Kingdom of Heaven. On the contrary, metaphysical speculation began with a vision of Chaos. What most attracted the ancient Chinese metaphysicians was not something that would transcend this Chaos, but the innermost essence of Chaos and that this essence remained hidden and mysterious. Insight and understanding emerged, for the person of understanding, out of this profound depth at the very heart of things. To traditional Chinese philosophers, the answer to everything about this world lay at the heart of Chaos. They called this place "Dao."

Chinese classical texts described Dao as worldly and non-worldly. It was "elusive and vague," yet in it were "the form," "things," and "the essence." Invisible, inaudible, and untouchable as it seemed, its natural course was something for people to view and to follow.[23] "[S]o large that nothing can exist outside it," it was also "so small that nothing can exist within it."[24] Although "enduring and long," it was "forever changing—alteration, movement without rest."[25] Such profound paradoxes constituted the ancient Chinese conceptions of Dao.

Such seemingly paradoxical but enchanting portraits of Dao had far-reaching impacts on the development of a most sacred and powerful form of Chinese discourse, namely the discourse on Dao. These descriptions defined what language should be used to address this ultimate state of the universe and the source of power. The language was to be a mix of two contradictory modes of expression: an indeterminate, speculative, and idealistic mode; and a determinant, analytic, and practical mode. The discourse on Dao became a conscientious and strategic play with these two modes of expression. The indeterminate, speculative, and idealistic mode was used when referring to the occult qualities of Dao. For instance, the followers of Confucius proclaimed that they had found the Dao or the Way to the Great Profundity, and that this Dao or Way was open to every believer. At the same time, however, they presented their Dao or Way in such a way as to make it appear more or less "elusive and vague" and, therefore, difficult to access, so it would open only for the most virtuous and persistent pursuers, such as Confucius.

The paradoxes between the two modes of expression of Dao as visible, distinct, constant and physical on the one side, and as invisible, all-embracing, ever-changing, and spiritual on the other, were akin to the Sphinx's puzzling riddles. Every speaker and preacher had to provide reasonable solutions to these riddles before he or she could profess to find the keys to the Dao as described by the ancients. The twelfth-century neo-Confucian solution, for instance, was to view the world of Dao as a vigorous interaction between two ultimate cosmic forces: the pervasive physical and vital Force (*Qi*) and the moral-spiritual Principle (*Li*), which the neo-Confucian Master Zhu Xi described as "pure, empty, and vast."[26] This view enabled the neo-Confucians to maintain their particularly equivocal form of discourse on Dao into the Middle Ages.

After the sixteenth century, the new school of Confucian empiricists called for substituting "empirical studies" for what they considered the "empty words" of neo-Confucian discourse. The Confucian empiricists proposed seeing Dao as no more than the way of concrete things.[27] The ancients' paradoxical observations on Dao as visible and invisible, manifest and subtle, near and distant, active and tranquil were explained by the empiricists as the assembling and dispersing of *Qi* (subtle matter and vital force) and by its other vibrant states of existence and movements.[28] Prominent empiricists such as Liu Zongzhou, Huang Zongxi, and Dai Zhen, however, continued to address the idea of Dao as something "filling the whole universe" and always "in the great process of evolutionary change."[29]

The tradition of Dao-discourse faced a crisis in the first half of the nineteenth century. The two complementary discursive trends within the Dao-discourse parted company as new generations of Chinese intellectuals became aware that the subject of Dao implied two separate sets of issues that ought to be addressed in separate forms of discourse. The first to realize this was an emerging school of scholars advocating practical statecraft. They saw Dao as primarily a social ideal characterized by moral-spiritual order and political and economic prosperity.[30] This school and the later agitators of the "self-strengthening" movement, which emerged after the second Opium War (1857–1860), introduced a set of statecraft and institutional issues (including taxation, commercial shipping, banking, a postal service, telegraph, mining, international law, and a parliament) into Dao-discourse that earlier generations would have considered marginal to the Confucian kingly way.[31] But the advocates of practical statecraft and the "self-strengtheners" continued to regard spiritual and moral cultivation as the most important and most legitimate subject matter for Dao-discourse. The old integrated discursive world of Dao was coming apart because the new interpreters of Dao required two concurrent lines rather than one line of discussion.

The last of the "self-strengthening" leaders, Zhang Zhidong, attempted to reconcile the new and the old sets of topics in his widely circulated *Exhortation to Learning*. The first part of his treatise, entitled "Internal Chapters," stressed selective retention of Chinese learning as the basis for "rectifying the mind." The second part, "External Chapters," elaborated on the use of Western devices such as schools, newspapers, railways, industry, and commerce to "create new modes of social practice."[32] At first glance, Zhang seemed to combine the two lines of discussion into one, with the traditional and idealistic line as his "internal chapters," and the relatively scientific and realistic line as his "external chapters." What Zhang really presented was a loose external alliance of the two trends of discussion, not an internal reunion of them, because his "external chapters" could not "rectify the mind" and his "internal chapters" could not "create new modes of social practice."

When such radical intellectuals of the late nineteenth century as Yan Fu, Tan Sitong, Kang Youwei, and Liang Qichao sought to start an internal dialogue between the two lines of discourse, they became the loudest voices for reform. Yan Fu eloquently showed how wealth and power conditioned the process of "Heavenly Evolution" toward moral perfection.[33] Tan Sitong and Kang Youwei suggested that such Western scientific concepts as "ether" and "electricity" affirmed the traditional Chinese perception of a universe that was essentially vital and ethical, after they equated ether to the "vital and humanistic *Qi*" and electricity to the "nerve, sense, and humanity" of the universe.[34] These arguments kindled the hope among Chinese that they could achieve traditional moral-spiritual ends by using Western learning as the means.

In the early twentieth century, the reformist discourse tradition was beginning to experience a scientific turn. In the first two decades of the new century, more than a hundred new periodicals commenced publication, each aiming to propagate Western science as the foundation of China's new order.[35] Those attempting a meaningful mediation between a scientific world and a traditional moral universe soon found themselves caught in a predicament. The scientific West was not making progress toward the ideal of "great harmony." Instead, it fostered a dirty, unjust world war (World War I). After his visit to Europe in 1919–1920, Liang Qichao returned to speak in sad tones:

> [T]hose who sang the glory of science's omnipotence all wished that once science succeeded the golden world would appear. Now it must be admitted that the efforts have been rewarded; a hundred years of materialistic advance have multiplied the aggregate efforts of the past three thousand years. Mankind, however, not only did not receive happiness [as a result of science] but also experienced many disasters, which it brought. [We] are like travelers lost in the desert; we see a huge black shadow in the distance and strive to catch up with it, thinking that it could be relied on as a guide. But after we catch up a little, the shadow disappears and we are in utter despair. Who is this shadow? He is none other than Master Science.[36]

In the ensuing mood of pessimism, Professor Zhang Junmai presented his controversial dichotomy between science and one's philosophy of life. Zhang identified the natural world with the most inanimate and stable version of Dao. In the realm of nature, things "all can be classified." There was an essential nature "running through all changes and phenomena" of any particular class of objects, so "a scientific formula for it can be discovered."[37] In contrast to his discourse on the natural world, Zhang used extremely vague phrases and elusive terms to describe the mind or the self as "precarious, subtle, refined, and undivided,"[38] "flowing past in an endless stream," and "changing ten thousand times in an instant."[39] He no longer spoke of nature and spirit in terms of the external and internal chapters of Dao. They were instead two entirely separate worlds.

Zhang's drastic solution to the paradoxes in the classical view of Dao as both natural and spiritual laws, his radical dichotomy between nature and spirit, only aggravated the spiritual crisis of those Chinese feeling "lost in the desert." His solution dismembered the all-embracing Dao. Even as Zhang tried to save the core of Dao, using his concept of the mind, he severed the link between the mind and the real world. Dao became a pure illusion that could never be realized.

In the China of the 1920s, the fate of the deep-rooted belief in the omnipotence and omnipresence of Dao depended on whether Dao could be reformulated in holistic terms. Intellectuals relying on traditional discourse were no longer fit for the challenge. The *zeitgeist* of the first decades of the century encouraged the emergence of patriotic and ambitious advocates of science to speak for the almighty Dao. In response to Zhang's speech, such defenders of a scientific universe as Ding Wenjiang, Wu Zhihui, Hu Shi, Ren Hongjun, Tang Yue, and Wang Xinggong reconnected nature and spirit, arguing that science was the sole path to the moral ideal of Dao.

A Scientific "Tower of Babel"

A distinctive feature of the pro-science group's rhetoric was their attempt to position themselves as the legitimate interpreters of Dao in the debate. Ding Wenjiang replied to Zhang with a provocative "declaration of war" against the metaphysician and assumed the role of protector of the holy tradition of the Dao of Chinese culture against the intruding evil forces of metaphysics:

> Metaphysics is truly a shiftless ghost—having mystified Europe for more than two thousand years and finding existence difficult there in recent years, it has now [masqueraded itself] and come to China to show off and deceive people.[40]

Other members of the pro-science group, including Wu Zhihui and Hu Shi, joined this holy war with much the same spirit of defending the tradition of Dao. They called on their supporters to fight against the "brokers" of Western metaphysics because the latter were trying to peddle the idea of "the Unknowable" (or the scientific unreachable).[41] Western metaphysicians were seeking an "exquisite excuse" to smuggle the Western concepts of God and the soul into China. Wu, for example, accused Zhang Junmai of having introduced "a variant of the concept of the soul," and of "hawking" Edward J. Urwick's notion of a "spiritual element," a deep faculty which was "always unknown, acting in the presence of circumstances which are never more than partially known."[42] The so-called "spiritual element," according to Wu, was just the original set of "perfunctory and narcotic words used by Western gentlemen in dealing with [the subject of] God."[43] As Hu put it, the real issue of the controversy became not whether science could settle the problems of human life, but whether Chinese should believe in the existence of God, spirits, and souls.[44]

The pro-science group took great care to play by the established rules of Dao-discourse at every stage of their campaign, demonstrating their concern for the legitimacy of their discourse. Their concerns for legitimacy were particularly evident in the measures they took to mediate and balance the two apparently opposed modes of discourse, which they employed to argue that: (1) their scientific observations best explained the traditional experiences of Dao; (2) science provided the most reliable channel to Dao; and (3) the scientific view of life was a great achievement of the moral state of Dao.

A "Mysterious" Materialistic Universe

In spite of the extremely atheistic and naturalistic overtones of their arguments, the pro-science group applied vague and elusive terms to complicate and even to mystify what their opponents were content to regard as a purely physical, mechanical phenomenon. Complicating and mystifying what was otherwise mechanical made it appear to be a modern version of Dao, just as legitimate as that described by the ancient sages, the neo-Confucianists, and the Qing empirical scholars. Wu Zhihui, a prominent defender of materialism, represented this tendency. In a widely read treatise, "A New Belief and Its View of Life and the Universe," Wu explained:

> [The Creation] was no other than to take so much "inconceivable" mass, possessing matter and force, and to make it into something. So many of such things were made into particles of electricity, and particles of electricity were made into atoms. Atoms became sun, moon, stars, mountains, rivers, grass, trees, birds, beasts, insects and fish.[45]

Wu seemed to be trying to draw his reader's view from heaven to earth by suggesting that the mystery of creating the real world and life could be explained as physical and chemical processes. At the same time, however, he mired his readers in another world of uncertainty through his subtle use of the words "inconceivable," "something," "so much," "so many," and "such." Wu's choice of words suggested that creating life remained a perplexing process and that it continued under the control of some fathomless and mighty power.

With regard to intuition, one of the most unknowable of all subjects to the defenders of metaphysics, Wu held that it was simply a product of reason:

> With careful employment of reason, we coerce certain kinds of sentiments to follow the regularity of nature. ... When certain kinds of sentiments are found to be in harmony with the heart and body, they are often left without examination and are relegated to the status of natural instincts. ... Our intuition is the kind of ability that has been passed down to us through innumerable generations' critical examinations conducted under innumerable circumstances.[46]

Thus, intuition was not irrational or unknowable at all but, once again, Wu chose an unspecific and indefinite term, "innumerable," to maintain a sense of mystery. What his anti-metaphysical account achieved was to exchange a qualitative sense for a quantitative sense of inconceivability. Although the act of intuition based on innumerable "practices" could no longer be seen as fantastic, it remained an inconceivable power, which crystallized innumerable generations of human wisdom.

To impress his reader further with a picture of the might of the mind, Wu played the subtle game of numbers again:

> Suppose we slice a hair into tiny pieces, then each piece has the capacity to accommodate four hundred billion atoms. Each atom, in turn, has electrons revolving around its core. An electron is about one hundred thousand times smaller than an atom. Each atom thus has its

own system; it contains the nucleus and electrons just like the solar system. Try to imagine how many these sorts of systems are needed to form a brain weighing three pounds and two ounces, plus five thousand and forty-eight cranial nerves.[47]

Wu used this sort of imagery to argue for the extreme complexity and subtlety of our thinking mechanism. So, he asked, "what is the need of any 'spiritual element' and the so-called soul, which never meets any real need anyway?"[48]

When describing the nature of the material universe according to science, Wu's language approximated even more closely the traditional discourse on Dao. As Wu put it, behind the manifold appearances, physical and spiritual, lay "one ultimate thing." He called it "the great Dark Mass," the name reminiscent of another more formulaic term, "the great Chaos," which Chinese have used to describe the primordial states of Dao and of the universe since the *Daode jing*.[49] Similar to the all-embracing Dao, his "great Dark Mass" also was at once "phenomenal and spiritual," "all-possessing and void," "temporal-spatial and transcendental," "orderly and chaotic," and "sensible and insensible". The ultimate thing was so inclusive that even if there were a God, Wu said, it was just a part of the "Dark Mass."[50]

The laws of such a "scientific" universe, therefore, must have had something of boundless magical power. Wu understandably spoke of scientific laws, such as causality and universal gravitation, as "divine" laws of his universe.[51] Other worshippers of science addressed these laws in similar terms: "[Causality] is absolutely universal in the world of experience"; "the lofty law of causality governs all his—man's—life"; "a view of life, as composed of both the knowledge of the facts and the general outlook on life, can never escape the magic circles of the two general laws of causality and the uniformity of nature."[52] The scientific law thus becomes, to use Wu's word, a "variant" of the concept of the omnipotent Dao.

Avenue to the Profundity of the Universe

Once the whole physical world was released from the curse of "dead matter," the defenders of science could make the lowly Cinderella of science a charming angel who held the golden key to the mysteries of the universe. Again, the two complementary modes of discourse—the determinant, analytic mode and the indeterminate, speculative mode—were adapted to construct the angel's two powerful "wings." On the one hand, the pro-science group recommended science as a reliable way for discovering the truth of Dao, by giving a narrow, inductivist account of the method of science. Ding Wenjiang said: "What we call the scientific method is no more than taking the phenomena of the world and analyzing them into kinds and seeking their order."[53] This simple and exclusively empirical explanation, characteristic of a scientistic approach to the scientific method, appeared to confirm rather than counter the deep-rooted view that Dao was observable and traceable.[54] Ding went so far as to suggest that even the "Confucian empiricists" had applied the same kind of method three hundred years earlier.[55]

The pro-science group also identified science with the spirit for finding truth. According to another eloquent defender of science, Ren Hongjun, "The scientific spirit, the spirit of searching for truth, is far-reaching and endless. With this spirit one could finally banish all prejudices and private wishes of the mind, having the mind come into direct contact with the lofty spirit of the natural world."[56] Although the pro-science group's empirical characterization of the scientific method implied that Dao was sensible and in good order, their stress on the spirit of scientific inquiry pointed to the other "lofty" and changeable side of Dao. Moreover, in regard to the scientific spirit, they returned to the traditional view that only virtuous, selfless, and persistent investigators could delve into the depths of the universe. With the wing of this far-reaching and endless searching spirit and the wing of the seemingly faultless procedure for discovering truth, the angel of science now could fly to contact the Dao of Heaven.

Imbued with this irresistible searching spirit, the pro-science group explored their opponents' territory: the realm of the unknowable. They saw that everything in it was not so "elusive and vague" as Zhang Junmai, Liang Qichao, and other dualists had suggested. Liang's "unanalyzable beauty," for instance, was simply a certain combination of lines, colors, and some other elements.[57] The advocates of science appeared primarily to be concerned with something really profound and something deeper in the world of Dao. They asked: What were those marvelous structures underlying what were perceived as mysterious beauties?[58] How did those extremely intricate temperamental, experiential, and environmental factors contribute to what Liang Qichao described as "zealous and irrational love"?[59] And what could be the secret formula for making life?[60] Questions about the secrets of life and spirit, which to their opponents seemed beyond the reach of any human inquiry other than metaphysical speculation,[61] thus became the special and technical arenas of science. The pro-science group could then approach a subject such as organic evolution as "a very complicated and very specialized issue." For Ding, "those who had never studied embryology, paleobiology, tectology, or genetics are not qualified to discuss it."[62]

Even when aggressively and assertively claiming to know more than their opponents, however, the pro-science intellectuals suggested that they still had a lot to learn. That suggestion enabled them to resist being placed at the very front of the stage of knowledge and to find cover behind a flimsy protective screen. They proclaimed that, as "men of very limited knowledge," they were simply presenting "what seems to be true" rather than truth itself.[63] They claimed to establish nothing but "hypotheses" that "could change at any time."[64] What they wanted was just evidence, "the humblest and the most justified request one can make."[65] Before a hypothetical view was fully proved, it had to be "open to question."[66]

The advocates of science assumed an ambiguous and uncommitted style when confronting the two profound subjects of traditional Dao-discourse, namely the origin of the universe and the very essence of human sentiment. The geologist Ding preferred to "put these issues aside and not discuss them for the time being" owing to their "empirical unverifiability."[67] The materialist Wu, on the other hand, assumed that the ultimate source of the universe was his "Dao," the so-called "great Dark Mass," but "if you are pleased to name it continuous creation [Zhang Junmai's terminology], you may; humorously to dub it an illusion of the mind is all right, too."[68] To the psychologist Tang Yue, beauty could be analyzed scientifically, but the immediacy of experience with beauty was "given. ... It cannot be analyzed, neither does it need to be. ... We might just as well call it 'a mystery'."[69] For Wu, his "great Dark Mass" was also analyzable, but it was such a Dao—"both the beginning without beginnings and the end without ends, and both infinitely large and infinitely small"—that "after its first nine tiers are respectively taken apart, there are still millions more. ... Science can only try to go into it as deeply as possible."[70]

Avenue to the Profundity of Life

The most decisive part of the campaign for scientism concerned the argument that science could govern a view or outlook on life. The pro-science group chose ambiguous terms, taken from the traditional sermonizing on Dao, and used them to justify their immediate transition from the realm of nature to the realm of morality. Ding appealed to the view that Dao was visible:

> True awareness of the pleasure and happiness of life can be acquired only when the manifold relations of the physical, biological and psychological realms are known. This kind of "vibrant" state of mind can be thoroughly enjoyed only by those who use the telescope to survey the abstruseness and mistiness of the heaven and by those who use the microscope to peer into the faintness and subtlety of the living world. How can this [state of mind] ever be imagined by those who sit meditatively talking about Buddhism or by those who speculate metaphysically?[71]

This passage stands as one of the most forceful and widely quoted arguments for science in the debate.[72] Its alluring assumption that scientific instruments such as the telescope and microscope could aid direct observation of the profundity of the universe and enhance one's enjoyment of life raised questions for readers with an exclusively scientific mindset.

The passage raised two questions. First, how could one possibly observe "the abstruseness and mistiness of the heaven" and "the faintness and subtlety of the living world," because the terms "abstruseness" (*xu*), "mistiness" (*mo*), "faintness" (*you*), and "subtlety" (*wei*) refer to the very obscure side of Dao that defies direct observation? Despite the apparent contradiction, this observation was perfectly acceptable to an audience familiar with traditional Dao-discourse, at least to the extent that the audience assumed that Dao was visible and open for everyone to see.

Second, how could this "scientific" observation have anything to say about the pleasure and happiness of life, which seem to be more a matter of one's view of life than a matter of scientific knowledge? For traditional Dao discourse, this may not have been a problem at all, however. From the perspective that Dao was both natural and moral, anything one meets in the external, real world could have implications for one's philosophy of life. Ding's claims, that true awareness of the pleasure and happiness of life come only through scientific inspection of the macrocosm and the microcosm, was difficult to verify, but it was equally hard to deny from the perspective of Dao. By exploiting these two "confusions" accepted in traditional Dao-discourse, the pro-science group was able to deprive the metaphysicians of their legitimacy to observe and explain life, because the metaphysicians could only "sit meditatively talking about Buddhism" and "speculate metaphysically."

Responding to the question about what meaning of life one could possibly grasp from scientific insight into "the abstruseness and mistiness of the heaven" and "the faintness and subtlety of the living world," Ren Hongjun quoted the testimonies of Isaac Newton and Joseph J. Thomson, a prominent physicist of the early twentieth century:[73]

> I do not know what I may appear to the world, but to myself I seem to have been only like a boy playing on the seashore, and diverting myself in now and then finding a smoother pebble or a prettier shell than ordinary, whilst the great ocean of truth lay all undiscovered before me. (Newton)[74]
>
> We climb to the top of the peak, and find that it reveals to us another more beautiful and more interesting view than any that we have yet seen and so it goes on. Our destination and the horizon are nowhere in sight. The greater progress science makes, the more inconceivable the magnificence of the Creation appears to us. (Thomson)[75]

Both citations ended with remarks about the incomprehensibility of the universe. What both scientists claimed to see, as the end of their significant scientific discovery, were profound views: the fathomless ocean of truth and the mountains of knowledge. The two passages brought the Chinese reader back to an "elusive and vague" vision of the cosmos, with a clear common implication: mankind was so petty and insignificant! Undoubtedly, that was what many Chinese preachers of Dao meant to say when comparing individual humans to the Great Dao, but Ding's question remains valid: How could this message be understood fully by those who had never used a telescope and microscope to see "the abstruseness and mistiness of the heaven" and "the faintness and subtlety of the living world"?

What the pro-science group tried to show their audience was by no means a gloomy, depressing scene. It was a bright sight of the great road to immortality, along which petty and insignificant humanity found itself merging into the immense, eternal flux of life. The pro-science group relied on the terminology of traditional Dao-discourse to build an extremely holistic view of the universe. For Wu, all living beings grew out of the same great "Dark Mass." The universe was in essence "a great living whole." With such a living whole, distinguishing its parts into yours and mine was meaningless because "I am the One, and so are you."[76]

Other advocates of science stressed the changeability of this great whole. Ding said the self was constantly interacting and interchanging facets with various environmental and physiological factors, so that "there is no clear, fixed, and universal dividing line between the 'self' and external objects."[77] The bounds of time, separating past from present and future, were also no longer clear or fixed when Tang emphasized that "the self is the product of many things that had gone before, and in turn the motivational force for many that follow after."[78] The fading vision of the self thus merged into the continuous stream of what the adherents of scientism called the "Great Self," which embraced the whole world and was immortal.[79] For Hu, the view of this Great Self was one of the greatest beliefs "founded on the commonly accepted scientific knowledge of the last two or three hundred years."[80]

With this "scientific" vision of the immortal Great Self, the pro-science group could join metaphysicians and moralists in a discussion about the meaning of life, culminating in a claim to a more positive feeling toward life and a greater sense of mission in this world. Tang's remark appeared especially compelling: How profound and inexhaustible could the meaning of one's life be from the view that the self is a "motivational force" for future generations![81] Wu conceived of life as a great theatrical act: "We build our theatre, script our play … with our brothers and sisters as the audience. … We might as well put on a good show," otherwise it would be only "self-deception."[82]

The conception of the immortal Great Self also allowed the pro-science group to speak about sagehood, a perfect state of transcendence of all worldly thoughts. By continuing to exploit the conventional notion of Dao as the ambivalent natural and moral law, Ren argued that the "far-reaching and endless" process of scientific searching for Dao could lead one to "banish all prejudices and private wishes of the mind," to "abandon fame, prestige, and concerns of social class," and eventually to "come into direct contact with the lofty spirit" of the universe.[83] This perfect state could be reached, however, only after one "acts upon exceedingly creative impulse and, meanwhile, exerts oneself to the utmost to fulfill one's duty to self-denial."[84] Thus, the "scientific" exploration, which started from investigating "the abstruseness and mistiness of the heaven" and "the faintness and subtlety of the living world" and moved to pursuing the profound meaning of life, ended with a religious call "to sacrifice the self for the survival and immortality of humanity."[85] Although this call was common to many earlier Chinese philosophies of life, for Ding, only the light of science could change one's religious impulse toward self-sacrifice from a blind instinct to a rational force.[86]

Science thus should be capable of and responsible for directing life. According to Wu, the scientific worldview must be able to provide the common ground on which to build mankind's philosophy of life, just as theism and belief in the immortality of the soul had united European philosophies of life for more than a thousand years.[87] In the face of the major choices in life between the bright and the dark and between salvation and degradation, the humble interpreters of science could not decline the responsibility to fight against metaphysics. For Ding,

> Metaphysics is a sworn enemy of science. As the spirit of metaphysics attaches itself to the body of Zhang Junmai, we as students of science cannot but knock it down. … We, of course, cannot expect that the view of life could be unified when all metaphysicians in this world have not died out. … The scientific method is almighty in the realm of knowledge. There is no fear that metaphysics will not finally surrender.[88]

This was not a purely intellectual debate *per se*. This was a "crusade" launched by the scientific "god" against the metaphysical "ghosts."

Conclusion

The above examination argues that we should understand the 1923 "science vs. metaphysics" debate as a modern extension of a centuries-long conflict between empirical and metaphysical trends within the Chinese tradition of discourse on Dao. The debate was not simply a head-on confrontation between modern Western modes of scientific thinking and traditional Chinese modes of metaphysical thinking. The advocates of science won, fundamentally because they succeeded in leading those who felt "lost in the desert" back to a traditional faith in the omnipotence and omnipresence of a spiritual and moral power. They were thus the more legitimate and enlightened successors to the tradition of the Dao-sermon. They brought novel and dramatic elements to this tradition, of course. After all, they had made science into a magical charm and a god.

The pro-metaphysics group also adopted the language of traditional discourse on Dao by appropriating both the empirical and the metaphysical modes of discourse in their arguments and by trying to keep them both in equilibrium. Their problem was that they separated the uses of these two modes for nature and spirit, as shown in Zhang Junmai's polar descriptions of the physical world and the mind. In so doing, the metaphysicians departed from the conventional usage of these two modes in Dao-discourse, which should be to establish and maintain a holistic world of Dao that, in Wu's words, was "phenomenal and spiritual," "all-possessing and void," "temporal-spatial and transcendental," "orderly and chaotic," and "sensible and insensible."[89] The result was that they deviated from the real goal of this discursive practice: to compete to be the interpreters of and spokespersons for the all-embracing Dao. In this sense, they came closer to a Western scientific mode of thinking than the pro-science group, but this did not help them to win the debate.

This case study supports a contextual approach to the rhetoric of science. Certain contextual constraints on scientific popularization seem to be universal. At least, science in the East has been faced with the same problem of maintaining "continuity" with an earlier intellectual and rhetorical tradition as Campbell and Gross have demonstrated in their case studies of these dynamics in the West.[90] Prelli's general observation—that reasonable and persuasive scientific discourse is "perceived as identifying, modifying, or solving problems that bear on a specific community's maintenance and expansion of their comprehension of the natural order"—remains valid here.[91]

Meanwhile, the case of the 1923 campaign in China that I have labeled *scientistic* suggests a new world of study for us. Here we see a different cultural tradition of intellectual concern and also a different world of rhetorical practice. Rhetoric is bound to play a greater role in scientific propagation in the less scientifically oriented Eastern cultures than it does in the Western hometowns of modern and contemporary science. It was not, however, the rhetoric of the Western scientific giants, nor even the rhetoric of their eloquent defenders in the West, that played the key role here. Superficially, Western science seems to possess inevitability, an unstoppable force that propels it to cross international borders and to destroy, mercilessly, everything it considers unscientific. Under that surface, however, Eastern champions of science have had to make cautious and persistent rhetorical efforts to establish the same "scientific" force. Scientific ideas must be rhetorically reconstructed so they will fit into the cultural structure of the dominant discourse before they can make their way into the dominant discourse of that culture.

Owing to this rhetorical need, that a scientific movement must adapt to a non-scientific tradition of cultural rhetoric, the movement and the consequent course of scientization in an Eastern culture becomes very different from those we have seen in the West, which had to meet the demand of a rhetoric appropriate to a Western context of intellectual discourse, whether it was neo-Platonic, theological, Baconian, Newtonian, or any other. The process of scientization seems to be set to follow the track of development of each culture. The scientific campaign is really an extension of a dialectical and dynamic form of cultural rhetoric. Only from this context of cultural and rhetorical tradition, not from the perspective of Western science as having a sacred mission to save the world, can we come to a deeper and more fruitful understanding of the nature and significance of the dissemination of scientific "gospel" in the East.

The rhetoric of science thus becomes a crucial key to understanding modern and contemporary intellectual histories. This is especially true for the East because scientization has constituted the core of modernization for Eastern nations. Our rhetoricians of science have a compelling and honorable obligation to explore such a key element in those processes.

In the China of the 1920s, the "game" of Dao-discourse persisted even into the next stage of intellectual debate in which the debaters turned to fight for legitimacy to speak in the holy name of science. The Chinese communists and believers in the science of historical materialism, emerging around the turn of 1920s, joined the "science vs. metaphysics" debate when it was drawing to an end.[92] Posing as the final judge of this controversy, Chen Duxiu, a founder of the Chinese Communist Party, criticized many members of the pro-science group for their lack of understanding of the profound influences of socio-economic laws and forces on people's views of life.[93] In suggesting that one should view social-economic formation as the "final cause" of all religious, moral, ideological, political, and cultural practices, Chen appeared to be an even more thorough defender of material monism and the lofty law of causality.[94] All he recommended to begin with, it would seem, was nothing but economic causation, which seemed to be of the most material nature among the various possible "causes" of one's view of life. For Chen, only this perspective on material or economic determinism could "give objective, scientific explanations of all unscientific views of life," thus "leaving the metaphysical ghosts no way of escape."[95] This perspective, as the liberal Hu Shi admitted, had its ideological appeal, because it seemed to offer the alluring panacea of a "fundamental solution" to China's problems.[96]

In the following decades, Chinese communist doctrines that appeared to have a more fanatical bent for scientific determinism, and not the pro-science group's philosophies, emerged to represent scientific understanding of China's situation. In practice, the communist doctrines came to dominate the views of life of most Chinese peoples. The reasons for this outcome, of course, were complicated. From a rhetorical standpoint, we note that even the communist spokespersons continued to exploit the "game rules" of Dao-discourse. Despite his tendency to advance an economically deterministic interpretation of society and history, Chen Duxiu stressed that "causal relationships in a human society are extremely complex." Every society developed "in a particular time and space" and under such varied circumstances that an accurate prediction of its advancement was virtually impossible.[97]

As a group follows the tradition of Dao-discourse, it gets caught in the traps of the traditional, dominant language. Like the neo-Confucianists and the Qing empiricists, the adherents of scientism and the communists who succeeded them, in reality, did not make much fundamental change in the established power structures of Chinese discourse. Instead, they replaced an old vocabulary of authority with a new one. For instance, they substituted a scientific "god" for a metaphysical "lord," made the almighty "law of causality" take over from "Dao," and had great names in natural and social sciences, such as Newton, Einstein, and Marx, displace those of the Confucian, Daoist, and Buddhist sages. The "ghost" of traditional metaphysics was still very much in control of their scientific kingdom.

In the past several decades of practice of the so-called scientific socialism, China has witnessed floods of new forms of prejudice and dogmatism in the garb of scientific understanding and had experienced the craze of the worship of Marxist saints. The development of the Chinese communist movement and its final victory in 1949 steadily brought its leader Mao Zedong to the center of the sacred altar of science. Mao's doctrines, depicted by his followers as a perfect synthesizing of "the universal truth of Marxism—the highest ideology of mankind—with the concrete practice of the Chinese revolution," came to claim the most scientific as well as the most ethical and powerful system of thought in the history of China.[98] His feverish followers went so far as to believe that, if they followed the teaching of Chairman Mao, they would become all-powerful in themselves. This fantastical optimism was well expressed in the following titles of articles published in the communist dailies in 1966, the beginning year of the Cultural Revolution (1966–1976): "Man Heeds What Chairman Mao Says, Then Furnace Heeds What Man Says"; "Cotton Listens to Me If I Listen to Chairman Mao"; "Mao Zedong Thought Is the All-efficacious Golden Key"; "The Words of Mao Zedong Will Prove to Be True in Whatever Situation They Are Applied"; "Mao Zedong Thought Gives Me Inexhaustible Strength"; "Whoever Has True Command of Mao Zedong Thought Is the True Authority"; "We Are All-conquering and Ever-victorious by Creative Studying and Applying the Works of Chairman Mao."[99] Mao's thinking was the Dao or the Way. It is no wonder that one of the most popular catchwords in Mao's era was to march on or to follow "the broad road of Mao Zedong Thought."[100]

Two years after Mao Zedong passed away and the ultra-leftist Gang of Four—Mao's wife Jiang Qing, Zhang Chunqiao, Yao Wenyuan, and Wang Hongwen—became captive in 1976, the mouthpiece of the Chinese Communist Party, the *People's Daily*, raised the question: How did it happen that Marxism, which "in its essence is antithetical to obscurantism," had become a "new theology in China, even after the victory of the proletariat?" The author put the blame on the Gang of Four: "They borrowed the name of Marxism so they could enchain the population to their own cause."[101] One year later a key communist theorist, Zhou Yang, conceded that there was within the Party a tendency toward "simplification, dogmatization, and mythicization of Marxism."[102] From then on, scholars from inside and outside the Party have endeavored to probe deeply into the political, economic, social, and cultural roots of this tendency.[103] Regrettably, little attempt has been made to explore the problem of contemporary superstition from a rhetorical perspective. Today, when many Chinese scholars recommend following the true course of scientific enlightenment,[104] what they may need to reflect on is the language of their Dao-discourse.

Notes

The author thanks the editor and reviewers of the *Quarterly Journal of Speech* for their valuable comments and suggestions. A portion of this paper was presented at the 1998 International Communication Association conference.

1 T. S. Kuhn, *The Structure of Scientific Revolutions*, 2nd ed. (Chicago: University of Chicago Press, 1970); S. Toulmin, *Human Understanding* (Oxford: Oxford University Press, 1972); R. Merton, *The Sociology of Science: Theoretical and Empirical Investigations* (Chicago: University of Chicago Press, 1973); B. Barnes, *Scientific Knowledge and Sociological Theory* (London: Routledge and Kegan Paul, 1974); B. Barnes, *Interests and the Growth of Knowledge* (London: Routledge and Kegan Paul, 1977); D. Bloor, *Knowledge and Social Imagery* (Boston: Routledge and Kegan Paul, 1976); B. Latour and S. Woolgar, *Laboratory Life: The Construction of Scientific Facts* (Princeton, NJ: Princeton University Press, 1979); G. Holton, *The Scientific Imagination: Case Studies* (Cambridge: Cambridge University Press, 1978). For an extensive overview of the contributions of these and other philosophers, sociologists, and historians to the rhetorical turn in science studies, see C. A. Taylor, *Defining Science: A Rhetoric of Demarcation* (Madison: University of Wisconsin Press, 1996), 21–100. For a detailed account of the development of the rhetoric of science, see R. A. Harris, ed., *Landmark Essays on Rhetoric of Science: Case Studies*, second edition (London: Routledge, 2018 [1997]), 1–42. For a recent survey of scholarship in the rhetoric of science, starting with Philip Wander's 1976 definition, see also D. Gaonkar, "The Idea of Rhetoric in the Rhetoric of Science," *Southern Communication Journal* 58 (1993): 258–95; P. Wander, "The Rhetoric of Science," this volume [1976], 62–70. Harris provides a useful collection of landmark case studies within the field.

2 L. Prelli, *A Rhetoric of Science: Inventing Scientific Discourse* (Columbia: University of South Carolina Press, 1989), 122; A. G. Gross, "On the Shoulders of Giants: Seventeenth-Century Optics as an Argument Field," *Landmark Essays in Rhetoric of Science: Case Studies*, second edition. R.A. Harris, ed. (London: Routledge, 2018 [1988/1997]). 45–58, J. Campbell, "Scientific Revolution and the Grammar of Culture," *Quarterly Journal of Speech* 72 (1986): 351–76.

3 Scientific popularization is one of the prominent themes in rhetoric of science. For some important rhetorical studies of scientific popularization, see T. M. Lessl, "Science and the Sacred Cosmos," *Quarterly Journal of Speech* 71 (1985): 175–87; G. Myers, "Nineteenth Century Popularizations of Thermodynamics and the Rhetoric of Social Prophecy," *Victorian Studies* 29 (1985): 35–66; G. Myers, *Writing Biology* (Madison, WI: University of Wisconsin Press, 1990); C. Bazerman, *Shaping Written Knowledge: The Genre and Activity of the Experimental Article in Science* (Madison, WI: University of Wisconsin Press, 1988); K. Rowan, "Moving Beyond the What to the Why: Differences in Professional and Popular Science Writing," *Journal of Technical Writing and Communication* 19 (1989): 161–79; S. Shuttleworth and J. R. Christie, eds., *Nature Transfigured: Literature and Science 1700–1800* (Manchester: Manchester University Press, 1989); J. Lyne, "Bio-rhetorics: Moralizing the Life

Sciences," in H. W. Simons ed., *The Rhetorical Turn: Invention and Persuasion in the Conduct of Inquiry* (Chicago: University of Chicago Press, 1990), 35–57; M. W. McRae, ed., *The Literature of Science: Perspectives on Popular Scientific Writing* (Athens, GA: University of Georgia Press, 1993); A. G. Gross, *The Rhetoric of Science* (Cambridge, MA: Harvard University Press, 1996); J. T. Battalio, *The Rhetoric of Science in the Evolution of American Ornithological Discourse* (Stanford, CT: Ablex, 1998); L. Ceccarelli, *Shaping Science With Rhetoric: The Cases of Dobzhansky, Schrodinger, and Wilson* (Chicago: University of Chicago Press, 2001).

4 E. A. Burtt, *The Metaphysical Foundations of Modern Science* (Atlantic Highlands, NJ: Humanities Press, 1952; original work published 1924).

5 See Chan Wing-tsit, ed. and trans., *A Source Book in Chinese Philosophy* (Princeton: Princeton University Press, 1963); A. Watts, *Tao [Dao]: The Watercourse Way* (New York: Pantheon, 1975); A. Waley, *Three Ways of Thoughts in Ancient China* (Stanford, CA: Stanford University Press, 1982); A. C. Graham, *Disputers of the Tao [Dao]: Philosophical Argument in Ancient China* (La Salle, IL: Open Court, 1989).

6 *A Source Book in Chinese Philosophy*, 26. Lao Zi traditionally was considered an older contemporary of Confucius; however, scholars have found convincing evidence to suggest that *Daode jing* was written after Confucius and that Lao Zi probably lived during the fourth century B.C.E. See Fung Yu-lan, *A History of Chinese Philosophy*, trans. Derk Bodde, vol. 1 (Princeton: Princeton University Press, 1983).

7 Zhuang Zi, "Tian Dao," *Zhuang Zi* (Changchun: Wenshi, 1993), 250–72; Liu An, "Yuan Dao xun," *Weinan Zi* (Beijing: Huaxia, 2000), 1–22; Yang Xiong, "Wen Dao pian," *Fayan* (Jinan: Shandong Youyi, 2001), 51–68; Guo Xiang, "Tian Dao zhu," *Zhuan Zi Guo Xiang zhu* (Taipei: Xinxin, 1965), 5, 11; Ge Hong, "Dao yi," *Baopu Zi* (Beijing: Zhonghua, 1985), 151–67; Wang Tong, "Wang Dao pian," *Zhong shuo*, SPPY ed., vol. 354 (Taipei: Zhonghua, 1965), 1–7; Han Yu, "Yuan Dao," *Han Yu xuanji* (Shanghai: Guji, 1996), 263–77; Zhang Zai, "Tian Dao pian," *Zhang Zai ji* (Beijing: Zhonghua, 1978), 13–5; Wang Tingxiang, "Dao Ti pian," *Wang Tingxiang ji*, vol. 3 (Beijing: Zhonghua, 1989), 751–55; Wang Fuzhi, "Tian Dao pian," *Zhang Zi zhengmeng zhu* (Beijing: Zhonghua, 1975), 49–59; Jin Yuelin, *Lun Dao* (Shanghai: Shangwu, 1940); Feng Youlan (also romanized as Fung Yu-lan), *Xin yuan Dao* (Chongqing: Shangwu, 1945); Tang Junyi, *Yuan Dao pian*, 3 vols (Hong Kong: Xinya, 1973).

8 Zhang Liwen and others, *Dao [The Way]* (Beijing: Zhongguo Renmin Daxue, 1989), 4–10.

9 Cited in A. F. Wright, "The Chinese Language and Foreign Ideas," in *Studies in Chinese Thought*, ed. A. F. Wright (Chicago: Chicago University Press, 1953), 268–303; cited material, 302, n. 8.

10 See, for example, Chen Shaoming, Shan Shilian, and Zhang Yongyi, *Bei jieshi de chuantong: Jiandai xixiangshi xinlun* [An Interpretation of Tradition: A New Approach to the Modern History of Thought] (Guangzhou: Zhongshan, 1995); Liu Dachun and Wu Xianghong, *Xinxue kulu: Kexue, shehui, wenhua de dazhuangji* [A Painful Journey to New Learning: A Clash Among Science, Society, and Culture] (Nanchang: Jiangxi Gaoxiao, 1995); D. W. Y Kwok, *Scientism in Chinese Thought 1900–1950* (New Haven: Yale University Press, 1965).

11 Zhang Junmai, "Renshengguan [A View of Life]," in *Kexue yu renshengguan* [Science and a View of Life, hereafter *KYR*], ed. Zhang Junmai and Ding Wenjiang (Shanghai: Yadong, 1923; original work published in *Qinghua Zhoukan*, February 1923), 1–13 (4–9). For translation, see C. Furth, *Ting Wen-chiang [Ding Wenjiang]: Science and China's New Culture* (Cambridge, MA: Harvard University Press, 1970), 100.

12 Ding Wenjiang, "Xuanxue yu kexue [Metaphysics and Science]," in *KYR* (original work published in *Nuli Zhoubao*, April 1923), 1–30.

13 At the end of 1923, the bulk of the voluminous literature of the debate was collected into *Kexue yu renshengguan* [Science and a View of Life; *KYR*]. The collection, over 250,000 words, is the main source of my study. This collection is noteworthy because its compilers adopted an approach fashionable in earlier times in China and simply collected the relevant articles from the original sources and reprinted them without repagination.

14 Hu Shi, "Yinianban de huigu [A Review of the Past One and a Half Years]," in *Hu Shi wencun*, vol. 2, ed. Huangshan Publishing House (Hefei: Huangshan, 1996; original work published 1923), 359–64 (pp. 362–3).

15 Ding, "Xuanxue yu kexue," 1.

16 Li Zehou, "Ji Zhongguo xiandai sanci xueshu lunzhan [On the Three Intellectual Debates in Modern China]," in *Zhongguo xiandai sixiangshi lun*, rev. ed. (Taipei: Fengyun, 1990), 55–103 (p. 65).

17 L. Laudan, "The Demise of the Demarcation Problem," in *But Is It Science?*, ed. Michael Ruse (New York: Prometheus Books, 1996), 337–50 (p. 342).

18 Chen Duxiu, "Benzhi zuian zhi dapian shu [A Reply to the Charges Against Our Journal]," in *Chen Duxiu zhuzuo xuan*, vol. 1, ed. Ren Jianshu, Zhang Tongmo, and Wu Xinzhong (Shanghai: Renmin, 1991; original work published 1919), 442–43 (p. 443).

19 See, for example, Lin Yu-sheng, "Minchu 'kexue zhuyi' de xingqi yu hanu [The Rise of Scientism and Its Meaning in the Early Days of the Republic of China]," in *Zhongguo chuantong de chuangzaoxing zhuanhua*, ed. Lin Yu-sheng (Beijing: Sanlian, 1988), 264–8; Yan Bofei, "Lun 'Wusi' shiqi zhongguo de zhishi fenzi dui kexue de lijie [On the Chinese Intellectuals' Conceptions of Science in the May Fourth Era]," in *Wusi: duoyuan de fansi*, ed. Lin Yu-sheng (Hong Kong: Sanlian, 1989), 198–214.

20 Li, "Ji Zhongguo," 65.

21 Kwok, *Scientism in Chinese Thought*, 159.

22 Hu Shi, "Preface," in *KYR*, 1–33 (p. 2).

23 *Daode jing* (also *Tao Te Ching*, Chinese classical text), in *A Source Book in Chinese Philosophy*, ed. Chan Wing-tsit, trans. Chan Wing-tsit (Princeton: Princeton University Press, 1963), 139–76 (pp. 146, 150).

24 *Kuan-tzu* [The Book of Master Guan; Chinese classical text], trans. W. Allyn Rickett (Hong Kong: Hong Kong University Press, 1965), 168.

25 *The I Ching or Book of Changes* (Chinese classical text), trans. Cary F. Baynes, 3rd ed. (Princeton: Princeton University Press, 1977), 138, 546.

26 Cited in Fung Yu-lan, *A History of Chinese Philosophy*, vol. 2, 542–3.

27 Wang Fuzhi (also romanised as Wang Fu-chih, 1619–1692), great Confucian philosopher of the seventeenth century, is representative of this view. See *A Source Book in Chinese Philosophy*, 694–6.

28 For example, Wang Fuzhi, *Zhangzi zhengmeng* chu [Commentary on Master Zhang's Correcting Youthful Ignorance] (Beijing: Zhonghua, 1975; revision of the 1865 ed.), 1–28. See also I. McMorran, "Wang Fu-chih [Wang Fuzhi] and the Neo-Confucian Tradition," in *The Unfolding of Neo-Confucianism*, ed. Wm. Theodore de Bary (New York: Columbia University Press, 1975), 432–50 (p. 438). For a historical account of the rise of empirical scholarship (*kaozheng*) as a dominant form of Confucian discourse in the seventeenth and the eighteenth centuries, see B. A. Elman, *From Philosophy to Philology: Intellectual and Social Aspects of Change in Late Imperial China* (Cambridge: Council on East Asian Studies, Harvard University, 1984), 37–85.

29 Note, for example, the following famous sayings of Liu Zongzhou (also romanized as Liu Tsung-chou, 1578–1645), Huang Zongxi (also Huang Tsung-hsi, 1610–95), and Dai Zhen

(also Tai Chen, 1723–1777): "Everything in the universe is filled by a single Ether [*Qi*]. ... Heaven, by obtaining it, thereby becomes Heaven; Earth, by obtaining it, thereby becomes Earth" "In the great process of evolutionary change there is only the single Ether [*Qi*], which circulates everywhere without interruption" "Tao [*Dao*] is like 'movement'. The evolutionary operations of the Ether produce and reproduce without pause. That is why this process is called the Dao." Cited in Fung, *A History of Chinese Philosophy*, vol. 2, 640–53. Compare the neo-Confucian Zhu Xi, who said: "There is only one principle [*Li*] in the universe. Heaven receives it to become Heaven, Earth receives it to become Earth, and all those born in the universe receive it to become their nature. ... The evolutionary operation of principle is omnipresent." Zhu Xi, "Du daji [On Reading 'Great Principle of the Universe'']," in *Zhuzi daquan*, vol. 70, ed. Gao Shixian and Wu Rulin (Taipei: Zhonghua, 1985; reprinted from the 1532 ed.), 5b–7a (p. 5b).

30 Wei Yuan (1794–1856), a compelling speaker of the School of Practical Statecraft, made it explicit: "In all ages there is wealth and power without the kingly Way, but there is no kingly Way without wealth and power." Wei Yuan, *Mogu [A Silent Beaker]*, in *Wei Yuan ji*, vol. 1, ed. Wei Yuan's Works Editorial Board (Beijing: Zhonghua, 1976; revision of the 1878 edition), 1–81 (p. 36).

31 Professional statecraft and the institutional approach received early emphasis in the eighty-volume *Huangchao jingshi wenpian* [Compilation of Qing Essays on Statecraft]. The essays selected cover a variety of technical subjects such as the salt gabelle, grain transport, canal shipment, water control, military system, maritime defense, and the like. See He Zhangling and Wei Yuan, eds., *Huangchao jingshi* wenpian [Compilation of Qing Essays on Statecraft], in *Jindai Zhongguo shiliao congkan*, vol. 731, ed. Yunlong Shen (Taipei: Yunha, 1966; original work published 1826–1827).

32 Zhang Zhidong, "Preface to *Quanxue lun* [Exhortation to Learning]," in *Zhang Wenrang-gong chuanji* [Collected Works of Duke Zhang], vol. 5, ed. Wang Shunan (Taipei: Wenhai, 1980; original work published 1898), 14433. For a somewhat dated translation, see Zhang Zhidong, *China's Only Hope: An Appeal*, trans. Samuel I. Woodbridge (New York: Fleming H. Revell Company, 1900), 21–5.

33 Xiao Xiaosui, "China Encounters Darwinism: A Case of Intercultural Rhetoric," *Quarterly Journal of Speech* 81 (1995): 83–99.

34 Xiao Xiaosui, "From the Hierarchical Ren to Egalitarianism: A Case of Cross-cultural Rhetorical Mediation," *Quarterly Journal of Speech* 82 (1996): 38–54.

35 For a general review of the rising sentiment of scientism in China of the early twentieth century, see Kwok, *Scientism in Chinese Thought*, 1–30.

36 Liang Qichao, *You ou xinying* lu [Reflections on a Trip to Europe] (Hong Kong: Shanda, 1964; original work published 1920), 17–22. The translation is basically Kwok's, see Kwok, *Scientism in Chinese Thought*, 137.

37 Zhang, "Renshengguan," 8. Throughout this essay, the translation of cited Chinese texts into English is mine unless otherwise noted.

38 Zhang Junmai, "Zai lun renshengguan yu kexue bing da Ding Zaizhun [Further Discussion of a View of Life and Science, With a Reply to Ding Wenjiang]," in *KYR*, 1–98 (pp. 89, 92). Here Zhang made an allusion to one of the most profound teachings of the sage kings: "The human mind is precarious. The moral mind is subtle. Have absolute refinement and singleness of mind. 'Hold fast the Mean'." *Shu jing* [Book of history; Chinese classical text] (Shanghai: Guji, 1990; reprinted from the 1867 ed.), 53. According to Zhu Xi, the profound meaning of this famous saying constitutes the core of the learning of the Dao. "This is what Shun

transmitted to Yu. ... Since their time, one sage after another has handed down the tradition [of the Dao]." Zhu Xi, "Zhongyong zhangju xu [Preface to the Commentary on the *Doctrine of the Mean*]," in *Zhuzi daquan*, vol. 76 (Taipei: Zhonghua, 1985; reprinted from the 1532 ed.), 21b–23b (p. 21b); cf. Chan Wing-tsit, *Chu Hsi [Zhu Xi]: New Studies* (Honolulu: University of Hawaii Press, 1989), 321.

39 Zhang, "Zai lun renshengguan," 35, 19, 20, 22, 24.

40 Ding, "Xuanxue yu kexue," 1. Translation from Kwok, *Scientism in Chinese Thought*, 143.

41 Wu Zhihui, "Yige xin xinyang de yuzhouguan ji renshengguan [A New Belief and Its View of Life and the Universe]," in *KYR*, 1–165 (pp. 22–34); Hu, "Preface," 18–21.

42 Wu, "Yige xin xihyang," 27–8. Cf. E. J. Urwick, "Note to the Second Edition," *A Philosophy of Social Progress* (London: Methuen and Co., 1920), vi.

43 Wu, "Yige xin yang," 27–8.

44 Hu, "Preface," 23.

45 Wu, "Yige xin xinyang," 35. Translation based on Furth, *Ting Wen-chiang*, 120.

46 Wu, "Yige xin yang," 101–3. Other defenders of science took a similar view. See particularly Ding, "Xuanxue yu kexue," 14–5; "Xuanxue yu kexue, da Zhang Junmai [Metaphysics and Science, With a Reply to Zhang Junmai]," in *KYR*, 1–49 (pp. 40–2); Tang Yue, "Yige yiren de shuomeng [Dream-talks of a Derelict: Is Sentiment Above Science?]," in *KYR*, 1–10; Wang Xinggong, "Kexue yu renshengguan [Science and a View of Life]," in *KYR*, 1–18 (pp. 14–5). For their opponents' views on intuition, see Zhang, "Renshengguan," 5–6; "Zai lun renshengguan," 31–9; Fan Shoukang, "*Ping suowei 'kexue yu xuanxue zhizheng*' [A Critique of the So-called 'Debate on Science and Metaphysics']," in *KYR*, 1–24 (p. 17).

47 Wu, "Yige xin yeng," 31. Wu's words on the weight of the brain and the number of cranial nerves were hypothetical.

48 Wu, "Yige xin yeng," 32.

49 Wu, "Yige xin yeng," 7–9, 40. Cf. *Daode jing*, ed. Chan Wing-tsit, chap. 5.

50 Wu, "Yige xin yeng," 7–12, 10–12.

51 Wu, "Yige xin yeng," 14–23.

52 Ren Hongjun, "Renshengguan de kexue huo kexue de renshengguan [A Science of the View of Life or a Scientific View of Life]," in *KYR*, 1–10 (p. 7); Hu, "Preface," 28; Wang, "Kexue yu renshengguan," 16.

53 Ding, "Xuanxue yu kexue," 3, 20; "Xuanxue yu kexue, da Zhang," 12. According to Ding, "The omnipotence of science ... lies not in its subject matter, but in its method" (p. 20).

54 For other related accounts of the scientific method, see Wang, "Kexue yu renshengguan," 4–10; Tang Yue, "Kexue de fanwei [The Scope of Science]," in *KYR*, 1–8 (p. 2), Ren, "Renshengguan," 7–8. For a comment on Ding's insensitivity to the theoretical side of science, see Furth, *Ting Wen-chiang*, 111–2.

55 Ding, "Xuanxue yu kexue," 27.

56 Ren, "Renshengguan," 6.

57 Tang, "Yige yiren," 3; cf. Liang Qichao, "Renshengguan yu kexue [A View of Life and Science]," in *KYR*, 1–14 (pp. 8–9). Although Liang Qichao, who was responsible for the prelude to the debate, tried to mediate between the two parties, he insisted that human sentiments, especially the sense of beauty and love, could not be analyzed scientifically (pp. 8–9).

58 Tang, "Yige yiren," 3.

59 Tang, "Yige yiren," 6–9; cf. Liang, "Renshengguan," 9.

60 Wang, "Kexue yu renshengguan," 11–3.

61 See in particular Zhang, "Zai lun renshengguan," 50, 59–60.

62 Ding, "Xuanxue yu kexue, da Zhang," 14.

63 Zhu Jingnong, "Du Zhang Junmai lun renshengguan yu kexue de liangpian wenzhang hou suo fasheng de yiwen [Some Questions After Reading Zhang Junmai's Two Essays on a View of Life and Science]," in *KYR*, 1–8 (pp. 2–4).

64 Ding, "Xuanxue yu kexue, da Zhang," 11–2.

65 Ren, "Renshengguan," 8.

66 Hu, "Preface," 13–4.

67 Ding, "Xuanxue yu kexue," 13.

68 Wu, "Yige xin xinyang," 35.

69 Tang, "Yige yiren," 5–10.

70 Wu, "Yige xin xinyang," 150–1.

71 Ding, "Xuanxue yu kexue," 21. Based on the translation by Kwok, *Scientism in Chinese Thought*, 147.

72 See Hu Shi, *Ding Wenjiang zhuan* [Biography of Ding Wenjiang] (Haikou: Hainan, 1993), 71–2; also see Zhang, "Zai lun renshengguan," 117; Lin Zaiping, "Du Ding Zaizhun de Xuanxue yu Kexue [Having Read Ding Wenjiang's 'Metaphysics and Science']," in *KYR*, 1–40 (pp. 32, 36). According to Hu (pp. 71–2), Ding regarded this passage as the most interesting part of his "*Xuanxue yu kexue*" [Metaphysics and a Science]. Zhang Junmai and his sympathizer Lin Zaiping also cited this passage and believed that it represented one of the key arguments made by the pro-science group. Zhang, "Zai lun renshengguan," 117; Lin, "Du Ding Zaizhun," 232, 236.

73 Ren, "Renshengguan," 6.

74 Isaac Newton, quoted in S. D. Brewster, *Memoirs of the Life, Writings, and Discoveries of Sir Isaac Newton* (New York: Johnson Reprint Corporation, 1965; original work published 1855), 407.

75 The present version is my own translation. Ren cited Joseph J. Thomson's words in the Chinese language without indicating the source. The English version must appear somewhere before 1923 when Ren quoted it. To date I have been unable to locate the source, but I have found that the idea expressed in the quotation was a recurrent theme of Thomson's writings, where he had repeatedly expressed similar ideas on later occasions. For instance, "[I]t is the charm of Physics that there are no hard and fast boundaries, that each discovery is not a terminus but an avenue leading to country as yet unexplored, and that however long the science may exist there will still be an abundance of unsolved problems and no danger of unemployment for physicists." J. J. Thomson, *Beyond the Electron* (Cambridge, UK: Cambridge University Press, 1928), 9. "A great discovery is not a terminus, but an avenue leading to regions hitherto unknown. We climb to the top of the peak, and find that it reveals to us another higher than any we have yet seen and so it goes on." Quoted in G. P. Thomson, *J. J. Thomson: Discoverer of the Electron* (Garden City, New York: Anchor Books, 1966), 198. The author George Thomson footnoted the origin of this quote as follows: "Listener, January 29, 1930."

76 Wu, "Yige xin xinyang," 29–30, 100, 14.

77 Ding, "Xuanxue yu kexue, da Zhang," 30–5; cf. Zhu, "Du Zhang Junmai," 5–8; Tang Yue, "Xinli xianxiang yu yinguolu [Psychological Phenomena and the Laws of Causation]," in *KYR*, 1–15 (12–3); Hu, "Preface," 22–3.

78 Tang Yue, "Du le 'Ping suowei Kexue yu Xuanxue zhi Zheng' yihou [Having Read 'Critique of the So-called Debate on Science and Metaphysics']," in *KYR*, 1–10 (p. 9); cf. Wu, "Yige xin xinyang," 161; Ding, "Xuanxue yu kexue, da Zhang," 31; and Hu, "Preface," 27. This dynamic view of the self was first discussed in Hu Shi's widely read essay entitled "Buxiu, wo

de zongjiao [Immortality, My Religion]," in *Hu Shi xuanji*, ed. Ming Hu (Tianjin: Renmin, 1991; original work published 1919), 68–77.

79 Wu, "Yige xin xinyang," 161; Hu, "Preface," 27.

80 Hu, "Preface" 27.

81 Tang, "Du le," 9.

82 Wu, "Yige xin xinyang," 47–9; cf. 91, 145.

83 Ren, "Renshengguan," 6–7.

84 Wu, "Yige xin xinyang," 137.

85 Ding, "Xuanxue yu kexue, da Zhang," 38; cf. Hu, "Preface," 27. Ding (p. 38) defined religion as the "natural impulse" to sacrifice the self in the interest of the entire human race.

86 Ding, "Xuanxue yu kexue, da Zhang," 39–40.

87 Wu, "Yige xin xinyang," 23–4.

88 Ding, "Xuanxue yu kexue," 1, 4, 16. One participant in the debate noted the overweening tone in these statements and said they read like "the clamor of a punitive expedition." Lin, "Du Ding Zizhun," 3–4.

89 Wu, "Yige xin xinyang," 7–12.

90 J. Campbell, "Scientific Revolution" A. G Gross, "On the Shoulders of Giants."

91 L. Prelli, "A Rhetoric of Science."

92 For example, Chen Duxiu, "Da Shizhi [A Reply to Hu Shi]," in *KYR*, 33–42; "Preface," in *KYR*, 1–11; Deng Zhongxia, "Zhongguo xianzai de sixiang jie [The Current Tendencies of Chinese Intellectuals]," *Zhongguo Qinnian* 6 (November 1923): 2–6; Qu Qiubai, "Ziyou shijie yu biran shijie [The World of Freedom and the World of Necessity]," in *Qu Qiubai wenji*, political theory ed., vol. 2, ed. Qu Qiubai's Works Editorial Board (Beijing: Renmin, 1988; original work published in *Xin Qinnian Jikan*, December 1923), 294–309.

93 Chen, "Preface" "Ch'en Tu-hsiu's [Chen Duxiu's] Argument for Historical Materialism, 1923," in *China's Response to the West: A Documentary Survey, 1839–1923*, ed. Ssu-yu Teng and John K. Fairbank (Cambridge, MA: Harvard University Press, 1979), 249–51.

94 Chen, "Da Shizhi," 33–42; "Preface," 1–11.

95 Chen, "Da Shizhi," 34–5.

96 Hu Shi, "Duo yenjiu xie wenti, shao tan xie zhuyi [Study More Problems, Talk Less of 'Isms']," in *Hu Shi xuanji* (Original work published 1919), 93–7 (p. 97).

97 Chen, "Da Shizhi," 36–7; "Da Zhang Junmai ji Liang Rengong [A Reply to Zhang Junmai and Liang Qichao]," in *Chen Duxiu zhuzuo xuan*, vol. 2, ed. Ren Jianshu, Zhang Tongmo, and Wu Xinzhong (Shanghai: Renmin, 1991; original work published in *Xin Qinnian Jikan*, August 1924), 685–96.

98 Liu Shao-chi [Liu Shaoqi], *On the Party*, 5th ed., vol. 1 (Beijing: Foreign Languages Press, 1954), 9. This cited work was originally *Report on the Revision of the Party Constitution* delivered by the author in May 1945 to the Seventh Congress of the Communist Party of China. The author was then Mao's political associate. This report is credited with providing by then the most "scientific" account of the scientific character and superiority of Mao Zedong thought. According to Liu, "[Mao Zedong thought] has been formulated through the application of the Marxist world outlook and social outlook—dialectical materialism and historical materialism. In other words, it has been formulated on the solid foundation of Marxist-Leninist theories, by taking into account China's national traits, by profiting from the exceedingly rich experiences of modern revolutions and those of the Chinese Communist Party in directing the revolutionary struggle of the Chinese people, and by making a careful and scientific analysis of such experiences. It is the theory and policy for achieving the

emancipation of the Chinese nation and people. It has been developed on the basis of the interests of the proletariat and consequently the interests of the entire people, by applying the scientific method of Marxism-Leninism and by synthesizing China's history, social conditions, and all her revolutionary experiences. It is the only correct theory and policy to guide the proletariat and all the working people of China in their fight for emancipation" (p. 32).

99 Ma Wanxiang, "Ren ting Mao Zhuxi de hua, luzi jiuting ren de hua," *Liangning Ribao* (28 January 1966); Zhou Dazhi, "Wo ting Mao Zhuxi de hua, mianhua jiuting wo de hua," *Hunan Ribao* (27 January 1966); Bao Sien, "Mao Zedong sixiang shi wanling de jinyaoshi," *Zhejiang Ribao* (4 June 1966); Li Suqing, "Mao Zhuxi de shu yong dao nali nali ling," *Shanxi Ribao* (30 May 1966); Zhao Yulin, "Mao Zedong sixiang gei le wo wuqiongwujin de liliang," *Yejin Bao* (4 June 1966); Wu Zirong et al., "Shei zhangwo Mao Zedong Sixiang shei jiushi zhenzheng quanwei," *Shanxi Ribao* (28 May 1966); Yu Donghai, "Huoxuehuoyong Mao Zhuxi zhuzuo jiuneng gongwubuke zhanwubusheng," *Jilin Ribao* (10 July 1966).

100 For example, Editorial Board, "Zai Mao Zedong sixiang de daolu shang shengli qianjin [Successfully March on the Road of Mao Zedong Thought]," *Hongqi* 11 (August 1966): 19–21; Editorial Board, "Zai Mao Zedong sixiang de dadao shang qianjin [March on the Broad Road of Mao Zedong Thought]," *Hongqi* 13 (October 1966): 4–6; Editorial Board, "Yanzhuo Mao zhuxi kaipi de geming hangdao qianjin [Forge Valiantly Ahead and Keep to the Channel Opened up by Chairman Mao]," *Jiefangjun Bao* (26 July 1966); Zou Guozhen, "Huoxuehuoyong Mao zhuxi zhuzuo, yanzhuo geminghua dadao qianjin [Creatively Study and Apply the Doctrines of Chairman Mao, and March Along the Broad Road of Revolution]," *Dagong Bao* (10 August 1966); Wang Xiulan, "Mao zhuxi zhuzuo zhiyin wo zoushang geming dadao [The Works of Chairman Mao Show Me the Way of Revolution]," *Ningxia Ribao* (6 August 1966).

101 Xing Bisi, "Zhexue de qimeng he qimeng de zhexue [The Enlightenment of Philosophy and Philosophical Enlightenment]," *Renmin Ribao* (22 July 1978): 5. For critical discussion of this view, see V. Schwarcz, *The Chinese Enlightenment: Intellectuals and the Legacy of the May Fourth Movement of 1919* (Berkeley: University of California Press, 1986), 298–9.

102 Zhou Yang, "San ci weida de sixiang jiefang yundong [Three Major Thought Emancipation Movements]," *Guangming Ribao* (8 May 1979), 3. Zhou Yang was propaganda chief of the Chinese Communist Party before the Cultural Revolution (1966–1976).

103 For some important collections of these critical inquiries, see Feng Chi and Wang Yafu, eds., *Wusi fansi* [The Reflection on "May Fourth"] (Shanghai: Huadong Shifan Daxue, 1989); Lin Yu-sheng, ed., *Wusi: Duoyuan de fansi* [The May Fourth Movement: Pluralistic Reflections] (Hong Kong: Sanlian, 1989); Tang Yujie, ed., *Lun chuantong yu fanchuantong* [On Tradition and Anti-Tradition] (Taipei: Lianjing, 1989); Ju Xi, *Zhongguo de kexue jingshen* [The Chinese Spirit of Science] (Chengdu: Sichuan Renmin, 2000).

104 For example, Guo Luoji, "Sixiang yao jiefang, lilun yao chedi [Liberate Our Thinking and Have a Thorough Understanding of Theory]," *Hongqi* 3 (March 1979): 33–41; Ma Zhongyang, "Kang Sheng de 'fazhan lun' yu xiandai mixin [Kang Sheng's 'Developmental Theory' and Modern Superstition]," *Hongqi* 18 (September 1980): 23–27; Zhao Ziyang, "Zai jianshe he gaige de xinshidai jinyibu fayang wusi jingshen [Carry Forward the May Fourth Spirit in the New Age of Construction and Reform]," *Qiushi* 10 (May 1989): 2–5; He Zuoma, "Gaoju kexue qizhi, hongyang kexue jingshen [Hold High the Banner of Science, Carry Forward the Spirit of Science]," *Qiushi* 9 (May 1999): 5–9. See also Xing, "Zhexue de qimeng" Lin, *Wusi*; Feng and Wang, *Wusi fansi*; Tang, *Lun chuantong*.

18.
RACE AND GENETICS FROM A MODAL MATERIALIST PERSPECTIVE
by Celeste M. Condit

On September 9, 2005, science writer Nicholas Wade published an article in the *New York Times* stating that a version of a gene associated with enhanced brain size had been discovered to have been distributed differently across the globe. He wrote, "About 70 percent of people in most European and East Asian populations carry this allele of the gene, but it is much rarer in most sub-Saharan Africans."[1] This news article was based on two scientific essays published that month in the high-profile scientific journal *Science* by a group of scientists led by Bruce T. Lahn.[2]

The supposition of the research, that it revealed a genotype that predisposed people derived from relatively recent African ancestry to be less intelligent than people from other parts of the world, was immediately acted on by multiple research teams from white-dominated nations around the globe.[3] Several teams rapidly undertook experiments to confirm that people with the stigmatized version of the gene had either lower IQ or smaller brain size than those with the version found more frequently outside of Africa.[4] These research efforts rapidly and unanimously discredited Lahn's claim of a genetic connection between race and intelligence. As will be shown, however, the negative findings of this subsequent research were altogether predictable on a variety of scientific and historical grounds, raising significant questions as to why Lahn's studies were published in the first place. The argument here is that it was not a set of facts about the genetics of intelligence in different racialized bodies that drove the publication of the *Science* or *New York Times* articles, but rather a rhetoric of science that failed to take account of the material effects of embodied discursive matter.

At the theoretical level, this is to argue that an explanation based in idealist theories of knowledge is insufficient to account for the appearance of these articles, each of which represents itself as scientific fact. At the same time, however, explanations based in contemporary materialist theories of discourse are equally insufficient because they treat discourse reductively, as if it were little more than non-discursive physical matter. In short, whether driven by idealist or materialist presuppositions, contemporary theories of knowledge fail to articulate the impacts of the distinctive arrangements of discursive matter as it flows through both biological bodies and other media. This essay thus uses the reappearance of the discourse of scientific racism in *Science* and the *New York Times*

Celeste M. Condit. "Race and Genetics from a Modal Materialist Perspective." *Quarterly Journal of Speech*, Volume 94, Number 4, 2008, pp. 383–406.

as a case study to advance a more complex theory of materialist discourse, even as it uses that theory to account for the appearance of these articles within a historical circuit of scientific and public racism.

To accomplish this pair of objectives, I posit a modal form of materialism as an alternative to prevailing models of knowledge predicated on idealism or on existing forms of materialism. The latter are characterized as reductivist or physicalist because they efface the historical and valuative components of discourse and the distinctive and active force of human bodies. I then compare and elaborate on the implications of these alternative theories through a treatment of Lahn's original research published in *Science*, the *New York Times* coverage of those publications, *Science*'s subsequent quasi-retraction of those articles, and an analysis of the rhetorical strategy of that retraction in light of the historical positioning of science in late modern society. Drawing on this analysis, I con- clude by arguing for the desirability of both (a) reconstituting scientific practices so as to incorporate the effects of discursive material and (b) reconstituting critical theory to integrate the material effects of discursive and non-discursive matter, especially human bodies.

Idealism and Materialisms

The doctrine that the real or ultimately causative forces in the universe are "ideas" that stand outside the world of physical matter and appearance is frequently attributed to Plato. Although a wide range of idealist theories have been developed, idealism is under- stood here as the assumption that there are permanent forms that exist outside of human perception and language, but which language attempts to "convey," and which various methods of research may attempt to discover. This idealist account of knowledge is neither overtly expressed nor defended in most contemporary rhetorical theory, but as we will see, it plays a critical, if nevertheless contradictory, role in the grounding of sci- entific discourse.

The "idea" that racism might be established by scientific facts has been shown repeatedly to be false. Stephen Jay Gould and Jonathan Marks, among others, have docu- mented a pattern in Western science over the past century and a half whereby each round of new scientific technologies and their associated paradigms are presented as demonstrating that racism is scientifically grounded in biological facts, only to have the evidence for such claims subsequently rejected for its biased data selection, faulty calcu- lations animated by desire or ideological interest rather than mathematical precision, and selective pressure applied to the measurements made with different groups.[5] Accord- ing to the standards of science, the inability to demonstrate substantive racial differences through rigorous experimentation would seem to amount to a rather rigorous falsifica- tion of the claim to race-based biological inferiority. And yet, the discourse that claims a scientific grounding for racism lives on.

The recirculation of claims to scientific groundings for racism continues because discourses are not made of immaterial ideas, but rather of the material flows of symbols and images circulating through social spaces (televisions, books, posters, radios, com- puters, families, churches, telephones, etc.) and human bodies (including their neural networks). Karl Marx and Friedrich Engels prompted what was perhaps the first materialist understanding of discourse when they wrote, "The ideas of the ruling class are in every epoch the ruling ideas."[6] As has been noted repeatedly, they turned Hegel's idealist conception of the relationship between "spirit" and material history on its head by arguing that "[t]he ruling ideas are nothing more than the ideal expression of the dominant material relationships."[7]

Marx and Engels still used the German word customarily translated as "ideas" (*Gedanken*) rather than terms for "language" or "discourses." Consequently, the relatively vague and essentialist metaphor of "expression" emerged in the ontological gulf between the realm of ideas and that of physical matter. Since the late nineteenth century, a variety of theorists attempted to fill in the gap between "ideas" and "matter."[8] The source most important to the likely reader of this essay is the 1982 article by Michael Calvin McGee that argued that "[t]he alternative to *idealism* ... is to think of rhetoric as an *object*, as material and as omnipresent as air and water" and accordingly that "[d]scourse, even language itself, will have to be characterized as material rather than merely representational of mental and empirical phenomena."[9]

While there are many ways to read McGee's claims, the most prominent way in which his theory of rhetorical materialism has been developed could be described as a reductive materialism.[10] Because such approaches too directly appropriate the language and model of physics, they fail to account both for the distinctive and emergent properties of language, which create the phenomena we experience as "ideas," as well as for the distinctive properties of matter arranged in biological forms.

While the physicalist vocabulary of materialism is more and less visible in different theoretical formulations, it is explicit in the influential work of post-structuralist Gilles Deleuze, who writes that "the kinetic proposition tells us that a body is defined by relations of motion and rest, of slowness and speed between particles. That is, it is not defined by *a form or by functions*."[11] In short, Deleuze reduces all bodies to the same *form*less type:

> [W]e will not define a thing by its form, nor by its organs and its functions, nor as a substance or a subject. Borrowing terms from the Middle Ages, or from geography, we will define it by *longitude* and *latitude*. A body can be anything; it can be an animal, a body of sounds, a mind or an idea; it can be a linguistic corpus, a social body, a collectivity.[12]

Deleuze's writings are in no way univocal, and they have been fruitful for many purposes, yet his physicalist version of materialism has its costs, made most evident in Davi Johnson's recent application of this line of analysis to rhetorical theory and criticism when she writes that "[s]ubjects and objects are not defined by prior ontological distinctions; rather, they are articulated by the variant movements of these flows that combine and coagulate in accordance with their speeds or slownesses, accelerations, and decelerations."[13]

Johnson's essay is productive for the materialist theoretical tradition, because she accurately notes the difficulties materialists have had in dealing with the idea/matter binary. As she indicates, "even theories opposed to the idealist tradition cast matter as passive and reserve action for linguistic agencies."[14] Nonetheless, two features of her formulation are particularly problematic for effective rhetorical criticism: the elimination of ideological judgment and the sublation of time into space.

First, Johnson quite correctly indicates that a physicalist or reductive materialist perspective "requires rhetoric to abandon ideological judgment."[15] It does this because the movement of physical matter is presumed to have no value or ideology. Although one can map the various effectivities of different discourses that circulate, as Johnson does, a physicalist materialism offers no vocabulary or set of theoretical relations—neither in the drives of biological bodies nor in the "meanings" of discursive archives—that justify the choice of one discourse over another. A reductive materialism is thus incompatible with theories or motives that find ideological judgment to be either desirable or inevitable.

The second limitation of Johnson's reductive materialism is its denial of history. She lauds "highlighting geographical alternatives" and critiques the predominant historical materialism in rhetorical studies.[16] A reductive materialism discourages attention to temporality because the paradigm of physics conceives of things as universal, not as the product of a historical lineage. Objects are presumed to take the forms they assume at any moment solely as a product of the immediately surrounding forces (gravity, electromagnetism, and strong and weak forces, period). The subset of physical matter that appears in the form of biological beings, however, assumes that their forms are also due to their places in a lineage—the evolved templates they receive. Similarly, the effectivities of language (which include properties hazily identified by vague terms such as meaning, motive, intentions, values, ideology, etc.) emerge only from the varied exposure through time of specific collections of bodies to specific words in specific arrays.[17]

Johnson casts the physicalist version of materialism in a surface–depth binary that charts the physical properties of discourse as the valued surface and repudiates depth (as the form/function of biological bodies and the "ideas" through which discourse moves human bodies). She writes,

> The geographically oriented critic does not seek below the surface of discourse for hidden content or the prior intentions of a speaking subject, but stays at the surface, tracing connections and mapping dissociations. What were situated as hidden origins in the representational model become effects that arise from the surface of discourse like *froth, or mist.*[18]

Such physicalist versions of rhetorical theory may point us toward under-appreciated dimensions of discourse, but they are insufficient, because they presume that the causal force of discourse lies exclusively in the context of the immediate and local. Just as the energy/matter of an atom is presumed to function as the self-contained driver of its interaction with other atoms, so from this perspective we might presume that discourse can be understood as a self-contained driver of its interactions with other discourses.

A discourse that never circulated through a biological being, however, would be, if not inert, then at least something very different than it might be when words are understood to be driven and embodied by biological creatures. All the tremendous apparatus of the television industry, of the Internet, and of the cell phone would literally cease if biological bodies did not drive them. Even if one can imagine a day when humans are replaced by machines, the discursive networks of such machinery would be different in substantial ways. This is not to say that media do not matter. It is instead to say that the human body is a medium with specific properties that drive and shape discourse both in the moment and through time.

Post-structural rhetorical theorists such as Barbara Biesecker and Ronald Greene have shown the limitations of the conceptualization of biologically related terms that were key to pre-materialist rhetorical theories, such as "intention," "meaning," "value," and "situation."[19] Their work draws on an enormous body of psychological and philosophical literature that correctly discredits the idea that human actions are governed primarily by rationally based, fully self-aware, and programmatic choices that guide the selection of discourse by an actor.[20] Although these critiques rightfully identify limitations in the ways such concepts were formulated, they do not justify the wholesale dismissal of the role of the peculiar energies of bodies in the circulation of particular discourses. Rather than merely to discredit these key terms, therefore, they need to be reworked or replaced to articulate the activating energies of the non-unified, subconsciously driven, human animal.

In the case of the circulation of the discourse of genetic racism discussed in this essay, both Lahn (the geneticist) and Michael Balter (the science writer who composed *Science*'s treatment of the episode) declare themselves to be anti-racist.[21] Nonetheless, my analysis of the discourses produced under the signature of their bodies indicates that an activating component of Lahn's work was a motivation to reconfigure the existing racial dynamic in ways more favorable to himself, while Balter's body was strongly motivated to legitimate explanations of the patterns of the world that use a biological lens. Without bodies driven by such specific interests and desires, support for genetically based racial hierarchies would not have appeared in *Science* in 2005 and 2006. This is not to say that Balter and Lahn are either personally unique or culpable in these regards. Indeed, the works published under their bodies' names are produced by complex teams rather than by their bodies as singularities.[22] Although the collective character of the production of discourse complicates the outcome, it does not negate the role of bodies.

Marx's theory that interests drive the circulation of ideas is apt precisely *because* bodies are the kinds of things moved by interests—a characteristic that does not hold for atoms that are not structured into biological bodies.[23] To create a materialist understanding of discourse that explicitly accounts for these dimensions, rhetorical theorists might therefore want to develop a more careful analysis of the ways in which cultural and socio-political interests are in part the product of the interaction of (a) biological proclivities and (b) the sedimented history of discourses in bodies.

I characterize such a project here as a "modal materialism," a theory that action in the universe gains its character and influence from the interaction of the distinctive properties that arise when matter is arranged in different ways.[24] Modal materialism thus takes the canon of arrangement as integral to the ontology of being, holding that although all energy, matter, and action are constituted of physical energy/matter, different properties of matter and action emerge with different arrangements of matter/energy. This theoretical perspective suggests that there are minimally three

distinguishable modes of arrangement of physical matter that have characteristic properties. As indicated above, *physical being* is identified as universal and governed by laws
of localizable cause/effect. *Biological being* is distinguished by the emergence of a "self"
that manifests function through a time-linked chain of cause/effect that can be characterized as an activating and directed energy. Finally, *symbolic being* manifests non-local
(or multi-local) effectivity, which is often identified by the vague term "meaning." The
theoretical elaboration of such a perspective requires more space than is available here,
and so my primary goal in what follows is to illustrate the usefulness of such a perspective through an analysis of this most recent resurgence of scientific racism.[25]

Circulating "Race" as Genetic Flows

A discourse of race has flowed among the people born in Europe, who began increasingly to move around the globe from the fifteenth century onward.[26] This discourse was
pleasing to many Europeans because it elevated their status (symbolically and economically). It adeptly served as a self-justification of the force used to conquer and enslave
other groups of humans, without threatening the dissolution of social order among their
own genealogically and historically constituted group. Scientists in Europe, and later in
the US (where many European bodies flowed, complete with their European discourses)
articulated this racist discourse in several ways, but always within a steep hierarchy:
Europeans ("Caucasians") were the superior humans, portrayed either as in binary
opposition to all other races ("Whites" vs. "Coloreds") or on the top rung of a ladder
where Whites looked down on Black Africans ("Negroes") on the bottom rung, with
Asians ("Mongols") and Native Americans ("Indians") in the middle.

Two different arguments might serve to undermine the legitimacy of such a discourse. One might conclude that such discourse is not egalitarian, and therefore violates
important cultural values. Alternately, one might conclude that such discourse is empirically false. Ideological and scientific approaches place these two accounts at odds with
each other.

Ideological approaches argue that the truths produced by science merely echo the
words or normative interests of scientists or their society.[27] These words in turn are
understood as a function of the operations of an economic machine or a social structure.
On this account, whatever social group is dominant will inevitably proclaim itself
superior to others, regardless of the methods and evidence applied. Scientific evidence
will be created to confirm "common sense" assumptions about racial hierarchy, not
because of empirical facts about human bodies, but because of the material character of
society and its discourses.

A great deal of evidence supports the existence of such tendencies, and this essay
will add to that evidence in some ways. However, there is little comfort in such a
finding, for reductive materialist theories offer no basis on which to counter such
values or ideology. The most recent forms eschew critique altogether. More traditional
forms of ideological analysis may identify the biases that make a "common sense"
partial and interested, but because they maintain that discourse can only be self-
interested, they give no motive or method for someone to work against their own

interests. A framework that would enable us to mitigate genetic racism thus must add something to the reductivists' orientation.

Scientists own the other half of the value/fact divide, insisting that all evidence generated by "science" is factual and value free. When forced to face the history of how scientific evidence has been gerrymandered to ground racial hierarchies in biological difference, supporters of science literally temporize. They assert that findings in the past may have been impure or incorrectly handled, but that present methods and studies are above such biases. The scientific method—when properly followed—is advanced as a self-sufficient or at least self-correcting bulwark against bias. Past violations of the scientific method are thus dismissed as irrelevant to present practices. Current practices are presumed to be free of values and interests, because they are purified by "the method of science." Crucially, however, this method, though defended on the narrow grounds of the virtues of hypothesis-driven experimentation, extends its halo to any scientific observation or practice, as is evidenced by the fact that Lahn's research was not experimental, but it was defended as scientific nonetheless.

The debate about the relationship of race and genetics thus finds itself in a stale argumentative stasis. Ideological critics can point out the existence of racial bias, but they have no theory that would ground alternative practices (only a revision of whose interests should be dominant). Contemporary scientists, on the other hand, find themselves in the awkward situation of promoting racism in order to be faithful to science as it is constituted.

A superior option would be to redefine the practice of science in light of an understanding of the fuller complexities of human being. Scientific knowledge and understanding can only be constructed through words, symbols, and the associated diffuse interactions commonly called their "meanings" or "ideas." Words and symbols are inherently value laden because they are embedded as structures of relation in interest-laden biological beings. If scientific practice is to correct for its biases, it must account not only for the materiality of the physical and biological world it studies, but also for the materiality of the words and bodies in which science must be embedded.

Likewise, reductive materialist theories of language can be expanded to modal materialist perspectives, which understand words not solely as a product of structuring machines, but also as emergent interactions among inherently social bodies. As poststructuralist theories have established, identities do not come pre-constituted with bodies positioned in a particular social structure.[28] Instead, because identities emerge in social interactions, it is possible that something other than "self"-interest can drive discourse and action. The inherently discursive and interactive nature of our ideas opens the possibility of expanding the parameters of our identities. Because these ideas are embodied in biological bodies with localized drives, evading all bias remains impossible. The objective subject cannot live. Nonetheless, because humans are discursive bodies, and discourse exists both inside and outside physical bodies, inclusion and bias may be made greater or lesser. Such a perspective does not deny the activity of the social machine, but rather treats it as only one force among many.

This perspective both requires and permits us to account for the constraints imposed by the nondiscursive matter of the world, such as actually existing patterns of genetic variation. A modal materialism thus identifies the errors in research linking "race" to genetic variation as an interest-driven but meliorable mismatch between value-laden vocabularies and the patterns of genetic variation discernable to users of the vocabulary. The crux of the issue then can be understood as neither merely the question of whether there are biological variations among humans, nor merely whose interests are served by identifying such variations, but rather what *specific* vocabularies *do* when they *relate* discursive and non-discursive realities.[29] From such a perspective, applications of the lay vocabularies of "race" to human genetic variation fail both scientific tests such as precision and generalizability (i.e., cross-contextual utility), as well as public value criteria such as equal inclusion of the interests of differently situated human bodies. To understand precisely how this is so, and why biological scientists nonetheless repeatedly have reproduced these false and malign declarations, a close examination of the latest remake of the saga of biological racism is now in order.

Scene 1: Lahn Constructs and Circulates the Small Brain Allele for Sub-Saharan Africans

The global flow of human bodies has accelerated since the fifteenth century, and the patterns of the flow have changed. One of the bodies born neither in Europe nor the US came to bear the name "Bruce T. Lahn." Lahn's body was one that had felt the impact of racial contestation (more details in scene 3), and it came to inhabit the identity of "biologist" with the attendant discourses and class placements. Thus motivated and placed, Lahn was able to drive the publication of a pair of articles in *Science* that claimed to have identified a "signature of positive selection" with regard to specific versions of two genes related to brain growth (called "*ASPM*" and "*MCPH1*").[30]

The article that gained the most attention in subsequent publications began with the statement that "[t]he most distinct trait of *Homo sapiens* is the exceptional size and complexity of the brain."[31] It described *MCPH1* as "a critical regulator of brain size" and used statistical methods to identify "positive selective sweep," that is, recent evolution.[32] The article included a global map centered on Africa, which used tiny black and white pie charts to represent the relative presence or absence of the presumably favored genotype in the locations where the DNA was sampled. A lengthy caption charted the precise percentages of the genotypes at each of the sampled locations, and sub-Saharan Africa was the locale where this putative gene for large brains was identified as being relatively rare.

In like fashion, the second article highlighted the role of another gene, *ASPM*, in contributing to human brain construction. This article argued that one particular version of the gene "arose merely about 5,800 years ago and has since swept to high frequency under strong positive selection."[33] In this case, however, the world map visualized the absence of the putatively favored allele in both Africa and the Americas. It described the genotype as "notably higher in Europeans and Middle Easterners (including Iberians, Basques, Russians, North Africans, Middle Easterners, and South Asians), as compared with other populations."[34] The *New York Times*, and later *Science* itself, would preferentially reprint the maps and the racial profiling of the first article, but draw supporting claims from both alike, while ignoring, for example, the implication of the article about *MCPH1*, that Native Americans would have the highest percentage of "enhanced brain size."

These articles employed an emerging linguistic convention of contemporary biological science, which links human genetic variation to the social classifications of race. Empirical studies have shown that scientists in practice are sloppy in their usage of labels for human populations, employing no regular, well-defined, or orderly schema of terms to identify groups.[35] Nonetheless, though practice is erratic, a formal definition exists that has substantial currency. It identifies five "continental" "populations," which are identified with "race" in a heavily cited article by Neil Risch and his colleagues published in *Genome Biology* in 2002.[36] Risch et al. argue that human genetic variation can be equated with "race" because some statistical clustering programs fed global data about genetics produce five large clusters at one level of clustering resolution: Africans, Caucasians, Asians, Pacific Islanders, and Native Americans. Although they are regularly called "continental" groupings, none of the clusters is actually coterminous with a continent, a fact that signals the looseness of the match between the mathematical groupings and the labels applied to them. Further failures of the system of nomenclature are signaled by the inconsistent assignment of the enormous population of the Indian subcontinent, sometimes clustered with "Asians" and sometimes clustered with "Caucasians" (also labeled "Europeans"). A lack of data from Northern Africa, and the clustering of Ethiopians with Europeans/Caucasians rather than "sub-Saharan Africans," further muddies the groupings, as does the Hispanic population, and the relative invisibility of "Pacific Islanders" in "racial" category schemes in the US.[37] In spite of all of these mismatches between the genetic clusters, both scientists and members of the press seem to read the historically salient US social groupings of "Whites," "Blacks," "Asians," and "Native Americans" as matching four of these genetic clusters.

The existence of this Procrustean relationship between scientific discourses about continentally situated populations and lay discourses about race both motivated Lahn's selection of this data from a large corpus of results from his genome "sweep" and enabled and motivated the *New York Times* amplification of it for the public audience. Lahn, however, did not merely circulate the prior discourse of race, but rather rewrote the racial hierarchy according to the interests of his own body (whether he was aware of this or not). Instead of the ladder of Whites, Yellows, Reds, and Blacks, sometimes reduced to the binary of "Whites vs. non-Whites," Lahn proposed a scientific, genetic basis for a new hierarchy, most explicitly articulated in the binary of Asians and Whites vs. everyone else (but also sometimes appearing in the form of Blacks vs. everyone else). Neither Lahn's essays, nor those of the *New York Times* made that argument overtly. However, both articles employed this re-ordering of the historical hierarchy of races in empirically identifiable ways.

Lahn's statement that the presumably favored allele "first arose somewhere in Eurasia and is still in the process of spreading to other regions" sutured an alliance between Europe and Asia via the term "Eurasia," which was neither previously employed by standard scientific vocabularies of "populations" nor in the customary lay vocabularies of "race."[38] Lahn's discourse could have localized the allele's origin to one population (which was almost certainly the factual case), but instead it obscured the singular continent of origin in shared bi-continental frequencies. The rewriting of the older racial hierarchy is also evident in the choice to centralize Asia and Europe, even in the research article where the statistics and map show that the presumptively favored allele was most common in the Americas.

A social motivation for this rewriting of the racial hierarchy is embarrassingly obvious. Surrounded by Asian colleagues of superior performance and ability, the old White-dominated hierarchy was threatened. Rewriting the hierarchical ladder with Asians at the top—"Asian, White, Native American/Pacific Islander, Black"—lacks a certain appeal to Whites. Reordering the ladder with Native Americans at the top (followed by Whites/Asians, and Blacks), which would have been justified by the data of the *MCPH1* article, would likewise be unappealing and would additionally violate the common sense experiences of the typical (non-Native) American. The two binary options—"Eurasians" vs. everyone else and Blacks vs. everyone else—thus emerged as potential compromises to retain the superior position of Whites. They are constructed by selective focus on some of the data and by verbal choices that pair Whites with Asians. These new racial placements retain Whites in the dominant group, but accommodate the now difficult-to-ignore presence of bodies with recent Asian ancestry in the posts of the scientific hierarchy.

A reductive materialism has no means of accounting for this appeal. Having written the organic body and its drives out of being, there is no particular reason for one articulation to appear or repeat as opposed to another. The universality of the physical universe provides no template for biological and symbolic flows, which are always in the process of changing. If discourse is just streams of matter in indifferent relations, with no history and no bodies to appeal to, then Lahn's discursive formulation is nothing but pure contingency, like the accident of a meteor crashing into the earth. We can observe it, map it, and describe it, but we have no answer to the question, "Why?" In contrast, a multi-modal materialism enables us to acknowledge that Lahn's body has been carried along on the historical flows of discourse about race, but that the extended course of these flows has itself been partially a product of the activating interests of particularly formed bodies located (again by historical deposition) in places of power. Shifts in those depositions combined with Lahn's body's self-interested energies move him to the novelty of re-articulating the boundaries within the flow of those racial discourses.

Modal materialism also allows us to retain a modified category of truth, because it does not deny discourse its role in relating human bodies to each other and to the rest of the physical world. It need not deny that there are patterns of genetic variation, really existing in the world, because it insists that the work of producing "true" statements is not just a matter of identifying the existence or non-existence of genetic variation, but rather it is about how one matches up those patterns to discourses about them as the two become used in the world.

This approach requires systematic attention to the full material network of uses of a particular set of terms, which is a daunting task. Sometimes scientists attempt to limit this task by inventing technical vocabularies that they isolate from common sense parlance. In the case of discourses about genetic variation, however, the adoption of an independent, scientifically grounded vocabulary for human genetic variation has not occurred. The very utility of the scientific "findings" depend on their linkage to lay discourses of race, which is evident in the way the scientific findings were publicized in the *New York Times.*[39]

Scene 2: Nicholas Wade Reports in the New York Times

Nicholas Wade reported on Lahn's research in the *New York Times* on September 9, 2005.[40] The article employed a relatively technical style to support the claim that human evolution is "still a work in progress," though it also included potential objections by multiple researchers to the idea that the genetic variations involved were related to cognition. In describing the human groups involved, it employed word choices that mixed the more scientific vocabulary of "populations" with more lay terms such as "people": "About 70 percent of *people* in most European and East Asian *populations* carry this allele of the gene, but it is much rarer in most sub-Saharan Africans," and "The allele has attained a frequency of about 50 percent in *populations* of the Middle East and Europe, is less common in East Asia, and is found at low frequency in some sub-Saharan Africa *peoples.*"[41] In the third mention, Wade employed Lahn's unconventional term "Eurasia." This mixing of terms provided the audience a link between lay and scientific vocabularies, in case that anything more than the transfer of lay terms into the scientific vocabulary had been needed.

Wade also signaled that the research was about racial hierarchy by framing it as politically controversial. He quoted the director of the National Human Genome Research Institute Francis S. Collins and other researchers with regard to worries about how the papers would be "interpreted," noting that the research "could raise controversy because of the genes' role in determining brain size. New versions of the genes, or "alleles" as geneticists call them, appear to have spread because they enhanced brain function in some way, the report suggests, and they are more common in some populations than others."

An idealist account would hold that Wade, a science journalist, was simply reporting "scientific facts," a claim reinforced by his unusually dense discursive style and his extensive reference to "both sides" of the issue. But, as Sarah Wilcox's careful comparison of journalists' stories to scientific publications has shown, journalists do not report on all scientific research articles, even those about such controversial subjects as genetics and sexual orientation.[42] Instead, they select which scientific articles to circulate. Wade's decision to amplify a scientific discourse that supported racial hierarchies was a motivated act. Whether his choice was motivated by blatant racism, a fan's appreciation for genetics, or the hint of a controversy that sells newspapers, we cannot know, but the choice was not random or unmotivated, especially given substantial available reasons to believe that the presumptions that gave it widespread interest were not empirically true.

Meanwhile, Outside the Theater

The third scene of this story will reveal that the racial implications of Lahn's and Wade's discourses were demonstrated to be empirically false by several subsequent research efforts. Science, of course, is a discourse that permits error. What it does not condone is avoidable, predictable, or poorly informed error. A relevant question then is whether there was sufficient scientific reason to select and report these data as evidence of the evolution of human brain size across human populations.

Lahn's research was not experimental. It was not hypothesis driven, but data driven—a scan through a database of human DNA segments to look for genes that fit a statistical pattern. The discovered pattern was then forced into a post-hoc reconstructive explanation (brain size has increased in Asian and European populations). Several crucial facts indicate that there was a high likelihood that this reconstruction would prove false.

The suggestion that there could be a genotype that uniformly produces larger brain size among people of specific "racial" groups was predictably false, because dozens of scans of long stretches of DNA among multiple human groups have consistently shown that the genetic variability within large human groups is always greater than the genetic variability between groups.[43] The flow of genes has been clinal as humans spread out of Africa, but it has also been regional, as geographies and climates invented new alleles, and locally brecciated, as tribes warred, single individuals reproduced prolifically, diseases struck, and inventions flourished.

To define the distributions according to a socially defined, racialized category scheme required ignoring the well-established character of human genetic variation as clinal, regional, and brecciated. This is patently obvious within Lahn's own published data, which reports two different genetic variations that show two *different* geographical patterns, and thus invalidates the idea that there is a singular "racial" division relative to brain size. One study shows an elevated frequency among "Eurasians" but the other among "Americans" (at best perhaps "EuroAmerAsians"). At the very least, the choice to frame both studies within the claim that "Eurasians" have larger brains is false, *prima facie*, but the larger point is that no vocabulary as gross in its labels as "race" or "five populations" can accurately describe the existing complex patterns of genetic variation.

Note that this analysis locates both Lahn's and Wade's errors in the properties of the words they chose. It does not deny that there are patterns of genetic variation existing in the material world; it does deny that a vocabulary of "five populations" related to social groupings of race could be expected to describe these patterns of variation at a sufficient level of precision for scientific uses. The modal materialist's objection to Lahn's study, which focuses on the discursive matter employed, is thus different from the objections of the other scientists cited and quoted by Wade. These scientists focused on the sufficiency of the evidence of the linkage of the gene to brain size, not on the link to group labels. If this objection was designed to fend off charges of racism, it is a short-sighted strategy, because at this moment in history, it appears almost inevitable that variations in genes will be linked to variations in brain functions, and there will inevitably be some geographical patterning to such genetic variations. So it is not the identification of such genes per se that is problematic.

The scientific error lies precisely in the idea that substantial differences in brain size among human groups identifiable as "races" will be associated with specific genes. This will not be the case because there will be many variations that influence brain size or cognition, rather than only one or two, and each of these variations will contribute only small portions to any individual's total abilities (that is turning out to be a general rule of human genetics—common allelic variations contribute small portions of effects to any given capacity because many genes contribute to any capacity).[44] In other words, the normal range of brain capacity will not be substantially determined by any one genetic variation, because each individual's brain capacity is determined by an enormous number of genes (to say nothing of non-genetic factors). This individual variation will not add up to stable, measurably large differences among racial groups, because each of the contributing genes will have different geographical distribution patterns from each other (based on where they arise, genetic drift, founder effects, differential environmental inputs, etc.). Not only do the differences in Lahn's two articles provide immediate empirical proof, but these principles were well established and should have been known by Lahn's team, by the staff at *Science*, and perhaps by Nicholas Wade. The directed energies of interested bodies, however, led elsewhere.

Lahn's statistical methodology also contributed to the error. Simply stated, he employed statistics to examine changes through time and space in human genes, and he presumed that steep gradients of change indicated "evolution." However, it is well established that Africa harbors a much larger quantity of human genetic diversity than does the rest of the world, because humans have lived in Africa far longer than they have lived at other locations.[45] All the diversity that accumulated over the millions of years of human evolution exists in the populations in Africa. In contrast, when small groups of humans left Africa, they took with them only part of this range of diversity. This means that this original "founder effect" is confounded with what Lahn's methodology identifies as "signals of evolution."[46]

Even if this methodological fallacy did not disqualify Lahn's method, it points to a key discursive flaw of equating patterns of genetic variation with race. Sub-Saharan African populations are not self-identical to each other. Indeed, they are quite diverse when compared to other human populations spread across similarly sized geographic territories. Adopting the popular vocabulary of "races" thus creates an erroneous impression of equivalence in levels of genetic variation between groups that are not equivalent in their levels of variation. It thereby effaces these materially real and scientifically significant components of the patterns of genetic variation.

Finally, the way in which interests in racial hierarchy drove the publication of these discourses is evident in the extent to which they exceed their scientific evidence. Even were it true, Lahn's statistical analysis says only that one version of the human genotype—which is associated with brain size among other bodily effects—appears more often in non-Africans than in Africans. Nonetheless, his team, the reviewers, and Wade all assumed that the "evolved" allele produced "larger" brains that had greater function. Lahn's articles present no evidence at all on that issue. Their data only say that there is a difference in alleles. Several possible rationales indicate that the "evolved" allele might produce smaller brains. The human brain is the most energy-costly of the body's organs. As one moves to colder climates, a smaller brain may be advantageous to preserve the now more precious calories. Alternately, the human brain is postulated to have evolved its size due to intense human social interaction and competition. As humans left Africa, they no longer faced human competition for resources. Perhaps the larger brain was no longer necessary for survival. As humans left Africa, numbers of reproduction became a larger constraint than human competition. Perhaps the loss of mothers and children due to the large brain's inability to pass the birth canal led to selection for smaller brains but greater quantity of reproduction.

A variety of different evolutionary factors could have led one to assume that if there is a difference between Africans and everyone else, it is that Africans have larger brains. Likewise, the assumption that a larger brain is an "enhanced" brain lacks any direct evidence. Only social beliefs, engrained in brains through the circulation of social discourses about race, undergird Lahn's and Wade's claims. Lahn repeats the self-congratulatory notion that "[t]he most distinct trait of *Homo sapiens* is the exceptional size and complexity of the brain."[47] Lahn and Wade apparently presume that their racial groups are smarter than others. So they take evidence of difference in a brain-based genotype as evidence that the genotype common in their group is the one for a bigger, not smaller, brain.

On an idealist account, error in science may be forgivable, because science "moves forward" by making mistakes, by making hypotheses and testing them, and then declaring the hypothesized claim false.[48] In this case, however, the claim advanced by Lahn within the scientific circuit and amplified by Wade is grounded mostly outside of science, and such a link of lay and scientific discourse has already been falsified, many times.[49] As "an idea," then, Lahn's argument is false on its face, and should have been understood as false before its inscription. It should neither have been published by *Science*, nor publicized by Wade. But it is not just an idea; it is a discourse. And as such, it is not driven by a disembodied search for truth, but also by activating embodied interests, socially deployed, riding and redirecting well-established flows of discursive matter.

Scene 3: Science *Replicates the Scientist and Reports Failure to Replicate his Experiment*

Lahn's study prompted scientists in White-dominated nations worldwide (Canada, Australia, and the US) to attempt to confirm that the genotypic variations he detected were associated with lower brain size or lower brain function. None of these studies found a statistically significant association between the variables, and yet these disconfirmations of the racist assumptions were not circulated to the public by the *New York Times*.[50] The ambiguous way in which they were treated by *Science* itself is highly informative.

On December 22, 2006, about sixteen months after publishing Lahn's original work, *Science* published two articles by science journalist Michael Balter, one on Lahn himself and the other on Lahn's article.[51] The spatial relationship of the placement of the articles was striking. On page 1871, an essay promoting a vision of Lahn as an ideal scientist begins. It continues and concludes on page 1873. Between these two pages is a separate article in which *Science* reports the various failures to replicate and verify Lahn's thesis. A critic allowed categories such as "motive," "intention," and "interest" might say that the editors at *Science* appear to have felt a need to contextualize the disconfirmation of Lahn's work within a characterization of his efforts as an exemplar of science. Lacking such categories, there is only a most peculiar happenstance: an articulation that can be described in terms of likely effects, to be sure, and perhaps even mapped as a curious intersection of discursive flows, but there is no body (individual or institutional) with motives to promote such effects. Bodies, however, are present and active in many ways.

In the upper left corner of the first article is a color photograph of Lahn's body sitting in a chair in front of a lab bench. His hands are folded over each other on his lap, and his dark, slightly shaggy hair shines under the lights. His tan-yellow skin tone is darkened by the contrast with the yellow turtleneck he wears. The sidebar draws attention to his physical race and its deployment in Western projects; it reads, "Golden hands. Lahn's lab skills led swiftly to a University of Chicago post." In its dramatic opening, the article portrays the motives of this "slim and handsome" scientific knight as a "quest to understand the biology of human differences." He is "one of the fastest rising stars in genetics," who achieved tenure rapidly and garnered a major award for his "landmark" work. The romance is only heightened by the fact that he is "controversial," and a maverick who does not "follow instructions."

Lahn is quoted as describing himself as being "deeply traumatized" by the class privileges received by foreigners when he was growing up in China, and as having wondered whether there was a genetic basis for those differences. Further illustrating the embodiment of discourses of race (and class), and their global flows, the article indicates that when Lahn immigrated to the US, he changed his name from Lan Tian, because a janitor at McDonald's told him he looked like Bruce Lee. Just as the article moves into Lahn's early work at an MIT lab, the page ends, and the story of Lan Tian/Bruce Lahn is put into a temporal "hold" by spacing.

On the next page, the quasi-retraction is set in a different color, marking a different tone, titled "Links between Brain Genes, Evolution, and Cognition Challenged." This article summarizes the substantial accumulation of evidence that has refuted Lahn's original presumptions. It does so by combining definitive evidence with a non-definitive tone. Its author, Michael Balter, in e-mail communication, has said that the mix of material in the article was intended to meet the journalistic conventions for "balance" in covering an issue.

Visually signaling the departure from Lahn's original scientific publications, the top of the page features an altered version of the world map of the distribution of the frequency of the "supposedly favored *microcephalin* variant." Africa is no longer centered, as someone has *chosen* not to reproduce Lahn's map—a map to which *Science* holds the copyright—but to alter it by decentering the African continent. Balter attributes this choice to aesthetic preferences, indicating that the graphics department did not know the content of the article when they made this choice. These different motivations exert an influence counter to the previous flow, as the aesthetic choice to balance the photo by placing the major continental groups on each side and the ocean in the middle has the visual effect of attenuating the Africans vs. everyone else binary. The different interests of different bodies clearly make their impact felt. Nonetheless, these aesthetics do not expunge the hierarchy from the verbal text. Although it is the map of *MCPH1* (which isolates Africans and elevates Native Americans) that is reprinted, rather than the map of *ASPM* (which includes Native Americans and Africans both manifesting the non-favored allele), the embedded caption effaces the elevated frequency of the allele in Native Americans as it reads, "Provocative results. Allegedly favored variants are more common in Europe and Asia but may not be brain-related."

The opening paragraph indicates that the new research has "failed to correlate" the results with IQ, and Lahn is quoted as saying, "[W]e don't know what the variants do." The next paragraphs report the disconfirming studies, including Lahn's effort to establish the link between the genes and IQ in collaboration with Philippe Rushton, a Canadian psychologist noted for his claim that "African Americans have lower intelligence." The article quotes Rushton's concession: "[We] had no luck ... no matter which way we analyzed the data." The article then gives additional counter-evidence, including accounts of the other functions of the genes and the methodological objections to the study, though Lahn is also quoted as defending his methods. The last paragraph quotes Lahn's apparent concession to this barrage of withering refutation: "On the scientific level, I am a little bit disappointed. But in the context of the social and political controversy, I am a little bit relieved."

The article promoting Lahn as a scientist then recommences on the next page. The photo of Lahn on this page shows him standing high on a mountain, reprising the theme of his maverick independence with the caption "His way. Lahn survived a mountain hike on pickled eggs." His work on the controversial genes is then reintroduced, and it is admitted that "Lahn conceded that there was no real evidence natural selection had acted on cognition or intelligence." However, the article then immediately "balances" this concession by noting that the putative development of the new version of the gene arose "when the first art and symbolism showed up in Europe" and by restating the differences in distribution of the alleles in "75% or more of some Europeans and Asians Lahn studied, but in less than 10% of some African groups."

The article moves towards its conclusion by reframing the political dispute. Lahn is quoted as accusing others of starting with a political agenda and fitting evidence to it, with interviews from other scientists suggesting "that Lahn has shown courage," and that he should continue with the research, letting the chips "fall where they may." Surprisingly, given the evidence presented in the intervening page, the final paragraph concludes that "[t]ime, and further research, will tell if Lahn was right."

If science were simply the practice described in idealist accounts—a disinterested pursuit of the truth—then *Science* would merely have printed the refutation ("failure to confirm") of Lahn's premise. But that is not what they did. Instead, they embedded the refutation in a larger discourse about a human actor who embodied the scientific enterprise. One can best account for this as a *motivated* defense of their own institution and enterprise. If they have published apparently falsified data that fell squarely in a long line of discredited scientific defenses of racial hierarchy, does that not discredit their enterprise? Does this whole sordid episode not prove what the denizens of science studies have been loudly proclaiming when they argue that science is merely ideology dispensed via pipettes and beakers?

To shunt such a flow, *Science* fits Lahn—racial profile blazing—into the historic charactertype of the scientific hero on a solitary quest to battle ignorance and politics. Like Galileo and Darwin before him, Lahn is simply on a quest for truth. That noble quest is not always successful, but there is always a tomorrow. Consequently, Lahn's efforts to link a newly rising racial hierarchy to genetic evidence are not execrable, but rather laudable for rising above politics to follow the path of truth wherever it leads.

The idea that biology grounds racist hierarchies is a hypothesis that, apparently, can never be considered definitively refuted. Indeed, Balter has indicated that this is why he closed the refutative article with the statement that "[t]ime, and further research, will tell if Lahn was right." Three studies demonstrating a lack of linkage between the genetic variations and cognitive capacities are not enough. Somewhere, a more powerful study might someday be devised to demonstrate that there really is such a relationship. Given the appeal of the racial categories in which this putative relationship is (mis)framed, no matter how small the effect size of such a relationship, it will be taken, by bodies for whom it is advantageous, as providing scientific evidence of all the stereotypes of existing racist presumptions. Apparently, science, as currently configured, could only prove racism true. It can never prove racism false. This is the polar reversal of Popper's falsification doctrine. It arises, in large measure, because of the power of our common sense beliefs about race, and our inability to locate the aptness of a statement in the utilities of the relationship between statements and reality, rather than merely in the absolute truth or falseness of the statements or the existence or non-existence of reality itself. Only if the scientific method comes to understand its own always motivated discourse as part of its *material* is it likely to change this destiny.

In the mean time, replicating Bruce Lahn's body into the form of the independent scientist carrying his test tubes off into the sunset saves the body of *Science*/science from the embarrassment of racist motivation. Within three months, Lahn gracefully embodied the role in which he had been cast by publishing an empirically based concession titled "The Ongoing Adaptive Evolution of *ASPM* and *Microcephalin* Is Not Explained by Increased Intelligence."[52] As a good scientist, Lahn followed where his evidence led. Of course, in the mean time, both the script written and authorized by *Science* and Lahn's embodiment of it contributed to the rewriting of the racial hierarchy to include Asians, with their "Golden hands," into the dominant category.

There is no separating the activities of the bodies here from the rhetoric. The discourse is motivated and shaped by the differently situated bodily articulations of Lahn, Balter, and Wade (among many others). Although we cannot know all the nooks and crannies of their bodily motivations, and although stated intentions are not equivalent to the diffuse and even contradictory energies of real motivations, the latter nonetheless wield influence.

The point of emphasizing these motivations is not to shame individuals. Each of us can be only interested animals shot through with social discourses. The point of identifying the discursive motivations of these particular bodies is to show that there is no separation of what Johnson described as depth and surface when it comes to the material flows of meaning. The very selfish desires and interests of individual bodies activate and are reconstituted by the discourses they have absorbed, as well as those they recreate for particular contexts, but their "meaning" exists neither in the individual bodies, nor in the individual words. Although constituted through matter, the phenomenon traditionally called "meaning" is not a discrete object localizable a priori in a particular place in space–time. One cannot prefer surface to depth where there is neither. Instead, the meaningfulness of discourse exists in its widely distributed effectivities—a set of material arrangements indefinitely extended through space–time—in *Science* in 2005 and then 2006, in the *New York Times* in 2005 (as well as in at least nine other newspapers), and in the studies disconfirming the assumptions in Lahn's articles, which were dispersed in several journals (as well as in the present essay).[53] A particular, amalgamated pattern of presences and absences written in utterly entwined biological and discursive matter simultaneously constitute and move the flow of discursive effectivities.

Beyond the Scene: Race and Science in the Space–Time Continuum

The energies of individual bodies are crucial for fomenting the recirculation of scientific legitimations of racialized discourses, but the pattern becomes a historical flow with the duration and the ability to sustain itself as a discursive circuit only to the extent that the drives of the bodies are not singular, but rather reconstitute the drives, motives, and actions of many bodies similarly positioned. Science continually recreates a biological racism, in spite of the facts, because of longstanding commitments about who is a scientist, and what doing science is.

From its founding, the inventors of science and its early philosophizers modified the idea/matter binary as a material (experiment)/non-material (discourse) binary so as to define the activity of science as a mode of seeking truth that was opposite, and superior, to mere discourse. They aligned science with the material world of things and placed "discourse," especially discourse as a method, with the immaterial. One could engage in endless argument, or one could do science and control things. Francis Bacon, for example, introduced guided induction by saying that "the end which this science of mine proposes is the invention not of arguments but of arts."[54] He insisted that science was "not an opinion to be held, but a work to be done," and the ends and effects of these two different enterprises were notably different as well, "the effect of the one being to overcome an opponent in argument, of the other to command nature in action."[55] Bacon allowed verbally based modes of discourse such as existing methods of demonstration and the syllogism to have a place in "such as are matters of opinion" but not in investigations into "the nature of things."[56] In each case, science was placed on the side of the materially real (arts, work, things) and opposed to the realm of the immaterial (arguments and opinions).

This modification of the idea/matter binary preserved a fundamental ambiguity about the status of the conceptualizations—"laws" and equations—that constitute the perceived results of scientific endeavors. If these were representations of "ideas," they were ideas that existed not because of discourse, and only accidentally "in" discourse. Instead, these laws and equations existed because the method of science gave direct access to the real. This formulation often leaves scientists with a more or less covert idealist conception of the universe (with scientific laws standing as the true Platonic forms), which is a peculiar outcome for those who adamantly otherwise proclaim allegiance to a radical materialism.[57] Regardless of how explicitly this idealist view is adopted, the formulation also mandates that scientists must refuse to consider critical reflection on their own discourse as part of the practice of science. To reflect critically on one's own discourse would be to cross over to the discredited side of the binary. It would imply that one's scientific statements were not a pure product of the scientific method rather than in some part a product of disputation, opinion, or politics.

The place of science in society today remains anchored in the assertion that only the practices of science can give us access to the truths of the material realm, and that this is because science stands separate from immaterial "argument" and political opinion. Anything that threatens this binary hierarchy must be repaired, or the enterprise of science (including both its institutions and the status of the bodies of its practitioners) is threatened. Such a threat lurked in the promotion of a demonstrably false "scientific" defense of racial hierarchy by *Science,* the lead journal of the American Association for the Advancement of Science. Especially in light of the multiple disconfirmations, these articles could easily be taken by the opponents of science (bodies and their organizations who have something to gain from denying science its special social place) as a glaring example of how science is merely argument motivated by interest.

To respond to this threat, however, *Science*/science could not merely provide scientific proof. It had to step outside of those binaries in order to secure them. So it was, for example, that in speaking for *Science*/science, Michael Balter appealed to the purity of Lahn's motives (a quest for truth, not a political campaign), a third category that was neither pure idea nor pure matter, but rather embodied discourse/idea. In spite of the tremendous utility of the matter/idea (no-matter) binary in some applications, neither scientists nor critical humanists are able to accomplish their goals without recourse to a model of humans as beings whose actions are dictated by the forms and functions encoded in the conjunction of discourses and biological bodies. If we want a science that truly is a method for overcoming our biases, perhaps it is necessary to replace the matter/idea binary with a trinary that recognizes a fuller range of material arrangements—physical, biological, and symbolic.

Conclusion

Humanists (or "post-humanists") have struggled recently to bring together the implications of radically discursivist onto-epistemologies with the desire to "make a better world." Unlike the activist, the scholar ought not presume the luxury of assuming that the world is already fully known, and the best course of action obvious. It is the scholar's task—whether scientist or humanist—to seek what we do not yet understand and to invent better courses of action. What many humanistic scholars have long known, and most scientists have yet failed to recognize, is that values and interests cannot be inactive in the search for understanding, because they are inherent to the materiality of language in which knowledge must be constructed. They are not "froth" or "mist" with no discernible weight on matter. They have material effects on any search for understanding, knowledge, or truth. Only by recognizing this materiality can a scientist—or humanist—correct for the biases languages introduce.

While the experimental method can declare that a given hypothesis is false, this is an insufficient protection against bias, as the empirical record on race in science has shown.

The experimental method does not, in fact, erase the effects of the vast body of scientific observations that do not take the form of hypothesis-driven experiments; nor can it correct for the interpretive phase of either experimental or observational science, which is unavoidably linguistic.

A modal materialism may expand the vision of both humanists and scientists by recognizing rather than effacing all the different types of matter that are at play when human bodies sing and dance as they do. Gravity, sex, gender ... they do not all operate on identical rules. Reducing each to the other is disciplinary hubris. Physical laws, biological predispositions, and linguistic creations all contribute their modicum to our actions, and the three interact in dazzling ways. Discourse wins some pride of place because "knowing" is accomplished for humans so heavily through language. But what we know or understand is not solely a product of any one form of matter, but a product of the force of discourse in specific relationships with the other forces of the universe.

Notes

This essay is gratefully dedicated to Michael Calvin McGee, whose genius did not live long enough. Michael expressed high expectations for his students, which we were not able to fulfill in his lifetime. Both the high standards he modeled and his expectation that we could meet them continue to inspire us to these efforts.

1 Nicholas Wade, "Brain May Still Be Evolving, Studies Hint," *New York Times*, September 9, 2005, national edition, sec. A.

2 Patrick D. Evans, Sandra L. Gilbert, Nitzan Mekel-Bobrov, Eric J. Vallender, Jeffrey R. Anderson, Leila M. Vaez-Azizi, Sarah A. Tishkoff, Richard R. Hudson, and Bruce T. Lahn, "*Microcephalin*, a Gene Regulating Brain Size, Continues to Evolve Adaptively in Humans," *Science* 309 (2005): 1717–20; and Nitzan Mekel-Bobrov, Sandra L. Gilbert, Patrick D. Evans, Eric J. Vallender, Jeffrey R. Anderson, Richard R. Hudson, Sarah A. Tishkoff, and Bruce T. Lahn, "Ongoing Adaptive Evolution of *ASPM*, a Brain Size Determinant in Homo Sapiens," *Science* 309 (2005): 1720–22.

3 I use capital letters to designate all racialized groups, whether based on differences of color or ethnicity. The use of so-called "continental labels" requires capitals for some racial designations (typically based on ethnicity) but not others. Thus it is, for example, that *The Chicago Manual of Style* recommends capitalizing ethnic differences but leaving differences based on color in lower case unless "the writer strongly prefers" otherwise. In my judgment, the failure to capitalize "white" effaces the raciality of whiteness and to avoid that my "strong preference" is to capitalize all such distinctions. *The Chicago Manual of Style*, 15th ed. (Chicago: University of Chicago Press, 2003), 325–6.

4 C. Dobson-Stone, J. M. Gatt, S. A. Kuan, S. M. Grieve, E. Gordon, L. M. Williams, and P. R. Schofield, "Investigation of *MCPH1* G37995C and *ASPM* A44871G Polymorphisms and Brain Size in a Healthy Cohort," *NeuroImage* 37 (2007): 394–400; Nicholas Timpson, Jon Heron, George Davey Smith, and Wolfgang Enard, "Comment on Papers by Evans et al. and Mekel-Bobrov et al. on Evidence for Positive Selection of *MCPH1* and *ASPM*," *Science* 317 (2007): 1036a; and Nitzan Mekel-Bobrov, Danielle Posthuma, Sandra L. Gilbert, Penelope Lind, M. Florencia Gosso, Michelle Luciano, Sarah E. Harris, Timothy C. Bates, Tinca J. C. Polderman, Lawrence J. Whalley, Helen Fox, John M. Starr, Patrick D. Evans, Grant W. Montgomery, Croydon Fernandes, Peter Heutink, Nicholas G. Martin, Dorret I. Boomsma, Ian J. Deary,

Margaret J. Wright, Eco J. C. de Geus, and Bruce T. Lahn, "The Ongoing Adaptive Evolution of *ASPM* and *Microcephalin* Is Not Explained by Increased Intelligence," *Human Molecular Genetics* 16 (2007): 600–608.

5   Stephen Jay Gould, *The Mismeasure of Man* (New York: Norton, 1981); Jonathan Marks, *Human Biodiversity: Genes, Race, and History* (New York: Aldine de Gruyter, 1995); and William H. Tucker, "Burt's Separated Twins: The Larger Picture," *Journal of the History of the Behavioral Sciences* 43 (2007): 81–86.

6   Karl Marx and Friedrich Engels, *The German Ideology, Parts I and III*, ed. R. Pascal (New York: International Publishers, 1969; original copyright 1947), 39.

7   Marx and Engels, *German Ideology*, 39.

8   A proper defense of this claim would require a manuscript all by itself, but for some relatively contemporary examples, consider Louis Althusser, "Ideology and Ideological State Apparatuses (Notes Towards an Investigation)," in *Essays on Ideology* (London: Verso, 1984); Richard J. Bernstein, *Beyond Objectivism and Relativism: Science, Hermeneutics, and Praxis* (Philadelphia: University of Pennsylvania Press, 1983); Anthony Giddens, *Central Problems in Social Theory: Action, Structure, and Contradiction in Social Analysis* (Berkeley: University of California Press, 1979); Jack Selzer and Sharon Crowley, *Rhetorical Bodies* (Madison: University of Wisconsin Press, 1999).

9   Michael Calvin McGee, "A Materialist's Conception of Rhetoric," in *Explorations in Rhetoric: Studies in Honor of Douglas Ehninger*, ed. Ray E. McKerrow (Glenview, IL: Scott, Foresman & Company, 1982), 26, 25.

10 Maurice Charland, "Constitutive Rhetoric: The Case of the *Peuple Québécois*," *Quarterly Journal of Speech* 73 (1987): 133–50; and Ronald Walter Greene, "Another Materialist Rhetoric," *Critical Studies in Mass Communication* 15 (1998): 21–41.

11 Gilles Deleuze, *Spinoza: Practical Philosophy*, trans. Robert Hurley (San Francisco: City Light Books, 1988), 123 (emphasis added).

12 Deleuze, *Spinoza*, 127.

13 Davi Johnson, "Mapping the Meme: A Geographical Approach to Materialist Rhetorical Criticism," *Communication and Critical/Cultural Studies* 4 (2007): 32.

14 Johnson, "Mapping the Meme," 31.

15 Johnson, "Mapping the Meme," 45.

16 Johnson, "Mapping the Meme," 28.

17 The case of images and other symbolic systems is more complicated. Some of the issues are developed in Robert Hariman and John Louis Lucaites, *No Caption Needed: Iconic Photographs, Public Culture, and Liberal Democracy* (Chicago: University of Chicago Press, 2007).

18 Johnson, "Mapping the Meme," 31 (emphasis added).

19 Barbara A. Biesecker, "Rethinking the Rhetorical Situation from within the Thematic of *Différance*," *Philosophy and Rhetoric* 22 (1989): 110–30; and Greene, "Another Materialist Rhetoric."

20 Much of the relevant literature is summarized in Daniel C. Dennett, *Consciousness Explained* (Boston: Little, Brown & Company, 1991) and *Freedom Evolves* (New York: Penguin, 2004).

21 Lahn is quoted in Michael Balter, "Profile: Bruce Lahn: Brain Man Makes Waves with Claims of Recent Human Evolution," *Science* 314 (2006): 1871. All reference to Balter's statements about these articles are from e-mail messages, cited with his assent, September 27–28, 2007, and May 18, 2008.

22 In the conventions of their respective genres, the names of their bodies are assigned to the discourses under the assumption that they served as a kind of driving force and organizing node for

the production of this discourse. In the case of biology, the team leader's name comes last in the publication order as an indication that they organized the laboratory or research agenda.

23 For the present, interests might be understood as particularly configured congeries of biological drives.

24 I thank Jamie Landau for drawing my attention to the fact that Louis Althusser also described a modal materialism, though he did not develop the analysis in depth, and I do not share his interpretation of "ideas," among other divergences. Althusser, "Ideology and Ideological State," 40.

25 Preliminary efforts can be found at the Transilience Project website, www.gly.uga.edu/railsback/Transilience/Transilience.html/.

26 Martin Bernal, "Race in History," in *Global Convulsions: Race, Ethnicity, and Nationalism at the End of the Twentieth Century*, ed. Winston A. Van Horne (Albany: State University of New York Press, 1997), 75–92.

27 A wide variety of versions of this argument with regard to the functioning of science have been published. Some of the range is captured in the following: Alan G. Gross, *The Rhetoric of Science* (Cambridge, MA: Harvard University Press, 1990); Evelyn Fox Keller and Helen E. Longino, ed., *Feminism and Science* (Oxford: Oxford University Press, 1996); and Bruno Latour and Steve Woolgar, *Laboratory Life: The Social Construction of Scientific Facts* (Beverly Hills, CA: Sage, 1979).

28 Ernesto Laclau and Chantal Mouffe, *Hegemony and Socialist Strategy: Towards a Radical Democratic Politics*, 2nd ed. (London: Verso, 2001).

29 The relation of discursive and non-discursive matter is not representation, but rather a two-way street between flows and circuits of discourse and the other forms of matter in the world, based on more and less local utilities.

30 Evans et al., "*Microcephalin*," 1717–20; and Mekel-Bobrov et al., "Ongoing Adaptive Evolution of *ASPM*," 1722.

31 Evans et al., "*Microcephalin*," 1717.

32 Evans et al., "*Microcephalin*," 1717, 1719.

33 Mekel-Bobrov et al., "Ongoing Adaptive Evolution of *ASPM*," 1720. The articles actually trace haplotypes, which are co-occurring stretches of DNA, but the phrase "version of gene" or genotype probably captures the meaning for this readership more clearly.

34 Mekel-Bobrov et al., "Ongoing Adaptive Evolution of *ASPM*," 1721.

35 Pamela Sankar, Mildred K. Cho, and Joanna Mountain, "Race and Ethnicity in Genetic Research," *American Journal of Medical Genetics Part A* 143 (2007): 961–70; and Celeste Condit, "How Culture and Science Make Race 'Genetic': Motives and Strategies for Discrete Categorization of the Continuous and Heterogeneous," *Literature and Medicine*, 26 (2007): 240–68.

36 Neil Risch, Esteban Burchard, Elad Ziv, and Hua Tang, "Categorization of Humans in Bio-medical Research: Genes, Race, and Disease," *Genome Biology* 3 (2002): 1–12.

37 James F. Wilson, Michael E. Weale, Alice C. Smith, Fiona Gratrix, Benjamin Fletcher, Mark G. Thomas, Neil Bradman, and David B. Goldstein, "Population Genetic Structure of Variable Drug Response," *Nature Genetics* 29 (2001): 265–69.

38 Mekel-Bobrov et al., "Ongoing Adaptive Evolution of *ASPM*," 1722. They gave formulary attention to other potential causes.

39 The broader discourse about genetic variation and its links to race is complicated because of the insertion of the amelioration of "health disparities" as a potential usage, discussed in Condit, "How Science and Culture," 240–68.

40 Wade, "Brain May Still Be Evolving."

41 Wade, "Brain May Still Be Evolving" (emphasis added).

42 Sarah A. Wilcox, "Cultural Context and the Conventions of Science Journalism: Drama and Contradiction in Media Coverage of Biological Ideas about Sexuality," *Critical Studies in Media Communication* 20 (2003): 225–47.

43 Richard Lewontin, *Human Diversity* (New York: Scientific American Library, 1982).

44 See, e.g., Krina T. Zondervan and Lon R. Cardon, "The Complex Interplay among Factors that Influence Allelic Association," *Nature Reviews Genetics* 5 (2004): 89–100.

45 Ning Yu, Feng-Chi Chen, Satoshi Ota, Lynn B. Jorde, Pekka Pamilo, Laszlo Patthy, Michele Ramsay, Trefor Jenkins, Song-Kun Shyue, and Wen-Hsiung Li, "Larger Genetic Differences within Africans than between Africans and Eurasians," *Genetics* 161 (2002): 269–74.

46 David Goldstein, e-mail to author, February 17, 2006.

47 Evans et al., "*Microcephalin*," 1717.

48 This is the "falsification" account of science codified by Karl R. Popper, *The Logic of Scientific Discovery* (New York: Basic Books, 1959).

49 See Gould, *Mismeasure of Man*; Marks, *Human Biodiversity*; and Amy Sue Bix, "Experiences and Voices of Eugenics Field-Workers: 'Women's Work' in Biology," *Social Studies of Science* 27 (1997): 625–68.

50 Dobson-Stone et al., "Investigation," 394–400; Timpson et al., "Comment on Papers," 1036A; and Mekel-Bobrov et al., "Ongoing Evolution Not Explained," 600–8.

51 Michael Balter, "Profile: Bruce Lahn," 1871, 1873; and "Links between Brain Genes, Evolution, and Cognition Challenged," *Science* 314 (2006): 1872.

52 Mekel-Bobrov et al., "Ongoing Evolution Not Explained," 600–8.

53 Mildred Cho, "Natural Selection and the Lay Press: The Case of Lahn's Findings on Genetics and Cognition" (paper presented at the Translating ELSI Conference, Cleveland, OH, May 3, 2008).

54 Francis Bacon, "The Great Instauration (Translation)," in *The Philosophical Works of Francis Bacon*, ed. John M. Robertson (Freeport, NY: Books for Libraries Press, 1970), 249.

55 Bacon, "Great Instauration," 247, 249.

56 Bacon, "Great Instauration," 249.

57 See, e.g., Edward O. Wilson, *Consilience: The Unity of Knowledge* (New York: Alfred A. Knopf, 1998).

19.
SOCIOSCIENTIFIC CONTROVERSIES
A Theoretical and Methodological Framework
by Craig O. Stewart

The role of science in social controversies has perhaps never been greater. In the United States, there is continuing political debate over how evolutionary theory should be taught in public schools. President George W. Bush used his first veto to block federal funding for embryonic stem cell research. Lawrence Summers, former president of Harvard, continues to be a polarizing figure based on a speech in which he speculated that women are underrepresented in math and science fields due to biological differences between the sexes. In each of these cases, political controversies emerge over the meaning of science—Is evolution a settled fact or merely a "theory"? Does embryonic stem cell research destroy human lives? Are differences between women and men the result of biology or culture? Although the specific issues at stake are different in each of the controversies, what they have in common is the interweaving of discourses from a variety of sources, both scientific and social. The interwoven discursive texture of these controversies involves a multiplicity of participant roles, the interpenetration of public and scientific discourse, and the potential tensions between public and scientific reasoning and concerns (Goodnight, 2005).

In this paper, I argue for a theoretical and methodological framework for studying such controversies and their attendant discursive complexity. I begin by offering a conceptual definition for *socioscientific controversies*. I then discuss two traditional approaches to the intersections between public and scientific discourse—popularization and argument spheres—and their implications for the study of socioscientific controversies. Following this discussion, I describe Norman Fairclough's approach to critical discourse analysis (CDA) and argue for its utility as a methodological framework for research on the rhetoric of socioscientific controversies.

A CDA approach to socioscientific controversies offers a heuristic framework that rhetoricians and other qualitative researchers can use to investigate single controversies, to compare different controversies, or to situate multiple studies of controversy (Johnstone, 2008). CDA combines traditional discourse analysis' attention to the details of language with rhetoric's attention to the social uses of language, thus bridging these two sometimes disparate approaches to discourse about science (cf. Fahnestock, 2005). Further, by attending to the circulation and uptake of scientific discourse, CDA offers a

Craig O. Stewart. "Socioscientific Controversies: A Theoretical and Methodological Framework." *Communication Theory*, Volume 19, Number 2, 2009, pp. 124–145.

framework for understanding the multidirectional intersections of scientific and nonscientific discourse and incorporates attention to the reception of scientific discourse (e.g., Harris, 2005; Paul, Charney, & Kendall, 2001). This framework attends especially to how scientific discourse circulates beyond disciplinary boundaries and into other discourses, and theorizes how this socioscientific discourse may then lead to discursive change within and between spheres, or orders, of discourse. The CDA-based approach to socioscientific controversies is described in light of current work in the rhetoric of science and related fields and is illustrated through the analysis of a controversy over an evolutionary psychology study on gender and spatial cognition, which purportedly showed that women are superior to men at locating food items in a farmer's market.

Defining Socioscientific Controversies

The term *socioscientific controversy* draws on work in science education, sociology of science, and rhetorical studies. As described by science educators, *socioscientific issues* are "societal dilemmas with conceptual, procedural, or technological links to science" (Sadler & Zeidler, 2004, p. 5). Similarly, in the sociology of science literature, the term *science-based controversy* has been used to distinguish disputes over the political or social implications of science from those over the epistemological status of competing knowledge claims (Brante, 1993). Following Ziedler, Walker, Ackett, and Simmons (2002), I will use the term *socioscientific*, rather than *science-based*, to highlight the social and political nature of these controversies. Using Goodnight's (1991) account, we can describe controversies in general as "ubiquitous, temporally pluralistic, extended argumentative engagements constituted in the full range of communicative actions and enveloping communication systems and practices" (p. 2). Socioscientific controversies might then be described as extended argumentative engagements over socially significant issues and comprising communicative events and practices in and from both scientific and nonscientific spheres. Disputes that are important primarily within disciplines—such as debates over the use of one-tailed versus two-tailed tests of statistical significance—would be excluded from this definition, even though such disputes might take place in both public and technical forums. Some socioscientific controversies span decades, such as the ongoing debates over the teaching of evolution versus creationism or "intelligent design" in U.S. public schools. Others are relatively ephemeral, coming and going with the 24-hour news cycle. The case study in this paper explicates a relatively brief argumentative engagement over an evolutionary psychology study on gender and spatial cognition; this brief episode is a part of the significant ongoing socioscientific controversies over the role of biology in purported gender differences in cognition and behavior.

In terms of theorizing socioscientific controversies, Fairclough offers two important and related concepts. The first is the notion that controversies comprise not single communicative events, but *chains* of communicative events (Fairclough, 1995b). While any piece of discourse is situated in a communicative chain linking processes of discourse production and consumption, the study of controversies, as suggested by Goodnight's definition, must attend to these chains and the rhetorical processes that connect each link to the other. The second is that the links in this chain are composed of elements of different *orders of discourse*. That is, "genres, styles, activity types, and discourses" (Fairclough, 1992, p. 70) situated within "relatively stabilized configurations of discourse practices" (Fairclough, 1995a, p. 2).

Orders of discourse intersect in the context of socioscientific controversies both at the level of *intertextuality* and *interdiscursivity*. Intertextuality refers to the "property texts have of being full of snatches of other texts, which may be explicitly demarcated or merged in, and which the text may assimilate, contradict, ironically echo, and so forth" (Fairclough, 1992, p. 84; see also Solin, 2004). Thus we may find quotations from research reports, press releases, scientists, citizens, activists, and so on in the texts that constitute socioscientific controversies. Interdiscursivity refers to "the heterogeneous constitution of texts out of elements (types of convention) of orders of discourse" (p. 85). For example, Fairclough (1995b) shows how within an element of the media order of discourse, the "hard-news report," discourse practices from public and personal orders of discourse are drawn upon, creating a hybrid "public-colloquial discourse," which is evident in transforming official language to colloquial language, or in "chat shows" that combine discourse practices of public performance and private conversation.

In the context of socioscientific controversies, the interweaving and blending of orders of discourse are perhaps even more apparent. Beacco, Claudel, Doury, Petit, and Reboul-Toure (2002) show how "snatches of text" from scientists, members of the public, advocates, and others come together in media texts about controversial science issues, and how nonexperts draw on scientific sources to create their own arguments with respect to those issues. In the case of media discourse about controversial science, "journalists ... represent the discourse of many speakers *in their different social roles*" (Beacco, et al., 2002, p. 283, my emphasis). In other words, a topic that may originate in science, such as genetically modified organisms, when it is embedded in a social controversy becomes open to rhetorical (re)framing by citizens, politicians, and scientists. In this way boundaries between public and technical spheres are blurred, but not at the expense of one or the other; rather, a hybrid discursive space is created between the technical and the public (Moirand, 2003). Thus, in addition to the overt combinations of texts we will also find traces of discourse practices from different orders of discourse in the texts that constitute socioscientific controversies (Chouliaraki & Fairclough, 1999).

In the following section, I discuss two rhetorical approaches to understanding the intersections between public and scientific discourse: Popularization and argument spheres. I focus on these approaches because they are well-developed in the rhetoric of science literature and are relevant for theorizing socioscientific controversies. There are other approaches to controversies, such as those proposed by Gross (2005), but it is beyond the scope of this paper to provide an exhaustive review. I show how the popularization and argument sphere models are relevant to the CDA approach sketched above and how CDA extends these approaches to investigate socioscientific controversies.

Intersections between Scientific and Public Discourse

Popularization

Popularization of science refers to communications in which journalists or other communicators "translate" scientific reports into media for general, nonexpert audiences, and those in which scientists themselves communicate to such audiences. In both cases, there is often, at least implicitly, a translational or "didactic" model of communication that is unidirectional, moving from scientists on one end to the public on the other, with science writers, teachers, and so forth in the middle (Gregory & Miller, 1998). Similarly, Moirand (2003) characterizes the traditional model of science communication this way, in which the mediator is "a theoretical entity: institution + constraints of media [or other institutions] + journalist [or other mediator]" (p. 176), as shown in Figure 19.1.

Rhetoricians of science and other science communication researchers have paid a great deal of attention to the rhetorical task of accommodating/popularizing scientific discourse for lay audiences (e.g., Dowdey, 1987; Fahnestock, 1986, 2004; Hornig, 1990; Lievrouw, 1990; Rowan, 1989). Such analyses often begin with a report published in a scientific journal, such as *Science*, and then compare that article with subsequent accommodations published in, for instance, the "News section" of *Science*, or a newspaper or magazine article, to investigate differences in genre, grammar, and rhetorical structure (e.g., Fahnestock, 1986, 2004; Rowan, 1989; cf. Myers, 2003).

In a seminal essay, Fahnestock (1986) shows how the shift from scientific reports to accommodations represents a shift from forensic to epideictic genres. Scientific reports are forensic insofar as they are primarily, though not exclusively, directed toward epistemological or truth claims, whereas accommodations are epideictic insofar as they are directed toward the praise of science and scientists by appealing to either "the wonder" or "the application" of the scientific findings (p. 279). Thus, accommodated science is characterized by fewer hedges and qualifiers, and generally, more certainty in its presentation. Fahnestock (2004) finds that the core figures of argument in research reports in *Science* and *Nature* are retained in the accommodations published in the "news" sections of those journals, and that the accommodations can improve on the figuration, thus playing an important role in how the research becomes accepted as "knowledge."

Implications for Socioscientific Controversies

Popularization studies focus on only a small chain of communicative events, those linking discourses of science to particular popular accounts. They also imagine a unidirectional flow of discursive influence, from science to the public. Socioscientific

Figure 19.1 Representation of translational model of science communication.

controversies comprise a greater array of communicative events, however, and the flow of discursive influence is multidirectional. Science popularizations influence not only lay audiences but also scientists who are also influenced by social and political ideologies (e.g., Gregory & Miller, 1998). Other media such as blogs, press releases, or conferences held by interest groups, public forums, and the like further complicate the discursive landscape for public consumption of scientific discourse. Therefore, as Myers (2003) argues, traditional conceptualizations of scientific popularization need to be revised to include these varying orders of discourse and the tensions between them. In particular, studies of socioscientific controversies need to attend not only to changes in the representation of science in the public sphere, but also to the multiple communicative events and multidirectional flows of discursive influence, which constitute such controversies.

Argument Spheres

Another influential framework for understanding the intersection between scientific and public discourse comes from the work of G. Thomas Goodnight. In an influential essay, he outlines three "spheres" of argument: the personal, the technical, and the public (Goodnight, 1982). These spheres are "branches of activity—the grounds upon which arguments are built and the authorities to which arguers appeal" (p. 216). Argument spheres are characterized by how disagreements are dealt with. In the *personal* sphere, only informal argumentation, such as narratives and personal beliefs, may be required and the subject matter is considered to be of individual consequence. In the *technical* sphere, very specific rules of argumentation and standards of evidence, such as experimental research, statistical significance, and operational definitions, are required and the subject matter is rigidly defined as disciplinary fields. The *public* sphere "transcends" both the personal and technical by providing "customs, traditions, and requirements" for argumentation and taking on subject matter that has "consequences ... beyond the personal and technical spheres" (p. 220).

Goodnight (1982) argues that public deliberation may suffer because of the encroachment of technical and personal discourse into public discourse. For example, Farrell and Goodnight (1981) argue that a reliance on discourse practices from the technical sphere to the exclusion of those from the public sphere during the Three Mile Island nuclear incident sidelined the public and prevented it from engaging in reasonable discussion and action in response to these events.

Implications for Socioscientific Controversies

Unlike in the traditional model of science popularization, the flow of discursive influence is not unidirectional in the spheres schema. That is, while technical discourse may influence public discourse, the reverse is also true. Rowland (1986) argues that public encroachment into the technical sphere, by way of public opinion weighing into technical decision making, may have played a role in the *Challenger* space shuttle disaster. That is, public pressure to launch the shuttle may have overridden technical concerns about whether it was safe to launch. More positive public influence on the technical sphere is shown in the interventions of the activist organization ACT UP, which posed a success-ful "public" objection to the technical (i.e., medical) establishment with respect to HIV/AIDS in the 1980s. Specifically, ACT UP critiqued the appropriateness of scientific prac-tices such as double-blind studies, given the implications for those subjects from whom treatment is withheld in such studies (Brashers & Jackson, 1991).

Although the influence of argument spheres on one another has been characterized as encroachment, scholars have argued that some types of recurring controversies *bridge* different argument spheres. Social controversies bridge the public and personal spheres of argument (Olson & Goodnight, 1994). The public sphere creates the space for a social con-troversy owing to it being both "inclusive" and "contestable" (Olson & Goodnight, 1994, p. 250). In the public sphere, at least ideally, interlocutors are admitted with few exclusions and can challenge accepted norms of discourse. These challenges can be made both by those who seek to contest claims within these norms using discursive argumentation and by those who seek to engage in "nondiscursive arguments" that challenge the boundary between public and personal spheres by bringing into the public "aspects of life that are hidden away, habitually ignored, or routinely disconnected from public appearance" (p. 252).

Boyd (2002) argues that regulatory controversies bridge the public and technical spheres of arguments. In the regulatory controversy surrounding the approval of Olestra as a food additive, the Center for Science in the Public Interest (CSPI) subverted the technical norms of Food & Drug Administration hearings by offering anecdotal argu-ments, rather than arguments based on experimental evidence. Boyd argues that these "public" interventions on the part of the CSPI represent "out-law discourse" (Sloop & Ono, 1997) relative to technical norms, thus bridging the public and technical spheres.

Socioscientific controversies might be said to bridge the personal, public, *and* technical spheres of argument. However, these controversies—constituted in intertex-tual and interdiscursive formations—blur the boundaries between these discursive spheres to such an extent that bridges are not necessary, as texts and discourse prac-tices are interwoven across multiple levels. Further, the argument spheres identified by Goodnight may not always be the relevant ones, or, to put it another way, may be con-strued too broadly to best describe the relevant discursive practices in every contro-versy. As Myers (2003) states, only "from a great distance, does [technical] discourse seem to employ a single unified register" (p. 270). Fairclough's (1992) notion of orders of discourse offers a more flexible way to account for what discourse practices are rel-evant in context, how and where these practices intersect, and at what level discursive influence or change may be taking place. Goodnight's argument spheres are roughly equivalent to Fairclough's "societal" orders of discourse, which comprise other, more "local" orders that may be more relevant and productive for the investigation of socio-scientific controversies. For example, we might see the influence of discourse from evolutionary psychology, which is not necessarily representative of all scientific dis-course (much less of technical discourse) on certain media discourse practices—news reporting, blogging, and so forth—which are themselves situated between public and private orders of discourse (Fairclough, 1995b). Therefore, methodological attention to discourse practices at both macro- and microlevels are needed to account for the discourse of socioscientific controversies.

A CDA Approach to Socioscientific Controversies

In this section, I show how CDA, as articulated by Fairclough, can illuminate the rhetorical and discursive features of socioscientific controversies. This discourse analytic framework offers a systematic but flexible framework that can accommodate the singularity of individual cases without forcing controversies into a single model (cf. Goodnight, 2005). This method contributes to interdisciplinary theorizing of controversies in rhetorical studies in general and the rhetoric of science in particular. Gross (2005), for example, draws on critical theory, anthropology, and sociology to account for controversies over science and technology. CDA offers rhetoricians another critical social science perspective on controversies that attends specifically to language use at different levels and to its strategic and ideological functions.

Fairclough's approach to CDA is built on three layers of analysis: Text, discursive practice, and social practice (Fairclough, 1992). First, the *text layer* comprises the details of "vocabulary, grammar, cohesion, and text structure" (p. 75). Second, the *discursive practice layer* "involves processes of text production, distribution, and consumption, and the nature of these processes varies between different types of discourse according to social factors" (p. 78). This layer of analysis is central to the analysis of socioscientific controversies, as it is here where intertextuality and interdiscursivity are most relevant. And third, the *social practice layer* examines ideology, hegemony, and discursive change within and across orders of discourse. Drawing on Halliday's functional linguistics, within each of these layers, Fairclough argues that language can serve three primary discourse functions: *Identity*, which "relates to the ways in which social identities are set up in discourse," *relational*, which relates "to how social relationships between discourse participants are enacted and negotiated," and *ideational*, which relates "to ways in which texts signify the world and its processes, entities and relations" (p. 64). In the following section, I discuss in detail Fairclough's three-layered approach to CDA, particularly the discursive practice layer and intertextuality and interdiscursivity, and argue for each layer's relevance to the rhetoric of socioscientific controversies. Each layer of analysis will also be applied to the specific socioscientific controversy described below.

Science, Women, and Grocery Shopping

On August 26, 2007, *The Proceedings of the Royal Society B* published an evolutionary psychology research report online entitled "Spatial adaptations for plant foraging: Women excel and calories count" (New, Krasnow, Truxaw, & Gaulin, 2007, hereafter referred to as the *New et al. study*). The research reported in this article compared women and men in a way-finding task in a farmer's market. The participants "were led by a circuitous route to each of six food stalls, where they were given a food item to eat" (p. 2) and were asked to rate the food item on taste, frequency of consumption, and attractiveness of the stall. After completing the route, participants were taken to the center of the market and were asked to indicate with a pointer on a compass where each food item was located (they could not see the relevant stalls). The gender comparison found that the average error in pointing was 9 degrees less for women than for men, which "corresponds to a 27% improvement compared with men" (p. 3). Further, the experimenters found that self-reported sense of direction was significantly related to performance on the task. In addition to testing gender effects, the researchers tested whether caloric density of food items predicted accuracy on the way-finding task. They found that people, both women and men, tended to be more accurate the higher the caloric density of the food items. Other measures, such as liking food items or eating them often, were not related to performance on the task.

This research triggered a small socioscientific controversy, carried out through popularizations, media commentaries, and other text and talk about the study and its findings. These responses reveal some of the rhetorical effects of this research, as discourse from and about the study circulates in the context of controversy (e.g., Cherwitz, 1980). That is, they suggest how different audiences responded to this research and its representations by examining the various recontextualizations of texts and discursive practices, and the uses to which these recontextualizations are put. Thus, in socioscientific controversies, reception involves not only disciplinary audiences but also all those who encounter arguments from and about science, and how they resist or take up these arguments in social or political contexts (cf. Harris, 2005; Paul et al., 2001). Although this specific controversy was relatively limited, drawing commentary only over the course of a few days, it is embedded within longer, ongoing controversies over the role of biology and evolution in purported gender differences in cognition, language use, and other domains. The chain of communicative events constituting the controversy is illustrated schematically in Figure 19.2.

The figure shows three relevant orders of discourse for this controversy, which are represented by gray squares, corresponding to the discursive practice layer of analysis. Within each of these squares, the specific prior (on the left) and subsequent (on the right) texts that shape and are shaped by this socioscientific controversy are represented by white boxes, corresponding to the text layer of analysis. It is important to note that these are broad descriptions of macrolevel orders of discourse, but are more locally construed than in the technical-personal-public argument spheres model. Within the scientific order of discourse, itself a narrower order within the technical, we could further distinguish the orders of discourse of evolutionary psychology as a field, and of the *Proceedings of the Royal Society* as a journal. Likewise, in the media order of discourse, we could distinguish between the orders of discourse of newspapers and blogs and in the personal, between socially shared and individualistic representations (i.e., attitudes and beliefs) of gender and the relationship between these representations and discourse production and consumption. What I am calling the personal order of discourse refers to social cognitive aspects of discourse—what Fairclough (1992, p. 80) calls "member's resources"—the attitudes, beliefs, and values that shape and are shaped by individuals' interpretations and production of discourse, and the social knowledge that structures human communication (cf. Van Dijk, 2006). Further, these three are not always the relevant orders of discourse to shape and be shaped by socioscientific controversies. Other controversies may involve, for example, religious orders of discourse (comprising various religious beliefs and ways of talking about X) or political orders of discourse (comprising various political exigences like pending

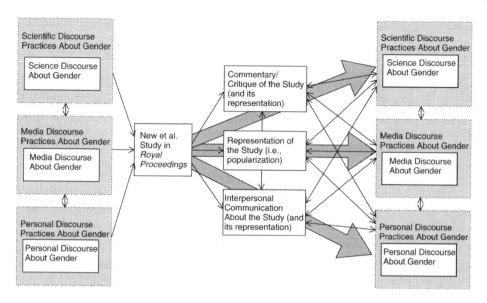

Figure 19.2 Schematic representation of socioscientific controversy over the New et al. study.

legislation or policy or electoral strategizing). The entire model is situated within the social layer, attending to potential ideological discursive influence and change within and across orders of discourse.

The general directional flow from left to right represents the temporal dimension of the controversy, the texts and discursive practices that precede the publication of the study on the left, and those that follow the controversy on the right. However, the chain of communicative events is not strictly linear. For example, consider a scientist who reads the New et al. study in the *Royal Proceedings*, and whose personal discursive practices (i.e., social cognitive representations) are influenced by this text. These practices would then shape specific utterances she might make subsequently in interpersonal communication with a colleague in rhetorical studies about the study. This text (the conversation) may then influence how this scientist would represent this study or others like it in future scientific texts that she might produce. This influence would then be traced from the New et al. study, right through the bottom gray arrow to Personal Discourse Practices, left to the Interpersonal Communication, and then right again to Scientific Discourse in the upper right corner.

In the middle of this model, the white boxes represent the specific texts that constitute the controversy—the study itself, media popularizations of the study, other public commentary and critique of the study (of which this article is an example), and interpersonal communication (i.e., everyday conversations) about the study. This part of the model represents the entextualization of the controversy. That is, these boxes represent the texts identified for analysis and thus will be the focus of the analysis that follows, with the exception of interpersonal communication. Due to the ephemeral nature of this kind of discourse, interpersonal talk about the study will not be analyzed, but it is important to note that this kind of discourse is an important element of science communication in general and of socioscientific controversies in particular.[1] The analysis pays particular attention to intertextuality and interdiscursivity. These concepts are represented by the arrows in the model, showing the potentials for borrowing text and discursive practices across texts and orders of discourse. In sum, this analysis will show how the texts comprising this controversy are shaped by texts and discursive practices from scientific, media, and personal orders of discourse (which is why these boxes are not embedded within single discursive practice boxes). Although each layer of analysis in Fairclough's scheme is discussed separately below, these are overlapping rather than discrete analytic categories, and each layer builds on the other: Analysis of discursive practice relies on text analysis, and analysis of social practice relies on analysis of discursive practice.

Text Layer

As described above, scholars investigating accommodations or popularizations of science for public audiences have paid a great deal of attention to texts and the textual differences between scientific research reports and media representations of these research reports (e.g., De Oliveria & Pagano, 2006; Fahnestock, 1986, 2004; Rowan, 1989; see Calsamiglia, 2003, for an overview of this sort of work in discourse analysis). Likewise, researchers have examined how experimental research reports are structured at the textual level (e.g., Atkinson, 1999; Bazerman, 1987; Gross, Harmon, & Reidy, 2002). Such studies show the three discourse functions operating in the text layer in scientific and science-based discourse: The identity function, in constructing the scientist or expert; the relational function, in constructing a didactic relationship between a knowledge deliverer (either a scientist or a mediator) and knowledge receivers (members of the public); and the ideational function, in constructing "reliable" knowledge. In the context of socioscientific controversies, the possible constructions within these functions are more varied along with the discursive and social practices that are involved in such controversies.

Both the scientific and media discourse about the New et al. study make similar ideational constructions regarding gender by presupposing sexual dimorphism, or that women and men are biologically, psychologically, and behaviorally distinct from one another, and this presupposition is evident at the level of text analysis. Indeed, New et al. state as much in their introduction: "In certain cases … ancestral men and women would have faced distinct spatial demands; in these cases, we should find that the resultant cognitive mechanisms are sexually dimorphic" (p. 1). Despite this claim, we might expect scientific discourse to be cautious, featuring hedges, qualifiers, modal verbs, and so forth, to construct scientific claims as being contingent on data (Fahnestock, 1986). In the above quote, we see examples of modal verbs, *would* and *should*, suggesting less certainty than would be the case if "would have" were deleted and "should" were replaced with "will." Such modalities are characteristic of how the article represents the relationship between theories and observations about gender and evolution. However, such caution is not characteristic in the article's representation of observed gender differences. Hedges such as "in general" and "on average" occur only rarely, representing such difference as absolute, rather than as differences between averages, around which there is a great deal of overlap between women and men. These ideational constructions of women and men as objects of research serve important relational functions as well, as will be discussed in the following sections.

Although some media popularizations of the New et al. study, such as that in *The Economist*, use similar modalities to describe evolutionary theory, others did not. For example, the *Daily Telegraph* reported, "[t]oday, a scientific study says that over many thousands of years evolution has designed women to excel when it comes to hunting down the most fulfilling food" (borrowing the word *excel* from the title of the New et al. report) and the *Daily Mail* reported: "While men developed the acute sense of direction needed for hunting, women mastered the art of gathering food such as fruits and berries." Overall, the textual representations of claims regarding evolutionary theory do differ in ways that we might expect as this discourse is recontextualized from a scientific order of discourse into a media order of discourse; however, the representations, and underlying assumptions, of claims about gender differences do not seem to differ greatly between these orders of discourse. These textual constructions would likely influence personal orders of discourse for different audiences (scientific and nonscientific) and may reflect the influence of both personal and media orders of discourse on science, as will be discussed below.

Discursive Practice Layer

Within the discursive practice layer, Fairclough is especially interested in intertextuality and interdiscursivity as they relate to the production, distribution, and consumption of discourse. As described above, intertextuality refers to the creation of texts through the combination of specific prior texts, as in the use of quotations in news reporting. Interdiscursivity refers to the borrowing of more general discourse practices, rather than of specific prior texts, from one order of discourse within another.

Intertextuality and interdiscursivity across orders of discourse are central to understanding socioscientific controversies, since such controversies are constituted in the blending and interweaving of texts and discourse practices. That is, a chain of communicative events drawing on texts and discursive practices from only one order of discourse would not constitute a socioscientific controversy. The controversy over the New et al. study includes, crucially, recontextualizations in the form of popularizations, but also chains out into other texts—newspaper editorials, media commentary, blog posts, and so forth. In these new contexts, intertextuality and interdiscursivity are used, both strategically and unconsciously, to create arguments about gender, shopping, and spatial cognition, which combine scientific, media, and personal texts and discourse practices.

As noted in the text analysis above, the research report in the *Royal Proceedings* rarely hedged its representations of differences in the spatial cognitive abilities of men and women. Scientific discourse practices ordinarily tend to favor more cautious representations. However, as critical scholars show (e.g., Condit, 1996; Fausto-Sterling, 2000; Lancaster, 2003), even within scientific orders of discourse, culturally dominant ways of describing women and men—as distinct from one another, rather than as groups with substantial overlap in interests and abilities—seem to override scientific caution in describing variable and contingent group differences and are in fact institutionalized in the research practices of sexual science. In other words, from a critical perspective, it would be naïve to suppose that the research questions and hypotheses posed in this study emerged only as they related to theory or data-based exigences in the scientific order of discourse. Discourse practices from personal and media orders of discourse, that is, personal beliefs about gender, media representations of the competence of men at grocery shopping and other domestic tasks, as well as scientific orders of discourse, shape the textual representation of the New et al. study that appeared in the *Proceedings of the Royal Society* at the level of interdiscursivity. That is, the ideational representation of gender in the journal draws on practices from other, nonscientific, orders of discourse.

The role of interdiscursivity can also be strikingly seen in how news media (re)framed arguments from the New et al. study. While news media discourse practices tend to emphasize the effects and implications, rather than the processes, of science, such choices in the framing of scientific research are not neutral, either substantively or ideologically. The frame favored in the popularizations, as instantiated in headlines and lead paragraphs, is based on stereotypes about women and shopping, and suggests that the implication of the study is that "science" shows such stereotypes to be true: "Why women are better at shopping than men" (*Daily Telegraph*), "Women really are better than men at shopping" (*The Economist*), "Women are born to shop, experts say" (*Daily Mail*). Indeed, as developed in the lead paragraphs in the *Telegraph* and *Daily Mail*, this finding not only confirms the stereotype, but has the additional application of providing justification for men not to shop for food: "Men who hate supermarkets now have the ultimate excuse to leave it to their mothers, wives or girlfriends" (*Telegraph*); "Men who hate trawling the shopping centres now have the perfect excuse to stay at home" (*Mail*). These frames reflect news media practices favoring sensationalism and familiarity relevant not only to the interpretation of science but also the interpretation of other social and political discourses (Bennett, 2003). These (re)framings of scientific discourse also make it plain that this discourse not only accomplishes ideational constructions of gender (of women and men as objects of research about which claims can be made) but also relational constructions (of how women and men should behave socially in relation to one another).

Socioscientific controversies, like other controversies, open up opportunities to challenge authoritative claims. These challenges can be accomplished with intertextual configurations that construct dialogue with science and/or its media representations, constructing agonistic relations between different interlocutors and scientists. In news discourse, this is most often accomplished by including critical quotations from either scientists or nonscientists, although the identities of these sources would need to be constructed as authoritative according to journalistic practices. For example, an article about the New et al. study published in the *Sydney Morning Herald* concluded with the following:

But Dr Monica Minnegal, a senior lecturer in anthropology at the University of Melbourne, was sceptical [sic] about suggestions that implied humans had stopped evolving. "To reduce everything to what happened on the savanna way back then is for me problematic," she said.

With respect to the identity, relational, and ideational functions of discourse, socio-scientific controversies allow for more diversity of constructed identities to participate authoritatively, more opportunities for relational constructions placing these identities in conversation with scientists, and, consequently, more counterclaims and critiques to inform the interpretation of science. New media technologies, such as blogs, facilitate the proliferation of socioscientific controversies, affording opportunities for nonjournal-ists to create their own intertextual dialogues to either critique or to take up scientific claims within a socioscientific controversy. This is especially important when mass media outlets do not include alternative voices or perspectives in their representation of science.

An example of how intertextuality can serve these discourse functions in contro-versy can be seen in the way that feminist bloggers recontextualized figures and data to challenge the interpretation of scientific discourse offered by scientists or science jour-nalists. For example, a blogger on Salon.com uses such recontextualizations to reframe a seemingly large relative effect as a small absolute effect: "While the study reports that women were 27 percent better than men at pointing out the correct direction, the absolute numbers are not as shocking: Men tended to be off by 33, women by 25" (www.salon.com/2007/08/23/nuts_and_berries/ [Link updated and accessed 8 August 2019—RAH]). Recontextualizing figures describing sample sizes offers another way to critique science methodology, based on the assumption that large sample sizes are required to make generalizations about large groups of people: "The evidence for this amazing claim? A survey of 45 men and 41 women at six gatherings of a farmers' market (averag-ing seven of each gender at each market)" (www.thefword.org.uk/blog/2007/08/more_improbably). These recontextualizations serve identity functions, constructing the bloggers as credible critics of science, and ideational functions, referencing specific bits of text (the numbers reported) in order to resignify them as supporting different claims or as providing counterevidence to the claims offered by the study's authors and/or science journalists (cf. Fairclough, 1992, p. 60).

The challenges to science afforded by the recontextualization of figures primarily target methodological practices from scientific orders of discourse. Other types of intertextuality, such as recontextualizing larger chunks of text, either by hyperlinking to or reproducing parts of a representation of science, allow interlocutors in socioscientific controversies to juxtapose scientific claims with challenges to the assumptions underlying those claims. These challenges may draw on a variety of orders of discourse. For example, a blogger entitles a post on the New et al. study, "Women evolved for supermarkets! More bollocks from the world of 'science'." The post links to the *Tele-graph*'s article, reproduces seven paragraphs in the blog post itself, and juxtaposes the science journalist's interpretation of the study, drawing discourse practices from media (hyperlinking and quoting practices in blogs), personal (ironic criticism), and scientific (offering alternative hypotheses) orders of discourse:

OH GIVE ME A BREAK.

This kind of shit is really summed up by the first sentence of the article. Evolutionary psychology, the perfect excuse for men to act like assholes. This [finding] "probably has its origins in the African savannah"? That is more likely than it being, oh, something to do with social conditioning, the fact that women still tend to do the great majority of food shopping for their families, and might therefore simply have had more practice at it somewhat more recently than the days of our distant ancestors? That's not even worth mentioning as a theory.

This is what happens when I read the Daily Telegraph at the tea shop. (realcdaae.livejournal.com/325763.html)

In socioscientific controversies, intertextuality not only allows for journalists to juxtapose competing scientific claims with one another or with discourse from citizens, activists, politicians, and so forth, but also for the latter to construct dialogic relationships between themselves and scientists and science mediators in new media contexts.

Socioscientific controversies comprise multiple points of view, and intertextuality and interdiscursivity as described above allow not only for critique but also for people to take up scientific evidence uncritically to support their own position. In the present case, this kind of taking up of scientific discourse involved interdiscursivity more so than intertextuality. That is, taking up discourse about the New et al. study as positive evidence in cultural discourse about gender was accomplished less with the recontextualization of specific bits of text, but rather with reconfiguring the arguments of the study within more general media and personal discourse practices. This is evident in how science journalists framed their popularizations, situating the study squarely in stereotypical discourses about women and shopping. Others similarly used this study to support their suppositions about women, men, and shopping, incorporating discourse about the study into personal anecdotes about gender and grocery shopping, emphasizing women's efficiency and men's incompetence at food shopping. For example, an editorial accompanying the *Telegraph*'s popularization situates the scientific discourse within narrative descriptions of the author and her husband's different modes of shopping for food. Similarly, a blogger situates discourse about the study within "common sense" notions of how women and men shop:

Any women [sic] that has ever asked her husband or significant other to do the grocery shopping knows how true this [finding] is. Most women can go into the grocery store, find exactly what is on the list, and even save a few dollars, all in under an hour. Most men go in, having completely forgotten the list at home, and just start buying. ... The scariest part is seeing the groceries unloaded and realizing that you are just going to have to go back yourself and get what you REALLY needed. (www.regentstreet.me.uk/2007/09/13/women-make-better-shoppers/ [Link broken as of 8 August 2019—RAH])

Through interdiscursivity, scientific discourse becomes part and parcel of cultural discourses about gender.

Social Practice Layer

The social practice layer in Fairclough's framework is primarily concerned with ideology, hegemony, and power. Drawing primarily on Althusser, Fairclough (1992) defines "ideologies [as] significations/constructions of reality (the physical world, social relations, social identities), which are built into various dimensions of the forms/meanings of discursive practices, and which contribute to the production, reproduction or transformation of relations of domination" (p. 87). The discursive instantiations of ideologies are "located both in the structures (i.e., orders of discourse) which constitute the outcome of past [discursive] events and the conditions of current events, and in events themselves as they reproduce and transform their conditioning structures" (p. 89). Despite science positioning itself as outside of politics and ideology, critics from a variety of perspectives have shown how scientific orders of discourse are highly ideological (see Longino, 1990, pp. 194–214, for a review). As has already been discussed, ideology shapes scientific practice by defining particular objects of study, in this case, gender, and how to go about studying those objects, by assuming gender dimorphism and seeking out statistically significant mean differences between genders (e.g., Condit, 1996).

The following blog comments reveal that at least some audience members are well aware of the ideological implications of the socioscientific controversy surrounding the New et al. study, which have to do with the construction of social relations between men and women:

> I don't quite understand, if men are supposed to be better navigators then why are they unable to pick up things from supermarkets? Or is it that somehow men are very conveniently good at the things that mean that they're clever, rational, and meant to be in charge of things, but not good at the things … that means [sic] they need to do stuff sometimes? Can anyone help me with that? (Comment 2, punkassblog.com/2007/08/23/lost-in-the-supermarket/) You're not reading the hilarious subtext which is "men are fucking idiots." Evolutionary psychology is fascinating to me. (Comment 6, readcdaae.livejournal.com/325763.html)

The particular "female advantage" in spatial cognition reported in the *Proceedings of the Royal Society* can be, and was, taken to mean that women are better suited to the domestic task of shopping for groceries. "Male advantages" in spatial cognition and other domains of evolutionary psychology rarely amount to similar suitability to domestic tasks but, rather, suitability to relatively privileged tasks (map reading, etc.). Even if the particular finding was framed as a "male disadvantage," as suggested by the second quote above, this negative framing still justifies men avoiding a particular domestic chore (i.e., sometimes it pays to be a fucking idiot). Thus, as these comments argue, this scientific discourse as it works its way through the chain of communicative events can support male hegemony and privilege.

But this hegemonic discourse is not without its challenges. As we have seen, the context of socioscientific controversy enables interlocutors to reject mass mediated interpretations of scientific discourse, and to cast doubt on the scientific research itself. In other words, socioscientific controversy creates opportunities for interlocutors from a variety of constructed identities to critique the claims for science using various ideational representations. These ideational challenges can often be substantive—such as by reframing the 27% difference between women and men in absolute terms, recontextualizing the numerical figures describing the sample size (highlighting the relatively small sample size), and by challenging the connection between purported evolutionary contexts and contemporary society. Such challenges, instantiated in the discursive practice layer, are relevant also to the social practice layer, as they challenge the discursive authority of science outside of scientific orders of discourse and, indeed, challenge claims within the scientific order of discourse. In other words, these examples show how intertextuality and interdiscursivity are related not only to processes of "text production, distribution, and consumption" but also to ideological struggles between orders of discourse.

Although socioscientific controversies afford opportunities for robust criticism of scientific discourse in nonscientific orders of discourse (news media, blogs, interpersonal conversations), hegemony can be seen in the influence, or lack thereof, on scientific discourse from these orders of discourse. For instance, evolutionary psychology still tends to represent women and men as completely distinct biological entities. Intertextual influence—that is, reference to specific texts from the socioscientific controversy in the form of quotations or citations—is unlikely to appear subsequently in the scientific order of discourse. Generally, scientific orders of discourse include only a limited number of possible identity constructions, construct primarily didactic relationships with external participants, and validate only certain types of ideational claims about the world.

However, the discourse of socioscientific controversy can certainly influence scientific orders of discourse in a variety of ways. In a study of a controversy over a conference paper purporting to show that homosexuality can be "cured," criticisms emerging in media orders of discourse influenced the scientific order of discourse by influencing scientists to explicitly attempt to shut off and delegitimize such criticisms in the context of the study's subsequent publication in a scientific journal (e.g., by dismissing this as the discourse of "the street"). Although direct intertextual influence from outside sources was easily excluded by the scientific order of discourse, interdiscursive influence was evident in shifts in the discursive representation of the study in the journal, responding to criticisms about participant selection, possible malingering by participants, and so forth, that emerged in the context of the socioscientific controversy (Stewart, 2008).

With respect to the controversy over the New et al. study, as noted above, scientists talk with nonscientists, and also read (and write for) newspapers and blogs, which will bring their attention to certain research reports that they might not have otherwise read, and these texts will also shape, at least in part, their interpretations of the research. The discourse comprising this controversy (and others like it) helps to shape how or whether scientists working in the field of evolutionary psychology represent the New et al. study in subsequent scientific discourse and how scientists working in other fields think and talk about evolutionary psychology in general. The local order of discourse constituting evolutionary psychology would likely exclude direct intertextual influence, but the broader scientific order of discourse may be influenced such that the evolutionary psychology order embedded within it is marginalized. Along these same lines, discourse practices in the media and personal orders of discourse may be influenced such that subsequent studies on gender may be treated more skeptically by journalists, or scientific claims about gender are more easily resisted by individuals, thereby reducing the hegemonic influence of evolutionary psychology on other orders of discourse. This kind of change in the arrangement of discursive power within and between orders of discourse is neither simple nor sudden, and would not be accomplished in response to any single socioscientific controversy; however, conceptualizing such controversies using Fairclough's framework posits that such discursive change is at least possible and provides clues as to how it might happen (Chouliaraki & Fairclough, 1999).

Conclusion

The analysis of the controversy over the New et al. study makes the following moves that distinguish the CDA approach from popularization and argument spheres approaches. First, it approaches the New et al. research report not as an absolute starting point, but investigates how this technical discourse draws on prior nontechnical discourse practices. As shown in the text and discursive practice sections above, the New et al. report tended to treat gender differences as absolute and stable, rather than as variable and contingent, drawing on ways of talking about gender that are consistent with social discourse practices rather than technical ones. In other words, compared with typical popularization studies, it looks backward to consider potential—especially ideological—influences on technical reports, and not just forward to how these reports are translated for public audiences. This analysis also shows that the technical sphere is not as uniform as might be imagined and that the blurring of discursive boundaries is evident in each link in the communicative chain. Furthermore, in the discursive practice section, in addition to considering how information is changed as the study is popularized, it investigates the ideological implications of these changes and how, further down the chain, different interlocutors take up bits of text and discourse practices to challenge science and scientists or to reinforce existing assumptions about gender. Finally, in the social practice section, it considers how the discourse comprising this controversy—and others like it—might go on to circulate back into and influence scientific, media, and personal texts and discourse practices.

Although not all socioscientific controversies will look exactly the same in this framework, it does suggest that they will necessarily involve the interweaving of texts and discourse practices from different orders of discourse. These controversies reveal how scientific and nonscientific orders of discourse "are potentially experienced as contradictorily structured, and thereby open to having their existing political and ideological investments become the focus of contention in struggles to deinvest/reinvest them" (Fairclough, 1992, p. 70). Discourse from and about the New et al. study was taken up by different audiences—reporters, media commentators, bloggers—using a variety of discursive practices. While some interlocutors appropriated this discourse to support stereotypical representations of gender, others resisted this discourse in various ways, revealing and challenging the ideological commitments of the New et al. study in particular and of evolutionary psychology in general. This kind of analysis shows the circulation of scientific discourse through controversy and some of the strategies that different audiences can employ to use scientific discourse to attempt to reinvest ideologies about gender in media or personal orders of discourse or to deinvest the same ideologies as they are manifest in scientific orders of discourse.

It is worth considering, in conclusion, where CDA fits in rhetorical studies of controversy more generally. Goodnight (2005) argues that science and technology controversies vary along so many dimensions that each one potentially represents "a singularity" and that scholars should therefore "leave the field of controversy study open, and not a little unorganized—without decisive categories, unreduced to predictive processes (initiation, development, resolution, and revision), and free from genre constraints" (p. 26). There is a tension, however, between favoring bottom-up analyses of controversies, each drawing on a theory or method only as suggested by the individual case, and top-down analyses, showing how each case can be explained by a general theoretical framework or predictive model, "perhaps by channeling [one's] observations through the philosophy of a prominent social theorist" (Ceccarelli, 2005, pp. 30–31). Fairclough's CDA framework is a methodology that mediates between bottom-up and top-down analyses of controversies. It is necessarily grounded in the analysis of texts and discourse practices as they are constituted in particular cases, addressing the need to account for the unique composition of individual controversies. At the same time, it links these micro- and mesolevel analyses to macrolevel analysis of broader social functions and processes (in Fairclough's [1992] framework, through a Foucauldian theoretical lens). Other frameworks drawing on other social theorists (e.g., Gross, 2005) focus on macrolevel analysis without explicitly connecting social analysis to the analysis of language and discourse practices. Fairclough's (1992) approach to CDA is a framework that explicitly links social theory with "attention to concrete instances of practice and the textual forms and processes of interpretation associated with them" (p. 61). It therefore offers a worthwhile framework for the study of socioscientific controversies in particular and should be part of the ongoing conversation on theory and method in controversy studies in rhetoric and communication.

Note

1 For example, Southwell and Torres (2006) find that media exposure to science is positively related to perceived ability to understand science, which predicts self-reports of conversations about science. In a study of perceived risks of skin cancer, higher media exposure to skin cancer information led to higher perceived societal risks, but this effect was attenuated by higher self-reported interpersonal communication about skin cancer (Morton & Duck, 2001). Studies such as these show that interpersonal and media communication are intertwined in the context of socioscientific issues. We might expect that greater consumption of media discourse about science leads to more interpersonal conversations about socioscientific issues, which in turn influence the effects of subsequent media discourse on individuals' perceptions of these issues. It is therefore important to include interpersonal communication as part of the chain of communicative events in socioscientific controversies. Although it would be ideal to be able to analyze instances of

contemporaneous interpersonal communication about the New et al. study in this paper, archives of such conversations, of course, do not exist as they do for media discourse about the study. While focus group or interview data could be collected and analyzed, this discourse would necessarily be produced in contexts and for purposes designed by the researcher and not the discourse participants, and would be only artificially connected to the other discursive data in this analysis.

References

Atkinson, D. (1999). *Scientific discourse in sociohistorical context: The philosophical transactions of the Royal Society of London, 1675–1975*. Mahwah, NJ: Lawrence Erlbaum Associates.

Bazerman, C. (1987). Codifying the social scientific style: The APA *Publication Manual* as a behaviorist rhetoric. In J. S. Nelson, A. Megill, & D. N. McCloskey (Eds.), *The rhetoric of the human sciences: Language and argument in scholarship and public affairs* (pp. 125–144). Madison: University of Wisconsin Press.

Beacco, J.-C., Claudel, C., Doury, M., Petit, G., & Reboul-Toure, S. (2002). Science in media and social discourse: New channels of communication, new linguistic forms. *Discourse Studies*, **4**, 277–300.

Bennett, W. L. (2003). *News: The politics of illusion*, 5th ed. New York: Longman.

Boyd, J. (2002). Public and technical interdependence: Regulatory controversy, out-law discourse, and the messy case of Olestra. *Argumentation and Advocacy*, **3**, 91–109.

Brante, T. (1993). Reasons for studying scientific and science-based controversies. In T. Brante, S. Fuller, & W. Lynch (Eds.), *Controversial science: From content to contention* (pp. 177–191). Albany: SUNY Press.

Brashers, D. E., & Jackson, S. (1991). "Politically-savvy sick people": Public penetration of the technical sphere. In D. W. Parson (Ed.), *Argument in controversy: Proceedings of the seventh SCA/AFA conference on argumentation* (pp. 284–288). Annandale, VA: Speech Communication Association.

Calsamiglia, H. (2003). Popularization discourse. *Discourse Studies*, **5**, 139–146.

Ceccarelli, L. M. (2005). Let us (not) theorize the spaces of contention. *Argumentation and Advocacy*, **42**, 30–33.

Cherwitz, R. A. (1980). The contributory effect of rhetorical discourse: A study of language-in-use. *Quarterly Journal of Speech*, **66**, 33–50.

Chouliaraki, L., & Fairclough, N. (1999). *Discourse in late modernity: Rethinking critical discourse analysis*. Edinburgh: Edinburgh University Press.

Condit, C. M. (1996). How bad science stays that way: Brain sex, demarcation, and the status of truth in the rhetoric of science. *Rhetoric Society Quarterly*, **26**(4), 83–109.

De Oliveira, J. M., & Pagano, A. S. (2006). The research article and the science popularization article: A probabilistic functional grammar perspective on direct discourse representation. *Discourse Studies*, **8**, 627–646.

Dowdey, D. (1987). Rhetorical techniques of audience adaptation in popular science writing. *Journal of Technical Writing and Communication*, **17**, 275–285.

Fahnestock, J. (1986). Accommodating science: The rhetorical life of scientific facts. *Written Communication*, **3**, 275–296.

Fahnestock, J. (2004). Preserving the figure: Consistency in the presentation of scientific arguments. *Written Communication*, **21**, 6–31.

Fahnestock, J. (2005). Rhetoric of science: Enriching the discipline. *Technical Communication Quarterly*, **14**, 277–286.

Fairclough, N. (1992). *Discourse and social change.* Maiden, MA: Blackwell.

Fairclough, N. (1995a). *Critical discourse analysis: The critical study of language.* New York: Longman.

Fairclough, N. (1995b). *Media discourse.* London: Arnold.

Farrell, T. B., & Goodnight, G. T. (1981). Accidental rhetoric: The root metaphors of Three Mile Island. *Communication Monographs, 48,* 271–300.

Fausto-Sterling, A. (2000). *Sexing the body: Gender politics and the construction of gender.* New York: Basic Books.

Goodnight, G. T. (1982). The personal, technical, and public spheres of argument: A speculative inquiry into the art of public deliberation. *Journal of the American Forensic Association, 18,* 214–227.

Goodnight, G. T. (1991). Controversy. In D. W. Parson (Ed.), *Argument in controversy: Proceedings of the Seventh SCA/AFA conference on argumentation* (pp. 1–13). Annandale, VA: Speech Communication Association.

Goodnight, G. T. (2005). Science and technology controversy: A rationale for inquiry. *Argumentation and Advocacy, 42,* 26–29.

Gregory, J., & Miller, S. (1998). *Science in public: Communication, culture, and credibility.* Cambridge, MA: Perseus Press.

Gross, A. G. (2005). Scientific and technical controversy: Three frameworks for analysis. *Argumentation and Advocacy, 42,* 43–47.

Gross, A. G., Harmon, J., & Reidy, M. (2002). *Communicating science: From the 17th century to the present,* New York: Oxford University Press.

Harris, R. A. (2005). Reception studies in the rhetoric of science. *Technical Communication Quarterly, 14,* 249–255.

Hornig, S. (1990). Television's NOVA and the construction of scientific truth. *Critical Studies in Mass Communication, 7,* 11–23.

Johnstone, B. (2008). *Discourse analysis,* 2nd ed. Cambridge, MA: Blackwell.

Lancaster, R. N. (2003). *The trouble with nature: Sex in science and popular culture.* Berkeley: University of California Press.

Lievrouw, L. A. (1990). Communication and the social representation of scientific knowledge. *Critical Studies in Mass Communication, 7,* 1–10.

Longino, H. E. (1990). *Science as social knowledge: Values and objectivity in scientific inquiry.* Princeton, NJ: Princeton University Press.

Moirand, S. (2003). Communicative and cognitive dimensions of discourse on science in the French mass media. *Discourse Studies, 5,* 175–206.

Morton, T. A., & Duck, J. M. (2001). Communication and health beliefs: Mass and interpersonal influences on perceptions of risk to self and others. *Communication Research, 28,* 602–626.

Myers, G. (2003). Discourse studies of scientific popularization: Questioning the boundaries. *Discourse Studies, 5,* 265–279.

New, J., Krasnow, M. M., Truxaw, D., & Gaulin, S. J. (2007). Spatial adaptations for plant foraging: Women excel and calories count. *Proceedings of the Royal Society: Biology,* [online]. doi: 10.1098/rspb.2007.0826. Accessed September 12, 2007.

Olson, K. M., & Goodnight, G. T. (1994). Entanglements of consumption, cruelty, privacy, and fashion: The social controversy over fur. *Quarterly Journal of Speech, 80,* 249–276.

Paul, D., Charney, D., & Kendall, A. (2001). Moving beyond the moment: Reception studies in the rhetoric of science. *Journal of Business and Technical Communication, 15,* 372–399.

Rowan, K. E. (1989). Moving beyond the *what* to the *why*: Differences in professional and popular science writing. *Journal of Technical Writing and Communication*, **19**, 161–179.

Rowland, R. C. (1986). The relationship between the public and the technical spheres of argument: A case study of the *Challenger Seven* disaster. *Central States Speech Journal*, **37**, 136–146.

Sadler, T. D., & Zeidler, D. L. (2004). The morality of socioscientific issues: Construal and resolution of genetic engineering dilemmas. *Science Education*, **88**, 4–27.

Sloop, J. M., & Ono, K. A. (1997). Out-law discourse: The critical politics of material judgment. *Philosophy & Rhetoric*, **30**, 50–69.

Solin, A. (2004). Intertextuality as mediation: On the analysis of intertextual relations in public discourse. *Text*, **24**, 267–296.

Southwell, B. G., & Torres, A. (2006). Connecting interpersonal and mass communication: Science news exposure, perceived ability to understand science, and conversation. *Communication Monographs*, **73**, 334–350.

Stewart, C. O. (2008). How a media controversy can influence a scientific publication: The case of Spitzer's "reparative therapy" study. In B. Johnstone & C. Eisenhart (Eds.), *Rhetoric in detail: Discourse analyses of rhetorical talk and text* (pp. 255–278). Amsterdam: John Benjamins.

Van Dijk, T. A. (2006). Discourse, context and cognition. *Discourse Studies*, **8**, 159–177.

Zeidler, D. L., Walker, K. A., Ackett, W. A., & Simmons, M. L. (2002). Tangled up in views: Beliefs in the nature of science and responses to socioscientific dilemmas. *Science Education*, **86**, 343–367.

20.
PRESENCE AS A CONSEQUENCE OF VERBAL-VISUAL INTERACTION
A Theoretical Approach
by Alan G. Gross

In *Chaïm Perelman*, Ray Dearin and I contend that presence transcends the isolated effects that Perelman and Olbrechts-Tyteca catalogue; we contend that there is a global form, a synergy of effects in which "to be persuaded is to live in a world made significantly different by the persuader" (151). In "Presence as Argument in the Public Sphere," I extend this form of presence from the verbal to the visual. In this essay I attempt to further the analysis of presence, to offer a systematic account of the verbal-visual interaction on which it depends, to offer, in effect, a genealogy of presence. I contend that an account so broadly based is essential if we are to explain the mystery of verbal-visual presence, to explain what is, in fact, the central mystery of Perelmanian presence, the transformation from the perceptual into the argumentative and narrative. According to *The New Rhetoric*, presence is based on the fact that "the thing on which the eye dwells, that which is best or most often seen is, by that very circumstance, overestimated." Initially, then, presence is perceptual; its effect is "to [fill] the whole field of consciousness." But according to Perelman and Olbrechts-Tyteca, such is the nature of presence that what is "at first a psychological phenomenon, becomes an essential element in argumentation" (116–18). As we shall see, this formulation is insufficient when dealing with geology, as it is a science in which argumentative subserves narrative presence: One of the goals of geological argument is an account of the history of the earth.

There is another problem in dealing with geology, indeed, with most texts in the sciences. Although for Perelman and Olbrechts-Tyteca presence is the product of verbal interaction alone, this cannot be true of any work in which information-bearing images contribute significantly to meaning. Indeed, I believe it is a fair criticism of the rhetoric of science that it has so far largely ignored or slighted these vital semiotic resources. Bazerman's *Shaping Written Knowledge*, Prelli's *A Rhetoric of Science*, Moss's *Novelties in the Heavens*, Condit's *The Meanings of the Gene*, and Ceccarelli's *Shaping Science with Rhetoric*—none of these major works in the rhetoric of science analyze a single visual. My *Communicating Science*, written with Harmon and Reidy, and Fahnestock's *Rhetorical Figures in Science* do feature scientific visuals, though they do not by any means treat them as semiotic equals.

Alan G. Gross. "Presence as a Consequence of Verbal-Visual Interaction: A Theoretical Approach." *Rhetoric Review*, Volume 28, Number 3, 2009, pp. 265–284.

Nor is it possible in the pursuit of a theory of verbal-visual interaction to have recourse to the literature in the field of visual rhetoric. For the last quarter-century, rhetorical critics and theorists have lived with the uneasy realization that the rhetorical tradition, which dealt more or less adequately with its typical focus, public address, was seriously challenged when confronted with the visual, whether in its pure form, as in photography or architecture, or in its mixed modality forms: manifestations as diverse as cartoons, graphic novels, film, and scientific articles and monographs. In a pioneering consideration of the problem, Sonja J. Foss presents a three-stage model of visual comprehension, one that "moves from identification of a function or functions communicated by an image, to assessment of the fulfillment of that function by the image, and finally an evaluation of the legitimacy of the function" (Peterson 21). Peterson praises Foss's schema because it "provides a vocabulary tailored, in particular, to visual elements" (20). Peterson objects, however, to Foss's first step, "identification of a function"; for Peterson this step presupposes that perception is unproblematic (22). Peterson offers an alternative schema that quite properly focuses on the process of seeing. Unfortunately, neither Foss nor Peterson provides us with a theory of visual communication. Without such a theory, as Peterson correctly opines, critics are forced to treat "a primarily visual text (painting, coin, cartoon, and so forth) as though it were a speech" (19–20). Examples abound. An exemplary anthology, *Visual Rhetoric*, abundantly illustrates the problem. It consists almost entirely of attempts to apply rhetorical theory as traditionally understood to texts in which meaning is the consequence of verbal-visual interaction, texts for which it most assuredly was not meant.

Such attempts do nothing to further the goal of a theory specific to verbal-visual interaction. It is no wonder that Cara Finnegan, writing in 2004, exhibited concern that "if visual rhetoric is *visual* rhetoric, and verbal rhetoric is *rhetoric*, then the iconophobic dominance of text remains unquestioned, and visual rhetoric is forever subordinated to the traditional artifacts of public address" (244). It is no wonder that in 2007 Lester Olson noted after a thorough review of the literature that "we [still] do not have a substantive treatise that might accurately be described as a theory of visual rhetoric" (14).

This essay is meant as a first step in the correction of that omission. It is an attempt to provide rhetorical critics with a semiotic and cognitive genealogy of presence, a key concept within the rhetorical tradition; it is an attempt to explain presence as a consequence of verbal-visual interaction. It is hoped that this effort will be viewed as critically useful, that its illumination of the argumentative, narrative, and rhetorical structure of my exemplary text, Alfred Wegener's *Origin of the Continents and Oceans*, will be seen as a new beginning for the communicative analysis of scientific texts, indeed, of any text that is not exclusively verbal. First I outline Dual Coding Theory (DCT), a theory of verbal-visual interaction. Then I illustrate the theory, showing how it creates an argument and transforms that argument into a narrative appropriate to a historical science, geology. Finally, I show that while Wegener uses his visuals with rhetorical intent, this use transgresses the permissible limits of disciplinary communication.

The Genealogy of Presence

A genealogy of presence in texts in which meaning is a consequence of verbal-visual interaction requires recourse to theories that are broader in scope than rhetorical theory as traditionally conceived. It requires Wolfgang Köhler's Gestalt theory to account for our perceptions and C.S. Peirce's semiotics to account for their interpretation. Both theories have the distinct advantage of a built-in visual bias. Gestalt categories that apply flawlessly to the visual apply only awkwardly to other modes of perception; moreover, Peirce himself acknowledges a visual bias in his thinking: "I do not think I ever reflect in words. I employ visual diagrams, firstly, because this way of thinking is my natural language of self-communion and secondly, I am convinced that it is the best system for the purpose" (qtd. in Leja 97). Such a bias leads to difficulties when we try to incorporate the other senses in a general hermeneutic of presence. But they suit my current purpose exactly, the illustrative analysis of a theory of verbal-visual presence in a single work, Wegener's *Origin*.

Presence has its beginnings in the patterns of perception our sensory systems produce, organized in accord with the "laws" of Gestalt psychology. Köhler and his followers were certainly mistaken when they hypothesized that perceptual processes were actually organized along Gestalt lines, hard-wired into the brain (1947). Given the current state of our knowledge of such processes, it would probably be best to regard the Gestalt "laws of organization [as] opportunistic guides to the viewer as to what will afford desired visual information" and to support the view "that they probably vary widely in level, speed, and power" (Hochberg 291). In one plausible accounting, there are six Gestalt principles. According to *figure-ground*, we see objects automatically as shaped, framed against a shapeless background, one that may, in fact, also have a shape, though we do not perceive it as such. When this background actually does have a shape—as in the case of the cell structure of tables or the latitude-longitude coordinates of maps—we can direct our attention alternately to it and to the foreground of data elements. We see a second Gestalt principle in operation, *good continuation*, when we complete in our mind's eye the rectangular shape of a whiteboard despite the fact that the man standing in front of it is partially blocking our view. Scientific tables are characterized by a third Gestalt principle, *enclosure*; on the other hand, relationships among the contents of their cells are highlighted by means of the fourth principle, *similarity and contrast*. A fifth principle, *proximity*, groups adjoining letters of the alphabet into words, even in an early Greek manuscript where there is no actual separation (Hochberg 260–61). A final and overriding principle is *Prägnanz*, the perception of an overall Gestalt. When we arrive home after a long journey, what we see is not windows, doors, and roof but the house we live in.

Gestalt patterns are meaningful only insofar as they participate in a system of value-laden differences. Saussure articulates this principle for language:

> In all these cases what we find, instead of *ideas* given in advance, are *values* emanating from a linguistic system. If we say that these values correspond to certain concepts, it must be understood that the concepts in question are purely differential. That is to say they are concepts defined not positively, in terms of their content, but negatively by contrast with other items

in the same system. What characterizes each most exactly is being whatever the others are not. (115)

Saussure's principle applies generally to any semiotic system. For example, traffic signals and electrical wiring diagrams also rely for their interpretation on value-laden differences. To differentiate these systems from languages, let us call them codes.

Patterns of perception made potentially meaningful according to Saussure's principle are interpreted as Peircian symbols, icons, or indexes. Patterns recognized as verbal are understood as symbols, whose relation to their objects may be, but need not be, arbitrary. Alphabets are systems of wholly arbitrary signs; ideograms are symbols that are not wholly arbitrary. Patterns recognized as non-verbal are understood either as symbols, icons, or indices. An icon is a sign that depicts; a photograph or a drawing of a microbe is an icon; an index is a sign whose relation to its object is causal or indicative. Geiger-counter readings are causally linked to the external world; in a photograph an arrow pointing to a cell nucleus is merely indicative. To avoid ambiguity, let us call this latter category of signs deictic.

For the purposes of exegesis, Peirce's categories are insufficiently fine-grained to capture all meaningful transactions within a system of signs. Accordingly, to interpret the verbal, I borrow from linguistics, narrative theory, logic, and rhetorical theory—analytical perspectives that are, I judge, compatible with his semiotics. I single out as linguistic a semantic concern for the relationship between words and the world, a syntactic concern for the legitimate combinational possibilities of words in sentences, and a pragmatic concern for the effect of natural-language utterances on interlocutors.

Utterances also partake in larger systems of meaning, organized either in chronological sequences or according to logical operations. There are two types of chronological sequences: those that are repeated without change and those that are unique. The first we call processes; the second, narratives. I single out as logical the following operations: definition, classification, implication/inference, and generalization by induction. Definition operates by genus and differentia. A chair is an article of furniture designed for sitting; it has a back and four legs. The genus is furniture; the differentia, designed for sitting, having a back, having four legs. Classification operates by division; it creates hierarchies of categories, each level of which has the same cognitive status within the system specified: For example, the animal kingdom can be divided into creatures with and without backbones. Implication is a property of propositions whereby to commit to one is to commit to another. If all men are mortal, then by implication, all Armenians are mortal. Inference is the psychological process by which this implication is realized. Induction is generalization from a necessarily limited set of instances: from the genetics of some peas to the genetics of all peas, from the genetics of all peas to all genetics.

I single out as rhetorical the three traditional canons that are the sources of persuasion in oral and written communication: the invention of arguments that however persuasive would not pass muster in formal logic; the arrangement or organization of discourses with persuasion in mind; and style, the systematic use of persuasively significant variations in the means of expression. Traditionally, invention is subdivided into three forms of appeal: *logos*, appeals from reasoning; *ethos*, appeals based on the trust that the author creates in the reader; and *pathos,* appeals to the emotions of the auditor or reader.

I now move from the verbal to the visual. While we see images, we do not ordinarily see words; rather, we see through them to their underlying concepts. This is what reading means. The verbal and the visual also differ in the way they are organized. Words are ordered in sequential hierarchical structures composed of combinations of smaller units linked by systematical internal connections. A paragraph is composed of a sequence of sentences, composed of sequences of clauses and phrases, composed of sequences of words, composed of sequences of letters. Images, on the other hand, are ordered into synchronous hierarchies or nested sets. A face is composed of a nested set of eyes, eye-brows, nose, mouth, teeth, ears, brow, and cheeks. When organized into larger units, moreover, words never entirely lose their separate identities; the components of images, on the other hand, tend to lose their separate identity as they become embedded or nested. We see a face, not its components; we see, not an intricate nesting of various Gestalts but, as a consequence of *Prägnanz,* a single Gestalt. The verbal and the visual are also processed differently. Words are processed sequentially; in contrast, images can be processed not only sequentially but also in parallel and simultaneously.

Images differ from words in one other important respect: They are subject to semiotically relevant spatial transformations. They can be rotated on their axes: Subjected to this transformation, topographical surfaces reveal geological depths. Three-dimensional objects may also be projected onto two-dimensional surfaces; we do so when we create a map. One image, moreover, may be superimposed on another, an effect achieved when lines of latitude or longitude are applied to maps. In addition, a sequence of visuals may be animated; this is how temporal progression is routinely represented in films (Clark and Paivio 151–52).

Other transformations are possible. Some take place within a particular category of sign. For example, a photograph of an eye may be used to construct a drawing of the eye, a shift from one iconic mode to another. Some transformations involve a shift from one category of sign to another. A series of measurements may be used to construct a line graph, a shift from the symbolic to the iconic. The iconic may also be transformed into symbolic: Photographs of *an* eye may become a diagram of *the* eye. Finally, the iconic may be transformed into the indexical: A chest x-ray may reveal the cause of a persistent cough. Thomas Sebeok makes the essential point about the plasticity of the Peircian categories:

> In general, it is … inane to ask whether any given subject "is," or is represented by, an icon, an index, or a symbol, for all signs are situated in a complex network of syntagmatic and paradigmatic contrasts and oppositions, i.e., simultaneously participate in a text as well as a system; it is their position at a particular moment that will determine the predominance of the aspect in focus. ("Iconicity" 1433n)

As Gérard Deladalle points out:

> [W]e must insist … on the functional character of these distinctions: what is an index in one semiosis may be a symbol in another. Take, for instance, the symptom of an illness. … If this

symptom is referred to in a lecture on medicine as always characterizing a certain illness, the symptom is a symbol. If the doctor encounters it while he is examining a patient, the symptom is an index of an illness. (19–20)

The contention of Sebeok and Deladalle that context is central to semiotic interpretation is a generalization of Saussure's principle that meaning is constituted by difference.

Allan Paivio's Dual Coding Theory (DCT), on which I will rely in the remainder of this essay, takes the differences between the verbal and the visual seriously into account. Why DCT? Indeed, why theory? If my goal were no more than a plausible exegesis of an instance of verbal-visual interaction, theory might be regarded as superfluous. But my goal is a hermeneutics that is also psychologically real, an exegesis supported in principle by evidence derived from a program of experimentation in cognitive psychology, governed always by the actual constraints and affordances of perceptual and cognitive processing. While it remains true that "virtually nothing is known about either the logic or the psychology of scientific hypothesis formation and confirmation," a lack of substantial progress toward a worthy goal does not mean that we must remain satisfied with ungrounded exegetical practices (Wilson and Sperber 586). Because DCT insists on psychological adequacy, it keeps our exegeses honest. DCT is also useful because it has heuristic potential. First, it gives us a criterion for choosing from a wide array of tools those that work together coherently in the exegetical task DCT sets for us—the creation and communication of meaning by means of verbal-visual interaction. More generally, DCT reorients rhetorical criticism in the direction of a pressing exigency: the fact that while dealing with solely verbal texts has been the rule in rhetorical criticism, in the real world such texts are the exception.

This high praise for DCT does not mean that it can be employed as is; for exegetical purposes it must be amended. On DCT's verbal side, I have added linguistics, logic, and narrative theory; on its visual side, I have added Gestalt theory to organize perceptions and Peirce's semiotics to interpret them. For all of these components, however, the criterion of psychological realism raises the epistemic stakes. It is now insufficient that they be compatible with DCT; instead, they must be integral; they must actually constitute DCT's fine-structure. At this point in the progress of cognitive psychology, it is true that we cannot, as a general rule, meet this standard. Gestalt Theory does meet it; Peirce's semiotics does not. But the principle will continue to hold that as cognitive psychology advances, so should the hermeneutics of verbal-visual interaction.

Figure 20.1 presents us with a model of verbal-visual interaction. At the top of the diagram, verbal and nonverbal stimuli enter *our sensory system* and, by means of representational connections, are channeled into either the verbal or the nonverbal associative system, two separate processing units linked by referential connections. At the bottom of the diagram are the verbal and nonverbal responses that are the output of the model. These constitute everything human beings do to create and to communicate meaning. By means of associative connections in varying configurations and of varying strengths, the system as a whole represents, from one perspective, memory and, from another, the organization of knowledge in the brain. As Paivio says, "knowledge is memory" (27).

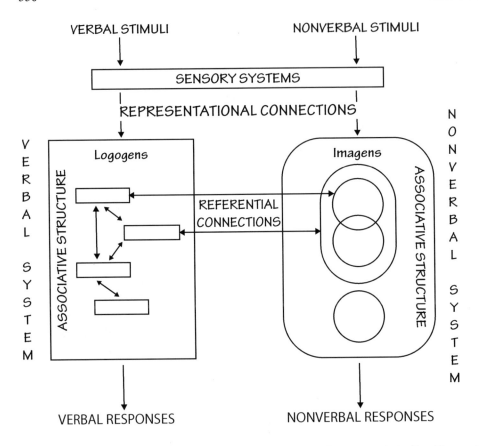

Figure 20.1 A Model of Verbal and Visual Processing According to Dual Coding Theory. From
        Paivio, 34 (Figure 3.1). This diagram shows the representational units and their refer-
        ential (between-system) and associative (within system) interconnections.

In this theory we store the verbal as logogens, the nonverbal—shapes, sounds,
actions, and visceral sensations related to emotions—as imagens. Logogens are not
words; imagens are not images. These terms are used "to distinguish the 'dormant'
verbal and non-verbal representational units from their consciously experienced verbal
and non-verbal images and their behavioral expressions." While imagens are analogous
to what they represent, this is not true of logogens, which are stored in various modalities: "auditory, visual, motor, haptic [that is, those related to the sense of touch]" (37).
Unless they are activated, a process that "occurs via pathways that connect representational units to the external world and to each other," isolated logogens do not mean.
Meaning involves "the juxtaposition of a logogen and referentially related imagens or
associatively related logogens" (41).

For Paivio, all links—those between logogens and imagens considered separately
and those that join logogens to imagens—are associational. For Paivio, therefore, the
links among linguistic components we characterize as syntax, semantics, and pragmatics are at their most basic level simply strong associations. Similarly, the logical
operations of definition, classification, implication/inference, and generalization by

induction at their most basic level mirror strong associational links. This is equally true of the realizations of temporal succession from which narratives are built. Analogously, in the imagens association system, what the Gestalt psychologists call laws of pattern perception, Paivio must attribute at their most basic level to the strength among associations that allows us to recognize patterns as patterns, and, subsequently, as objects or events. To turn Paivio's theory into a systematic hermeneutic capable of detailed exegesis, I need to employ rule-governed patterns from Gestalt psychology, Pierce's semiotics, linguistics, logic, and narrative theory. No theoretical damage is done, however, if what I call rule-governed patterns are regarded merely as strong associational links.

Combining Gestalt psychology, Peirce's semiotics, and Paivio's Dual Coding Theory, I have outlined a process by which the interaction of the verbal and the visual leads from perception to meaning. In so doing, seemingly, I face a difficulty: Surely, a theory of meaning and a theory of presence are not the same. This difficulty, however, is only apparent. In *Chaïm Perelman*, Ray Dearin and I defined a "superordinate" form of presence as the "cumulative effect of interactions" among arrangement, style, and invention (135). But to say this, I think, is the equivalent of saying that while rhetoric's function is, in Aristotle's words, "to see the available means of persuasion in each case" (1355a), the effective employment of these means in a particular case creates by the operation of *Prägnanz* the single Gestalt that is the psychological equivalent of presence, the rhetorical concept at issue. In persuasive texts to trace the genealogy of presence is to reveal it as the synergy of "all the available means of persuasion." In this essay I solve the mystery of presence in Wegener's *The Origin of Continents and Oceans* by showing how the synergy of all of the available verbal and visual means of persuasion create an overarching perceptual, argumentative, and narrative Gestalt.

The Structure of Wegener's Argument

By both historians of geology and geologists, Wegener has been routinely called the father of the theory of Continental Drift, a scientific revolution with a place in geology as important as Copernican heliocentricity in astronomy. Others had suggested continental drift as a cause of the current configurations of the earth's surface, but it was Wegener's *Origin* that created a lively and durable conversation and controversy among the community of geologists (Schwarzbach). The structure of Wegener's provocative argument is inductive, a movement from the specific to the general. By means of words and images, he attempts to convince his readers of what was then a startlingly counterintuitive claim: The earth is "not a solid body … but exhibits flow and is subject to" continental movements, the wandering of the earth's crust, and probably also the displacement of its axis (164). He attempts to convince readers that its continents and islands, once joined into one massive body of land, Pangaea, drifted apart over many eons "like pieces of a cracked ice floe in water" (17).

To make his difficult argument, Wegener relies on a confluence of inductive inferences drawn from very different classes of evidence: "The determination and proof of relative continental displacements," he asserts, "have proceeded purely empirically, that is, by means of the totality of geodetic, geophysical, geological, biological, and paleoclimatic data. … This is the inductive method." (167). This confluence among classes of evidence transforms Wegener's argument into what English philosopher William Whewell calls a consilience of inductions. Surprise is a crucial element in making this consilience convincing. For example, recounting the geological and paleontological evidence for climate change that is best explained as an index of drift, he says: "The prodigious number of facts which can be utilized in this way as fossil evidence of climate shows surprisingly [*überraschenderweise*] that in prehistoric times most parts of the earth had very different climates from those of today" (126; see also 91).

While there is some discomfort among philosophers concerning the incorporation of surprise, a psychological effect, into any theory of confirmation, neither Whewell, the theorist of consilience, nor Wegener, its practitioner, has any scruples in so doing (compare Laudan; Fish; Forster). After all, if the theory that the continents are fixed in place is presupposed, then the converging evidence for drift is bound to be surprising. Moreover, this surprise is the psychological correlative of an underlying epistemological phenomenon: the avalanche of converging evidence that decisively undermines the received theory and at the same time supports its competitor. The degree of surprise incident on consilience corresponds roughly to the degree to which the theory under attack fails.

Because Wegener wishes to make continental drift—a phenomenon that his readers cannot experience—as present for them as possible, it is unsurprising that virtually all of his inductions have a strong visual component: Wegener moves constantly between Paivio's verbal and his nonverbal system. An induction from geophysics, the subject of chapter 4, exemplifies Wegener's practice. In this chapter a host of individual measurements is transformed into the curve shown in Figure 20.2, created from a base of

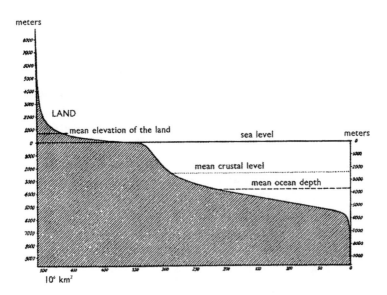

Figure 20.2 Hypsometric Curve of the Earth's Surface (According to Krümmel). From Wegener, 35 (Figure 7).

measurements that subdivides the surface of the earth into one kilometer squares and subsequently arranges this data in order of height above and below sea level (35–36). The significance of the graph lies in its suggestion that the earth is divided into two layers, an impression reinforced by the strong Gestalt contrast between the relatively light sial forming the "mean elevation of land," and the relatively heavy sima, the "mean ocean depth." This coded representation of Cartesian space transforms Wegener's data into an iconic depiction of the earth's surface, a depiction with indexical implications. If a light sial "floats" on a heavy sima, drift is possible. In this interaction between the verbal and the visual, conceptual presence is made palpable.

In Figure 20.3, while Wegener maintains the same graphic code, he transforms the curve from Figure 20.2 so that its bimodal distribution is visually unequivocal. This is effected by superimposing the bimodal solid curve on its dotted normal counterpart: a striking Gestalt contrast. The implication is indexical: Because bimodal distribution is real, continental drift may be real. As a consequence of its transformation from the iconic to the symbolic, Figure 20.3 has become conceptually transparent. This is in accord with Bertin's insight that "the most efficient constructions are those in which any question, whatever its type and level, can be answered in a single instant of perception, that is, IN A SINGLE IMAGE" (146). Bertin is clearly talking about *Prägnanz*, a conceptual *Prägnanz*.

In Figure 20.4, the solid curve is transformed into its mechanical counterpart, an iconic schematization with indexical implications. Its components are differentiated by a visual code: In this diagram the crust is divided into sial, represented by diagonal hatching, and its underlying sima, represented by the dotted area. The horizontal hatching above the sima represents the ocean. Gestalt contrast designates the components; their interaction is suggested by Gestalt proximity.

Figure 20.4 also has a symbolic dimension. It is a model that stands for *any* continental edge. This symbolic transformation is consistent equally with the data and with drift theory. To see drift, we need only to animate the model within the context of the earth's evolving geology. If this is done, what has been presented as the state of the earth at any one time will be transformed into its changing state over time.

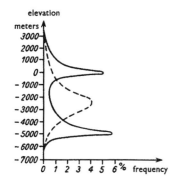

Figure 20.3 The Two Maxima in the Frequency Distribution of Elevations. From Wegener, 36 (Figure 8).

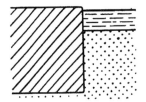

Figure 20.4 Diagrammatic Cross Section Through a Continental Margin. Horizontal hatching = Water. From Wegener, 36 (Figure 9).

Wegener Transforms his Argument into a Narrative

Because geology is also an historical science, Wegener's inductive argument for drift must be transformed into a narrative of drift, a sequence of events that represents the unique past of the earth. This transformation is foreshadowed early in Wegener's monograph. In the series of maps reproduced in Figure 20.5, Wegener reconstructs the earth's history during three successive geological epochs: the upper carboniferous (about 310 million years ago), the eocene (around 58 million years ago), and the lower quaternary (about 1.5 million years ago). As we move from epoch to epoch, the white space always in the foreground functions in accord with the first principle of Gestalt: It gradually emerges as the present configuration of continents and oceans. In addition, the land mass that was to become South America drifts away from western Africa by the length of the Atlantic Ocean and, simultaneously, rotates about sixty degrees clockwise to achieve its current configuration. These three maps—three snapshots in a sequence that can achieve its full effect only when animated—are not pictures of the earth; rather, they are conjectures as to its development over geological time. They presage the narrative that can be responsibly told only after the argument that will support it has been diligently constructed. They are indexical only in intent.

In Figures 20.6 and 20.7, the visual hypothesis presented in Figure 20.5 is tested against iconic representations of the actual geology of the continents of Africa and South America and the Oceanic rift between them. The map of western Africa in Figure 20.6 depicts strike, the horizontal direction of a stratum, rendered visible by means of the Gestalt principle of contrast and rendered meaningful as part of a cartographic code. Two indications of strike are relevant to the argument in favor of drift: an older, northeastern strike parallel to the upper reaches of the Niger south-west of Tombouctou (Timbuctu, in present-day Mali) and a newer one, just visible in the lower right-hand corner of the map, just east of Annobon Island. The direction of these strikes and those in South America will support a narrative in favor of drift if, when they are brought together, they fit exactly, like the pieces of a jigsaw puzzle.

Figure 20.7 is also an iconic representation that maps strike directions, this time in South America. These also have been rendered visible by means of the Gestalt principle of contrast and rendered meaningful by means of a cartographic code. To see the conformity between the two western African strike directions and these, a conformity essential to Wegener's narrative, we must rotate the map sixty degrees

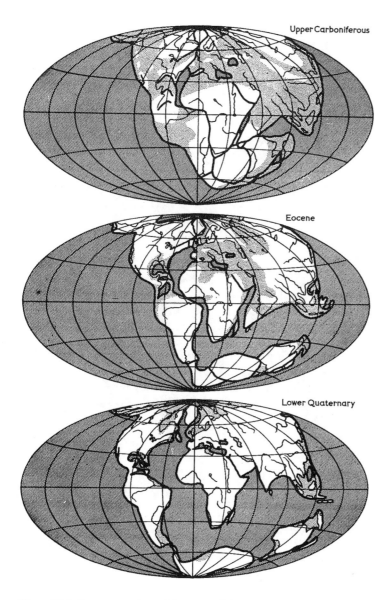

Figure 20.5 Reconstruction of the Map of the World According to Drift Theory for Three Epochs. Hatching denotes oceans, dotted areas are shallow seas; present-day outlines and rivers are given simply to aid identification. The map grid is arbitrary. From Wegener, 18 (Figure 4).

counterclockwise in order to take "into account the large angle through which South America must be turned in our reconstruction." As a result of this epistemologically significant rotation, "the direction of the Amazon becomes exactly parallel to that of the upper course of the Niger [the line just above Tombouctou], so that the two strike directions coincide with the African ones" (66). As a result, the two maps fuse into a single *Prägnanz*, a metonym for the theory. The iconic has now been transformed into

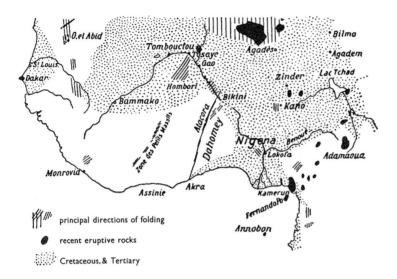

Figure 20.6 Strike Directions in Western Africa (According to Lemoine). From Wegener, 65 (Figure 16).

the indexical, the map into the cause of one of its features, a feature that drift theory has made significant.

Toward the end of his monograph, the transformation from indexical argument into indexical narrative, foreshadowed in Figure 20.5, is realized in the fine structure of Wegener's prose. Logical operators, emphasized in this excerpt, simultaneously drive argument and narrative:

> If the basalt layer under the granite was really specially fluid as assumed, *then* as the Atlantic rift opened wider progressively, this layer would have had to rise up here, subsequently flowing steadily out from both sides; it would first have formed the whole ocean floor, and would still today form the greater part of it. As the rift opened up progressively wider, the ability of even this material to flow *must finally have* become inadequate, and the underlying dunite *must have been* exposed as windows in the basalt. (211–12; italics added)

Wegener's narrative has a dual structure. Each of its episodes is related conceptually to every other: Each instantiates a geophysical process. As the repetitive chronological sequence develops, however, a second, unique structure manifests itself, one that is specifically narrative. On one level, the geophysical processes cycle and recycle; simultaneously, on another level, a plot unfolds from which emerges the unique configuration of the earth's oceans and land masses. Out of argumentative presence its narrative counterpart emerges.

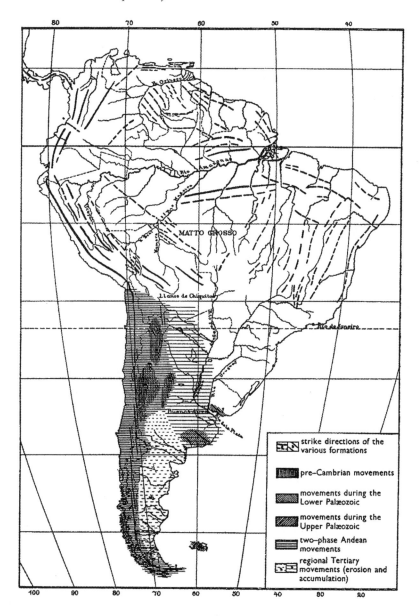

Figure 20.7 Diagrammatic Tectonic Map of South America, According to Keidel and J. W. Evans. From Wegener, 67 (Figure 17).

From Science to Advocacy

So far I have assumed that there is no discrepancy between what Wegener asserts about the history of the earth and what can legitimately be inferred from the visuals from which his assertions derive; I have assumed that the verbal and the visual are fully compatible. This assumption must now be interrogated. In fact, Wegener's narrative was systematically undermined for most of the geologists in his audience because, throughout *The Origin*, he exhibited a confidence in his hypothesis that his visual evidence did not support. This overconfidence is embodied in his manipulation of the rhetorical categories of style and arrangement, a manipulation with a *pathotic* valence: His was an argument that generated heat as well as light. For example, concerning the continental configuration displayed in Figures 20.6 and 20.7, he said:

> By comparing the geological structure of both sides of the Atlantic we can provide a very clear-cut test [*scharfes Kontrolle*] of our theory that this ocean region is an enormously widened rift whose edges were once directly connected, or so nearly as makes no difference. This is because one would expect that many folds and other formations that arose before the split occurred would conform on both sides, and in fact their terminal sections on either side of the ocean must have been so situated that they appear as direct continuations of each in a reconstruction of the original state of affairs. Since the reconstruction itself is necessarily unambiguous [*zwangsläufige*] because of the well-marked outlines of the margins and allows no scope for juggling [*keinen Spielraum für eine Anpassung*], we have here a totally independent criterion [*einem ganz unabhängigen Kriterium*] of the highest importance [*von grö ter Bedeutung*] for assessing the correctness [*der Richtigkeit*] of drift theory. (61)

This verbal swagger, of which many additional examples may readily be adduced, transforms Wegener from a scientist into an advocate. This advocate's stance leads him systematically to slight his opponents' arguments by means of dismissals so curt as to foster skepticism about their motive: "[T]hese objections, so far as they are not just misunderstandings," he asserts, "mostly involve mere side-issues whose solution would have little significance for the basic concepts of drift theory" (96). At times Wegener goes further; he ignores his opponents' arguments altogether: "We shall refrain here from citing the literature in support of our statements. The obvious needs no backing by outside opinion, and the willfully blind cannot be helped by any means" (133; see also 97, 213). This diminution of his opponents' presence can be visual as well as verbal. Wegener literally sweeps these opponents under the rug: He buries opposing arguments and their refutations in footnotes (99n; see also 100n, 104n, 113n, 120n, 210n; 215–26n). His treatment of Ökland is a dramatic instance of such interment. In the text Öklund's views seem to accord with drift theory. Only from the footnote do we learn that he actually rejects drift theory in favor of sunken-continent theory, ignoring, so Wegener asserts, its "geophysical untenability [*Unhaltbarkeit*]" (103n). In this case, Gestalt foreground and background have been flagrantly manipulated in the interest of advocacy.

Wegener's was a modest success. His monograph was translated into French and English and his theory was adopted by a few, for the most part Continental, geologists. Its reception in England, and especially in the United States, however, was largely negative, even hostile (LeGrand 55–69). The most plausible explanation to date for this relative failure is that of historian Naomi Oreskes. She traces the early rejection of continental drift, especially by the American geological community, to two interlinked preferences. The first is a methodological preference for evidence that appears to be independent because its source, instrumental readings, has apparently eliminated the subjective judgment of the observer (304). The second is the identification of false but useful theories with the truth. Uniformitarianism—the belief that the continents and oceans were always more or less as they are now—"was ·enabling. It enabled [American geologists] to interpret field evidence in a consistent and logical way" (314). To these explanations of the American resistance to drift, I would like to add a third: Wegener's systematic violation of the norms of scientific argument, exhibited most dramatically in the contrast between what his visuals equivocally suggest and what his words unequivocally assert. For many geologists, what was present in *The Origin of Continents and Oceans* was this contrast, not Wegener's theory.

Conclusion

The exegesis of the principle of presence was chosen deliberatively as an exemplification of a new theoretical outlook. It is Perelman and Olbrechts-Tyteca who make it clear that presence originates in human psychology, a move that I interpret as an endorsement of explanations of its origin within a framework provided by cognitive psychology. But my analysis of Wegener's *Origin* is designed to illustrate the general superiority of a theory of verbal interaction founded on cognitive psychology, on the affordances and constraints of human cognition: This analysis is designed to illustrate what a good theory enables us to *see*. Only the employment of such a theory, I believe, can avoid the unwelcome subjectivity interpretive license otherwise affords; only in this way can textual analysis advance as our understanding of human cognition advances.

From this point of view, the exegesis of the genealogy of presence in Wegener's *Origin* constitutes a model for what must be done if textual analysis is to become a science, not in the narrow sense of the English word, but in the wider sense of the German *Wissenschaft*, a reasonably accurate translation of the Aristotelian *epistēmē*, the serious study of anything. In my view, Aristotle's *Rhetoric* was the first step in this direction. It is a mistake, I believe, to interpret the *Rhetoric* as *doxa* on the grounds that the material of rhetoric is *doxa*. In my view, the *Rhetoric*, rightly viewed, is an *epistēmē* of *doxa*; it is a view I share with Edmund Husserl and Martin Heidegger. While Husserl does not mention the *Rhetoric*, he refers to the commonplaces and commonplace arguments that form the substantive core of that work: "[W]e seek in vain in world literature for investigations that could serve as preparatory studies for us—investigations that might have understood this task as that of a science in its own right (a peculiar science to be sure, since it concerns the disparaged δοξά [*doxa*], which now suddenly claims the dignity of a foundation for science, επιστημη [*epistēmē*])" (155–56). In *Being and Time*, Heidegger says of Aristotle's treatment of the emotions in the *Rhetoric* that it is "the first systematic hermeneutic of the everydayness of Being with one another [*die erste systematische Hermeneutik der Alltäglichkeit des Miteinanderseins*]" (138). Heidegger gets it exactly right.

Note

1 I would like to thank Richard Enos and Michael Zerbe for all of their help.

Works Cited

Aristotle. *On Rhetoric: A Theory of Civic Discourse.* Trans. George Kennedy. New York: Oxford UP, 1991.

Bazerman, Charles. *Shaping Written Knowledge: The Genre and Activity of the Experimental Article in Science.* Madison: U of Wisconsin P, 1988.

Bertin, Jacques. *Semiology of Graphics: Diagrams, Networks, Maps.* Trans. W. J. Berg. Madison: U of Wisconsin P, 1983.

Ceccarelli, Leah. *Shaping Science with Rhetoric: The Cases of Dobzhansky, Schrödinger, and Wilson.* Chicago: U of Chicago P, 2001.

Clark, James M., and Allan Paivio. "Dual Coding and Education." *Educational Psychology Review* 3 (1991): 149–210.

Condit, Celeste Michelle. *The Meanings of the Gene: Public Debates About Human Heredity.* Madison: U of Wisconsin P, 1999.

Deledalle, Gérard. *Charles S. Peirce's Philosophy of Signs: Essays in Comparative Literature.* Bloomington: Indiana UP, 2000.

Fahnestock, Jeanne. *Rhetorical Figures in Science.* New York: Oxford UP, 1999.

Finnegan, Cara A. "Review Essay: Visual Studies and Visual Rhetoric." *Quarterly Journal of Speech* 90 (2004): 234–56.

Fish, Menachem. "Whewell's Consilience of Inductions—An Evaluation." *Philosophy of Science* 52 (1985): 239–55.

Forster, Malcolm R. "The Confirmation of Common Component Causes." *PSA: Proceedings of the Biennial Meeting of the Philosophy of Science Association* I (1988): 3–9.

Foss, Sonja K. "A Rhetorical Schema for the Evaluation of Visual Imagery." *Communication Studies* 45 (1994): 213–24.

Gross, Alan G. "Presence as Argument in the Public Sphere." *Rhetoric Society Quarterly* 35 (2005): 5–21.

Gross, Alan G., Joseph E. Harmon, and Michael Reidy. *Communicating Science: The Scientific Article from the 17th Century to the Present.* New York: Oxford UP, 2002.

Heidegger, Martin. *Being and Time.* Trans. John Macquarrie and Edward Robinson. New York: Harper and Row, 1962.

——. *Sein und Zeit.* Tübingen: Max Niemeyer Verlag, 1972.

Hochberg, Julian. "Gestalt Theory and Its Legacy: Organization in Eye and Brain, in Attention and Mental Representation." *Perception and Cognition at Century's End.* Ed. J. Hochberg. San Diego: Academy, 1998. 253–306.

Husserl, Edmund. *The Crisis of European Sciences and Transcendal Phenomenology.* Evanston: Northwestern UP, 1970.

Köhler, Wolfgang. *Gestalt Psychology: An Introduction to New Concepts in Modern Psychology.* New York: New American Library, 1947.

Laudan, Larry. "William Whewell on the Consilience of Inductions." *Monist* 55 (1971): 368–91.

LeGrand, Homer E. *Drifting Continents and Shifting Theories.* Cambridge: Cambridge UP, 1988.

Leja, Michael. "Peirce, Visuality, and Art." *Representations* 72 (2000): 97–122.

Moss, Jean D. *Novelties in the Heavens: Rhetoric and Science in the Copernican Controversy.* Chicago: U of Chicago P, 1993.

Myers, Greg. *Writing Biology: Texts in the Social Construction of Scientific Knowledge.* Madison: U of Wisconsin P, 1990.

Olson, Lester C. "Intellectual and Conceptual Resources for Visual Rhetoric: A Re-examination of the Scholarship since 1950." *The Review of Communication* 7 (2007): 1–20.

Olson, Lester C., Cara A. Finnegan, and Diane S. Hope, eds. *Visual Rhetoric: A Reader in Communication and American Culture.* Los Angeles: Sage, 2008.

Oreskes, Naomi. *The Rejection of Continental Drift: Theory and Method in American Earth Science.* New York: Oxford UP, 1999.

Paivio, Allan. *Mind and its Evolution: A Dual Coding Theoretical Approach.* Mahwah, NJ: Erlbaum, 2007.

Perelman, Chaïm and Lucie Olbrechts-Tyteca. *The New Rhetoric: A Treatise on Argumentation.* Trans. John Wilkinson and P. Weaver. Notre Dame: U of Notre Dame P, 1969.

Peterson, Valerie. "The Rhetorical Criticism of Visual Elements: An Alternative to Foss's Schema." *Southern Communication Journal* 67 (2001): 19–32.

Prelli, Lawrence J. *A Rhetoric of Science: Inventing Scientific Discourse.* Columbia: U of South Carolina P, 1989.

Saussure, Ferdinand de. *Course in General Linguistics.* 1916. Trans. Ray Harris. Ed. Chales Bally, Albert Sechehasye, and Albert Riedlinger. La Salle, IL: Open Court, 1986.

Sebeok, Thomas A. "Iconicity." *MLN* 9 (1976): 1427–56.

——. "Indexicality." *Peirce and Contemporary Thought: Philosophical Inquiries.* Ed. Kenneth Laine Ketner. New York: Fordham UP, 1995. 222–42.

Van Waterschoot van der Gracht, William A. J. M., et al., eds. *Theory of Continental Drift: A Symposium on the Origin and Movement of Land Masses Both Inter-Continental and Intra-Continental, as Proposed by Alfred Wegener.* Tulsa, OK: The American Association of Petroleum Geologists, 1928.

Wegener, Alfred. *Die Entstehung der Kontinente und Ozeane.* 4th ed. Braunschweig: Friedrich Vieweg und Sohn, 1929.

——. *The Origin of Continents and Oceans.* 4th ed. Trans. J. Biram. New York: Dover, 1966.

Whewell, William. *Selected Writings on the History of Science.* Ed. Y. Elkana. Chicago: U of Chicago P, 1984.

Wilson, Deirdre and Dan Sperber. "Pragmatics and Modularity." *Pragmatics: A Reader.* Ed. Steven Davis. New York: Oxford U P, 1991. 583–95.

21.
NETWORKS, GENRES, AND COMPLEX WHOLES

Citizen Science and How We Act Together through Typified Text
by Ashley Rose Mehlenbacher and Kate Maddalena

Introduction

In 2011, a massive tsunami resulting from a 9.0 magnitude earthquake crashed over a ten-metre-high seawall and devastated the already stricken Fukushima Daiichi nuclear power generation site. Some five years after the multi-reactor failure, the crisis at the site continues, and the environmental, health, and safety risks borne of the disaster continue to be debated and studied. Nuclear disaster has been attended to for decades in scientific and science studies literature, of course. For social studies of science, both the accidents at Three Mile Island and Chernobyl provide important cases for understanding the social construction of risk (Goodnight, 1982; Wynne, 1992), risk and crisis communication, and the inevitability of disaster in technoscientific modernity (Beck, 1992). However, as the disaster at Fukushima unfolded, new possibilities for responding to the disaster and its risks did as well. We can characterize these possibilities in terms of technological affordances that provided new ways of organizing people, information, and knowledge-making practices, namely through networked technologies. For example, Twitter spread news as it unfolded and Wikipedia allowed for various information to be documented (Mehlenbacher & Miller, 2016). New media forms and their affordances do not exist in material form alone, but also within the rhetorical possibilities we imprint on them. To better understand how the material affordances of new media are taken up, a rhetorical account helps document the exigencies to which we respond, the situational constraints of our responses, and the forms or patterns that constrain our possible utterances (cf., rhetorical situation in Bitzer, 1968; Miller, 1984, 1992; Vatz, 1973).

To productively engage and entangle these areas of study we first explore a number of intersecting literatures in an effort to productively align and challenge theoretical constructs that help us understand where and how we find possibilities for utterance, information sharing, knowledge production and sharing, and ultimately scientific research within networked new media forms. Bringing together the work of Rhetorical Genre Theory (RGT) and Actor-Network Theory (ANT) in rhetorical studies of science and social studies of science, we offer an illustrative theoretical account of useful and

Ashley Rose Mehlenbacher and Kate Maddalena. "Networks, Genres, and Complex Wholes: Citizen Science and How We Act Together through Typified Text." *Canadian Journal of Communication*, Volume 41, Number 2, 2016, pp. 287–303.

complex analytical strategies and theoretical entailments we have uncovered at the inter-sections of these fields. Building on our previous work in this area (Mehlenbacher & Maddalena, 2015), we suggest by way of a case study that these new forms and possibil-ities are complicated by new technologies and new genres.

Exploring the Integrated Fukushima Ocean Radionuclide Monitoring (InFORM) Network as our case, we investigate how Actor-Network Theory and Rhetorical Genre Theory highlight different aspects of the network and its actors. InFORM is a Cana-dian research network that studies radiological risk in coastal seawater in the Pacific Ocean following the disaster at Fukushima Daiichi Nuclear Power Plant (FD-NPP), which released radionuclides into seawater through atmospheric and water-based con-tamination. Models predicting the arrival of these radionuclides, InFORM argues, include a great deal of uncertainty. Given uncertainty in models, InFORM works to collect on-the-ground—or, rather, in-the-ocean—data to monitor arrival times and contamination levels of seawater along the Canadian pacific coast. Data collection is accomplished with the use of a sampling kit and the labour of academics and citizen scientists. In this article we explore how InFORM reveals a complex case of actors, agents, and networks that formed in response to uncertainties in the aftermath of the Fukushima nuclear disaster.

In the pages that follow, we review pertinent literature in rhetoric of science, tech-nology, and medicine in both Canadian and U.S. contexts, as well as intersecting work from science studies broadly conceived. We focus specifically on ANT and RGT perspec-tives as a means to describe how networks are produced by (and produce) objects, or "complex wholes," that act suasively. We then turn to the InFORM network as a response to the events at Fukushima and focus very narrowly on the tool that InFORM citizen scientists use to sample ocean water for the purpose of data collection. Our ana-lysis yields several insights about how ANT and RGT complement each other. The concept of the material "complex whole" (Mol, 2003) allows us to see a data-collecting instrument as a genre in itself; the concept of rhetorical genre may allow us to conceptu-alize agents and their agency more completely. Finally, we see the combined method as an argument for the uptake of Rhetorical Genre Theory in science studies, a turn being taken in the rhetoric of science, but that remains mostly absent from broader science studies.

Science as Social Action

When the 2011 Tōhoku earthquake and tsunami hit the coast of Japan, natural disaster and modern risks combined in the cascading failures at the Fukushima Daiichi nuclear generation station. Three of six reactors at the site were badly damaged, and as the situ-ation unfolded a great deal of uncertainty drove speculative discourses and proleptic rea-soning. Will the reactors meltdown? What does *meltdown* mean anyway? Will radiation reach foreign coasts? (For examples of such discourse, see Kinsella, Mehlenbacher, & Kittle Autry, 2013) While some efforts to dispel fear focused on informing publics about nuclear science and engineering in energy production through broadcast media and direct encounter (Ionescu, 2012), others used this event to create an opportunity for publics to help inform scientific research (Mehlenbacher 2016, Mehlenbacher & Miller, 2016).

Canada's Integrated Fukushima Ocean Radionuclide Monitoring (InFORM) Network is one example of a project involving citizens in the production of scientific knowledge. A press release from August 2014 describes the project, led by chemical oceanographer Jay Cullen at the University of Victoria, as a "new marine radioactivity monitoring network that will engage scientists in Canada and the US, health experts, non-governmental organizations—and citizen scientists along the British Columbia coast" (University of Victoria, 2014). As the press release continues, and as the project unfolds, the complexity of the network begins to unfold. Constituting the network is not only the human actors—the organizational actors—but also a multitude of materialities; geographies; conceptual and theoretical constructions and norms; and textual productions. The shape of coasts, patterns of habitation and points of access, ocean currents and wind patterns, roads and transportation systems, scientific methods, scientific training, training and reporting documentation, and scientific tools are central to the construction and reconstruction of the InFORM network, or similar enterprises.

What spurred such a complex network is of significant rhetorical interest because the exigence is likewise complex. A lack of information about the condition of the Fukushima nuclear site generated much speculation. Such a lack of information and reliable data from which to draw conclusions generates an exigence to which InFORM and others (Mehlenbacher & Miller, 2016) respond by developing strategies to collect and interpret data on their own. InFORM takes up the particular problem of radionuclides in the Pacific Ocean, saying "an urgent *end-user demand* for quality, timely, monitoring data that can be used to estimate public health risks associated with the presence of FD-NPP derived radionuclides in the marine environment and to *provide citizens with reliable information* so that they may minimize their exposure to potentially harmful levels of radiation" (InFORM, 2015, emphasis ours). Data collection alone, as the emphasized phrases indicate, is not the sole response of InFORM. Rather, we see here that collecting and producing data for citizens is cited as an important part of their work. Such a move to provide publics with data about resulting contamination from the Fukushima disaster is not unprecedented (c.f., Mehlenbacher, 2014; Mehlenbacher, 2016; Mehlenbacher & Miller, 2016), but this is an important trend in rhetorical responses worth noting. Part of the rhetorical situation to which InFORM and other radiation contamination sensing projects respond is an exigence for publicly available and useable data. Or, perhaps, we might say a continuing exigence. In early April 2015 the first traces of radioactive material originating from Fukushima were detected in seawater off the coast of British Columbia. Reports in the mainstream media covering the findings cite the InFORM project's Jay Cullen, who discusses the significance and some of the science behind the findings (see, for example, Stueck, 2015). Media coverage highlights the continuing exigence to which InFORM responds.

With a general sense of the exigencies—the need for information, for data, for publicly accessible and useable data (Mehlenbacher & Miller, 2016)—we can look more closely at the composition of the response. Though there are many kinds of rhetorical objects produced by the InFORM network we could theorize, many of them appear to fall into traditional categories of scientific genres, including proposals, lab notebooks, or instructions and procedure manuals. These traditional genres of science communication have been studied in their various forms and fall into what we might describe as "internal" genres of science communication. As one might expect, where there are internal genres there are also external, and we could explore how newsletters, newspaper articles, and press releases are used to share scientific knowledge. We could also explore emerging genres of science communication found on the web as unique objects of study: the website (where resources, news, and affiliates are detailed and a blog is housed); the blog itself with its multimodal embedded genres, such as video and images; social media sites, including Facebook and Twitter, put to work for sharing; community computing for data production; or even the forum for citizen scientists to discuss their work (see Mehlenbacher, 2016; Mehlenbacher & Maddalena, 2015; Mehlenbacher & Miller, 2016). All of these are interesting and worthy of study, certainly, but we are specifically interested in attending to the rhetorical situation by examining the intersection of the material and semiotic, exemplified in data collection genres.

Residing at the nexus of human actors, organizations, geographies, norms, and texts are the tools used to collect data: sampling kits. For citizens to participate in the InFORM network's coastal monitoring for radionuclides there needs to be some mechanism whereby water samples and data are collected and returned to the academic team for processing. Providing self-contained kits and sampling instructions means prescribing and proscribing what counts as data, and importantly what counts as good data. Sampling kits, then, become objects rhetoricians of science and science studies researchers broadly can use to understand complex configurations of scientists, citizens, and socio-discursive and also material objects, including geographies.

Actor-Network Theory, which we will consider momentarily, can tell us much about how these sampling kits function within a network. We can theorize relationships and their effects through a "flat ontology" in ANT that helps us understand the interactional effects among humans and non-human objects. Such an approach has been usefully employed to study cultures of science and scientific knowledge production in a variety of contexts by science studies scholars in Science and Technology Studies. Related science studies in the field of Rhetoric of Science have sometimes employed such terminology, but often approach cultures of science and scientific knowledge production using the rhetorical tradition as a foundation for critical concepts. Each approach offers important perspectives to help understand the complex systems of scientific knowledge production and changing cultures of science we find in the case of InFORM. To better articulate this point we now turn to some of the previous work that helps build the framework we use to investigate InFORM.

Intersecting Literatures

To begin mapping out rhetorical deployment of Actor-Network Theory, and where that intersects with rhetorical deployment of Rhetorical Genre Theory, we first look to the study of Rhetoric of Science, Technology, and Medicine (we, in fact, begin this work in Mehlenbacher & Maddalena, 2015, which offers the foundation for our work here). As rhetorical studies of science and technology expand to include health and medicine (Keränen, 2013), we find productive conversations already bringing together ANT and rhetorical theories. Rhetoric of health and medicine in the U.S. has recently recognized ANT and related Latourian approaches as a useful language for rhetorical studies of health. Studies of medicine provide examples of the successful blending of disciplinary lenses, i.e., combinations of ethnographic work and textual analysis, to "get at" discursive and socially constructed objects and experiences in health. Christa B. Teston's (2009) method is such an approach; though her work does not explicitly reference Actor-Network Theory, she writes a grounded-theory study of documents' roles in cancer care decision-making that notes similar entanglements between genre, phenomenon, and action in healthcare, examining "the ways that [the standard of care document] rhetorically excludes and includes ways of seeing and doing" (p. 346). Teston claims that medical practitioners must balance patient experience and institutional expectations via documentation to categorize and produce actionable phenomena. Annemarie Mol (2003) theorizes patients' bodies as "complex wholes": network effects (i.e., objects) in themselves that are also points of intersection for multiple other networks. We employ Mol's concept of a "complex whole" later to conceive of how material objects may come together to constitute instantiations of genres.

As Mol and others argue, once networks produce objects, those objects are able to become actors in other networks, and the problem of agency arises. S. Scott Graham (2009), in a consideration of how medical practitioners establish phenomena, uses ANT and theories of rhetorical/material action to discuss the once-contested disorder fibromyalgia and the multiple subject positions enacted by patients and professionals to effect "change in the status quo" (in this case, the acceptance of fibromyalgia as a legitimate medical disorder). The ability to effect such changes is how Graham defines the term "agency," and we take Graham's definition as our own in a later discussion of issues of agency. Many of the critical questions in these texts become questions of social construction, ontology, and ethics: who or what is the patient, and what constitutes the patient's body? What suite of symptoms constitutes a given disorder, and whose experiences establish that phenomenon? Ultimately, the responses to those questions depend upon a separation between subject and object positions. Scholars who employ an ANT framework to describe networked action must also inevitably deal with the fact that ANT requires that no such separation be theorized (see Read & Swarts, 2015)—that is, ANT requires "symmetry" between what other frames might categorize as object, subject, and/or agent—what Graham (2009) calls "actor-actant symmetry." Graham notes that rhetorical scholars deal with this conflict by incorporating rhetorical theories of agency with the "flat," or symmetrical, frame of ANT, most notably Carolyn R. Miller (2007), who sees rhetorical agency as a *"kinetic energy* of rhetorical performance" (p. 147, emphasis original) and Ronald Greene (2004), who theorizes agency as work. The combination of ANT and genre approaches presents us with new questions about how (rhetorical) agency is enacted by (material) objects. The consideration of genre can lead, we maintain, to a more robust conception of agency in social studies of science more broadly.

All told, ANT has proven a productive alliance for rhetorical studies of health communication, an area of research with intersections along rhetorical studies of science and technology. Another important feature of ANT is that it has been used as a frame for rhetorical action, but it is often paired with a theoretical language that can account for distinctions between rhetorical actants and subject entities adequately (Graham, 2009; Greene, 2004; Miller, 2007). Sarah Read and Jason Swarts (2015), writing for scholars in technical communication, for example, have recently paired ANT with network analysis, proposing that network analysis is a way to "understand the form and mechanism of [network] connections as a subset of possible connections within a networked space" (p. 15). Similar to Read and Swarts, we find ANT productive in terms of rendering networks—and the objects enchained in and produced by those networks—visible, but lacking in terms of how networks stabilize and maintain. More importantly, we also want to know what invisible social factors determine the activation of new networks.

How do we talk about pre-existing, "example" networks that influence the activation of new ones? What ANT provides is a way to reveal complexity in some entity—a system, situation, case, an object, et cetera—an actor. But if we want to attend not to the attributes that constitute the actor but the rhetorical worlds from which actors draw their persuasive power, we must return from flat ontologies to rhetorical axiologies in an effort to determine how we construct our scientific epistemologies. Or, rather, we must return to axiologies with the actors we found in flat ontologies. A particularly useful way to understand these rhetorical dimensions is through Rhetorical Genre Theory because genre studies provides a language to talk about rhetorical decisions as social actions.

Rhetorical Genre Studies are especially pertinent to Canadian studies of science, health, and medicine. Judy Segal (2000) explains, "rhetoricians of science are not easily distinguishable from genre rhetoricians [in Canada]" (p. 66). In Canada genre has been a critical framework favoured by those studying and teaching the rhetorical nature of science, technology, and medicine (e.g., Artemeva & Fox, 2010, 2011; Artemeva & Freedman, 2001; Freedman & Smart, 1997; Giltrow & Stein, 2009; Graves & Graves, 2012; Schryer, 1994; Schryer, Lingard, & Spafford, 2007; Segal, 2002, 2007). Further, Canada has been central to the development of genre studies, with the 1992 "Rethinking Genre" colloquium and the Genre 2012 conference, both held at Carleton University. Genre studies broadly describes a multidisciplinary area of research that continues to gain traction in discourse studies around the world, from three early traditions (Hyon, 1996) to emerging Brazilian and Scandinavian traditions (Miller & Mehlenbacher, 2016). Genre studies have been especially insightful ways to study knowledge-making and knowledge-sanctioning practices in scientific, medical, technical, and other professional discourses (Artemeva & Fox, 2010, 2011; Bazerman, 1988; Berkenkotter, 2001; Berkenkotter & Huckin, 1995a; Bhatia, 1993, 1995; Devitt, 1991; Geisler, Bazerman, Doheny-Farina, Gurak, Haas, Johnson-Eilola, Kaufer, Lunsford, Miller, Windsor, & Yates, 2001; Schryer, 1994, 2000; Schryer & Spoel, 2005; Spinuzzi, 2003, 2004; Spinuzzi & Zachry, 2000; Swarts, 2006; Yates & Orlikowski, 1992; Zachry, 2000). Given the attention to genre as a rhetorical concept for understanding how epistemic work in science and medicine is conducted through recurrent situations and typified rhetorical responses, it is valuable to engage this approach once again. However, we diverge from genre studies traditional objects of analysis—texts, in the broadest semiotic sense of the term—to study a material-semiotic genre, the sampling kit. But before we make the case for this genre we ought to pause and define more carefully the concept of genre.

By genre we mean a rhetorical concept that describes "typified rhetorical actions based in recurrent situations" (Miller, 1984, p. 159). Our definition of genre thus departs from more common notions of the term where the classification of texts within a pre-defined set is a primary concern. Attention to taxonomy and classification draws on a kind of formalist tradition found in a good deal of literary scholarship, but here we are rather concerned with a kind of pragmatic tradition that understands genres as products of discourse communities (Miller & Mehlenbacher, 2016). For scientific genres we can say writers, usually scientists, "find in existing models the solution to the recurring rhetorical problems of writing science" and "As these solutions become familiar, accepted, and molded through repeated use, they gain institutional force. Thus though genre emerges out of contexts, it becomes part of the context for future works" (Bazerman, 1988, p. 8). Understanding genre in this way means genres, as Amy Devitt, Anis Bawarshi, and Mary Jo Reiff (2003) suggest, "become less transparent and more constitutive, less the means of classifying texts and more the sites at which language's social character can be understood" and thus "genres are as material as the people using them" (p. 542).

But still we remain in the realm of language, written and spoken, and the notion of discourse remains somewhat restricted. It seems, we speculate, easy to imagine genres of writing, such as the novel or a poem, speech, such as a eulogy, painting, such as portraiture or in another sense of genre, Flemish Baroque, video games, such as the role-playing game, and of course television series, films, and theatre, et cetera. Creative works are familiar grounds for genre discourse. Even non-creative written works such as patient medical-history forms (Devitt et al., 2003), scientific articles (Bazerman, 1984; Berkenkotter & Huckin, 1995b; Gross, Harmon, & Reidy, 2002), grant proposals (Ding, 2008; Tardy, 2003), et cetera, have been characterized as genres. Charles Bazerman (1988) helps us understand where rhetorical attention to scientific genres in particular has been drawn when he writes "Knowledge produced by the academy is cast primarily in written language—now usually a national language augmented by mathematical and other specialized international symbols" (p. 18). Our science, medicine, and other professional genres are spaces where we can explore the concept of genre and understand how written communication shapes knowledge production, but still we wish to extend our vision beyond written text. To that end, we will turn to sampling kits for a more expansive account of scientific genres.

Integrating Approaches

We now take an integrated approach to our example case: the InFORM sampling kit. Our approach contributes to ongoing work that reveals productive alliances between genre and ANT and articulates ways of knowing through non-discursive, typified rhetorical actions in recurrent situations (following Miller, 1984, on genre). As communication scholars, and rhetoricians in particular, continue to integrate concepts with broader science studies, and science and technology studies in particular, (see, for example,

Hasian, Paliewicz, & Gehl, 2014), key concepts from both traditions must be put into conversation, and we attempt to address some of those concepts in the following analysis.

Complex Wholes and Systems

One way to uncover sampling kits as objects within the InFORM knowledge-producing network is to understand something of the object's nature. We could, of course, talk about objects as "quasi-objects," as Bruno Latour (2002) argued, taking up the work of Michael Serres, in *We Have Never Been Modern*. Quasi-objects are not merely dumb objects to which we ascribe meaning, but rather are those that remind us of the reciprocal relationship between material forms and construction of social norms and understandings. Moving through, and thus acting in and upon, the world, quasi-objects remind us of the rather jejune object-subject distinctions of modernity. But objects in this tradition, and even the idea of ANT "actors" pose something of a problem to the particular aspects we wish to explore here. To call an object an "actor," as proposed in the first ruminations of Latour's now-famous theory, is to ignore the problem of scale, that is, the fact that most actors are in fact networks themselves. Several approaches to networks and networked objects could offer language for such an understanding. We could, for example, take John Law's (2002) concept of the network-object and its famous example of the Portuguese war ship, which helps to render "invisible" or ephemeral work more visible for analysis. Instead, we have chosen to turn to Mol's (2002) *The Body Multiple: Ontology in Medical Practice*, which considers the problem in terms of "complex wholes," such as patients' bodies in healthcare systems when the body is at once an object of knowledge, a point of negotiation for the establishment of a phenomenon, and a subject position. Mol's methodological territory is applicable to most considerations of the intersection of experience, mediation, and epistemology. What we learn from Mol is that "objects" are indeed a matter of scale, dependent upon what level of configurations is attended to. It is well and good to claim that reality—or social reality, if you like—is a system of interdependent, contested, dynamic, relational effects, but at what point do these effects start to hang together with stability? When can we name them and use those names as components of larger sets of relations? And what do we render invisible by taking a relational effect and calling it an "object"? Mol's concept, the "complex whole," helps us see the separate objects that compose a sampling kit as one object in concert. The kit, like Mol's body multiple, is at once a group of objects and one object; at different levels of configuration, any of these objects may be activated by more than one network (of action).

InFORM's network is a complex whole with several potential levels of configuration to choose from in terms of a focus for analysis. For example, we might choose to analyze from the perspective of global ecologies, at which scale InFORM itself might be seen as one self-contained actor that influences others, or even fades into a larger actor of "policy" at the global scale where policy actually affects ecology. Moving to a finer-grained scale, we could look at InFORM as a (again self-contained) network of organizations: funders, universities, nongovernmental organizations (NGOs), and the like. That scale would allow us to talk about a network of political economy. But we want to focus on data collection genres and knowledge making, and so we narrow our focus once again and see two levels of configuration that might be productive: 1) a network of academic knowledge making that interacts with a network of "non-academic" activists and citizen scientists, and 2) a network of humans, instruments, and environmental features.

Both the academic/citizen scientist network and the human/instrument/environment network share a particularly important actor as a node: the sampling kit. The sampling kit is a complex whole itself, but for our purposes we take it as a self-contained object in the network that includes the scientists of InFORM and the citizen scientists who deploy the kits for data collection. A straightforward ANT approach to the sampling kit would maintain that it was a powerful actor, an object that produces inscriptions (data) that can then be translated and circulated in the knowledge-producing and policy-producing networks we list above. However, the ANT account is lacking from a rhetorician's point of view. We maintain that part of what gives the sampling kit its power is the fact that it is also a rhetorical object of a certain type that both academic and citizen scientists recognize: an instantiation of a data-collecting genre.

Rhetorical Objects

Our claim—that the sampling kit is the instantiation of a genre—requires some unpacking. First, we establish the sampling kit as a rhetorical object. That is, it is a semiotic object, a "readable" text, which acts suasively on its user. The kit is a very simple assemblage of bucket (for scooping water), funnel (for pouring water into bottle), crated water bottle (for containing water), green shipping container (for shipping the sample for analysis), and a shipping label (also for shipping the sample to a lab for analysis). While there are certain traditional rhetorical objects within the kit (namely texts) we are interested in strategically overlooking them for the moment. Kits are sent already assembled to InFORM volunteers, and sampling activity is reported on the InFORM blog in the form of reportage-style posts, a citizen-science feature page, and a more formal "results" page (InFORM, 2015). Many posts feature photography of the sampling kits in action (InFORM, 2015).

Written text is pervasive in the project, as is true for most scientific work. What is especially interesting for this citizen science project is the way that written text is used to communicate among scientists, citizen scientists, and broader audiences. Newsletters offer information about data collection and analysis, data collect methods, how analysis is performed once data is sent into INFORM scientists, and even short profiles of scientists and citizen scientists are offered. Each page of InFORM's website is a potential site for analysis in terms of emerging genres of science communication, including a blog, informational videos, and data collections (cf., Mehlenbacher & Miller, 2016). While rich textual rhetorical resources are offered by InFORM, we are especially interested in those objects that may be overlooked by our rhetorical vantage. If we imagine rhetoric in Aristotelian terms, "the faculty of discovering in any particular case *all* of the available means of persuasion," (Kennedy, 1991, p. 36, emphasis ours) then we might move beyond language and even texts more broadly construed. Taking an expansive view of Kenneth Burke's (1969) conception of rhetoric as "symbolic means of inducing cooperation" (p. 43), and expanding the domain of symbolic production to the level of cultural phenomenon—which is, of course, not new; cf., Barthes' (1972) *Mythologies*—our expansive engagement allows us to refigure our rhetorical lens and grasp new modes of persuasion and associated cultural phenomenon.

Rhetorical Genre Theory in concert with Actor-Network Theory allows us to look beyond more traditional objects of rhetorical inquiry and see materials as making arguments by rhetorical enchainment. We can find some provisional justification, or at least some metaphorical alignment anyway, in Miller's (1994) case for genre as a rhetorical concept when she writes that "Calling a genre a 'cultural artefact' is an invitation to see it much as an anthropologist sees a material artefact from an ancient civilization, as a product that has particular functions, that fits into a system of functions and other artefacts" (p. 69). Specifically she provides us with a way to understand how sampling kits function as suasive complex objects through their typified response to a recurrent rhetorical situation, through their patterning. Using a similar approach and seeing objects as inseparable from their rhetorical associations, we look at the materials of the kit itself and see a genre (a data-collecting genre) in a larger genre system (a scientific knowledge-producing system).

The kit is found at the interface between what we might call the arhetorical ocean—or, rather, perhaps the ocean to which we are unattuned—and obvious rhetorical human organization and perception. Sampling ocean water is an action that does not immediately produce written text as such, but the sampling kit's configuration ultimately renders the sampled water into a kind of readable text. More importantly for the present analysis, the component parts of the kit have syntactic and semantic effects on users and work together (rhetorically) to convince the user to act. The crate inside the box is a syntactical arrangement, and the bucket's relationship to the user's hand and the water can be seen, similarly, as a material syntax. Semantically, the simplicity of the kit allows for little confusion in terms of meaning making: the bucket is for scooping, the funnel for pouring in, the bottle for containing, and the green shipping container and label for mailing. Arguably these components are already material genres, and our expectations around them combine in a composition to create a new, meaningful object (cf., semiotic text or cultural artefact) through an arrangement of context, text, and recurrence. These components would not make the same argument taken separately; scoop, store, and send are effectively unified in the kit under one social action: "sample" or "collect data." Volunteers who have joined the InFORM community will recognize the sampling kit as a typified object used for a particular action in a recurrent situation. The online InFORM community references the kits in text and image; via the text-based network of the blog, volunteers' conceptions of what the kit is and what it is for are maintained and reinforced. Having established the kit as a rhetorical object, we can then move to argue that it is an example of a data-collecting genre. Where we locate the notion of sampling kits as genre is in their rhetorical shape and function. Recurring rhetorical opportunities are responded to by the typified action, indeed rhetorical action, of collecting samples through kits for the purposes of inscription. What this means for the genre user is that they are moved to respond in particular ways and understand their role within the larger data collection process through the lens of scientific discourses.

Further, we should consider how the progression of data (or, rather, sample) collection moves through analysis to become the data through which we know. In some ways the apparatus of a citizen science project such as InFORM un-boxes methods and approaches to analysis and representation that would perhaps otherwise be obscured from publics. InFORM provides not only an overview of methods, including both how gamma spectrometry is used and even how a gamma spectrometer works. Beside a photo labelled "A disassembled germanium detector with exposed germanium crystal and electrical connections through which the voltage gradient is applied," a description on the InFORM website reads: "This gamma spectrometer has been taken apart so that you may see the large crystal of pure germanium metal and two electrodes inside. When a photon hits the crystal, it produces a tiny electrical current." (InFORM, 2016). So the efforts to look inside the "black box" that Latour and Steve Woolgar (1979) told us about almost 40 years ago seem to be intensified in at least this citizen science project. We also find that the presentation of data through InFORM's online platform (its website) allows those who have collected samples to learn something of the outcome of the analysis. All of this, of course, is part of a changing rhetorical landscape and new rhetorical opportunities.

Data collection is a highly rhetorical activity because it provides the initial crafted response to the situation. Indeed, this crafted response shapes how subsequent inscriptions will be produced; thus we find that the rhetorical possibilities for inscriptions are shaped by the initial decisions about what data will be collected, by whom, and how that data will be shared. In this sense we could say that other instruments could be understood in the context of material-semiotic data collection genres, including tagging devices that geolocate animals or an app that identifies a birdsong and logs data into a census database. While it is certainly possible to suggest expanding *genre* to include these cultural artefacts, it may extend the concept beyond its intended design, if you will allow the metaphor, which is not a new problem for the concept of genre. Indeed, genre in formalist traditions, such as literary studies, certainly did not account for the kind of pragmatic rhetorical work that Miller (1984) advocated for in her formulation of what constitutes rhetorical genres. What we are suggesting is that genre can help us understand another part of the scientific knowledge-making process, and specifically it can help us understand typified suasive responses to recurrent situations.

Agency and Extensions

Whether rhetoric, and rhetoric of science and technology specifically, benefits from cross-pollination with the field of science studies is a current question among U.S. scholars of the rhetoric of science and technology. A recent debate between rhetorician Leah Ceccarelli (2013) and philosopher-sociologist Steve Fuller (2013) in the pages of *Rhetoric and Public Affairs*, and later at the Association for the Rhetoric of Science and Technology 2014 National Communication Association meeting, has renewed some of these debates and reminds us that the chasm between rhetorical studies of science and technology and should-be allied fields remains great. This is, of course, bad business for rhetoricians, but it is also bad business for science studies. Rhetoric is a dirty business dealing in moving epistemological, ontological, and axiological targets. And this, we want to suggest, is especially important as rhetoric of science and technology and science studies are thinking not about science and society, but science and societies. Both fields must come to terms with different epistemological, ontological, and axiological commitments of those societies, or publics, not in a relativistic tradition but in a pragmatic tradition concerned with complex negotiations among scientists, publics, and the material world we so precariously inhabit.

Our analysis of the sampling kit employs the concept of genre to explain how non-human objects might achieve agency in networks, an explanatory problem that arises constantly in purely "flat" actor-network arrangements common to science studies/ studies in science, technology, and society (STS). Graham's (2009) definition of agency, "the process of instantiating change in the status quo" (p. 379), is closest to the one we operationalize here, via the concept of genre change. Our version of agency derives from pre-existing (and rhetorical) notions of what things are and what they are for. That is, like Miller (2007), we see agency as a product of rhetorical construction that reflects post hoc application and not an a priori status. The blended method we employ to better see how such agency operates suggests that rhetoric, at least in the form of genre theory, has much to offer science studies through its articulation of suasive appeals.

Informed Actions and Agency

Rhetoric's long-standing attention to what Aristotle called artistic proofs might draw our attention away from what seems inartistic—artless science invested in the program of discovery, not invention (Miller, 1979)—but the distinction between artless and artful obscures the complicated interaction of discovery and invention at work in the process of data collection. As Miller reminded us in 1979, and decades of scholarship in rhetorical studies of science elaborated upon,

> Reality cannot be separated from our knowledge of it; knowledge cannot be separated from the knower; the knower cannot be separated from a community. Facts do not exist independently, waiting to be found and collected and systematized; facts are human constructions which presuppose theories, (p. 615)

and, importantly to our questions of typification and recurrence, "We bring to the world a set of innate and learned concepts which help us select, organize, and understand what we encounter" (p. 615). When we understand such concepts of organization to our rhetorical activities, whether discourse or other modes of persuasion, we are indeed engaging in artful construction. When we decide to craft a text or speech into a particular genre or when we deploy a complex object in the service of knowledge construction, including later inscription, we engage in persuasive activities. As Miller (1984) suggests, genres are not important simply because they tell us about different forms but rather "what ends we may have," including the ability to "eulogize, apologize, recommend one person to another, instruct customers on behalf of a manufacturer, take on an official role, account for progress in achieving goals" (p. 165)—and, perhaps, collect data and share it with a broader community.

ANT's contribution to the blended-theory approach presented here is to give us a map (or a multitude of possible maps) of possible locations for analytical focus. The Latourian way of seeing does not allow us to exclude any actors as unimportant or outside of our scope, and so we consider things that we may not otherwise see. The very simple, even rudimentary, sampling kit is an example of just such an actor: it may seem liminal or negligible from the point of view of a "traditional" rhetorician. The kit is not a "traditional" text, rather it is a stop along the way to producing the text. By flattening our ontology, however, we see the kit as an actor on equal footing with the scientists, volunteers, and texts included in the network. With ANT, *we find the kit*. When we revisit the kit from a rhetorical point of view, we see that its very simplicity *persuades volunteers to act*. In fact, the kit may be a rhetorical agent.

With Actor-Network Theory we have located the kit, and genre helped us to understand syntax(es) by which the kit persuades its user to (re)produce knowledge by collecting data and contributing to an epistemology grounded in scientific thinking. Genre, as a concept, also helped us explore how objects participate in, perhaps even direct a good deal, of this knowledge making through typification of rhetorical response. If an object is the sum effect of a group of networked actions, then genre allows us to talk about how the networked object is/acts as an object in another network: it is recognized, the recognition is suasive, and the object is taken up, as a whole, as an actor. So genre, as a pre-existing network of social expectation, also helps explain how objects such as instruments gain a kind of agency unto themselves.

Put another way, when we want to learn something about the material world we learn through a combination of rhetorical lenses, relational interactions, and acts by material objects. InFORM reveals the complex ways we can come to understand modern technoscientific risks (Beck, 1992) through a combination of science, citizen science, and the innovative science communication that results from this new rhetorical landscape that involves both experts, non-experts, and materialities that persuade us to act and act upon us. Questions remain about the agency of objects, the agency of non-experts and publics, and even the agency of experts or scientists to persuade and act. As we continue to explore how science communication is changing it seems evident that the complexity of our topic will increase as the complexity of our technoscientific knowledge and risks, and their intersections with broader material, geographical, social, and discursive landscapes increase too. As InFORM's work, and the whole problem of nuclear risk, remind us, C.P. Snow's (2012) two cultures problem persists, but there are great efforts to find a bridge for it. Our theoretical vantage for examining how science communication is changing will likewise require such adaptability. Bringing together ANT and genre we hope to explore one possible way to explore multiple intersecting forces through which and by which we communicate.

References

Artemeva, Natasha, & Fox, Janna. (2010). Awareness versus production: Probing students' antecedent genre knowledge. *Journal of Business & Technical Communication, 24,* 476–515.

Artemeva, Natasha, & Fox, Janna. (2011). The writing's on the board: The global and the local in teaching undergraduate mathematics through chalk talk. *Written Communication, 28,* 345–379.

Artemeva, Natasha, & Freedman, Aviva. (2001). "Just the boys playing on computers": An activity theory analysis of differences in the cultures of two engineering firms. *Journal of Business and Technical Communication, 15,* 164–194.

Barthes, Roland. (1972). *Mythologies.* New York, NY: Farrar, Straus and Giroux.

Bazerman, Charles. (1984). Modern evolution of the experimental report in physics: Spectroscopic articles in physical review, 1893–1980. *Social Studies of Science, 14,* 163–196.

Bazerman, Charles. (1988). *Shaping written knowledge: The genre and activity of the experimental article in science.* Madison, WI: University of Wisconsin Press.

Beck, Ulrich. (1992). *Risk society: Towards a new modernity.* London, UK: Sage Publications.

Berkenkotter, Carol. (2001). Genre systems at work: DSM-IV and rhetorical recontextualization in psychotherapy paperwork. *Written Communication, 18,* 326–349.

Berkenkotter, Carol, & Huckin, Thomas N. (1995a). *Genre knowledge in disciplinary communication.* Hillside, NJ: Lawrence Erlbaum Associates.

Berkenkotter, Carol, & Huckin, Thomas N. (1995b). News value in scientific journal articles. *Genre Knowledge in Disciplinary Communication: Cognition/Culture/Power* (pp. 27–44). Hillsdale, NJ: Lawrence Erlbaum Associates.

Bhatia, Vijay K. (1993). *Analysing genre: Language use in professional settings.* London, UK: Longman.

Bhatia, Vijay K. (1995). Genre-mixing and in professional communication: The case of "private intentions" v. "socially recognized purposes." *Explorations in English for Professional Communication.* Hong Kong: Department of English, City University of Hong Kong.

Bitzer, Lloyd F. (1968). The rhetorical situation. *Philosophy and Rhetoric, 1,* 1–14.

Burke, Kenneth. (1969). *A rhetoric of motives.* Berkeley, CA: University of California Press.

Ceccarelli, Leah. (2013). Controversy over manufactured scientific controversy: A rejoinder to Fuller. *Rhetoric & Public Affairs, 16*(4), 761–766.

Devitt, Amy J. (1991). Intertextuality in tax accounting: Generic, referential, and functional. In C. Bazerman & J. Paradis (Eds.), *Textual dynamics of the professions: Historical and contemporary studies of writing in professional communities* (pp. 336–335). Madison, WI: University of Wisconsin Press.

Devitt, Amy J., Bawarshi, A., & Reiff, M.J. (2003). Materiality and genre in the study of discourse communities. *College English, 65,* 541–558.

Ding, Huiling (2008). The use of cognitive and social apprenticeship to teach a disciplinary genre: Initiation of graduate students into NIH grant writing. *Written Communication, 25,* 3–52.

Freedman, Aviva, & Smart, Graham. (1997). Navigating the current of economic policy: Written genres and the distribution of cognitive work at a financial institution. *Mind, Culture, and Activity, 4*(4), 238–255.

Fuller, Steve. (2013). Manufactured scientific consensus: A reply to Ceccarelli. *Rhetoric & Public Affairs, 16*(4), 753–760.

Geisler, Cheryl, Bazerman, Charles, Doheny-Farina, Stephen, Gurak, Laura, Haas, Christina, Johnson-Eilola, Johndan, Kaufer, David, Lunsford, Andrea, Miller, Carolyn R., Windsor, Dorthy, & Yates, JoAnne. (2001). IText: Future directions for research on the relationship between information technology and writing. *Journal of Business and Technical Communication, 15,* 269–308.

Giltrow, Janet, & Stein, Dieter. (2009). *Genres in the Internet: Issues in the Theory of Genre.* Amsterdam, NL: John Benjamins.

Goodnight, G. Thomas. (1982). The personal, technical, and public spheres of argument: A speculative inquiry into the art of public deliberation. *Journal of the American Forensic Association, 18,* 214–227.

Graham, S. Scott. (2009). Agency and the rhetoric of medicine: Biomedical brain scans and the ontology of fibromyalgia. *Technical Communication Quarterly, 18*(4), 376–404.

Graves, Heather, & Graves, Roger. (2012). *A strategic guide to technical communication.* Peterborough, ON: Broadview Press.

Greene, Ronald W. (2004). Rhetoric and capitalism: Rhetorical agency as communicative labor. *Philosophy and Rhetoric, 37*(3), 188–206.

Gross, Alan G., Harmon, Joseph E., & Reidy, Michael S. (2002). *Communicating science: The scientific article from the 17th century to the present.* Oxford, UK: Oxford University Press.

Hasian Jr, Marouf, Paliewicz, Nicholas S., & Gehl, Robert W. (2014). Earthquake controversies, the L'Aquila Trials, and the argumentative struggles for both cultural and scientific power. *Canadian Journal Of Communication, 39*(4).

Hyon, Sunny. (1996). Genre in three traditions: Implications for ESL. *TESOL Quarterly, 30,* 693–722.

Ionescu, Tudor B. (2012). Communicating in Germany about the Fukushima accident: How direct encounter beat media representations. *Environmental Communication: A Journal of Nature and Culture, 6*(2), 260–267.

InFORM (Integrated Fukushima Ocean Radionuclide Monitoring). (2015). Integrated Fukushima ocean radionuclide monitoring network web site. URL: http://fukushimainform.ca/ [June 2015].

InFORM (Integrated Fukushima Ocean Radionuclide Monitoring). (2016). *Gamma spectroscopy.* Integrated Fukushima ocean radionuclide monitoring network web site. URL: http// fukushimainform.ca/methods/gamma_spectroscopy/ [February 2016].

Mehlenbacher, Ashley R. (2016). Emerging genres of science communication and their ethical exigencies. In B. Vanacker & D. Heider (Eds.), *Ethics for a digital age* (pp. 3–18). New York, NY: Peter Lang.

Mehlenbacher, Ashley R. (2014). *Hacking science: Emerging parascientific genres and public participation in scientific research* [Dissertation]. Raleigh, NC: NCSU Institutional Repository, Dissertations.

Mehlenbacher, Ashley R., & Maddalena, Kate. (2015). Harnessing agency for efficacy: "Foldit" and citizen science. *POROI: An Interdisciplinary Journal of Rhetorical Analysis and Invention, 11*(1), 1–9.

Mehlenbacher, Ashley R., & Miller, Carolyn R. (2016). Intersections: Scientific and parascientific communication on the Internet. In Randy Allen Harris (Ed.), *Landmark Essays in Rhetoric of Science: Case Studies,* second edition (pp.239-60). London: Routledge, 2018 [2016].

Kennedy, George A., (trans.) [Aristotle] (1991). *On rhetoric: A theory of civic discourse.* New York, NY: Oxford UP.

Keränen, Lisa. (2013). Conspectus: Inventing futures for the rhetoric of science, technology, and medicine. *POROI: An Interdisciplinary Journal of Rhetorical Analysis and Invention, 9*(1), 1–9.

Kinsella, William J., Mehlenbacher, Ashley R., & Kittle Autry, Megan. (2013). Risk, regulation, and rhetorical boundaries: Claims and challenges surrounding a purported Nuclear Renaissance. *Communication Monographs, 80*(3), 278–301.

Latour, Bruno. (2002). *We have never been modern.* Cambridge, MA: Harvard UP.

Latour, Bruno, & Woolgar, Steve. (1979). *Laboratory life: The construction of scientific facts.* Princeton, NJ: Princeton University Press

Law, John. (2002). Objects and spaces. *Theory, Culture & Society, 19*(5–6), 91–105.

Miller, Carolyn R. (1979). A humanistic rationale for technical writing. *College English, 40*(6), 610–617.

Miller, Carolyn R. (1984). Genre as social action. *Quarterly Journal of Speech, 70,* 151–176.

Miller, Carolyn R. (1992) Kairos in the rhetoric of science. This volume [1992], 184–202

Miller, Carolyn R. (1994). Rhetorical community: The cultural basis of genre. In A. Freedman & P. Medway (Eds.), *Genre and the new rhetoric* (pp. 67–78). London, UK: Taylor and Francis.

Miller, Carolyn R. (2007). What can automation tell us about agency? *Rhetoric Society Quarterly, 37,* 137–157.

Miller, Carolyn R., & Mehlenbacher, Ashley R. (2016). Discourse genres. In A. Rocci & L. de Saussure (Eds.), *Verbal communication* (pp. 269–286). Berlin, DE: De Gruyter Mouton.

Mol, Annemarie. (2003). *The body multiple: Ontology in medical practice.* Durham, NC: Duke University Press Books.

Read, Sarah, & Swarts, Jason. (2015). Visualizing and tracing: Articulated research methodologies for the study of networked, sociotechnical activity, otherwise known as knowledge work. *Technical Communication Quarterly 24*(1): 14–44.

Schryer, Catherine F. (1994). The lab vs. the clinic: Sites of competing genres. In A. Freedman & P. Medway (Eds.), *Genre and the new rhetoric* (pp. 105–124). London, UK: Taylor and Francis.

Schryer, Catherine F. (2000). Walking a fine line: Writing "negative news" letters in an insurance company. *Journal of Business and Technical Communication, 14,* 445–497.

Schryer, Catherine F., Lingard, Lorelei, & Spafford, Marlee. (2007). Regularized practices: Genres, improvisation, and identity formation in health-care professions. In C. Thralls & M. Zachry (Eds.), *Communicative practices in workplaces and the professions: Cultural perspectives on the regulation of discourse and organizations* (pp. 21–44). Amityville, NY: Baywood.

Schryer, Catherine F., & Spoel, Philippa. (2005). Genre theory, health-care discourse, and professional identity formation. *Journal of Business and Technical Communication, 19,* 249–278.

Segal, Judy Z. (2000). What is a rhetoric of death? End-of-life decision-making at a psychiatric hospital. *Technostyle, 16*(1), 65–86.

Segal, Judy Z. (2002). Problems of generalization/genrelization: The case of the doctor-patient interview. In R. Coe, L. Lingard, & T. Teslenko (Eds.), *The rhetoric and ideology of genre: Strategies for stability and change* (pp. 171–184). Cresskill, NJ: Hampton Press.

Segal, Judy Z. (2007). Breast cancer narratives as public rhetoric: Genre itself and the maintenance of ignorance. *Linguistics and the Human Sciences, 3,* 3–23.

Snow, Charles Percy. (2012). *The two cultures.* Cambridge, UK: Cambridge University Press. (Originally published in 1959)

Spinuzzi, Clay. (2003). *Tracing genres through organizations: A sociocultural approach to information.* Cambridge, MA: MIT Press.

Spinuzzi, Clay. (2004). Four ways to investigate assemblages of texts: Genre sets, systems, repertoires, and ecologies. *The 22nd annual international conference on design of communication: The engineering of quality documentation* (pp. 110–116). Memphis, TN: Association for Computing Machinery.

Spinuzzi, Clay, & Zachry, Mark. (2000). Genre ecologies: An open-system approach to understanding and constructing documentation. *ACM Journal of Computer Documentation, 24,* 169–181.

Stueck, Wendy. (2015). Radiation from 2011 Fukushima nuclear meltdown in Japan detected on B.C. coast. *The Globe and Mail.* [24 March, 2016].

Swarts, Jason. (2006). Coherent fragments: The problem of mobility and genred information. *Written Communication, 23,* 173–201.

Tardy, Christine M. (2003). A genre system view of the funding of academic research. *Written Communication, 20,* 7–36.

Teston, Christa B. (2009). A grounded investigation of genred guidelines in cancer care deliberations. *Written Communication, 26*(3), 320–348.

Vatz, Richard. (1973). The myth of the rhetorical situation. *Philosophy and Rhetoric, 6,* 154–161.

University of Victoria. (2014). *UVic oceanographer leads new radioactive monitoring network* [Press release]. URL: http://communications.uvic.ca/releases/release.php?display=release&id=1427 [June 2015].

Wynne, Brian. (1992). Misunderstood misunderstanding: Social identities and public uptake of science. *Public Understanding of Science, July*(1), 281–304.

Yates, Joanne, & Orlikowski, Wanda J. (1992). Genres of organizational communication: A structurational approach to studying communication and media. *Academy of Management Review, 17,* 299–326.

Zachry, Mark. (2000). Communicative practices in the workplace: A historical examination of genre development. *Journal of Technical Writing and Communication, 30,* 57–79.

INDEX

Printed in the United States
by Baker & Taylor Publisher Services